THE ONCE AND FUTURE
GREAT LAKES COUNTRY

McGill-Queen's Rural, Wildland, and Resource Studies Series

Series editors: Colin A.M. Duncan, James Murton, and R.W. Sandwell

The Rural, Wildland, and Resource Studies Series includes monographs, thematically unified edited collections, and rare out-of-print classics. It is inspired by Canadian Papers in Rural History, Donald H. Akenson's influential occasional papers series, and seeks to catalyze reconsideration of communities and places lying beyond city limits, outside centres of urban political and cultural power, and located at past and present sites of resource procurement and environmental change. Scholarly and popular interest in the environment, climate change, food, and a seemingly deepening divide between city and country, is drawing non-urban places back into the mainstream. The series seeks to present the best environmentally contextualized research on topics such as agriculture, cottage living, fishing, the gathering of wild foods, mining, power generation, and rural commerce, within and beyond Canada's borders.

THE ONCE AND FUTURE
GREAT LAKES COUNTRY

An Ecological History

JOHN L. RILEY

McGill-Queen's University Press

Montreal & Kingston · London · Chicago

© McGill-Queen's University Press 2013
ISBN 978-0-7735-4177-1 (cloth)
ISBN 978-0-7735-4388-1 (paper)
ISBN 978-0-7735-8981-0 (ePDF)
ISBN 978-0-7735-8982-7 (ePUB)

Legal deposit third quarter 2013
Bibliothèque nationale du Québec
Reprinted 2013
First paperback edition 2014
Reprinted 2015, 2020

This book has been published with the help of a grant from Furthermore: a program of the J.M. Kaplan Fund.

Printed in Canada on acid-free paper

Funded by the Government of Canada   Financé par le gouvernement du Canada   Canada   Canada Council for the Arts   Conseil des arts du Canada

We acknowledge the support of the Canada Council for the Arts.
Nous remercions le Conseil des arts du Canada de son soutien.

Library and Archives Canada Cataloguing in Publication

Riley, J.L. (John L.), 1950–, author
The once and future Great Lakes country : an ecological history / John L. Riley.

(McGill-Queen's rural, wildland, and resource studies series; 2) Includes bibliographical references and index. Issued in print and electronic formats.
ISBN 978-0-7735-4177-1 (bound). – ISBN 978-0-7735-4388-1 (paper) –
ISBN 978-0-7735-8981-0 (ePDF). – ISBN 978-0-7735-8982-7 (ePUB)

1. Human ecology – Great Lakes Region (North America) – History.
2. Great Lakes Region (North America) – Environmental conditions – History.
I. Title. II. Series: McGill-Queen's rural, wildland, and resource studies series ; 2

GF512.G74R56 2013   304.2'09713   C2013-903656-3   C2013-903657-1

Set in Minion 10.5/14 by Pata Macedo

CONTENTS

ACKNOWLEDGMENTS

An ecologist cannot help but read history differently. This seemed a risky proposition at first, and I appreciate those who shared the risk, especially the George Cedric Metcalf Foundation, which awarded me a Metcalf Fellowship in 2007–08, and the Nature Conservancy of Canada, which afforded me the same licence. In particular, I thank Sandy Houston and Ruth Richardson of the Metcalf Foundation and John Lounds of the Nature Conservancy, and I also sincerely thank the Dalglish Family Foundation, the George Cedric Metcalf Foundation, the McLean Foundation, and the J.M. Kaplan Fund for their financial support of McGill-Queen's University Press in publishing this work.

I offer my thanks to Mary Lynne Armstrong, Pegi Miller, and the staff of the Shelburne Carnegie Library for borrowing materials for me from far and wide, to the Bower and Laverty families for the histories they have entrusted to the Dufferin County Museum Family Archives, and to Steve Brown of the Dufferin County Museum for access to those archives. Donna Holmes helped guide me through local Mono history, and Barb Dickson in the Land Surveys Branch of the Ontario Ministry of Natural Resources afforded me very pleasurable access to their Peterborough archives. I have benefited from discussions on many other fronts, including with Rob Ross of the Paleontological Research Institute, Ithaca, NY; Gord McBean of the University of Western Ontario; Leonard Munt of Haida Gwai, who shared his recollections of York Region; Mark Stabb of the Nature Conservancy of Canada, who offered insights on the Ottawa valley and Niagara River; and Dan McKenney of the Canadian Forestry Service. I particularly thank Colin Anderson and Jessica Hawkes of the Nature

Conservancy of Canada, and Judie Shore, John Taylor, and Barb Konyi for their support with maps and illustrations. Warm thanks are extended to all of those whom I have cited and quoted, and who will know by their inclusion how much I appreciate their contributions. Uniquely helpful have been my conversations with a number of fellow Brodie Club members: Kevin Seymour and Jock McAndrews of the Royal Ontario Museum, and Ed Addison and Harry Lumsden, formerly of the Ontario Ministry of Natural Resources.

Early drafts were kindly reviewed by Andrew Stewart, Strata Consulting, whom I thank in particular for his guidance on archaeology and paleoecology; Wasyl Bakowsky of the Ontario Natural Heritage Information Centre; Jack Imhof of Trout Unlimited Canada; and Graeme Wynn of the University of British Columbia. The support and advice of Ramsay Cook, professor emeritus of history at York University, was especially meaningful to me, as was his challenge that every geography deserves to have its ecological story told. The editorial advice of Sylvia Barrett, Colin A.M. Duncan, Mark Abley, and Curtis Fahey was very much appreciated. Despite the good advice and direction, a work like this must contain errors of both omission and commission, and responsibility for these is entirely my own.

Finally, my family and my partner, Katherine Lindsay, did all they could to encourage me, far beyond anything reasonable, for love.

A NOTE ON MEASUREMENTS AND CURRENCIES

A wide range of antiquated and modern imperial and metric units and currencies are cited.

Antiquated / Nautical	Imperial	Metric
	acre	0.4 hectares
arpent (Fr.)	0.85 acres	0.3 hectares
	square mile (640 acres)	259 hectares
	pound (lb.)	0.45 kilograms
	ton	1016 kilograms
	foot	0.3 metres
	yard	0.9 metres
brasse (Fr.)	5.5 feet	1.7 metres
fathom (Eng.)	6 feet	1.8 metres
chain (Eng.)	66 feet	20.1 metres
arpent (Fr.)	191.8 feet	58.5 metres
league (Eng.)	2 miles	3.2 kilometres
lieue (Fr.)	2.4 miles (3 miles in early 1600s)	3.9 kilometres
minot (Fr.)	1.1 bushels	39 litres
sous (Fr.) 1534	$0.005 US/CAN 2013	
écu (Fr.) 1640	$30 US/CAN 2013	
£ (Eng. pound) 1767	$30 US/CAN 2013	
£ (Eng. pound) 1830	$20 US/CAN 2013	

FOREWORD

Ramsay Cook

Several years ago Sandy Houston of the George Cedric Metcalf Foundation asked me if I would look at a manuscript on the early environmental history of Canada. I readily agreed, because in a somewhat desultory way I had been working on a similar subject for almost a decade. What surprised me and piqued my curiosity was that John Riley, the author, was not an historian with whom I was familiar. Moreover I was told that he had drafted a complete manuscript in a year with the support of the Metcalf Foundation, a rather unusual funding agency for an historian. There were more surprises to come.

First surprise: Riley was not a professional historian but rather the senior science officer at the Nature Conservancy of Canada, a scientist with a long and distinguished career both as a public servant and as an activist citizen in the conservation movement. Here is one example: he was undoubtedly the key player in the successful campaign to save the Oak Ridges Moraine from threatening urban sprawl. The second surprise was to discover that Riley had read and assimilated a huge volume of original sources, as well as a pile of published works, essential to writing the history of the environment of the Great Lakes region beginning with the earliest contact of Europeans and Native people and continuing into the nineteenth century. This literature, composed by explorers, cartographers, merchants, missionaries, and travellers, had often been consulted by earlier historians but rarely with Riley's qualifications and his focus on the environment. The third and most important surprise was the realization that being trained as an environmental scientist rather than as a professional historian had armed him with exactly the qualifications necessary to write a fully informed study of the region's environmental past, its present, and its future prospects.

As a practical naturalist he had restored and re-wilded his Mono Township farm, scaled cliffs, descended into caves, paddled canoes, camped, watched birds, identified trees, fish, mammals, and insects. He could explain why it is important to distinguish a marsh from a swamp and a bog from a fen. "One of the more transcendent rites of spring," he writes lyrically, "is to canoe Minesing swamp in full flood, beyond the hackberry levees into the deep clear waters in the fen, where you can see beneath your canoe, under several feet of water, crystal red pitcher plants." As a scholar and public servant, he had learned, either directly or through his many scientific friends, about archaeology, ecology, climatology, biology, natural history, paleobotany, entomology, animal behaviour, and even North American history. He knew that a heronry identified near Lachine by Champlain in 1611 still exists, thanks to the Nature Conservancy of Canada, and he understood the recent fate of the nine-spotted ladybug. All of this experience and scientific knowledge rested on a passion for the environment and a profound Darwinian understanding that "nature never repeats itself."

Once I had read the first draft of Riley's study I discovered something else about the author: he was endlessly willing to read more, to revise and reshape and improve his manuscript. At the mid-point of this process he let me know that he had just bought a set of the *Jesuit Relations* (seventy-two volumes) and was discovering its rich rewards! It has now all come to fruition in this extraordinary book entitled *The Once and Future Great Lakes Country*.

The puzzle now is this: can this book be categorized? It is certainly a history of the environment in its many parts: natives and newcomers, trees, birds, mammals, fish, flowers, trees, grasses, and insects. At the same time, it is a detailed history of environmental change brought about by the various actors in that environment. It is also contemporary history, a recounting of campaigns to save important parts of our shrinking natural environment, and of government policies devised to protect and even restore natural spaces in a globalized world. In addition it is a balanced assessment of environmental change. And the author himself is occasionally present: we have glimpses of a man rebuilding his farm house, planting trees and flowers, planning conservation goals, negotiating with politicians, always looking for ways to improve the health of the environment.

Riley offers a deeply disturbing account of the depredations of the past. But just as often he expresses a well-argued conviction that there are many realistic reasons for a more positive assessment about where we are going. Since nature never repeats itself, we cannot expect to return to a past earthly paradise, but carefully devised conservation and re-wilding measures can bring a new, more livable world. "It will not help to defend a status quo that never really existed," he writes. But Riley is no Pollyanna. The challenges remain daunting: population growth, climate change, habitat destruction, and invasive plants, fish, insects, and pathogens. Nor does he underestimate the destructiveness of human greed that drives people to favour short-term growth of production and consumption over long-term environmental health and stability. And so the cautious optimism that brings this marvellous book to a close: "The Great Lakes country may well be anomalous on the modern stage, with cause to be both glad and fearful. As William Shakespeare wrote four centuries ago, 'Nature's bequest gives nothing, but doth lend.'" *The Once and Future Great Lakes Country* suggests that the "once" points to the route that the inhabitants of this region can choose to ensure a "future" that, like nature, does not repeat its past.

The final result is something much richer than a conventional work of environmental history. John Riley has written the book I once thought I might write and I am now glad that I was too slow off the mark. His knowledge, practical experience, and determination make this a singular work that combines historical scholarship, scientific understanding, and subtle, low-key advocacy. It could not have been written by a mere historian or a mere scientist.

April 2013

The Fifth Line: A Farm Just Like Thousands of Others

Every county and township in Great Lakes country has its Fifth Line. It may not be called the Fifth Line, but it is always the same, an old trail or road allowance that was never worth opening because the hills were too steep, the river too wide, or the swamp so final.

The Fifth Lines remind us that, out beyond our imposed dominion of roads, cities, and fields, there still beats the true heart of the land. When my grandmother died and left her faraway grandson a small sum, I was young and determined to find a piece of land that would anchor me to some place local and particular – somewhere other than the city where I would have to earn my way. My partner and I knew the back roads of Great Lakes country better than most. Its valleys and woodlands attracted us, and so did its lakes. As life often unfolds, however, my partner thought some place near the farm where she grew up would be best, and so it was there we bought a derelict, and thus affordable, farm. It fronted on the Fifth Line of Mono Township, in the high country between Lake Ontario and Lake Huron, near the midpoint of the Niagara Escarpment. It was a good place for two naturalists, a restoration project crying out for cheap labour. The sign said, "Not a through road," which, for those so inclined, usually means "Now it gets interesting."

The place had few so-called improvements. A perimeter fence to keep the cattle in. A handful of splendid sugar maple around the buildings, and a horde of aggressive Manitoba maple planted in windrows by some unsuspecting hand. There was a farmhouse with the usual additions to the back; the roof was shot, the windows cracked, and the dirt basement open to groundhogs. The bank barn had a collapsed mow floor and its doors were off. On the upside, it was a place of simple construction where I could work without any serious investment in skill or tools.

Behind the fields was a threadbare bush. It had a few massive beech and maple that pre-dated settlement, but it was grazed to the bone and the springs and stream were all tracked into mud. Unlike nearby woods, with their show of spring flowers, this one did not have a single trillium or any other member of the lily family – the cattle take them first – and not a single tree seedling.

But these concerns paled in comparison to the big picture. The hills of Mono have a sky as big as the prairies. They look down on the Nottawasaga valley where it fans out onto the Alliston flats just south of Georgian Bay. On the northeast horizon is ancient *Wendake*, or Huronia. To the south lie the Oak Ridges and, from the high ground on the farm, you can look right over them into Toronto, an hour distant on excellent roads. In the early 1800s, when the farm was first settled, it took days to get here on foot through forest and swamp.

The story of the land in Mono repeated itself remorselessly across all of northeast North America over the past four centuries. The winds of change blew hard and have scarcely abated. The story of Nature writ large on the wider landscape – of collapse and restoration – I see through the lens of a farm that is just like a thousand others. What lessons survive from the days of epic contest for this place? What events so aligned that the conquest of a continent gave rise to land uses and land-tenure ideas that would entice unprecedented numbers of cross-ocean migrants, and change the place more totally, more rapidly, than anything in the 10,000 years before?

The First Owners

In the mid-1800s, emigration was akin to salvation itself. The urge to take up land, in an era when agriculture mattered, grew to a pace never seen before. The mindset was European and it would take another century for people to stop speaking of *emigration* and use the word *immigration* instead. Then, like now, both words were code for fresh labour lured by the promise of gain. In particular, in those days, it meant first-time ownership of unoccupied land by farm families who could turn sheer hard work into personal gain and, at the same time, directly profit those who had come earlier and had orchestrated the treaties, surveys, and disposition of the land.

At the beginning of the 1800s, the Native peoples of central Ontario were mostly Algonquian-speaking Ojibwa Missisauga. The treaty that divested them of their Mono land interests was signed on 17 October 1818. The Natives who signed it were never owner-occupants of Mono. Rather, they too were recent arrivals, some from the north and others from lands they had already surrendered. Five headmen, including William Yellowhead, or Musquakie, after whom Muskoka is named, sold to the Crown a principality of 1,592,000 acres for a yearly annuity of £1,200 sterling. It is almost certain that Musquakie was never in Mono, unless he had passed through on the old Nottawasaga trail while hunting. The place was the Missisauga's by conquest of the Iroquois, but any personal connection to it was thin at best.[1]

These Ojibwa and others had moved into the area following the ethnic cleansing of northeast North America in the 1600s, which was primed by smallpox and then prosecuted by the Iroquois, armed with Dutch and English weapons. A thousand Iroquois descended on the Huron northeast of Mono in 1649, and the nearby Petun soon after. In the next decade, the Iroquois spread their terror as far afield as the Mississippi, James Bay, Lac Saint-Jean, the St Lawrence, and the Carolinas, eliminating, absorbing, and displacing the Native allies of the French.

The Petun, or *Tianontati* (meaning "there the mountain stands"), were the closest to Mono, living in nine towns on the south-facing slopes and lake terraces below the Niagara Escarpment. They farmed, and traded their manufactured chert edges and their namesake tobacco. In 1636 the Jesuit Jean de Brébeuf asked the Huron where dead souls went and was told that the "village of souls" lay west beyond the Petun in the cliffs and caves of the escarpment. The Iroquois killed, abducted, and expelled the Petun. This warfare, following as it did on the heels of new diseases, triggered one of the longest periods of wilderness regeneration in world history, with hardly an acre broken for corn or cleared for farming for a century and a half. No wonder the land looked like the forest primeval when settlers arrived in force in the 1800s.[2]

First Nations never settled in Mono. Mono lies on the high ground that is called the Ontario Island, the first land to show above the ice as the last glacier decayed. It was a cool upland of deep forests, through which a few main trails connected the Huron, Neutral, and Petun. Two years after the land treaty in 1818, the township was surveyed by Sam Benson. One of the leading surveyors of his day, Benson was paid in land to lay out the bush lots, township by township. His notes from the front of our 100-acre parcel on Mono's Fifth Line say "maple beech hemlock," and then exactly the same for the back line. In payment, Benson got 3,000 acres of Mono. One-seventh of the township was reserved for the crown and another seventh for the Church of England;

the rest was for eager newcomers from a depressed, religiously intolerant, war-torn, and worn-out northern Europe. The surveys and land sales across Great Lakes country – an area as large as France and the United Kingdom combined – were a tour de force conducted with military precision, in the true self-interest of the elites of Canada and the United States.[3]

One of this elite was George Goodhue, the first "owner" of our farm. He was American born and came to London, Ontario, in 1820. London grew into the district capital, and Goodhue grew with it. He was councillor, village president, merchant, distiller, ash dealer, postmaster, banker, and magistrate. His emporium on Court House Square sold everything the settlers wanted and bought everything they had to sell. In 1831 he married the daughter of John Matthews, member of the House of Assembly for Middlesex. In 1842 his pro-reform ideas – or rather those of his father-in-law – helped him become member for Canada West. One obstacle to his political rise, however, was the approval of the local Methodists and, accordingly, Goodhue attended a Methodist meeting and poured his purse out on the table, reported at $50. The nomination duly followed.

Goodhue profited from the Rebellions of 1837–38 by acquiring some of the lands confiscated from the rebels. By the 1840s, he was a major land speculator. He bought land and he sold land, and foreclosed on mortgages on which he charged an interest ranging from 6 per cent in good times to 24 per cent in the years after the New York bank panic of 1857. When he died, he had land in nine counties, and his estate was enormous. In the *Dictionary of Canadian Biography*, F.H. Armstrong offers this summation: "Goodhue was neither better nor worse than any of the other Upper Canada pioneer merchants who rose to wealth as their region opened up. London was one of the last areas of the province to be settled, however, and in his case the memory of his great wealth and the tales of the harshness of his business activities have not yet died. Indeed, the legend of Goodhue as a sort of tight-fisted Midas has become deeply rooted in western Ontario folklore."[4] We may take it for granted that Goodhue, like the Native vendors before him, never visited Mono, certainly not the 100-acre parcel he bought for £32 from the crown on 21 August 1846 and sold to James Bower almost immediately.

The Newcomers

James Bower was born in Ireland in 1808, the son of William Bower, who had been a sergeant in the English army when Napoleon was defeated at Waterloo in 1815. They were Protestants in a Catholic Dublin. Following Waterloo, William was pensioned off, and he and his family migrated to Upper Canada in 1831 in the company of a former captain, Peter Montgomery, and his family. The two families travelled together, likely via Halifax and York, and settled in Newmarket, which at the time was the northern terminus of Yonge Street.⁵

Young James worked as blacksmith for Samuel Lount, the reform leader who led one of the rebel marches on Toronto in 1837, and who was hung for his effort. It was British policy to stabilize their colonies by attracting pensioned military men and their families with free land grants. William Bower, Sr, did not take up his grant right away but his friend Montgomery did, on lot 24 in Mono, on the Fifth Line east of Hurontario Street, which was the first road built from Lake Ontario to Georgian Bay.

Unlike his father, James was definitely in the market for land. He took up his grant near Collingwood, fifty miles northwest of Newmarket, and began his settlement duties, clearing the land and building a cabin. The story of his annual hike was told by his son James, Jr: "To make the trip back and forth between Newmarket and his homestead, he took as nearly as possible [a] direct line to Hurontario Street ... [and] followed it north to his homestead ... The western part of the trip was made by the aid of a pocket compass from one settler's clearing to another." This took him by way of the Montgomerys in Mono and, at a neighbour's, he made himself "acquainted with my mother [Dorothea Laverty] ... His acquaintance with my mother having ripened into an engagement, they decided to make the trip to Toronto to get married ... The ceremony was performed by the late Bishop Strachan of the diocese of Toronto. The only way to get there was to walk, and walk there and back they did, settling on lot 19 in the sixth concession of Mono, the place given to my mother as her marriage portion. Later my father sold his homestead ... and, in 1841, purchased the adjoining 100 acres ... [one lot east] for the sum of £60."

Bower's father joined them in Mono. The story has it that his father and Peter Montgomery had to hike to York to pick up their military pensions and that one time, while Montgomery was doing this chore for both of them, he was robbed on his way home. Another story has it that William Bower, Sr, was killed by a falling tree while rousting cattle out of the bush at the age of 104.

James was thirty-seven, with two children and another on the way, when he bought a third 100 acres - our place - due west of his other lots, this time from the land speculator Goodhue. His first two lots were all hill and dell but this one, with its front on the Fifth Line, was on higher ground, and more than half of it was level tableland. It was the first time the lot ever had an owner-occupant.

James and his boys cleared ninety acres and put them to the plow. Huge rocks, put there by the glacier, had to be moved. The Bowers may not have carved and cut the stones with the skill of the faraway Inca, but they moved them all the same – and of their own volition. In 1849 James built a one-and-a-half-storey fieldstone cottage, and then a barn and shed. He put up rail fences and watered the cattle in the springs. A photograph of the Bowers in the Dufferin Museum shows a dour set to their faces. It was likely the first time they had faced a camera.[6]

Dorothea Bower, born in 1816 in County Armagh, Ireland, was the first white girl raised in Dufferin County. When she was three, her family emigrated. Their Atlantic crossing took nine weeks and many lives, including those of her mother and brother. The survivors made their way to York and drew their lot for land in 1821. They worked their way north from Mono Mills up the Seventh Line. Dorothea's grandfather stumbled while fording the Nottawasaga and broke the family china they had carried all the way from Ireland. Near the 20th sideroad, they built their cabin, where Dorothea grew up with her siblings and the occasional Missisauga as playmates.[7]

Dorothea bore James Bower seven children. The eldest, William, married Elizabeth Coleman and, in 1866, bought the Fifth Line farm from his father for $700. James built a retirement cottage at the top of the driveway. More than a century later, a related Coleman named Elmer parsed the situation in these words: "James was at last on the height of land, master of all he surveyed." He died in 1885, "aged 77 years and 6 months," and was buried in the cemetery at the crossroad one farm north. Dorothea died a year later, "aged 78 years."[8]

Over time, the links of descendant land ownership mesh together into chain mail of local design that can be penetrated only by close relatives and, in truth, by few of them. The records are all of names, dates, and payments, nothing about the land. William the younger sold the farm to his eldest son in 1902, who farmed it for ten years and then retired to his grandfather's cottage at the top of the driveway, having sold the farm to his daughter Dorothea's husband, "R.J." McCutcheon. One of their six children, Luella, was born in 1910. It was a close-knit neighbourhood. Elmer Coleman, friend and schoolmate of Luella's brother Bert, married Luella in 1935 in the front parlour. Bert built a rockery to celebrate the occasion. After Dorothea died in 1953, the farm left the family, first to John Hetherington for $2,700 and then, after he died and the place went downhill, to the hockey player "Red" Horner, who ran it to stockers.[9]

When we first saw the place, a deceptive gold of cemetery spurge covered the fields. Digging out the basement yielded a few old glass inkwells and a copper school seal, all dating from when Elsie Thompson roomed here while she taught at the one-room school opposite the old Anderson place the next line over. James Bower had also built the Anderson's stone house, and Elsie had to cross the Anderson fields to get to school, in a way reminiscent of the trek that had once taken young James Bower by Dorothea Laverty's place, and with the same result – Shelly Anderson and Elsie were married, and Elsie moved from one Bower-built house to another.

Sixty-five years after Bower settled the place, and sixty-five years before we arrived, Mono's forest cover was down to about 10 per cent. The wind began to carve blowouts and raise dunes in overused fields. Descendants of those who had cut down the trees started planting them again in 1915 and, in 1925, the local council resolved "to purchase some wastelands being sold for taxes; same to be used for reforestation." A year later, 35,000 trees were planted. William Bower was among those planting trees that year. In 1949 Shelly Anderson persuaded the local school board to volunteer students to plant trees, which they did every spring for twenty years. Erosion was stopped on thousands of acres, and forest now covers more than a third of Mono. The soils are healing, wildlife is returning, and the streams are running clear again.[10]

An Earthly Paradise

The Great Lakes country – our first wild west – now supports a population of more than forty-five million and a shared annual economy of more than $1 trillion. It is a place that is open to the continent, and now to the world, more of a crossroads than anything separate or insular. From west to east are Chicago, Sault Ste Marie, Sudbury, Detroit, Cleveland, Kitchener-Waterloo, Hamilton, Buffalo, Toronto, Rochester, Kingston, Montreal, and Quebec City. Farther east, twice this many people occupy the Atlantic seaboard. One of the world's most egalitarian and wealthy societies evolved in the Great Lakes region, and it was there that North American manufacturing and consumerism were invented and perfected, and where a new post-industrialism is emerging. There is a massive $350-billion annual cross-border trade but deep down it is a region of quiet wealth. Amusements are built for visitors and newcomers, but most of its wealth is invested in youth, education, physical comfort, and modern enterprises both within and beyond the region.

Today, the migration of people and the manufacture of land ownership remain as defining industries. Over the next twenty-five years, for example, the number of residents in the Toronto area will increase by more than three million to a total of eleven million, requiring new construction about the size of Greater Boston. Well over half of Canada's growth in population will occur here. Migration is different now only by degree, and by place of origin. Just as in the 1800s, land companies negotiate for lands that are once again undefended, this time by their low value as farmlands. The landscape continues to be fractioned into ever smaller – and now tiny – parcels. And, as before, the profit flows to the agencies and companies expediting the migration and construction. The names change, but the results are the same. The modern version of the land treaty is the "option to purchase," and the modern face of the old land companies the "official" or "comprehensive" plan. Modern forensics says to "follow the money" but, in this case, we will "follow the land," and its environmental consequences.[11]

This book is about Great Lakes country, *le pays d'en haut* of New France, and its various arrival coasts and corridors linking it east, west, and north. It has nurtured humans for thousands of years, and it is where we hope to live for thousands more. Before the arrival of Europeans, it was a land of diverse Aboriginal peoples, successful hunters, fishers, harvesters, artisans, and traders, many of them belonging to farming nations. In the first part of the book, The Land and What Happened to It, Aboriginal land use is explored, in particular as a guide to an ancient circle of relations that is of increasing interest today. After European contact, the region suffered an extraordinary period of disease, warfare, and genocide – followed by a century and a half of ecological wilding. It then suffered the birth pains of our modern states, whose settlement and industrial occupation we take such pride in. Many nations called this place home, and many nations contested it. Today, two nations – Canada and the United States – have cohabited it in peace for a remarkable two centuries.

The second part of the book, Voices of Nature Past, revisits the trauma that occurred as the result of our assumption of the region's lands and waters, fish and wildlife, and forests and prairies. It gives voice to its first peoples, visitors, explorers, and surveyors, who left us first-hand accounts of a series of profound ecological transformations. At centre stage are the world's largest freshwater seas – *les mers douces* they were called. Nowhere else on Earth is there so much fresh water in the planet's livable temperate zone. To the north is the mineral-rich boreal country of the Canadian Shield; and to the south the lower lakes, with their warm and fertile Paleozoic plains, moraines, and shores. It is an extraordinary endowment of immense geopolitical importance, and its natural capital will continue to make it a magnet for human endeavour.

Two arms of the ocean reach Great Lakes country up the corridors of the Hudson and St Lawrence rivers, and another connects to James and Hudson bays. Beyond the lakes, into the continent, other well-watered lowlands lead south and west to the Ohio and Mississippi rivers, and the prairies, all of them corridors of power and culture, now and for thousands of years past (Fig. 1).[12]

A hundred years after contact, the first permanent white settlement beyond the Atlantic tides at Montreal and Albany was Detroit, the achievement of the French explorer Antoine de Lamothe Cadillac. His report home in 1701 was rhapsodic: "This country, so temperate, so fertile, and so beautiful it may justly be called the earthly paradise of North America." It was, of course, customary for adventurers to sing the praises of their discoveries but, in this case, Cadillac put his claim to the test and brought his own wife and family, and others, all the way from the St Lawrence to settle. The English echoed Cadillac's opinion soon after they defeated the French. In 1759 the army officer William Lee wrote of the land around Niagara: "It is filled with deer, bears, turkeys, raccoons and, in short, all sorts of game. The lake affords salmon and other excellent fish. But I am afraid you will think I am growing romantic. Therefore, I shall only say it is such a paradise and such an acquisition to our nation that I would not sacrifice it to receive the dominion of any electoral prince in Germany."[13]

The book's third section, Nature's Prospect, poses the emerging questions. How does the Great Lakes country today compare to the paradise of Cadillac and Lee? The Native founders had achieved a modest, stable level of material and spiritual accomplishment, and the newcomers' mission was nothing less than to convert the place into a new and better Europe. We have harvested, grown, and orchestrated resources far beyond anything contemplated, and are now committed to a second remarkable migration, with more than 80 per cent of us now living in cities and towns, the exact opposite of a century ago. This reorganization of matter and energy to meet the just-in-time needs of intensifying city-states is, at current scales, similarly unpredictable and unprecedented. Major costs of all kinds, including environmental and social costs, are paid forward by both city-states and donor countrysides, in precarious imbalance.

The modern landscape is sponsored by affordable hydrocarbons, which we can thank for the comfortable bubble in which we are currently domiciled. The changes that come with cheap energy extend far beyond urbanization, however, and we struggle to understand them in our daily lives. How will cheap food, climate warming, and globalization play themselves out? How long can they co-exist with some semblance of social equality, cultural diversity, and native ecology? On balance, the evidence to date across Great Lakes country suggests that we have reinvested well. In comparison with a century ago, there is now more forest cover, cleaner water, recovering native biota, and an improved quality of life. It is nothing like the original "paradise," but there are many new and ambitious environmental policies and pursuits, restoring some of the region's ecological integrity even while we intensify development in some parts of it. We see around us, finally, some signs of homegrown maturity in our home place. Restoration is taking hold. Slowly, the natural geography and a new commonwealth appear to be reasserting themselves. In this good fortune, Great Lakes country may well be anomalous among regions of the world, and we have reason to be careful as a result.

The old stories help us frame and measure the pace of change as we are now experiencing it. Like every generation, we think that the changes happening now are greater than ever before, but this place has gone through much more massive transformations in the past. Great Lakes country was almost totally different in 1800 from what it was in 1600, and then totally changed again in 1910. It will be a different place again by 2050.

The changes that occur in Nature, large and small, come on relentlessly like waves on the shore. Human nature, by contrast, looks for security, and every generation projects its own illusions of stability, based on its own fears and flight responses. Charles Darwin left us a famous metaphor, the "entangled bank," in the last paragraph of On the Origin of Species: "These elaborately constructed forms, so different from each other, and dependent upon each other in so complex a manner, have all been produced by laws acting around us." Natural selection was the law that he described, the engine of irreversible change. An unavoidable corollary of natural selection is that Nature never repeats itself. Indeed, Nature cannot repeat itself. Some may find this unsettling but, given the near total change that this place has witnessed, and will again, equally as many should find in it comfort, and a new respect and humility.[14]

PART ONE

THE LAND AND
WHAT HAPPENED TO IT

CHAPTER ONE

The Land beyond Memory: Before 1500

The Fifth Line follows the crest of one of the horseshoe moraines that ring the Ontario Island and back on to the Niagara Escarpment, the white necklace of limestone cliffs that shapes the Great Lakes basin. Here the cliffs are deep in forest, redolent in ferns – more ferns than anywhere else around – and both dangerous and inviting. From the high ground of the Fifth Line, the land falls away to the south and east; sometimes, when the lands below are deep in mist, Mono seems to sit high on the shores of an inland sea, as it once did long ago.[1]

Elba Cave

In the spring of 1990, I got a note from Greg Warchol of the Toronto Caving Group about a cave just discovered by spelunkers along the escarpment in Mono. Writing that "there are no signs of vandalism and minimal signs of traffic," he sent along photos of a cave floor littered with bones. At ground level its entrance was easy to miss, a dark hole about three feet wide, dropping off into thin air. It was a natural trap for the unaware, and a refuge for others.

Greg said they would get me into the cave, and I asked Howard Savage to join us. "Doc" Savage was the retired pediatrician who set up the archaeo-osteology laboratory – the bone lab – at the University of Toronto; he was in his eighties. As we worked our way down, feet first, little brown bats flew up in our faces. We left the ladder at thirty feet and edged down another forty-five or more between sheer walls and wedged blocks, our sputtering headlamps leading us to the cave floor. I mapped the cave, Doc collected bones, and we escaped unharmed, three bags full.

Back in Doc's lab in the old Borden Dairy building, the bones – more than six hundred of them from twenty mammal species, and from frogs, toads, and birds as well – were slowly identified. The most interesting were marten bones, a species cleared out of the area 150 years ago. Dating showed they belonged to an individual that had roamed the escarpment 570 years before present (BP). The bones had just been sitting on the surface. Perhaps another visit was in order.[2]

Jock McAndrews, the renowned paleoecologist at the Royal Ontario Museum (ROM), joined us for the second crawl. Once inside, we carefully dug through the bones and breccia on the cave floor, collecting each stratum so Jock's lab could identify the pollen grains that had rained down over the years. The pollen in the bottom layer turned out to be jack pine and balsam fir, clues to a kind of early pine-fir woodland that no longer occurs in the area.

We collected more bones, of course, and a few weeks later Doc was surprised to find two half femurs from an adult pika, a mammal long gone from eastern North America and now a resident of tree-line talus slopes in the Rocky Mountains. The bones were documented and then sacrificed to an isotrace dating technique that revealed they were 9,780 years old. These pika had been an early arrival, just after the last glaciers (Fig. 2).[3]

We looked deeper into the pika story. Pika bones had been found before, in the 1950s, when a machine operator in a quarry south of Mono, near Rattlesnake Point, had cut into a cave. He bagged the bones and sent them to the ROM, where they sat untouched until paleontologists Rufus Churcher and Roberta Dods inspected them in the 1970s. They were the bones of an extinct species of giant pika and, without dates, were assumed to be ancient, predating the last glacier. Elsewhere in the east, pika bones had also been found in caves from West Virginia to Maryland, but they too had not been dated and were assumed to be ancient. The bones from Mono were large. Were they the giant pika? Their size and age made it clear that they were, according to paleontologists Jim Mead and Fred Grady, who also concluded that giant pika had to be added to the long list of species that perished soon after the last glacier receded.[4]

The surprising find of a new Holocene extinction prompted Jock and a motley crew of us to return to a small lake close to the cave the next winter. Using its thick ice to lever against, we pulled a core of sediments from the lake bottom. The goal was a continuous pollen record right back to the time of deglaciation. We could not quite reach bottom, but we did get back to 10,430 years BP – the same millennium as the pika – so we could infer what the place looked like at the time. It was a thinly treed woodland of spruce, pine, fir, and birch, interrupted by rocky cliffs and talus slopes, perhaps analogous to today's tree-line habitats in the Rockies. This is, of course, an ecosystem drastically different from what is here today – and gone now for 8,000 years, its member species moved on, mostly north, in the wake of the receding ice. What was the landscape like back then? What wildlife was here? What humans?

Between the High Ground and the Inland Seas

When the climate warmed at the end of the last ice age, the southern edges of the ice sheets were awash in meltwater. The water found its way through myriad channels and impoundments, into a shifting puzzle of early great lakes, which drained off in different directions as the weight of the ice was lifted from the Earth's mantle and the land rebounded upward. The waters released were immense, and the Earth's oceans rose by 375 feet. Land was soon revealed above the water and ice, and grew larger and larger as the water drained off. Across thousands of miles, the postglacial landscape looked like the bottom of an old gravel pit or quarry just after spring melt.

The high ground of Mono – part of the Ontario Island – was one of the early places to be free of ice, and the water from Mono and from lands to the north carved out a deep spillway that drained south in volumes sometimes as great as what flows over Niagara Falls. The meltwater sorted and resorted the fresh, nutrient-rich glacial deposits, and added them to the shape-shifting logic of old shores, lake bottoms, and stratified drift.

About 17,000 years BP, these meltwaters drained into a proto-Lake Erie called Lake Maumee, which flowed south through Ohio to the Mississippi, following an ancient lowland corridor from the lower Great Lakes to the centre of the continent. For 2,000 years, this lake was fifty feet or more higher than today's level. Water also flowed to the Mississippi by way of Lake Michigan, south through the Illinois River valley. Then, some time after 14,500 BP, the waters of proto-lakes Erie and Ontario found a new and lower outlet to the east, down the Mohawk River and Lake Champlain valley to the Hudson River and the Atlantic. These lowlands became the corridors through which many species migrated first and fastest after the last ice age and, later, they were also the corridors that linked the Native cultures within and beyond the region. The Great Lakes country was a blank slate, a tabula rasa, of ice and water, and migration and succession, at continental scales, rendering it always as much a crossroads as a destination.

At the same time, a vast precursor to both lakes Huron and Michigan was forming. This lake – Lake Algonquin – drained east past Lake Simcoe across the Carden limestone plain and, from there, down the contact line between the hard-rock highlands and the soft-rock lowlands (between Precambrian and Paleozoic) into Lake Ontario, the Hudson, and the Atlantic. A few centuries later, the St Lawrence valley suddenly cleared of ice and the north Atlantic surged in, creating a huge inland sea – later named after Champlain – over much of eastern Ontario and Quebec, and the Ottawa and Lake Champlain valleys. As the land rose and sea levels fell, this left behind another broad lowland corridor, connecting the Great Lakes to the Gulf of St Lawrence.[5]

By 11,600 BP, the decaying glacier still occupied Lake Superior and points north, and the lakes downstream were at their lowest levels. Lake Huron was between a hundred and three hundred feet lower than present, for two millennia. Lake Erie was a hundred feet lower. As a result, southern Lake Huron and western Lake Erie were high and dry, and Georgian Bay was separated from Lake Huron by a bridge of land between the Bruce peninsula and Manitoulin Island.[6]

Native peoples have origin myths that involve floods and invoke a post-glacial landscape of rising and falling lakes, and shifting outlets. The Bruce-to-Manitoulin land bridge, the subject of Native myth, has now been mapped with underwater sonar. As in the myth, there are cliffs, relict beaches, and water-falls, all now underwater. Echoing even earlier events, other Native myths tell of the Atlantic Ocean rising after the ice left, flooding rich coastal valleys.[7]

The landscape could hardly have been more different, a scene of shifting, drowned, and emerging shores, worked and reworked by water and wind. In total, in the Huron-Erie basin, there was a 600-foot difference in water levels between 16,400 and 12,300 BP; and in the Ontario basin, there was a 350-foot difference in water levels between 15,800 and 13,400 BP. Soon after they were clear of ice, the shores of the Great Lakes had open vistas and plentiful fish and game. Hunters were working the land by 14,000 BP, and almost all the land they and their descendants occupied were the water-worked lands that lay between the high-water and low-water levels of these fluctuating lakes. It was to this part of the landscape that the Paleoindians came. Later on, these were also the lands, with their sorted lighter soils, that could be most easily cleared and farmed. They were, in fact, almost the only part of the landscape that was occupied and settled by Natives. And it is also in this zone that the vast majority of us still live (Fig. 3).[8]

The meltwaters that drained through Mono flowed south along the Niagara

Escarpment, at right angles to the slope of the land because the water could not flow downhill to the east, where the lowlands were still full of ice. So it flowed south instead, over-spilling into successive valleys as it worked its way south. Where the channel nicked the Niagara Escarpment, which had been buried by glacial sediments, it uncovered it and re-deposited the materials downstream in deltas. The escarpment geologist Walter Tovell called those deposits the "great gravel train," in honour of the sand and gravel industry that is its beneficiary. (Privately, he used the term "great gravy train.")

I hiked and drove the spillway with Walter, admiring its muscular effects on the land and visiting its rarities, like Scott's Falls and Lavender Falls, where the escarpment rock layers are all exposed. It was under the Lavender Falls that I first saw the famous Fossil Hill chert, which was mined for the manufacture of stone-age edges and points. Walter retired to Mono about the same time that archaeologist Peter Storck, also of the ROM, was connecting these chert exposures with the Paleoindians and their ancient fishing and hunting. All the Paleoindian sites that Storck studied were in that zone between the high ground and the high-water levels of the early lakes, in open terrain that Jock McAndrews characterized, based on pollen cores, as a "spruce-parkland ... with groves of trees growing in sheltered locations and ... a patchwork of open areas of grasses and sedges in more exposed and drier habitats."

In his *Journey to the Ice Age*, Storck provides a remarkable window on the culture of the Paleoindians. When he began his work there were only fifty early Paleoindian artifacts from Ontario, only a few of them the serious fluted spear points used by big-game hunters. Storck started looking for what might have been ancient game trails that led down to the shores of old Lake Algonquin, sites "overlooking possible fording places where caribou might have crossed narrow bodies of water at the southern ends ... of the lake." Two of his early finds were just north of Alliston on the old Lake Algonquin beaches. Next was the Fisher site, also on an old beach but farther north, overlooking the main Lake Algonquin. By 1978, he had more than tripled the previous archaeological finds of fluted points, unearthing 156 of them as well as another 1,400 other tools. The Fisher site turned out to be a point factory that exported knapped chert products across the region. It was, in Storck's words, "one of the most productive early Paleoindian sites in all of North America."

Archaeologist Andrew Stewart studied these finds and concluded that the Fisher factory site had both primary knapping areas that handled the rough chert nodules, and secondary fluting areas where the final spear points were made. This suggested a more complex manufacture than was first thought.

John Tomenchuk, tool expert at the ROM, also found different patterns on the stone edges that were used to cut meat, bones, or fish, and concluded that the Fisher site was just as important for its inshore fishing as it was for its chert and its access to caribou. Evidence was thin, however, because bones do not persist as well as stone and there were no bones at the Fisher site. From that period, caribou bones had only been found at a few Paleoindian sites in northeast North America – north of Detroit, in the Hudson valley, in southern New Hampshire and Maine, just north of Boston – and not yet north of the lakes.[9]

Storck started a dig in 1979 on a Lake Algonquin beach southeast of Lake Simcoe, at Udora. By 1987, his team had exhumed the largest collection of identified animal bones from any early Paleoindian site in eastern North America. There were caribou, arctic fox, and snowshoe or arctic hare, dating between 11,300 and 10,400 BP. So, finally, here there were Paleoindians, their prey, their tools (points, scrapers, and net sinkers) *with* a date, all together on the shore of old Lake Algonquin. Caribou were the favoured prey, but the Paleoindians' attraction to sites depended as much on their ready access to tool-grade stone and to abundant fish, waterfowl, and plants in lakeshore settings, which sustained them for millennia before anyone farmed in the region.[10]

There were additional resources to the east. Lake Algonquin later flowed down the Ottawa valley into the saltwater Champlain Sea, which was at its highest levels about 13,800 BP. Its shores offered access to north Atlantic species, and fossils have been found of cod and capelin, four seal species, and five species of porpoise and whale. Whale bone and teeth were trafficked as far inland as central Michigan. Just like the freshwater lakes, the shores, deltas, and estuaries of the Champlain Sea attracted the attention of Paleoindians.[11]

We do not know whether or not Paleoindians were few in number, but what we do know is that they were in Great Lakes country before 14,000 years ago, and that they were expert tool-knappers, hunters, fishers, gatherers, and traders. Spruce parkland dominated the scene, and caribou was the game of choice. Their spear points seem right for even larger animals, like the spruce-eating mastodon, but so far only other types of tools have been found in association with mastodon bones in the region, such as along Lake Michigan before 14,000 years ago and east at the Hiscock site in Genesee County, New York. Paleontologist Daniel Fisher has identified nineteen sites where there may be indirect evidence of mastodon butchering and underwater meat storage. So far, there is only circumstantial evidence of mastodon hunting here. It *is* known, however, that the Great Lakes country just after the last glacier was decidedly different from anywhere else on Earth.[12]

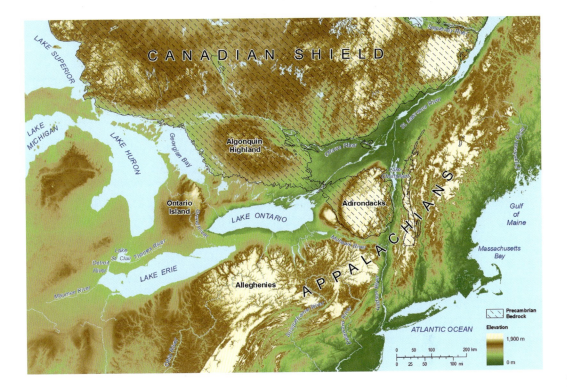

FIGURE 1

The Great Lakes country and its open corridors to the sea and to the western interior:
rich watered lowlands nested among less hospitable uplands.

FIGURE 2

Bones of twenty mammal species from the last nine thousand years were found in Elba
Cave, along the Niagara Escarpment, including the now-extinct eastern pika, a sibling
species of the pika in the Rocky Mountains today. (Sketch, J.L. Riley; image courtesy
A.D. Wilson)

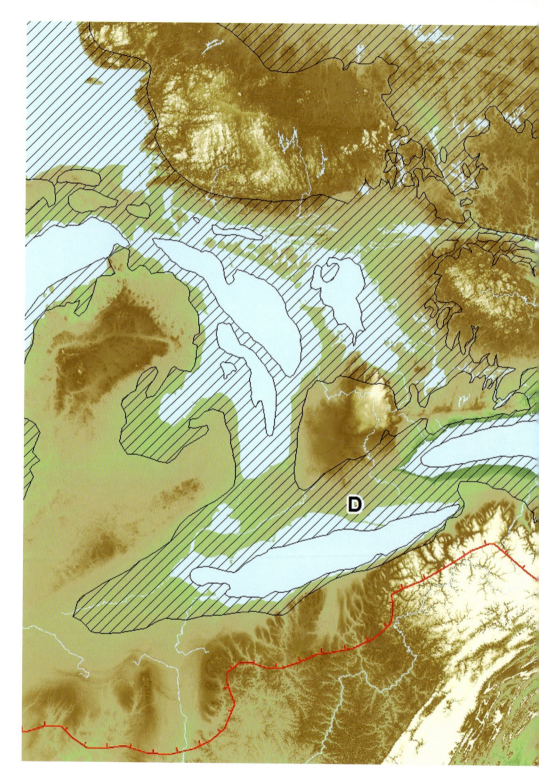

FIGURE 3
The Great Lakes, St Lawrence, and Mohawk-Hudson were, at different times, either overfilled or emptied as the melting glaciers drained away. The land between the

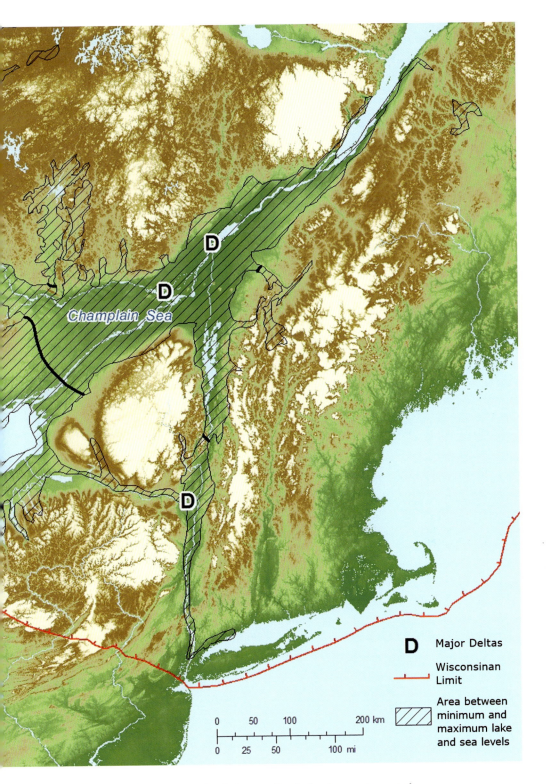

Champlain Sea

D Major Deltas

Wisconsinan
Limit

Area between
minimum and
maximum lake
and sea levels

0   50   100   200 km

0   25   50   100 mi

highest and lowest water levels is cross-hatched, where water sorted
and smoothed the land on which Native farming and fishing was focused.
(Note south limit of the last glacier in red, and some large deltas as D.)

FIGURE 4

Natives manufactured sophisticated goods throughout Great Lakes country, as illustrated by these Late Shield Archaic grave goods (1500 BC) from a richly endowed grave to the south of Lake Nipigon. (Canadian Museum of Civilization, s98–277)

FIGURE 5 [right top]

Some of the native homelands about 1500. The Iroquoian-speaking nations are noted in black; the Algonquian speakers in red. (After Heidenreich 1972, Tanner 1987)

FIGURE 6 [right bottom]

Great Lakes country in the 1500s and 1600s.

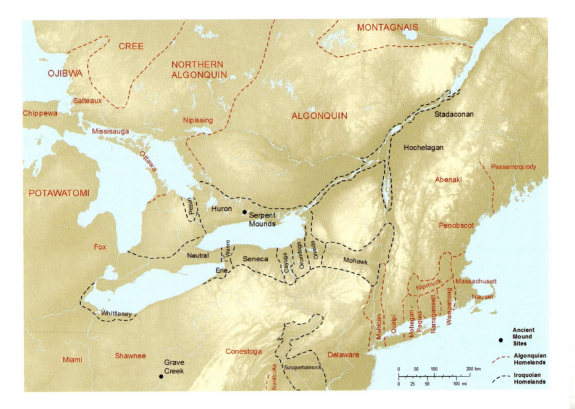

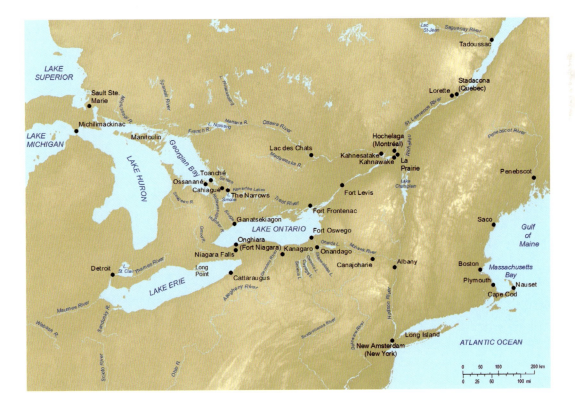

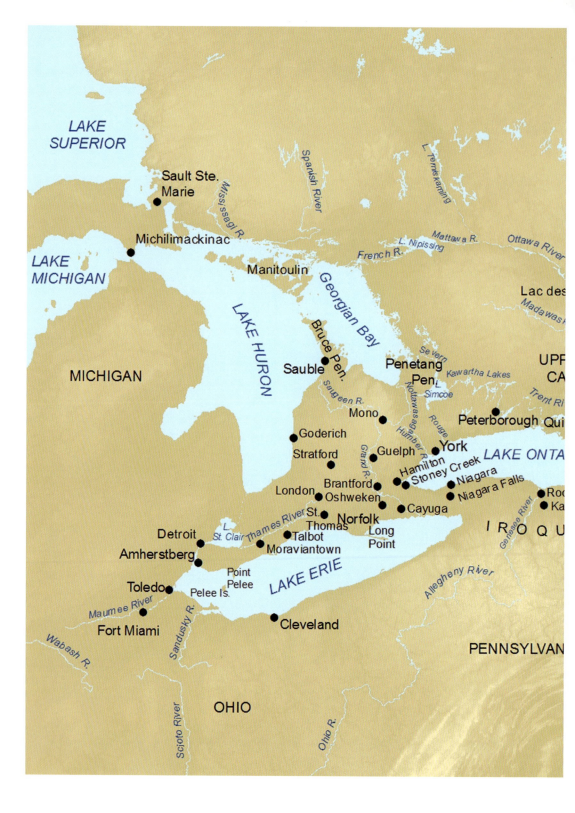

FIGURE 7 Great Lakes country in the 1700s and 1800s.

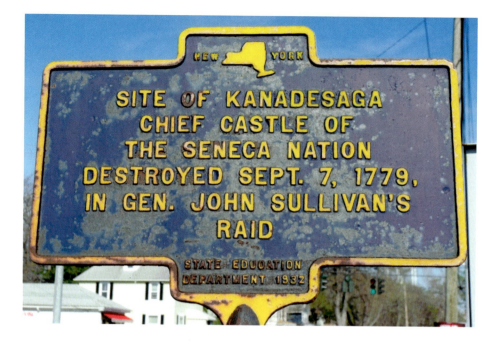

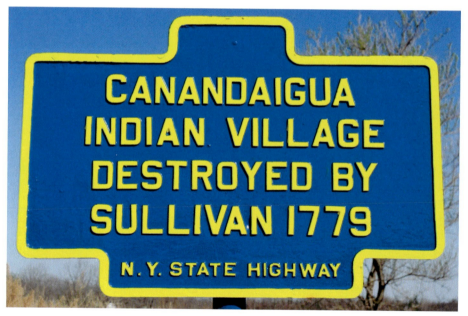

FIGURE 8

New York State highway signs celebrate Sullivan's military campaign to eliminate the Iroquois. (Images, J.L. Riley)

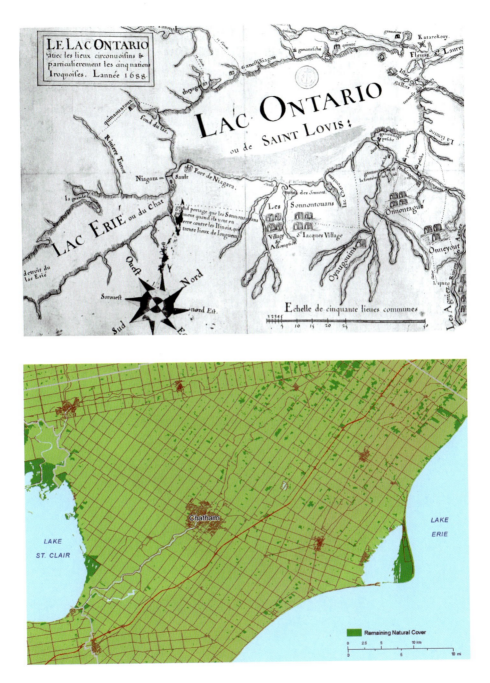

FIGURE 9
Some of the major Native trails in Iroquoia were mapped in 1688 by the Jesuit Pierre
Raffeix (and redrawn by J.B.L. Franquelin in 1688). (Courtesy Service historique de la
défense, Paris; image from Harvard Map Collection)

FIGURE 10
Typical settlement road network in the lower Great Lakes region, Chatham-Kent, Ontario.

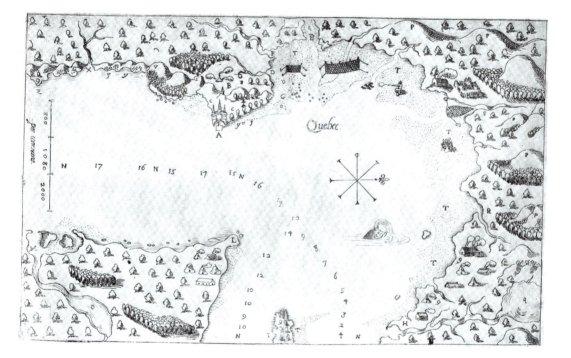

FIGURE 11

Champlain was a trained illustrator who made good use of aerial views, such as this one of the Quebec narrows in 1608, also illustrating two kinds of Native fish weirs. (Champlain Society; Biggar 1925, vol. 2, 24)

FIGURE 12 [right]

Rattlesnakes were abundant in the Niagara Gorge, even at the Cavern of the Winds, the ultimate tourist destination at the base of Horseshoe Falls, about 1840. (Based on drawing by Colonel J.P. Cockburn) (Niagara Falls Public Library)

The Passenger Pigeon. N.Y.
(columba migratoria)
(Pin Kneed)
MALE   FEMALE

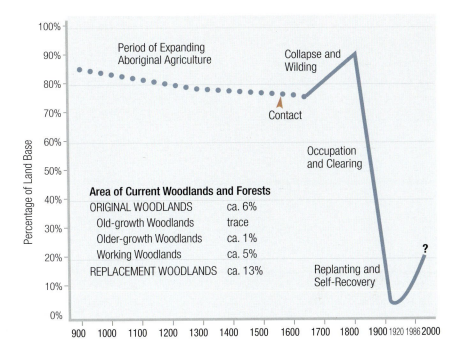

FIGURE 13   [left top]
Passenger pigeons roosting among beech nuts, as drawn in the 1840s by pioneer naturalist William Pope, Norfolk County, Ontario. (William Pope Collection, Toronto Reference Library)

FIGURE 14   [left bottom]
The highlands of Mono about 1900, cleared and converted to European pasture, grazers, and farm crops. (Dufferin County Museum and Archives, P-2964)

FIGURE 15   [above]
The extent of forest has changed dramatically in the past millennium around the lower Great Lakes.

from the Camp on the heights above Queenston

FIGURE 16 [left]
The upland forests of the Great Lakes and St Lawrence were walls of woods separating Native nations centred on the lowlands. Their threatening aspect was illustrated by William Bartlett about 1842. (J.L. Riley's collection)

FIGURE 17 [above]
Elizabeth Simcoe sketched the black oak savanna along the crest of the Niagara Gorge at Queenston, above the lower Niagara River, in 1793. (Archives of Ontario, F47-11-1-0-90)

FIGURE 18

Frances Anne Hopkins sketched one of the many timber rafts on the St Lawrence, about 1860. As Harold Innis put it, "industrialism was poured into moulds of wood," and timber from Canada fuelled the Industrial Revolution in Europe and America. (Royal Ontario Museum, 962.37)

Overkill, Overchill, Over-Ill, and a Comet

Time travellers to the Great Lakes region would have seen a spectacular bestiary at that time, one that had mastodons and mammoths up to ten feet tall at the shoulder; woodland muskox; shrub ox; fugitive deer and stag moose; flat-headed and long-nosed peccary pigs the size of small deer; the short-faced bear, a superb predator twice the size of a modern grizzly; the tapir; the wild horse; giant beaver the size of a bear; the dire wolf; and ground sloths the size of cattle.[13]

The early Paleoindians, or Clovis, saw twenty mammal species disappear. The die-off was fast and widespread. In 1876 the naturalist Alfred Russell Wallace described how the Americas had become, after the die-off, "a zoologically impoverished world, from which the hugest and fiercest and strangest forms disappeared." The largest mammals vanished first and the smaller ones, like the giant pika, a little later. Many birds were also lost, from raptors to passerines.[14]

Other, more widespread species were spared, such as caribou, bear, and muskox. Some of them, like bison, elk, and moose, survived the last glaciation in Alaska and began their increase in numbers southward during the Clovis era, and before the end of the mammoth, horse, and others. Caribou and bison presumably grew in numbers to occupy some of the habitat left vacant by the great die-off. Fossils of bison place them in both southern Ontario and upper New York at this time. Later still, about 11,500 BP, cougar arrived from Central America.[15]

The focus of early naturalists was the charismatic megafauna, the mastodon and mammoth, whose bones still show up with some regularity. In 1768 the Scottish anatomist William Hunter reviewed the fossils from along the Ohio River and concluded that the mastodon had been a carnivore and a direct threat to early man! "As men we cannot but thank heaven that its whole generation is ... extinct." The geologist Charles Lyell scanned the record of extinctions in 1832 and agreed, adding, "We wield the sword of extermination as we advance." Later in life, Lyell would also blame a climate change, and so did others who worked on cave bones in the 1870s.[16]

Did man or climate cause the great die-off? For some time, the debate has tilted toward human "overkill." The geoscientist Paul Martin updated Hunter's case in the 1960s, saying that humans were a "new and thoroughly superior predator, a hunter who preferred killing and persisted in killing animals as long as they were available." Others demurred, saying that "the evidence ...

may never be adequate to unequivocally convict." Martin said there could have been as many as a million Clovis Paleoindians descended from as few as a hundred founding individuals over the course of twenty generations, and that "they could have caused the mass extinctions without ever even reaching their theoretical population maximum." The ecologist Charles Kay added that large numbers of Clovis were not needed to explain the overkill if animal numbers were low and the hunting success of the Clovis was high. Hunting likely revolved around killing by gut wounds, he said. "If you gave me 100 stone-tipped spears, I would guarantee 95 dead mammoths."

Kay postulated a landscape that had many predators and limited prey, even before the Clovis arrived as possible super-predators. This accords with the very few archaeological finds of any massed Clovis hunting. Only a few spear points have ever been found with the bones of animals, and fewer than a fifth of Clovis sites in the entire United States show evidence of any game hunting. All of those that do involve bison or mastodon. In the northeast, there are even fewer sites, and the subject is even more speculative. Some researchers point to the six other extinction events in the last ten million years in North America, long before the arrival of man. Others cite the extinctions perpetrated by the Polynesians when they occupied New Zealand or Easter Island. And so the debate goes, dancing around the question of just how relentless might have been the appetites of the "noble or ignoble savage," as it is parsed by anthropologist Shepard Krech.[17]

Recently, an extraterrestrial explanation has been added, not unlike the explanation for the earlier demise of dinosaurs. A comet may have hit the Laurentian ice sheet 12,900 BP, truncating entire ecosystems and triggering a deep freeze. Geologists Richard Firestone and Peter Schultz argue that the clues for this lie in a "black mat" of sediment that has been found at more than fifty sites stretching from Canada to Mexico. This mat of soot and charcoal is a diagnostic mix of extraterrestrial iridium, nanodiamonds, and other exotics. As Schultz puts it, "the object would have exploded over North America or slammed into it, or both, shattering and melting ice sheets, sparking extreme wildfires, and fueling hurricane-force winds." Dust and debris launched into the atmosphere would have shrouded the Earth, blocked the sun, and caused temperatures to plummet, triggering a mass die-off. The black mat, Firestone and Schultz found, lies just above the last spear points of early Paleoindians and the last bones of the mammoths. Could this be the answer – a major impact and extinction event followed by the immigration of different animals in its wake?[18]

This "overchill" hypothesis, in competition with the idea of "overkill," may or may not stand the test of time, but it does explain the well-documented global cooling at that time, called the Big Freeze or Younger Dryas. Another idea entirely, the "over-ill" hypothesis, is that some novel pathogen wiped out the animals. Or all three phenomena may have been in play. There could have been a kill-off by Paleoindians *and* a global freeze caused by comet impact, *compounded* by new pathogens or by toxic emissions from the comet. Still others, however, maintain that the Big Freeze was the result of shifts in water circulation in the north Atlantic. Whatever the cause, it lasted about a millennium and when the climate warmed, the sun shone on a very different continent.[19]

The Great Greening

After the Big Freeze the ecology of the region changed again, just as dramatically but more slowly. At the height of the last ice age, the trees, plants, and animals of northeast North America had their refuges far to the south. The oaks and hickories were south and west of the Appalachians, and beech held on in the cool loess hills of the southern Mississippi. White pine and hemlock waited out the glacier on the continental shelf off the Carolinas and then spread back from there. Chestnut was one of the last to budge from its refuge on the Gulf coast. They were all veterans of twenty or so successive glacial cycles, moving and removing their ranges each time. Ice ages were the norm, for 80 to 90 per cent of the time, with interglacials – like this one – the brief interludes between them.[20]

We now live with an interglacial flora and fauna that, despite its appearance of stability, has never been static. The postglacial landscape was like a blotter or petri plate that differentially absorbed and advanced different species depending on the ability of their propagules to grow, and the resistance of the land and climate to that movement. The well-watered lowlands around the lakes warmed and greened more quickly than the drier, colder uplands behind them – the Appalachians, Adirondacks, Alleghenies, and Canadian Shield (Fig. 1). The lowlands held the waterways by which fish and other aquatics moved from the Mississippi and elsewhere into the Great Lakes. They were also the routes by which plants and insects moved first and farthest. Among plants, hardy windborne species moved faster than cold-sensitive fruit-bearing ones that relied on animal transport. Birch beat chestnut. At best, the region's flora and fauna had a few millennia of relative equilibrium before European contact, but even then it was a work in progress.[21]

Variability across Great Lakes country is extreme. Travelling south from the raw mixed conifer forests of the Canadian Shield, the earliest French arrivals all remarked on the more lush broadleaf forests and prairies up the St Lawrence and around the lower Great Lakes. To English observers coming from the south, it was just as obvious that the lowlands were richer than the uplands around them. Native peoples had long appreciated the lowlands, and settled and farmed them – the only part of glaciated North America to support an advanced Native agriculture.[22]

We know from the pollen left in lakes and bogs that the vegetation that first took hold after the glacier melted was not forest but, rather, a shore, dune, and plain vegetation of willows, birch, alder, juniper, sedges, and grasses. The arrival of spruce turned the open country into an open spruce parkland between 14,000 and 12,000 years ago, perhaps like some of the terrain near Hudson Bay today. Jack pine, red pine, and balsam fir followed, and white pine arrived about 11,000 years ago. White pine peaked around 8000 BP, and was then followed by increases in oak, beech, hemlock, elm, ash, and maple, as the modern forest took shape. The climate warmed markedly from 8000 to 5500 BP, during a postglacial climatic optimum called the Hypsithermal, when it was about as warm as the industrially warmed climate of today. In that period species spread farther north and some, like red pine and white elm, still hold on in remote northern sites as disjuncts. About 1400 AD, a "Little Ice Age" settled in. This cooling froze in its tracks the first European settlement of North America, by way of Iceland and Greenland, and it reached its coolest between 1645 and 1715. It then warmed slowly until, by about 1850, modern carbon emissions started to bring the climate within the ambit of human influence for the first time.[23]

The Native cultures of the northeast evolved in tandem with these changes. The late Paleoindian and Archaic hunters and gatherers, who harvested in family groups or clans in the period from 11,000 to 3000 BP, continued to hunt caribou but took increasing advantage of more varied fare, such as deer and moose and, as the climate warmed, arrivals like nut trees and fruit shrubs. They continued their reliance on fishing and, as early as 5000 BP, installed permanent fish weirs, such as at the Narrows between lakes Simcoe and Couchiching, and on the Charles River in Boston. By 4000 BP, Native fishers were using weirs, spears, gaffs, hooks, lines, and nets, all of sophisticated manufacture.[24]

Families banded together seasonally when fish were plentiful, such as sturgeon in the spring and whitefish in the fall. Shellfish and wild rice also were taken in season, the latter in such quantities that it supported settlements nearby, such as at Cootes Paradise on Lake Ontario until 800 years ago and on the Fox River near Green Bay until 300 years ago. Families dispersed to hunt in the winter and maintained satellite camps near predictable food sources like the fish weirs and deer runs they constructed, and the pigeon roosts, nut groves, and sugar bushes they frequented.[25]

For the hunt, they chipped stone darts, knives, and scrapers, and polished and grooved stone axes, as well as adzes for working wood. They ground slate lances and knives and carved bone chisels, hooks, needles, combs, and beads. The spear and *atlatl* were the hunting tools of choice, but the bow and arrow was invented in the Midwest around 500 AD and spread far and fast. Copper ware from Lake Superior, the Bay of Fundy, and elsewhere is found at sites from this time on, and Atlantic conch shells begin to show up too (Fig. 4). Trade grew. Formal burials began.[26]

Corn and Culture – The Garden

When the Great Wall of China was begun in 200 BC, central North America was long settled. Nations were raising their own monuments. People were more numerous than later, and their confidence reached its zenith in the middle Mississippi and Ohio valleys, where their ceremonial mounds and geometric earthworks still grace so many terraces and promontories. They left us a tantalizing legacy of artistic renderings in media as diverse as shell, bone, clay, terra cotta, copper, mica, meteoric iron, flint, quartz, obsidian, soapstone, and argillite, as well as pearl jewellery and sophisticated textiles.[27]

Standing at Serpent Mounds near Peterborough, Ontario, one cannot help but muse about the mound builders and the farming culture that enabled them (Fig. 5). Spread across half a continent, mound sites by the hundreds marked a distinct new level of cultural achievement. At Serpent Mounds there are eight mounds in addition to its 200-foot-long namesake mound. Seventy-four burials have been found in the serpent, interred with copper from Lake Superior, silver from northeast Ontario, and shells from the Gulf of Mexico. Built from 70 BC to 300 AD, Serpent Mounds is one of many northern mounds stretching from Rainy River to Lake Huron and the St Lawrence. The Manitou Mounds on Rainy River number seventeen and are up to twenty-five feet tall; they were started about 300 BC and occupied since then into historic times. It is only one hundred and twenty miles from the Manitou Mounds to the upper Mississippi, and trade was active with nations there.[28]

Two hundred miles south of Serpent Mounds is Grave Creek, West Virginia. From the top of the largest burial mound in the Ohio valley, you look out over a rich bottomland set within high valley walls. The mound is 70 feet tall and 300 feet around, and originally had a wide moat and satellite bastions and ridges. It was the most complex site of the Hopewell-Adena culture from 250 to 150 BC, and it took three million baskets of earth to build the main mound. When treasure hunters opened it in 1838 they unearthed tombs with offerings of copper and shell beads. A saloon was built on it in 1860 and, soon after, a state penitentiary was erected right across the street.[29]

The same era brought mastery to the domestication of open-ground crop plants, which was done by annual seed harvest and by replanting year after year, selecting for better plants, larger seeds, and quicker germination – the requisites of a useful crop plant. Farmers domesticated sunflower, purslane, artichoke, chenopod, knotweed, and new varieties of squash, likely all native species of the floodplains they lived in. They were domesticated long before Mesoamerican crops like corn and beans were imported.[30]

Between farming and gathering, and hunting and fishing, it was the latter that generated the most energy for the time invested. However, food from hunting and fishing was perishable, and hence the importance of gathering and storing durable foods. From 4,000 to 1,000 years ago, Native land care opened up the forest, dried the ground, and focused on mast and fruit – acorns, walnuts, butternuts, chestnuts, beechnuts, hickory and hazel nuts, and other fruits and berries. Together, the open terrain, crop fields, and mast and fruit attracted white-tailed deer, turkey, raccoon, squirrels, and passenger pigeon, which the Natives hunted. In this system, humans were the key, taking both the forage and the forager. It had all the hallmarks of a robust ecological strategy, and it endured for millennia.[31]

The fields, meadows, wildlife, and woodlands were an interconnected production system, a low-energy-input system that was adopted by those living near the Great Lakes by about 300 BC, when Hopewell trade goods also began to appear north of the lakes. It was a time of sophistication and plenty, based on farming, hunting and fishing, and trade and ceremony, the latter evidenced by the pearl blankets, sculptures, and pottery that people interred in their earthworks.[32]

The epicentre of that Mississippian culture was Cahokia, located across the river from modern St Louis. Cahokia was the largest city north of Mexico, with more than 120 mounds. The central mound, at 100 feet tall, is the largest earth monument in the Americas, twenty-two million cubic feet of earth that were moved by hand, to stand as testament to the urban elite that governed it. As many as 20,000 to 30,000 people lived there in plastered and painted polewood homes with thatched roofs, and there were even more living nearby, farming, gathering, and manufacturing in support of the city. Woodhenges served as its astronomical calendars, and its plazas were planned around formal buildings and around manicured sports fields where the game of *chunkey* was pursued with passion. Cahokia was in its apogee from 1050 to 1300 AD, after which it dispersed and declined, its floodplain fields and woodlands exhausted. However, the culture of farming and of towns, mounds, and palisades had spread across North America's heartland. Standing on top of Monks Mound at Cahokia leaves one in little doubt that the proto-Iroquoians who settled the Great Lakes and St Lawrence had roots in the ancient corn culture of the Mississippi.[33]

Tobacco arrived early in Great Lakes country, about 500 BC, but farming matured only a thousand years later, as cultivars of corn were gradually selected for colder, northern sites. A form of eight-row corn was grown as far north as the Detroit area and the Grand River in southern Ontario by 500 AD. Corn was the mainstay of farming by 1000 AD, and was later acclimatized as far afield as northern Lake Huron and the Atlantic seaboard. A masterpiece of Native culture, corn was bred in southern Mexico more than six thousand years ago; biologist Nina Federoff at Pennsylvania State University has called it "arguably man's first, and perhaps his greatest, feat of biological manipulation."[34]

By 1100 AD, the holy trinity of corn, beans, and squash – the three sisters – had arrived south of Lake Ontario, and by 1300 AD the trio were complemented with sunflower for oil and tobacco for smoking. Farm clearings grew and so too did soil erosion, as evidenced by a decline in bottomland elm pollen and by the deposition of charcoal layers in bottomland sediments. North of the lakes, corn, sunflower, tobacco, longhouses, and villages were common by that date, and beans and squash arrived between 1300 and 1430 AD, coincident with a tripling in population, as the new crops began to provide the balanced nutrition needed for a year-round diet based on farming. For example, a diet of corn alone is deficient in the requisite animo acids lysine and tryptophane, which are abundant in beans and squash. Grown together, some of the crops were tall, like corn, while others climbed on corn, like squash and some beans. Some of the crops were net users of soil nitrogen, and others were net fixers of nitrogen. Squashes also helped shade out weeds and keep soils cool, and – given that some herbivores are inhibited by the compound cucurbitacin that they produce – may even have lent fields some immunity from foraging.[35]

Modern agriculture does not focus on the farming of multiple, complementary crops in the same fields, set among productive open woodlands. But Central America has its *milpa*, where corn fields might have a dozen crops growing together – beans with corn, squash climbing on sunflowers, and ground crops like amaranth with shrubs like avocado. The term *balanoculture* is used for a culture of oak and acorn flour, and in Spain there is the *dehesa*, the oak savannas from which cork, acorns, tanbark, and charcoal are taken, while the grassland beneath supports cattle or, when acorns are plentiful, pigs. There were also acorn cultures in California, and there still are the *jhum* land rotations of the Indo-Burmese mountains, with long cycles of croplands, villages, managed woodlands, and hunted wildlands. Worldwide, and in the New World, this was once the norm. "Polyculture" is a word used to distinguish it from its antithesis, monoculture, and conversational English comes closest with words like "gardening" and "horticulture."[36]

In 1669 the Sulpician Bréhant de Galinée described a Seneca village set in the midst of fields five miles in circumference. In 1799 Major John Burrowes described Seneca fields of "about 100 acres, [of] beans, cucumbers, simblens [squash], watermelons, and pumpkins in such quantities [as] would be almost incredible to a civilized people." Two days later, he saw another 150 acres: "Some corn stalks measured eighteen feet and a cob one foot and a half long. Beans, cucumbers, watermelons, muskmelons, cimblens are in great plenty." This was an advanced horticulture.[37]

Arthur Parker knew as much as anyone about Native farming in his day. Parker was born in 1881 on the Cattaraugus Seneca reserve on Lake Erie. He was the first archaeologist at the New York State Museum, and in 1910 he interviewed Native elders north and south of the lakes, itemizing their many cultivars of corn, of different colours and sweetnesses, grouped within broad classes of soft corn, flint corn, sweet corn, and pod corn. He recorded fourteen kinds of beans, the ancestral type being the "cornstalk bean," and five kinds of squash, several melons, and all manner of fruit, root, berry, nut, and sap plant. Crop plants were so important that Parker noted how a goal of some Iroquois raids, "according to many of the old Indians, was to get new vegetables."[38]

The most thorough compilation of Aboriginal uses of plants in the region has been done by Charlotte Erichsen-Brown, who describes a "sophisticated agriculture." Hardly a native plant went untested or unknown as either a food, fibre, or medicine. This demanded a true knowledge of specifics, on which success depended, and the list of useful species was longer than those it excluded: onions, serviceberries, hog-peanut, groundnut, milkweed, New Jersey tea, bergamot, mayapple, sumac, groundcherry, gooseberries, currants, raspberries, arrowhead, bulrush, cattail, blueberries, nannyberry, and so on. Indeed, the distinction between the wild and the cultivated was one of degree only, and it is likely that even wild plants like sweet flag, wild plum, Canada onion, wild rice, walnut, and pawpaw were deliberately selected for superior types.[39]

Each plant had its story. Sassafras created such a stir when it arrived in Europe that traders crossed the Atlantic just to harvest it. Early Virginia exported as much sassafras as tobacco. In 1716 the Jesuit Joseph-François Lafitau "discovered" ginseng at Kahnawake, on the St Lawrence, and began ginseng's long overharvest for the China trade. It was a Mohawk woman who showed Lafitau the ginseng, because plants were the particular domain of women. When the Stadaconans saved the explorer Jacques Cartier and his men from scurvy in 1536, by giving them leaves from the *annedda* tree, it was two women who went to gather it. Species by species, their special uses were known. The Menominee used to say, "Powerful are the things we use," about how the things we know about nature define us.[40]

Stone Age Land Stewardship

When I was young there was a stream behind our home north of Toronto, and the local priest began an archaeological dig in the late 1950s on the same south-facing slope as our place. Fossil post holes were all that remained of the native longhouses, which were located about the same distance above the stream as our house. I was impressed. The priest let me keep a beautiful crenulated potsherd that was later Woodland or early Huron, from some time before 1500 AD. A school was later built on the site, and a baseball diamond.[41]

By 1350 AD, the Iroquoians of the lower Great Lakes were in full occupation. There followed, after 1400 AD, a gradual consolidation of peoples into the Wendat (Huron), Petun (Tobacco), Attawandaron (Neutral), and St Lawrence nations north of the lakes. Earlier, for example, there had been widespread Huron settlements north of Lake Ontario from the Niagara Escarpment in the west to the Bay of Quinte, and north to Georgian Bay and the Trent River system. By the historic period, the Huron were condensed into the area north and west of Lake Simcoe. Their former hunting areas and fishing and gathering camps were still in regular use, but their earlier settlements were vacated (Fig. 5).[42]

In southwest Ontario, the Native settlements toward the west end of Lake Erie and north to the Thames regrouped into forty or so Neutral towns east of the Grand River and on the Niagara peninsula. The Neutral were a federation of nations, and they remained in loose association with Iroquoians who still resided in the southwest, for example, the Whittlesey in villages near Toledo and Cleveland. Originally, the Iroquoians along the St Lawrence River were established from eastern Lake Ontario downriver to the narrows at Quebec, and south up the Richelieu River to Lake Champlain. However, by the time of European contact, they too had gathered into two large fortified centres, with a few dozen satellite camps. South of the lakes, the Iroquois Five Nations also consolidated away from Lake Ontario on the till plains and valleys of the Finger Lakes and the Genesee and Mohawk rivers, where salmon, eel, and sturgeon were plentiful and where there were good growing conditions and ready access to chert deposits and hunting grounds.[43]

The denser settlement clusters meant greater distances between them and, whether it was the cause or the effect, factionalism grew apace, reinforcing the differences. Defence became more important and palisades were built around larger townsites that were increasingly located on higher ground with access to water. In these nation clusters, individuals were highly valued, as were children. Mothers took long breaks between children and prolonged their breastfeeding. A family of three children spaced well apart was the ideal, which we now associate with high levels of socialization and affluence. Food was not the sole constraint and the accepted style of warfare likely minimized fatalities. At the same time, though, human sacrifice was practised, and on the increase, as the remains in townsites show, peaking after 1500 AD.[44]

Farming was an expert activity focused on carefully chosen lands, which also influenced the selection of townsites. Clearing trees with stone axes or by girdling or fire, and working the soil with wooden tools, were major investments of energy, so loose, well-drained soils with sparse trees were preferred. Sandy loams were the preference of Huron farmers, and were also the choice of the Neutral and of the Iroquoians in eastern Ontario. In Iroquoia, the well-drained soils grew woodlands of oak, beech, butternut, and, southward, hickory, walnut, and chestnut. South of Lake Erie in Pennsylvania, Native settlements were centred on oak, hickory, and chestnut woodlands and clearings, themselves perpetuated by Native land practices.[45]

A climatic warming took place as this farming expanded from 900 to 1400 AD. Called the Medieval Warming, it reinforced the shift in vegetation toward open woods and prairies. Natural succession is slow and takes generations to equilibrate; and during this period, succession was also driven by Native practices - clearing, firing, and coppicing - that favoured an open terrain and desirable mast trees, right through to the time of European contact, when oaks were quantitatively the most important trees in the eastern broadleaf forest.[46]

It has been calculated that just over 5 per cent of Ontario south of the Canadian Shield was directly converted by Native settlement and farming, an area about the same extent as all the sandy uplands near water that were arable using Native methods. The Natives, however, likely extended those impacts to three or four times that area of land, primarily through firing the land to keep it clear and improve wildlife habitat, and by regular coppicing of trees to ensure a steady supply of small stems for firewood and pole-wood. This was an occupied landscape.[47]

To complete this circle, maintaining non-forest habitat increased the favoured prey of hunters, which included browsers and mast feeders like white-tailed deer and elk; omnivores like black bear; mast and ground feeders like turkey, ruffed grouse, passenger pigeon, and geese; and grazers like rodents and lagomorphs, and bison south of the lakes. The wildlife helped keep the land open and, along with fish, were avidly taken, with only a few competing predators like wolf and lynx. As a result, the hunting, fishing, and farming were excellent in Great Lakes country, and significant food reserves were expertly stored in pots, baskets, and pits against future needs. At the time of European contact there was a durable ecological balance between humans and landscape. This is not to be confused, however, with an entirely peaceful co-existence.[48]

The Native Estate

At the time of contact, Great Lakes country was home to multiple nations belonging to two great lineages, the Algonquian speakers to the north, east, and west, and the Iroquoian speakers in the south. The Algonquians included the dispersed peoples of the Canadian Shield and the northern Appalachians, as well as the settled nations of the Midwest and Atlantic seaboard. They almost entirely surrounded the Iroquoians of the Great Lakes, St Lawrence, and Susquehanna (Fig. 5).

Civility within nations was coordinated by civil headmen, guided by custom, consensus, and clan mothers, but each clan also had its war lord. While external conflicts were common, the goal was not to eliminate an enemy or burn down its towns. Archaeologist James Tuck describes the period 1000 to 1500 AD as "devoid of drastic population shifts, conquests and ... annihilation." Raids and counter-raids were for honour and pride, based on personal enmity and revenge, and for the abduction, enslavement, and adoption of women and children – to replace lost ones and acquire goods and crops. In retrospect, the differences between the lineages and nations seem minor, but they were never reconciled in favour of their broader best interests, and were exploited to their disadvantage.[49]

The Algonquians in the north – the Algonquin (Nipissing and others), Cree, and Montagnais – and the northeast – the Webanaki (Micmac, Passamoquoddy, Abenaki, and Penobscot) – were hunters, fishers, and gatherers renowned for their ability to live off the land. Their dispersed family groups also gathered seasonally for harvest and trade. South along the Atlantic were the Massachusett, Mahican, Nipmuck, Narragansett, Quiripi, and Mohegan-Pequot. Along with those in the west – the Potawatomi and Ojibwa (Chippewa, Missisauga, and Saulteaux) – these peoples lived in towns and villages and were expert farmers as well as hunters, fishers, and gatherers. Isaack de Rasieres, the secretary of the Dutch colony of Manhattan, described the nations along the Atlantic in 1627: "Their government is democratic. They have a Chief Headman who they choose by election."[50]

Similarly, the Iroquoians had their own nations, kinship clans, and sister languages. The Iroquois, or Five Nations, occupied the Mohawk valley, Finger Lakes, and Niagara frontier (Iroquoia), and were a confederacy, from east to west, of the Mohawk, Oneida, Onondaga, Cayuga, and Seneca. West of Iroquoia were the Wenro, Erie, and Whittlesey, and to the south the Susquehannock and Tuscarora. North of the lakes were the St Lawrence Iroquoians and, on the Ontario peninsula, the Huron and Neutral confederacies and the Petun. The highlands around and between them were well known to them and were defended as their proprietary hunting and fishing territories as well as strategic buffers.

The Iroquoian nations relied on their polycultures of multiple crops to complement their hunting, fishing, and gathering. This required an accepted division of labour. Men cleared the land, hunted and fished, built houses and palisades, and traded and warred. They made tools and weapons, and constructed canoes, those in the north of birch bark and those in the south of heavier barks like elm and chestnut. Women planted, tended, harvested, and stored crops; processed foods, fibres, roots, and medicines; and clothed and nurtured their families. Nets were a shared labour, the women gathering nettles and hemp stems to roll and twist into cord on their thighs, the men weaving nets from it, and the women processing and storing the men's catch of fish. Animal husbandry focused on dogs, bear cubs, ducks, and geese, all raised for food. Some fields were shared; others were individually posted with clan symbols or personal glyphs. Farming was a successful investment of energy, even during the coolest part of the Little Ice Age between 1600 and 1730. At times, corn accounted for half the carbon intake of the Huron but it was often less, because of droughts or crop failures two or three times each decade. Overall, an ancient circle of relations was respected: a cycle of first using and then drying fish and corn for late-winter staples, followed by fall and winter hunting that slowly declined as winter wore on, when dried foods became the mainstays until the first welcome spring runs of fish.[51]

The domain of the Iroquoians was largely coincident with the range of eel in the interior of North America. The only fish honoured as a clan totem of the Iroquois, the eel matured in the Lake Ontario basin and in the St Lawrence and Ottawa rivers before migrating to the mid-Atlantic to spawn. Queen's University ecologist John Casselman says that, at the time of contact, half of the fish biomass was eel, a species with six times the caloric value of any other. They numbered as many as twenty-five to fifty million in Lake Ontario in 1600, and were taken with spear, net, weir, and hook – and even through the ice where they balled up together to overwinter in the mud.[52]

Stake and stone weirs, and stream funnel-channels, were built into rivers, lakes, and estuaries, and were near-industrial modifications that automated the fish harvest. With these, the Natives became, in essence, filter feeders themselves. For example, there were "stone dams" on the Delaware River for harvesting shad, and Georgia archaeologist Thomas Neumann describes how they became fixed over time. "Many of the river channel islands along the Atlantic seaboard represent silted-in, rock-based fish weirs." In the west, in 1670, the Jesuit Jacques Marquette saw a massive fish weir on the Fox River near Green Bay, made "by driving down large stakes in two brasses of water [eleven feet], so there is a kind of bridge ... for the fisherman who, with the help of a small weir, easily catch sturgeon and every other kind of fish." These were expert interventions, parallel to the Natives' use of snares, drives, and fire in their management of wildlife and habitat.[53]

Native towns were clusters of longhouses, which required much bark and small-caliper poles and ties. The Jesuit Jean de Brébeuf described Huron longhouses as "bowers ... covered with cedar bark [and] large pieces of ash, elm, fir or spruce ... some two brasses in length [eleven feet], others of twenty, of thirty, of forty [220 feet]." Mohawk longhouses in the 1640s were described by one of their first guests, Adriaen Van der Donck, as "never more than twenty feet wide" and made of "hickory saplings" curved over and covered with "the bark of ash, chestnut and other trees ... In their castles [palisaded towns], they frequently have twenty or thirty houses ... Some of them ... [are] a hundred and eighty yards long ... They crowd an astonishing number of persons [in them] ... Towns ... usually have woodland on the one side and corn lands on the other sides." When the Jesuit Joseph Chaumont visited Onondaga in 1655, he found the streets "carefully cleaned" and the town surrounded by multiple palisades of upright trees reinforced with bark and withes, and with raised fighting platforms. Such villages were prone to fire. At Onondaga, a longhouse caught fire and "in less than two hours, more than twenty of them were reduced to ashes."[54]

In Huronia, north of today's Toronto, towns were occupied on a cycle of ten to twenty years or so of declining soil fertility and increasing distance to wood, which was needed daily. Others lasted longer, an average of twenty-five years for Onondaga townsites. In addition to water access, defensibility, and suitable soils, sites were also chosen for access to firewood and pole-wood. Using stone tools, the men girdled, burned, and felled trees to make fields, and cut and hauled wood and bark. A town was moved, said the Jesuit Jacques de Lamberville in Onondaga in 1682, only "to have firewood in convenient proximity, and to secure fields more fertile ... Carts are not used here ... [and] the labor ... is consequently harder ... [They] render reciprocal aid to one another ... [or] are freed from that obligation by giving food to those whom they have employed."[55]

At the time of contact, the population of Iroquoian-speaking peoples was small but substantial. In the east were the Stadaconans, with at least seven villages, and Hochelagans, with one large town. Both had a large number of fishing camps on the St Lawrence, and a combined population of at least 5,000.[56] In 1615 the Huron were estimated at more than 30,000 individuals in about thirty towns, an estimate still accepted today.[57] The Petun to the west numbered between 10,000 and 15,000.[58] The largest Iroquoian nation was the Neutral in the Niagara area, with over 30,000 in forty or more settlements. The first visitor to the Neutral, the Recollet Joseph de la Roche d'Aillon in 1626, described their territory as more developed than Huronia, with major trade in chert, corn, and tobacco. In all, the northern Iroquoians numbered as many as 80,000 individuals.[59]

To the south were the nations along Lake Erie and the Five Nations south of Lake Ontario (Fig. 5). Together these Iroquois numbered at least 20,000 to 25,000 in 1600.[60] South of them were the Susquehannock, and farther south the Tuscarora and Cherokee, likely beyond the range of regular trade. In 1636 the Jesuit Brébeuf estimated the total Iroquoian-speaking peoples at "more than three hundred thousand," but a figure of 100,000 or so Iroquoians in Great Lakes country is generally accepted today. Add to this an even less knowable number of Algonquians, at a minimum 30,000, which included the thousands north of the St Lawrence, at least 4,000 Potawatomi, and 10,000 Ojibwa, "more than three thousand" at Green Bay alone, as counted by the Jesuits in 1672.[61]

By 1600, the original population of Natives was almost certainly reduced by European diseases that had spread inland from the Atlantic coast before any Great Lakes Natives saw a European. Eastern North America was part of a single "epidemic region," and an entire litany of European contagions arrived before 1600, travelling fast and far before any face-to-face contact. This may help explain why the Huron consolidated their settlements on the Penetang peninsula in the 1500s, and why the Seneca did the same, gathering in four towns in the 1500s. No one knows.[62]

Whether diminished or not, in 1600 there were many thousands of land-clearing farmers, hunters, fishers, gatherers, artisans, traders, healers, leaders, and warriors pursuing culturally distinctive livelihoods throughout Great Lakes country, the world's largest freshwater transportation network. Nations traded easily throughout the region, and, together, they controlled access to central North America and had the advantage, when the newcomers arrived, of knowing how to farm, hunt, fish, travel, and war on their own home ground.[63]

The advantage was lost soon enough. The newcomers learned the Native languages and used them to advance their own interests. In exchange, the Natives mentored both the English and the French, canoed them across the continent, and built the east-west foundations of Canada and the United States. They introduced the warm-weather newcomers to winter and to the necessities of winter survival, such as snowshoes and toboggans. They showed them how to grow their crops, how to hunt and fish, how to make sugar from trees, and how to gain the furs they so single-mindedly wanted.

The Mohawk and the Huron

All the Iroquoian and Algonquian nations fell victim to the wars of foreign empires. From the northeast came the French, interested in fur, fish, settlement, and souls for Catholicism; and from the southeast, the Dutch, Swedes, and English, whose interests were fur, fish, and settlement – and freedom from Catholicism. At first, their similarities outweighed any differences.

They all brought metal, guns, trade goods, disease, and a radical new interest in land. In Great Lakes country, the Mohawk and the Huron stand out as particularly heroic and tragic. They shared an ancestral lineage but their minor differences were amplified by their alliances, the Huron with the French and the Mohawk with the Dutch and English. In the wars that followed, one of them lost and one of them won, but it made no difference in the end. Both lost their homelands, which then witnessed a sea change in ecology.

The Mohawk were poised between two ecologies, and traded between them: the southern forests and tidal waters of the Atlantic seaboard and the northern forests and fresh waters of the Great Lakes and St Lawrence. The Huron lived between two other ecologies: the Canadian Shield, rich in fish and wildlife, and a warm off-Shield terrain of good soils, excellent fishing, and fine hunting. These crossroad geographies conferred strategic importance on both nations.

The Mohawk country was richly suited to farming, fishing, and hunting, and was a major gateway between the Great Lakes and the Atlantic. From sea level on the Hudson, the Mohawk controlled the Mohawk valley, the upper Hudson, and the Lake Champlain corridor to the St Lawrence. They, and the Oneida, Onondaga, Cayuga, and Seneca, were bound in a confederacy and, under their Great Law of Peace, the *Haudenosaunee*, as they called themselves, reached consensus decisions based on formal debate in common council. Collectively, they could negotiate peace but decisions on war and internal affairs were taken by individual nations. Special measures could be put to the people as a whole but routine decisions were taken by headmen chosen by clan mothers. The Mohawk and Oneida had nine headmen each; the Onondaga, fourteen; the Cayuga, ten; and the Seneca, numerically the largest nation, eight.[64]

The Onondaga hosted the Five Nation council and maintained its *wampum* belts. Wampum were shell beads that were carved and woven into mnemonic devices to record council decisions. Belts of them were exchanged to codify treaties and as currency. Cadwallader Colden, an early settler and later lieutenant governor of New York, wrote in 1727: "*Wampum* is the current money … [of] the Indians: it is two sorts, white and purple; the [beads] … are wove as broad as one's hand, and about two feet long: these they call belts, and give and receive at their treaties as the seal of friendship." Wampum was manufactured on the coast and traded into the interior by the Mohawk and Susquehannock. Newcomers were quick to flood the trade with porcelain copies.[65]

The Mohawks produced a surplus of food for trade. To their first guest, Henry Hudson in 1609, they offered corn, squash, tobacco – and beads. In the 1640s Adriaen Van der Donck witnessed their trade in corn and the valley's abundant nuts, berries and fruit, which were the product of annual tending and burning. In 1643 the Jesuit Isaac Jogues commented how the Dutch found the land "quite suitable for use, cleared in former times by the *sauvages*, who tilled their fields there."[66]

At the time of contact, the Mohawk had three large fortified "castles." The Oneida had one; the Onondaga, two; the Cayuga, three; and the Seneca, four. The enlarged size of these new towns meant that they were more difficult to sustain and more (not less) vulnerable to threats like fire and disease. Fields had to be larger; those around the four Seneca villages, for instance, which were ordered burnt by the governor of New France, Jacques-René de Brisay de Denonville, in 1687, totalled between eight and sixteen square miles.[67]

To the north, on the Penetang peninsula of Georgian Bay, were the Huron. Until their contact with the French, the Huron knew of no culture materially superior to their own. They too were a confederacy of five peoples, who met annually to renew their consensus. They lived in thirty towns and villages, of which six were fortified, each of them more than twenty-five acres and with forty or so longhouses and populations of 2,000 or more. Each settlement was at the hub of its own fields, and at least 23,300 acres were in annual crop production. The largest town was Cahiagué, with 200 longhouses and a population of more than 3,000. It was "the fish spearing place," reliant on the ancient wooden fish weir at the Narrows on Lake Simcoe, which was itself as large a construction effort as a town and, by then, in continuous use for four millennia. The Huron fished as well for spawning whitefish among the islands of Georgian Bay and this key protein was dried, smoked, and stored in bark containers. In winter, they fished with nets through the ice.[68]

The Huron knapped their own tools and weapons, and were skilled potters, carvers, weavers, and skinners who made their own containers, clothing, smoking pipes, combs, awls, needles, and ornaments. Every species had its uses. There were the medicinals – as basic as emetics, diuretics, tonics, antiseptics, antiscorbutics – and various fibres to make different cords, woven into mats, nets, and baskets. Clothes were sewn from animal skins. True straight arrows fledged with feathers, and bows, shields, canoes, and snowshoes, were made to be both useful and beautiful.

The Huron traded their surpluses of food and goods, and their pottery has shown up in archaeological digs as far away as Rainy River, Lake Abitibi, and Lac Saint-Jean. In exchange, they got tobacco and chert from the Petun, tobacco and animal skins from the Neutral, and skins, dried fish, and meat from the Algonquians to the north. They traded for bison robes and copper from the west, and for marine shells and wampum from the southeast.[69]

Huronia was a hard-worked landscape. The annual crop cycle was just one part of a longer rotation of land clearance and pole-wood and fuel-wood harvest that was pursued more widely. Throughout the cleared uplands there were well-used lakes and streams and at least two hundred miles of trails that linked the towns and villages. Even longer trails led to their hunting grounds and to other nations, north along Georgian Bay, east along the Trent River, south from Lake Simcoe to Lake Ontario, and southwest to the Petun and Neutral along the Nottawasaga and Grand rivers.

Hunting, driving, and snaring game was training for manhood and practice for raids. Youth were kept busy learning to shoot and net birds, train dogs to track bears, raise geese, bears, and dogs for food, and pursue their vision quests. Life was hard but good. Samuel de Champlain damned it with faint praise: "Life is wretched by comparison with ours but [they] believe that none more excellent can be found." The modern Huron traditionalist Georges Sioui expresses it as a "circle of relationship," an exemplary ecology that linked the people to their land. Early on, Iroquoian society as a whole would be widely scrutinized because it adhered to customs that respected the individual, family, clan, and nation. In 1648 the Jesuit Paul Le Jeune wrote of their "goodness" and learning, and the Jesuit Joseph-Francois Lafitau, who lived among the Huron and Iroquois, wrote in 1718 of their "zeal for the public welfare ... There is a mutual adaptation of headmen and members of society, and a hierarchy such as could be desired in the best regulated state."[70]

It has been argued that this social contract, which seemed to hint at both individual rights and collective consensus, helped turn American heads toward independence. Benjamin Franklin was certainly familiar with the Five Nations. The Boston tea-partiers dressed as Mohawk to identify themselves as Americans. Colden began the elegies in 1727. "Each of these nations is an absolute republick ... governed ... by its own *sachems* or old men. The authority of these rulers is gain'd by, and consists wholly in the opinion the rest of the nation have of their wisdom and integrity." However, history proves, such academic admiration did not confer on the Natives any special place in the hearts of the newcomers. As historian Richard White says about American origin myths, Americans invented the Indian as they wanted the Indian to be, and dealt with them accordingly. It was only *after* their conquest that a more romantic view of them arose.[71]

The early anthropologist Lewis Henry Morgan was born in Iroquoia and acted as an attorney on behalf of Seneca land claims. His 1851 book on the Iroquois began the comparisons of Iroquois governance with that of ancient Greece and Rome. His retrospective praise of the "noble savage," which seemed to rest so easily in the American breast alongside its racism, was not echoed by early Canadian students of Native culture. In the 1800s anthropologists Daniel Wilson in Toronto, John W. Dawson in Montreal, and Horatio Hale in Clinton, Ontario, all rejected such expressions of cultural difference in favour of a broader view of "an undivided humanity" – of different "groups of human beings facing and solving problems in a distinctive and effective manner," as the anthropologist Bruce Trigger put it.[72]

This more prosaic appreciation has strengthened over time. Trigger wrote again in 1987: "The material culture of the northern Iroquoians was not impressive … Instead, the genius of Iroquoian culture is to be found in their psychological finesse, and the attention they lavished on social relations generally. A fundamental premise of Iroquoian life was a respect for individual dignity and a sense of self-reliance." This was governance by small numbers of unelected men and women but, for all that, it had the smell of liberty about it for newcomers, who had not yet had the faintest whiff of it from elsewhere. Native culture was – relatively speaking – egalitarian, and respectful of individuals, male and female. Their governance may have been rough but at least it was their own, not an ocean away in Europe, "a place where discord reigned and all the miseries of anarchy had long prevailed," in the words of one pillar of Albany society in the 1750s.[73]

The Native lifestyle attracted many. French youth became *coureurs de bois* living and trading far inland, and creating the Métis of North America. In 1670 these *coureurs* numbered 800, out of a total population of 9,700 in New France, about one in every family. Colden mused on the subject in 1727 about how difficult it was for the English "to persuade the people that had been taken prisoners … to leave the Indian manner of living." On the other hand, the naturalist Pehr Kalm noted in 1749 that the Natives "taken prisoners in the war always endeavoured to return to their own people again … though they enjoyed all the privileges … possessed by Europeans in America."

The appeal of the Native life waned soon enough, as the quality of that life declined. By then, too, life on the frontier may have been sufficiently libertarian that the twin urges for independence and profit could be as easily sated there as by going Native. Before long, the near-universal goal of newcomers would be land ownership, and the story of the Great Lakes country after 1500 is fundamentally the story of contact, disease, and extirpation, ushering in an era of protracted warfare over the land and massive ecological changes as a consequence.[74]

CHAPTER TWO

Stone Age Meets Iron – and Smallpox: The 1500s and 1600s

Mapmakers and *géographes* were among the intellectual elite of Europe in the 1500s and 1600s, and they served competitive, powerful patrons. Their maps were of immense value, and their interrogations of travellers yielded secrets that were coveted and traded in the same manner as modern military intelligence. Maps had evolved by slow increments from early Greek times, and then they matured overnight into the modern maps of Mercator, Champlain, and others, and framed the globe in a way that helped ignite European imperialism.[1]

The apparent competitiveness of nations masked an effort that was, in fact, multinational. Christopher Columbus was a Genoan sailing for Spain who by 1477 had already visited ports in England and Ireland to interview local sailors. Giovanni da Verrazano was a Florentine who explored for the French, and John Cabot was a Genoan sailing out of Bristol, funded by a Florentine bank in London. Explorers were a fraternity focused on the big questions of the day, such as: Was there a route to China other than by sailing south? The possibilities were all tested. Verrazano checked the coast of America from the Carolinas to Newfoundland in 1524. Ten years later, Jacques Cartier pushed up the St Lawrence to its saltwater limit and learned that he could travel inland "until one reaches a freshwater sea." Henry Hudson did the same up the Hudson River in 1609 (for the Dutch), and then as far south as he could in Hudson Bay in 1610 (for the English). By 1612, Champlain had Hudson's charts to incorporate into his own map of North America, a product of Europe's competitive pooling of geographic intelligence.[2]

The appetites of Europe's princes and merchants were also whetted by rumours of treasure. The fabled city of Sagana was said to lurk beyond the

St Lawrence; abducted Natives promised they could lead the French back to "a large city ... where there are many mines of gold and silver ... [and an] abundance of clove, nutmeg and pepper." In New England, the mythic city of Norumbega was somewhere up the Penobscot River. It was first mapped by Verrazano's brother Girolamo, who shared his maps with Henry VII of England in 1525 and Pope Clement VII in 1529. His maps of "Oranbega" were eventually corrected, but his "Arcadia" – of Greek myth – stayed on as Acadia.[3]

The question soon became: "What lay beyond the coasts?" And increasingly, the answer was: "Inland seas." Europeans at that time knew of no inland seas that were not saltwater, and they thought it was possible that there were saltwater connections leading farther west. It took until 1612 to map the inland lakes of the Iroquois and the great lowland corridors into them – the St Lawrence and the Hudson (Fig. 6). There were only a handful of obstacles to the free use of these gateway water corridors, the 225-foot rise in the St Lawrence to Lake Ontario, the 325-foot rise from Lake Ontario to the other Great Lakes, and the routes from the upper Hudson. And the trails around these had already been worn into the ground by millennia of Native use.

By 1500, there had undoubtedly been many unheralded crossings of the Atlantic – by Viking, Mediterranean, North Atlantic, and perhaps even Chinese sailors, but they left neither record nor rumour. In 1501 an adventurer from the Azores, Gaspar Corte-Real, sailed for the northwest passage but was stopped by ice. He abducted fifty or so Natives, whom he distributed as curiosities. A few of them were already wearing European trade goods, a broken gilt sword and two silver rings from Italy, when they were abducted. By 1600, there had been hundreds of profitable crossings for fish, whales, ivory, hides, and fur, leaving scarcely a trace in the public record.[4]

In 1524 Giovanni da Verrazano reported to the French king Francis I how he had coasted along the new continent from south to north, raised "the ensigns and arms of the King," and enticed the Natives with ornaments, glass beads, and the like, while abducting only a child or two. Of the southern coast of New England, he wrote ecstatically: "We frequently went five to six leagues into the interior, and found it as pleasant as I can possibly describe, and suitable for every kind of cultivation ... The fields extend for 25 to 30 leagues; they are open and ... so fertile that any kind of seed would produce excellent crops ... We found ... apples, plums, and filberts, and many kinds of fruit ... There is an enormous number of animals – stags, deer, lynx, and other species." He continued: "All along [the coast] we saw great fires because of the many inhabitants ... We took the small boat up [the Hudson] river to land which we found densely populated ... These people are the most beautiful and have the most civil customs that we have found on this voyage ... Their women are just as shapely and beautiful; very gracious, of attractive manner and pleasant appearance." Verrazano's New World was occupied, cleared, farmed, and cultured.[5]

Cartier

Ten years later, Francis I commissioned Jacques Cartier, a Saint-Malo seaman, to ship again for gold and a new way west. Cartier's narratives describe a Native culture in a state of shock. The Natives met the new boat people on the Gaspé in July 1534. Cartier wrote, "They numbered ... more than 200 persons, with some forty canoes ... Nothing above the value of five *sous*, their canoes and fishing-nets excepted." They had come from the narrows (*Kebec*) on the St Lawrence, where they had seven villages, one of about forty longhouses, and grew corn, sunflowers, tobacco, squash, and "beans of every colour." They built weirs to catch eel and other fish, and they visited the Gaspé each summer to net mackerel and hunt seals and porpoise. Cartier raised a cross and claimed the land by right of *dominium* over the infidels. The Stadaconan headman, Donnacona, protested and was seized, along with his brother and three sons. Cartier gave Donnacona a "hatchet and two knives" for two of his sons, dressed them in "shirts and ribbons," and sailed with them the next day for France, where the two youth were further educated in French manners that winter.[6]

The two brothers returned with Cartier to Stadacona the next year. Donnacona immediately visited Cartier's ship and retrieved his sons. After hauling up his ships in the St Charles River, Cartier learned that the St Lawrence was navigable upstream and populated, and he wanted to visit immediately. Donnacona was reluctant, however, and his two sons refused to guide them. He had questions. Why did Cartier beach his ships without permission? Why wouldn't Cartier enter into an alliance, which Donnacona would guarantee with his own sister's daughter? Why wouldn't Cartier leave a Frenchman in exchange for his two sons acting as guides? He got no answers and, a few days later, Cartier sailed upstream without guide or translator. At the Richelieu River, a village headman offered Cartier a young boy and girl, and he took the girl. He arrived at Montreal Island in October. "There came to meet us more than a thousand persons ... They brought us quantities of fish, and of their bread which is made of corn, throwing so much of it into our longboats that it seemed to rain bread ... It was fine land with large fields covered with the corn of the country ... as well as with beans ... [and] cucumbers and other fruits."[7]

The palisaded town of Hochelaga had fifty longhouses and more than fifteen hundred residents. Cartier read them the Bible but refused to eat with them. He climbed Mount Royal, saw the rapids above at Lachine, and then left. Back at *Kebec* his men were building a fort and mounting artillery to guard the ships. Cartier finally visited the town of Stadacona but again refused to eat with them. The Stadaconans persevered; a group of them volunteered for baptism but were refused. A trade was established – beads and ornaments for fish and eels – but the brothers who had wintered in France let it be known that what they were getting was worthless. That winter, Cartier ordered a cessation of contact, citing his fear of an illness that the Stadaconans had contracted. Scurvy broke out and twenty-five Frenchmen died, but they disguised it until March, when Cartier finally asked for help. They were promptly supplied with a cure. All in all, these were setbacks for diplomacy, made worse by outright offence. In May Cartier raised another cross and abducted Donnacona and nine others. With the exception of one girl, they all died. Donnacona survived four years. He won the confidence of Francis I, to whom he promised, if he was returned home, the secrets of gold and silver and spices – and of the fabled Sagana, which we now know as the Saguenay.[8]

Cartier's third voyage, in 1541, was for serious settlement; five ships were loaded with colonists, tradesmen, felon labourers, and stock. They arrived at Stadacona and told the new headman that Donnacona was dead but that the others were all great French lords. Cartier chose a site upstream, away from Stadacona, and then sailed for Hochelega, where he again visited for a day and left without any trade, intelligence, or good will. That winter, his colony was laid siege by the Stadaconans, and thirty-five French were killed. In June Cartier sailed for France and delivered a treasure of diamonds to Saint-Malo, where they were found to be quartz. Cartier was relieved of his command. A nobleman, La Rocque de Roberval, was put in charge, but the colony ran short of food the next winter. Fifty more died of scurvy, with no help this time from the Natives. In 1543 the colony was abandoned, and the Iroquoians closed the St Lawrence to European traders.

Jacques Cartier's narrative provides an unvarnished account of his intent, which was to enrich his king. A singular failure was the result. Historian Ramsay Cook writes of Cartier's failure that "his judgment, and therefore his representation, of these people was mortally flawed. They existed only in European terms, never in their own." It took sixty years – more than two generations – for a diplomat of the competence of Samuel de Champlain to again engage the Natives of the St Lawrence. By then, the Stadaconans and Hochelagans had vanished without a trace.[9]

What happened? The case has been made that the St Lawrence Iroquoians were expelled by the Algonquians, who wanted to control the French trade from Tadoussac. Others contend that they were dispersed by the Huron or Iroquois, who coveted the same trade. Still others argue that they simply withdrew to Huronia or Iroquoia after their encounters with the French.[10]

Disease might also explain the collapse – perhaps followed by war and withdrawal. New diseases had been arriving for decades, starting when an African slave arrived in Mexico with smallpox in April 1520. In the 1540s the Spanish explorer Hernando de Soto marched a thousand men, three hundred and fifty horses, and three hundred swine across the southeast United States, and a "scourge" or "pestilence" cleared the way for him, leaving some nations with as few as five out of a hundred alive by the time he reached them. The anthropologist Henry Dobyns has itemized the diseases brought to North America before 1560: smallpox in 1520; malaria in 1513; measles or typhoid in 1528; bubonic plague in 1545; typhus in 1549; mumps in 1550; and influenza in 1559. The effects of any single one of these cannot be underestimated. In the case of the St Lawrence, an "epidemic and plague" was raging in Saint-Malo when Cartier's ships left that port in 1534, and Cartier counted more than fifty deaths among the Stadaconans that winter alone.[11]

In the sixty years between Cartier and Champlain, Europe's use of the Gulf of St Lawrence exploded, to supply a protein-hungry Europe with cod as well as with oil from seals, walrus, and whales. Tadoussac, at the mouth of the Saguenay, was the saltwater terminus of an ancient Algonquian corridor into the interior, and the French and Basques adopted Tadoussac as their base. By 1550, there was regular traffic into Tadoussac and, by 1578, twenty to thirty vessels were whaling in the Gulf. Processing fish and oil meant time ashore, with the bonus of some trade in furs. Toward the end of the 1500s, there was the revival of an old technique that made fine felt out of the underfur of beaver pelts, to create the broad-brimmed hats that were the fashion statement of the day. The dictates of fashion were not to be ignored, nor their profits.[12]

Champlain

In 1603 King Henry IV conferred a monopoly on the trade to Aymar de Chaste. Samuel de Champlain was invited to join him, "at the king's pleasure," to "see and explore" New France. Champlain was from a naval family with its roots on the French Atlantic coast. His early career was blessed by France's great nation builder, Henry IV, who was raised a Protestant but who converted to Catholicism on threat of death, only to recant and then re-convert again. Champlain was also raised a Protestant but he too converted to the ascendant Catholicism when his king did. These were raw times. Force of arms was the prevailing right, and it was likely in the forge of France's religious wars that Champlain acquired the temper of a tolerant and successful leader.[13]

By 1603, Champlain had already served as an observer for the king in the Spanish New World and was an expert in surveillance and mapping. He was rewarded with a pension, and he also fell heir to the estate of a ship-owning uncle. His uncle had sent one of his ships to Newfoundland as early as 1570, and Champlain did his own research as well, questioning seamen and ship chandlers in various ports. So, at the age of thirty, he was a skilled agent trusted by his king, a *géographe du roi*.[14]

On arriving at Tadoussac, he immediately mapped it. A thousand Montagnais were there and he visited their camp three days later. The message for their headmen was presented by two Native sons just brought back from France. The French "desired to people their land, and to make peace with their enemies (who are the Iroquois) or send forces to conquer them." The headmen, "after smoking some time," replied that they were "content that his said majesty would populate their land and make war on their enemies." The parties then feted on "moosemeat ... bear, seal and beaver ... and great quantities of wild fowl." Thus was *entente* reached – settlement rights in exchange for military aid – a high-level pact not touching on details such as land ownership. In fact, no treaties with Natives dealing with land tenure were ever negotiated in New France.[15]

Champlain headed upstream past the abandoned sites of Stadacona and Hochelaga to the Lachine Rapids. This took him from the "cold" and "rocky" lands of the Canadian Shield to the "good and fertile" lands of the interior lowlands where, in addition to hunting and fishing, there was "grown a quantity of Indian corn" and many "oaks [and] wild fruit-bearing trees and vines." This was the same north-to-south pattern that he would see on the New England coast the next year: "the farther we went, the finer the land." He visited a fortified Algonquin camp at the mouth of the Richelieu River, where he gained some useful intelligence – up the Richelieu were the Iroquois and "a river that leads down to the coast," the Hudson.

Also, up the St Lawrence lay an inland sea "eighty leagues [190 miles] in length," with water at its far end that was *salubre* or "fresh" (translated misleadingly into English in 1615 as "brackish"), and a "waterfall ... a league in width" (Niagara), leading to yet another lake that was even longer and more *salubre*, and then another lake "so vast that they will not venture ... into the same." Natives also reported, Champlain wrote, "totally salty" waters far inland, and a salt sea to the north – "some gulf of this our sea" – Hudson Bay. Overall, the chain of great lakes offered the best prospect of "passage to China."[16]

When Champlain returned to France, he reported directly to Henry IV and published a narrative of his journey. He did this after his 1603 voyage and again in 1613 and 1619, and, as a result, his books read like field notes, fresh and original. They also gave him a voice in the court debate about colonization as a means to advance trade. The royal monopoly was passed to the entrepreneur Pierre de Monts and his partners, and they too asked Champlain to join them. Starting in 1604, they built fortified posts at the St Croix River in New Brunswick, unsuccessfully, and at Port Royal in Nova Scotia, successfully. In 1608 they were awarded one final year of monopoly, so they returned to the St Lawrence to enforce it and to set up a colony. The first of their ships to reach Tadoussac was boarded by Basque free traders and disarmed "for safety's sake." When Champlain arrived, he chose to negotiate rather than defend their rights, and focused instead on assembling a pinnace to sail upriver to the *Kebec* narrows, for "here begins the fine, good country of the great river." He picked a site below the heights, "covered with butternut," and set his men to cutting them, making planks, and raising a pallisaded habitation. Crops were planted and Algonquin joined them there that fall to pursue the annual eel harvest.[17]

No rituals for Champlain, like raising a cross. Instead, he concentrated on the politics and trade of the St Lawrence and the Gulf. He reaffirmed the French-Algonquian entente and, to fulfill its bargain in June 1609, Champlain, with his guns and a dozen Frenchmen, travelled with Algonquin warriors and a few curious Huron up the Richelieu to attack the Iroquois on Lake Champlain. Many turned back, but Champlain, two Frenchmen, and sixty warriors kept on, until they met two hundred Iroquois, who barricaded their position and waited. A single shot from Champlain's *arquebuse à rouet* left two headmen dead and another dying. Panic ensued, with volleys of arrows and more shots. Some fifteen Iroquois were killed, a dozen captured, and their corn and armour taken. Champlain returned to France that fall and recounted his exploits at court. He presented the king with gifts: a belt of porcupine quills, a pair of scarlet tanagers, and the head of a gar fish.[18]

Three months after Champlain's raid, and just eighty miles to the south on the Hudson River, occurred an event of equivalent consequence. The English navigator Henry Hudson, sailing for the Dutch, reached the upper Hudson and visited the Natives – also likely Mohawk – near present Albany. He called them "loving people," and his visit brought the Dutch and, eventually, their trade in weapons with the Mohawk. With these bookend voyages by Champlain and Hudson, the die was cast, geopolitically, for the northeast and its interior.[19]

The following June, Champlain and his allies killed eighty-five Mohawk at the mouth of the Richelieu. To mark the event, Champlain exchanged youths with his allies, sending the teenager Étienne Brûlé with an Algonquin headman in return for Savignon, the brother of a Huron headman. The alliance of the French and Algonquin was thus extended to the Huron, sealed with acts of blood and the exchange of sons. Also started was the tradition of Frenchmen living easily as Native sons, mastering the languages and serving in the *pays d'en haut*.[20]

Champlain further gained the Algonquin's respect by venturing up the Ottawa River three years later. He visited their villages, smoked their tobacco, and saw "their gardens and fields where maize was growing," and their pumpkins and beans, as well as the Old World peas they had already got in trade. At the Constance Bay sandhills, the Natives drew his attention to a "root which dyes a crimson colour, wherewith the Indians paint their faces and their trinkets." There still persists at Constance Bay two root plants long used for red dye, both at their *only* sites along the Ottawa and at the northern limits of their North American ranges. Champlain was a keen observer.[21]

At the end of this voyage, Champlain itemized the financial rewards of New France for the French Chambre du Commerce: the cod fishery; the salmon, sturgeon, eel, sardine, and herring; the whale oil and bones; the "marvellous" forests for masts, beams, joists, staves, planks, charcoal, pitch, and tar; the native hemp sails, ropes, and riggings; the mines and fur; and the corn and grapes. His report was a business prospectus and, to it, he added his magnificent maps of 1612 and 1613, which included all his discoveries as well as what he had learned from the Dutch and English. Yet unvisited, lakes Ontario and Huron and Hudson Bay were on the maps, only vaguely.[22]

In 1615 Champlain and Joseph Le Caron, a Recollet brother, met with the Algonquin and Huron near Montreal Island. Champlain was pressed about war plans and a visit to Huronia. They set out in two canoe parties, Le Caron in the first and Champlain the second – sixteen Frenchmen in all – up the Ottawa, across Lake Nipissing, and down the French River to Lake Huron, where they came across three hundred Algonquians, Ottawa of the Bruce and Manitoulin, who had canoed there to harvest blueberries for their winter supplies. Paddling south, they arrived at Huronia.[23]

The Huron Homeland

Champlain was matter-of-fact about Huronia, having witnessed similar settled nations along the Atlantic seaboard a decade earlier. "Here we found a great change in the country, this part being very fine, mostly cleared, with many hills and several streams." He visited its towns and villages and expressed a growing pleasure as he went, finally reaching Cahiagué, the largest of them. Champlain described the area he "visited on foot" as "twenty to thirty *lieues* [60 to 90 miles of] well cleared country where they plant much Indian corn ... [and] squashes and sunflowers ... This soil seems to me a little sandy but it is none the less good." Near Cahiagué, he visited the Narrows on Lake Simcoe, where a "great catch of fish takes place by means of a number of weirs." The Huronia that Champlain visited was stable, strong, and outward looking, several dozen towns and villages surrounded by tens of thousands of acres of cleared lands.[24]

Echoing Champlain's first impressions was Gabriel Sagard, a Recollet brother who visited Huronia eight years later. He arrived one midday in August, "the sun beating down perpendicularly on us," and he had to carry his gear a "great distance" to the town of Ossossané. He fell behind his companions and, hot and lost, sought out "shade under a tree in a fine large meadow." Two women finally found and gave him directions. It was a "well-cleared country, pretty and pleasant," with "open fields, very beautiful broad meadows." Huronia also revealed itself to Sagard as a well-governed nation that occupied a hard-worked landscape. Land ownership was clear; there were internal borders between its tribal lands, "just like the different provinces of France."[25]

Champlain was a guest at Cahiagué for two weeks. War preparations were on his mind. The plan was to attack the Iroquois again. This would be Champlain's third attack, and the Susquehannock, a sibling Iroquoian nation south of Iroquoia, let it be known that they too wished to join the raid. Their motive was retaliation – earlier that year the Mohawk, with three Dutchmen, had attacked them. Étienne Brûlé was Champlain's translator in Huronia and he agreed to join a party heading south to arrange for the Susquehannock to meet them. Brulé travelled there either by way of the Toronto Carrying Place or the Nottawasaga Trail, both of which led to Neutral country and, from there, south through what is now New York and Pennsylvania.[26]

The Huron-French war party headed east along the Kawartha lakes and Trent waterway, which "in times past were inhabited by Natives [Huron] who had since been compelled to abandon them out of fear of their enemies." On reaching Iroquoia, they attacked a well-fortified town that Champlain would later illustrate as having more than a hundred longhouses. It required a close siege and, finally losing patience, Champlain urged his allies to burn the town, which they refused to do. They waited four days for their Susquehannock allies, and then left two days before they showed up, returning with their wounded to Huronia for the winter.[27]

That winter Champlain travelled overland west toward the Niagara Escarpment and visited seven Petun towns there. He then headed north, likely to Owen Sound, to greet the Ottawa Algonquians whom he had met earlier picking blueberries on the east side of Georgian Bay. They too were hunters, fishers, farmers, and long-distance traders, "the cleanest [and] most industrious" he had met. In May Champlain returned to the St Lawrence by way of the Ottawa.[28]

The alliance deepened. For twenty years, it secured a safe route down the Ottawa to New France, and it temporarily stalemated the Iroquois. It raised Champlain's stock and in 1614 he and his partners were granted the trade monopoly – the Compagnie des Marchands. But growth was slow. Louis Hébert and his family arrived in 1617 and began to farm under a contract that guaranteed the sale of his produce to the company.

The year 1624 saw a treaty between the French, Algonquin, and Mohawk, and a truce between the Huron and the Seneca. These were mere deceptions, however, in a deeper war by any means, which had every party on full alert, seeking advantage. One element of this was the French deployment of missionaries to socialize and convert the Natives, to "fix the wandering *sauvages* ... with golden chains," as they put it. Early records of this were kept by the Recollets, two of them the unique reports of Gabriel Sagard in Huronia in 1623–24 and of La Roche d'Aillon with the Neutral in 1626–27. In 1625 the Jesuits displaced the Recollets and brought to New France a more zealous mission, insisting that only baptism could save a Native from the fires of hell and that the new diseases were "the justice of God." They kept excellent records – the *Relations* – which, fortunately for us, stray occasionally from their core message of needing more support for their aggressive harvest of souls.[29]

Meanwhile, the fur trade was good. The average number of furs shipped from Tadoussac rose from about 15,000 a year in the mid-1620s to over 30,000 in 1630. By 1635, the Huron were supplying 12,000 to 15,000 beaver annually, a major part of the trade. The Huron were also growing their trade with the Algonquin, the Petun, and the Neutral, and this required increased corn surpluses for trade. The new iron axes made land clearing easier, and the increase in production likely went to meet the external demands of trade. At the same time, domestic consumption rose, and more and more goods were given away at festivals to validate the status of the celebrants, or interred with the dead. Growth thus tipped the energy balance, and a crop failure, even for a single year, had more serious implications.[30]

Change came fast. Soon there was a decline in fur and the beginnings of a weapons trade. By 1630, beaver were gone from the Huron hunting grounds. Furbearers of all kinds were in decline in the Saguenay country. South of the lakes, the Iroquois traded with the Dutch on the Hudson about half as many skins as the Huron traded with the French and, by the 1640s, their supply was also declining. They would have to get their furs elsewhere. Dutch traders offered new goods to entice them and, by 1634, they were trading alcohol and, after 1639, muskets, powder, and lead, all contrary to official policy. English traders followed in lockstep, and firearms were soon part of a warrior's kit. The French exercised more control along the St Lawrence, intercepting more of the alcohol trade and trading guns with Native allies only if they converted to Catholicism – an estimated 120 individuals by 1648 – and only if they would travel all the way to the St Lawrence to acquire or repair them. This arms imbalance would come back to haunt the French.[31]

In 1629 Quebec fell to the English; Champlain had only sixteen fighting men to defend it. When it was returned to France in 1633, Champlain returned to Quebec. He built a chapel, expanded Quebec's defences, founded Trois-Rivières, and advocated a new attack on the Iroquois. A visionary to the end, in his last years he published another set of his *Voyages* and his magnificent 1632 map of northeast North America, covering all the Great Lakes country that the French had discovered: lakes Ontario, Erie, and Champlain as well as Lake Huron (*la mer douce*), Lake Superior (*le grand lac*), and the lands of the Huron, Neutral, Petun, and Iroquois. He died in 1635 on Christmas day and left his estate to the church. He was buried with honours and interred in an unmarked grave, reburied later in a place soon forgotten, and ultimately lost under old Quebec itself.[32]

First, Disease – Then, Extirpation

The pace of change escalated in the 1630s, and the new pathogens and weapons led directly, by 1650, to the collapse of entire nations and their domestic homelands. The Jesuits, newly arrived, set their sights on a permanent mission in Huronia. Influenza, measles, and other illnesses arrived soon after. The Jesuits carried disease to Huronia in their canoes in 1634; en route, Jean de Brébeuf wrote, "the contagion which spread among these tribes last year … suddenly seized several of our *sauvages.*" The contagion received equal billing in their *Relations* with their tough time on the Ottawa, where they carried their "canoes thirty five times and dragged them at least fifty," all amid an "infinite number of mosquitoes and gnats." For Natives, the pathogens were of more consequence.[33]

The Jesuits, like most Europeans, were already resistant to the diseases. They saw clearly, as in their 1637 *Relations*, that the "epidemic, which slaughters so many Huron, has not been communicated to the French." The Huron knew the Jesuits to be "the authors of their sickness." In their *Relations*, the Jesuits acknowledged their culpability, but Brébeuf told the Huron publicly to give up their dreams, marry for life, end their feasts, and stop their human sacrifices. The Huron refused, on the grounds that such changes would spell their end as a people. The deaths continued. They would have continued anyway, but what better confirmation of Jesuit blame? The Huron put the Jesuits on trial for witchcraft at Ossossané, and in the end it was only a direct intervention by the Huron headmen who were the leading beneficiaries of trade with the French that spared the Jesuits. Trade and profit trumped all else, a constant theme.[34]

At the same time, Native conflict escalated. In 1637 five hundred Iroquois, largely Mohawk, camped on the St Lawrence and intercepted the furs coming down to Quebec. They killed a Huron headman, which precipitated an avenging raid the next year, when three hundred Huron and Algonquin ambushed a hundred Oneida raiding northward. They took eighty captives to Huronia to execute, but the Jesuits insisted on baptizing them first, which infuriated the Huron. At this point, a new Jesuit headman arrived in Huronia, Jérôme Lalemant, his first posting outside France. His plan was to build an ambitious complex on the Wye River, a project that could not have been more irrelevant to the Huron. Nonetheless, work started and, by 1645, the fifty-eight Frenchmen at Sainte-Marie had a walled fort with four stone corner bastions and a church, hospital, cemetery, retreat, and a separate gathering place for "infidels."[35]

Native losses mounted. On the Niagara frontier, the surviving Wenro were unable to withstand the Seneca, and they moved to join the Huron and Neutral in 1638. It was at this point that the worst of the diseases arrived – smallpox. The Algonquin got it first and died in such numbers that the living could not bury the dead. Huron traders took it inland from Quebec, and thousands perished. The Jesuits baptized them as they died, at least a thousand that year by their own count. Lalemant took score in 1640: "In less than ten years they have been reduced from thirty thousand souls to ten thousand." Mohawk numbers dropped to 40 per cent of their earlier level (3,200 died). None were spared, and harvest failures made it worse. The combined regional effect of measles in 1634, influenza in 1636, scarlet fever in 1637, and smallpox in 1639 killed as many as two-thirds of the population in six years. Those who survived were a random selection – a third of all men, women, and children, and a third of all elders, farmers, hunters, healers, and artisans. They were refugees in their own homelands.[36]

The anthropologist Henry Dobyns puts the figure of those killed by European disease in the New World at 95 per cent of the total population within 130 years of contact. Others put the figure at 75 per cent mortality of Natives east of the Mississippi by 1800. Regardless, the devastation in the Americas was the greatest sudden collapse of human life and culture in human history. In absolute numbers, the losses in Central and South America and the southeastern United States in the 1500s were the greatest, but, proportionately, the trauma in Great Lakes country was equally as blunt.[37]

This vulnerability may be better understood one day. European resistance is not well understood either but it was almost certainly the result of natural selection by the various Eurasian plagues of the Middle Ages, causing, for example, the death of nearly three-quarters of England's population between 1348 and 1665. This selected for resistant immune systems and encoded that immunity into succeeding generations. Add to this the measured differences in immunity among peoples, specifically the higher degree of genetic homogeneity among Native immune systems as the result of the small number of individuals who originally arrived in the Americas. One positive aspect of this is that there are ailments with a genetic component, such as cystic fibrosis, that do not occur among Natives. On the other hand, Native North Americans have fewer human leukocyte antigens (HLAs), essential elements in immune function, and a more homogenous spectrum of HLAs, which increases the likelihood of a pathogen being passed from one vulnerable individual to another. Contagions may have been particularly virulent as a result.[38]

In hindsight, the technological advantages of European over New World nations were important, but perhaps not qualitatively so. Granted, advanced metallurgy meant advanced tools, weapons, and ships, and this conferred advantage – and so too did writing. At the same time, the New World enjoyed a greater mastery of crop breeding, farming, wildlife management, and, in some places, social governance. The key differences were not technological but immunological, involving susceptibilities to disease not understood then and barely understood now.

Life went on after smallpox, and the patterns of raid and trade continued. The Mohawk hunted and raided farther afield, using their firearms; they reported a kill of some two thousand deer in a single winter. The Neutral, without guns and soon to be victims themselves, sent two thousand warriors west beyond Lake Erie to attack a town. They killed and sacrificed many, and captured eight hundred. The capture of prisoners, for assimilation and labour, became essential after losing so many to disease. The Mohawk led the way, raiding for women, children, and furs. "They kill only the men and the aged women," the Jesuits wrote, "sparing ... the younger ones in order that they might dwell in their country and marry." These were now armed raids. In 1641 a war party of 350 Mohawk was said to have thirty-six guns. Two years later, they had nearly 300 guns and, the following year, they had guns and ammunition for 400 men. Trading with them were the English, Dutch, and Swedes north of Virginia, almost 16,000 of them by 1640. By contrast, New France had a population of only 400 by 1643, and was still slow to arm its Native allies, sending "a score of brave soldiers" to Huronia instead.[39]

The French did establish a military presence on Montreal Island in 1641, fronted as a religious enterprise. It immediately attracted Iroquois raids but their raids on Huron convoys became less successful, and a truce was arranged in 1645, marked by prisoner exchanges and a record number of exported furs. Both disease and crop failures were stressing the Iroquois and a new kind of warfare emerged, at a level of intensity distinct from the traditional raids for revenge, honour, and goods. The words total warfare, ethnic cleansing, and genocide are of recent origin, but, even before they were coined, the extirpation of weaker nations was an acknowledged part of European warfare, part and parcel of major advances in weaponry.[40]

In 1642 the Iroquois warriors attacked and burned a Huron village while the Huron warriors were away raiding Iroquoia. The next year, a raiding party of a hundred Huron was surrounded and destroyed. That year was a drought year in Huronia, and the Iroquois killed and abducted many Huron women and children as they worked their fields and foraged for food. In 1647 the Mohawk attacked the Susquehannock to their south, at the request of the Dutch, but, after that, they and the Seneca turned on Huronia again. Some suggest that their goal was again to intercept trade but the escalating pace of the raids, and the rising casualty numbers, argue that a more final solution was the objective.[41]

Negotiations and exchanges of prisoners and wampum continued, but war readiness was the order of the day. The Huron stayed at home in 1647, unwilling to have their men away trading. Some of the eastern Huron moved into villages farther west. As many as three thousand sought the protection of the Jesuits at Sainte-Marie; the records show a rise in baptisms but no special preparations for defence. Instead, there continued a corrosive spiritual duel of rites and rituals between the Jesuits and the Huron traditionalists.

That summer the Seneca attacked the Neutral and mauled a hunting party of three hundred Huron. Finally alarmed, the French sent a soldier in 1648 to take stock. The Huron had not traded the year previous and the few who had guns were short of powder and lead. Hundreds of well-armed Iroquois arrived and sacked one of the best-fortified Huron towns; Father Antoine Daniel sprinkled water on the Huron and urged them to fight, for which he was shot and burned in his church. This cost Huronia a tenth of its remaining population and severely disrupted its crop planting. Two hundred Huron canoed to the St Lawrence for supplies. There, they were enraged to find that the French were in peace talks with the Mohawk. In the face of this, the French dispatched to Huronia eight more soldiers, four more priests, a heifer, and a single small cannon.

A thousand Seneca and Mohawk, well armed, assembled north of Lake Ontario. Huronia was deep in snow when they arrived, undetected, in March 1649. They took a small town while it slept and then, the same day, sacked and burned the mission village of Saint-Louis and captured Jean de Brébeuf and Gabriel Lalemant. The Jesuit pair were stripped and forced to run a gauntlet of warriors, among them Huron who had been earlier adopted by the Iroquois, who took the lead in killing them. The next day the Iroquois attacked Sainte-Marie but were driven back. Loaded with spoils, they left for home.[42]

The Huron had lost another seven hundred. Within two weeks, they abandoned Huronia, burning their towns and dispersing north and west with whatever they could carry. The head Jesuit Paul Ragueneau ordered Sainte-Marie stripped and burned, "in less than one hour, our work of nine or ten years." The French rafted their one small cannon and their food, livestock, and tools to Gahoendoe (Christian Island), off the tip of the Penetang peninsula. As many as five thousand Huron left with them and, on the island, they built a stone fort around a water cistern (for the French) and a walled village beside it (for the Huron). At last they were safe but the Iroquois never attacked. Instead, they waited, chasing down Huron refugees and raiding the Algonquin and Nipissing.[43]

Soon starving, the Huron had to leave Gahoendoe to find food. The Iroquois picked them off and, in June, three hundred Huron set off with the Jesuits for Quebec, leaving everything behind, even the cannon. Weak as they were, they still tried to refuse to pay a toll exacted by their Algonquin allies on the Ottawa River, until the Algonquin strung up Ragueneau in a tree. Ragueneau offered a final benediction on the Huron, "a people wiped off the face of the Earth." Individuals survived, of course, on Île d'Orléans, near Quebec, and in refugee camps near western Lake Erie, Michilimackinac, and Green Bay. The largest concentration survived as assimilated Iroquois.[44]

Southwest of Huronia, the Petun and Neutral met the same fate. The Petun took to the offensive late in 1649, but an Iroquois war party evaded them and sacked and burned the main Petun town in their absence. Those remaining dispersed. This left the Neutral, a nation on good terms with its neighbours just two years earlier. In the fall of 1650, an army of a thousand Seneca, Mohawk, and Oneida destroyed a Neutral town and the Neutral retaliated, taking about two hundred Iroquois. That winter, a second Iroquois war party of twelve hundred destroyed another Neutral town and dispersed the rest. More than eight hundred fled west, and even more into the Ohio valley. Nothing survived of the Petun or Neutral nations.[45]

In the winter of 1651, the Dutch again urged the Mohawk to attack the Susquehannock. By then, however, the Susquehannock had been armed by the Swedes and they survived to make peace with the Mohawk in 1655. Meanwhile, the Mohawk and their Iroquois allies conducted a series of unprecedented, long-distance raids south to the Carolinas, west to the Mississippi, east to Tadoussac, and north to the Moose River and Lac Saint-Jean. Closer to home, they displaced their long-time rivals, the Mahican, from the Hudson River valley.[46]

This ethnic cleansing completely changed the Great Lakes country. The Ontario peninsula was left vacant of farming and Native land care, while other areas experienced new population pressures. Security was the refugees' goal, and the lands beyond Lake Huron and around Lake Michigan and the upper Mississippi were attractive, as the Jesuit Jacques Marquette noted in 1670 of the area just south of Green Bay, with its "beautiful plains and fields" where thousands of inhabitants could "raise corn ... in great abundance, [and] have squash as large as in France" and enjoy unmatched hunting and fishing. As many as fifty thousand residents and refugees lived together in a weak, new "village world," as historian Richard White calls it, nothing like their former nation states. Leadership and land ownership were in flux everywhere, with traditional customs sinking under the flood of refugee claims. Victorious, the Iroquoia homeland south of Lake Ontario stabilized temporarily, but the populous village world to the west – which was soon suffering from too many people working too few lands and overcrowding the fishing camps – invited new French ambitions to outflank the Iroquois, Dutch, and English in the interior.[47]

The Five Nations of Iroquoia were victors, but what had they won? After 1650, they soon realized that their trade with the Dutch was controlled by the Mohawk, and in 1653 the four western nations began talks with the French. The Onondaga welcomed the Jesuits and built a chapel, and the others followed. The western Iroquois also joined forces to attack the Erie nation, which ceased to exist as a result. The Mohawk grew alarmed, and they invited in the Jesuits as well. By now, the original thirteen Iroquoian nations of Great Lakes country were down to five – the Mohawk, Oneida, Onondaga, Cayuga, and Seneca – through disease and fratricide. Their subsequent story is a familiar tale of independent self-interest trumping any useful collective strategy, in this case about how to deal with the growing number of newcomers on their doorsteps.[48]

The expulsion of Native nations from the Ontario peninsula and around Lake Erie, combined with the relative collapse of Iroquoia as well, changed the ecology of the region. A culture of sophisticated, place-based farming and wildlife harvest was finished, as was its stewardship of the broader landscape for humans and wildlife alike. An enduring, collective endeavour was ended, leaving a rump of weakened Native nations and marginalized refugees. They could still pursue their dreams but, in reality, their roles were reduced to that of harvesters of natural resources and of well-paid extras in Europe's global war dramas. In both roles, their expert services would be competitively sought for another century and a half.

In Europe, nations were gnawing at the edges of their territories, and land was a limiting resource. In the New World, land – and how it was secured, cut up, and dispersed – would be the next great intervention. But until the bulk of migrants arrived a century and a half later, an unprecedented wilding took place. Under-hunted, the deer, passenger pigeon, and others increased to new levels (for a short time). Under-fished, the rivers and streams flowed with fish (for a little longer). Uncropped, uncut, and unburned, the open woods, meadows, and fields grew into old-growth forests. The results were as impressive to newcomers after 1800 as the native landscape had been to travellers in the 1600s. But it could hardly have been more different.

There are studies of the ecological impacts of war, including the effects of modern, mechanized, chemical, and nuclear warfare. However, less is made of the profound changes that can happen when the human hand is lifted from the land, such as on the Mayan peninsula or the Great Lakes country after 1650. Samuel de Champlain and the Recollet brother Gabriel Sagard were astonished by the open countryside of Huronia, as others were by many parts of the Great Lakes country and the St Lawrence and Atlantic seaboard, all the result of concerted Native enterprise over millennia. Settlers a century and a half later would see nothing of this.[49]

The New England

The Atlantic seaboard was the busiest of the arrival coasts and had some of the same first visitors as the St Lawrence. Champlain was sent in 1604 to survey the "coast of Norumbega" and, in short order, he debunked the myths of that city: "Those who mention it never saw it." The next year he landed at Saco Bay in southern Maine, the most northern farming site. Its towns were "surrounded by palisades" and by "cultivated fields" of corn, beans, squash, pumpkins, tobacco, and "nuts [and] vines." In fact, croplands dominate Champlain's drawings of Saco Bay, and of Plymouth and Nauset harbours farther south. His list of crops grew: a squash like cucumber, the pot-herb purslane, and the starchy root crop artichoke. Champlain sailed south again in 1606, looking for a warmer site than St Croix or Port Royal. He liked Saco Bay, where Natives has just "finished harvesting their corn." Their grapes were "as fine as those of France."[50]

The Algonquians of coastal New England pursued a culture of farming, fishing, hunting, trading, and craftsmanship similar to that of the Iroquoian nations west of the Appalachians. The coastal population south to the Susquehanna River was in excess of one hundred thousand at the time, by how much is not known, and the etchings by John White in 1585, and in Champlain's *Voyages*, are full of its towns and fields. Europeans were looking for safe harbours to settle but the risks were too great because the Natives were too numerous. The French explored but it was the English who persisted. Between 1602 and 1608, at least twenty-five crossings were made to the New England coast by the English, none of them settling.[51]

In that decade, England was overrun by plague. Almost forty-five thousand died in London alone. On 4 November 1605 twenty barrels of gunpowder were discovered beneath Westminster, laid by Catholics to blow up the Protestant king James I and his parliament. By luck, the king was away that day sanctifying Lancelot Andrewes as bishop. Andrewes was the leader of the great national project of the day, the King James Bible, which was widely sold and which conferred on the English, says historian Benson Bobrick, nothing less than "the right and capacity of the people to think for themselves." It also consecrated England to its imperial future, its first page stating its licence: "God said, let us make man in our image ... and let them have dominion ... over all the earth." The same decade was as cold as it got in the Little Ice Age, and poor crops were the norm. "Frost fairs" were staged on the frozen Thames. The Globe theatre premiered *Hamlet*, *Othello*, and other creative views of the world beyond England's shores. By 1610, there were two hundred English ships working the New World and other nations had hundreds more. In the 1500s, English interests had focused on the Avalon peninsula of Newfoundland, claimed for Queen Elizabeth I in 1583, but that interest quickly shifted south, and reports of those visits were avidly received.[52]

Captain Bartholomew Gosnold sailed to Cape Cod in 1602, and his ship chaplain, John Brereton, wrote a book about it that went through two editions in 1602. "In comparison," he reported, "the most fertile part of all England is but barren ... [We saw] meadows very large and ... even the most woody places doe grow so distinct and apart, one tree from another, upon greene grassie ground ... as if ... artificial." The people were "exceeding courteous, gentle ... Of a perfect constitution of body ... and destitute of edge-tooles or weapons." To the Natives, the ship crews must have looked like inferior, blanched specimens of humanity, but they had iron and iron edges and, for people who had only copper, in amounts too small to be much more than ceremonial, the new metal trade justified the social intercourse that was required of them.

Uninhabited islands that looked safe to settle were carefully noted, in particular for their "oakes ... cedars ... beech, elme, hollie, walnut trees in abundance ... hastlenut trees, cherry trees ... sassafras trees ... divers other fruit trees." A promotional "treatise" was part of Brereton's book, urging England to "plant" settlements on the coast. He cited Jacques Cartier's nephew about a great lake in the interior with "salt" water.[53]

The next year, Martin Pring came on behalf of the merchants of Bristol to collect sassafras to cure "the French poxe," or syphilis. He noted the same flora, fauna, and crops, as well as fruits such as "peare-plum" (serviceberry) and "a white kind of plum" (beach plum). In 1605 a book about a voyage by Captain George Weymouth was published; on an excursion inland he too reported the open country. They "marched up into the countrey ... for the space of some three miles, having but little wood, and that oke like stands left in our pastures in England."[54]

The Atlantic coast between the Hudson River and the Gulf of St Lawrence was home to a dozen or more Algonquian nations (Fig. 5). There was one confederacy around Cape Cod, consisting of the Nauset (with thirty settlements), the Massachusett (several dozen), and the Wampanoag. To the north was the Abenaki confederacy of the Passamaquoddy, Penobscot, and others. Their towns were sheltered in the river valleys, some of them sprawling for miles, with crop fields around them and ready access to many other permanent satellite camps for hunting, fishing, and gathering, such as those near the tidal flats, estuaries, bird colonies, and cranberry bogs. Their buildings were arched ridge poles sealed tight with bark, "warmer than our English houses," William Wood claimed. "In their planting ... they exceed our English husbandman." Wood, a resident from 1629 to 1633, also described the open countryside: "There be likewise in diverse places near the plantations great broad meadows, wherein grow neither shrub or tree."[55]

Another resident was the Cambridge-trained theologian Roger Williams, who wrote his *Key into the Language of America* in these same years. His findings that Native peoples had their own land-tenure system were not well received, and he was banned from Boston. Natives were, he said, "very exact and punctuall in the bounds of their lands ... and I have knowne them to make bargaine and sale amongst themselves for a small piece or quantity of ground: notwithstanding a sinfull opinion amongst many that Christians have [a] right to heathens land." He admired their civility; their conflicts were "farr less bloudy and devouring than the cruell warres of Europe."[56]

The coast was soon clear enough to settle. Smallpox – or hepatitis – made its appearance in 1616 and, over the next three years, killed eight or nine of every ten Natives. They "died in heapes as they lay in their houses." The Pilgrims arrived in 1620 and their governor, William Bradford, would later recount how their hunger that December drove them to search the abandoned Native villages "and digging up found in them diverce faire Indian baskets filled with corne ... A spetiall providence of God ... or else they might have starved." God made "room for us," he said, and the disease did not touch them. Was there any point to land treaties after such an expression of God's will? A treaty was signed nonetheless and the peace held for fifty years, aided again by smallpox in 1633, when half the remaining Natives died. Finally, the last of the Natives rebelled but they were too few, too late. European dominion came quicker here than elsewhere.[57]

Miantonomo, the Narragansett headman in 1642, stated what was clear to the Natives, for which he was executed. "Our fathers had plenty of deer and skins and our plains were full of game, as also our woods, and of turkies, and our coves full of fish and fowl. But these English have gotten our land, they with scythes cut down the grass, and with axes fell the trees; their cows and horses eat the grass, and their hogs spoil our clam banks; and we shall all be starved."[58]

New Netherlands and New Sweden

History slides easily over the Dutch, but the Dutch had an indelible influence on how the land was occupied. In 1624 the West India Company built posts on the Delaware and Connecticut rivers and at Fort Orange (Albany) at the tide limit on the Hudson, in Mohawk country. Within two years they were at war with the Mohawk and - savaged - they withdrew to Manhattan. Changing tactics, they began the direct purchase of land from the Natives and thus opened the southern gateway to the Great Lakes. One of the purchases, by Kiliaen van Rensselaer, an Amsterdam jewel merchant, was a million-acre patroonship centred on Fort Orange. Among themselves, however, the Dutch still insisted they had "discovered" the place and had taken possession "in the right of their discovery," as stated by Adriaen Van der Donck.[59]

Van der Donck, a young doctor of law, arrived in 1641 to administer Rensselaer's colony of a hundred settlers around Fort Orange. There were fewer than fifteen hundred Dutch colonists at the time, most of them in New Amsterdam (New York). Van der Donck helped negotiate a treaty with the Mohawk in 1645, and he was rewarded with twenty-four thousand acres on the lower Hudson, including what is now the Bronx. By age twenty-six, he was a Manhattan merchant, and opposed to his governor's taxes. He carried an appeal to The Hague to protest the taxes and to generate investment, but he failed at both and instead spent his time writing a treatise about the New

Netherlands. He returned in 1653 and died two years later. In 1664 the English admiral Richard Nicholls sailed into New Amsterdam and ended the Dutch dream. The settlers stayed, however, and were the group in closest ongoing contact with the Iroquois and, later, the most avidly anti-English force in the American Revolution.

By 1663, New France had scarcely 3,000 residents, compared with 8,000 in New Netherlands and 30,000 in New England. South of New Netherlands was New Sweden, with a population of less than a thousand. The Dutch took it in 1655, and the English in 1664. New Sweden was in the lower Delaware valley, where the Lenape or Delaware lived, and their treatment set the tone for future land dealings. In 1681 the Quaker William Penn was granted the Delaware by royal charter, to pay off a debt the English owed his father. In 1683 he wrote, "The country is in soyle good, aire serene ... & sweet from the cedar, pine & sarsefrax ... The people; they are savage ... but they have great shape, strength, agility; and in council (for they observe ... property & government) grave." Penn signed a treaty for their land in 1686, but there was no map attached to it. As time went by, and more newcomers arrived, the Lenape welcome wore thin.[60]

Penn's treaty festered for fifty years, at which time a new treaty – the Walking Treaty – was proposed to map, as relinquished lands, those lands that could be surveyed up the Delaware River in a day and a half. Unbeknownst to the Lenape, the English had prepared and, at dawn on 19 September 1737, three fit men set out on an endurance race upriver, which ended with one of them covering fifty-five miles. On this basis, the English claimed a million acres. In the face of Lenape outrage, the English in Philadelphia asked the Iroquois to evict the Lenape, offering in return to make the Iroquois the vendor of choice for the English in such transactions in the future. In 1742 Canasatego, the Onondaga chief, did the deed, chiding the Delaware: "How came you to take upon you to sell land at all? We conquered you. We made women of you. You know you are women and can no more sell land than women."

Thus the Iroquois took on the role of real estate agents for the English, and the Delaware began their retreat, an exodus of biblical proportions that did not end for some of them until 1792, in the heart of Great Lakes country, ironically not far from the Iroquois in southwest Ontario. More of this later, but the pattern was set – the conquest of lands directly or by secondary conquest of lands already taken by European, with private or Native-backed land deals on the side and, finally, direct government involvement, if and as needed.[61]

Filling in the Map

Farther north, meanwhile, the Iroquois were unrelenting in their raids, and New France was fearful. In 1660 alone, seventy French and forty-four Native allies were killed, and scores captured. The next year the governor asked Pierre Boucher, a hero of New France who had saved Trois-Rivières and Quebec from the Iroquois eight years earlier, to champion New France to the new Sun King, Louis XIV. The court was impressed and asked Boucher to write a general prospectus, his *Histoire véritable et naturelle*, which, like Champlain's in 1632, combined a geography of New France with practical advice, such as: "The people best fitted for this country are those who can work with their hands."[62]

In 1663 Louis XIV declared New France a royal province and, over the next few years, sent eleven hundred soldiers. He also invited more than eight hundred women to emigrate, *les filles du roi*, and New France doubled in population to more than six thousand in the next decade. In 1666 Alexandre de Tracy was dispatched with a force of thirteen hundred up the Champlain valley to the Mohawk valley, where he burned five Mohawk towns. This was part of a new French policy to contain the English and their allies. Another part of the policy was to install Jesuits among the Iroquois, and a new colony of Iroquois Catholics near Montreal – the French valued them for "the intelligence they give in time of war," Cadwallader Colden would later write. To the north, Jesuits were sent toward Hudson Bay to assess its prospects, but they came back with news of a land "dry, barren and sandy, and the mountains ... with only rocks, or with little stunted trees." (Not all Jesuit intelligence was welcome. Louis Nicolas worked throughout New France from 1664 to 1675 but he was more interested in travel and commerce than conversions, and few of his writings were published by the Jesuits, neither his "*histoire naturelle*" nor his companion "*Codex*" of drawings of plants, animals, and people.)[63]

The adventurer René-Robert Cavelier de La Salle arrived in New France in 1667. His interests were also secular, and in 1669 he set off to find the river the Iroquois called the Ohio. He took with him the Sulpicians Dollier de Casson, a soldier-turned-priest, and Bréhant de Galinée, to map the trip. They reached the Seneca nation, "about six days journey" from the Ohio, but were persuaded to turn back. They returned by way of Niagara, where Galinée heard, reported, and mapped Niagara Falls (without seeing it) – "one of the finest ... waterfalls in the world." Near Burlington Bay, La Salle was either struck down by fever or, as reported by Galinée, fled for Montreal "at the sight of three large rattlesnakes."

Despite this fumbled start, the two Sulpicians carried on, to become the first Europeans to visit all of the Great Lakes. They canoed along lakes Ontario and Erie, along Lake Huron to the Mackinac Islands at the mouth of Lake Michigan, to Sault Ste Marie at the mouth of Lake Superior, and back to the St Lawrence by way of the French and Ottawa rivers. The Great Lakes were all connected. It was these two, not La Salle, who declared the *Act of Taking Possession of the Lands of Lake Erie*, claiming the territory by right of discovery. Their key discovery was the strait, *le détroit*, by which Lake Huron discharged into Erie. Here they came across a "god of stone," where travelling Natives camped, paid homage, and inscribed their tribal glyphs. The French took their axes to it and "threw it into the water."[64]

About the same time, Seneca from south of Lake Ontario reoccupied a site on its north shore, near the mouth of the Rouge River. Their village, Ganatsekiagon, was on the high ground above the first rapids where the Rouge and Little Rouge Creek meet, and where there were defensible slopes and good fishing. Galinée wrote on his map that "it was from here that Mr. Perray and his party camped to enter [portage to] Lake Huron ... the road is very fine." He was referring to Jean Peré and Louis Joliet, who used the portage in 1669 on their way to Lake Superior to find copper. A Sulpician mission was established there the same year.[65]

In 1675 the Recollet Louis Hennepin arrived in New France, on the same ship as the returning explorer La Salle and Bishop Laval. La Salle brought with him a royal land grant on Lake Ontario, to establish a "bulwark against the incursions of the Iroquois," and Hennepin was posted to this new Fort Frontenac, named for the French governor. By 1678, La Salle was ready to try again, this time to explore the Mississippi, first visited five years earlier by Marquette. Hennepin was drafted as reporter, and, that winter, he and fifteen others sailed to the mouth of the Niagara River, where they were greeted by Seneca who supported them with whitefish caught there. They palisaded their supplies, waited for La Salle, and visited Niagara Falls – a "wonderful downfall ... outrageous noise ... So rapid ... that it violently hurries down the wild beasts," a harvesting role well known to the Natives below. Hennepin's sketch of the falls has sixteen Frenchmen viewing it from the west side of the gorge. He drew conifers ringing the river and cliffs, as did other early visitors, where there are none today, and thin broadleaf cover beyond. "The trees are but few, and chiefly firrs and oaks," he wrote.[66]

La Salle joined them briefly around Christmas, and, in January, they portaged their gear above the falls and laid the keel of the first ship above

Niagara, the *Griffon*. They tried to trade with the Seneca, "especially for brandy," but the Seneca reaction was swift and the French had to retreat to the *Griffon*, afraid to live on shore. La Salle returned in July and they sailed west on Lake Erie, and up the Detroit and St Clair rivers, where they stopped to survey the passage into Lake Huron. "Lake Huron falls into this St. Claire by several canals ... interrupted by sands and rocks. We sounded all of them, and found one at last ... but were forc'd to drop our anchors near the mouth of the lake ... The wind turning southerly, we sail'd again; and with the help of twelve men, who hall'd our ship from the shoar, [we] got safely ... into the Lake Huron."[67]

A storm chased them north to Michilimackinac, where the Jesuits and the refugee Huron, Petun, and Ottawa welcomed them and showed off their corn and crops. They sailed for Green Bay and, after loading the *Griffon* with furs, La Salle sent it back to Niagara to exchange them for supplies. The *Grifffon* vanished. La Salle canoed to southern Lake Michigan and the Illinois River. Before La Salle turned back, he sent Michel Accau and Antoine Augel on to find the Mississippi, along with Hennepin. Setting out in February 1680, they were soon taken prisoner by the Sioux and marched endlessly across a "vast plain," which the Natives set on fire to hunt bison. Luckily for them, Daniel Dulhut, who traded with the Sioux, exchanged some goods for them, and returned them to Michilimackinac. Hennepin made his way home via Long Point, Niagara Falls, and the St Lawrence, and shipped for France. His narrative was published in January 1683, reprinted twice, and translated into Italian, Dutch, German, and, under his supervision, English. He was famous, and it went to his head. A second and third fictional account followed, ensuring infamy for Hennepin, who never returned to New France.[68]

In the same year that Hennepin's *New Discovery* was published, the Baron de Lahontan arrived in New France, a seventeen-year-old with a fine title but no estate. At the time most Canadiens were tenant *habitants* living on feudal land grants to seigneurs or the church. Annual rents, work levees, mill rates, and licences to hunt, fish, and log were their lot, and, to this, the church added its tithes, pew rentals, and fees for baptisms, marriages, and burials. These were legacies of the *ancien régime*, and 90 per cent of the population remained unschooled and illiterate through the first century of New France. Newcomers like Lahontan loved the place.[69]

In the spring of 1684, Lahontan joined an unsuccessful military foray to punish the Iroquois. He then spent two years around Montreal and Lake Champlain as an avid student of Native life. He signed up for another failed raid on the Iroquois, and was then assigned a troop of soldiers to venture north, starting from Dulhut's post on the St Clair River. He sent men overland to Niagara from there, who reported that the old Neutral country was vacant and wilding: "March'd ten days, fifty leagues, without seeing a soul." At Michilimackinac, he too took note of the Native "corn and beans ... [and] citruls [squash] and melons." They reached the Mississippi in March 1689 and, by July, Lahontan was back in Montreal, and appointed assistant to Governor Frontenac. Various misadventures trailed him to France and back, engaged him to the governor's god-daughter, and then chased him to Newfoundland and Holland. He drifted around Europe and, in 1703, published the work that made him famous. His were not the words of a cleric or a promoter but, he said, of "a savage myself, and that makes me speak so favourably of my fellow savages." Lahontan wrote about life and liberty in the wilderness, "the finest days of my life." This was a radical tonic for readers tired of Europe's miseries. Within seven years, more than fifteen editions of his book were printed in four languages.[70]

Lahontan's *Dialogues* with Adario, a Huron, expressed a philosophy that was reviled by the Jesuits as "dangerous" but would later influence thinkers like Jean-Jacques Rousseau and be called, in recent years, an "accurate picture of aboriginal American ideology" by the Huron philosopher Georges Sioui. Lahontan's praise of the Native was a direct criticism of Europe. "Tis vain to remonstrate to them [the Natives] how useful the distinction of property is for the support of a society. They brand us for slaves ... whose life is not worth having, alleging that we degrade our selves in subjecting our selves to one man [the king] ... [and] that ... all our sciences are not so valuable as the art of leading a peaceful calm life ... [and] to run well, to hunt ... to work a canoo, to understand war, to know forests ... and to be able to travel a hundred leagues ... without any guide." However, Lahontan was doing no favour to Natives by so significantly understating their interests in land and goods. Ironically, the baron spent much of his own life trying to recover property that had once been attached to his family title in France.[71]

The emphasis here has been on first-person accounts of the Native economy, land use, and ownership. The second part of the book will let these same first voices describe the natural world as they saw it. True, they often wove into their narratives some telling threads of cultural bias and self-promotion. For instance, Lahontan idealized *le bon sauvage* as cover for his critique of France. However, he and others were also first-hand, wide-eyed witnesses to a completely new world, and where their accounts corroborate one another, about physical phenomena such as places and peoples, crops and towns, and species and landscapes, they are no doubt trustworthy.

CHAPTER THREE

Wilding the Land with War: The 1700s

We can only touch on this period the way an impressionist painter might, barely colouring some foreground characters and framing their background. In this light, the overall picture is of warfare and wilding, collapsed land care, and an end to the original ecology of the place. It would take both space and time for it to take on its new wildness, and conflict guaranteed both.

In 1687 the kings of England and France were on friendly terms. This meant nothing in the New World. New France's governor, Denonville, led an army of seventeen hundred French and four hundred Natives south of Lake Ontario. A year earlier, he had ordered a brilliant overland strike against the English on James Bay, and an attack on the Seneca might similarly reverse the English tide. However, his army practised no stealth and the Seneca had time to reach Albany, rearm, and set an ambush. A hundred Frenchmen and uncounted Natives were killed. The French regrouped and turned on the town of Kanagaro but the Seneca burned it first and left only their corn fields, which the French spent five or six days destroying, "with our swords," wrote Lahontan. The French retreated with a few dozen Natives for the king's galleys (Fig. 7).[1]

In 1689 fifteen hundred Iroquois warriors retaliated. They laid waste the Montreal countryside, killing twenty-four French and abducting eighty. The same year, France and England declared war but again it had nothing to do with North America. A Dutch Protestant, William of Orange, had been invited to take over as the king of England from the Catholic James II, who fled to France. More than ever, overseas interests were worth investment and, before the war ended, the French had been driven from James and Hudson bays again.[2]

How capricious were the shifting loyalties? In 1696 Governor Frontenac led the French and their converted Iroquois Catholics around Montreal in another attack south of Lake Ontario. Again, the Onondaga were forewarned, and, on a tree, they painted a picture of the French army and laid beside it a bundle of 1,434 rushes, a precise count of the number of its soldiers. Then they fired their town and left. The French razed their corn fields and turned on the nearby Oneida, who were largely French sympathizers already converted by the Jesuits. The scorched-earth tactics left the people homeless, starved, and exhausted, and left the land to go wild.[3]

The French continued to project their influence westward. Antoine de Lamothe Cadillac founded the first European settlement above tidewater in North America, in 1701, bringing his own wife and child, and other families, to what is now Detroit. He invited the Huron and Petun refugees in the area to settle nearby, which they did, taking on the name Wendat, or Wyandot, again. After 1700, many of the Natives who had been displaced westward once more moved east to the Ohio valley and the west end of Lake Erie, forced by food shortages in the west and encouraged by the French at Detroit. This gave form to a multi-ethnic village world and a new western confederacy.[4]

The French and English were at war again by 1702. The Iroquois asked for neutrality and many of them began to rebuild, this time not the palisaded, attack-prone "castles" of former times but smaller homes separated by family fields, like those of the newcomers. The Iroquois were few, the Onondaga down to a single site, "about 2 or 3 miles long, yet the scattered cabins on both sides of the water [in today's Syracuse] are not above 40 in number ... so that the whole town is a strange mixture of cabins, interspersed with great patches of high grass, bushes and shrubs, with some pease, corn and squashes."[5]

The English kept the Iroquois by their side. A sensational London visit was orchestrated in 1710 for the "Four Indian Kings" – one of them the Mohawk Sa Ga Yeath Qua Pieth Tow, grandfather of Joseph and Molly Brant. They took in cultural highlights like cockfighting and learned how the English adored John Churchill, the Duke of Marlborough, for his brilliant leadership of their armies on the continent. At a performance of Shakespeare's *Macbeth*, the crowd chanted until the chiefs were invited to sit on stage, where they no doubt understood Macbeth's words, "blood will have blood." They met Queen Anne and were painted in full regalia by John Verelst. They saw in England a landscape totally owned and occupied. What could they have thought? Within two years, the English were building Fort Hunter in the Mohawk valley west of Albany, as proof of the alliance. Queen Anne presented the Mohawk with a new chapel and with silver communion plate and a common prayer book translated into Mohawk.[6]

Shielded by the alliance, the Five Nations extended their hand to others, notably to a small sibling nation, the Tuscarora, who were fleeing English settler attacks in the Carolinas. They joined as a non-voting member of a new Six Nations. At the same time, protected by the alliance and by Fort Hunter, settlers pushed up the Mohawk valley. By the 1730s, there were four thousand of them in the area, mostly Dutch and German, with about five hundred Mohawk just to their west.

Cadwallader Colden passed judgment on these settlers in 1727: "The meanest people of every nation ... [They had] industry in getting money, and they sacrificed every thing other people think honourable." Perhaps true, but also perfectly consonant with the world they came from. A few of them became honourable men, nevertheless. William Johnson, a young Irishman, arrived in 1738 to take care of an estate in the Mohawk valley which his uncle, Admiral Peter Warren, had bought from the widow of a New York governor for £110. Johnson was Catholic at a time when Catholics were being dispossessed of their land in Ireland, and his uncle instructed him to convert before taking up his post. He thus learned early to be morally adept, and to navigate between Catholic and Protestant, English and Irish, and, after learning to speak Mohawk, between the English and Iroquois. This was the new normal in North America, the "middle ground," as historian Richard White calls it, of shifting allegiances and mixed marriages. The fur trade was built by middlemen and Métis, and Johnson was a master of the middle ground.[7]

Johnson led an astonishing life as trader, soldier, and real estate and treaty agent. As Colden said, "Johnson is the most considerable trader with the western Indians ... All the ... Indians do the westward stop at his house and there were supplied, and ... few or none were seen [by the merchants] at Albany." Johnson differed from Colden's description of the mean settler only by degree, and the honour he achieved was less as a settler than it was as a middleman.[8]

Based on the Mohawk's trust, Johnson was appointed "Colonel" of the Six Nations by New York Governor George Clinton. King George made him a baronet for fighting the French. His liaisons were as chaotic as his times. His first partner was a young German émigré, Catharine, who died in 1759. Johnson then brought under his roof the Mohawk Molly (Mary) Brant, already with child. In due course Johnson would father more than fifteen children with at least five women, four of them Mohawk, and he was said to have sired many more, such as the great-grandfather of the poet Pauline Johnson. His profligacy grew with the telling but, in Iroquoia, Molly Brant was his "Lady Johnson," the chatelaine of Johnson Hall and partner in his role as adopted Mohawk. In his will he called Catharine his "wife" and legitimized their children's inheritance, and he called Molly his "housekeeper" and left their eight children with farms, land, and money.[9]

Modern upstate New York and Pennsylvania were Indian territory, Johnson's domain, but the Native nations were weak and unable to resist British expansion. To counter it, the French reinvested in Fort Niagara. The British countered with Fort Oswego, at the other end of Lake Ontario. The French then built a post at what would become Toronto. These were outposts, not settlements, and in the absence of Native care the land grew wilder. Around Detroit it was different and, by 1750, its farms had spread and its 483 settlers and 33 slaves raised both native crops and wheat, barley, oats, peas, peaches, pears, and apples, and had 3,370 head of livestock. At Detroit, land care was re-established, but in the European manner of the St Lawrence.[10]

Astute observers in these years included the botanists John Bartram and Pehr Kalm, and we will return to their observations later. Both were correspondents of Carl von Linnaeus, the Swedish classifier of flora and fauna, and they collected specimens for him. Bartram was the first New World-born botanist, a nurseryman and exploring naturalist. Self-taught, he shipped hundreds of plants to England and was appointed the King's royal botanist, with pension. His travels took him to Lake Ontario and the Onondaga capital where, in those days, the Onondaga still maintained the council and wampum of the Six Nations, in a longhouse "80 feet long, and 17 broad."[11]

Kalm came to America already elected to the Swedish academy of sciences. He enjoyed regular contact with Bartram, Cadwallader Colden, Benjamin Franklin, and others in British's coastal colonies and with Jean-François Gaulthier, the royal physician in Quebec. These were individuals who shared a philosophy described by Kalm as "the use of natural history, of the method of learning ... to make a country powerful." Science on the march. Early in his visit, Kalm interviewed the oldest Swedes in the former New Sweden and heard them lament "the great decrease in eatable fowl" and the "decrease in fish," which they put down to forest clearing, overhunting, overfishing, and mill dams. To them, by the 1740s, the changes were already "as between day and night."[12]

The Seven Years' War and Attempted Extirpation

In the sixty years leading up to 1750, the British and French were formally at war for half the time, and preparing for war the rest of the time. By 1754 they were at it again, and one of the opening salvos involved an British Army major, George Washington, whose men ambushed a French detachment in Ohio country, killed its leader, and were in turn defeated. In the east, a British battle victory triggered the 1755 expulsion of Acadians to Quebec and Louisiana. In the same year, a conference of eleven hundred Iroquois, Missisauga, and Delaware (Lenape) was hosted by William Johnson and Mohawk headman Hendrick to renew their war alliances. These actions were all peripheral to Great Lakes country, but the Great Lakes were the prize.

When war was finally declared in 1756, it was global in scale, pitting Britain, Prussia, and Hanover against France, Austria, Sweden, Saxony, Russia, and Spain. In North America, imperial expansion was the goal. On Lake Ontario, Fort Oswego changed hands twice. In 1758 Fort Frontenac (Kingston) and the Ohio valley fell to the British. Native grievances were rekindled; for example, the Delaware would be mollified only if Johnson himself would reconsider the Walking Treaty, forced on them by the Iroquois two decades earlier. In the west, the Native village-world remained uncommitted, and a new pan-Nativism was on the rise.

The main theatre was the St Lawrence and Lake Ontario. In 1759 a thousand Iroquois were led by Johnson to Fort Niagara, along with three thousand British under John Prideaux. They arrived in front of the fort and, when Prideaux stepped in front of a mortar and had his head blown off, Johnson assumed command. His Iroquois ambushed twelve hundred French marching in relief, and took 150 scalps and 100 prisoners. Niagara promptly surrendered. Johnson gave his word that the Iroquois would plunder the fort but treat the defeated French honourably, which they did. Only three Iroquois died in the campaign, and fewer than 60 British. *Le pays d'en haut* was thus severed from the St Lawrence. The role of Natives was decisive.

In September 1759, after a three-month siege led by James Wolfe, Quebec City fell to the British. That winter, the victors were themselves under siege, praying that it would be British reinforcements that arrived first the following spring. They were, and the French army retreated upstream. That summer Johnson led seven hundred warriors to the St Lawrence and persuaded another eight hundred French allies to join them. Together they marched on Montreal and the Catholic Mohawk from Kahnawake, long-time partners of the French, marched as his personal bodyguard. They met the British General Jeffery Amherst along the way, at the surrender of Fort Lévis. Unlike Johnson at Niagara, Amherst would not permit any Natives to plunder Fort Lévis, on the grounds they were too savage. The Natives got the message, and fewer than a third of them continued on to Montreal to accept the final French capitulation. Thus expired New France. So too ended, for a while, the centrality of the Iroquois. As General Thomas Gage put it, "North America in the hands of a single power robs them of their consequence, presents & pay."[13]

The news of France's defeat and Amherst's insult did nothing to placate the western tribes. They were further offended by the British haste to take advantage. Amherst quickly issued a monopoly over the Niagara portage, and Johnson warned him: "There appears to be a universal jealousy amongst every nation [which] will never subside whilst we encroach within the limits which, you may recollect, have been put under the protection of the king." Amherst demurred: "It never was my design to take an inch from them, unless when the necessity ... obliges me to." Necessity, it turned out, was whatever Amherst thought fit and, among other things, it meant an end to the supply of gunpowder to the Iroquois. By this time Amherst had been in the Americas a total of three years, never west of Oswego. In 1761 he used the phrases "entire destruction" and "extirpate them root & branch" three times in letters to Johnson, who protested to the powerful London Board of Trade, arguing instead for "diplomacy and generosity."[14]

Among the western tribes, a confederacy was taking shape. A Native prophet, a Delaware named Neolin, revealed himself in 1762. "The land on which you are, I have made for you, not for others ... Drive from your lands those dogs in red clothing." In 1763 the confederacy's war chief, Pontiac, led a full assault by nine hundred warriors - Ottawa, Ojibwa, Missisauga, Potawatomi, Wyandot, and others. Nine of the eleven English forts on the Great Lakes were taken, and Detroit and Pittsburgh were laid siege. Two thousand settlers were killed, and many more evacuated.[15]

In response, William Trent, commander of the Pittsburgh militia, began spreading smallpox. "We gave them two blankets and an handkerchief out of the smallpox hospital. I hope it will have the desired effect." In July, Colonel Henry Bouquet wrote to Amherst committing himself "to inoculate the Indians by means of blankets." Amherst approved, and urged him "to try every ... method that can serve to extirpate this execrable race." A major snowfall ended Pontiac's war on 29 October, and the next day a messenger arrived with the news that France and Great Britain were again at peace, and that no help would come from the French. Pontiac and his army dispersed, and General Amherst was recalled to London, never to return.[16]

The next year, British forces were massed to attack Pontiac but Amherst's plan for a race-war was changed, under Johnson's influence, into a demonstration of British power instead. Even so, Pontiac retreated to the Maumee River, and the Potawatomi and many Wyandot and Delaware also shifted west. Johnson convened a council of nations at Fort Niagara, and two thousand came. Johnson gave them presents and cash totalling the fantastic sum of £38,000, excluding the cost of £25,000 for the month-long council. Johnson's influence was at its zenith at the very time that the influence of Natives was at its lowest. Pontiac's rebellion was a final, failed attempt at Native sovereignty. They would instead soon become expert at what the British now required of them, their land rights.[17]

Land and the Royal Proclamation

How would the land be settled? Each of the individual British colonies or provinces, as well as New France and the Hudson's Bay Company, had different arrangements with the Natives. For instance, in 1742, the lieutenant governor of Pennsylvania followed up on the Iroquois' earlier services in evicting the Delaware, and signed a treaty with the Iroquois Six Nations to buy from them the lands along the Susquehanna River. This fiction was based on the earlier attempt by the Mohawk, acting for the Dutch, to conquer the Susquehannock. By this deceit, the Susquehannock nation ceased to exist. As with the Delaware, the land had nothing to do with the Six Nations except that it could be claimed by right of conquest, and thus sold.[18]

Two years later, both Virginia and Maryland similarly treated with the Six Nations to extirpate their presumed land rights (by conquest) in exchange for goods worth £100 sterling. The signatory was the same Canasatego, the Onondaga headman who had helped the English displace the Delaware and Susquehannock. At one point, Canasetego berated the bickering provincial commissioners: "We are a powerful confederacy; and by your observing the same methods ... you will acquire fresh strength and power." Benjamin Franklin, signatory to the U.S. constitution, was at that council taking notes.[19]

Establishing a paper trail was the preferred British approach and, by 1750, there were many experts in such treaties. William Johnson was the "Indian agent" of choice and he supported Native interests in selling land. Many

Iroquois, including Johnson's protégé Joseph Brant, Molly's brother, saw the benefits. By the age of thirteen, in 1755, Brant had already fought under the Mohawk Hendrick against the French. He and his mentor, Johnson, acknowledged Native land ownership as the basis for its sale. "Each nation," Johnson wrote, "is perfectly well acquainted with their exact original bounds, the same is again divided into due proportions for each tribe [clan], and afterwards subdivided into shares to each family, with all [of] which they are most particularly acquainted, neither do they ever infringe upon one another." It was the same in the north; in 1761 Alexander Henry noted on the Ottawa River how "the Algonquins ... claim all the lands on the Outaouis as far as Lake Nipisingue; and that these lands are subdivided between their several families, upon whom they have devolved by inheritance."[20]

By contrast, the French held to the ancient code of crown rights, that the land was theirs by right of discovery, conquest, and occupation. This was the case with Cartier on the Gaspé in 1534 and at Montreal in 1535, Casson and Galinée on Lake Erie in 1669, and Dulhut west of Lake Superior in 1679. The claim to the "lands of Lake Erie," for example, took "possession in the name of their king, as of unoccupied territory." Crown rights meant there was no need for treaties. The British, however, played it both ways, entering into treaties when they served even while accepting other parties' rights by conquest, such as those of the Dutch and Iroquois.[21]

The Iroquois were active players in all this, and their leaders, such as the Mohawk Hendrick in 1754, understood the implications: "After we have sold our land we in a little time have nothing to shew for it; but it is not so with you ... They will say we were fools for selling so much land for so small a matter." Nevertheless, land sales grew. Astutely, the Mohawk began to lease it and benefit directly from tenant revenues. The first leases were to Canadiens around Kahnawake on the St Lawrence, followed by leases in Iroquoia. The leases built relationships between settlers and Natives but, as historian Alan Taylor notes in *The Divided Ground*, "leasing alarmed the colonial elite as a double threat: to their designs on Indians lands and to their control over common whites." Johnson defended the practice: "If the Indians are ... the proprietors of their lands ... they certainly can give preference to whom they like." In his own dealings, Johnson's code of practice was based on council meetings, sworn interpreters, and notarized documents. Liquor and creative surveys were not his way. Even so, he came to own as much as six hundred thousand acres of land personally. His approach also had legal backing. In 1757 the king's legal advisers rendered the Pratt-Yorke opinion, which validated "the right of any English subject to acquire land from any Indian who would sell or give it to him, and the right to enter upon it and possess it."[22]

The imperial elite had other ideas. Such transactions were to cease. A Royal Proclamation to this effect was issued by George III in October 1763. It embodied two principles. First, weakly stated, "Nations or tribes of Indians ... should not be molested or disturbed in the possession of such parts of our dominions and territories as, not having been ceded to or purchased by us, are reserved to them." Second, and more emphatically, all cessions of land would be the exclusive domain of the "crown." The first of these was an acknowledgment of the reality of the territories beyond the influence of settlement, such as Pontiac's western confederacy. The second was the legal formula for securing those same lands by treaty. While not an issue in the north or the west, where there were very few whites, there was a steady press of newcomers south of the lakes looking for land, and many of them already had it by virtue of private land sales and leases. The Proclamation asked these settlers to "remove themselves" but, of course, this did not happen.

The Proclamation also mapped the "Indian territory" reserved to them, west of the Appalachians, the same as mapped in the treaty that ended the Seven Years' War. This "Proclamation line" was the western extent of the thirteen existing British colonies. All the lands east of it were deemed to be occupied by conquest, private deals, settlement, or coercion, and were exempt from the Proclamation. This exemption was also extended to the two new provinces of Quebec and Nova Scotia. West of the line was Indian territory, the first-ever recognition of Native territory in British law, and an immediate source of resentment among frontier residents. Maps were serious business for people hot for land and, inflaming matters further, in 1774, the British altered the boundary of the new province of Quebec to include the unceded Native lands south of the Great Lakes.[23]

The Proclamation's bottom line was to prohibit private land sales or leases by Natives. In this way, the Natives were "under our sovereignty," the Proclamation said. The motive was money. The British authorities needed the revenues from land sales to pay the costs of administering their provinces, and, later, the American authorities would need the same revenues to pay the debts incurred in fighting the British and to backstop their infant currencies. In all of this, land was key. The authority to secure, sever, and sell land was the equivalent of printing money.[24]

The Proclamation was one of the grievances fuelling the American Revolution, particularly for the Dutch, who had a long history with Johnson and the Mohawk. They hosted "patriot" gatherings within a month of William Johnson's death in 1774 to inflame anti-Proclamation and anti-Native sentiment. After the Revolution, however, the new elite, including those of Dutch origin, quickly adopted the part of the Proclamation that stated it was only *they* who had the right to treat for Native lands. This sense of "racial entitlement," as historian Alan Taylor calls it, set the stage for American aggression and the "Indian wars" to come. America's military tradition was founded on the suppression of Natives in the century between its revolution and its civil war.[25]

A more respectful British policy emerged from the same Proclamation and helped sustain the military partnerships, especially with the Iroquois, that would defend the Canadas against invasion after the revolution. Not once was there a case of serious military conflict between Europeans and Natives within the modern borders of eastern Canada. Natives and whites were allies in the defence of Canada against the Americans, just as in earlier times Natives had helped to defend New France against the English. The Natives still ended up with only a few small reserves, but by more civil means.[26]

Whose stories should be told? In 1760 Johnson nominated Joseph Brant to a scholarship at Moor's Indian Charity School in Connecticut, the precursor to Dartmouth College. Brant arrived there on horseback and was treated as a gentleman, learning enough in two years to begin a life of self-education that would see him act as attorney and even as translator of the Bible. In 1765 Brant married Margaret, the daughter of an Oneida headman, whom he met while on a war party orchestrated by Johnson to deal with (yet again) the Delaware. They settled in his father's modern home in the Mohawk valley, where he wore broadcloth and ran a store. They had two children, a son, Isaac, and a daughter, Christina.[27]

In 1769 Brant, accompanied by his wife and son, guided New Jersey-born Richard Smith on a tour of the Mohawk and Susquehanna valleys to inspect a land grant that Smith had just acquired south of the Mohawk homeland. As the trip progresses and Smith realizes that his guide is also a farmer and landowner, and educated, he mentions Brant more often in his diary. In the old Susquehannock homeland, Smith saw the remnants of Native life there: abandoned corn fields and orchards, deer fences, lands cleared by firing, and tombs, "one of them a flat pyramid about 3 feet high." Even by the time of Joseph Brant's youth, the traces of Native culture were fading, and the land was wilding. A long war over land was soon upon them, and Brant would be the Iroquois war chief.

Forty Years of War for the Canadas

In the years bracketed by the American Revolution and the War of 1812, the Canadas and the Indian territory between the American states and the Great Lakes were the scene of perpetual conflict between American republicans and British loyalists. The Native warrior was, once again, by turns trusted and needed, and reviled and feared. Forty years of guerrilla war, and war by other means, repeatedly swept the land of its inhabitants and let nature assert itself as wilderness.

The Thirteen Colonies rebelled against absentee governance. Their tax protests reached iconic status one night in December 1773 when seven tons of British tea were tipped into Boston harbour. The colonials dressed as Mohawk for the occasion, to signify that they were American and libertarian – like the Mohawk. The following year, smallpox broke out in Boston, killing whites and Natives alike, and spread west into Six Nations country. During the revolution, a patriot army failed in its march on Montreal and Quebec when smallpox caught up with it, saving the Canadas. Inoculations for smallpox had been introduced from Turkey to England in 1718, then to Boston in the 1720s, and some say the success of the revolution turned on the order by George Washington, later, to conduct the world's first mass inoculation of an army in 1778.[28]

William Johnson died months before the American Revolution began. The British named Joseph Brant as secretary to the superintendent of Indian affairs. The rebels also wooed both Joseph and Molly Brant. Brant's old master from the Charity School, Eleazor Wheelock, pressed him to side with the rebel cause but Brant's reply was that Wheelock himself had taught him to "honour the king." The rebels said they were a federation of nations, like the Six Nations, gave the Mohawk wampum and gifts, and asked only for neutrality. A rebel aide noted, "The Indians understand their game, which is to play into both hands." Of course, they had to play the hand they were dealt; by this time, the Mohawk numbered only four hundred, surrounded by more than forty thousand settlers.[29]

In 1775 Brant brought four of the Six Nations to the British side and then sailed to England to look for support. Like his grandfather before him, he was introduced to the king, this time George III, feted and showered with gifts, and painted in oils by George Romney. He was initiated as a Mason. While he was away, three thousand rebels invaded the Mohawk valley. They played on the pool table in Johnson Hall and helped themselves to William Johnson's famous collection of Indian artifacts. Brant returned the next summer, fought with the British on Long Island, and then worked his way up the Susquehanna valley to rally the Iroquois.

Brant led a brilliant guerrilla campaign against the rebels, perfecting the age-old raiding tactics of the Iroquois. But only a fifth of Brant's "Volunteers" were Mohawk. The rest were white loyalists who dressed as Natives. Brant armed and fed them, harboured their families, and led them back to their original homelands to fight. He had command of four hundred and fifty at the battle of Oriskany in 1777, where about four hundred rebels were killed. In early 1778 his Volunteers killed 340 rebels on the Susquehanna. In September, they raided the Mohawk valley, destroying sixty-three homes, as many barns, and all the mills. Three settlers were killed. The Volunteers took Cherry valley, killing thirty and capturing seventy. Brant was introduced as the genius of frontier warfare, essential to Canada's defence, when he met the British governor, Frederick Haldimand, in Quebec in 1779.[30]

It was brutal and personal. William Johnson was dead a full three years when John Adams, the revolutionary leader and second president of the new republic, wrote: "The family of Johnson, the black part of it as well as the white, are pretty well thinned ... They deserve extermination." Theft, revenge, and vilification were the rule, both during and after the war.[31]

Another Campaign, Another Treaty

The American Revolution split the Six Nations. Most Oneida and Tuscarora, and many Seneca, backed the Americans, while others supported Brant and the British. However, the American general George Washington made no distinctions and wanted them all gone, "not merely overrun but destroyed ... Our future security will be in ... the terror with which the severity of the chastisement they receive will inspire them." His strategy was "pushing the Indians to the greatest practicable distance from their own settlements and our frontiers ... throwing them wholly on the English."[32]

In August 1779 General John Sullivan prosecuted Washington's orders with five thousand men. They made a clear run for the Genesee valley and torched forty-eight Seneca towns and villages, and corn fields and orchards, one of them with fifteen hundred fruit trees. Chenussio (Genesee) itself had 128 houses, many of them large and elegant, in Sullivan's words, "almost encircled with a cleared flat, which extended for a number of miles, covered by the most extensive fields of corn, and every kind of vegetable ... The corn was

collected and burned ... which method we have pursued in every other place."
Sullivan then retraced his steps and eliminated any Cayuga he had missed on
his outward leg. Women and children were targeted in what was called the
"squaw campaign." (Even American General James Clinton acknowledged
that the Iroquois "never violate the chastity of any woman," and Brant always
claimed "he made no war upon women and children.")[33] The destruction was
complete, Sullivan guaranteed the U.S. Congress. "We have not left a single
settlement or field of corn ... nor is there even the appearance of an Indian on
this side of Niagara." To this day, it is said there are more signs along New York
highways celebrating Sullivan's attempted genocide than any other event in
state history (Fig. 8).[34]

Loyalty to the British was thus hardly unexpected. Brant and his men
took Sullivan's march to heart and resumed their raids the following February,
again in the Mohawk valley. A force of fifteen hundred led by Brant and by
John Johnson, William's son, cleared every white settlement out of the valley
west of Schenectady. Brant burnt his own home village of Canajoharie, which
the republicans had occupied. Between this campaign and Sullivan's, only
two Native towns were left in old Iroquoia, Seneca settlements that were both
visited, in the winter of 1781, with smallpox.[35]

Of course, most of the Natives were non-combatants, and homeless. Two
hundred Mohawk headed north for Kahnawake, led by John Deserontyon.
Five thousand Iroquois fled to the Niagara frontier. Two-thirds of them
were women, children, and elders. Fort Niagara became a refugee camp, and
Governor Haldimand struggled to support them. He knew that they – and the
white loyalists who were also arriving by the thousands – represented the only
chance for a future British presence in central North America. The Niagara
camp, "The Bottom," degenerated into a horror of shanties, taverns, and
brothels. The Americans set up a camp for displaced Oneida near Schenectady;
it was more of the same, but with smallpox as well. At Niagara, there was little
to share, and jealousies were rife. The senior Mohawk clan mother, Molly
Brant, worked to calm the people; her influence was "far superior to that of all
their chiefs put together." Many died and, ten years later, human bones could
still be seen littered about the fort. The offers by Haldimand of land grants
began to look attractive. For his own part, Brant took up a farm upriver of Fort
Niagara and, his first and second wives having died, married again, this time
to Catharine Croghan, a Mohawk clan mother.[36]

Haldimand got word in 1782 that the war was ended and that a peace treaty
would follow. There were 100,000 British subjects in the Canadas, outnumbered

by 2.5 million Americans. For those who had resisted the new republic, there would be no quarter given. Brant began to look for a home for his people. He attended the U.S. Continental Congress on behalf of the Six Nations, and asked for a land settlement. He failed, for obvious reasons – the end of the war meant that everyone was obliged to declare himself either a patriot or royalist or, as the Canadian narrative has it, rebel or loyalist. For everyone with a home, family, or property, whether Native or white, the choices were brutal. The first white loyalist refugees arrived at the Niagara River and the St Lawrence in 1778 and, eventually, roughly one in twenty-five of the white inhabitants of the former Thirteen Colonies, and likely well over three-quarters of their resident Natives, left for the north and west.

The Treaty of Paris of 1783 was a diplomatic coup for the new United States. Benjamin Franklin was one of its negotiators and he went so far as to baldly request that Britain make a "voluntary offer of Canada" as a conciliatory gesture. Language was drafted to this effect but, in response to an unrelated matter (Gibraltar withstood a Spanish siege), British interests firmed and a boundary was pencilled down the centre of the Great Lakes and St Lawrence. This ceded a vast territory to the Americans and was seen as an act of betrayal by everyone in the Canadas – who had not lost any of their lands in the interior during the revolution and who still held Detroit, Niagara, Michilimackinac, and Oswego. Haldimand wept: "My soul is completely bowed down with grief at seeing that we (with no absolute necessity) have humbled ourselves so much as to accept such humiliating boundaries. I am heartily ashamed and wish I was in the interior of Tartary." Native allies were devastated; the British general Allen MacLean reported how Joseph Brant charged that "England has sold the Indians to Congress." To distract Native anger, MacLean released eighteen hundred gallons of alcohol to the Natives at The Bottom in Niagara.[37]

The treaty required the American Congress to "recommend" that the states compensate loyalists for their losses of land and property. However, the states refused to repeal their Confiscation Laws and their Laws of Attainder. Instead, they accelerated the confiscations. In the same way that the Royal Proclamation had validated the Thirteen Colonies' right to their land by conquest, the new thirteen states applied a similar "right by conquest" to their former neighbours' lands.[38]

The best map of North America at the time was one compiled and published in London by the Virginian John Mitchell. An early edition of his map was used by English authorities when they issued the Royal Proclamation, and it was his map's fourth edition in 1775 that was appended to the Treaty of

Paris. This is arguably the most important map in the history of the region, the first broad-scale land-tenure map of northeast North America. Called the "red-lined map," it included a new southern limit for the Canadas, a new international boundary, and the western limits of the former British provinces. Still unmarked (and unceded) was the Native territory between them. It was for these Native lands that a highly aggressive war by other means soon began.[39]

Empire States

The American Revolution left the land south and west in Great Lakes country open for business and it quickly filled with settlers, ushered in by rapid-fire land deals. By 1780, whites outnumbered Natives in upper New York State by fifteen to one. Numerical superiority soon turned to moral superiority, and both the real and fictitious atrocities of the war years were blamed on the Natives. This in turn justified the unilateral usurpation of their land; in 1782 New York State, without benefit of treaty and in defiance of the U.S. Congress, confiscated 1.5 million acres of Cayuga and Onondaga land to raise funds to pay off its soldiers.

In 1784 the New York legislature moved to monopolize land transactions by asserting its right, as the natural successor of the British crown, to the exclusive control of all sales of Native land. Speed was of the essence because six of the thirteen states had original "royal charters" that established them from "sea to sea." New York was not one of them, but Massachusetts was and it was looking to expand west. At the same time, the U.S. Congress had its own designs. Again, the issue was money. The Articles of Confederation granted no authority over Native territories, nor did they confer on the federal government the power to raise taxes, even in support of its currency. The states were in no better shape; they had to pay off the debts they had incurred in raising armies to fight the revolution. Land, and its sale, was the easiest way to finance the new nation and its states.

The strongest wartime ally of the United States, the Oneida, was the first challenge. They lived on lands reserved by Congress "for their sole use and benefit." Numbering only six hundred at the time, the Oneida adapted well, building a buffer of dependent settlements on their east side. They granted lands to influential New Yorkers and entered into lease agreements that brought a steady income. New York State did not approve, however, and adopted the pretence that the Oneida were being duped by white land jobbers. Clearly, they needed state assistance and New York Governor George Clinton offered it freely. Congress argued that this was a federal matter but Clinton acted, and won the Oneida lands as a result.[40]

He did so by means of council and treaty. Both state and federal agents initiated rival councils with the Iroquois at the same time and place in late 1784. When talk at the federal council got serious, Clinton seduced the Natives with free alcohol. Federal officers moved to impound the liquor but the state sheriff arrested the federal officers for theft. Meanwhile, spokesmen for the Iroquois declared that they were sovereign and should be treated as equals, but the federal agents were clear. "It is not so. You are a subdued people." Two days later a treaty was signed and, the next day, Pennsylvania got its own treaty extirpating all Iroquois interests in return for $5,000 in goods. Six of the Natives who signed were held as hostages until the following spring.[41]

Later in 1784, after plying an Oneida headman with rum, a speculator got a deed to other Oneida lands. The Oneida protested and the state again stepped in to "protect" them, and required them to sell to the state a tract five times larger. The Oneida came back with a proposal to lease the land instead, but Clinton informed them that the state would be unable to protect them if they did not sell their lands outright. The next day the Oneida signed, guided by their clan mothers, who wanted peace and food relief. A tract of 460,000 acres was sold for cash and for the food left over from the council. The historian Alan Taylor adds it up: "During the next two years, New York sold 343,594 acres in the cession for $125,955, dwarfing the $11,500 paid to the Oneida."[42]

The pattern was set. The next Oneida land deal, a lease of five million acres, also inspired a state intervention. The deal would have given the Oneida a large reservation, prime fishing sites, and cash of $16,500 over fifteen years. Petrus, speaking for the Oneida, cited the U.S. guarantee of their land rights and said they were "determined not to sell any of their lands." Clinton stepped in again, and the legislature vetoed the deal. Two more years of negotiation got New York a treaty for the same lands, owned outright, for less.[43]

The treaties in the 1780s were made easier by widespread crop failures, due to record low temperatures, as much as four degrees colder than the 225-year average. The cold lasted five years, the result of light-shielding dust injected into the atmosphere in 1783 by volcanic eruptions at Laki, Iceland, and at Asama, Japan. Life was hard everywhere. The year 1793 then brought disease to the U.S. capital of Philadelphia, killing five thousand – one in every ten. Not sure of its origins, some blamed the passenger pigeons: "When the pigeons continue with us all the winter ... such winters are often followed by malignant epidemics." Other doctors were prescribing pigeon dung as a remedy for other disorders. Treaties did not make the headlines of the day.[44]

The state treaties rolled west but, to stall their advance and to protest the U.S. failure to meet the terms of the Treaty of Paris to compensate loyalists, Britain held on to its Great Lakes forts. In 1791 Fort Miami was built on the Maumee River to maintain a strong alliance of Native nations and guard the southern approaches to Detroit. Detroit was a growing trade centre, port to a dozen ships of fifty tons or more, and service hub for the western tribes, which numbered many thousands locally, such as those living in a "continuous village for a number of miles" along the Maumee. Not far away, in the same year, Pennsylvania laid claim to its last "triangle" on Lake Erie, in a treaty settled for $15,640. New American forts followed.[45]

Late in 1791, President Washington sent another army west. The Natives encircled it on the Wabash and, in a daring attack, killed over 690, suffering only 60 casualties. This was history's greatest Native victory over U.S. forces, and the Natives filled the dead soldiers' mouths with dirt to mock their lust for land. Revenge came in 1794 when General Anthony Wayne systematically pushed the frontier to the Maumee River and defeated the Natives at Fallen Timbers (near modern Toledo). The British at Fort Miami refused to help the fleeing Natives, and their dead went uncounted. Wayne destroyed nine towns and imposed a treaty on ninety Native signatories from a dozen tribes, who ceded most of Ohio, and Detroit and Chicago, in exchange for "goods."[46]

Before this final campaign, one group of Delaware made it north of the lakes, descendants of those who were forced off their land by the Walking Treaty of 1737 and by the Iroquois. They had joined a Moravian mission in 1768, led by David Zeisberger, who chronicled their painful retreat westward. For example, about ninety of them were massacred by American militia in one incident in 1782. Finally, ten years later, Zeisberger asked for help from William Dummer Powell, a loyalist judge who lived beside the Wyandot mission on the Detroit River. Powell asked the Indian agent Alexander McKee where they might settle and, in April 1792, they boarded boats and canoes and worked their way up the Thames River to a new home they would call Fairfield, not far from other refugees, including the Iroquois on the Grand River.[47]

The Wyandot, former Huron stock, were among those who ceded their American lands in 1795, and were finally relocated to Kansas, where they had to buy land from other refugee Delaware. North of the lakes, they sold their land interests in 1790, except for their old mission on the Detroit River and a reserve on the Canard River. The former they sold in 1800 for £300 in merchandise, and the latter was split, in 1881, among its forty-one final families, to stay or sell as they pleased.

By 1800, the Empire State of New York was fully grown, west to Lake Erie and north to the six-square-mile reserve left for the St Regis-Akwesasne Mohawk on the 45th parallel. State revenues from land sales between 1790 and 1795 showed a net profit of more than $1 million, *after* the full cost of surveys, councils, treaties, purchases, and annuities. This, in turn, set the stage for private enterprises like the Ohio, Scioto, and Holland land companies and the Pennsylvania Population Company to make even more profit. In 1790 the state of New York was America's fifth-largest by population, lagging behind Virginia, Massachusetts, Pennsylvania, and North Carolina. By 1820, New York was the colossus of American states, its most populous, and its leader in both wealth and exports, subsidized in large part by its Native land transactions.[48]

North of the Lakes

The American Revolution forced an exodus of migrants north of the lakes, and the British administration knew it was not ready. In 1776 Henry Hamilton was appointed to govern western Canada's largest settlement, and he described Detroit before the influx: "The industry and enterprising spirit of the [British] traders of this post so far outgo the [French] Canadians that I am persuaded the latter will in a very few years be dependants on ... the former ... The straight ... [is] plentifully stocked with variety of fine fish ... yet not one French family has got a seine ...The soil is so good that great crops are raised by careless & very ignorant farmers." There were, of course, no markets as yet for any increase in production, but Hamilton was as ambitious for growth as the elites south of the lakes.[49]

Frederick Haldimand took over as governor in 1777. He was a military man with long service fighting the French and the Americans. In the aftermath of the revolution, his goal was to hold on to the British posts on the lakes, to serve as the necessary arrival camps for refugees, Native and white alike. He also moved quickly to legitimize a land-tenure system that could accommodate the refugees and adhere to the Royal Proclamation. Not all the refugees could wait; some Seneca, Cayuga, and Onondaga elected to stay on reserves near Buffalo, New York, while some Oneida privately bought land on the Thames River north of the lakes.[50]

There were about a thousand Ojibwa Missisauga on the Ontario peninsula north of lakes Erie and Ontario - hunting, fishing, farming, and trading - and they were soon the object of Haldimand's ambitions. In 1781, in return for 300 suits of clothing, the Missisauga sold the land on the west bank of the Niagara River from Lake Erie to Lake Ontario. The same year, the Ojibwa sold the island of Michilimackinac to the British, not knowing that the authorities in London would cede Michilimackinac – and all the Great Lakes forts – to the Americans two years later.[51]

Other treaties were signed with the Missisauga in 1783 and 1784 – for the Bay of Quinte area on the north shore of Lake Ontario, and for the land down the St Lawrence to the Ottawa River. The treaties specified the lands and the payments; one of them had a one-time payment of clothing for all families, guns for the unarmed, powder and ball, twelve laced hats, and red cloth for twelve coats. Haldimand held one township on the Bay of Quinte for the Mohawk who had recently migrated to Kahnawake. The clan mother Molly Brant joined them there, living herself in government housing in Kingston on a pension of £100 sterling a year.

White loyalists began arriving, and the British supplied them with land, and the tools to work it. These were difficult years; 1787 and 1788 were hot "hungry years" that dried up the crops and streams. The winter of 1790 was so hard that the deer in some places were almost wiped out by wolves. The king's storehouses were opened and emptied. Despite it all, the loyalists took root. Patrick Campbell, a Scottish farmer who travelled up the St Lawrence in 1791, was full of praise: "I now passed all the French settlements, and entered that occupied by ... loyalists; and though it is but eight years since the first tree was cut down in this district, they do not fall much short of having as much of the land cleared as the French who have been more than a hundred years in possession. The cause of this ... [is] the tenure of the land." Campbell was comparing the seigneurial tenant system of the French and the fee-simple ownership of the English.[52]

More refugees were created when, under Jay's Treaty of 1796, the British undertook again to vacate their lake posts. As a result, Haldimand ceded Fort Oswego to the Americans, who proceeded to expel the Natives there, most of them to Canada. Withdrawal from the other garrisons followed; Fort Niagara moving to Fort Erie, Michilimackinac to St Joseph Island, and Detroit across the river. The Great Lakes and St Lawrence would be the new border.

Detroit presented a unique problem. Claimed by the French through conquest, it had been settled by Native refugees following the Iroquois wars and then by French soldiers, traders, farmers, and voyageurs. Both shores were occupied. There were six windmills, three watermills, and 320 farms on the east shore alone. Following French practice, a series of narrow lots ran back from the shores, and, in the first twenty years of British rule, both sides of the Detroit River were resurveyed, severing the strip lots into occupied front lots and new back lots. However, many more lots would be needed after July 1796, when Detroit's military and most of its merchants and residents evacuated the west bank to resettle on the Canadian side of the river.[53]

In anticipation, in 1790, the Indian agent Alexander McKee signed a treaty with thirty-five headmen of the Ottawa, Ojibwa, Potawatomi, and Wyandot, paying them £1,200 for 1,344,000 acres of land stretching east to Catfish Creek, and reserving two sites for Natives on the Canadian shore. By evacuation day, almost all the Canadian shore from Point Pelee to Lake St Clair, and the hundreds of new back lots, had been surveyed and sold. The new land went to loyalists and to administrators. McKee, himself a loyalist, took compensation of £3,000 in 1788 for his American losses, which he converted into real estate, eventually controlling a hundred square miles of southwest Ontario. Land speculation was the growth industry of the day.[54]

A priority for Haldimand was the settlement of the Iroquois loyalists led by Joseph Brant. Brant considered the possibility of the Bay of Quinte, where his sister was, but he also weighed the benefits of remaining closer to the western tribes and chose instead a "tract of land consisting of about six miles on each side of the Grand River … from the River La Tranche [or Thames] into Lake Erie." In March 1783 Haldimand promised them the land "granted to them by a deed." First, however, a land treaty was legally required and, by then, the Missisauga had the land by virtue of conquest, having themselves expelled the Iroquois, who had earlier expelled the Neutral. Such a land grant would bring the Iroquois back again, and the superintendent of Indian affairs, John Johnson, Sir William's son, emphasized to Haldimand just how uneasy the Missisauga were at the thought of the Iroquois being granted their land. "They are so numerous, they will overrun their hunting grounds," as had happened before.[55]

Haldimand's agents settled with the Missisauga in 1784 for two and a half million acres extending from Niagara along the Lake Ontario shore as far as Burlington Bay, northwest from there to the Thames River, then downstream on it to a line straight north from Catfish Creek on Lake Erie. The price was £1180/7/4 and "presents," in return for "all that tract or parcel of land … together with the woods, ways, paths, waters, watercourses, advantages, emoluments and hereditaments, whatsoever." Some of the Missisauga left. Others were allowed to stay.[56]

Later that year, Haldimand made the promised grant to the Six Nations. Surveys would be done later. The land grant to the Six Nations was the largest to any loyalists. Sixteen hundred Iroquois loyalists took up the grant immediately, and more followed. They spaced their six nations along the river from its mouth – the Delaware and Cayuga first, and then the Onondaga, Seneca, Tuscarora, and Oneida. The Mohawk settled farthest upstream at Brant's Ford (Brantford), at the upper limit of navigation on the Grand and on the closest overland routes to Lake Ontario and the Thames. Brant invited others to take up land there as well. Some were white veterans who had fought with his Volunteers, some had useful farming skills, and some had Native wives and children. For doing so, Brant faced various charges, as well as serious internal rebuke and an assassination attempt. Some families left to join the Quinte Mohawk but Brant persevered, and the settlement at the ford prospered.[57]

The Grand was – and still is – a majestic river rising on the Ontario Island and full of inviting river meadows, oak slopes, prairie crests, and, close to its mouth, big waters and marshes. Patrick Campbell, the Scottish farmer, visited a few years later and called it "the finest country I have as yet seen ... none are more so in all America ... the soil rich." The Mohawk were, he said, "better and more comfortably lodged than the generality of the poor farmers in my country ... They have a deal of crop, and excellent cattle, inferior to none I have seen in the province."[58]

The years between the American Revolution and Jay's Treaty were ones of violent disruption, of terrorism and counter-terrorism, and of refugees and expulsions. The war for the Great Lakes country was prosecuted aggressively by Americans and British alike. Fundamentally, it was about land, and the competing claims of its usurpers, aggravated by the fresh insult of daily casualties. The undeniable outcome of their pincer movement was compared by a Delaware of the day to a pair of scissors, the two blades of which appear as if they would harm each other but in reality harm only "us, poor Indians, that are between them. By this means, they get our land."[59]

Brant and Simcoe

Joseph Brant, commissioned by the king as "Captain of the Northern Confederate Indians," was also a master of land transactions, and it was land and compensation that occupied his attention on his second visit to England in 1785. He was again entertained by the king, George III, whose hand he would not kiss – he kissed the queen's instead. More pomp and circumstance but no commitments. Brant accepted compensation for the Mohawk losses in the American Revolution, £15,000, including £1,112 for himself and £1,206 for his sister Molly. He was also granted a pension of five shillings a day for life, and he left for home with canaries, a parrot, and a monkey.[60]

In 1791 the Canadas were divided into upper and lower provinces. John Graves Simcoe was appointed lieutenant governor of Upper Canada and arrived by way of Quebec the following July. He too was a resolute defender of empire, sensitive to the infamy of the Treaty of Paris cession of the Indian territories to the United States. On this he was clear: "Upper Canada is not to be defended by remaining within the boundary line." His ambitions ran to a second fort, modelled on Fort Miami, on the Mississippi. However, peace and stability had to be the priorities. His "most material concern … is the management of the Indian nations … to counteract the machinations and encroachments" of the United States. Whites in Upper Canada numbered only ten thousand in 1791, and there were ten times as many south of the lakes.[61]

Brant was Britain's ally but he never missed a chance to extract American counter-offers. He toured the Iroquois homeland in 1792, visited New York City, and dined with President Washington in Philadelphia. Word of this soon got to Simcoe, who noted: "Brant … said that the offers of Congress … were a township for himself, as much lands as he chose for the Indians, and a guinea a day for himself for life." Needless to say, other Mohawk considered his conduct disgraceful. They would have heard the stories, verified only later, that Brant had taken secret payments from the American secretary of war.[62]

Brant bought land for himself from the Missisauga at Burlington Beach, beside Lake Ontario. At the other end of the beach strand lived his Welsh friend from the Mohawk valley, Augustus Jones, who was the province's deputy surveyor and married to the daughter of a Mohawk headman. Brant and Jones rode their horses together on the strand, and it was Jones who was asked to conduct the survey, seven years later, of the limits of Haldimand's 1784 treaty with the Missisauga. The survey started in January 1791, headed northwest from the mouth of a stream near Brant's house on Burlington Bay. The survey line crossed the Grand River on its way to the Thames, and that line – the Jones Line – was the northern limit of the lands ceded by the Missisauga and granted to the Six Nations.[63]

It was left to Simcoe to deliver the substance of Haldimand's promises. As soon as he had Jones's survey, he expressed surprise at its size.

"The extent of this grant was unknown to me until at a public council Captain Brant produced the promise under the hand of General Haldimand." Even so, Simcoe issued a "patent," signed 14 January 1793, that clearly set out its boundaries, up "the said [Grand] river as far as the same has been purchased by us ... of the said Mississague nation."[64]

What was less clear were the legal rights granted. It was *not* an outright grant of land ownership, Simcoe wrote: "Indian nations were precluded [by the Proclamation] from the sale or letting of their lands ... [which would] annul the intent of his majesty's government in making a permanent provision for the maintenance of the Indians ... and leave them at the mercy of the land jobbers." Just as Natives had learned in New York State, they were not to sell or lease their lands. Brant, however, had sufficient influence to have the patent set aside, and added a plea for sympathy. "The Indian hunts being worn out and their people ... yet not being sufficiently advanced in agricultural arts to maintain themselves, the letting of their lands appeared ... the most reasonable mode of making provision for their women, old men, and children."[65]

Brant's legal case was for equity - for "lands granted to the Indians as fully as to the loyalists." The Six Nations, he said, "were not always to be fools because they have once been such." Their lands were large enough for themselves and for others, and leases would bring steady revenue. Brant also pursued land sales, and obtained the power of attorney from thirty-five headmen to do so. Simcoe suggested a compromise: sell the land to "such persons as the king's government should approve" and "place the money in the British funds, giving the annual interest to the Indian proprietors." Brant "seemed to acquiesce in this idea," Simcoe reported, and such was the approach taken. Brant and the Six Nations understood leases, fee-simple title, annuities, and interest payments, and wanted to use them all. (It took until 1973 for Brant's legal opinion to be upheld by the Ontario High Court; their fee-simple lands could be sold or leased as they pleased.)[66]

On this basis, Brant acted as attorney for the Six Nations and arranged the sale of fully half the original grant, five townships. Speculators offered a total of £85,332, an average of fifty-seven cents per acre, and an annuity of over £5,000 a year. This was far more than Natives had ever received from government treaties or land sales, and seventy times more than the Missisauga had got for their tract of land - four times larger - only five years earlier.[67]

Simcoe balked, again citing the original intent that the "people of the Six Nations and their heirs [have] the full and entire possession ... always." However, in 1797, Simcoe was replaced by his deputy, Peter Russell, whom

Brant was soon able to unnerve. He met with U.S. and French officials in Philadelphia and spread rumours about that he would "march his Mohawks to assist in effecting a revolution, & overturning the British government in the province." He did not have to go that far, but, to make the point, "Colonel Brant accompanied by three hundred warriors waited upon President Russell [and] extorted from the Council a declaration that they would confirm the past [land] sales, and ... assent to their future disposition," as recounted by Chief Justice Powell. The following February, Brant attended council and his sales were approved. With this, Brant sold 352,000 of the 570,000 acres of the original Grand River land grant. More would follow.[68]

On their way back from Philadelphia the year before, Joseph Brant and John Deserontyon had met New York officials in Albany and done some business on the side. They signed away the last of the original Mohawk lands south of the lakes for $1,000 and $600 respectively. Brant claimed, "I have never appropriated a dollar of money belonging to my nation for my own use," but many thought otherwise. His estate on Burlington Bay was formalized as a grant of 3,450 acres in 1798, and he built one of the finest homes in Upper Canada, a Georgian mansion where he served the best fare, on the finest plate. Patrick Campbell's description of Brant's hospitality was typical: "Two slaves attended the table, the one in scarlet, the other in coloured clothes, with silver buckles in their shoes, and ruffles ... We drank freely after dinner, port and Madeira wines." At times, Brant's household had more than twenty servants and slaves.[69]

Brant was Anglican and a devotee of cultural adaptation by the Mohawk. As soon as his band of loyalists arrived on the Grand, the Mohawk Chapel was built. To establish its historic lineage, the chapel was invested with the silver communion service and Bible that Queen Anne had given to the original Mohawk valley chapel after Brant's grandfather visited London in 1710. Cultural change was not always reciprocated, however. Brant proposed the severance and sale of lots; the authorities refused. Brant wanted to keep a registry of their lands; authorities discouraged it. Brant helped complete a Mohawk translation of prayer books; this was encouraged.[70]

Joseph Brant died at his home on Burlington Beach in November 1807. He had taken the full measure of life, much in the mould of his mentor William Johnson. It was Brant who had led the resistance by the Iroquois and loyalists, and prolonged the instability that gave nature more time to go wild. His wife, Catharine, appointed their son John to assume his father's mantle but he died without issue, and she had to choose a second heir, this time her daughter's son William Simcoe Kerr, whose great-grandfather was, of all people, William Johnson himself.[71]

The War of 1812, the Final Cessions, and Progress

Not all wars have ecological consequences. The War of 1812, though locally bloody and personally grievous, took place even while settlers kept arriving. It was a sideshow to the Napoleonic Wars in Europe, and seizing Canada had the smell of manifest destiny about it, as U.S. Secretary of War William Eustis said: "We can take the Canadas without soldiers." The grounds for optimism were that 80 per cent of the 65,000 people in Upper Canada in 1811 were from south of the border, or their descendants. Even the British commander, George Prevost, doubted that more than a third of his militia were to be trusted. Both sides underestimated the bitterness of the dispossessed loyalists and the loyalty of the peaceful Canadiens.[72]

The United States declared war on Britain and its dependencies in June 1812. In July General William Hull invaded Upper Canada from Detroit. He courted the Six Nations on the Grand, with no success, and so did the British lieutenant governor, Isaac Brock, with more success. The northern Six Nations, with their annuities from land sales invested in English banks, were asked to fight their southern Six Nations brethren, whose annuities were invested in American banks. The western tribes under Tecumseh had no such annuities.

Brock struck fast. Michilimackinac was taken in July by a raw crew of troops, voyageurs, and Natives, and soon afterwards Hull retreated to Detroit and surrendered it, in fear of the "northern hive of Indians" and Brock's claim that they were "beyond my control." At the same time, Hull ordered the U.S. fort at Chicago abandoned. A second American army was lost on the Niagara River in October, when two hundred Natives counter-attacked at Queenston Heights, helping force the surrender of a thousand Americans. Mohawk chief John Norton led the allies, aided by William Kerr, Joseph Brant's son-in-law, and John Brant, his son. Brock was killed in the action, and great emotions were at play in Canada. The key was guarding the supply lines from Lower Canada, and British-Canadian forces repelled various attacks on the St Lawrence.[73]

The following October the British withdrew from Ohio and Detroit. Pursued up the Thames by the Americans, the western war chief Tecumseh and his one thousand warriors pleaded unsuccessfully for General Henry Procter to resist. Finally, they turned to fight at the Delaware village, Fairfield.

Procter, as witnessed by Major John Richardson, "mounted on an excellent charger, and accompanied by his personal staff, sought safety in flight," and the troops and Natives fought on. Tecumseh was shot, and the Americans "made razor strops of his skin." This was the last time the Iroquois and western nations fought together, and it marked the end of the western confederacy.[74]

Two American armies marched west from Niagara in 1813. The first was stopped by a night attack at Stoney Creek that took a hundred Americans prisoner, and the second was stopped at Beaver Dams, where more than four hundred Iroquois attacked the Americans, causing 75 casualties and so much fear that 460 Americans surrendered to 50 irregulars called the "Green Tigers." Norton, Kerr, and Brant were again the Native leaders. They saw action the next year at Chippewa, where they faced their New York brethren directly. After that, only a few of them rallied for the final standoff at Lundy's Lane, or to harry the last American army, which attacked from Detroit in October and almost reached the Grand before outrunning its supplies. The total war casualties from 1812 to 1814 were about twenty-eight thousand, the majority dead from disease. This was less than half the casualties of the single-day battle of Waterloo, where Napoleon was defeated in 1815. In Great Lakes country, the war ended where it began, except for the rise of nationalism on both sides of the border, particularly in Canada, where the pillage and burning by American armies inspired a new depth of enmity. What had been, in the words of historian Alan Taylor, "a porous borderland of shifting identities," hardened into one of the globe's most durable borders. The lasting consequence has been two centuries of peace, and a region free of the effects of modern warfare, which scar much of the rest of the globe.[75]

In 1830 the Six Nations ceded the site of Brantford. Five more tracts were sold in the following decade. A company was formed in 1832 to build shipping locks on the Grand and some portion of the Six Nations trust fund was invested in that. In 1840 it was resolved to move the Six Nations to a single tract south of Brantford, all the rest to be sold and the proceeds put into the trust fund. Six headmen signed the documents but it took until 1847 to move everyone to that final tenth of their original land grant. By then, their trust fund was about $800,000. In 1848 the land remaining was parcelled out in 100-acre parcels to 325 families – Native, white, black, and Métis. At that time, fully half of the families farmed and owned oxen or horses. The land clearing and farming peaked in the 1890s. Ohsweken was its main town, boasting stores, factories, churches, schools, and medical offices. The Six Nations settlement on the Grand was a uniquely resourced success in cultural adaptation.[76]

The year 1847 saw the final cession of Algonquian lands in southern Ontario, those of the Ojibwa on the Bruce peninsula. Their treaty established that, if there were land sales on the peninsula, "the proceeds of the sale ... [would be] for the use and benefit of the said Ojibway Indians." For the first time, in the last of the southern treaties, the revenue from the survey and sale of land would flow to Natives. That year also marked the beginning of the flood of European potato-famine refugees, with more than eighty thousand arriving in Upper Canada, almost two-thirds of them children, "surplus" they were called. Sick and starving, almost as many again died on route and in quarantine. Migration to the region has not abated since.[77]

Two dates stand out, 1800 south of the lakes and 1850 north of the lakes. These are the respective dates when newcomer populations exceeded the number of pre-contact Natives by a factor of more than ten. South of the lakes, migrant settlers flooded in on the coattails of early land cessions. In Upper Canada, the influx came later, reaching only a quarter of the southern population by 1840, about 450,000. North and south, these dates mark the rising tide of land clearing, burning, and turning, and the end of the long wilding. The year 1850 also marked the end of preferential British trade duties for Canada and the start of closer continental trade links.

Americans were eager for new land, on their own frontiers or northward, offering opportunities, for example, to George Goodhue of London, who traded in lands in Mono and elsewhere. Early on, the American public was persuaded of Canada's possibilities by such individuals as the clergyman John Ogden in his *Tour* of 1794. Equally encouraging were the British who wrote home enticing others to join them. Neither, however, inspired nearly the numbers that the potato famines did. The total population north of the lakes passed a million in 1852, doubling in a decade. Eighty-three per cent of this population was rural, with the rest in urban centres, almost exactly the reverse of today.[78]

John Langton was an Englishman who came by choice. Of merchant stock, he took his degree at Cambridge and arrived in 1833. He was lured by a book of *Travels* by Isaac Weld, and he urged his family to come. He had bought 400 acres on Sturgeon Lake, northwest of Peterborough, where the chain of Trent waterways was sure to profit him. He should have known better, having personally been on the world's first inter-city rail run from Liverpool to Manchester in 1830. For fifteen years on the lake, he enjoyed the company of six settlers in total – five with university or college educations, and a sixth just with money. They had profit on their minds, "lots and concessions being the only subject of conversation here." Land, and its acquisition and sale, was the basis of wealth in the 1800s, whether by treaty, survey, farming, logging, water power, railways, or pure speculation.[79]

Langton's Peterborough neighbourhood was called by some "the most polished and aristocratic in Canada." Notables included Langton's sister Anne (the artist), Samuel Strickland, Thomas and Catharine Parr Traill (Strickland's sister), and Dunbar and Susanna Moodie (another Strickland sister). Their literary output on the subject of life in Upper Canada was published in London for an eager market. Strickland worked for the Canada Company, and that company's promotional book, by Tiger Dunlop in 1832, was a most endearing portrait. So too was Patrick Shirreff's farm report on the region in 1835 and Anna Jameson's *Rambles* in 1837. The Great Lakes country was a well-advertised destination.[80]

Their reports were of frontier prospects, and of entrepreneurs. Langton wrote about "Mr. Purdy the miller, a Yankee ... [who built] the largest mill-dam in the world" in the town of Lindsay. His dam impounded the Scugog River into the present Lake Scugog – "it raises the water seven feet and makes a navigable communication where none before existed, for thirty-seven miles back. It destroys seven mill sites and overflows 11,000 acres of land." Purdy's grant indemnified him from any claims by landowners who were flooded upstream, and in 1838 the aggrieved parties hacked his dam apart and flooded all the farms and mills downstream. Upper Canada was a wild west. Most of Langton's original neighbours left, "not fit for this country," and second-generation settlers arrived, "as confident and high in hopes as their predecessors." They were migrants of necessity rather than choice, less educated and even more hard-working. In 1849 Langton took up the square-timber trade, rafted logs down to Quebec, and then entered politics.[81]

By this date, the number of Natives from the Atlantic to the Great Lakes had declined to eight or ten thousand, perhaps 5 per cent of their number in 1600. In the south, their ecological influence no longer extended far beyond their reserves. Today, however, they are again a force for change. On the Grand, for example, and beyond it, the Six Nations is a wealthy community, with major real estate, cigarette, and gambling interests. The anthropologist Dean Snow notes: "The longhouse survives as an institution, just as the clans survive, having persisted through expulsions, epidemics, wars, adoptions and hostile outside government policies. Their belts, their languages, their games, their cuisine, their dress, their characters, their humor, and their fundamental sense of community all survive ... The Iroquois are dynamic and human ... reinventing themselves yet again." Their territory is also distinct, a wooded green island surrounded by farm monoculture and exurban development, easily spotted on satellite images. Today, some of the finest examples of our remaining natural ecosystems are on Native reserves, a subject we will return to later.[82]

The details of the ecological wilding that took place in the two centuries before 1850 are the subject of later chapters. By 1850, from the landscape's point of view, the original Native footprint was little more than a trace. The force that superseded all others was that of the European migrant, who set out to build a new Europe in the wilderness - and did.

CHAPTER FOUR

Manufacturing the Land: The 1800s

The end of the War of 1812 was marked by an inexplicable punishment meted out globally, a "year without summer." The world economy was squarely based on agriculture, and there were four killer frosts across the Great Lakes country in June, July, and August 1816. The cause – not then understood – was an eruption of the Earth's second largest volcano, at Tambora, Indonesia. The abiding issue of the day was domestic security – of food, home, and land.[1]

Peace settled deep into Great Lakes country. Elsewhere, military thinkers would talk about "war as politics by other means," inaugurating the modern path to total warfare. However, the cost and carnage of the Napoleonic Wars also made it politic to seek the same ends while avoiding outright warfare, especially on one's own land. Thus, "politics as war by other means" took root, and so too did the modern entente, which promotes "law as war by other means" and deploys laws and constitutions to the same ends. The word "lawfare" has been coined for this, and a state of lawfare has long existed (and been perfected) in Great Lakes country. Land, property, and ownership are at its core, and the manufacture of land is one of its defining tactics. What did this new, lawful manufacture of land do to the ecology of the region, human and otherwise?[2]

North of the lakes, the occupation proceeded quietly. Some of the treaties, like the 1818 Lake Simcoe-Nottawasaga Purchase, included lands that were not part of the personal experience of their Native signatories. Pathos began to enter the talks; a headman at that treaty begged for a doctor and made no mention of hunting or fishing rights. Some of the early treaties were for sites of military importance, like the lands between Lake Couchiching and the Penetang peninsula, home to many Natives although none of them the original Huron.[3]

For similar military reasons, the Missisauga along northwest Lake Ontario were asked to treat for their lands in the 1790s. They retained Joseph Brant as their agent but he asked for too much. A decade later, however, this postponed treaty and the treaty that dealt with the adjacent purchase of Toronto and its portage to Lake Simcoe were looking problematic. The construction of Dundas and Yonge streets was underway and the Missisauga protested their survey and construction (by Augustus Jones), making new negotiations prudent. In 1805 William Claus, deputy superintendent of Indian affairs and another grandson of William Johnson, completed the re-surrender of Toronto. (In 2010 it was purchased again, for $145 million.) The lands along Lake Ontario west to Burlington were also surrendered, for £1,000 sterling and the right to fish at the mouth of the Credit River, as well as a bush lot for Mrs Brant and ongoing use of Burlington Beach – recall that Brant's home was at the north end of the beach.[4]

The British kept to the letter of the law but tightened its terms, for example, by replacing one-time payments with annual payments. This reduced the upfront costs and allowed annual land sales to cover the yearly payments. Even those could be chiselled; for instance, in southwest Ontario in 1818, an agreement was reached to buy the Huron Tract, more than 1.8 million acres west of the Grand, from the Thames north to the Sauble, for an annual payment of £1,975, half in goods and half in funds, with two small reserves. However, this was judged too much, and was revised down to £2/10s per capita yearly payment to a maximum of 140 persons, with no reserve, for the southern half, and for the northern half, £1,100 annually split 460 ways, with four reserves. Wording was added to reduce the annuity if there was a decline in population, but none was added to reflect any growth in numbers. By such creative means, authorities continued to recognize the status conferred on Natives by the Royal Proclamation, even while pursuing the Proclamation's approved method of extirpating that status.

American authorities followed the same practice of negotiated treaties as long as their military weakness required it. They also agreed with the British that the lands secured by discovery (as mapped by the Proclamation) would require no treaties. In addition, in 1823, the U.S. Supreme Court extended the doctrine of discovery westward and confirmed that those people who were so discovered had only a right of occupancy. "Conquest gives a title which the courts of the conqueror cannot deny," concluded Chief Justice John Marshall.

At the same time, he urged a gentle patronage. "Humanity, acting on public opinion, has established as a general rule, that the conquered shall not be wantonly oppressed." So said the court, but forced "removal" was soon the lawful means, under the Indian Removal Act of 1830, by which Natives were displaced west of the Mississippi. By differing means, the Americans and British achieved the same end – a lawful land monopoly.[5]

These are primal matters, to which jurisprudence seems unlikely ever to bring reconciliation or remedy, to either possessors or the dispossessed. The question here is, Did the differences in legal approach north and south of the lakes result in the lands and waters being treated any differently? It seems not. The acquisition and manufacture of the land itself, and its sale and conversion, were the ecological determinants, not law or policy. After the War of 1812, the majority of migrants moving to Canada were still from the United States. They came in search of cheap land and economic opportunity, rather than in preference for one civil authority over another. North America represented freedom *from* authority. On both sides of the lakes, the price and productivity of land was as good a predictor of its ecological trajectory as either nation's laws.

It is remarkable, notes historian Robert Surtees, that "the angry Indian frontier of the American experience, with its thousands of American and Native casualties, was not repeated north of the Great Lakes." Why? First, the Iroquois had eliminated their sibling nations north of the lakes, and were emboldened to defend their lands to the south. Second, the French occupied much of the vacated territory and built co-dependent relations with the remaining and displaced Natives, independent of treaties. There were few whites in Upper Canada and its "Indian agents" were able to assure the Natives that it would be "many years ... before any settlement [would] come near to your villages." There was less fear of an influx of militant settlers than was the case south of the lakes. Finally, the Missisauga were few in number and coexistence was their goal. They were Algonquians, and they considered their agreements as formal peace treaties that implied long-term mutual support over and above any land sales, trusting that they would benefit in proportion to their acquiescence.[6]

Malthus and Migration

In England the apocalyptic poet William Blake wrote *Jerusalem* in 1804, lamenting Britain's "dark satanic mills" and dreaming of a "green and pleasant land." Thomas Malthus was in his prime as a political economist. He gained notoriety with his claim that population growth would outpace material production. At that point, he said, population would be kept at subsistence levels by famine, war, and disease. He mused about tying wages to the bare cost of living and he discouraged charity. Malthus helped set the stage for a century of tough justice, which would be protested in England by Charles Dickens and others. All that stood between the educated world and disaster was self-restraint, contraception, and the education of misery. Only by late marriage and moral restraint might the condition of mankind be, albeit mildly, mitigated.[7]

Malthus acknowledged emigration as "a slight palliative" that might reduce these pressures temporarily. "The parts of America settled by the English" were, he said, the best of a poor lot, as "an asylum for its redundant population." Life was cheap. The Napoleonic Wars demanded ever larger armies and navies. When war was on, all able-bodied men were needed; when war ended, they were all surplus. Cholera hit London and Paris in 1832 and 1849, killing twenty thousand in London alone. Then, in 1846, a potato famine devastated northern Europe, most appallingly in Ireland and the Scottish highlands.[8]

At the same time, Britain was aggressively privatizing its lands by depopulating rural areas where the "landlord" held the land but the tenants had ancestral rights to farm. This "inefficiency" in the old feudal system had prompted "enclosures" as early as medieval times but, by the late 1700s, they also fit hand-in-glove with new laws to pacify the rebel Scots Highlanders. The land rights of crofters were extinguished, their houses fired, and their lands given to loyalists, most of them absentee Londoners who liked the higher profits from the more tractable Cheviot sheep. The 1813 Policy for the Improvement of the Highlands made these practices law, and northern England, Ireland, and Wales were similarly "improved." Emigration became state policy and the choice of millions.[9]

Thus was a former commonwealth privatized by force of law. Since feudal times, land had been owned by the crown and entrusted to others. Tenants enjoyed rights of occupation in exchange for loyalty, produce, or payment. Converting such lands to outright ownership expanded the pool of transferrable wealth – and England led the way. The manufacture of private land was exported on the coattails of empire and it put an end to nearly all the land-tenure systems it encountered. It was a direct export to North America, where Native lands were similarly enclosed by force of law. Firing Native villages was standard practice both at home and abroad.

In North America, however, there was so much land, so many newcomers, and so much scope for profit from land that the result was a much more egalitarian outcome than in Europe. The reorganization of land in Britain detached people *from* it, while the reorganization of land in North America attached people *to* it, most of them for the first time. The Irish visitor "C.H.C." was one of many who noted: "There is no doubt but that Canada is the country for the poor man. It is the country where the hard working immigrant, without the consolation of any other earthly possession beyond health, stands a better chance of succeeding, than he ... with five hundred pounds ... who means to live idle." Emigration was subsidized, and forced on felons. Destinations like Australia had their felon founders, and the Americas had their Puritans, Dunkards, and loyalists, none of them welcome at home. It was Joseph Banks, the naturalist and president of the Royal Society, who introduced the idea of shipping convicts to Australia in 1779. It would take up the slack created by the American Revolution, which had slowed the shipments of felons across the Atlantic.[10]

It was a harsh world. Consider just how similar was the lot of a newcomer and a Native. A British farm tenant is forced from his home by his government and told that there is land he can own outright across the Atlantic, in the province of New York – land now cleared of its Native tenants (as they too had been cleared). The farmer migrates and invests a generation of labour in those lands, at which point the American Revolution dispossesses him, again without compensation. He is told that there are *new* lands in the Canadas, vacant of any competitors for title, and free. He moves north and settles on property legally sold by the Six Nations, such as that in Waterloo, only to have *his* descendants two hundred years later told that their land title is again in question – this time by Natives whose ancestors never lived anywhere near his land. Whose land?

Or consider the Missisauga, who considered themselves the owners of southern Ontario, having defeated the Iroquois in three battles in 1696, just as the Iroquois had earlier conquered the Huron, Petun, and Neutral. After a period of relative peace, their grandchildren are told that they must sell their land to the British to provide a homeland for the Iroquois, their ancient enemy. On doing so, they have the choice of migrating elsewhere or joining a reserve. They choose to join the Six Nations on the Grand, but the Six Nations are land-rich and cash-poor, and decide to sell most of the lands granted to them, against the advice of the government. Two hundred years later, the Six Nations go after the local non-Native municipalities for a share of development charges on the same lands that they had earlier insisted on selling. Whose land?

It is hard to know which story is more pathetic or more deserving. The modern analogue is the migration of refugees worldwide, a perpetual reminder of the human impulse to expel or encamp the excess peoples of overcrowded landscapes. Its root cause lies perhaps in the innate human hunting-and-gathering impulse, which motivates individuals to hunt and gather competitively the land itself. Still, the parcel-based property rights enjoyed by the majority of its citizens became the stabilizing foundation of North America's early economic success.

The popular press picked up on the ideas that Malthus expounded. One London magazine put it plainly in 1822: "The modern doctrine of population has actually frightened the good people of this country out of their senses; and men and women, boys and girls, have been flying for years past in every direction ... to escape." In the decade after 1830, even before the potato famines, almost seven million people fled the British Isles. This practice of state-encouraged emigration was called "shovelling out the paupers," and it led to a population exodus that was unparalleled globally until the modern era.[11]

The Land Companies

North America's first companies were chartered offshore to import fur, fish, and anything else they found, and to enforce their monopolies. The first of them, the Compagnie des Marchands (and Compagnie des Cent-Associés) and the Hudson's Bay Company, owned vast tracts but did not sell land. The land companies that came later did so almost exclusively, partnering with the state after the state secured the land, and making fabulous profits and imprinting a new land-tenure system. What was the most profitable way to sell the land as quickly as possible? Public land-grant offices were the first means but their role was soon privatized. Privatization would also build the moneyed class that a new colony needed. Simcoe was objective on this score: "The companies to whom these lands are sold are unrelenting in their efforts ... [to] allure future emigrants from whose numbers alone they can expect remuneration."[12]

The Canada Company was chartered in 1825 to colonize Upper Canada. Its attractions were good ships, low fares, farm tools, and cheap land. It had 2.5 million acres it had bought for £341,000, half of it the Huron Tract on the east shore of Lake Huron and the other half crown reserves scattered across Upper Canada. John Galt, the Scottish novelist and biographer, was the company's founder. He personally chose the site for its headquarters and called it Guelph in honour of the royal family. Galt hired Samuel Strickland as "engineer" in 1828, and it took Strickland little time to realize, after doubling his money on two properties, that "land speculation is one of the surest and best means of making money in Canada."[13]

Newcomers, then as now, complained of their lot. They pointed to the sharp business practices and suspect accounts of the Canada Company. For example, the company's original purchase price was spread over sixteen years and paid directly to the executive branch of Upper Canada, the Family Compact, rather than to the public accounts of the elected assembly. This was common knowledge and helped fuel the Rebellions of 1837–38.[14]

The public face of the Canada Company was William "Tiger" Dunlop. As a youth he was part of a literary clique at the University of Glasgow but his father was bankrupted by a mill failure and he had to join the army. He was a twenty-one-year-old army surgeon when he first served in Canada in 1813, manning the field hospital at John Crysler's farm on the St Lawrence, where twelve hundred defenders held off an army of four thousand Americans. There were more than seven hundred casualties and, the next summer, Dunlop was in Niagara attending to the wounded at the equally bloody Lundy's Lane.

Bush life appealed to Dunlop. After a posting in India (where he got the name Tiger) and some time in London with the likes of Samuel Taylor Coleridge, he accepted Galt's invitation to return to Canada in 1826 to assist him with the Canada Company. His first "dive" into the bush was in the company of Joseph Brant's son John and the surveyor Mahlon Burwell, laying in the line to Lake Huron (now Highway 8) and the lots along it. Where their line reached Lake Huron, they founded Goderich. Somehow, between surveying lots and building roads, and surviving Galt's resignation in 1829, Dunlop managed to write a charming solicitation for the Company, *Statistical Sketches of Upper Canada*. Unlike some of the other guides of the time, it reads not like an extended complaint by an inconvenienced tourist but, rather, like an engaging account by a long-time resident.

Resident he was, in his "Castle Gairbraid" on the heights above Goderich and Lake Huron. From it he visited "nearly every township" in Upper Canada and shared his advice: "If you have no money to throw away, and wish to have snug quarters for yourself and your family next winter, you will not stay one hour in Quebec ... for by dawdling about Quebec, Montreal, Kingston and York, you will spend more money and lose more time than ... might have lodged and fed yourself and family during the first and worst year of your residence in the new world. The Canada Company has an agent at Quebec for the purpose of forwarding emigrants ... and any emigrant ... may ... thus be transported to the head of Lake Ontario more cheaply and expeditiously than ... were he to make his own bargain." What could be more reasonable?

When you get here, Dunlop continued, "apply at the office of the Canada Company or the crown commissioner, where you will receive every information as to the lands most suitable to your circumstances and views, and learn the terms on which they are willing to sell." The company's terms? Payment over five years, at 6 per cent interest. Clear four acres a year. Build a house by the second year. Then you get the deed. Even better, "in the Huron Tract there are no reserves of any kind; and as for absentee proprietors, the Company's regulations compel all its settlers to clear about three and a half per cent of their land annually for the first seven years." This meant that a settler, who had to clear the road in front of his own land, did not have to do the same for absent neighbours.

"If you have no particular motives to induce you to settle in one part of the province more than another, I would recommend to you the Canada Company's Huron Tract ... The first time the Huron Tract was ever trod by the foot of a white man was in the summer of 1827. If the tide of emigration continues to set in as strongly as it has done, in ten years from this date [1842] it may be as thickly populated as any part of America ... Who then are to go to the Canadas? ... All who cannot support themselves comfortably by their labour at home."[15]

Thus was it done. Hundreds of thousands of land parcels were marketed. Colonization companies were pioneered in New France but they were perfected by the British. John Galt would later found the British American Land Company in Lower Canada, where he was deeded 800,000 acres in the Eastern Townships for £120,000. Between 1815 and 1855, about one million newcomers from Britain and Ireland arrived in Canada, most of them landing at Quebec, most of them Irish. The majority of the U.S. arrivals landed at New York and Boston and, between 1820 to 1850, numbered about 2.5 million, about 60 per cent of them British and Irish and 25 per cent German. A great many of them made their way to the Great Lakes country, on both sides of the border.[16]

The land companies exercised immense political influence. Eventually Dunlop left the Canada Company and ran for office in 1837 on a reform ticket against the company's James Strachan, son of the Family Compact's bishop. Dunlop's platform? "That faction commonly called the Family Compact has been the great check to Canada's prosperity and the cause of nine-tenths of the disaffection which has disturbed its peace." The election in Goderich was a brute contest to see who could physically defend the hustings, the raised voting platform in the square, against their opponent's attacks. The military showed up to man the polls, so the Canada Company changed tactics and brought in illegal voters instead, winning by 159 votes to 149. An investigation followed, which threw out 58 Canada Company votes and put Dunlop into the legislature, where he was outspoken – and ignored. A promised investigation into the Canada Company never materialized. Land and profit, then as now, were too important to debate.[17]

Some land companies were set up to serve particular ethnicities. Alexander Macdonnell, an army chaplain, persuaded the British government in 1804 to grant 200 acres to every Scots soldier he could bring to a new Glengarry on the St Lawrence. About 160,000 acres were allotted. Everyone knew their story, even the governor general, George Prevost, who noted their "deep disgust in finding their friends or themselves stripped of their little farms [in Scotland] to make way for sheep-farmers." They arrived by family group, led by their Highland patriarchs. Among the first were eighty-four Macdonnells. More than two thousand arrived in the first decade. They received no financial aid. Even so, when asked to do so, they formed the Glengarry Light Infantry Fencibles to fight with the British in the War of 1812. Many of North America's Scots had their start in Glengarry.[18]

Another land company was that of Archibald McNab, head of the River Tay McNabs of Scotland. To escape his debts he fled to Canada in 1822 and negotiated for land in the Ottawa valley for his clan. Each family would get 100 acres, and McNab himself 1,200 acres. On this basis he piped his first crop of Scots off the boat in 1825 and led them up the Ottawa to Lac des Chats, where they faced scant provisions and a demanding laird. McNab assigned to them debts for anything spent on their behalf, and they worked for him if they could not pay, with their land titles held as collateral. His holdings were vast, as described by an Irish visitor in 1844: "Thousands and thousands of acres of unfrequented pine forests … wherein the foot of the white man never treads, with the exception perhaps of the migratory forester." While his clan went without, McNab hosted parties and curried favour. Petitions began to pile up but they went unheeded until the Rebellions of 1837–38, when his clan refused to heed his call to arms. The land agent in Perth investigated, and soon agreed that their pleas were justified. McNab offered to sell for £9,000, settled for £2,500, and they finally got their land titles. McNab left the country and died in France.[19]

The Talbot settlement followed the same pattern but on a grander scale and to better effect. Colonel Thomas Talbot was private secretary to Lieutenant Governor Simcoe, and, when he toured the north shore of Lake Erie with Simcoe, he saw its promise and he returned in 1800 with a field officer's grant of 5,000 acres and a side deal that, for every settler he located on fifty of those 5,000 acres, he would be entitled to another 200 acres. Talbot would be sole magistrate of the transactions, and he alone would keep the records. He arrived at what would become Port Talbot in 1803 and built his "castle," a rambling set of log cabins, on the bluffs a hundred feet above the lake. "The scenery is woodland broken here and there by clearings formed into beautiful fields," ran a description of the time. Through a cabin window, Talbot dispensed his justice to those brave enough to seek it. By 1821, he owned 65,000 acres and was lord of all he surveyed – a settlement renowned for its excellent roads and prosperous farms. He fended off all administrative interference by visiting London, and he died and was buried at his castle in 1853.[20]

Others did the same for less. In 1823 Peter Robinson, a Malthusian and member of the Family Compact, brought almost six hundred emigrants from the depressed south of Ireland to Lanark, and in 1825 the British Parliament granted him £30,000 to bring another 2,000 to Upper Canada, giving them free land, tools, stock, and provisions to get started. Tiger Dunlop, on behalf of the Canada Company, challenged this generosity as unfair government interference in the land business.[21]

There was never any doubt that the New World was an incomparable opportunity for the labouring poor of Europe. James Bower of the Fifth Line of Mono was one such migrant, and so was Peter Kastner, who settled near Stratford. Kastner was a shoemaker who arrived on his lot on 18 June 1832 with three dollars and a family of eleven, including his mother and father and a child born on route. In ten years, he had a house, a barn, a cobbler's shop, a distillery, and livestock. Exclusive of the shop and distillery, he was worth three thousand dollars.[22]

The Shock Troops of Settlement

The region's first modern land surveyors learned their trade in the military campaigns of the British against, in turn, the Dutch, French, Natives, and rebels. George Washington got his surveyor's commission from the College of William and Mary and worked as county surveyor for three years prior to his service in the British army. He clearly understood "the want of accurate maps of the country," and after his service he returned to surveying and land speculation, the pursuit of many gentlemen of the day. Between 1749 and 1799, he surveyed over two hundred tracts and held title to some sixty-five thousand acres at thirty-seven sites.[23]

The Dutch engineer Samuel Holland served in the British navy under Captain James Simcoe (father of John Graves Simcoe) off Louisbourg in 1758, where he met and trained the future explorer James Cook in mapmaking. They served with distinction in charting the St Lawrence River in 1759, and, following the successful river assault on Quebec City, Holland was asked to produce a map of the lands around Montreal and Quebec, which was released as the *Murray Atlas*. He then proposed to extend the survey to all the British provinces and, on that basis, was appointed surveyor general of the Canadas in 1764. He would take no increase in salary and would provide his own survey equipment. He would, however, accept payment in land.[24]

His first project was the Detroit area, to re-survey the old seigneurial tracts and issue new land certificates. His next challenge was the new loyalist settlements, starting with fourteen townships along the St Lawrence above Montreal. He would later open up areas like the Eastern Townships in Quebec, where surveys began in 1792. The land surveyors were in regular, direct contact with the Natives, and their maps would become essential components of land treaties. In fact, they worked hand-in-glove with their associates at "Indian Affairs."

In 1785, as a member of the Legislative Council, Holland introduced a law to standardize the business of land surveys. All surveyors would be tested before their appointments, against survey monuments built to strict specifications, for example, for distance and compass direction. Their standard would be the 100- or 200-acre lot, and they would lodge their field books with the surveyor general when they died. South of the lakes, the federal government's Land Ordinance of 1785 similarly grounded its surveys, beginning in Ohio, laying out the standard western template of square-mile lots grouped into six-mile-square townships. A U.S. surveyor general was appointed in 1796.[25]

Surveyors were the foot soldiers in the manufacture of land. Their weapons were the theodolite for sighting angles, a sixty-six-foot chain, a telescope, compass, and level, and an axe and gun. By 1795, when Upper Canada's land registry was set up, their instructions were clear, to record "the kind and quality of the soil and timber, entering each kind of timber in the order of its relative abundance." Their notes and diaries are some of the best eyes through which to see the land as it was. Surveyors like Samuel Benson, Augustus Jones, Hugh Black, Mahlon Burwell, William Chewett, John Stoughton Dennis, Joseph Fortune, John Galbraith, William Hambly, Patrick McNiff, John Roche, Frederick Rubidge, David Smith, John Stegmann, and Samuel Wilmot live on today in the fabric of the land itself.[26]

Many were military men, and among the few professionals in the region. The result was as intended, a paramilitary regularization of the land into rectilinear parcels. It was like printing money, and it preceded by many years the mints in the United States (1792) and Canada (1858). In Upper Canada, the currency was clear: civilian loyalists got 100 acres plus 50 for each family member; military privates got 100 acres and 50 for family members; non-commissioned officers 200 acres; warrant officers and lieutenants 500 acres; captains 700 acres; those more senior 1,000 acres plus; and surveyors a few thousand acres for each township plan. The Church of England and the crown each got one-seventh of all land. Tracts of land both large and small were additionally dispersed to satisfy the flood of petitions and pleas from "the particular friends of government" which dominated executive agendas. Once granted, all subsequent sales were at the going rate.[27]

There were also bonus offers. In 1787 Holland's deputy was authorized to grant an extra 200 acres to those who "improved their lands," and refuse it to those who had "doubtful principles and reputations." This loyalty test sparked a sharp reaction, and no wonder. Cash was rare and the abuse of land grants was commonplace, and resented. As reported by the surveyor general of Upper Canada, by 1826, eight million acres of land had been granted but less than a million and a quarter had gone to regular settlers. The rest went to friends, officials, and surveyors. Five million acres were held by speculators. In addition, three million acres were reserved for clergy and crown. Essa, west of Lake Simcoe, was a typical township. Twenty-eight per cent went to clergy and crown, and 60 per cent to absentee owners, including 5 per cent to its surveyor. Only 12 per cent was available for bona fide settlers. To give just one example, Chief Justice William Dummer Powell and his family accumulated 12,800 acres in land grants, by no means a rarity. The aim was clear, to establish a "just aristocracy" as Simcoe called it, financed by land sales.[28]

Land and farming were central to the economy of the region but its governments were dominated by lawyers and administrators only peripherally attached to rural life. The Rebellions of 1837-38 north of the lakes were fully vindicated by John Lambton, himself an earl and aristocrat, who was sent to report on it in 1838. He had nothing good to say for the "petty, corrupt, insolent cliques" – the Family Compact in Upper Canada and the Château Clique in Lower Canada. "This body of men possessed almost all the highest public offices [and] wielded all the powers of government ... the bench, the magistracy, the high offices of the Episcopal [Anglican] Church, and a great part of the legal profession ... [and] the chartered banks." Clergy reserves, in particular, had retarded the rate of land sales and economic growth. He acknowledged this tenet of the failed rebellions and the clergy reserves were sold as a result, and at a great profit.[29]

Roads Make It Permanent

The Native trails of Great Lakes country were ancient and well developed. They followed the logic of the land, the path of easiest footfall and shallowest river ford. The Great Iroquois Trail led from the Hudson up the Mohawk, and west through the Finger Lakes to Niagara and Detroit. North of Lake Erie, another road led west from Niagara and the head of Lake Ontario to the ford on the Grand (later Brant's Ford) and on to the Thames and Detroit. From Detroit there were routes west to Lake Michigan and Chicago, and north to Michilimackinac and Sault Ste Marie and, from there, to Green Bay and the Mississippi. Others headed south, to the Susquehanna, Delaware, and Ohio, and north to Lake Champlain. Today's expressways and interstates follow the same routes.

Some of them were international and others domestic, linking the Native towns and waterways in a bimodal network of canoe and foot traffic. No other monuments testify so clearly to the central role of the Great Lakes as a crossroads and hub, and they outlasted their founders everywhere. The Iroquois Trail was upgraded to a King's Highway in the 1660s, and the English, French, and Americans all fought over it. In the end, Iroquoia was razed by soldiers marching on Iroquois roads. The Finger Lakes trail is now Highway 41, and Clover Street (Highway 65) follows Seneca trails north to the Ridge Road, from Rochester to Lewiston, and from there to the Niagara portage, itself now Military Road (Highway 265), to the mouth of Cayuga Creek.[30]

As early as 1688, some of Iroquoia's main highways were mapped by the Jesuit Pierre Raffeix, who also mapped the roads from Lake Ontario, at Ganatsequiagon (mouth of the Rouge) and Theyagon (mouth of the Humber), north to Lake Simcoe and Lake Huron (Fig. 9). In 1791 the surveyor Patrick McNiff mapped the "trails" in southwest Ontario. For example, there was "a plain and good path" from the Thames to an "old Indian village" at Rondeau, which was "a great resort of Indians in the spring of the year [for] fish and fowl." Several roads converged on Pelee and the Thames. The roads were well worn and trafficable; Lieutenant Governor Simcoe's party rode their horses over the Toronto portage. As a result, settler trails followed them closely, like the Davenport Road in Toronto, the Hockley Valley Road up the Nottawasaga, the Warsaw Road in Peterborough, and the Great North Road from Parry Sound. Others, like Yonge Street and Highway 400, were straightened versions of them.[31]

Any road was soon rutted and muddy from horses and wagons, and, before earth moving and gravel, the cheapest material to stabilize a roadbed was wood. One observer wrote: "Whole hecatombs of trees are sacrificed to form a corrugated causeway of their round trunks, laid side by side, over which wagons can be slowly dragged or bumped, any attempt at speed being checked by immediate symptoms of approaching dissolution in the vehicle." The historian Kathleen Lizars described the corduroy logs as "from nine inches to two feet in diameter, not squared, flattened, or even straight, and often far apart." Next came plank roads. The planks were a minimum of three inches thick, preferably oak (but even pine was used) and laid across rows of length-wise sleeper logs. Plank roads like the one from Cobourg to Rice Lake were fast and smooth when they were new, but wagon wheels and horseshoes soon wore them out, and frost and water finished them. Settlement roads were the ubiquitous complaint of all travellers.[32]

North of the lakes, each land grant required its recipient to clear the road allowance at its front and build and maintain the roads or bridges along it. Winter roads were the easiest to travel but even then it was the landowner who was expected to level the snow along their section. The effort required was incredible; in Mono, one section of road had to climb the Niagara Escarpment inside the road allowance and needed massive rocks moved to do so. The effort was also seriously frustrated by the vacant clergy and crown lots and company lands left untended. All this was enforced by one of Upper Canada's first acts of Parliament. There were exceptions, roads maintained at public or company expense: military roads like Dundas, Danforth, Talbot, Kingston, and Penetanguishene, and survey roads like Hurontario, Huron, and Garafraxa. Along a few of them, like the Durham road, land was granted free in exchange for clearing and maintaining it – an early example of privatization to offset the costs of infrastructure.[33]

Upper Canada's Parliament also allowed township "pathmasters" to force farmers to work on roads and bridges beyond the fronts of their own farms, proportional to the assessed wealth of the farmer. Enforcement was a night-mare, even after landowners were allowed to pay cash in lieu of labour, an early form of property tax. Another solution was privatization. Starting about 1825, the busiest public roads were franchised - "turnpiked" - and barred with tollgates. On some there were tollgates every four or five miles; even pedes-trians and animals were charged. There were five tollgates between Oshawa and Uxbridge, as well as tolls for bridges and ferries. Yonge Street was a country road and its first tollgate was at Bloor Street. There was another at Hogg's Hollow, and another at Langstaff. Protests were commonplace. In the Rebellions of 1837–38 Samuel Lount and his seven hundred rebels gathered at the Bloor tollgate, a fine place for an insurrection. In 1890 sixty-three farmers in Woodbridge and Kleinberg destroyed two tollgates, and several of them were shot by the toll-keeper. A tollgate on the Cobourg-Port Hope turnpike was burned in protest. As late as the First World War, Cobourg was circled by five tollgates, and the last of them disappeared from Ontario only in 1926.[34]

Any map of the region today shows the indelible imprint of its roads, one of the densest rural road grids in the world (Fig. 10). At the same time that land in England and Europe was being assembled into larger blocks owned by fewer individuals, the United States and Canada were dissecting the land and dispersing it in small parcels to thousands of individual owners, tightly joined by roads. On each individual land parcel, families were distributed along innumerable roads, clearing forest, plowing prairies, draining wetlands, hunting, fishing, and damming, and, if they were lucky, they could keep a small bush lot for fuel-wood. Ecologically, en masse, the best soils and best-watered lowlands were converted from their natural systems, lot by lot. Society in the New World - and the landscape - were forever different as a result.

Land Rights in Canada

Neither the French nor the English recognized Native land rights. France simply imported and imposed the feudal system of pre-revolutionary France. The Compagnie des Cent-Associés was set up in 1627 to own French North America and it lasted until 1663, when New France was designated a French province. The formula throughout was the same - "no land without a *seigneur*." Land was assigned to a landlord who, acting as a "good father," could assign it to others in return for *foi et hommage* (loyalty and tribute). The assignees were tenants or habitants, who made payments to the seigneur for the right to a part, *une roture*, of his land. At first, land rights changed hands only by favour or by censure but eventually they were sold, and habitants could buy and sell *rotures* and become seigneurs. To dampen the speculation this caused, a land-transfer tax was imposed.[35]

By 1663, the Compagnie had assigned seventy seigneuries along the St Lawrence from Quebec to Montreal. The fifty of them located outside the towns were often hundreds of square miles in size. From 1667 to 1760, another 150 rural seigneuries were conceded upstream of Montreal on the St Lawrence and Ottawa, and downstream to Tadoussac. "The more important the individual the larger the grant," as geographer Cole Harris has said. The earliest of them were surveyed by *rhumb de vent*, a line drawn perpendicular to a given point on the river, and this system became standard along the St Lawrence, Detroit, and Red rivers. Where this became engrained over time, and where subgrants and divisions for inheritance were made, a unique pattern of thin, linear properties arose, anchored by homes and villages and churches all along the water.[36]

Feudalism required subservience or enforcement, both of them problematic on a frontier. There was always work in the *pays d'en haut*, and this was an accepted outlet, so much so that a new people evolved – the Métis. By law, any trade with Natives was allowed only by prior licence, with duties paid on returns, so both licences and duties were avoided by all who could. Such laws, and the seigneurial system itself, did little to create transferrable wealth or inspire innovation.[37]

The wealth of the seigneurs varied. Some had long waterfronts, good soils, and vast backcountry lands, and were paid annual rents and tributes, as well as fees for fishing, cutting, pasture, and milling. Then there was income from the sale or re-sale of *rotures*, or from other legal services. In a cash-poor economy, however, much of the income was in-kind and many seigneurs were of more modest means, little better than their habitants. Of even more modest means were the Natives, as noted before the Supreme Court of Canada in 1887: not in "six hundred concessions of *seigneuries* ... can be found even an allusion to, or a mention of the Indian title" to land. (The British condoned the seigneurial system after their conquest in 1760 but gradually undermined it with legal surveys and land titles, and abolished it in 1854.)[38]

The British saw treaties as the means to expedite land transactions, not as a legitimization of land rights. The Royal Proclamation treated New France and the Maritimes, and the thirteen British provinces to the south, as prizes of discovery and exempted them from the niceties of treaties. Treaties were pursued for the remaining lands in Great Lakes country, aggressively so south of the lakes under both the British and Americans. Like the Americans, Canada too claimed "the absolute exclusive right to extinguish the Indian title either by conquest or by purchase." In practice, however, it would proceed with more civility, reflecting both an unwillingness and an inability to impose and a self-identification with the common-law notion of "peace, welfare and good government." This phrase was British imperial boilerplate and served with honour in the Royal Proclamation and in the Quebec Act of 1774, the Constitutional Act of 1791, and the Union Act of 1840. It appeared again in Canada's constitutions, the British North America Act of 1867 and the Constitution Act of 1982, as "peace, order and good government" (POGG), and with the same intent, a strong legal authority based on negotiated consensus, an appropriately deferential and collectivist framework for a small developing nation.[39]

"Peace, order and good government" also conveyed a respectful tone, befitting a place that was more refuge than battlefield, a place for the homeless and the defeated, Native and European alike. There were, and still are, issues of broken promises and compensation that warrant remedy. Of these, the most pressing are the issues of poverty and landlessness, and the degrading Indian Act of 1876. In another class entirely are the claims of wealthy nations like the Six Nations, whose land grant on the Grand is a very different story of power and self-interest.[40]

The mechanics of "POGG" as it relates to land remain largely intact. The provinces have legal authority over land and its use, as they did before Confederation. Prime Minister Wilfrid Laurier's Commission of Conservation, which he established in 1909, built on this by drafting model legislation for provinces to adopt to guide municipal governance and land-use planning. In Ontario these are the Municipal Act and the Planning Act, under which Ontario can establish policies that every municipality must respect in their decisions. Decisions that are not consistent with provincial policy can be appealed to an appointed (and much maligned) board of adjudicators, whose decisions are rarely changed by government.[41]

These acts both drive and regulate modern land and development rights. They govern the use and parcelling of land in Ontario, and they stand as a collective statement of what to develop and what to leave on the land over the next twenty-five years as the province tries to accommodate four million more newcomers. Few residents have any familiarity with the mechanics of this engine of development, but its "provincial policy statements" are the critical documents that will define the future ecology of Ontario. They are avowedly committed to rapid and intensive growth but also include policies that "natural features and areas shall be protected for the long term," as places where "development and site alteration shall not be permitted."[42]

In Great Lakes country south of the lakes, development pressures have moderated since historic peaks, with a few city-state exceptions. Nature is on a slow mend, promoted by many agencies, groups, and individuals. North of the lakes, this renewal is also well advanced but it does so in the face of fantastical growth that is proposed for its city-states. However, Canada's approach to land rights, by which private rights are subordinate to collective permissions, has now been confirmed by successive political regimes – which have decreed that the best of what is left of nature will remain. We will return to this later, to consider the ill-twinned destinies of nature and the city-state.

Land Rights in the United States

Land cessions south of the lakes were neither peaceful nor orderly. Both the British and Americans treated with those who were willing to sign, and took other lands without treaty, and disbursed both to newcomers as fast as possible. By this means, a greater proportion of citizens acquired rights in land than was ever the case in Europe. The American identity started with the possibility of land ownership, and property owners were soon the majority, outnumbering the elites and urban dwellers. Property thus acquired a unique claim on American affections, including a claimed right to the use of private land for any purpose as long as it did not deprive others of their equal rights on their own properties. Early on, such rights were a notably sensitive matter for those who had taken over the lands of evicted white loyalists. The U.S. Constitution of 1787 did not recognize any rights to compensation for loyalists, ignoring the treaty that settled the revolutionary war. No reference was made to "property" or "compensation" at the time that loyalists were still being relieved of their property.

With a speed that was not lost on loyalists, a constitutional amendment was adopted in 1791 to make it clear that individuals *then* could not "be deprived of life, liberty or property, without due process of law; nor shall property be taken for public use, without just compensation." Later, another amendment clarified that no state could "deprive any person of life, liberty, or property, without due process of law." Notwithstanding that "property" included slaves at that time, a great canon of law has developed around this, dealing with land rights and their place in the United States.[43]

For a settled landscape, its ecological integrity hinges largely on the balance struck between the individual right to use and develop land, on the one hand, and the community's right to a public interest in its use, on the other. Until the early 1900s, individual rights largely prevailed. Landowners could not be forced to leave lands undeveloped simply to accommodate community wishes. These were "takings" and thus "compensable." Even so, New York City started to regulate, or "zone," districts for different land uses, and in 1922 Supreme Court judge Oliver Wendell Holmes said that they had the right to do so. However, he added, "If regulation goes too far, it will be recognized as a taking." On this equivocating basis, New York City went ahead, and in 1926 the Supreme Court approved its plan to separate residential from industrial and commercial uses. Zoning has since been used throughout the United States to frame urban development and set boundaries beyond which development should not occur. But it was not used for environmental purposes for another fifty years.

In 1987 the Supreme Court considered the case of the California Coastal Commission and tried to balance its environmental land-use zoning against previous findings of "compensable takings." It also looked at the South Carolina Coastal Council from that point of view in 1992, and it set a new threshold – whether such regulations left landowners with no "economically beneficial use." Only at that point, which remains in dispute, are environmental land-use regulations compensable. Still, in the real world of modern development, community approvals have increasingly required solutions that compensate the *community* for development. This has grown into an almost mandatory requirement for open-space set-asides as "dedications" (or "cash in lieu"). A grey area still remains, however, between such local land "exactions" and public policy "takings" in support of broader landscape conservation.[44]

Joseph Sax, author of a reflection called *Mountains without Handrails*, quotes justice George Sutherland from 1926: "Until recent years, urban life was comparatively simple; but with the great increase and concentration of population, problems have developed, and constantly are developing, which require, and will continue to require, additional restrictions in respect to the use and occupation of private lands." Despite this, the property-rights movement has again gathered strength since the 1980s, arguing for the rights of private owners *despite* any collective interest in reducing pollution, caring for water, or protecting wildlife or habitat. From this perspective, even the Endangered Species Act or Clean Water Act are claimed to constitute "takings."[45]

The U.S. Supreme Court continues to seek out the "reasonable" but, so far, concepts like ecological sustainability or the conservation of nature have not met the test of community acceptance, at least not to the degree that they must if they are to be used to validate land-use restrictions. In 2001 the state of Massachusetts expressed (and mapped) an exemplary vision of the lands in the state that, if retained in a more or less natural condition, would sustain the native species and natural landscapes of Massachusetts. But the state governor could only release this *BioMap Project* as advice. In 2005 the Harvard Forest and dozens of other groups tabled a *Wildlands and Woodlands Vision* for the same area. Both efforts are aspirational rather than regulatory – and less likely to be realized as a result.[46]

The constant over the last three centuries has been the land and its use and development. What has changed has been the shift from the discrete and identifiable to the intensive and systemic. In the 1800s there was an agreed-on synonymy between place-based industrial development and land development. Major industries developed land as a means to increase productivity, such as the town of Paterson, New Jersey, in 1831, for textiles, firearms, and locomotives; the town of Menlo Park, New Jersey, in 1876, for Thomas Edison's electrical-appliance industry; the Corning Glass Works in the Finger Lakes in the 1870s; the Oneida Community and its flatware industry; Eastman Kodak and Bausch and Lomb in Rochester, for optics and photography; and Milton S. Hershey's "model town" in Pennsylvania in 1903. To make shoes, Thomas Bata built Batawa, Ontario, in the 1930s. Now, by contrast, land development can occur almost anywhere, linked by transportation and transmission networks that are themselves systemic.

What has also changed are the international standards. Thomas Adams was a Scottish lawyer who was secretary of the first "Garden City" in Letchworth, England, in 1900. He was recruited by Canadian prime minister Robert Borden in 1914 to bring the new urbanism to Canada. Adams served as adviser to the Commission of Conservation and, in 1917, laid the plans for the Garden City of Témiscaming, Quebec. Kimberly-Clark followed with the town of Kapuskasing, Ontario, in 1922, and the Aluminum Company of Canada with the Garden City of Arvida, Quebec, in 1925. When the commission faltered, Adams left for New York City to serve from 1923 to 1930 as its director of regional planning. The first U.S. Garden City was Radburn, New Jersey, in 1929. The elastic variations on Garden Cities did much to inspire the next template, the "suburbs" that still dominate. They began in

Canada with Don Mills, built by E.P. Taylor in 1954 in Toronto. Upscale examples include Frank Stronach's Magna campus in Aurora and all the new planned satellite cities. It is this car-based suburban-city that the modern land company has mastered.[47]

The Modern Land Company – Just One Story

Jonathan Baker left Pennsylvania with his father in 1797. They paused near Stoney Creek on the Niagara peninsula and then set out on the "trail of the black walnut" – the trail travelled by farmers in search of rich lime-based soils. It took them to Vaughan Township in 1801, just west of Yonge Street, where they settled quietly. Soon after 1816 they built a bank barn and parked in it the Conestoga wagon that had brought them. They also built a forge and harness shop, and sugar shack, and kept it all together into the 1990s.[48]

We would go there as children in late winter, hoping that Amos Baker, the family patriarch, would flick some maple taffy on the snow for us. His horses walked from tree to tree and he tipped the maple sap into the tank they pulled. They cut any windfalls for firewood and sold it to people like Pierre Berton in Kleinberg. Amos's daughter, Mary, went to my high school and was top student in her senior year, and then returned to the farm.

A bush like the Bakers' was a rare thing in Vaughan and when a Parkway Belt Plan was declared by Ontario Premier Bill Davis in 1978, with his bush in it, Amos Baker warranted a special clause saying that, whenever he wanted, the province would buy the bush and conserve it. Ostensibly the plan was to protect some open space around Toronto, and people thought it meant no subdivisions, unlike the land all around it.[49]

The years passed and Amos's brother Isaac, who ran the harness shop, passed on. Amos asked the province to buy the bush but nothing was done. I remember one day when Charlie Sauriol, the conservationist who spearheaded the purchase of more than five hundred natural areas in Ontario, approached me with an assistant deputy minister in tow. We had a good chat about the Baker bush and met with senior bureaucrats about money, but nothing was done.[50]

Years later, the Ivey Foundation supported Ontario Nature in a survey of the best woodlands left in southern Ontario, to build the case for conserving them. I asked Brendon Larson, who did the fieldwork, to look at the Baker bush. He concluded that it was "the most mature deciduous woodland in the district." The bush was the first place north of Lake Ontario, sixteen miles away, where forest birds like the scarlet tanager, wood thrush, and pileated woodpecker still bred. Some of its maples were over 250 years old. It was magnificent.[51]

When Amos died, his son Paul farmed for a few years, took out a few oak to make ends meet, and then sold the farm for development. People were shocked but they should not have been. The Bakers were surrounded. The so-called Parkway Belt had been developed into a new, toll-gated 407 expressway, a new power corridor, and a new Toronto rail by-pass. Paul had no farm neighbours left, and no local co-op or mill. The community had abandoned him.

The MacMillans had a farm in the same "block" as the Bakers. As with almost every "block plan" brought forward by developers and city planners, it would end up at an Ontario Municipal Board hearing to tidy up any last-minute details. Lyn MacMillan and I sat down with Mayor Lorna Jackson of Vaughan in 1998 and asked what we could do. We decided that we would be one of those last-minute details, and I formally asked to be a participant in the hearing.

The board hearing commenced. We spoke in opposition to the development of Baker's Woods, as it was called, or to houses too close, or roads through it. Any approval to sever, develop, and sell land is serious business, equivalent to printing money, so we spoke respectfully, but to little effect. Fortunately, there are backrooms other than those frequented by hearing officers. Sympathetic civil servants told me where there were unspent government funds, and one of Lyn MacMillan's sons played squash with one of the government party's fundraisers. The information was passed along and a deal was struck to buy the bush and thereby remove the hearing's main issue, the clearing of the woods for housing, a right that should not have been actionable in the first place.

About this time, I was walking the edge of the bush. I stubbed my toe on a hidden tree stump, clean-cut at ground level, with its top painted black to hide it. I looked up and, sure enough, there was a gap where a tree had stood. A little farther and there was another gap, and another stump. I notified York Region's tree by-law inspector, Leonard Munt, and by the time he was finished, he had found seventy-five trees immaculately removed from the edge of the Baker's Woods. The idea was to shave off its edge to make space for home lots.

Charges were laid under the tree by-law against Metrus Development. Each tree was a separate offence and the fine was $385,000, the largest in Canadian history. News spread and the politicians were upset ... not that the trees had been cut but that the largest developer in Canada might be offended. Apologies were extended and charges dropped, if the developer would make a $20,000 contribution toward planting some trees. Of course, the developer, Fred DeGasperis, agreed. Lyn MacMillan, the mayor, and I visited him soon after and unsuccessfully argued that he could make more money if Baker's Woods was the centrepiece of his project rather than its undeveloped leftover.

In the zone of assimilation around Toronto, land is now so expensive that consultants and lawyers fight over every inch of it. They argue about things like where the "drip-line" is. A drip-line is where a raindrop would fall, on a still day, from a tree's outermost leaf. A metre beyond that and you have a standard limit of development in some municipalities, even though it is well known that what remains is insufficient for a large tree's roots. We argued for a thirty-foot setback and the hearing officer made it half of that. A six-year-old standing in the rain could tell you where the drip-line is but, as it happened, it took a dozen public servants, consultants, and others to locate it, one person with stakes and the rest of us arguing. Lawfare politely waged, lot by lot, is thus pursued, both for and against nature.[52]

Months later, people gathered to celebrate the bush's protection. The Bakers would return to Pennsylvania with more than $20 million and the original Conestoga wagon. At the event I asked *Toronto Star* reporter Gail Swainson to quote me saying nice things about the role that Fred DeGasperis, the owner of Metrus, had played in saving the woodlot. She asked him about it directly and his response was guarded – it was the first time he had been complimented like that. As unlikely as it was, DeGasperis went on to do good deeds for the Oak Ridges, but more of that later. Suffice it to say that he is one of a long line of individuals dating back through three centuries in Great Lakes country, from Boucher and Johnson to Brant and McKee, whose fortunes were tied to the land and its manufacture.

Over the past two centuries, the players and the rules have changed but the fundamentals are the same. The ability to secure, sever, and sell land remains the tried and true path to wealth. Its justification is still migration, although redevelopment and intensification are now also cited. The existing landowners are again invited to leave, happy with their payments. Today, the farms are cleared again, this time of their topsoil as well, and are severed into lots that are smaller than ever, and, by this formula, growth itself becomes the primary agent of growth. Building the new city-state creates employment as long as the building continues. Henry Ford's formula for economic stability was to "pay the workers enough so they can buy their own cars," but only a very few, if any, of those working in the building trades can buy a new home on the old Baker farm.

The legal construct of the Earth as property - alienable, divisible, and disposable - has served us well. When every frontier was still ahead, and when the need to hunt, gather, and farm was so deeply engrained in our genetics that any other behaviour was suicidal, it was the ethical thing to do. Now, however, with all our modern wealth, knowledge, and technology, this is no longer the case and, in many respects, we are now venturing beyond, to rediscover an ancient and common interest in the land, a theme we will return to in Part Three of this book.

It is the consensus of scientists worldwide that the primary cause of the decline of nature and its many creatures has been land fragmentation and habitat loss - a loss by a thousand cuts. If you ask the same scientists to imagine the scale and dimensions of the worst possible assault on a landscape, the following tactics would emerge, based on global experience. First remove any vestige of original Native stewardship from the most productive lands. Then remove the Native people themselves. Survey and sever the land into an unnatural grid of small land parcels. Build roads to each parcel and install a strong, industrious family on each one. Arm each family with a mission to succeed and the tools to clear, drain, farm, hunt, fish, and dam. Then repetitively harvest the standing biomass of the remaining native ecosystems on the other, less productive parts of the landscape. And to guarantee the outcome, accomplish all of this in less than three centuries, to avoid any deep affection for the native land that might creep in over a longer period.[53]

This was the story of the Great Lakes country. We will now turn, more particularly, to the fate of its wildlife, forests, and other special places.

PART TWO

VOICES OF NATURE PAST

CHAPTER FIVE

Taking the Wildlife: 1500–1900

Everyone who came early to North America witnessed its superabundant wildlife, its brilliantly coloured birds, its astonishing numbers of fish and game, and, above all, the breathtaking phenomenon of the passenger pigeon, which accounted for a quarter of all the birds in eastern North America. "Blue meteors," some called them. A "biological storm," said the ecologist Aldo Leopold.[1]

Champlain saw them in "an infinite numbers" on the New England coast in 1605 and, in 1625, Sagard reported another "infinity" in Huronia. Two centuries later, a flight over Lake Ontario was measured as eighty miles long by Irish traveller Isaac Weld. Another over Ohio in 1806 was estimated by ornithologist Alexander Wilson as a mile wide and two hundred and forty miles long, more than two billion birds. Yet another over Niagara in the early 1860s was measured with care, and calculated later at 3.7 billion birds. The link between them and the mast, or nut, trees was clear. Henry Small wrote in 1866 that pigeons showed up in force "about once in four or five years," coinciding with the years of heavy beechnut production, "the same seasons the black squirrels are most abundant." They swept the oak woodlands clear – as John Muir wrote, "thousands of acres perfectly clean of acorns in a few minutes."[2]

They nested in massive roosts throughout the Great Lakes, Appalachia, and the Atlantic seaboard. In the 1640s Van der Donck described an Iroquois hunt. "When they find the breeding places of the pigeons, [they] frequently remove to those places with their wives and children, to the number of two or three hundred in a company, where they live a month or more on the young pigeons, which they take after pushing them from their nests with poles and sticks."

In 1782 the pioneer Horatio Jones attended a Seneca hunt at a Genesee roost. The nestlings were taken when the adults left to feed. "Several hundred men, women and children gathered in ... the pigeon woods" and "cut down the roost trees ... and each day thousands of squabs were killed." They were cooked, dried, and smoked for eating and for winter stores, "packed in bags or baskets for transportation to the home towns."[3]

Settlement increased the harvest. Samuel Thompson, in 1834, called the roost near his farm in Huronia a marvel. "Men, women and children went by the hundred, some with guns, but the majority with baskets, to pick up the countless birds that had been disabled by the fall of great branches of trees broken off by the weight of their roosting ... The women skinned the birds, cut off their plump breasts, throwing the remainder away, and packed them in barrels with salt." A roost on the Bruce peninsula was described in the *Paisley Advocate* on 28 April 1876: "Immense flocks ... have begun building ... The place is visited by scores of persons who are shooting the pigeons, and all the shot in Owen Sound and Southampton seems to have been fired away as a telegram has been received in Paisley asking for a supply." London's William Sherwood Fox told how his father said that the noise of the pigeons was like the "falls at Niagara as heard by one standing on the footway behind the heavy curtain of falling water."[4]

A veteran pigeon-netter reported that the largest roost he ever saw, south of Mackinac Island in Michigan, extended "twenty-eight miles, averaging three or four miles wide ... The old birds never feed near the nesting, leaving all the beech mast, etc., there for their young, many of them going a hundred miles daily for food." A roost in New York State stretched from Oneida County to Jefferson, thirty miles long by three miles wide. One in Pennsylvania was more than sixty miles long. By this time the pigeon was a cash crop shipped to market by rail and steamer. In 1878 the public finally rose in alarm to protect one of the last great roosts, in Petoskey, Michigan, but it was too late and a million and a half birds were killed. The last of them died in 1914 in a cage at the Cincinnati Zoological Gardens. Aldo Leopold raised a monument to its passing in 1947.[5]

A species of such preponderant biomass exerts a deep influence on a landscape. The pigeon consumed vast quantities of mast and fruit, and redistributed vast quantities of germinating nuts and seeds in its feces. Acorns, hazelnuts, beechnuts, chestnuts, and maple keys were favoured, but the pigeon was an omnivore, ingesting whole seasons of grapes, cherries, strawberries, currants, wild rice, blackberries, and corn – in fact, all the food plants that

Natives had also collected or grown, a mutually beneficial co-dependence. Pigeons also fed on the eruptive outbreaks of forest caterpillars and leaf defoliators. "One office of the pigeon seems to be to protect the oak forests," noted the Reverend William Peabody of Massachusetts in 1841.[6]

The archaeologist Thomas Neumann has detailed this co-dependence of Native land care (in aid of mast, fruit, and crops) and the fauna that were encouraged by that land care and that were, at the same time, the preferred game of the Natives. The passenger pigeon was one of these, and central to the Native economy. Bird bones do not last long as artifacts but, in Ontario, pigeon bones are found at the majority of archaeological sites, often in good numbers, and in Onondaga sites they are as well represented as any other bird.[7]

Other species also show up in the early records in biblical proportions. Isaac Weld said it was common practice to call certain years the pigeon year, bear year, or squirrel year, based on their numbers. In some years bear headed south and arrived at Lake Ontario or Erie, or the St Lawrence, and swam for any shore they could see. "Prodigious numbers of them are killed in crossing the St. Lawrence by the Indians, who had hunting encampments ... the whole way along the banks of the river." In squirrel years like 1796, Weld noted how black squirrels migrated from the south "towards Niagara River ... and at its narrowest and most tranquil part ... upwards of fifty thousand of them crossed the river in the course of two or three days." In 1832 Tiger Dunlop commented on the "unaccountable migration of certain animals of this continent. Squirrels, weazles, mice, moles, &c., appear in great numbers for a month or six weeks, and then as suddenly disappear." There was a black squirrel outbreak in 1828, following a vole irruption the year before, of which Dunlop said, "from that date ... to the present, February 1832, not a single solitary individual of the species has been seen." In 1830 "the Talbot settlement [on Lake Erie] was invaded by an army of weazles, which boldly entered the houses."[8]

After three centuries of attentive harvest, the native wildlife of Great Lakes country is a shadow of its former self. Where wildlife was once abundant and muscular on the land, the faint modern irruptions of boreal passerines heading south when their crop trees fail, or of owls in winter, go largely unnoticed. We have worked hard to be independent of nature – independent of our place in the world, so to speak – and to reduce and remove and restrict it. Today, even the hint of abundance, like deer in Pennsylvania, or raccoons in Toronto, or Canada geese, or opossum moving north, makes us nervous. The first instinct is that these are possible vectors of disease, rather than likely indicators of health and plenty.

By 1600, Europe's wildlife had been reduced to penury over millennia. Eastern North America achieved the same in less than a handful of generations. The pace of change was astonishing – and still is. C.H. Douglas Clarke, Ontario's provincial wildlife director, wrote about this in 1964: "If we can actually see the skeletonizing of the land and the filling in of the waters, then it is impossible for us to reach a state of normal adaptation to the environment." Such is the subject of this chapter, the observed changes in nature's estate, in the observers' own voices.[9]

The Atlantic Arrival Coast

The early reports were not always clear about what was being seen. The naming of species was the special role of naturalists, who were using field collections, comparative descriptions, and standard names to begin the global catalogue of life. The title "naturalist" was a high compliment in its day. It had been in use since 1587, and Carl von Linnaeus and Charles Darwin both called themselves naturalists. For them, it meant that the world and its phenomena could be explained by natural causes – "by laws acting around us," as Darwin said. This was long before the word "scientist" came into use in the late 1800s to describe the same people documenting their observations of nature, and testing their explanations against those observations. In those days it was enough for travellers to list their finds and collect what they could. This was perhaps the era of our greatest sympathetic curiosity about nature. The novelties of the Americas, and at the same time of Asia and Africa, poured into Europe as the rewards of empire.[10]

The Atlantic seaboard was busy by 1602, when Gabriel Archer listed what he recognized, such as the "great store of cod-fish" and the "sculls [schools] of herrings, mackerels and other small fish in great abundance." Then there were others, "in our own English tongue of no name," such as the herons and geese and "pengwins" (great auk). Archer's ship chaplain, John Brereton, added more, worth repeating given the coast's modern condition: cranes (likely whooping and sandhill); seals (likely harbour seal); otter; "luzernes" (lynx); and "wilde-cats, very large" (cougar). There were "fowles ... of infinit store," likely the heath hen, the east-coast prairie chicken of the open coast, no doubt served at the Pilgrims' first Thanksgiving and now extinct.[11]

Champlain's notes on the Atlantic seaboard in 1604 and 1605 were limited. He remarked on horseshoe crabs up to "a foot in breadth and a foot and a half long" and the rafters of turkey that congregated "when their corn is ripe ... in the summer." In 1606 he wrote, "All the harbors, bays and coasts from Saco onward are filled with every kind of fish ... and in such abundance that ... there was never a day or night during which we did not see and hear more than a thousand porpoises passing alongside ... chasing the smaller fry." Among the gifts he took home for the king's amusement were a caribou, a young moose, a hummingbird, and five Canada geese.[12]

North, on the Maine coast in 1605, James Rosier reported on "raine-deer, stagges, fallow-deere" (caribou, possibly elk, and white-tailed deer). Samuel Purchas soon published a list of Abenaki words that included *coribo* and *moosur*. For someone coming from England, where there were no such animals, these were useful names. The same Samuel Purchas reported on other voyages, including one by Thomas Hanham in 1606, noting "red deere [elk], and a beast bigger, called the *mus*" (moose), "deer, red and fallow" (elk and white-tailed deer), and "deer with hornes and broad ears" (moose). Slowly, a vocabulary emerged.[13]

William Wood was an observer on the coast in the 1620s. In his 1634 *New England's Prospect*, he wrote, "The chief thing [Natives] hunt after is deer, mooses and bears; it grieves them more to see an Englishman take one deer than a thousand acres of land. They hunt likewise after wolves and wildcats, raccoons, otters, beavers, musquashes [muskrat]." They corralled the deer in "hedges a mile or two miles long ... and made narrower ... by degrees, leaving only a gap of six foot [where they] shoot the deer." Wolves were "so numerous ... there is little hope of their utter destruction" and, he wrote, the "most injurious ... [was] a rattlesnake, which is generally a yard and a half long." An "expert" fishery was conducted with lances and hooks, and with nets made of hemp "stronger ... than ours." The cod were "larger than in Newfoundland" and "[Atlantic] salmon ... plenty ... Sturgeon be all over the country ... some of these be twelve, fourteen, eighteen foot long." Contemporaries saw Natives whaling off Maine, spearing them "with a bone made in [the] fashion of a harping iron fastened to a rope."[14]

The reports were graphic. Thomas Morton lived on the coast in the 1620s, and he told how the bear was "a tyrant at a lobster, and at low water will downe to the rocks, and groape after them with great diligence." Roger Williams wrote about the Massachusett hunting turkey, geese, and cranes; they "lay nets ... and catch many fowle upon the plaines and feeding under okes upon akrons [acorns]." He witnessed their falconry, explaining that the Natives had tame hawks ... "about their houses to keep the little birds from their corne," and was struck especially by the "millions ... of blackbirds."[15]

Henry Hudson thought he had found a Northwest Passage in September 1609 when he saw the wide estuary of the Hudson River. "We sailed up the river 12 leagues," and where it shallowed south of today's Albany, he was invited onshore by a headman. He visited one of their granaries: "Well constructed of oak bark ... [with] a great quantity of maize or Indian corn, and beans of the last year's growth; and there lay near the house, for the purpose of drying, enough to load three ships ... The land is the finest for cultivation that I ever ... set foot upon, and it also abounds in trees of every description." A contemporary, Emanuel Van Meteren, said the same. "In the lower part of the river they found strong and warlike people; but in the upper part they found friendly and polite people, who had an abundance of provisions, skins, and furs, of martens and foxes, and many other commodities, as birds and fruit, even white and red grapes."[16]

Adriaen Van der Donck described the Hudson and Mohawk valleys in the 1640s. The Natives were "much engaged in hunting," and sometimes as many as "one to two hundred drive over a large district of land and kill much game," also using fences that "narrow at their terminating angles, wherein they drive multitudes of animals." They fished collectively, too, with seines. Trade was brisk: "80,000 beavers are annually killed in this quarter ... besides elks, bears, otters, deer and other animals." Cougar were rare but the bison "plenty ... towards the southwest"; the deer "incredibly numerous"; the moose and elk well "known to the people of Canada"; and the wolf "numerous." He also listed "wildcats," fox, racoon, mink, hare, muskrat, black and flying squirrels, groundhog, skunk, and others "for which we have no names." There were two kinds of eagle, one called "white-heads"; turkey, which were "common ... all over"; a hummingbird that "sucks its nourishment ... like the bees"; cranes in "great numbers"; swans "dressed in white"; and pelicans. He too listed the salmon and sturgeon ("plenty in the rivers"), lamprey ("large as a man's leg"), and smelt and cod ("very plentiful"). Rattlesnakes he saw personally, "on Long Island."[17]

The bounty was soon taken for granted, and less frequently reported, as if it were no longer news. Van der Donck was one of those who took it for granted. "There are some persons who imagine that the animals of the country will be destroyed in time, but this is unnecessary anxiety."

Cartier and Champlain

Jacques Cartier was an experienced transatlantic traveller before his 1534 voyage to the Gulf of St Lawrence, and he recorded only the oddities, such as Funk Island, off Newfoundland. "It is so exceeding full of birds ... each of our ships salted four of five casks, not counting those we were able to eat fresh." Cartier had made straight for Funk Island to take on provisions, as did every ship of the day. A few casks each and, by 1844, the flightless great auk, the North Atlantic's equivalent of the penguin, was extinct. A polar bear was also seen feeding on the island, "white as a swan," and south of its modern range.[18]

Cartier came again the next year. On the north shore of the Gulf near Anticosti Island, there were a "great number" of walrus, and off the Saguenay, a beluga fishery. The Natives took eel and mackerel, using "large vessels ... in which they place their fish ... and on these they live during the winter." He was hyperbolic about the fishery: "The richest in every kind ... that anyone remembers having ever seen or heard of ... mackerel, mullets, maigres, tunnies, large-sized eels and other fish ... [and] as good smelts as in the river Seine. In spring ... lampreys and salmon. Up above Canada are many pike, trout, carp, bream and other freshwater fish."[19]

Cartier listed the birds he thought "the same as in France," such as "swans, white and gray geese, ducks, drakes, blackbirds, thrushes, turtle-doves, wood-pigeons, goldfinches, tarins, canaries, linnets, nightingales, sparrows," and "larks, pheasants, partridges." He also noted elk, deer, "bear and ... otter, beaver, marten, foxes, wild-cats, hares, rabbits, squirrels" and, on Lac Saint-Pierre, "muskrats ... wonderfully good to eat." The ship captain Alfonse de Saintonge would write in 1542 about the St Lawrence: "Fowle in abundance, as [also] bustards, wild geese, cranes, turtle doves ... and many other birds." Abundance was the standard refrain.[20]

Samuel de Champlain was an exceptional observer. On his St Lawrence voyage in 1603, he distinguished the animals he was "unacquainted with" from those he was. He listed the bear, hare, porcupine, fox, beaver, otter, and muskrat but, most carefully, the four ungulates – moose, caribou, white-tailed deer, and elk. His names for these ungulates cycled through several iterations as he sorted them out, male and female, young and old, and he admitted his difficulty.[21] Five years later, Champlain built his *Abitation* near the old Stadacona, and he sketched two different kinds of Native eel and fish weirs at the mouths of the Saint-Charles and Moulin rivers (Fig. 11). Eel fishing in the fall provided both Natives and newcomers with "manna" that lasted until mid-winter. Upstream in 1611 he toured the Lachine Rapids and marked two heronries on his map, one of which is still there today, on an island protected as a nature reserve. His *Voyages* were full of detail.[22]

Champlain's canoe trip to Huronia in 1615 threaded the islands along the east coast of Georgian Bay. The lake trout were "as much as four and a half feet long, and the smallest ones seen are two and a half feet." So too the "pike of like size and ... sturgeon, a very large fish." The Huron "make nets for catching fish in summer as in winter, when they usually catch fish under the ice by a line or with a seine." On his raid down the Trent, the Huron drove the deer into the river and speared them from their canoes. There were, he said, "many cranes as white as swans" – whooping cranes. He hunted that winter in Huronia, noting its "swans, white cranes, geese, ducks, teal, thrushes, larks, snipe, geese." He recorded the Natives' traps and snares, and the details of a deer hunt, which used fences each side of which was "fifteen hundred paces." By this means they took 120 deer in thirty-eight days, a unique record of the efficiency of a Native deer drive.[23]

One day before the frost came that year, Champlain chased "a certain bird which seemed to me peculiar, with a beak almost like that of a parrot, as big as a hen, yellow all over, except for its red head and blue wings." Many have mused about his observation, which invites the conclusion that he was chasing a stray Carolina parakeet, another once plentiful species now long extinct, the last one dying at the Cincinnati zoo in 1918. May the fashion of feathered hats never return.[24]

The French Religionists

The Recollets and the Jesuits reached the St Lawrence in 1615 and 1625 respectively. In 1623 the Recollet Gabriel Sagard arrived in the Gulf, and complained of the whales, which were "very tiresome to us and hindered our rest by their continual movement and the noise of their spouting." He reported polar bear on Anticosti Island. In Huronia, he spent most of his time in town and reported less about the land and its resources than about its domestic life and social customs. However, he did fish off the Georgian Bay islands, where the Huron set their nets at night and hauled out the next morning "monstrously large" lake trout, sturgeon, pike, and *assihendo* (whitefish), the latter a key source of oil. He also took note of the lake herring, gar, and *einchataon* (burbot), and the turtles, snakes, toads, and frogs – especially the edible turtles and bull frogs.[25]

Sagard kept lists of the birds he saw: the cardinal, hummingbird, goldfinch, red-headed woodpecker, bald eagle, turkey, Canada goose, cranes, swans, partridges, raptors, and others. The "infinite" passenger pigeons fed on acorns and, on the roost, "allowed themselves to be knocked down by blows of stones and poles." There were mammals too: the moose ("very rare in Huronia");

caribou (the Natives "gave us a foot"); deer ("more plentiful in the province of the Neutrals"); and the wolf, fox, squirrels, chipmunk, hare, lynx, marten, bear, beaver, muskrat, and porcupine.[26]

La Roche d'Aillon, another Recollet, walked in 1626 from Huronia to the Neutral country at the head of Lake Ontario. It was "incomparably larger, more beautiful, and better than any other of all these countries. There is an incredible number of deer [cerfs], which they do not take one by one ... but making three enclosures in a spacious place, they run them all ... [and] take them ... [They] have this maxim ... that they must kill all they find, for fear ... that if they do not take them the beasts would go and tell the others ... There is also a great abundance of ... elk [eslans], beaver, wild-cats and black squirrels [and] wild geese, turkeys, cranes and other animals, which are there all winter." In 1640 Jérôme Lalemant visited eighteen Neutral towns and villages; they "greatly excel in hunting deer [cerfs], elk [vaches], wild cats, wolves, black squirrels, beaver and other animals of which the skin and the flesh are valuable ...They have also multitudes of wild turkeys, which go in flocks through the fields and the woods."[27]

The Jesuit Relations from 1632 to 1655 detail much of the natural history of the Great Lakes and St Lawrence. In 1632, for example, at Paul le Jeune's landfall at Tadoussac, there was "a great white eagle near its eyrie. Its head and neck were entirely white, the beak and feet yellow." A skilful Montagnais was harpooning eels from a canoe – "three hundred in one night" – and their weirs on the tidal flats were "capable of holding five or six hundred eels." The eels were used in particular for "travel food," because of their superior caloric value. The Relations tracked the eel harvest around Quebec City: "forty thousand eels" in the three months before October 1646. By 1670, "fifty thousand barrels ... [of eels] were caught in three months of every year" in the lower St Lawrence.[28]

A fine overview of the St Lawrence was part of the 1663 Relations, the work of the traveller Charles Simon. Entering the St Lawrence "from the sea are whales, blowers, gray porposes, sturgeon, salmon, barbel, shad, cod, herring, mackerel, smelt and sea-wolves [seals]. The banks sometimes appear entirely covered with the last named ... The abundance of all these fish passes belief." The cod were "so vast" that "ships are quickly filled with them." The smelt sometimes covered the riverbanks "to a depth of about a foot." And so on. Upstream it was different again, two kinds of pike and two of perch, catfish and beluga, and eel so "very abundant" that "one fisherman ... caught in a single day, in his weir, five thousand." Again, downstream of Quebec, at Île aux Coudres, there were caribou (élans) "in great abundance," and l'Isle-aux-Grues was "quite overrun" with geese and ducks. Upstream, the islands in Lac Saint-Pierre abounded with "deer and wild cows [elk] ... in herds ... [and] moose swimming," and were "all wonderfully stocked with fish of every species."[29]

The Jesuits had active missions in Iroquoia from 1654 to 1708. Jean de Quens witnessed an elk drive south of Lake Ontario in 1654, which "killed eighteen *vaches sauvages* in less than an hour." Nearby, the *Relations* also record the Onondaga eating elk, deer, wildcats, bear, and beaver, and netting pigeons where they flocked around the lakes in the spring. The Onondaga fished with spears and weirs, even through the ice, and took the sturgeon with hatchets. There were perch, bass, catfish, salmon, pike, and eel, the latter speared by the hundreds – up to a thousand by a single man in an evening. In 1656 the Jesuit Claude Dablon saw the Oneida using in-stream weirs to "catch at the same time the eels, that descend, and the salmon, that always ascends." The Jesuit Pierre Raffeix would describe Cayuga country as "almost uninterrupted plains" – the "swans and geese are very abundant ... and in spring one sees nothing but continual clouds of all sorts of wild fowl." He wrote that the Natives killed "annually more than a thousand deer [*chevreuils*]" and used "snares" to catch "pigeons, from seven to eight hundred being often taken at once."[30]

On his way to Iroquoia from Montreal in 1654, Simon Le Moine remarked on the "*prairies*" east of Lake Ontario, "a resort for all nations" where he saw herds of elk (*vaches sauvages*) "sometimes ... four or five hundred of them together." On his return, he wrote, "herds of twenty cows leap into the water ... and our men, for sheer sport, kill some of them with their hatchets." The following year, Joseph Chaumont passed the same way and saw whole "herds of cows or deer [elk, *vaches*, and deer, *cerfs*] swimming from isle to isle. Our hunters cut them off ... and lined the entire shore with them, killing them as they pleased." The same "vast prairie" had "an incredible number of geese."[31]

Today, vastly reduced, what remains of the "prairies" east of Lake Ontario are the Chaumont barrens – or unforested limestone plains. Elk preferred this habitat, and Champlain's map of 1632 also noted elk between the Ottawa valley and Kingston, where there are also limestone plains. Much later, Ottawa city clerk William Lett would write that elk preferred "the southern shore of the [Ottawa] river," where there are limestone plains and where they persisted as late as 1840. They held out until 1869 in the Alleghenies south of the lakes. The popular chronicler of game animals, Ernest Thompson Seton, was appalled by the elk hunt in the 1800s – the vast majority taken "for the joy of seeing the great creatures fall in dying agony." Since 1900 there have been repeated efforts to restore elk, with limited success so far.[32]

Bréhant de Galinée was the first European to winter on Lake Erie. He did so near Port Dover in 1669, on the Norfolk sand plain, a *paradis terrestre* and a "great hunting ground" for elk, deer, bear, cats, racoon, and beaver. The land was "watered by rivers and rivulets filled with fish and beaver ... [and] we saw there at any one time more than a hundred deer in a single band, herds of fifty or sixty elk, and bears fatter and of better flavor than the most savory pigs of France." As well, he wrote, the Natives caught "a great deal of fish" at the mouth of the Niagara River and enjoyed "very good hunting" on the "dry prairies" along the Grand River. Pierre Charlevoix, the Jesuit traveller, would also note in 1721: "There are a great number of bears in this part of the country, and last winter more than four hundred were killed on Point Pelee alone."[33]

On his way north along the Lake Huron shore, Galinée mapped the "great hunting grounds" on Manitoulin and its offshore islands. He visited the *sault* on St Marys River and saw the skill involved in fishing from canoes, using long rods with hoopnets. The rapids were "so teeming with ... whitefish ... that the Indians could easily catch enough to feed 10,000 men ... Each weighs six or seven pounds but it is so fat and delicate that I know of no fish that approaches it. Sturgeon is [also] caught in this river, close by, in abundance." In 1670 Nicholas Perrot also visited Sault Ste Marie and that winter Perrot and some Algonquin "got more than two thousand four hundred caribou [*élans*] in their hunt on ... the island of the Ottawas [Manitoulin] ... using only snares." Caribou at their southern limits may have been in decline even then from hunting and, in 1647, from a "disease" that "made them vomit blood" and remain "still while they were pursued."[34]

By 1669 and 1670, the Jesuits Jacques Marquette, Claude-Jean Allouez, and Claude Dablon were establishing missions west of Lake Michigan, where "beautiful plains and fields ... as far as one can see" led to the "great river named Messi-Sipi." There were thousands living there: "all of these nations have their fields of corn, squash, beans and tobacco," and "fine hunting ... of buffalo, bear, elk, turkey, ducks, geese, pigeons and cranes." Game was so plenty that "one can kill what he chooses." At Green Bay, "more than three thousand" Potawatomi hunted amidst "clouds of swans, geese and ducks ... seeking in autumn the wild rice." The rice beds were spectacular and the waterfowl so abundant that the Natives "stretch nets for them with such skill that, without counting the fish [caught], they ... catch in one night as many as a hundred wild fowl." Like Galinée the same year at Detroit, these Jesuits found, beside the massive Native fish weir on the lower Fox, "a rock shaped by nature in the form of a human bust," which "the Natives honor, never failing to offer it some sacrifice in passing." They too cast it into the river, "never to appear again." Another paradise on earth, by 1670 already vulnerable to Iroquois attacks and Jesuit missions.[35]

The Jesuits did not publish the work of Louis Nicolas, although he offered exceptional detail and drawings – unique for a Jesuit – of the harvest and use of plants and animals in New France. Walking across Iroquoia in 1670, he too had seen the *vastes prairies* south of Lake Ontario, "where the grass was almost a quarter of a pike high [five feet]" and "as far as the eye could see." He sketched the bison, the *pichikiou* or *boeuf sauvage*, and remarked how the newly armed Natives were eliminating it from its eastern haunts "with no regard for future needs."[36]

The Recollets returned to New France in 1670. The Recollet Louis Hennepin was assigned to La Salle in 1678 and put in some time waiting for him at Fort Frontenac. The Cayuga who had moved there fed him and his party on "elks and roe-bucks," and, nearby, he raided an island gull colony and took "four baskets" of eggs to use "in omelets and pancakes." He spent the winter at the mouth of the Niagara River, where the Natives took "an infinite quantity of whitings [whitefish], sturgeons and all other sorts ... They cannot get over this huge cataract [and] the quantity taken here is incredible ... There are salmon-trouts [lake trout] of fifty or sixty pound weight." Along Lake Erie, he said, "we staïd some time to kill sturgeon, which come here in great numbers, to cast their spawn on the side of the lake. We took nothing but the belly ... and threw away the rest."

On Lake Ontario, Hennepin wrote, "the most considerable fishery ... is that of eels, which are very large, of salmons, and salmon-trouts, and white fish." The lake trout spawned on cobble shoals along the north shore, which were dredged away in the 1800s by a fleet hauling out gravel for construction projects. Hennepin described fishing "nets made of nettles" that were "forty or fifty fathoms long," which the Natives "put in a great canow, after they cast it in an oval form in convenient places ... They take sometimes four hundred white fish, besides many sturgeon."

The country along the Detroit and St Clair rivers, Hennepin wrote, was "stock'd with stags [elk], wild-goats [deer], and bears ... Turkey-cocks and swans are there also very common." On Long Point his party took venison and fowl, and a bear – "we liv'd for a hundred leagues upon the game that we kill'd in this place." Later he saw rattlesnakes in the Niagara Gorge where, he said, they were "very common ... during the great heats, and lodge in holes all along the rocks." This was the first of many reports of rattlesnakes at Niagara.

On their return along the south shore of Lake Ontario, he wrote, "We wanted then neither powder nor shot, and therefore we shot at random all that we met, either small birds, or turtles, and wood-pigeons, which were ... in so great numbers, that they did appear in the air like clouds."[37]

The Secular French

The French court asked Pierre Boucher to report to it on New France, based on his thirty years living there. His 1664 *Histoire véritable et naturelle* takes his readers first to the Gulf, tempting them with the cod, salmon and oysters, and coal and plaster that could be had there. The ungulates were well known to Boucher: moose (*orignal*) were "the most widely distributed"; *caribou* were distinct, with "hoofs ... [that]do not sink in the snow" and in numbers as far south as Trois-Rivières; elk (*vaches sauvages*) "go in herds" though "none are to be seen below ... Trois-Rivières"; deer (*cerfs*) were absent below Montreal but plentiful above it; and bison (*bufles*) were present far in the interior.

Systematically, Boucher goes through the animals and their distribution, along with the novelties, like the "cats and rats ... brought from France." There were "extraordinary numbers" of belugas in the lower St Lawrence, for example, and, in Lake Ontario, "salmon, sturgeon, catfish and eels ... [in] prodigious quantities." Huronia a decade after its evacuation, he said, was still open country "almost all cleared as France is" and "crowded with waterfowl" and deer, "turkeys and other feathered game," and with a special fishery, "through the ice ... for herring, which abound." He was clear about what he knew. "In the Great Lakes, there are quantities of fine large fish of different kinds that have not yet any names ... but still are delicious eating." And then there were the mineral springs, the oil springs, the lead mine, the copper – in short, the opportunities.[38]

In 1683 the young Baron Lahontan was eighteen and on the loose around the St Lawrence. He was quick to notice the habitants working the eel fishery, copying the Native weirs. "At low water they stretch out hurdles to the lowest water-mark ... Between the hurdles they place at certain distances [weirs] called *ruches* [and] as often as the tide comes in, the eels ... croud in ... [and] When 'tis low water, the inhabitants take out these eels, which are certainly the biggest and the longest in the world. They salt them up in barrels."

Lahonton was a true hunter-gatherer, and an early adopter of Native ways. He spent a winter on snowshoes hunting for "elks" north of Montreal where "the herds are largest in the beginning of spring ... We took fifty-six ... and might have kill'd twice as many if we had hunted for ... the skins." They also took deer and caribou using the Natives' techniques. In 1686 he shot "an infinity" of fowl in the marshes of Lake Champlain, including snipe, rails, ducks, geese, and teal. Along the lake they blasted the pigeons on their roosts, a bird "so numerous in Canada" that "the bishop has been forc'd to excommunicate 'em oftner than once." They set their dogs on two wolverines (*carcaioux*), trapped two hundred and fifty otter, and then went bear hunting. He witnessed "the stupidity of the wood-hens [spruce grouse] which sit upon the trees in whole flocks, and are kill'd one after another without ever offering to stir." The experiences that winter deeply affected him.[39]

In 1687 Lahontan canoed the north shore of Lake Erie. At Long Point, he reported, "we frequently saw flocks of fifty or sixty turkeys, which run incredibly fast upon the sands." Soon they were in the strait between lakes Huron and Erie, and drove whole "herds of harts [elk, *cerfs*] and roe-bucks [deer, *chevreuils*]" into the water and killed them from their canoes. "I cannot express what quantities of deer [game, *bêtes fauves*] and turkeys are to found in these woods and in the vast meads [*prairies*] that lye upon the south side of the lake ... [where] we find wild beeves [bison, *bœufs sauvages*] upon the banks."[40]

Also on the south side of Lake Erie, likely near Cattaraugus, Lahontan caught sturgeon "six foot in length," and later, at Michilimackinac, he saw the "vast sholes of white fish" that both the Natives and French relied on. The Natives also caught "trouts as big as one's thigh ... not only with hooks, but with nets." The Native nets at Michilimackinac were also admired that year by Henri Joutel, one of La Salle's men: gill nets twelve hundred feet long and two feet deep, set to depth with stone weights and cedar floats. Like others, Lahontan drew up lists of what he saw, separating those not known from those that were, and those in the north from those in the south.[41]

In 1694 Antoine de Lamothe Cadillac was officer-in-charge at Michili-mackinac. Four years later he sailed for France to lobby for a new post on the strait between lakes Huron and Erie. In 1701 his Detroit project was set in motion. "At the entrance to Lake Erie," Cadillac wrote, "to the south-south-west, are boundless prairies ... It is there that these mighty oxen [bison], which are covered with wool, find food in abundance ... I sent ... some hides and wool of these animals ... to make trial of them, and it has been found that ... the hides may be very usefully employed, and the wool used for stockings and cloth-making."

"Of stags and hinds [elk, *cerfs* and *biches*], they are seen in hundreds, roebucks [deer, *chevreuil*] black bears, otters and other smaller fur-bearing animals; the skins of these animals sell well ... Game is very common ... wild geese and all kinds of wild ducks. There are swans everywhere ... [and] quails, woodcocks, pheasants, rabbits ... There are so many turkeys that 20 or 30 could be killed at one shot. There are partridges, hazel-hens, and a stupendous number of turtle-doves." The cranes were "grey and white" and "the savages value the latter greatly, on account of their plumage, with which they adorn themselves." He saw "birds of rare beauty ... of a beautifully red fire color ... I have seen others of a sky blue color with red breasts ... A pleasant warbling proceeds from all these birds, especially from the red ones with large beaks." A novelty entirely was the marsupial opossum: "The female has a pouch under her belly which opens ... [and] if the mother finds herself pressed, she quickly shuts them up in pouch and carries them all away." Then just a southerner, opossum now ventures north as far as Green Bay and the Ottawa valley.⁴²

Collectors and Traders

Some visitors came for the sole purpose of studying nature, and the naturalist Pehr Kalm was one of them. Arriving on the Atlantic seaboard in 1748, he noted how "several gentlemen ... asserted that during their life they had plainly found several kinds of fish decrease in numbers every year." The following June he sailed up the Hudson River and, "on the whole passage we met porpoises," he wrote. (Porpoise sightings in the Hudson are now tracked as rarities.) Kalm wintered in Albany when it was the leading fur-trade centre, getting 80 per cent of its beaver from Canadien smugglers and shipping more than 40,000 furs a year. Brandy was the trade item of choice, and wampum was made locally by whites. "The avarice, selfishness and immeasurable love of money of the inhabitants of Albany are very well known throughout all North America."⁴³

Near the mouth of the Mohawk, he wrote, "sturgeon abound ... leaping high up into the air." The locals jacklighted them and, using spears from boats, left the shores "covered with dead." In the same area, Kalm saw "immense numbers of wild pigeons ... in which we found a great quantity of the seeds of the elm," their local crop in June, and he noted that "in May the seeds of the red maple" were favoured. "Their flesh is the most palatable of any bird's flesh I have ever tasted."⁴⁴

At Niagara in the fall of 1750, Kalm stated that there were "such abundant quantities of dead waterfowl ... below the fall, on the shore, that the garrison of the fort for a long time live chiefly upon them ... They find also several sorts of dead fish, also deer, bears and other animals which have tried to cross."

Kalm's party killed three rattlesnakes on the portage around the falls. "In the beginning of autumn ... they gradually gather here from all directions and creep into the ... [gorge]; and when in the spring it gets warmer they come out again ... [and] by the hundreds. It was asserted that about six hundred ... had been killed this spring in this neighbourhood." Kalm sent two Native boys down the gorge and they came back with "twenty fine eals" caught by hand. Kalm was on the east side of the gorge and it was somewhere on the bare, wet limestone there that he, or the boys, collected a new species of shrub St John's-wort for his mentor Linnaeus, who named it after him. It has only been collected one other time in New York State, also at the falls, proof that Kalm had a keen eye.[45]

Kalm witnessed the harvest of porpoises and eels on the St Lawrence below Quebec. He noted the predator-prey relationship between them, and how the fish weirs caught both of them. He itemized the fur trade at Quebec: from the north came beaver, *orignacs* (moose), *cariboux,* bear, wolf, lynx, marten, fox, wolverine, and muskrat; and from the south came bison, elk, deer, otter, cougar, fox, raccoon, lynx, bobcat, and squirrels. "Many of [the traders] settle among the Indians far from Canada, marry Indian women, and never come back."[46]

A few of the traders left narratives. Alexander Henry was one of them, working out of Albany to supply the troops who were mopping up French resistance in 1760. After Montreal surrendered, he headed west in search of new markets "thrown open to British adventure." He canoed up the Ottawa and, at Lake Nipissing, caught "in two hours ... as much fish as all the party could eat" – bass, sturgeon, pike, and *masquinonge*. At Michilimackinac the Ottawa grew corn, which they "mashed and dried ... [and] a bushel, with two pounds of fat, is reckoned to be a month's subsistence" for a voyageur – a corn pemmican. It was expensive, so Henry instead fished that winter for "white fish ... a delicious and nutritive food ... here in astonishing numbers." They weighed "from six pounds to fifteen" and the Natives "cure them ... in the smoke, and lay them up in large quantities." He saw women at the Sault using the fur of hares, of no trade value, "cutting it into narrow strips, and weaving these into a cloth, of the shape of a blanket, and of a quality very warm and agreeable." Pigeons were "in great plenty" and he learned to sugar the maples. Henry was a student of the Algonquians, a key to his success as a trader.

Just a few more observations from Henry. In 1764, near Michilimackinac, he killed a cougar, "which animal sometimes attacks and carries away the

Indian children." Along the North Channel of Lake Huron he enjoyed the Native delicacy caviar, "the roe of the sturgeon, beat up, and boiled, and of the consistence of porridge." Near the French River, he almost stepped on a rattlesnake, and would have shot it except his Native companions called it "grandfather" and let it go. This was the great Laurentian North of Great Lakes country, and Henry learned it well.[47]

It was at this time that Jonathan Carver, the New England military surveyor, also travelled west. He too wrote how "the banks of the River Detroit [were] excessively fruitful, and proper for cultivation of wheat, Indian corn, oats, and peas. It has also many spots of fine pasturage." Like Hennepin earlier in the *Griffon*, he had difficulty sailing the channel exiting Lake Huron: "There is a bar of sand, which prevents those that are loaded from passing over it." His schooner had to offload, cross, and reload again. Carver wrote that the western Erie islands were "infested with rattlesnakes" and had a "greater kind of all these reptiles ... particularly of the water snake ... which amounted to myriads." The endemic Lake Erie water snake is now listed by law as both threatened and endangered.[48]

The Scottish trader Robert Dickson reported on Green Bay in 1793. The "Canadians" living there had "horned cattle and a number of horses" that "run wild," evidence of an "indolence" that belied the rich soils of the area, where the Natives were raising "corn, squashes, potatoes, melons & cucumbers ... and very well flavoured tobacco." Dickson reported more favourably on the wildlife farther west, where the "vast plains ... feed vast droves of buffalo and elk."[49]

Land Appraisers

The land trade gave rise to appraisal specialists, some of them working on their own and some for others. Two such appraisers were Richard Smith south of the lakes, and Patrick Campbell to the north. Smith set out in 1769 to inspect his own land grant near Otsego Lake, on the height of land south of the Mohawk valley. Deer and bear were abundant, and the Natives used "deer fences." He saw a set of elk horns, "the length of each ... 4 feet." The fishing in Otsego Lake was for brook trout and lake trout ("the common and the salmon trout"), pickerel, pike, perch, catfish, eel, sucker, and shad, and the bait he used for fishing was "pidgeons flesh or guts." On his way up the Susquehanna River, he saw the Oneida and Tuscarora use a brush weir weighted with stones to conduct a successful "shad fishery," followed by "an equal division of the fish."

Eighty years later, in 1848, Susan Fenimore Cooper would once again take stock of the wildlife around Otsego: all the bear, beaver, wolf, cougar, moose, and deer had been eliminated by 1810.[50]

The region was a war zone in these decades and the wildlife may have recovered briefly as a result. John Graves Simcoe reflected that "in consequence of the Indian warriors, who are the best hunters, being so often … [at war] … the encrease of deer &c. has been prodigious." In upper New York State in the 1780s, "the deer ran as plenty as sheep ... We killed them as we wanted them." In the Niagara area, Daniel Servos was a fur trader at Niagara in the 1780s. "The furs bought by him ... were the elk, deer, bear, marten and others, but no beaver. The beaver had been extirpated ... [and there were] no beavers in the memory of man. Deer, bears, wolves, foxes and porcupines were plentiful, also wild cats and panthers [cougar]. The last named savage animal prowled about until 1854, when the last one seen was shot two miles from Niagara. The woods swarmed with squirrels – black, red and grey – and wild turkeys ran or flew in great flocks."[51]

The fishery remained strong, as noted in 1792 by the Scottish land appraiser Patrick Campbell. "On the borders of Lake Ontario ... fish are caught in freshets in the spring ... in such numbers." At Hamilton Bay, "I saw several Indians of the Messessagoe nation fishing for pickerel, maskanongy, pike and other kinds of fish," using spears with "two prongs each about six inches long." On the Grand River, an "abundance of fish are caught ... particularly in spring; such as sturgeon, pike, pickerel, maskanongy, and others." And at the mouth of the Niagara River he saw "1008 [fish] caught at one hawl of a seine net, mostly ... white fish, and a few herrings; the former weighs at an average about two pounds. I [also] saw ... the sturgeon ... many of them weigh from thirty to forty pounds each. In place of a back-bone, they have only a large sinew full of gristle, of which the best isinglass may be made [for making glue]. The fishing here continues from ... October to ... May, and I have been told that 6000 have been caught in a day."[52]

Campbell visited Niagara Falls and underestimated its height at "149 feet 9 inches." The projection of Table Rock over the British side of the falls was "50 feet 4 inches." Before it collapsed into the gorge in 1850, Table Rock was the best place to view the falls. Horse-drawn carriages could turn around on it, and the souvenir trade was brisk. It was always wet with mist, so wet that the botanist Thomas Nuttall collected the carnivorous horned bladderwort on it in 1818. At the other end of the Horseshoe Falls, Goat Island was, Campbell said, "so overrun with rattlesnakes that it is dangerous for any person to walk through it, until a parcel of swine were put on it ... Hogs are so fond of snakes that if they once get a hold, should they be so hard bitten with a strong rattlesnake to make them squeal, yet they hold fast until the snake is devoured."[53]

The Lieutenant Governor and His Wife

Simcoe sleighed from Niagara to Detroit in the winter of 1793. The land between the Grand and the Thames was "frequented by immense herds of deer" hunted by the Natives using a "fence of stakes." His party camped at a Native cemetery full of "painted hieroglyphics ... denoting the nation, tribe and achievements of the deceased." There also were paintings of men "returning from battle with scalps, and animals ... well drawn, especially a bison ... The most remarkable were men with deer's heads." The totemic narrative was still strong.[54]

Farther down the Thames, Simcoe's party encountered the Delaware. Their Moravian priest, David Zeisberger, assured Simcoe of their loyalist credentials, and produced his copy of a 1749 royal document guaranteeing them freedom of worship. Zeisberger had kept a diary from the previous summer when he and his brethren had come up the Thames, far enough to be "again in the bush, our own masters," as he put it. They had had "a supper of turtles [spiny softshells] taken on the way." The Delaware, like their ancestors on the Delaware River, "made a fish-dam here and got so many that the whole town for a time had enough to eat and more." They did this every year and a later diary entry said, "Fish are now coming up the river in schools, the children and those older were busy catching a great quantity, so that through the week the whole town eats nothing but fish."[55]

Zeisberger also commented on farming amid the wildlife. The year 1796, he wrote, was "a year quite apart by itself ... There were early frosts, which have kept on, but since we made good use of planting time, the corn ripened in good season. With game, too, it has been unusual. Raccoons, squirrels, bears, wolves, and wild turkeys came in great number, and did great harm to the fields, here indeed not so much, for the Indians scared them away, but among the white people they ruined whole fields ... All sorts of vermin came from the south, tried to get over the river, and were drowned, whole heaps of which could be seen."

Simcoe expressed his pleasure with the Delaware and then continued on the Native trail west. "To the south [was] a range of spacious meadows. Elk are continually seen upon them, and the pools and ponds are full of fish." He inspected the British garrison at Detroit, paid his respects at Bloody Ridge (where Pontiac had slaughtered the British), and then turned east, visiting along the way the future site of London at the forks of the Thames, "a capital situation," his journal noted.

The lieutenant governor's wife, Elizabeth Simcoe, was an astute diarist and an able artist. Her first impressions of Quebec City in 1791 had nothing to do with nature but focused instead on the city's busy winter social season. There was news of her husband and the fighting south of the lakes. And gossip. An earthquake. Moccasins from the Huron village nearby. The day after Christmas, Upper Canada became a province, and she was wife of its first lieutenant governor.[56]

Three days after landing at Niagara-on-the-Lake, she set off for Niagara Falls, "the grandest sight imaginable." She viewed it from Table Rock and wrote, "It is said there are many of these snakes near it" (Fig. 12). She reported "a stuffed rattlesnake ... killed near Queenstown in the act of swallowing a black squirrel. The snake measured 5 feet six inches long & had seven rattles." She also told how the crew building the military road in the Dundas Valley west of Lake Ontario "kill rattlesnakes every day ... [and] Captain Smith sent two of the snakes in a barrel that I might see them, they are dark & ugly & made a whizzing sound by shaking their rattles." Later on, she reported the news from Augustus Jones that "7 hundred rattle snakes were killed near Burlington Bay this summer. They live in caves & in very dry weather go down to the lake to drink."[57]

Mrs Simcoe loved the whirlpool below the falls. "The current is so strong that eddies are formed in which ... trees carried down the falls [spin around] upright. Vast rocks surround this bend of the river & they are covered with pine & hemlock." At night "the fires the Indians had made ... for the purpose of spearing fish had a picturesque appearance." The Niagara Whirlpool lies in an ancient fork in the Niagara bedrock gorge, where the river is trying to erode its way down a deep, sand-filled channel called the St David's buried gorge. This channel is a rare break in the cliffs of the gorge, and was where snakes came out of the gorge after wintering there. The Thompson farm was at the head of the whirlpool in the 1800s and historian Hazel Mathews wrote: "In the Whirlpool below the Thompsons was a large den of rattlers of uncommon size. Whereas the Indians set fire to dry leaves in order to kill the snakes when they were emerging from hibernation, the settler made war upon the snakes with ... hogs. Some five hundred were killed in one day by an organized expedition in the gorge."[58]

Today, the Massasauga and timber rattlesnakes barely survive south of the lakes. They are largely finished north of the lakes too, with the Massasauga holding out only in the swamps, bogs, and shores around Georgian Bay, and at Wainfleet bog near Fort Erie and the Ojibway prairie in Windsor. The timber rattler held on in the Niagara Gorge until August 1941, when the last one was killed. No one talks about reintroducing them despite many suitable sites and the modern absence of free-range hogs.[59]

Mrs Simcoe witnessed the fishery at the mouth of the Niagara. A "great many whitefish ... are caught here from October till April." She described "sturgeon ... about six feet long ... and infinitely better than those which go to sea. Cooks who know how to dress ... them make excellent dishes from sturgeon. The 5th Regt. have caught 100 sturgeon & 600 whitefish in a day in nets."[60]

On reaching York, she canoed the harbour. The estuary of the Don River was "covered with rushes, abounding with wild ducks & swamp black birds with red wings." An eighteen-year-old naval lieutenant, Joseph Bouchette, had surveyed the harbour in 1793; the "immense coveys of wild fowel ... were so abundant as in some measure to annoy us during the night." She canoed up the Don, with its "fine butternut" and its "bald eagle ... on a blasted pine." There were "millions of the yellow & black ... swallowtails [butterflies] & heaps of their wings lying about." Of the salmon, she wrote, "The rivers & creeks on this shore abound with [them] ... swimming in shoals around the boat." These were Atlantic salmon, which came up the St Lawrence perhaps ten thousand years ago and settled into Lake Ontario as a permanent and migrating resident, spawning in all its streams but unable to scale Niagara Falls into the lakes above.[61]

Pigeons "darkened" the York skies and built their nests "where there are plenty of acorns." Mrs Simcoe noticed, however, how they left the acorns in the vicinity of the nests "till the young ones can leave their nests & then [they] scratch the acorns up for them." At Niagara too, they were "in such numbers that besides those they [the Natives] roast & eat ... they salt the wings & breasts ... in barrels."[62]

Most of the Natives Simcoe met were refugees who had spent time in transit camps like The Bottom. To make matters worse, there was deep snow in the winter of 1794 and the deer hunt failed. The local Missisauga "almost starved," she said; "a great many of their women & children come to our windows every day for bread which we cannot refuse." It was boom and bust, and the next fall she got word from Augustus Jones that, along Yonge Street, "the Indians killed over 500 deer in a month within a fence of 7 miles." Mrs Simcoe came to admire the Natives, particularly the Iroquois, she said, who "never appear to make one motion that does not effect the purpose they intend. There is always an appearance of distinction." She also trusted their medicines. When her husband "the Gov" was ill and "without proper attendence," she turned to "a root – I believe it is calamus," a tonic that "relieved his cough in a very short time."[63]

One of the Simcoes' guests was François La Rochefoucauld, who had fled the French Revolution. In 1795 Mrs Simcoe and he climbed into the Niagara Gorge. "The descent is very difficult," he wrote, "perpendicular steps, hewn out of trees, caverns, and projecting rocks. I frequently crawled along on both hands ... and thus I toiled a mile and a half to reach the foot of this stupendous cataract." He reported other highlights as well. "We assisted at a fishing ... upwards of five hundred fish were caught, among which were about twenty-eight or thirty sturgeons, small pikes, whitings, rock-fish, sun-fish, herrings, a sort of carp ... salmon, trouts." And, of course, "the neighbourhood is much infected with rattle-snakes, yet none ... were ever bitten."[64]

Travel Writers

The Canadas were fertile ground for travel writers, and their offerings, appealing as they did to an emerging moneyed class in Britain and the United States in the 1790s, were well received. One such writer was Isaac Weld, an Irish gentleman whose writings' popularity can be attributed in part to the feeling of "spreading desolation" across Europe, where war was almost a constant in the years between the French Revolution in 1789 and the Battle of Waterloo in 1815. Weld inspired many to emigrate to Upper Canada, including John Langton.[65]

In his 1799 *Travels* Weld makes the usual comments about the fish in the St Lawrence and Lake Ontario, reflecting that "if the fisheries were properly attended to, particularly the salmon fishery, the country would be even more enriched thereby than by the fur trade." He was overly optimistic to think that either the fish or the fur would last. In the Niagara Gorge, Weld crawled to the foot of the falls. "I advanced within six yards of the edge of the sheet of water, just far enough to peer into the caverns behind it; but here my breath was nearly taken away by the violent whirlwind that always rages at the bottom of the cataract."[66]

At that date the thickness of the water column as it passed the lip of the Horseshoe Falls was about twenty-five feet. It was a force of nature, a falls on the move, eroding back by about four feet each year. By comparison, the present recession rate is only a few inches each year, because so little water falls over it. In 1894 the flow was 270,000 cubic feet per second. Now, from

November to March, the current is just 50,000 cubic feet each second, and the rest goes to hydro turbines. Most of the water is put over the falls during the summer tourist season – until the evening light show is over – after which the falls are turned down again. Overall, 25 per cent of the water is assigned to the falls, and the rest is for power. The flow will decline even further after the Canadian tunnels and turbines are upgraded to use their maximum allowable flow, matching similar upgrades on the U.S. side. Tourists still visit the falls by the million, and their astonishment is still genuine even if they are only seeing a fraction of what early visitors saw.

Like others, Weld recorded the "great numbers" of "fishes, squirrels, foxes and various other animals ... carried down [the falls], and consequently killed. A dreadful stench arises from the quantity of putrid matter lying on the shore, and numberless birds of prey, attracted by it, are always seen hovering about the place." It has been estimated that, in that era, at least a hundred fish passed over the falls each second, an impartial sampling of the superabundant wildlife of the region. The modern gorge is antiseptic by comparison.[67]

Weld headed for Fort Erie, where the Seneca still grew corn, none "less than eight feet in height [and] between the rows ... gourds, squashes and melons." He joined them in a squirrel hunt with blow-guns; they "never ... miss their aim at the distance of ten or fifteen yards." Weld sailed west, until wind drove his party on to Point Abino, of which he wrote: "The mounds of sand ... are truly astonishing; those next to the lake ... are totally devoid of verdure; but others, situated behind them ... are covered with oaks of the largest size" – as they still are today. Weld went bear hunting and slept "under the shelter of one of the steep sand hills." There was "a large covey of spruce partridge" or spruce grouse, now gone from the region south of the Canadian Shield and Adirondacks. (Point Abino is privately conserved today, and still the site of the finest oak-clad sand dunes on the Erie coast, famous for its cathedral-like feel and its displays of spring wildflowers.)[68]

Tacking three days west, Weld's ship anchored off Middle Island, one of the western Lake Erie islands, "all covered with ... fine timber ... [of] oaks, hickory trees and red cedars," he wrote. "The islands are dreadfully infested with serpents and on some of them, rattlesnakes are so numerous that in the height of the summer, it is really dangerous to land: it is now late September [and] a couple of them, of a large size, were killed." On Middle Island, the brave Isaac Weld wounded a snake with "its belly a vivid orange" (a harmless northern redbelly) and confronted a "hissing snake" (an eastern hognose). "The shores swarm with gulls," as some of the shores still do.[69]

The English diarist John Maude toured through Iroquoia to Niagara Falls in 1800. He fished at the "junction of the Mud and the Conhocton Creeks. Mr. Patterson is the only person possessed of a seine-net ... At the first haul we took twenty-two Oswego bass, two suckers, and one perch; second haul, seventeen bass, two suckers, and one perch. The Oswego bass [were] on an average three lbs each." He made much of the snakes and he too was sure that hogs were the antidote. "The hog certainly prefers the rattle-snake to all others." At Niagara Falls, he noted, "bears live in the clefts of the rocks below the falls, as do also wolves; and ...rattlesnakes, which are found in great number and extraordinary size ... one having twenty-four rattles."[70]

George Heriot came to Lower Canada in 1792 as a clerk and, by 1799, was deputy postmaster general of Canada. His watercolours and descriptions of the Canadas were soothing bromides that included many details. In 1802 eighty men worked at eight trading posts on the north shore of the Gulf of St Lawrence, "for peltry with the savages, and also for the salmon, whale, seal and porpus fisheries," still in business after two centuries of harvest. His "white purposes" were belugas, which they caught with "snares" and reduced to "upwards of a barrel of oil" each. The St Lawrence beluga is now scarce and threatened, an attraction for tourists but toxic to eat.[71]

Heriot painted the waterfalls around Quebec, almost all of them dammed for power by then. The Huron at Lorette still had two hundred acres in corn and lived, he said, "in almost uninterrupted harmony and tranquillity." The Mohawk at Kahnawake were also farming, raising hogs and poultry. The St Lawrence was lined with farms, towns, convents, monasteries and mills, and overall, he wrote, the "wild animals ... [have] become extremely rare, not only from the immense numbers that have been killed, but on account of the increase of settlements and population."[72]

On Lake Ontario Heriot witnessed a "productive salmon and sturgeon fishery in ... Duffin's Creek." As well, "the river Humber ... the Tobyco, the Credit, and two other rivers ... abound in fish, particularly in salmon." Lynde Creek, just west of Whitby, teemed with salmon; they were killed "with a pitchfork from a log stretched across the creek." From Heriot's perspective, the wildlife (and especially the fish) were still plentiful, and others agreed. William Kirby of Niagara wrote about these years that "the Two, Four and Eight-Mile creeks ran in full streams of water out of the tree-shaded swamps, and in the spring ... shoals of fish, pike, muscalonge, suckers and others, almost choked the streams as they pressed up them to spawn. Later on ... the white fish came in endless shoals to the lake shores, and were caught in seines and eaten fresh, or salted and smoked for use. In short, twenty-five years [of immigration] has sufficed to turn the wilderness of woods into a rural paradise, where all things goodly grew for the use of man."[73]

For the Use of Man: The 1800s

The wildlife was in decline by 1800 but newcomers with no experience of earlier times still found it plentiful. Native commentators had a longer time frame and, by 1806, the decline of the Credit River fishery was clear to the Missisauga. The headman, Quinepenon, described how the "waters on this river are so filthy & disturbed by washing with sope & other dirt that the fish refuse coming into the river as usual for which our families are in great distress for want of food."[74]

William Cronon, the scholar of New England's early ecology, sums up the situation by 1800. "New England in 1800 was far different from the land the earliest European visitors had described. The Indians ... were reduced to a small fraction of their former numbers ... Large areas particularly of southern New England were now devoid of animals ... [and] beaver, deer, bear, turkey, wolf and others had vanished. In their place were hordes of European grazing animals which constituted a heavier burden on New England plants and soils ... [Its] forests still exceeded its cleared land in 1800 but ... the remaining forest had been markedly altered by grazing, burning and cutting. The greatest of the oaks and white pines were gone, and cedar had become scarce."[75]

Within a few years, the same occurred westward. In 1800 John Maude was near Bath, in upper New York, praising the promise of its timber trade. He walked the "E side of Mud Creek, through white pine, hemlock, oak, yellow [red] pine, &c. The white pine exceeded any that I had yet seen ... Mr. B. had measured one, when a log, two hundred and two feet." As the forest was cut, the wildlife was taken. James Fenimore Cooper, who lived in the Susquehanna headwaters after 1825, recorded its victims, starting with the passenger pigeon. "If the heavens were alive with pigeons, the whole village seemed equally in motion. Every species of fire-arms ... was [in use] ... None pretended to collect the game, which lay scattered over the fields in such profusion as to cover the very ground with the fluttering victims."[76]

North of the lakes, Tiger Dunlop was promoting land sales but it was too late by 1832 for him to pitch its superabundant wildlife. Instead he sold it on libertarian grounds. "There have arrived in the province within these three last years perhaps 15,000 English agricultural labourers; and it is no very great stretch of the imagination to suppose that every twentieth man of them when at home, was a poacher." In Canada, hunting "would be ... an honest, respectable and useful mode of making the two ends of the year meet." Bring your poaching skills to the New World. There were deer "in great abundance." Bear might take your pigs, so hunt them. "Otters are abundant," and so too fox, raccoon, and squirrel. The wolf had a bounty on its head and "will soon be extinct." There were ruffed grouse, spruce grouse, snipe, woodcock and bobwhite, and geese and swans that could be hunted when migrating through.[77]

"Two summers ago," Dunlop wrote, "a stream of [pigeons] took it into their heads to fly over York; and for three or four days the town resounded with one continued roll of firing ... Every gun, pistol, musket, blunderbuss and fire-arm ... was put [to use] ... The constables and police magistrates were on the alert, and offenders, without number, were pulled up ... till at last it was found that pigeons, flying within easy shot, were a temptation too strong for human virtue to withstand – and so the contest was given up, and a sporting jubilee proclaimed." Fishing was still good and Dunlop emphasized in particular the "pickerel, maskanonge, black and white and rock bass," and the brook trout. Salmon, sturgeon, whitefish, and herring were the real "articles of commerce," and "the monarch ... is the Mackinaw [lake] trout ... which seldom weighs less than twenty ... and in some rare instances ... ninety pounds... Every settler ... ought to bring out a seine net with him." With such sage advice was depletion fuelled.[78]

Every fall the salmon crowded into the streams feeding Lake Ontario, and they could not have been easier to catch. In Wilmot's Creek east of Toronto in the 1820s, as told by Samuel Wilmot, Canada's pioneer fish nurseryman, "they were so plentiful ... men slew them with clubs and pitchforks – women seined them with flannel petticoats." To the west, in 1831, the Irish sportsman Thomas Magrath spent six weeks with the Missisauga at the mouth of the Credit. "At night the shore was brilliant with the fishing lights in the canoes ... My brother and I speared one hundred and twenty salmon of a night; but they are now becoming less numerous in consequence of the number of saw-mills erected, the profusion of sawdust on the water, and the multitudes of oak staves annually floated down the river." The Atlantic salmon was doomed. Within twenty years, there was one sawmill for every 700 people in New York State, and one for every 600 people in Ontario (one for every 300 in York and Norfolk counties).[79]

Hunting near Adelaide, west of London, Upper Canada, Magrath confessed his "mistake in supposing that the woods afforded the best sport – quite

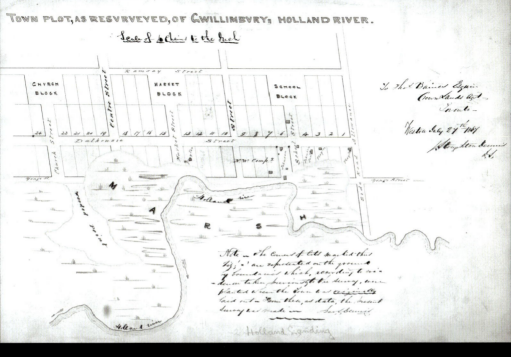

FIGURE 19

One of Upper Canada's alternate capitals, St Albans, was laid out at the direction of
Lieutenant Governor Simcoe at the terminus of Yonge Street at the Holland River, on
a native campsite and prairie. (Archives of Ontario, C295)

FIGURE 20

Gathering wild lupines in High Park, now downtown Toronto, was a family affair in 1918. The prairie was ended with herbicides but is now being revived with ground fires, shrub removal, and wildflower planting. (Photo John Boyd; Library and Archives Canada PA071052)

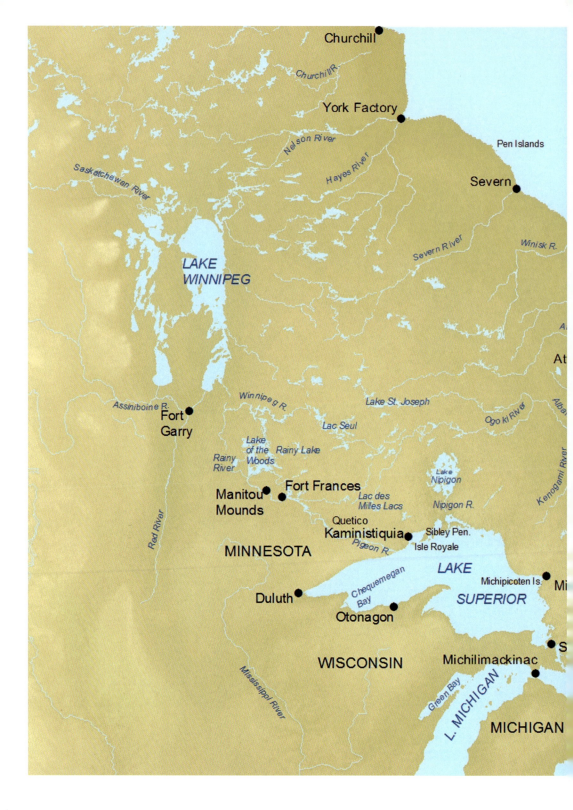

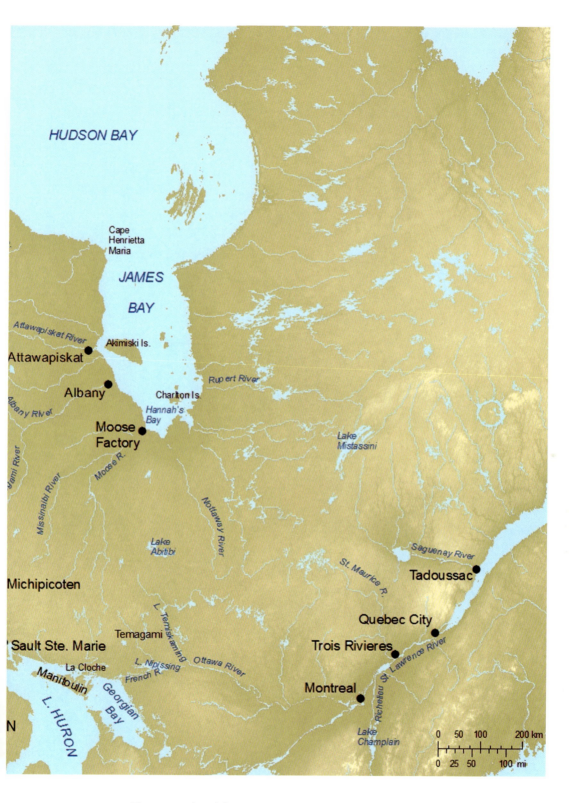

FIGURE 21 The geography of the Laurentian and Hudsonian landscapes of the old Canadas.

Parks and Protected Areas

Other Conservation Areas

Future Lake Superior Biosphere Reserve

Lake Superior Marine Conservation Area

Lake Superior Drainage Basin

ONTARIO

LAKE SUPERIOR

MICHIGAN

| 0 | 50 | 100 | 200 km |

| 0 | 25 | 50 | 100 mi |

FIGURE 22 Much of Lake Superior's shores, waters, and backcountry have been conserved, and constitute an unofficial international biosphere reserve of global significance.

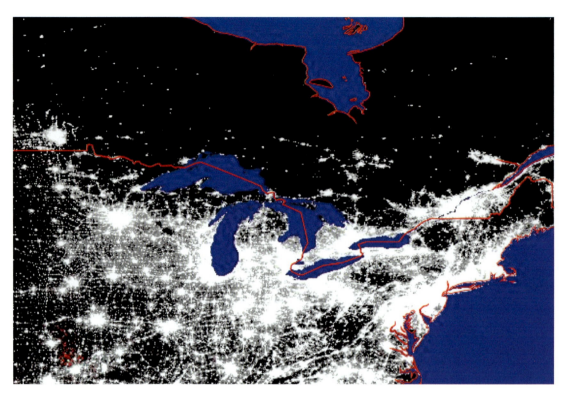

FIGURE 23

The modern night sky of Great Lakes country is an artifact of the new city-states and the incandescent waste of energy. (US NOAA National Geophysical Data Center)

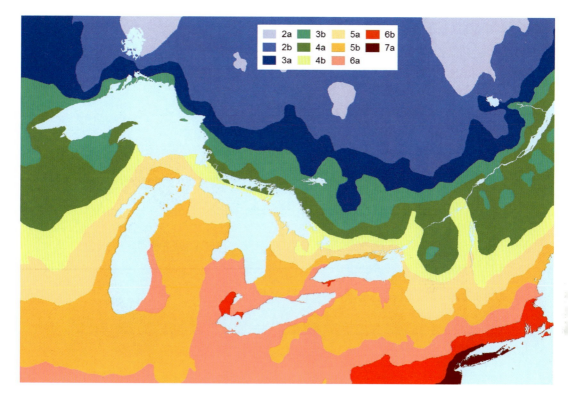

FIGURE 24

Vegetation hardiness zones illustrate the topography, corridors, and challenges facing organisms as they adjust to climate change.

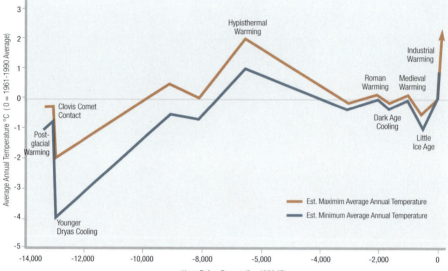

FIGURE 25

The climate of Great Lakes country has changed dramatically over the last fourteen thousand years, illustrated here as a graph of maximum and minimum annual temperature estimates.

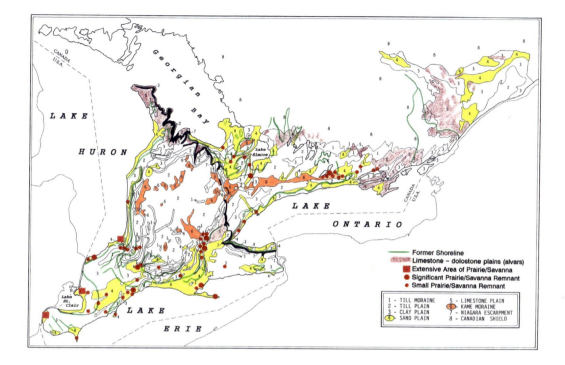

FIGURE 26

The oak woodlands, savannas, and prairies of the Ontario peninsula corresponded with
the centres of Native settlement. (After Bakowsky and Riley 1994)

FIGURES 27 a and 27 b
Wasaga Beach, on Georgian Bay, attracted up to a million bathers annually in the 1970s.
Now, piping plover are nesting on the beaches again. (Wasaga image, J.L. Riley collection;
plover image, Ann Brokelman)

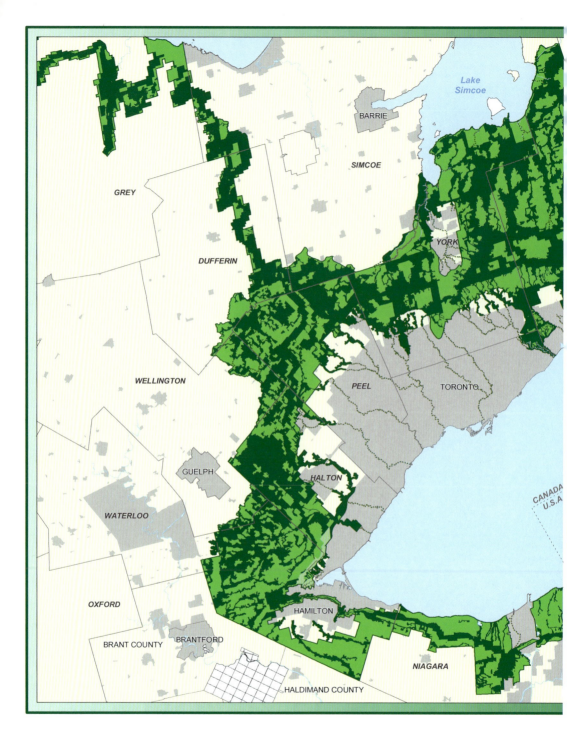

FIGURE 28

The natural systems of south-central Ontario are protected by supportive land-use regulations, as in the natural-heritage system (in dark green) for the Niagara Escarpment, Oak Ridges, and Greenbelt. (Ontario Ministry of Municipal Affairs and Housing)

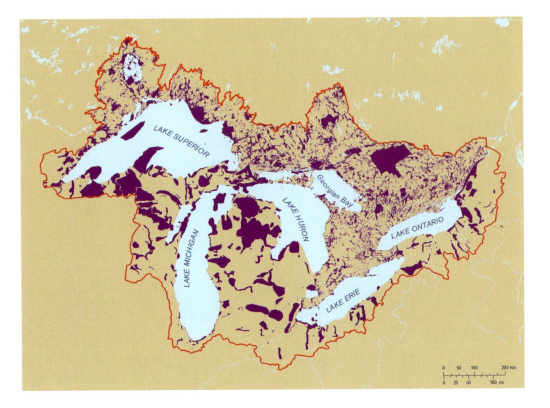

FIGURE 29

A conservation blueprint for Great Lakes country. (Nature Conservancy of Canada)

the reverse; in them you have nothing but bears, wolves, deer, turkeys, partridges; whilst the cleared land abounds with birds too numerous to mention ... woodcock, snipe, partridge, quail, very large, and the meadow lark [and] plover also." Bobwhite, he said, become more "abundant as the clearing advances." Magrath also pursued his sport elsewhere in Upper Canada. "For river shooting, the Nottawesaga, which runs into Lake Huron, is the best duck river I have ever met. Twenty pair a day ... [is] a common day's sport. Here are to be found, in great numbers, the large black ducks." In Toronto in 1831, he and his brothers shot a bear and "frequently brought home from twelve to fourteen brace [of woodcock]."[80]

Richard Rorke was an Irish Quaker who, in 1834, took up 200 acres in Tecumseth, southwest of Lake Simcoe. He was "young ... and ... there were no game laws that I had heard of yet." He was disappointed initially because, he said, "it did not appear that any large game could be found." However, he soon learned that the Innisfil Creek swamp was its local refuge. The bear went for the settlers' pigs and Rorke recounts a half-dozen bear chases in the swamp. The fur, meat, and fat were much appreciated. Wolf were in decline, "shy of man" and "never any danger." He spent all his free time hunting and, in forty-four years in Tecumseth and Collingwood townships, he saw only six wolves at large. He trapped many others, of course, especially on the expanding sheep farms. As well, he said, "we in the Beaver River Valley had our river to resort to and it proved for a length of time an almost inexhaustible magazine of ... the finest and largest trout, until the milldam at the mouth of the river put an end to trout fishing in that stream forever."[81]

John Langton advertised the Kawartha Lakes to his father in England in 1833. "Our fish are the bass, the maskinonge – a most excellent species of pike, as fat almost as an eel – and the eel itself; the sunfish ... [and] the white fish above and salmon trout below. The bass is our staple ... if you are on the lake, tie a line baited with a piece of red cloth round your wrist and proceed on your journey, and ... before you have got a quarter of a mile you will feel your prize." He went on. "We have abundance of venison, which is becoming more plentiful as the clearings increase, affording them more food ... Partridge and rabbits are pretty plentiful ... Ducks in ... tens of thousands frequent the rice beds at the mouth of Scugog. These, together with a bear, two wolves, martens, racoons, muskrats and squirrels, are my only acquaintances as yet." Wildlife remained relatively abundant on the edge of the Canadian Shield.[82]

Patrick Shirreff's farm survey in 1833 started with few comments about wildlife. No mention of deer in Canada, for example, but he did take note of the turkey and partridge on the Chatham plains; the ducks "in vast numbers" on the Detroit River; the bald eagles on the lower Thames; and the prairie chicken that "abounds" on the White Pigeon prairie in Michigan. When he arrived on the prairies of Illinois, he was finally confronted with abundance – cranes, swans, ducks, and geese; hundreds of "prairie-hen"; partridges so tame they were "killed with stones"; deer, which were "frequently seen"; and woods that "abounded with green coloured paroquets [Carolina parakeet] ... in flocks of six or seven." By comparison, he was shocked by what he had seen in the east: "I have seen more game in half-an-hour in Scotland than I saw in all my wanderings in Canada."[83]

Resident Naturalists

Charles Fothergill was an English Quaker who came to Upper Canada in 1817. An expert naturalist who had published a checklist of English birds, he settled in Port Hope, where he ran a general store and was postmaster, justice of the peace, and distiller. He moved to York to become king's printer and his newspaper, the *Weekly Register*, carried his nature column and got him into politics. He represented Durham in the legislature, started a museum, corresponded with John James Audubon, criticized the Family Compact, and died penniless in 1840.[84]

Fothergill gives us some of the first systematic records of wildlife in Upper Canada. He loved Rice Lake and its ricebeds, and he bought 1,200 acres at the mouth of the Otonobee River, "Castle Fothergill," where he did most of his shooting. He knew his birds in the hand and reported more than a hundred species at Rice Lake from 1820 and 1822, for example: the loon (a "common bird"); "wild swan" ("not very common"); wood duck ("extremely common"); ring-necked duck ("very common"); bald eagle ("not uncommon"); hawk owl ("more numerous in the fall"); red-headed woodpecker ("one of the commonest and most noisy birds"); northern shrike ("by no means uncommon"); and fourteen warblers. Upper Canada, he said, likely "produces many other birds belonging to this charming [warbler] family – so engaging and so useful." He knew the rufous-sided towhee, which "breed on the oak plains of the Rice Lake every spring."

He reported an eastern ratsnake in Prince Edward County, nine feet long and climbing a tree to feed on young birds in a nest. He noted, in the Scugog and Rice Lake areas, fisher, mink, otter, wolf ("rather too numerous"), lynx, bobcat, and moose. "Towards Lake Erie ... black squirrels are more numerous than on L. Ontario – and sometimes appear in such numbers as to seem ... almost incredible ... A member of the house of assembly assures me that in the vicinity of Fort Erie ... 1100 black squirrels were killed in one day ... Every 6 or 7 years ... the squirrels become so numerous as to cross the river Niagara in thousands."

Fothergill reported that a colleague in the legislature, from near the Burford Plain, told him of an elk that "weighed upwards of 900 lbs. when killed. Their race in Canada was destroyed only a few years ago by Indians now living who killed them all one winter in which there happened to be a deep snow crusted on the top." Elk hung on until 1840 south of Ottawa River, until the early 1850s near Collingwood, and until about 1870 in the Alleghenies and Algonquin highlands.[85]

William Pope was another resident naturalist, a lad of twenty-three when he first visited Upper Canada. He returned in 1842, settling in Norfolk County. He was an artist, "unique in his time," the artist J. Fenwick Landsdowne has said, and his watercolours and diaries are full of detail (Fig. 13). For instance, there were frosts in May and June 1834 that "destroyed all ... the beechnuts, acorns, hickory nuts, butternuts, hazelnuts and all the wild fruit of every description ... The squirrels are necessarily driven to ... robbing the fields ... The same with the wild turkey." In 1842 there was a rare abundance of different mast and the hogs took all of them, "living through the winter upon them." This made for good pork but poor oak regeneration.

In summer, Pope wrote, the passenger pigeon sought out "a particular kind of plant that ... flourishes in these parts [toothwort] ... the white crisp roots of which afford them a great part of their subsistence." By September, he said, there were pigeons "from one end of the country to the other ... Prodigious quantities are killed and yet to all appearance their number are not lessened even in the slightest degree." Pope commented on how pigeons modified regeneration. "The woods are now full of young beech trees which have sprung up this spring – some pigeons which I shot had some of those nuts in their crops." Beech regeneration in such densities, in the absence of pigeons, no longer occurs. The turkey, Pope observed, eat "the wild fruits and berries, beech mast, chestnuts, hickory and butternuts, acorns, Indian corn and grain. They also eat insects and grass ... and sometimes young frogs and other small animals." So abundant were they in their roosts, "their dung was strewed beneath the trees in considerable quantities."

Pope's comments on the wolf are refreshing. It was, he wrote in 1845, "particularly pleasant and agreeable to have a dozen of wolves in full pursuit of you at night when two or three miles from any habitation. The spirit-moving chorus of their mellifluous voices growing nearer and nearer ... is particularly fine and grand, and will not fail to pierce the soul ... Yet I could never learn that the wolves at any time ventured to make an attack on man."[86]

The Stricklands, Jameson, Kane, and Others

Upper Canada's resident writers all commented on the wildlife. Sam Strickland, for example, travelled widely for the Canada Company. In 1831 he hunted the St Clair marshes. "By three o'clock P.M. bagged eleven brace of wild ducks and blue-winged teal." On the same trip, off the Bruce peninsula, an Ojibwa "bartered with us, giving us fresh salmon-trout [lake trout] for whiskey and apples. One ... [was] no less than seventy-two pounds." That same year Strickland sold his property on the Otonobee and bought land in the bush near Lakefield, where he encountered wolf and lynx. He also reported a "wolverine" but he described a lynx, a mistake perhaps explaining other such reports of wolverine, such as in Uxbridge in 1808.[87]

By 1852, Strickland reported, the deer were "not now nearly as numerous ... [Twenty-five years ago] a trapper ... and four of his companions passed my house on a small raft on which lay the carcasses of thirty-two deer – the trophies of a fortnight's chase near Stoney Lake. I once had seventeen deer hanging up in my barn at one time." The wolf, he had learned, was "not nearly so ferocious as the European animal, nor ... quite so large." Strickland was by then familiar with the eastern wolf, which still persists today, distinct from the larger gray timber wolf of the north.[88]

Strickland's sister Catharine Parr Traill commented on the dearth of game in the newly wild, dense bush. "Almost all wild animals are more abundant in the cleared districts than in the bush." In her 1855 "cookery-book," the *Canadian Settler's Guide*, she focused on the game in settled areas, like grouse, groundhog, black squirrel, and pigeon. The fish were still varied, like perch, muskellunge, eel, salmon, whitefish, and bass, and, she assured readers, there were "no laws restricting the poor man from casting his line into the water or launching his night-canoe." Well, there were laws but there was no enforcement. A law had been passed in Upper Canada in 1807, "for the preservation of salmon," prohibiting the use of nets in the streams north of Lake Ontario. It was ignored and, in 1836, a petition to Parliament by 185 citizens would state that the "salmon fishery ... was in danger of annihilation." The law was notional only.[89]

The Irish travel writer Anna Jameson explored Upper Canada in 1837, on her own, when she was forty-two. Her goal? "My business here is to observe." Her wildlife observations were infrequent but, for example, she wrote about the marshes in Toronto Bay, "intersected by inlets and covered with reeds [and] the haunt of thousands of wild fowl, and of the terrapin [softshell or snapping turtle] ... and as evening comes ... the fishing boats gleamed along the surface of the water, for thus they spear the lake salmon, the bass and the pickereen."[90]

A farmer west of Port Talbot told Jameson that "the wolves ... during the last winter ... had carried off eight of his sheep and thirteen of his brother's." In severe winters, she reported, bears in "great number ... carry off the pigs and young cattle." She boarded a steamboat in Detroit headed north. "We passed a large and beautifully green island, formerly called Snake Island, from the immense number of rattlesnakes which infested it. These were destroyed by turning large herds of swine upon it, and it is now ... called Hog Island" (now Belle Isle). It was July, and Lake St Clair had "innumerable flocks of wild fowl ... and here and there the great black loon was seen diving."

At Sault Ste Marie, the fishery had reached industrial scales. "Vast quantities are cured," Jameson wrote, "and sent down to the eastern states. Not less than eight thousand barrels ... last year." Returning east along the North Channel, she entered the Mississagi River, where Natives had "crammed [Alexander Henry] with a porridge of sturgeons' roe. The river is still famous for sturgeon." She then attended the annual payment of treaty goods at the east end of Manitoulin, where farming was well underway and the soils were "rich and good."[91]

Jameson ended her "summer rambles" in a twenty-five-foot canoe on the east coast of Georgian Bay, a "delightful run among hundreds of islands; sometimes darting through rocky channels so narrow that I could not see the water on either side of the canoe, and then emerging ... through vast fields of white water-lilies; it was perpetual variety, perpetual beauty, perpetual delight." In 1852 the world traveller Edward Sullivan would similarly gush, "No less than 36,000 islands ... the finest freshwater archipelago in the world." (In 2004 the coast was designated a World Biosphere Reserve and, today, more of its shores and islands are protected from development than anywhere else on Lake Huron.) From there, Anna Jameson's return to Toronto was all standard fare and easy going, with Yonge Street actually "macadamised" close to Toronto by then.[92]

In 1845 the Irish-born artist Paul Kane went on a painting excursion to "Owen's Sound" and, from there, to the Saugeen River on Lake Huron, where treaty negotiations with the Ojibwa were underway. "The land hereabouts is excellent but ... the inhabitants subsist principally on fish, which are taken in great abundance." He also reported an active deer fence. Kane then canoed for two weeks along the east coast of Georgian Bay where, as he said, he "threaded a labyrinth of islands of every size and form ... enchanted with the beauty of the ever-varying scenery, as we glided along."[93]

Wildlife around the Bay of Quinte, east on Lake Ontario, were mentioned in the notes of Cannif Haight, a native Upper Canadian born to Quaker loyalists. He remembered the springtime jacklighting for pike, pickerel, and "a maskelonge or two." By the 1830s, he said, bear and wolf "had ceased to be troublesome"; there was a $4- bounty for each wolf's head. "Netting wild pigeons" was a popular sport, and some of them were caged and taken out "as we wanted them."[94]

Thomas McIlwraith, the early ornithologist, wrote about the pigeons in 1854, "the year of the cholera." At the west end of Lake Ontario, in the spring, there were flocks "every hour of every day passing to the west. The summer was unusually warm, and ... the birds seemed weak ... Vast numbers were killed, till ... a rumor got abroad that eating ... pigeons caused the cholera." He also recorded the regional demise of the whooping crane, by then "hardly known in the east," and the prairie chicken, its "days ... numbered" (gone by 1897). Bobwhite were "greatly reduced and in need of the protection [of law]" and turkey were "more hunted as they become more rare." The bluebird was "seldom seen," driven out by the house sparrow, a newcomer that arrived about 1875. He also reported the arrival of barn owls from the southwest ("in the last few years") and of loggerhead shrikes ("two individuals shot in April 1860 ... not observed prior").[95]

Charles Weld was a younger half-brother of Isaac Weld and, in the 1850s, he revisited the places that Isaac's 1796 *Travels* had taken him. He wrote about the timber rattlers at Lake Champlain, where they still hang on today. "Their favourite playground is the sunny side of Tongue Mountain, near Rattlesnake Island, where they pull the reptiles from between the rocks by their tails and, snapping them to death, carry them off in baskets as trophies ... They had killed, in one day, the incredible number of 1100."[96]

Writing at Walden Pond in Massachusetts, David Henry Thoreau was one of the first to ask, "Is it not a maimed and imperfect nature that I am conversant with?" In 1855 he checked off the particulars of William Wood's 1634 *Prospect* against what he saw around him. "The nobler animals have been exterminated here, - the cougar ... lynx, wolverine, wolf, bear, moose, deer, the beaver, the turkey, etc. – [and] I cannot but feel as if I lived in a tamed and, as it were, emasculated country." Of the birds, he wrote, "eagles are probably less common; pigeons of course … heath cocks all gone … [and] more owls then, and cormorants … [and] sea-fowl … and swans." The oaks, firs, plums, and tulip-trees were all less abundant. Even "the streams are, perchance, somewhat shrunk." For Thoreau – as it is for many of us – the nature that is immediately at hand is fascinating enough and worthy of record. But he knew he was witnessing nothing like what people two centuries earlier had seen. He wished that he had known "an entire heaven and an entire earth," but it was too late.[97]

For some time longer, in the remote uplands and in the wilds of the Canadian Shield, the animals persisted. On the path to domestication, by way of clearing and plowing, there was a delay of about fifty years from south to north. In 1864 Thomas Mason could write from Dysart Township, just south of the present Algonquin Park: "We have plenty of … bears, wolves, beavers, otters, fishers, martins, minks and muskrats and wild cats and a great many more … The deer are also numerous. A very splendid animal [is] of the elk breed, many of them weigh 200 pounds each, but the only animal the hunters fear is the wild cat. Some of them measure 6 feet in length and have claws the length of a man's finger … I am happy to say these animals are not numerous." But the cougar was still around in 1864 and would persist another fifty years.[98]

One of the last places to be settled south of the Shield in the east was the Bruce peninsula, jutting north into Lake Huron. Dry rocklands dominate its uplands. On its east side is an escarpment cliff, and the other side tips gently under Lake Huron. Like much of Manitoulin, Killarney, and Lake Superior, its stories are maritime tales of isolated ports and camps, and of wrecks like the steam-wheeler *Bruce Mines* in 1854, the *Regina* and *Jane Miller* in 1881, and others. Many early travellers, like Paul Kane, avoided it entirely by crossing its base.

This was Ojibwa land, and some of it, like the Fishing Islands, was surrendered as late as 1885. As early as 1831, however, the Fishing Islands were home to ship captain Alexander MacGregor. Historian Norman Robertson recounts how, in 1834, MacGregor made a deal with a merchant in Detroit "to catch and deliver … a quantity of fish of not less than three thousand barrels annually, the company at the same time agreeing to take as many more as [he] could secure. The price … was one dollar per barrel." When they spotted a shoal of whitefish or herring, they took them with seine nets, enough "to fill five hundred or a thousand barrels" from each haul. Soon his success was the envy of Goderich, and his fishing rights were granted to a company of cronies, including Tiger Dunlop. Fishing was still big on the Huron coast late in the 1800s, with lake trout up to seventy-five pounds and whitefish up to twenty, but it soon faded.[99]

In 1890 there were 152 boats and 15 tugs registered to fish in Georgian Bay. They had, as James Hamilton reported to the Royal Canadian Institute in 1893, "738,600 fathoms of gill nets" – a thousand miles of them. Fishing around the bay's islands was intense. "The channels between them are the chosen breeding grounds for the whitefish ... [and] for the large lake trout, sturgeon and other fish," wrote Hamilton. "Many tons of fish are unlawfully taken in bays and rivers, and on shoals, where if allowed to spawn, they would add many thousand fold to their kind." The fishermen came from everywhere and the fish were shipped everywhere, particularly south. There was no enforcement and Hamilton called it as he saw it, "wholesale destruction." Royal commissions were appointed in 1892 and 1906 to investigate the Georgian Bay fishery, "the most valuable freshwater fishing ground in the world," but nothing came of them.[100]

The Advent of Sport

When the novelist John Richardson of *Wacousta* fame returned to his native Canada in 1838, he came as a sports reporter for *The Times* of London. For game, he said, the Detroit River "is almost without equal .... Bevies of quail ... Snipe is so common in the marshes that a sportsman ... [can] bag as many couple as he can well carry home. The woodcock abounds ... and one has only to cross the water into Michigan to find the prairie hen." There was "turkey shooting, deer shooting, and duck shooting," and all the fish you could take, not "*à la* Walton" but with "net and spear." He loved the lower Thames River, where it was all marsh, "a forest of tall rushes affording shelter and nutriment ... to myriads of wild ducks of every description ... As you at length issue into the lake, the surface ... is seen darkened ... with huge flocks of these migratory birds."[101]

In 1866 the *Canadian Handbook and Tourist's Guide* was published in Montreal. It was written by a recent arrival, Henry Small, not in the spirit of discovery or to convey any practical details for emigrants, but rather for the amusement of the tourist and sportsman. There were reduced wildlife numbers everywhere by then but his guide overlooks this, like any good tourist guide.

Here is a sampler. In the Gulf of St Lawrence, "the Bird Rocks [off the Magdelenes] are tenanted by large numbers of gannets, puffins, guillemots, auks and kittiwakes … several schooners [at a time] loading up with eggs." On the St Lawrence, Lac Saint-Pierre had "good pike fishing, and enormous quantities of eels … also good duck shooting." The Thousand Islands were great "for pike, maskinongé, black bass, doré, &c. … A maskinongé which weighed 49 lbs, was nearly 8 feet in length." At Rice Lake there were "maskinongé of the largest size … one that weighed upwards of 30 lbs. … [and] thousands of wild ducks … [and] partridges, quail, and game birds … on the wild rice." West of Lake Simcoe the "passenger pigeon congregates in thousands to breed … probably the abundance of beech mast … attracting them." The Holland Marsh had "good snipe-shooting … in the peat-bogs." Fishing in Nottawasaga Bay had an "average daily take [that] exceeds 2000 fish, weighing from 1 to 40 lbs. each [which] are carried principally to the Toronto market." The Lake St Clair marshes were "the finest duck-shooting ground in the world." Long Point had "ducks of all kinds, and geese [and] wild swans." Burlington Bay "abounds in pike, bass, perch and eels," and the Credit "headwaters … swarm with speckled trout."[102]

The human mind is not good at registering the loss side of the change ledger. Ecologists call this kind of retrospective amnesia the "shifting baseline syndrome," by which a diminished resource is passed on to a new generation for whom it becomes, in turn, their original estate. In Small's case, he did not mention animals like deer or turkey - or Atlantic salmon - a testament to how soon we forget. He put an impressive spin on the situation but the wildlife clock was ticking down. In 1856 a law was adopted in Upper Canada, after it was promoted by the "sportsmen of Toronto," to prohibit the hunting of bobwhite between February and October. The first law to protect bobwhite in Ohio dates from the following year. Bobwhite continued its decline, worn down by shot and net. In 1868 Ontario passed an Act for the Better Protection of Game in Ontario but there was still no enforcement. Today, bobwhite is an endangered species. Thus we manage, with good intentions, to draw down our natural capital.[103]

Extirpation and Extinction

What happens when you remove most (and in some cases all) of the dominant fauna - the passenger pigeon, turkey, Canada goose, trumpeter swan, spruce grouse, prairie chicken, bear, elk, moose, bison, lynx, cougar, raptors, snakes, whitefish, Atlantic salmon, lake trout, and ciscoes - from the richest temperate freshwater landscape in the world over less than two centuries? And then simultaneously reduce to life-support levels the numbers of most other native vertebrates? What happens when you remove so many species, in such numbers? The result is what we have around us today.

Most of these species interacted within the orbit of a woodland-grassland ecology that was maintained at high levels of productivity by clearing, firing, grazing, and wildlife interactions. In their absence, the land drifted into different kinds of habitat, mostly closed-canopy forest. The landscape then suffered the trauma of one of the most thorough agricultural conversions in world history, most of it still in non-native habitats as a result. The Native polyculture was mechanized into a non-Native monoculture. Paul Catling, at the University of Ottawa, comments. "Large and abundant vertebrates that are now extinct or threatened have contributed to extensive environmental heterogeneity" in the past, and "this heterogeneity increased biodiversity. Loss of these vertebrates has major impacts on the species left behind."[104]

The billions of passenger pigeons themselves constituted as many as half the total number of birds now summering in the contiguous United States, and as many as still fly south out of Canada each fall. People thought they would never end. Towns like Hartford, Michigan, could ship by rail "three boxcars of birds daily for forty days," from just one place. At their peak, pigeons occupied, *each year*, as much as 8 per cent of the landscape with their roosts and feeding areas, and consumed the acorns of hundreds of thousands of oak *each day*. Where they landed, their sheer weight broke trees and opened up the canopy. The ground under their roosts could be covered with as much as a foot of feces, leaving a distinct signature of death and rebirth. Alexander Wilson reported in 1814 thousands of acres devoid of any live vegetation, with all the trees either standing dead or fallen. At the same time, the fecal rain enhanced nutrient availability, and pigeons daily dropped vast quantities of seeds at those prepared sites.[105]

"Fruit eaters have long been known to defecate seeds with improved germination and growth as compared with those that have not passed through a digestive system," Catling reminds us. The seed dispersed by pigeons, and their opening of forest canopies, spread mast and berries into every available niche and, as a result, mast and fruit species were more abundant than today. Herbivores like the squirrels cached seed – so widely and forgetfully that they too helped regenerate them. High numbers of herbivores could, as a result, perpetuate their own preferred habitats. Pigeons located their nests where there was abundant mast exposed at the time of spring snowmelt. They selected for particular species. For example, white oak was highly abundant in pre-settlement forests and this may have been because the acorns of white oaks germinate in the fall and were thus not available to pigeons in the spring, an advantage they had over the red and black oaks. As well, the broken branches and tipped trees in the roosts contributed dry fuel that extended any ground fires, which in turn encouraged the oaks with thicker barks, like white, bur, and black oak, and knocked back the red oak.[106]

These circles of relationship added heterogeneity and diversity to the landscape, which in turn encouraged particular species. Pokeweed, also called pigeonberry, could become abundant, and ginseng was another predictable responder. In retrospect, the record is too sketchy to understand the implications of the loss of even a single species like the passenger pigeon, let alone the composite impacts of losing all the major herbivores at the same time.[107]

Consider the elk. In 1632 Champlain mapped the preferred elk haunts on the limestone plains of eastern Ontario and, in 1654, Le Moine saw large herds of elk on similar plains east of Lake Ontario. Galinée saw herds of fifty and sixty elk on the Norfolk sand plain in the winter of 1669, and in 1670 Dablon reported them in herds of "four and five hundred" along the Fox River. Grazing by elk undoubtedly helped define the original prairies and limestone plains, as cattle define their pasture, but, again, this was just one of many species. Take the caribou, grazing in such numbers that Nicholas Perrot and friends could snare twenty-four hundred on the open plains of Manitoulin in 1670. Or the bear, which is an omnivore and can eat as many as two hundred thousand berries in a day and disperse that seed anywhere within a day's walk. For large fruits like the pawpaw, the black bear (and Natives) may have been the only dispersal agents, but their ranges no longer coincide and pawpaw is likely on its way out unless it is deliberately propagated and dispersed.[108]

The changes that occurred here as a result of the species extinctions caused by radical climate cooling twelve thousand years ago can only be vaguely imagined. The record in Great Lakes country after 1600 gives us a clearer – but still incomplete – picture of the massive changes arising from a comparable suite of modern extinctions and extirpations. It is unarguable that our present woodlands, prairies, and wetlands are far less diverse and robust than they were four hundred years ago, just through the removal of key vertebrates. Add to this the elimination of the many species-habitat interactions that similarly enhanced diversity, and then add our own modern simplification and homogenization of the landscape.

The result was near total loss. Steward Udall, the U.S. secretary of the interior in the 1960s, put it bluntly. "It was the intoxicating profusion of the

American continent which induced a state of mind that made waste and plunder inevitable. A temperate continent, rich in soils and minerals and forests and wildlife, enticed men to think in terms of infinity rather than facts, and produced an overriding fallacy that was nearly our undoing – the myth of superabundance."[109]

The Greatest Freshwater Fishery on Earth

In Great Lakes country, the myth of superabundance lasted longest where it was least visible, under water. The Great Lakes fishery followed the same plot as its lands: a sustainable Native harvest rapidly forced into a near-total collapse of biomass, followed by extirpations and invasives. What we have today, as a result, is a freshwater system that is totally different and fundamentally vacant in comparison with when we took it over.

Warning signs came early. In 1857 Richard Nettle, superintendent of fisheries in Lower Canada, made a plea for the protection and artificial propagation of brook trout and salmon, and Samuel Wilmot did the same in Upper Canada. Wilmot was a farmer and merchant east of Toronto who grew up on Wilmot's Creek. He began restoring the salmon himself, hatching them out at home in 1866. This grew into the Newcastle Hatchery, the first effort to restore Great Lakes stocks. By 1881, however, even Wilmot saw the end: "I cannot disguise from myself that the time is now gone by forever for the growth of salmon and speckled trout in the frontier streams of Ontario." For his efforts, Wilmot suffered vigilante attacks, uninterested judges, and cowed juries.[110]

The Great Lakes is also arguably the best-studied fishery in the world. Originally dominated by eel, trouts, ciscoes, and sculpins, it had 159 native species in countless numbers. The first attempt to measure the fishery put its harvest at 28.5 million pounds in 1868. The harvest grew fivefold within twenty years to 146.25 million pounds, a free-for-all to satisfy an insatiable market. From 1916 to 1940, it averaged 112 million pounds per year, and then dropped to present levels less than half of that. Eleven native fish were extinct. By the 1950s, the devastation was obvious and there was a rote palliative: "No single factor led to the decline of native fish species in the Great Lakes." However, the common thread was the abuse of the Great Lakes as a natural system. For example, there was an international Great Lakes Fishery Commission in place by 1955 and no one can remember a time when scientists were not calling for laws to prohibit ocean-going cargo ships from dumping their ballast waters into the Great Lakes. However, it was only in 2006 in Canada, and 2008 in the United States, that this finally happened. Now the ships clean out their ballast tanks in the open Atlantic. Too little, too late. By this and other means, more than 185 new, non-native aquatic organisms have been introduced, many of them both successful and highly virulent.[111]

Lake Ontario once had eighty-one species of native fish. Ten have been extirpated and others eliminated as species abundant enough to be harvested for commercial sale. Atlantic salmon reached Lake Ontario up the St Lawrence, and eel migrated upstream to Lake Ontario as well – and still make the attempt. However, new species took advantage of the ship canals built up the St Lawrence and from the Hudson to Lake Erie. The re-plumbing was for commerce, with no thought for ecological consequences. The parasitic sea lamprey got into Lake Ontario through the St Lawrence canals in the 1830s, and above Niagara Falls through the Welland Canal in 1921. Fortunately, a unique lampricide was discovered to control them. The Atlantic rainbow smelt got into Lake Erie in the 1920s, and the non-native alewife got into Lake Ontario in 1873 and Erie in 1931. The Welland Canal was also the route into Lake Erie for white perch, after it got into Lake Ontario through the Erie Canal in 1952. The native Atlantic salmon was one of the few species that did not use the Welland Canal, nor was it helped on its way by fishermen or agencies – odd, given the persistent stocking of other non-native salmon since the 1870s.[112]

The Atlantic salmon was a dominant fish in Lake Ontario and the St Lawrence. Settlement, logging, and dams warmed and blocked the streams, and mills dumped their waste bran and sawdust into them. By 1898, the salmon was finished in Lake Ontario. By the 1960s, the lake trout was commercially extinct, and the lake sturgeon collapsed after 1880, down to a catch of about five thousand pounds a year by 1960. A sturgeon can live more than one hundred and fifty years and a female takes at least twenty years to mature. Even then she spawns only once every four or five years. It was listed as threatened by New York State in 1983, and it was big news in 1995 when a seven-foot sturgeon was caught in eastern Lake Ontario. Then, in 2004, one was caught off the Niagara River. River divers have now found numerous sturgeon in the deep waters of the lower Niagara and, as a result, the U.S. Fish and Wildlife Service is actively stocking sturgeon in lake estuaries. Ontario finally put a fishing ban in place in 2008 but no restoration has started yet. Habits die hard.[113]

The eel fishery, Hennepin wrote, was "the most considerable fishery" on Lake Ontario and the St Lawrence. Eel made up half of those areas' inshore fish biomass, says John Casselman at Queen's University. For the past half-billion years, young glass eels and elvers in the Atlantic have sought out freshwater in which to mature, leaving their breeding grounds in the Sargasso Sea to do so. Casselman has calculated that 30 to 50 per cent of the overall fecundity of the entire Atlantic species rested on the Lake Ontario–St Lawrence eels. Their four-thousand-mile journey was one of the longest migrations in nature but, in the last fifty years, eel numbers have dropped more than 90 per cent, their passage blocked by hydroelectric dams on the St Lawrence. Eel ladders were installed and, at first, a million eels a year climbed them. The numbers are now less than fifteen thousand a year, because the grown eels that try to return to the Sargasso Sea are minced in the hydro turbines. Population recruitment in Lake Ontario is now less than 1 per cent of what it was in the 1960s. The power companies are experimenting with ways to help eels get by the dams, both up and down, and are stocking them in Lake Champlain and the Thousand Islands. Casselman warns, "The eels are sending us a message and I hope we're listening."[114]

In Lake Ontario itself it was profligate fishing, along with rising water temperatures, bottom sedimentation, and pollution, that ended its fishery. Overharvesting continued even while stocks were collapsing. For example, there was no commercial fishery in the United States for whitefish after 1975 but Canadian fishermen were still taking 225,000 pounds in 2001. In the same year, Canadians were taking 25,000 pounds of eel and had an "allowable" quota seven times that much. This was wishful thinking – there has been no significant eel fishery on the U.S. side of Lake Ontario since 1983. Only in 2004 was the eel fishery finally banned in Lake Ontario.[115]

Pacific Ocean chinook salmon were imported to Lake Ontario in 1878. This was followed, over the years, by ten more alien salmonids, including rainbow trout, brown trout, and five Pacific salmon. Most were introduced before 1960 and some of them have been supported ever since. Attempts were even made to introduce them into Hudson Bay.[116]

Lake Erie once had eighty-four native fish species. Six have been extirpated. Its harvest peaked in 1900, at 3.5 tons per square mile, seven times the productivity of Lake Ontario. From 1915 to 1971, the catch held steady even though the types of fish changed totally. Its lake trout was finished long ago and, by 1965, its whitefish and lake herring were virtually gone. The once abundant blue pike was declared extinct. The Eurasian carp was intentionally released in 1878 in Lake Erie and 3.6 million pounds were harvested twenty years later. It uprooted aquatic plants and ruined most marshes, and quickly got into Lake Ontario and beyond. The non-native smelt was planted in Lake

Michigan in the early 1900s and got into Lake Erie in the early 1940s. By 1952, 375,000 pounds were caught and, by 1961, the catch was 12.8 million pounds. In 2000 the Lake Erie catch was still 7.1 million pounds. Overall, the Erie fishery was transformed totally, from herring, blue pike, and whitefish to yellow perch, walleye, smelt, and carp.[117]

By the 1960s, scientists were seeing other changes. The dams in the St Lawrence controlled water levels in Lake Ontario and ended its ancient cycles of high and low water levels. Wild rice disappeared and aquatic vegetation thinned. The astonishing flushes of mayflies and other insects that fish eat were a thing of the past. The water chemistry shifted, with increases in nitrogen and phosphorus from human sources causing algal blooms that depleted the oxygen. Overall, the lakes became eutrophic, overly rich in nutrients. An oxygen-depleted "dead zone" showed up in Lake Erie. Industrial chemicals such as PCBS, DDT, mirex, dioxin, and endocrine-disruptors started causing fish declines and behavioral abnormalities, as well as compromised immune systems and gender changes. A leading scientist, Henry Regier, spoke up in 1968. "As ecologists we simply cannot take seriously the prediction that the human population in the Lake Erie basin will increase from about 10 million to 24 million in 2020." He added, "It is quite inconceivable to us that North Americans will remain so ignorant of ecological principles."[118]

The international agreements on water quality, which were intended to stop things like mercury pollution, were not enforced. The Great Lakes subsidize the industrial wealth of two great nations by receiving and flushing its wastes. By 1990, it was official: "The zero discharge goal for persistent toxic chemicals established in the 1978 Great Lakes Water Quality Agreement ... will not be achieved in the foreseeable future." Success was something for another day.[119]

The easier problems were tackled. Major efforts have reduced pollution from municipal sewage, detergents, and fertilizers. Billions were spent on a 50 per cent reduction in phosphorus by the mid-1980s. Scientists began to anticipate the lakes becoming oligotrophic, or lacking in nutrients and rich in oxygen, but what happened instead was an increase in the arrival of new invasives. As late as 1973, a U.S. researcher would state that the "invasion of new species ... has not been particularly damaging in Lake Erie." The wake-up call came in the 1980s when ship ballast from the Baltic or Black Sea brought to Lake St Clair the zebra mussel, which started a whole cascade of changes. Because they ingest suspended solids, pollution, and phytoplankton, they cleared the water column and increased light penetration. Forage invertebrates changed as a result. Zebra mussels quickly invaded all the Great Lakes and became so abundant that they soon constituted their own new substrate type. Then the quagga mussel showed up in Lake Erie in 1989, again from ballast. Also a filterer, it soon spread to all the Great Lakes. Then came the round goby, a small fish from the Black Sea, to Lake St Clair in 1990. It out-competes other native fish that are the normal forage of larger fish, and can survive in degraded waters and spawn more frequently.[120]

Biologists Adele Crowder and John Smol at Queen's University have summarized the changes. "The most important stresses are not cyclic. Instead, they are events that exceed the tolerance of the ecosystem, such as extreme high and low water levels, heavy sedimentation caused by development, the introduction of a new contaminant, or the invasion of a rapidly proliferating, exotic species. [The basin has] experienced almost continuous change and will continue to." There is no status quo. The problems feed on themselves. For example, type-E botulism is a native bacteria that lives on lake bottoms and is normally quite subdued. It is now being filtered and concentrated by zebra and quagga mussels that are then consumed by round gobies. These are eaten by loons and other fish-eating birds, which die as a result. Non-natives can thus cause change far beyond the simple displacement of native species – they cause fish and waterfowl disease, excess algal growth, and even the decline of the native, shrimp-like amphipods at the bottom of the food chain. Meanwhile, there are also measurable increases in the concentrations of industrial chemicals like flame retardants, pharmaceutical hormones, and plasticizers, all unanticipated. What does the shortage of food and forage mean for fish? Why are phosphorus levels increasing again, even though inputs are under control? Is it inevitable that western Lake Erie will have blankets of toxic blue-green algae as it had in 2009? What about recent invasives like viral hemorrhagic septicemia (vHS), a global fish killer?[121]

A pattern emerges. We do not direct or manage change, but instead react to change that is now so rapid that researchers can't keep up with it. In the absence of any shared goal, perhaps we might default to a matter of principle – to restore the native diversity of the Great Lakes, to the degree it is possible. The Great Lakes contains a fifth of the world's surface fresh water and we treat it like a carnival fish pond. There is a growing interest in the native species in the lakes, particularly Lake Superior, which is still more or less intact. Lake Superior is the only Great Lake with strong natural reproduction by lake trout and it still contains seven fish that have been extirpated from the other lakes;

these could be the focus of future restoration efforts. For some, it is too late. Three of the Great Lakes' ciscoes are extinct but, for others, restoration remains possible. More of this later.[122]

The water levels in the Great Lakes are manipulated to serve the twin gods of power generation and shipping. Shores are armoured everywhere; two-thirds of those on the Niagara, Detroit, and St Clair rivers are artificially hardened. Dams regulate the water levels in Lake Ontario and Lake Superior. Lake Ontario has seen its cycles of water levels tamed, so that waters no longer flood its backshores and enrich its wetlands. Lakeshore marshes that were rich and diverse only forty years ago are almost devoid of aquatic plants. Water levels in Lake Michigan and Lake Huron are exploring new lows and some residents are convinced that the ship channel carved through the natural sills at the exit of Lake Huron, which Hennepin first described in 1679, is the problem.[123]

Everyone in Great Lakes country has witnessed their own local changes. For example, the last forty years have seen four major surveys of fish in the lower Rouge River estuary on Lake Ontario, and its fish changed radically every time, with new ones appearing, like Pacific salmon, and natives dropping out, like the eel. Scaled up to the basin as a whole, this story of early native abundance and use, destroyed by libertarian overharvest and mismanagement, and soured by extinctions and invasives, is unequalled. Yet we rarely acknowledge it, seldom teach it, and never mourn it. If this is what happened to the fish and wildlife of the region, what happened to the habitats they relied on, the native forests and the other ecosystems of the region?[124]

CHAPTER SIX

Clearing the Wood: 1500–1900

Mono was a wall of wood when Sam Benson surveyed it in 1820. He tallied the dominant trees on each 100 acres. In the east half of Mono he listed 910 trees – sugar maple, 28 per cent; beech, 28 per cent; and hemlock, 24 per cent – the trees of a closed-canopy forest. There were a few cedar, basswood, and elm, and a handful of pine, birch, and tamarack. There were no oak, hickory, walnut, or butternut, trees that like the open and are intolerant of deep shade. Mono woodlots are the same today, although hemlock is rarer, stripped long ago for its bark. By 1843, there were a few scattered clearings. Forty years later, more than 80 per cent of Mono's forests were gone. By 1910, it was all over, its sandy highlands grazed down and blowing. Tree planting – to heal the land – started in Mono in 1915 (Fig. 14).[1]

When I was with Ontario Nature, the Ivey Foundation funded us to survey what remained of the woodlands of southern Ontario. Biologist Liz Snell had already calculated the historic losses of wetlands – 70 per cent cleared and drained. The U.S. Great Lakes states had lost the same 70 per cent of their wetlands. That single statistic had galvanized conservation in Ontario, justifying a provincial policy of no-development in wetlands that is still in place and working well.[2]

Had we been just as thorough clearing our upland forests? After the great wilding, 90 per cent of southern Ontario was wooded. Some of it was lowland swamp and we knew that 70 per cent of that had been cleared. The surprise was that the losses on the uplands were even greater. By 1910, Snell calculated, 94 per cent of all upland woodlands had been cleared and converted to farming. Only 6 per cent remained with original forest soils intact – the trees had been cut but the soils not plowed. The same assault rolled across southern Quebec, northern New York, Ohio and Pennsylvania, and southern Michigan. The leftovers became our farm bushes, downsized, down-aged, species-poor, and see-through, after a century of cutting every decade or so (Fig. 15).[3]

On the upside, since that low point about 1910, Ontarians have replanted or allowed trees to restore themselves on 13 per cent of the land, including 9 per cent of its uplands. This was done largely on privately owned farmlands. In Mono tree cover more than tripled in the last century, typical of many locales across the south half of Great Lakes country. What emerged in that time was a new consensus that this was the right thing to do, made possible because hydrocarbons and hydroelectricity provided cheap, clean alternatives to fuel-wood and coal. Farmers focused their crops on the best soils, built fences to protect the woods and waters, got inexpensive trees from public nurseries, and took pride in the result.

Even so, the net loss of woodlands since settlement was more than 80 per cent in the Great Lakes lowlands. The bulk of what we replanted was put into row-on-row monoculture, mostly of conifers, that mirrored our farming. Nature has forgiven some of this, and a few of the plantations are infilling with native species from neighbouring woods. It is the original woodlands – the 6 per cent unplowed – that support most of what is left of the region's forest diversity. We sometimes even tell ourselves that those "6 per cent woods" are some true facsimile of what was once here.

Well, not quite. As part of the same survey, ecologist Brendon Larson took up the search for the best and oldest of the "6 per cent woods." We reviewed all the available surveys and polled the naturalist community for leads. Then he went looking. Now it is important to recall that the trees in Great Lakes country are long-lived. For example, hemlock, white pine, sugar maple, and beech can live more than 450 years; red pine and white cedar 400 plus; white oak 550 years or more; and red oak 300 plus. Given all this, it was shocking to learn that a federal forest inventory had calculated the average age of a forest stand in southern Ontario between 47 and 53 years, less than for anywhere else in the Great Lakes or boreal forests – and a fraction of the age of a mature tree.[4]

The search was intense but, in the end, it did not find a single acre of upland forest in southern Ontario that had remained intact through the clearances. There are such stands on the southern Shield and in the Alleghenies and Adirondacks but, in the southern lowlands of Great Lakes country, not an acre of old-growth forest. The oldest ones we ended up calling "older-growth," forests that might look something like their forebears if we could leave them alone for a century and could protect them from forest pathogens for a century, neither of which is likely.

Fortunately, the best of the recovering, older-growth woodlands still meet many of the needs of their dependent wildlife. Forest-interior specialists like the ovenbird and veery hang on, but are declining – by as much as 50 per cent in the last twenty-five years. Also fortunately, there is now a growing acreage of public and private woodlands on the landscape that will not be cut in the next century. We are finally putting some of our lands on life support, a radical change for a society that, not too long ago, saw them serving only "for the use of man."[5]

Under Native Management

What did the earliest visitors say about the forests? Again, the standard refrain was abundance. In 1535 Cartier called the country around Stadacona on the St Lawrence as fine "as it is possible to see, being very fertile and covered with magnificent trees of the same varieties as in France, such as oaks, elms, ash, walnut, plum, yew, cedars, vines, hawthorns bearing a fruit as large as a damson." The pines were remarkable, and upriver near Hochelaga the woods were "full of oaks," "the most magnificent trees in the world." There were "so many vines loaded with grapes that it seemed they could only have been planted by husbandmen." Of course, Cartier visited those same "husbandmen" – the Hochelagans – who, he acknowledged, "cleared the land."[6]

In 1603 Champlain described "the whole region" downstream of Quebec as "covered with conifers [*sapin, cyprez*] and birch, a most unpleasant land." By contrast, the "grapes, pears, hazelnuts, cherries [and] currants" started near the narrows at Quebec. Upriver he called the lands around Lac Saint-Pierre "the most pleasant we had yet seen; the woods are very open, so that a man may easily go through them." There were *noyers* of two kinds, likely butternut and bitternut hickory, and islands rich in "grapes, walnuts, hazelnuts, and a ... fruit like chestnuts, cherries, oaks, aspen, poplars, hops, ash, maple, beech" but "very few" conifers. Champlain coasted the New England shore the next two years and described the same shift from closed northern forests to open southern woodlands. Near Saco Bay, there were "fine oaks and nut-trees, with cleared land and abundance of ... fine grapes" and, inland, woods that were "very open [and] abound in oaks, beeches, ashes and elms." There was also the *sassafras.*[7]

In 1609 Champlain was back on the St Lawrence. The islands in the Richelieu River were "covered with oaks and butternuts" and he reported chestnut on the shores of Lake Champlain. On Mount Royal, he described an old Native field and the young woods around it full of plum, butternut, cherry, and vines. Champlain understood the link between broadleaf trees and fertile soils, but he also took note of the sandy soils that were easy to farm and grew valuable pineries. On his trip up the Ottawa River in 1613, he mapped its islands, rapids, and portages (on one of which he lost his astrolabe), and took note of its "great forests," in particular its pines and cedars and, on its islands and shore, its butternut, grapes, and "fine open woods." Around Lac des Chats, "the lands ... are sandy and covered with pines ... [and] burned down by the Indians." At the time of forest clearing two hundred years later, the Ottawa valley was one of the world's great pineries. Some are left today, such as Gillies Grove in Arnprior, where Ontario's tallest white pine grow and date back to at least 1800, no doubt germinated on the heels of an early fire.[8]

In Huronia in 1615, Champlain described an open country with an "abundance of *vignes* [grapes] and *prunes* [plums], which are very good, raspberries, strawberries, small wild *pommes* [hawthorn or crabapple], *noix* [walnut] and ... *figues* [mayapple]." Common trees were the oaks, elms, and beech. Champlain canoed down the Kawarthas and Trent River through former Huron territory. Here again, he offered up his standard code phrase for good land – "vignes & noyers," and noted, "One would think the trees had been planted for ornament [*par plaisir*]." At the east end of Lake Ontario, he said, there were "*prairies* with an endless quantity of game, and many vines and fine woods, and a great number of *chastaigners* [chestnuts]."[9]

In 1623 Sagard reported the same open countryside in Huronia, and he made a useful survey of its plants, listing the oaks, beech, maple, cherry, basswood, cedar, spruce, and even the pitcher plant and tiger lily. The Huron boiled oak acorns to eat them: "quite good," he said. In 1640 the Jesuit Jérôme Lalemant said of the Neutral country that it was "fields and woods" and its fields all "corn, beans and squashes in equal plenty." He saw "chestnuts, of which they have plenty, and wild apples, a little larger than [in Huronia]." It too was open countryside.[10]

Later, in 1665, the Intendant Jean Talon would again describe the northern forests downstream of Quebec City as "overloaded with trees which make of it one forest which ... chokes beautiful and rich production." However, at Baie-Saint-Paul in the 1690s, Le Roy de la Potherie would brag about the pine, describing them as "the finest masts in Canada ... [and] inexhaustible." The cold climate made them "close-grained and gives them a stronger tension [and] better quality." The red pine were more than thirty inches in diameter, he said, and there was "a saw-mill there where they sometimes make twenty thousand planks a year." Of these same forests Lahontan would say in the 1680s, "The whole country [is] a continued forest of lofty trees ... The price of wood is almost nothing in comparison with the charge of its carriage." This was the Laurentian forest, the total forest. Like Champlain, Talon noted the shift to open woodlands upstream, to the south and west.[11]

When Galinée wintered on the north shore of Lake Erie in 1669, he echoed Champlain's earlier code of plenty, referring to "an abundance of fruiting trees, and grapes so plentiful that one could live on them." His party gathered "walnuts and chestnuts, which were there in great quantity. We had ... in our granary 23 or 24 *minots* [bushels] of these fruits, besides apples, plums and grapes." They made red wine that winter and, overall, the country was "open, interspersed with beautiful meadows." Thirty years later, Hennepin would use similar language to describe the land between lakes Erie and Huron: scattered "groves and forests ... made up of walnut-trees, chestnut-trees, plum-trees and pear-trees, loaded with their own fruit and vines."[12]

Lamothe Cadillac described the Detroit area around 1700. "The woods are mixed ... white oak, red, walnut, elm, white wood [basswood], mulberry, cottonwood, chestnuts, ash." They were "as straight as arrows ... and almost without branches except near the top, and of enormous size and height." "One tree ... is unknown to me ... its leaves are a vivid green ... it flowers in the spring, and ... the flowers are white [magnolia or tulip-tree] ... Another tree ... is well defended, the prickles ... pierce the wood like a nail; it bears a fruit like kidney-beans [honey locust]. There are also citron-trees ... the same in form and color as the citrons of Portugal, but ... sweeter and smaller [pawpaw]." Westward, the wood thinned. Coasting the west shore of Lake Huron, the Jesuit Henri Nouvel reported "poor lands ... without any fine timber ... nothing but small firs and other wretched trees." And at Green Bay, there were only groves dotting the prairies, "nothing but elms, oaks and similar trees ... [and] vines, plum-trees and apple-trees."[13]

There were notable shifts from open woodlands to closed forests remarked on throughout the region. For example, the Carrying Place portage between Lake Ontario and Lake Simcoe was a route La Salle took at least four times in the 1680s. It was a good climb, which La Salle exaggerated for his home audience as "over the crest of very high mountains," known locally and more modestly as the Oak Ridges. Captain Pierre Pouchot described them in the 1750s: "We more frequently find pine and cedar on account of its vicinity to mountains [which] are covered with fine timber." Already the pine was moving in. By 1764, when Alexander Henry travelled it, he wrote, "The whole country was a thick forest." Today, the Carrying Place crosses the largest broadleaf forest on the moraine, at Happy Valley, no longer an open woodland. Wilding, in the absence of Native care, was largely a shift to dense, closed forest, with the decline in diversity that went with it.[14]

New Engand, Iroquoia, and the Wilding Forest

Much of northern New England before settlement was forested in spruce, beech, balsam fir, cedar, yellow birch, sugar maple, and hemlock. Most newcomers headed south for the warmer, open countryside, so open in the 1630s that, as noted by Roger Williams, fuel-wood was an issue; and so, when Natives were asked why the English had come, they said that it must have been "to remove to a fresh place for the wood's sake." William Wood also wrote of a landscape still open fourteen years after smallpox put an end to Native land clearing. "Whereas it is generally conceived that the woods grow so thick that there is no more clear ground than is hewed out by labor of man, it is nothing so, in many places diverse acres being clear so that one may ride ahunting in most places ... There is no underwood, saving the swamps and low grounds that are wet."[15]

Open woodland also prevailed in Iroquoia. Harmen van den Bogaert arrived at Fort Orange in 1630 as an eighteen-year-old barber-surgeon, and he reported on a trip west in the winter of 1634. Mohawk country was "sparsely wooded" and, farther west, the Oneida woods were "mostly oak" and "full of birch wood and flatlands cleared for sowing." This was an open countryside mixed with woodlands of pine, oak, and walnut, and with a young re-growth of birch pole-wood.[16] Van der Donck wrote of Mohawk country in the 1640s that "they who cultivate the land ... clear off the land ... by cutting down the trees and collecting the wood into great heaps and burning the same." There was wood in "abundance": chestnut (used for nuts and bark); sycamore ("handsomer than the linden"); tulip-tree (for canoes and flooring); and ashes, maples, basswood, birch, poplar, "sapine" (hemlock), willow, sassafras, persimmon, wild cherry, and crab apple. "The mulberries are better and sweeter than ours," he wrote, and there were "several kinds of plums, wild or small cherries, juniper, small kinds of apples, many hazelnuts, black currants, gooseberries, blue India figs [*Opuntia*], and strawberries ... blueberries, raspberries, black-caps ... artichokes, ground-acorns, ground beans, wild onions and ... other ... roots and fruits known to the Indians, who use the same." This was a rich southern buffet.[17]

When Lahontan visited the Seneca homeland, he too noted the rich woodlands, "replenish'd with oak, wall-nut and wild chestnut." The whole country around Lake Erie, he said, was "deck'd with oak-trees, elms, chestnut-trees, walnut-trees, apple-trees, plum-trees and vines." Claude Dablon spoke of the Onondaga country as "almost entirely of chestnut and walnut" and other nut trees, with "apples" (likely pawpaw) and the "universal plant" (sassafras). Pierre Boucher summarized Iroquoia, in general, as having "hardly any" conifers but, rather, "only fine forests of oak, chestnut, walnut, beech, lime, mulberry," and "abundant" fruit trees.[18]

Sixty years later, in 1743, the botanist John Bartram rode and canoed up the Susquehanna, and then down to Onondaga country, noting the major trees and the collectibles like ginseng and maidenhair fern. On the high ground, the forest trees were "so close to one another ... it seems almost as if the sun had never shone on the ground." These were closed, old-growth forests. Bartram's party got their horses through it and descended to the Onondaga capital, where Bartram saw "oaks, hickery, white walnuts, plums and some apple trees," and also "good land producing sugar maples, many of which [were] tapped to make sugar." The rise to the east of town was "good limestone land, producing sugar maple, elms, beech and some white pine." The slopes to the west were treed with "linden, elm, sugar maple, white walnut, oak, hickory and chestnut, besides ginseng." Many of these trees need open ground to establish and they were likely only one generation removed from the more open conditions of a century before.[19]

The botanist Pehr Kalm reported in 1749 that the woods near Albany and the mouth of the Mohawk were mostly cleared and settled. However, near Saratoga Springs the farms thinned and Kalm saw sassafras, chestnut, and mulberry, as well as "hemp ... in abundance near old [Native] plantations." He saw "the American elder and the wild grapevines only in places where the ground had been somewhat cultivated ... and [where] lime trees [basswood] and white walnut trees were most numerous." It was still open but it was wilding. Between the Hudson River and Lake George he saw "woods [of] red and white pine ... white and red oak grew abundantly among the pines but were small." This was young forest, closing in on formerly open land. "I did not see a single sugar maple," said Kalm, a remarkable statement given the frequency of the tree today. Sugar maple is only slowly adventive on open ground, but then it dominates.

On horseback between Lake Champlain and Montreal, Kalm described low wet forests and marshes along with "high mountains, rising remarkably above the rest." These were the Monteregian hills, which crest above the clay plain and include Mount Royal itself. The lowland, he said, was "very fine and rich, and when the woods are cleared and the ground cultivated, it will probably prove very fertile." (It has since become the leading farm region in Quebec.) Kalm reported a brisk trade in ginseng, with farmers complaining that Natives were gathering ginseng instead of helping them with their harvest. He travelled with the physician and naturalist Jean-François Gaulthier, and they made detailed notes of what they saw, including the salt-tolerant plants along the St Lawrence tide-line, which he knew from Europe, and the bearberry, which "the Indians, French, English and Dutch ... call ... *sagackhomi*, and mix the leaves with tobacco" for smoking.[20]

In 1769 the estate appraiser Richard Smith passed through Albany and along the Mohawk. He travelled by wagon through William Johnson's estates, and it was the "rich bottoms" that attracted his eye; above them were "pine barrens both stony and hilly." The valley bottoms south near Otsego Lake had "a deep black mould all the way" and, finally on his own land at Otsego, Smith called it "one of the finest bottoms in the world ... of birch, sugar maple, wild cherry, black thorn, butternut, elm white and red, iron wood." He was describing an early-succession mosaic of trees, "easily cleared." The ground above it, by contrast, was "chiefly tall beech, sugar maple and hemlock; not an oak or hickory was seen" – the ancient, highland walls of wood (Fig. 16).[21]

In late May, Smith followed an "Indian path" into the former Susquehannock lowlands. There were already settlers in the "rich pasture land cleared long since by the Indians, the remains of their corn hills yet to be seen." Other settlers were in the "orchards ... planted by the Indians" even though their graves were still visible. Much of the land was open, or had been "destroyed by fire," as Smith termed it, but there was fine timber nearby, the same trees with the addition of chestnut, sycamore, and shellbark hickory. One oddity was a birch "26 feet in circumference." These were diverse forests growing on formerly open Native lands.[22]

In 1782 the missionary David Zeisberger trekked along the Clinton River in southeast Michigan. "We found many traces that a long time ago an Indian town must have stood on this place, for we saw many holes in the ground

... [for] keeping their corn ... [and] little hills where corn had been planted, but where now is a dense wood of trees two to six feet in diameter." French travellers in northern New York could still make out "the remains of orchards, and even of ancient clearings." Frederick Pursh, the Russian botanist, would notice in 1807 the white pines, aspens, and magnolias overtaking the abandoned Cayuga clearings at Ithaca, and the surrounding "oak timber mixed with pine." The clues were in the trees. Thomas McKenney, head of the Bureau of Indian Affairs, could still make out the Oneida "castle" in 1826, by then "a grove of butternut trees, large and very beautiful." The signs of Native care were growing faint but they were still there.[23]

The New Wild North of the Lakes – and New Markets

After its conquest of New France, England's navy pressed its interest in Canada's timber. The Royal Navy was nicknamed "England's wooden walls" and deservedly so, given the immense volumes of wood it consumed. In 1775 the navy had 270 ships-of-the-line and the British government ordered governors James Murray and Guy Carleton to secure all the oak and pine in Canada for ship hulls and masts. The French had tried this as early as 1683 but there were too many trees to enforce it. The new orders were also resisted by Lieutenant Governor Simcoe in Upper Canada, because settlers had to cut down the trees or leave the land uncleared and "forfeit their grant." Orders were amended to set aside surveyed tracts of oak and pine, and thus guarantee a supply for the defence of empire.[24]

The oak and pine in Great Lakes country were without equal. Even so, they were cleared within seventy-five years, barely outlasting the wooden ship itself. The average ship-of-the-line required three to four thousand oak trees, immense timbers of specific shapes that were carved to fit. As warships grew, by necessity, so did their masts, until the standard for a pine mainmast was forty inches through at the base and a hundred and twenty feet tall, and perfectly straight. Tree size began to mean something, and was soon recorded.

The historian Arthur Lower listed some of the mast trees. "In 1808 Hugh Gray stated that white pine masts had been brought down to Quebec 120 feet long and four feet in diameter ... In 1846 Bonnycastle described ... red pine that he had seen and measured near Barrie, Ontario ... 200 feet high and girthed 26 ... In 1862 a white-pine plank was exhibited by the Canadian government at the London Exhibition ... 50 inches wide by six inches thick."

England had no such trees and it faced a decade of Napoleonic blockades that kept it from the forests of the Baltic. In 1803 England imported 10,000 loads of square timber from Canada (each load was fifty cubic feet) and 287,000 loads from Europe. By 1811, England was getting more timber from Canada than from Europe, and by 1820 there were 275,000 loads coming from British North America and only 65,000 from Europe and elsewhere. By then, a London group had a sawmill beside Montmorency Falls, "the largest in America," with "76 saws constantly at work."[25]

Patrick Campbell's 1792 survey took stock of Upper Canada when it was at its most wilded. "The country along the [Lake Ontario] coast and about the Bay of Kenty ... [is] mostly of hard wood of a fine growth and very stately ... Into the country ... about six miles ... the wood [is] mostly hickory, straight and almost of equal thickness for forty feet to the branches ... Here are great quantities of chestnuts, and some butt[er] nuts." Hickory, chestnut, and butternut grow in full sun, and such woods could have formed only on once-open ground. In Niagara, he wrote, the land between Lake Ontario and the escarpment, which is now fruit country, was "heavily timbered [with] oak, walnut, chestnut, butternut, hickory, mapple or sugar wood, ash, pine, and ... others." The crest of the escarpment had "a much lighter soil ... thinly timbered, and all of oak."[26]

In 1792 Lieutenant Governor John Simcoe and his wife, Elizabeth, left Quebec for Upper Canada. At the mouth of the Jacques Cartier River, she said, the slopes had a "park-like appearance," a "fine turf with large trees scattered over it." Upstream of Montreal she noticed the change in bedrock at the Thousand Islands, with "pine or oak growing on a grey rock ... variegated by ... different mosses." The hemlock was "a more immense height than English people can suppose," and the "strawberries ... as well flavored as the best scarlet strawberries in ... England." She was cautiously measuring what she saw against her tame English home but, by the time she exited this way in 1796, she would mention nonchalantly a "wild kind of shriek ... it was the painters (so they call panthers)." These in fact were cougar.

At Kingston, Mrs Simcoe's spirits began to rise. She walked one evening "in a wood lately set on fire ... You have no idea of the pleasure of walking in a burning wood ... I think I shall have some woods set on fire for my evening walks. It keeps the mosquitoes at a distance." This got more ink in her diary than the investiture of her husband as lieutenant governor the next day. She described how a forest was cleared: "The heavier timber is cut through the bark ... This kills the tree, which in time the wind blows down. The stumps decay in the ground."[27]

They sailed for Niagara and set up camp by the village at the rivermouth on "very dry ground ... in parts covered with oak bushes." The river banks were "covered with wood a hundred feet in height," and the common trees were "oak, chestnut, ash, maple, hickory, black walnut." Travelling to the falls, she wrote that "a fine turf leads on to the woods" and that the crest of the escarpment at Queenston was "a fine dry healthy spot" where the Queen's Rangers could raise their tents among "the large oaks." She sketched this setting, an open oak wood kept clear by drought and burns (Fig. 17). Thirty years before, the British army ranger Robert Rogers had described the same slopes as "thinly timbered with lofty oaks," as if they were "artificially transposed."[28]

There were novelties on the river shores, the fringed gentian and cardinal flower, and Elizabeth Simcoe was botanist enough to know that there was nothing like the milkweed back home in England. Captain Henry Darling showed her his stuffed animals, and she learned about sweet grass from Joseph Brant. Her tastes ran to the comestibles – to the cranberries and roasted chestnuts the Natives brought. The lieutenant governor's work soon took him west; in February he and six officers and twenty soldiers left Niagara and, above the escarpment, headed for the Thames River across "plains of white oaks and ash" until they met with forest again along the Thames. Near the Delaware "castle," their guides showed them "a spring of an oily nature, which upon examination proved to be a kind of petroleum," like the "burning" springs seen south of the lakes by the Jesuits.[29]

When France declared war in 1793, Simcoe had to entertain the possibility that the United States would join the French and attack Canada. Removing his capital from the border was imperative, and so too were preparations for possible naval action. Simcoe had seen the "valuable country" around Toronto and, he said, its harbour was "admirably adapted for a naval arsenal and dockyard." The site had been purchased from the Missisauga six years earlier as a military precaution. The surveyor Alexander Aitkin had inspected the site in 1788, noting its "timber mostly oak and pine for upwards of a mile above the [shore]." A survey in 1793 laid out Simcoe's "city of York" at the east end of the harbour in a "grove of fine ... large oak."[30]

Simcoe and his party sailed to York in 1793. Its bay was "beautifully clear & transparent" and Elizabeth soon visited "the peninsula," which the Toronto Islands were at that time. She found its meadows "very pleasing," covered with cottonwood, wild vines, and beach peas. "The Indians esteem this place so healthy that they come & stay here when they are ill." The Simcoes rowed east to "the high lands [where] the shore ... has the appearance of chalk cliffs but I believe they are only white sand ... We talked of building a summer residence there & calling it Scarborough."[31]

Simcoe soon turned his attention to the portage to the north, which had been purchased at the same time as York and which also offered options in the event of an American attack. He and four officers, on horseback and with four Natives, set off up the Humber River on the "long pine ridge" and, from there, the route was "chiefly wooded with maple, bass[wood], beech, pine and cedar." They climbed the Oak Ridges - a "very uneven ground ... [with] some very fine yellow pine [red pine] and black birch [black cherry]." These are trees of open sites, by then beginning to infill. Soon they descended into the Pottageville swamp, which they pushed through with canoes "where it would be impossible to walk without their support, it being a quagmire." In the swamp was the Holland River and, downstream, they came to Lac La Clie or Lac Taronto, which he named Lake Simcoe in honour of his father. On this outing, forests were not Simcoe's focus.[32]

When the French nobleman La Rochefoucauld stayed with the Simcoes in 1795, he wrote that the Niagara portage on the Canadian side was "extremely sandy ... covered with oaks, chestnuts and fine hickory trees, and such parts as are better watered, bear ... ash and maple trees." As Campbell had also noted, the land between the lake and the escarpment "mountains" had "old and beautiful trees ... of a size unknown in Europe." Near Kingston he was thrilled to see a state-of-the-art sawmill set up by a loyalist from Connecticut; it had "thirteen saws going; a log fifteen feet in length was cut into boards in thirty-seven minutes."[33]

In 1797 Isaac Weld came up the St Lawrence, which had ship locks by then, around the Long Sault rapids. "The pines in this neighbourhood are far more majestic than on any other part of the St. Lawrence." He admired the Thousand Islands, "beautiful in the highest degree," and at Queenston he remarked on the oaks and their "immense size." He climbed down the Niagara Gorge on "Mrs. Simcoe's ladder" and described the cliffside "pines and cedars hanging over your head ... with their heads downwards, being suspended by their roots." (Ecologists Doug Larson and Peter Kelly at the University of Guelph dated these escarpment cedars by counting their rings, and found some a thousand years old, and one of them 1,320 years, the oldest tree in eastern North America. Crooked and useless, they are one of the only pristine "forests" left.)[34]

George Heriot's *Travels* from 1799 to 1806 are notable for the number of times he mentions oak, pine, and other woodland trees, compared with his less frequent references to maple and its dense-forest associates. The trees around the Bay of Quinte were "oak, elm, hickory, maple and pines." Toronto was "cloathed with spreading oak." Between Burlington and Niagara, the streambanks were "covered with pine-trees of a large growth." Along the lower Oswego, the trees were "white and red oak, and chestnut." The timber at "the mouth of the Genesee consists chiefly of white and red oak and chestnut" and, at Buffalo Creek, "red pine," "white oak-trees near its mouth," and "large oak timber without any underwood." On Wolfe Island and the nearby mainland, "the timber ... is red oak, butternut, maple, ash, elm and small pine." The shipyard in Kingston built with "red cedar or oak." The trees above Niagara Falls on the Canadian side were "the oak, the ash, the beech, fir, sassafras, cedar, walnut, and tulip-trees," and the outlet of Lake Erie was "cloathed with oak, ash, chestnut, apple, and cherry-trees." Overall, Heriot described "immense tracts of woods, filled with oak." Around Lake Ontario, he mentioned oak twelve times, pine and chestnut three times, and maple twice. Open woodlands were still the norm.[35]

About the land clearing, Heriot was clinical. "The mode of commencing a settlement is by cutting down the smaller wood, and some of the large trees, collecting them into heaps, and burning them ... The remaining trees are girdled [and] after passing a harrow over the soil ... the grain is sown, the harrow is again used, and thus left without any further trouble, the newly-cleared ground yields a copious increase. A stranger is here struck with sentiments of regret on viewing the number of fine oak-trees which are daily consumed by fire, in preparation for cultivation."[36]

The Botanists

Botany had an early start in New France. The colony's first botanist was Michel Sarrazin, who arrived in 1685 and stayed until his death in 1734. He lived near the Plains of Abraham in Quebec City, and he collected and dried plant specimens, some of which he sent to the new Muséum d'histoire naturelle in Paris. In 1742 Jean-François Gaulthier inherited his post as royal physician, as well as his collections. He too corresponded with European scholars and sent his finds back to France. In 1749 Gaulthier helped Pehr Kalm on his Quebec visit, collecting around Quebec City and no doubt encountering the two plants that Carl von Linnaeus would name in honour of New France's botanists, the pitcher plant *Sarracenia* and the wintergreen *Gaultheria*.[37]

In 1806 André Michaux embarked from France "to collect seeds and young trees ... [for] the national nurseries of France." Botanists of the time made detailed notes, such as Michaux's around lakes Ontario and Erie. "Basswood [is] most abundant in Genesee [country] ... In some districts it frequently constitutes two-thirds, and sometimes the whole of the forests. The sugar maple, the white elm and the white oak are trees with which it most frequently associates." In western Pennsylvania, he saw "large forests, nine tenths of which consisted of white oaks." Today, basswood and white oak rarely dominate any of our woods. At Niagara Falls, "the river," he said, "was bordered with arbor vitae" (white cedar), and there were also the magnolia tree, the Kentucky coffee-tree, and the black maple, the latter also "a large part of the forests of Genesee." His *Flora boreali-americana* was for many years the most complete flora of eastern North America.[38]

The English botanist Thomas Nuttall spent thirty years in America, travelling through Great Lakes country in 1810. On his way to Lake Erie he described all that was new to him: the honey locust and hellbenders, beach peas and newts, cottonwood and soapberry, hop trees, and moonseed. He visited the Lake Erie prairies ("like an ocean") and was much taken with the "prairie blackbird," the bobolink. Sailing northwest he reached the Fox River on Green Bay in September. Around the lakes he collected twenty species of plants new to science, two of them endemics restricted solely to the Great Lakes, the dwarf lake iris and the Huron tansy. Nuttall's *North American Sylva* was the first attempt to describe all the trees of North America.[39]

John Goldie apprenticed as a gardener at the Glasgow Physic Garden and learned enough to want to join the ranks of globetrotting botanists. He landed in Halifax in 1817. His method of study was to travel by foot and he walked from there to Quebec. He shipped his collections home but they were lost at sea. He then walked to New Jersey, whose pine barrens afforded "many rarities to the botanist." Again he shipped his specimens but again they were lost at sea. His finances failed and he worked the summer of 1818 as a labourer. Another shipment of collections was lost. Back to labour and, by June 1819, having "amassed about 50 dollars," he set off for the Canadas. (At year-end he returned to Scotland with only the collections he could carry, but still they included fourteen species new to science. He had a good eye.)[40]

That June, Goldie walked up the St Lawrence from Montreal, past the "thickly settled" French lowlands and Glengarry, which had "all the appearance ... of Scotland." He hiked over the "solid rock" of the Frontenac Axis, where the mosquitoes and black flies left him "besmeared with blood." He took a day in Kingston to forward his gear to York by steamboat, and then was off again. Beyond the Bay of Quinte he was "completely into the bush," each house "7 or 8 miles distant from the last." On 25 June, he came to the Rouge River. "Before mid-day I passed a creek which lay very low ... All the declivity on the east side was completely covered with *Penstemon pubescens* such a quantity of which I never expected to see in one place – For a number of miles today I passed through barren sandy pine woods, which it is probable will never be cleared." Cleared they were, of course, and are now part of Toronto. The *Penstemon*, or beardtongue, is an indicator of open ground and the slope on the east side had burned in 1802. Goldie crossed the Rouge at its first riffle, immediately below the site of the abandoned Native village of Ganatsekiagon. This same location, when it was surveyed by David Smith in 1793, was marked off as "230 acres of land set apart for His Excellency Major General Simcoe, to complete his military allowance." It was a strategic site, and well chosen by the Simcoes.[41]

John Galbraith would survey the lower Rouge in 1833. The slope that Goldie had described as open in 1819 had a "scattering ... of pine and oak with an almost impenetrable thicket of briars, hazel and other sorts." It was reforesting rapidly. The mature oak in the valley went to build ships at the mouth of the river, and the pine was also shipped. By 1861, there were forty-five sawmills and gristmills on the Rouge tributaries and two-thirds of the bush in the lower townships was gone. By 1942, only 4.2 per cent of the watershed was left in tree cover. Regeneration was fast, however, and was accelerated in 1954 by Hurricane Hazel, which flushed all the houses, orchards, and roads into the lake and instilled a new respect for nature. In 1991 the superb oak highlands between the lower Rouge and the Little Rouge, Simcoe's old land grant, became the core of the Rouge Park, Canada's largest urban park, and in 2011 the government of Canada announced its interest in creating a new national park in the Rouge.[42]

After crossing the Rouge, Goldie walked on to York through "a pine barren ... similar to ... [those in] New Jersey." He later walked the south shore of Lake Erie, where the land was being cleared but where there were still "immense quantities of that beautiful tree the *Liriodendron tulipifera* [tulip-tree] ... The common size of the stem at bottom is 3 to 4 ft diameter and it continues ... to the height of from 40 to 60 ft without a single branch." The "botanical productions" of Great Lakes country impressed this well-travelled botanist, and he later returned to settle.[43]

In the early 1800s there were many learned visitors. Another of those who took up the Linnaean challenge of discovering new species was Constantine Rafinesque. He journeyed through Iroquoia to Niagara Falls, Lake Champlain, and Ohio, and even to Richard Smith's Lake Otsego. He knew the naturalists of his day, and he wrote for the learned societies of Europe. His was a fine-grained interest in the minutiae of nature, and he seldom wrote about the land; the discipline of *ecology* would be framed only at the end of the century. However, he did return regularly, between 1802 and 1833, to the New Jersey pine barrens with its "sandy pine woods and gravelly plains." He saw the Albany pine barrens cleared and he saw the Hudson and Mohawk valleys transformed by the Erie and Champlain canals, by railroads, and by "3 cities and 20 villages within a circle of 12 miles radius ... Albany has already 25000 population, Troy 15000, Schenectady 8000."[44]

Success and Succession

To comprehend the colossal energy that was expended to reduce these wilded forests to farm, field, and bush, we need to reflect on what happened in the century and a half after Native land care ended. On the lands that Native peoples had cleared, burned, and tended, there were now closed-canopy forests that had flourished for a century and a half. On the lands that had stood as upland walls of wood between Native nations, the forests were that much older and denser. In 1798 James Kent visited the Oneida country along the Genesee Road, which had been clear and under Native care for centuries. "The forests were majestic, the timber tall, thick & enormously large ... like a high, impervious wall." Artists of the day, like the famed William Henry Bartlett in his 1842 *Canadian Scenery*, illustrated the same walls of wood (Fig. 16).[45]

Doctor John Howison came from Scotland in 1821 and was near the St Lawrence when he had his forest epiphany. "I had never before experienced the sublimity of a *real* forest, nor witnessed a succession of trees of such magnitude and beauty. Immense oaks grew so close to each side of the road that the intervening space was merely wide enough to permit the passage of the calash ... There is no difficulty in explaining the ... aversion with which the Canadians regard trees." (By contrast, the Agricultural Society of England gave an award that year for the individual who planted the most trees in England.) Howison spent some time in Glengarry, where "clumps of immense oaks ... [and] piles of blazing timber sent forth columns of smoke which enveloped the forests." The rings of one felled oak dated it "at least two hundred and sixty-seven years," he wrote, and "its size was very moderate when compared with that of many others which grew beside it and which ... I judged to be five or six hundred years old."[46]

Iron edges, which had been the core trade in the early days, were even more important in the new forest. The felling axe was the most important tool for settlers. Two men with a team of oxen could "junk" (as the cutting and piling was called) about three or four acres a year. Most of the land was far from any mill or market, and so most of the timber was burned. Of the rest, the wood cut for heating and cooking far exceeded any wood cut for lumber. The geographer David Wood calculated that, just for household fuel, "Ontario would have required [in 1842] over 1,500,000 cords, or the yield from about 80,000 acres of woodland ... During the 1840s, the fuel-wood demand would have required ... about one million acres." William Cronon documented the equivalent demand in New England: "A typical household probably consumed as much as the thirty or forty cords of firewood each year ... more than an acre of forest every year."[47]

The axe was followed by the plow. The earliest ones used in the New World were made of wood and metal, little better than the wooden hoes and spades of the Natives. The iron moldboard plow, however, brought brute force to farming, turning under ancient natural soils for the first time and making monoculture possible. Invented in China and manufactured and traded first by the Dutch, it attracted inventive minds to the challenges of efficient farming. Even Thomas Jefferson worked on the problem and, in 1794, he came up with his "moldboard of least resistance," but it was still iron and brittle. In 1837 John Deere perfected the self-scouring steel plow, and made manufacturing history. Faced with the axe - and the plow and seed drill - the land would offer no further resistance.

Individual settlers were at the mercy of a foreign geography when they arrived, and some of their heroics were incredible, and wasted, as James S. Graham pointed out in the 1820s. "Although no axman, he [my grandfather] set about clearing fifty acres of this valuable timberland for farming purposes. After the timber was destroyed, he found the soil had little value. Had he been more experienced, he might have chosen fifty acres of hardwood land which ... would have produced a rich, fertile soil." The energy of many thousands was thus blunted on the land itself, especially those who found themselves unknowingly landed on its uplands, barrens, and swamps.[48]

The choice of land was critical. Tiger Dunlop travelled Upper Canada as a land agent in the 1820s, and his *Statistical Sketches* offered specific advice. The best soils for plow-based farming were on the interior uplands, and not on the water-sorted lowlands near the lakes and rivers, for which Native farming had been suited. He understood the attraction of the lowland plain, "because the trees being at a distance from each other, after the manner of a gentleman's park in England, it is easily cleared ... [and] makes beautiful pasture." However, he insisted, "land is rich and lasting just in proportion to the size and quantity of timber which it bears; and, therefore, the more trouble he is put to in clearing his land, the better it will repay the labour he has expended." Dunlop was pushing land sales in the Huron Tract, of course, but he was correct nonetheless and its heavy lime-rich soils have stood up well to a century of farming.[49]

The oak, hickory, and hazel plains and woodlands occupied by the region's Natives and their wildlife had lighter soils that could be cleared and farmed with the tools they had. In the early days, they were also highly desirable: New York politician and farmer George Geddes wrote in 1859: "The 'oak lands'... that belt of land, once covered with oak and hickory, is the true wheat land, while the beech and maple lands are best adapted to grazing, and the pine lands are generally well suited to both grain and grass." The advice might differ but it hardly mattered. All of it would be completely cleared before long.[50]

Tree diversity was much sought after. The Irish settler Thomas Magrath described the land he settled in 1832 at Adelaide, between London and Lake Huron: "Maple, beech, butternut, elm, white ash, hornbeam, a sprinkling of oak, and some cherry and basswood; all indicating a prime soil ... The knowing ones ... say it will give wheat forever." There were other benefits from clearing and burning. Magrath could collect and sleigh his excess ash to the nearest ashery. "The pot-ash manufacturers have an exorbitant profit, and think it is well worth their while to follow and attend on new settlements." By this formula, the highland till plains and moraines of southern Great Lakes country were cleared, and a durable agriculture ensued, with a skim of back-line woods left for fuel-wood, sugar, and timber.[51]

Patrick Shirreff came to Great Lakes country in 1833 to document its farm potential for his younger brother. Coming in through New York and the Hudson, he was most impressed by the industry of the region. Agriculture was religion, wheat was its church, and the conversion was well underway. He took careful note of its soils. The Genesee flats had "alluvial soils, with scattered aged trees ... cleared by nature ... chiefly in grass, affording the richest pasturage I ever saw." After reaching York, a striving town of eight thousand, he headed east with the Kingston mail. Close to York, "the soil, for ten miles down the margin of the lake, is poor sand covered with pines." Beyond that the soils were "free loam" and "the vegetable mould in [the] forest was five inches deep." (He also took note of new arrivals like the "way-thistle .... known in the states by the name of the Canada thistle." It was an early invasive, the object of noxious-weed laws, and Americans still call it the Canada thistle because it came by way of Quebec.)[52]

Shirreff later crossed the plains in the mid-reaches of the Grand River, "chiefly oak openings" with every tree "small and stunted." West again, the raised banks of the Thames upstream of Delaware were also "oak openings," grading downstream into "plains" and "prairie." Near Lake Erie he saw the pawpaw and chestnut, which "seems to occupy the place of the pine," and at Colborne, in Norfolk County, he reported that a local iron-works needed coke to process "bog-ore" from a nearby marsh. "The company would clear any farmer's woodland for the coke it produced." Any local demand was considered godsent.[53]

The general succession on the sorted sediments of lower elevations around the lower Great Lakes was from its native unforested state to closed forest, and then to modern farm monoculture, in two centuries. This played itself out across the region. For example, George Head was an Englishman who spent four months in the region in 1815. He travelled deep into the heart of ancient Huronia a hundred and sixty years after Native land care had ceased, and all he saw was forest, where Champlain and others had seen open fields. Even with a "gang of Canadian axe-men" he could make no impression on the forest, and gave up after seven days.[54]

The largest forest left in Huronia is Awenda Park. Paleoecologists Jock McAndrews of the Royal Ontario Museum and Elliott Burden of Memorial University have pulled cores from lakes in Awenda to interpret the pollen record, and archaeologist Roberta O'Brien surveyed the park and collected 17,000 artifacts. What they found was that Native farming had begun about 1450 AD, in a forest dominated by maple, beech, and hemlock. After 1450 corn and weed pollen were deposited in the lakes from active crop fields. O'Brien discovered six occupation sites ranging from a half-acre to eight acres within a mile of Awenda's lakes. Toanché, one of them, was where Champlain entered Huronia, where Brébeuf called home, and where Brulé was executed. It was a town set among open fields and meadows. O'Brien would find only traces of flint corn, beans, squash, and sunflower, and the bones of harvested animals.

We have few descriptions of Huronia in the century and a half after its demise, but the pollen record is clear. White pine and oak took over the old fields and meadows. The tree canopy closed gradually, the soils accumulated organic matter and moistened, and maple and beech settled back in. Two of the larger maples at Awenda date from 1725 and 1770. The forest became the "home bush" of the Becks, who ran a lumber mill in Penetanguishene. They took out the overstorey white pine and the furniture-grade oak, the pine by 1890 and the oak by the 1960s. It then became a park and, today, the old Huron villages rest under maple, beech, and ash, with a few other trees. It has all the look of an older-growth forest but, in fact, it is a post-agricultural, post-clearance forest, like many of the modern woodlands in the region.[55]

Central Ontario

Central Ontario attracted a remarkable band of settler-writers, and forests drew their attention as much as anything. John Langton came early to the Kawarthas and his land on Sturgeon Lake, he wrote in 1833, had a "beach lined with cedar, hemlock, birch and pine, and immediately behind that … oak, maple and basswood." He worked hard to clear, burn, and turn his land, and wrote little else about it other than its value for re-sale. He saw one way to profit and, in 1849, he took up the square-timber trade, rafting logs down to Quebec for export. At the same time, Robert Harrison, east of Peterborough, was cutting the old pines that had their heads high above the incoming broadleaf forests. From "a pine tree little more than three feet in diameter … we cut eleven twelve foot saw logs [and] the top end of the top log was a foot in diameter." One was "seven feet six inches in diameter." Moving a single stem took a "mast gang" of every available hand and "twenty-two span of spirited, active, powerful horses." It was dangerous work hauling up and down hills, he said, "surcharged with the spirit of daring amounting to fascination."[56]

Samuel Strickland arrived in 1825 and took work on the farm of a loyalist at Darlington on Lake Ontario. He married a daughter of the house and, the next year, settled on 200 acres in Peterborough near his new brother-in-law. Peterborough at the time was a single cabin and Scott's sawmill. Strickland was soon clearing and burning. "In the month of July," he wrote, "the whole country at night appears lit up by these fires." That fall his wife died. He persevered with the clearing, re-wed the next year, and, in 1828, joined the Canada Company. He bridged the rivers at Guelph, helped survey the Huron Tract, and earned the right to offer advice. "The best land is timbered with oak, ash, elm, beech, bass-wood and sugar-maple. A fair mixture ... is best, with here and there a large pine ... Too great a proportion of beech indicates sandy or light loam: a preponderance of rock-elm is a sign of gravel or limestone." His advice was the same as Tiger Dunlop's: "The soil is of excellent quality when timbered in the manner described."[57]

Strickland was an admirer of fine trees. Superabundance was ending and a relic forest giant was noteworthy. For example, in the upper Thames, he saw a cherry with a "circumference as high as I could reach [of] ten feet seven inches." Along the Maitland at Goderich were "natural meadows" that had clumps of "magnificent" sycamores, one of them a hollowed shell that Strickland, Dunlop (a large man), and eleven others could stand in. The largest tree between Galt and Guelph was the Beverly oak, its diameter eleven feet and its "trunk rising ... sixty or seventy feet before branching off." Strickland built his house in Goderich of cherry-logs, "little inferior to mahogany either in appearance or durability," and he saw a farm near Sarnia "fenced with black walnut rails ... a pity that precious material like this should be used for such purposes."[58]

In 1831 Strickland left the Canada Company and took up land twelve miles farther up the Otonabee near Lakefield. To "penetrate a lot of two hundred or more acres, in its original state, is always an herculean labour." Then came the clearing and ashing. Potash was a staple of the settler economy. "Several things should be considered before the emigrant attempts the manufacture of this article. Firstly, his land should be well-timbered with oak, elm, maple and bass-wood. Secondly, it must have a stream of water, near which he may erect his works." Potash salt, or potassium carbonate, had long been used for making soap and glass but, in the 1800s, it was also made for export, for use in the manufacture of military explosives. For many settlers it was the only cash that could be had from clearing the bush and, from 1810 to 1840, it brought about $40 a barrel, four times the price of a barrel of flour and three times a barrel of whisky.[59]

The advice from Tenche Coxe, potash booster and published economist, was clear. "The settler in making his clearing must take care to burn the brush and wood in such manner as to preserve the ashes. Out of the wood ashes, thus saved, he should make as much pot ash, or pearl ash, as he can; and he should dispose of this for ready money, strong clothing, axes, spades, ploughs or such other things for his farm or family." Potash was the leading item shipped on the Erie Canal in its first twenty years. Thus were great forests reduced to the caustic chemicals of industry.[60]

Later on, Strickland grew nostalgic. "What a difference a few years make ... With the aid of a compass or by following the course of some unknown stream, with much toil and difficulty we made our way back for miles, through dense forests, swamps and creeks ... or launch the light bark-canoe on some distant lake. We travel the same route twenty-five years afterwards, and the forests have bowed their lofty heads – the swamps are drained – the rivers bridged, and the steamer ploughs the inland wave, where shortly before glided the canoe." No place on Earth had been occupied and transformed so quickly. With the same speed as south of the lakes, his Huron Tract went from no settlers at all in 1826 to twenty-seven thousand in twenty-four years.[61]

The year 1832 was a banner one for Strickland's sister Catharine. She met her husband, Lieutenant Thomas Traill, married, and migrated to join her brother near Lakefield. His letters had prepared her for what they faced. The Traills fled through Lower Canada, spurred on by a cholera outbreak there. She loved the St Lawrence and "its thousand islands, which present every variety of wood and rock." They arrived in Cobourg in August and took a light wagon north. The slopes north of Lake Ontario were "bold forests of oak, beech, maple and bass-wood, with now and then a grove of dark pine." They crossed the Rice Lake plain, ferried the lake, and walked the last three tough miles up the Otonobee. "Every few yards our path was obstructed by fallen trees, mostly hemlock, spruce or cedar, the branches of which are so thickly interwoven that it is scarcely possible to ... force a passage." Beyond the riverbank, broadleaf trees prevailed, "such as bass-wood, maple, hickory, butter-nut, oak, beach and iron-wood, which trees always indicate a more productive soil than the pine tribe." Her interest in nature brought fresh detail to her writing.[62]

Along the Kawarthas, where Champlain had made no note of pine, Traill said, "The pines are certainly the finest trees ... [and] being so much loftier than the other trees, are sooner uprooted, as they receive the full and unbroken force of the wind in their tops; thus it is that the ground is continually strewn with ... huge pines." In the winter of 1833, the Traills engaged to supply a mill "with five hundred pine logs ... twelve feet in length, and not less than sixteen inches in the square ... A fine clean pine will yield from five to six [of these] logs; the largest of these will frequently measure from three to four feet in diameter; but no difference is made in price between the very large and those that are just within the limits." The logs were boomed in the river and rafted downstream: "Five or six such rafts pass down in one day."[63]

The economy was all farm and family. "Where there is ... a convenient sugar-bush ... the making of sugar and molasses is decidedly a saving; as young children can be employed in emptying the troughs and collecting fire-wood, the bigger ones can tend the kettles ... and the wife and daughters can finish off the sugar." Another task was to pull the weeds from the new fields: the native wild raspberry, gooseberry, and strawberry, and the "vile" fire-weed and the "great pest" sumac. "I have been obliged this spring," Traill wrote, "to root out with remorseless hand hundreds of sarsaparilla plants, and also the celebrated ginseng, which grows abundantly" – and which is now, of course, an endangered species.[64]

Traill was an ecologist before the word "ecology"was invented. In nature, there is "change but not loss," she would reflect. "Here lies one of the old giants of the forest at our feet. The earth has sustained it year after year ... through the network of cable-like roots and fibres. Never idle were those vegetable miners ... taking and selecting only such particles as were suited to increase the woody fibre and add to the particular qualities of the tree ... But while the tree had been receiving, it had also ... given back to the earth fresh matter, in the form of leaves, decayed branches and effete bark and fruitful seed. It had purified and changed the gases that it had first inhaled, and deprived them of the properties that were injurious to animal life."[65]

Catharine's sister Susanna married retired naval officer and writer Dunbar Moodie in 1831 and they too arrived in 1832. They settled first near Cobourg and then in the bush at Lakefield. Her initial feelings were those that "the condemned criminal entertains for his cell," and her 1852 book *Roughing It in the Bush* was a sad lament for her reduced station in life. There was little to like about the bush. The burning of wood piles "haunted me in my dreams," and the logging bees were "noisy, riotous, drunken." She was thrilled, however, with a canoe trip to Stoney Lake. "Most of these islands are covered with huckleberries [blueberries, and] ... grapes ... cranberries, blackberries, wild cherries, gooseberries and ... currants." She named one island Oak Hill, for its "abundance of oak-trees."[66]

Dunbar understood the social levelling of life in the bush. "Alone, a man may fell the trees on a considerable extent of woodland; but without the assistance of two or three others, he cannot pile up the logs previous to burning. Common labours and common difficulties produce a social unity of feeling among backwoods-men ... Every tree that falls beneath the axe opens a wider prospect, and encourages the settler to persevere in his efforts to attain independence." Not everyone could meet the challenge, however, and the Moodies sold up and settled in Belleville in 1839, where Dunbar served as sheriff. It was from their new home that Susanna would write *Life in the*

Clearings, a more affectionate look at the comforts of a Canadian society newly emerged from the bush. She revelled in the replacement of the wild shores with stone wharfs and warehouses. By 1853, the valley slopes around Belleville were "a beautiful prospect ... fine trees which have grown up since the ax first levelled the primeval forests." Her country visits were by choice and therefore charming, such as to the Oakhills at Rawdon, where a "clean little country inn" put on a good dinner. Around Belleville, by then, the conversion was complete.[67]

Travel Writers and Settled Sons

The travel writer Anna Jameson arrived in Toronto in the winter of 1837. "What Toronto may be in summer, I cannot tell," she wrote. "Its appearance to me, a stranger, is most strangely mean and melancholy. A little ill-built town on low land at the bottom of a frozen bay." She was not one to gloss things over. The tangled shore was "a mere swamp ... the birch, the hemlock and the tamarack trees ... growing down to the water's edge." She saw the backcountry by sleigh, travelling "for miles" through "melancholy pine" and noticing only a "bald-headed eagle ... [on] a blasted pine." Soon winter lifted, however, and by June she was exclaiming that "the wooded shores of the lake are very beautiful, and abounding in game." And heading west, she was eager for "the pine forest, which extends with little interruption for about forty miles to Hamilton."[68]

Jameson tallied the various woodlands she passed. From Woodstock to Ingersoll along the Thames, the land was "covered with hard timber, as oak, walnut, elm, basswood," but between Ingersoll and London she passed "seven miles of pine forest ... and then ... some miles of open flat country, called the oak plains." She wondered about succession, how "a different species springs up spontaneously in its place." At St Thomas she visited a furniture factory; the "black walnut, a tree abounding here ... [is] more beautiful in colour and grain than the finest mahogany; and the elegant veining of the maple-wood cannot be surpassed."[69]

After visiting Colonel Talbot at his "eyry" above Lake Erie, Jameson entered the "road dividing the township of Howard from the Harwich township." It was one of "those terrific corduroy paths" and led through "dark pine forest, and ... rank swamp." Farther on, "the overhanging foliage ... shut out the sunshine ... and we travelled on through a perpetual gloom ... The timber was all hard timber, walnut, beech and bass-wood, and oak and maple of most luxuriant growth." "I cannot look with indifference," she confided, "far less share the Canadian's exultation, when these huge oaks, these umbrageous elms and stately pines, are lying prostrate, lopped of all their honours, and piled in heaps ... or standing, leafless, sapless ... having been girdled and left to perish."[70]

The travel writer Edward Sullivan, visiting Upper Canada in 1850, also felt sympathy. "There are three ways of clearing in Canada ... the first by setting fire to the forest and trusting providence to extinguish it; the second method is by 'ringing' or dividing the bark all round, which causes the trees to die immediately; the third is by cutting them down altogether; this latter operation is performed ... when the snow is four or five feet deep, and a stump of a corresponding height is left. I don't know which of these three ... gives the country the most desolate ... appearance."[71]

The English sportsman and naturalist Ross King left us one of the most sympathetic images of the wilded forest, in 1866. "The grand forests present a more striking appearance than anything else to the eye of one just arrived from the Old World. No one entered their shadows or tread their long-drawn vistas of tall grey stems, spanned by over-arching roof of dark leaves, without the idea of a vast cathedral involuntarily rising in the mind. Like ruined columns, huge prostrate trunks lie strewn around, some but newly fallen, others moss-grown and verdant ... while many show only a dark line of decayed vegetable mould, the last ... vestige of their former stateliness."[72]

Canadian writers were less impressed. Born in 1825 near the Bay of Quinte, Cannif Haight put it baldy. "The muscular arm of the sturdy pioneer had hewn its way into the primeval forest, and turned the gloomy wilderness into fruitful fields ... Wood, save the large oak and pine timber, was valueless, and was cut down and burned to get it out of the way." This was the near unanimous view, which had not changed since his grandparents' experience on their own first farm, made worse by the failure of British supplies to reach them when they arrived as loyalists, and by the taste of the basswood buds they had to eat to survive. But their hardships had faded by 1830, in proportion to the demise of their forest. By then, "a genuine content and a hearty good will, one towards another, existed in the older parts." Yet in the back bush, where there was still "the boundless continuity of the shade," the trees remained "a standing menace."[73]

For Haight, the year 1830 marked "a new order of things" in Upper Canada. There were finally "laws to protect society, encourage education and foster trade." In 1830 Upper Canada had 91 post offices and 132 public schools. York had three churches and a population of 2,860. There was the Bank of Upper Canada, with capital of £100,000 and reported deposits of £1,600,000. Upper

Canada College opened its doors in 1830, with an endowment of 60,000 acres of public land. The Welland and Rideau canals were opened in 1830, and there were four lighthouses on the lakes. There were 429 sawmills. Twelve miles of Yonge Street were paved. Beginning in 1831, ministers of faiths other than the Church of England were permitted to conduct marriages. Haight was one of the new natives, for whom there was no doubt at all that this was progress.[74]

Samuel Thompson was a settler from England who later became editor of a Toronto newspaper and of *Hansard*. He arrived in York with his brother in September 1833 and, for £20, they bought a location ticket for 200 acres and headed north to Holland Landing to get the boat to Barrie. From there they walked west on a line cut to the Nottawasaga River, beyond which the trail faded. Hugh Black had surveyed this line in 1822: "Pine plains, pine plains, pine plains." To the south, Sam Benson had surveyed Essa in 1820: a sand plain of "white and yellow [red] pine." Thompson was more eloquent. "There is something majestic in these vast and thickly-set labyrinths of brown columnar stems averaging a hundred and fifty feet in height ... and from one to five in thickness, making a traveller feel somewhat like a Lilliputian Gulliver. I have seen a solitary pine nearly five feet thick and somewhere about a hundred and seventy feet in height."

These were the great pineries of the Simcoe lowlands. Today, only a few persist, themselves Lilliputian in comparison, at the Camp Borden military base and the Beattie Pinery south of Alliston. The Beattie Pinery has the only pine of any size and they date back to the great fire of 1849 or slash fires in the 1870s. In 1954 the Beatties were asked by Ontario for their red pine, to use as pylons to build the Burlington Skyway, because they were the biggest left in the province. They took out one or two hundred stems that were ninety feet long and still eight inches in diameter at the top – big by modern standards but less than half the size of the trees Thompson saw.[75]

Thompson settled near Sunnidale, "close to a large cedar swamp." This was the edge of Minesing, one of the largest swamps in the region, today more than three-quarters of it a nature reserve. In those days, the only benefit Thompson saw was that he could get "government contracts for corduroying or causeway-ing the many swampy spots" along the roads. There was no trail when they came: "The surveyor's blaze is the sole distinctive mark between the adjoining lots and your own; there are trees innumerable – splendid trees ... As you see no chance of conveying them to market for sale [they] must be consumed by fire ... You may 'some day' have the opportunity of selling them in the shape of potash, 'when there is a road out' to some navigable lake or river."[76]

Thompson made some novel observations. "Clearing by fire was sure to be followed by a spontaneous growth, first of fire-weed or wild lettuce, and secondly by a crop of young cherry trees, so thick as to choke one another. To test the matter, I scooped up a panful of black soil from our clearing, washed it, and got a small tea-cupful of cherry-stones. The cause of this surprising accumulation of seed was not far to find. A few miles distant was a pigeon roost ... To these pigeons we were, doubtless, indebted for our crop of young cherry trees." The pigeon's role in dispersing fruit, and fertilizing it, was known even then.[77]

In the Huron Tract, Thompson "saw a white oak that measured fully twelve feet in circumference at the butt and eighty feet clear of branches." Yet, he said, "we send our pine cross the Atlantic as if it were the most valuable wood that we have, instead of being, as it really is, amongst the most inferior. From our eastern seaports, white oak is shipped in the form of [barrel] staves chiefly, also some ash, birch and elm. But what about the millions of tons of hardwood of all kinds which we destroy annually? ... Why not warm ourselves with the coal of Nova Scotia, of Manitoba, and ... of the Saskatchewan, and spare our forest treasures for nobler uses?"[78]

The Maw of the Market

In the first half of the 1800s the shipyards of Europe and the Americas were the largest non-agricultural industries in the world. The weaponry was metal but the muscle was wood. Oak and pine were as crucial to navies as oil is today. Interest in Canada's wood grew after the American Revolution, and even more after the United States and France became "most favoured" traders in 1800. The St Lawrence was an obvious option and Britain soon guaranteed both contracts and preferential tariffs. Buyers set themselves up in Quebec to purchase anything coming downriver as well. The traffic downriver from Vermont - timber, staves, and potash - gained momentum but it was in 1806 that the inland trade got serious, when the New Englander Philemon Wright got a contract to deliver an Ottawa River raft of timber to Quebec City by the end of July.[79]

Wright and his partners assembled their raft near the mouth of the Gatineau River and began, in June, the 175-mile journey to Quebec. The raft broke up on the Long Sault Rapids, and they spent a month assembling it again. They were too late to meet their contract but in November Napoleon's continental blockade of the British Isles began, and Wright's raft was of much more interest. This ushered in a half-century of timber rafting to saltwater ports, and the business of winter logging fit hand-in-glove with summer farming. Many individuals took up rafting, like Langton in the Kawarthas. A raft of two thousand to twenty-four hundred timbers was worth roughly $12,000 in the middle of the 1800s. A raft of valuable, lightweight pine could hold afloat a good load of heavy oak. Prices climbed and, later in the century, the same raft was worth over $100,000. The Ottawa valley was so thoroughly logged as a result that today it would be nearly impossible to assemble from that entire woodshed the timber for a single such raft (Fig. 18).[80]

How was wood tenure to be imposed? Who had the right to dam and drive what rivers? Who would collect fees for licences? Tenure systems were devised *de novo*, and the Ottawa District was a pioneer administration: licences were issued and paid for at Bytown, based on estimated limits and harvest levels; stumpage fees were paid on a quarter of the estimated harvest, and bonds were posted for the rest; volumes were measured when the logs were boomed in Bytown; and accounts were settled when the rafts made it to Quebec. Lower Canada enacted Canada's first timber regulations in 1805, regulating the rafts on the St Lawrence. Fifteen years later, Upper Canada brought in a duty on timber imported from the United States. Finally, in 1827, regulations in Upper Canada required loggers to buy licences and pay stumpage fees. The systems were all gamed, and beyond enforcement.[81]

Between 1845 and 1849, however, Britain rescinded its low duties on lumber and wheat from Canada, as well as Canada's preferential access to British ports. Along with the potato blight, a general economic recession took hold in Britain, eroding the colonial system and ushering in U.S. competition. The epic industrialism of the United States, centred in the northeast, took full flight and, as economist Harold Innis put it, "industrialism was poured into moulds of wood." The United States was the ascendant market, and U.S. import duties were finally overcome by a reciprocity agreement in 1854. At that point, *The North American Assault on the Canadian Forest*, as historian Arthur Lower called it in his book of that title, took root and American demand for cheap wood and paper has been an active, negotiated file between Canada and the United States ever since.[82]

Dominant players began to emerge. Some, such as William Price, had roots in Royal Navy procurement monopolies. By the 1840s, Price, had expanded beyond the St Lawrence, built nine sawmills in the Saguenay country, and established a vast export business. The Canadian lumberman John Booth was a legend on the Ottawa River. His mill at Bytown got the contract for

Canada's first Parliament buildings, and it could cut six hundred thousand feet of lumber a day. It was the American trade that dominated, made possible by new canals and railways. The Erie Canal reached Buffalo in 1825, and the Welland Canal opened in 1830. The Richelieu Canal opened in 1843, completing the water route from the St Lawrence to the Hudson. Oswego, where the Erie Canal reached Lake Ontario, imported less than two million feet of lumber from Canada in 1840 but, ten years later, was shipping more than sixty million feet. The first canal west into the Mississippi basin was opened in 1845, linking Lake Erie to the Wabash River. Trade became north-south, and the last year in which timber exports to England exceeded those to the United States was 1867. Twenty years later, there were fourteen Canadian rail lines delivering wood to ports on Lake Ontario and Lake Erie. Eight rail lines to Lake Huron did the same. U.S. railways like the Baltimore and Ohio Railway picked up the wood at Buffalo, Rochester, Detroit, and Chicago; at least eight railways connected the northern forest to the Atlantic seaboard. Booth himself built rail lines east to Vermont and west to Georgian Bay. The forest was the essential feedstock of industry.[83]

Both Canadians and Americans cut timber on both sides of the lakes and, for all, the traffic was largely stateside. In 1890 President William McKinley, from Buffalo, signed into law a bill that removed the tariff on logs from Canada but raised the tariff on sawn lumber to about 50 per cent. In retaliation, Ontario passed a law the next year that any pine cut on public lands had to be sawn in Ontario. None of this constrained the flow of hardwood or wood from private land, however, and milling was a scalable industry, on which the fates of communities turned. George Grant, at Queen's University, wrote in 1882: "The mill-privileges of the Grand River were a perilous temptation to shear it completely ... [and] the banks have been shamefully denuded ... If municipal councils would but realize that a manifold source of wealth is wasted ... they would carefully guard these natural resources." However, such censure did nothing to slow the trade, trumped by the clearer logic of profit.[84]

Catharine Traill spoke of it almost as a psychosis, observing that the settler "wages war against the forest with fire and steel." She mourned its outcomes. "There are scarcely any hedgerows here, and ... [there is] a sad want of clumps of trees for shade and shelter also, about the homesteads. With the early settler ... 'Down with it' was the universal motto. Many persons have wasted and burnt timber to the value of the fee simple of their estates."[85]

Truth be told, rural settlers could not keep the old forest giants. They were just too dangerous when they were not embedded in a continuous forest.

Thomas Magrath, the Irish settler, stated as much in 1831: "A wise settler will take care not to leave any trees standing close to the site of his intended mansion; a friend of mine ... having just completed his roof, was sitting under it ... when a tremendous crash, from a falling tree of great dimensions, laid the entire edifice level with the ground." Even Traill knew the dangers: "The taller the tree the more liable it is to being uprooted by storms." She offered an alternative: "Leave several acres of forest in a convenient situation, and chop and draw out the old timbers for fire-wood, leaving the younger growth." This became the norm, and most settlers retained a section of bush to supply their fuel-wood.[86]

Volumetrically, timber and fuel-wood consumed less forest biomass than burning the wood to clear the land. However, all of this was soon eclipsed by industrial demand. Historian Hazel Mathews wrote about one such industry: "The whole Kaatskill region was covered by a continuous forest of hemlock ... Trunks measured 4 feet in diameter were common, and many measuring up to 12 feet and standing as tall as 150 feet ... It was the bark peelers who in the 1830s and thereafter swarmed over the mountains to ... strip them of their bark ... to supply the tremendous quantities of tan bark required by the tanning industry." Another hemlock heartland lay east of Georgian Bay, and the towns of Parry Sound, Bracebridge, and Burks Falls were largely founded on their tanneries, now long gone. Hemlock is slowly reviving itself in our forests.[87]

The tanning industry and the iron, glass, paper, and chemical industries used massive volumes of wood. For example, Pittsburgh boasted of the wood coming down the Allegheny River in 1870, claiming "annual flows upwards of 10,000,000,000 feet ... Pittsburgh furnishes forty-six percent of all the glass, sixty-eight percent of all the steel, and thirty-eight percent of all the iron manufactured in the United States." This massive demand for wood continued until coal took over as a fuel and chemical feedstock, and it remained strong until oil and gas finally displaced it. The tanning and wood-chemical industries could use almost any lignin that could be shipped and boiled, and some foresters called these clear-cuts the "chem cuts," unlike any cutting before or since.[88]

The Horror

In the 1830s, the eastern Ontario judge Jacob Pringle lamented: "Each tree of the forest was an enemy to be attacked and got rid of as soon as possible." Anna Jameson added: "The pity I have for the trees in Canada shows how far I am yet from being a true Canadian." Richard Bonnycastle, the royal engineer and painter, put it bluntly in his 1842 guide to the Canadas: "Trees in America are regarded with a sort of horror." By the 1850s the lament was getting louder. [89]

Any laws were about trade, not cutting, and were to little purpose. "Great embarrassment was caused by the squatters and timber miners in the late 1850s and 1860s," it was reported. Timber miners posed as settlers, made their down payments, cleared the land, and sold it. A commission was appointed in 1863 to enquire into the destruction of the forest; it failed to report, but a later commission would write that "the history ... has been that of 'cut out and get out.'"[90]

It was wildfire that helped tip the balance. Fire had made it possible to clear the land but that same fire was too much of a risk as soon as settlement reached a certain density. Where there were few settlers, wildfires were barely noticed. For example, James Hamilton reported that, one summer in the late 1840s, "an extensive fire began in the Lake Superior country, and advancing easterly, ran along the north shore [of Lake Huron] ... over an area of five hundred miles in length and one hundred in width." Little property damage was reported but "the smoke materially interfered with navigation on the lakes."[91]

Attitudes changed as the risks to settlers increased. Samuel Thompson wrote that "1870 will long be remembered as the year of the Ottawa fires ... Wind from the south-west fanned into flames the expiring embers of bush-fires and burning log-heaps throughout the counties of Lanark, Renfrew, Carleton and Ottawa. No rain had fallen there for months previously, and the fields were parched to such a degree as ... to render buildings, fences, trees and pastures so dry that the slightest spark would set them in a blaze." Some soils were "burned so deeply as to render farms worthless." More than two thousand people fled into Ottawa, and three inches of ash fell on the town. Prime Minister John A. Macdonald (in Ottawa) wrote a letter to Premier J. Sandfield Macdonald of Ontario (in Toronto), laying the blame: "We are recklessly destroying the timber of Canada, and there is scarcely a possibility of replacing it." Of course, forests were a provincial jurisdiction and not his responsibility. The next year, Ontario sold at auction the largest timber licences it had ever permitted, for 3.2 million acres on the north shore of Lake Huron. The reality was that timber sales were a vital source of revenue for the province.[92]

The link between settlement and wildfire was brought to a head by the first railways. Steam locomotives were on the Mohawk and Hudson Railway by 1831, the Champlain and St Lawrence Railway in 1836, and the Ontario, Simcoe and Huron Railway in 1853. The German traveller Johann Kohl would write in 1854, as he sat on the new train from Toronto to Lake Simcoe: "We rose by a succession of zig-zags up first one and then another of the 'oak ridges' ... Fire appeared to have been very active in these woods, and great tracts were burnt down on each side." The sparks belching from the locomotives were, of course, the cause.[93]

That same year, Charles Weld was on a ship heading north on Lake Champlain when his trip was interrupted by wildfire. To avoid it, he embarked by rail to Ogdensburg on the St Lawrence. "During the entire distance (120 miles), with the exception of clearings, where the black ruins of the settler's homestead told how fiercely the fire had blazed, we passed between burnt brushwood and charred trees. At every station ... [there were] crowds of terrified men and women ... The whole countryside was wrapped in flames and smoke ... The forests to the north of the river were on fire for many miles, and the conflagration was fast spreading." The combination of slash left by logging, wooden buildings, and ignition by steam locomotives was deadly.[94]

Fires were more common in some areas than others. Ecologist Steve Varga searched out the historic accounts of fire in the *Wiarton Echo* and found that there were major slash fires on the Bruce peninsula every year or two from 1879 to 1932. Many were late-summer fires that got away from settlers who did not wait for winter to burn their brush, but others were the same natural fires that had long maintained the dry rock barrens of the Bruce. Timberman Robert Lymburner surveyed the results of the cuts and burns on the Bruce in 1920: "There is no timber of value other than firewood ... on the whole peninsula."[95]

Andrew T. Drummond, the Montreal banker, spoke to the Montreal Horticultural and Fruit Growers Association on the subject in 1878: "No person who has visited the Saguenay district, the upper Ottawa, the shores of Lake Superior, and the Albany River country, can be blind to the fact that forest fires have been a source of vast ruin." Fire protection, he said, was part of the price of a civil society. Others, such as Robert Bell of the Geological Survey of Canada, were even more blunt. The great pineries that had once stretched from the Ottawa to Lake Superior were almost "entirely destroyed" by fire and, except for "small groves," had been replaced by other species. The losses were "almost incalculable" and of "serious national consequence."[96]

The issues of fire, logging, railways, and public safety were thus conflated. By 1915, half of all forest fires were caused by railways. More than 85 per cent of the lands burned were cutovers, grasslands, or barrens. Only 15 per cent was uncut forest. The fires on densely settled lands were readily suppressed but remote areas were another matter and there were new rail lines in areas of active logging. Terrifying fires ensued. The 1911 fire between Porcupine and Cochrane killed 70 people, and the 1916 fire between Haileybury and Cochrane killed 250. The following year there was an Ontario Forest Fire Prevention Act and a new troop of patrol-and-control rangers paid for by levies on timber licences. The advent of fuel-oil locomotives ended the large rail fires and, by 1927, there were new statistics – 90 per cent of fires were not caused by railways. Blanket fire suppression has now been in place across the region for eighty years, another imposed regime, like land tenure and roading, that has deep ecological consequences, largely ending the earlier era of pineries, woodlands, and prairies.[97]

The Reconstruction

Forest conservation became an economic concern. A Nova Scotia military officer, N.W. Beckwith, wrote in the *Canadian Monthly* in 1872 that "destroying a forest because we want timber is like smothering a hive of bees because we want honey ... We are wasting our forests, habitually, wickedly, insanely, and at a rate which must soon bankrupt us in all that element of wealth." A recession began the next year and, by 1877, timber exports had dropped by 40 per cent. The argument was made that exporting logs was the same as exporting jobs and, in 1898, Ontario required that all timber cut on public lands be processed at home.[98]

Economics also directed the responses south of the lakes. In 1872 New York State retained the lawyer Verplanck Colvin to complete "a survey of the Adirondack wilderness." Two years later, he wrote: "Unless the region be preserved essentially in its present wilderness condition, the ruthless burning and destruction of the forest will slowly ... creep onward ... and vast areas of naked rock, arid sand, and gravel will alone remain to receive the bounty of the clouds [water] and be unable to retain it." Businessmen did not want the source waters of the Erie Canal to dry up and, in this, they had joint cause with a growing number of recreationists who visited and invested in the Adirondacks. The response was to withdraw public lands from sale in 1883 and, two years later, establish the Adirondack Forest Preserve, to be "forever kept as wild forest lands." It remains to this day the largest protected area in the contiguous United States.

The protection of the Catskills soon followed, in response to similar concerns. Businessmen pointed to "industry's dependence on a steady supply of water power, which only healthy forests could provide." The public was also nervous about New York's drinking water, and conserving the Catskills became a *cause célèbre*. Harvard botanist Charles Sargent chaired a public commission, and wrote: "The merchantable timber and the hemlock bark were long ago cut, and fires have more than once swept ... the entire region, destroying the reproductive powers of the forest as originally composed and ruining the fertility of the thin soil ... A stunted and scrubby growth of trees is gradually repossessing the hills, which, if strictly protected, may sooner or later develop into a comparatively valuable forest." When the New York State Forest Preserve was created in 1885, it also included the Catskills, still forever wild today as a 700,000-acre park.

North of the lakes, a report tabled by the Ontario Fruit Growers Association in 1879 stated: "How much depends on the judicious planting of forest trees, their presence producing abundant rainfall, preserving and distributing moisture and thereby forming a preventative against drought and devastating floods." At its meeting in 1880, the association heard Benjamin Gott of Arkona bitterly deplore the "merciless havoc made upon them (our forests) for the base and meager considerations of the present ... If something is not speedily and effectually done ... we shall ... find ourselves compelled to forever inhabit a dismal treeless waste and an unfruitful region."[99]

Two years later, the first-ever congress of North American foresters was held in Cincinnati and in Montreal. Its first recommendation was in support of reserves of public land for the application of modern forestry. The idea gained ground in Ontario through the work of a clerk in the Ontario Crown Lands Department, Alexander Kirkwood, who put out a pamphlet in 1886 called the *Algonkin Forest and Park*, concluding with a blunt appeal: "The commissioner of crown lands who establishes Algonkin forest and park will be cherished in the warmest corners of many hearts."[100]

A commission was struck in 1892, chaired by the same Kirkwood. It recommended a "forest reservation and national game preserve" to maintain water supplies, preserve primeval forest, protect wildlife, experiment with forestry, and provide for health and recreation. Algonquin Park was founded the next year. Thomas Gibson, first park secretary, wrote: "No railway ... approached its borders; no travelled highway ... led to it. There was not a cross-road hamlet within its boundaries; not a post-office, church or school ... [However] the lumberman has been long at work." Protection turned out to be a movable feast. William Saunders, scientist and director of the Experimental Farm in Ottawa, would complain bitterly: "Commercializing the game in the park progressed from one thing to another ... the rangers destroyed the muskrats because they injured the marsh growth, the beaver and the porcupine because they destroyed trees, the otter and the mink because they ate fish, the fox, fisher and marten because they killed partridge, and the wolves because they killed deer." (The experiment with forestry continues to this day, under the Algonquin Forest Authority, and the park is a wounded giant, with 78 per cent of it reserved for logging and with a spreading cancer of roads that are extended yearly, for the sole use of loggers and a new generation of truck-based Algonquin who can hunt and fish as they wish.)[101]

By 1900, deforestation was also linked in Canadians' minds with water issues and local climate. In 1879 Toronto engineer Kivas Tully attributed the lowering of Lake Ontario water levels to forest clearing, and in 1904 he documented a coincident decline in precipitation and lake levels, and an increase in temperatures, and linked them all to deforestation. In the face of public concern, aggressive tree planting, or "farm forestry," was adopted, led in Ontario by Edmund Zavitz. Of Niagara loyalist stock, "E.J.," as he was called, taught forestry at the Guelph College of Agriculture before serving as deputy minister of forestry. Planting trees was his cause, and his motivation lay all around him in the "waste lands" he described in an influential 1908 report.[102]

"In 1904," Zavitz wrote, "the municipal assessors' returns gave less than fifteen percent of woodland for all the settled townships" in southern Ontario. Two-thirds of what remained was lowland swamp, which meant that only 5 or 6 per cent of uplands remained unbroken. Zavitz surveyed the moraines and sand plains that had formerly been oak woodlands, pineries, and prairies (and even earlier Native hunting grounds). Cutting and grazing had degraded many of them, and their reclamation was a social imperative. They could not, he wrote, "properly support social organizations such as schools and churches. The state cannot afford to allow citizens to live and develop under the enforced conditions existing in many of these waste areas."[103]

The situation was, if anything, worse on the Canadian Shield to the north. In 1909 Canada set up a Commission of Conservation to advise on the nation's natural resources, and it conducted the first modern forest survey in Ontario. Clarence "C.D." Howe (later Canada's "minister of everything") and forester James White, both at the University of Toronto, surveyed the lands north of the Trent River and Kawarthas. Governments had already spent ten million dollars on dams and canals in aid of logging and settlement. "The sequence of this mismanagement is everywhere the same," they wrote. "The removal either of the best or of all timber, without disposing of the debris, leaves a slash which is invariably subject to fire." Clear-cutting upset the water balance and caused "extremes" of drought and flood. The wild Kawartha forest had been "a magnificent pinery" but, of the million acres they studied, only 700 acres remained uncut in 1912. "A few seed trees remain but not enough to re-establish the crop on a commercial basis," they reported. "The whole area has been burned ... [and] nearly two-thirds of the area have been burned over two or three times and are practically ... beyond natural recuperation." In the year 1912 alone, 175,000 acres burned, often burning the soil right off the rocks, creating a "man-made barren." The marshes "upon which the farmers are dependent ... were burned to the depth of two feet, the roots of the grasses being completely killed."[104]

Two-thirds of the study area was privately owned, a quarter of that by timber companies. The rest was public land licensed to lumbermen. The thousands of settlers who saw their streams and soils disappear were collateral damage. "Not only have many farms been abandoned ... but a considerable number that ought to be abandoned remain occupied by those who lack the means and energy to move, thus forming a poverty-stricken community." What was recommended was "the removal of this degenerating population" and, to this end, their lands were bought for back taxes, many "at the rate of about 17 cents per acre." These lands, which should have never been granted to settlers in the first place, would live to see another day as recovered timber lands owned and licensed by the government on a maximum-allowable-cut basis. But the "magnificent pinery" of the early days would not return.[105]

Other Ontario "waste lands" were the Norfolk sand plain, the Huron fringe, the Simcoe sand plains, the Thessalon sand plain, and the eastern Oak Ridges. The province could not reforest these lands alone and, in 1911, it passed the Counties Reforestation Act, asking local authorities to help. Zavitz's work led directly to the establishment of public tree nurseries in each of these areas, providing affordable seedlings that inspired a tree-planting tradition that eventually stocked tens of thousands of acres of provincial forest, a hundred thousand acres of county forest, and many hundreds of thousands of acres of private and conservation-authority land.

The same happened south of the lakes. In 1906 Harvard philosopher William James penned *The Moral Equivalent of War*, pushing for the conscription of youth to remind them of "man's relations to the globe he lives on." New York Governor Franklin D. Roosevelt began to fund tree planting in 1929, and in 1930 the state started purchasing marginal and abandoned lands to reforest. Men made unemployed by the Great Depression were hired and, when he became president, Roosevelt extended the program nation-wide. Fourteen thousand Ohioans, for example, worked in the Civilian Conservation Corps planting trees, flood-proofing streams, and slowing erosion. The Appalachian strip mines were a focus, as were the "chem cuts" of upland Pennsylvania.

In the same period it was finally conceded that vast areas of New England, earlier cleared for farms, were better left to forest, and the word "New Englandization" – synonymous with forest re-wilding – entered the vernacular of ecologists. This astonishing "explosion of green," which continues today, was popularized by Bill McKibben in a 1995 article in the *Atlantic Monthly*. McKibben's story is also prophetic if we recall the historic lag between major landscape changes south and north of the lakes. Affluence and the retreat of farming to the best farm soils resulted in what he called "the great environmental story of the United States, and in some ways of the whole world." This was the return of forest to 90 per cent of New Hampshire, 80 per cent of Vermont, and 60 per cent of southern New England.[106]

North of the lakes the pace of conservation quickened later, after the Second World War. This was a war in which more than a million Canadians served abroad and it soon dawned on leaders that nothing would be the same in the future. Hundreds of thousands of experienced men, most of them from farm families, would be returning from a devastated Europe to a stripped, eroded, and financially depressed rural Ontario. The provincial government retooled in 1941 and brought in Frank MacDougall as deputy minister of lands and forests, a military man and graduate forester. A national advisory committee on reconstruction was set up the same year.

In 1941 the Guelph Conference was held to discuss *Conservation and Post-War Rehabilitation*. This gathering brought together the best forestry, farming, wildlife, and naturalist minds of the time, and organizations that continue their work today, like the Federation of Ontario Naturalists, the Ontario Federation of Anglers and Hunters, and the Royal Canadian Institute. Its report on the "old Ontario" was blunt. "All the renewable natural resources of the province are in an unhealthy state. None of these natural resources will restore themselves under present conditions, and the need for far-reaching measures of restoration and conservation is acute." The report addressed the losses of forest and wildlife, flooding, desiccation, erosion, pollution, water, and soils. The goal was clear: "Replacing the unplanned individualistic exploitation of the past hundred years by planned management based on knowledge and recognizing public as well as private interest."[107]

Based on this approach, Arthur Richardson was asked to conduct a "type" survey of the Ganaraska watershed north of Lake Ontario, to set a standard for such reports region-wide. He identified the lands that should be conserved, and bought and planted, and the manpower and funds needed to do so. At the same time, John Irwin, a forester and Toronto book publisher, kept up a dogged critique of Ontario forest practices. "If I may speak with moderation, I would say that our treatment of the forests of Canada represents the ultimate in callous stupidity, and a flagrant abuse and breach of trust on the part of our elected representatives, for which we the people must accept our share of responsibility."[108]

Three years after the Ganaraska report was tabled, and taking its recommendations to heart, Ontario combined its approaches with those of the Grand River Commission Act of 1938, the Muskingum Watershed Conservancy in Ohio, and the Tennessee Valley Authority, and passed the Conservation Authorities Act of 1946, mandating communities that shared watersheds to pursue their own conservation priorities while drawing on provincial funds and advice to do so, under Richardson's direction. This soon evolved into thirty-eight "conservation authorities" covering most of southern Ontario and the built-up areas of the north.

The first goal was to secure major river valleys, which had been prime real estate at the time of the original land grants and dam permits. These would be priorities for tree planting and for erosion and flood control. Funds raised locally were matched by the province, and this formula slowly and quietly yielded the largest purchase of private conservation lands in Canadian history, more than 360,000 acres. Local funds were difficult to raise, of course, and private individuals like Richard and Beryl Ivey of London were pivotal to this success, aided by conservation groups like the Nature Conservancy of Canada, founded in 1962 and led after 1966 by Charles Sauriol.

In recent years Ontario public agencies have backed away from their support for conservation and tree planting. However, that work remains a matter of deep public commitment, and a growing number of land trusts, fish and wildlife groups, and tree foundations continue it, partnering with conservation authorities and others. It is crystal clear, as it was sixty years ago, that there is much to do. Before the shutdown of public tree nurseries in the 1990s, more than one billion trees were planted on the private lands of Ontario, and another billion on its public lands. A program autopsy written at the time stated that this unparalleled effort fell "well below the potential for afforestation." Parts of the Great Lakes lowlands are greening and have 30 per cent tree cover again, but there are still tens of thousands more acres to restore. Agencies, organizations, and individuals know what to plant and where, but, despite the best efforts of "big picture" plans and "conservation blueprints," the effort falls short. Our lands and waters continue to be, in places, "degenerating," to use Zavitz's term, and "unhealthy," in the words of the Guelph Conference.[109]

The Cut Continues

Whether they were owned publicly or privately, standing trees invited cutting. As timber in parts of the region became scarce, and cutting more contentious, parts of it were set aside as parks. One such fragment was Rondeau, on the north shore of Lake Erie. Declared a park in 1894, it was described by its first park ranger, Isaac Gardiner, as "probably the largest and finest block of timber left in this section of the province." Gardiner added that "it is doubtful whether any other part of America of equal area could present a greater number of distinct species, or a more splendid growth of individual trees."

On special assignment in 1908, Zavitz went to Rondeau Park to mark its "merchantable timber." He warned the politicians that any cutting would cause a public outcry, but it took a storm of protest to stop it. By then it was half cut. William E. Saunders wrote in desperation: "The Rondeau devastation is the prize demonstration of incompetence on the part of our 'save the park' managers." Rondeau Park was cut again over subsequent decades, even after its forest was designated a "nature reserve" within the park. In the 1970s, the rationale given was that it was too dangerous to have large standing trees within falling distance of public trails. Finally, in July 1998, a fluke downburst with winds gusting to 110 miles per hour finished off the Rondeau forest, leaving half its remaining trees dead and reducing its standing biomass by 83 per cent.[110]

The largest of Canada's deep-south woodlands is Backus Woods, on the Norfolk sand plain. It was the home bush of the Backus family, who cut it only modestly for the family mill. Just a thousand acres, it has Canada's finest stands of trees like black gum and tulip-tree, and supports more rarities than any other Ontario woodland, like the hooded warbler, the Acadian flycatcher, chestnut, and ginseng. Many trees date from the 1700s; one black gum is more than four hundred years old. The family sold it to the local conservation authority in 1956. The temptation to log it for profit was too much, and the threat to cut Backus went public in the 1980s. It took a terrific clamour to stop it, and Backus was put under an agreement that prohibited cutting in exchange for the proceeds from a million-dollar endowment. This lasted until the end of the agreement in 2010, when the threat of cutting was renewed. This time a private conservation group, the Nature Conservancy of Canada, had to ask its supporters to step forward and buy back Backus from its public owner.[111]

These are the exceptional woodlands, which the public cares about. Away from the public eye, private-land forestry is largely business as usual, conducted on an ad hoc basis by cutters who persuade individual landowners that it is time to thin the bush again to raise some cash. Some have updated their pitch, saying that a young forest is fast-growing and healthy but an older forest is slow-growing and over-mature. Sometimes it is portrayed that it is an owner's duty to cut their bush. As a result, the majority of private woodlots are cut too often, regenerate with fewer species, and never reach maturity. Forest birds tell the story and the birds that live in deep forest interiors are barely hanging on, this at a time when there is no serious cutting for fuel-wood. Imagine if the old demand for fuel-wood returned.[112]

The geography of how we deplete our physical substrates shifts as each targeted resource is depleted, and we – the omnivore – shift our appetites to new resources, new sources of energy, protein, and fibre, and new continents. We are obsessive in our focus and almost invariably invasive, regardless of culture or creed. Perhaps a few cultures and a few mountain or island enclaves aspire to some level of self-restraint but even they are expected to fall to the seductions of modern techno-materialism. The human mind operates within the gestalt of its known domain, focusing forward on the targets that promise rewards – hunting, gathering, securing. When the target, no matter how important, is depleted, the loss is almost instantly immaterial, and new targets come into focus. This behaviour, coupled with the shifting baseline syndrome, sits deep in our Paleolithic limbic systems and drives us, by hunger and desire, to comfort or flight.

These "animal spirits," as the economist John Maynard Keynes called them in the 1930s, fuel our conversion of the complex natural world into the simple and useful. If and when they are satisfied or diverted, the naturalist E.O. Wilson contends, our love of nature, or "biophilia," can then rise to the fore. Settlers were in rational horror of the wilded forests. We were heroic in clearing them, and learned to appreciate them only when they were gone, as we gained comfort and affluence. There is not a single old-growth forest on the southern Ontario peninsula, for example, and yet we now have good reason to be optimistic that we are saving many of the fragments that are left. The same human ability to focus forward, and to get pleasure from anticipation and reward, is now helping to conserve nature. We are a domineering species, and our history on this landscape underscores just how muscular we once were.

We could be domineering again, on behalf of nature, and we will return to this subject later.[113]

Times are tough for nature. As society deepens its commitment to its new city-states and to their citizens' creature comforts, the focus slides away from the supportive landscape. It is increasingly taken for granted that citizens themselves must take on more of the non-urban responsibilities, on behalf of the public in general. Whether it is tree nurseries, fish hatcheries, species recovery, or nature reserves, citizens are stepping forward. Public agencies, for the most part, are eager to encourage the new doers, remove any barriers, and provide expertise and incentives. As a result, the region now has private nurseries, hatcheries, and restoration projects that are bringing back the turkey, trumpeter swan, Atlantic salmon, and elk, and the native trees, shrubs, and wildflowers. Regulations like species protection and tree-cutting bylaws help, but it is financial incentives, such as untaxing nature, that are the most positive influences. In Ontario and Quebec, for example, the private owners of woodlands, wetlands, and significant natural areas can reduce their property taxes in exchange for keeping their lands natural: small steps toward a full recognition of nature's contribution to society.[114]

The magnificence of our ancient woodlands will never be seen again. The best of our remaining woods may well remain in place, and some may look good in another hundred years, but most of them will just continue to get cut every decade or so. Quantitatively, however, we are more than holding our own. For every acre of woodland or wetland lost these days, there is more than an acre established, some assisted and some not. We are gaining forest cover, partly the result of public policy but more so the consequence of shrinking farms and of alternative fuels and building materials. Slowly and volumetrically, the region is growing a new woodland heritage.

There are unsung heroes. The Krugs of Bruce County, Ontario, were famous for their furniture, and Bruce Krug was responsible for their bushlots and for supplying their sawmills. He and his brother Howard were keen naturalists and decided early on to go gentle on their own woods and to plant their open fields. The Kinghurst forest, about seven hundred and fifty acres, had been in their family since the 1880s. They cut it selectively until the 1920s and, during the Second World War, let its rock elm go to the navy. About two hundred trees were taken after a bout of tent caterpillars in the 1970s. For all that, it is still one of the finest older-growth forests in southern Ontario, and the Krugs donated it to Ontario Nature in 1998. Bruce's direction was, "Just leave it alone."[115]

Our own bush in Mono was worked far too hard for far too long. The cattle did the most damage. When we came, there was not a seedling left. Or a single plant of the lily family, or toothwort, or yew. The springs were deep wallows. Now it has been fenced and left alone for thirty years. The saplings are thick again and the springs have healed. The yellow birch is back and the butternut is spreading. Turkeys have returned and hang around the beech trees, but the beech is now dying and they are looking for other food. We planted thousands of trees, many of them to buffer the old bush, about half of them oak. These are good things. We will let the bush grow free for as long as we can, and thousands of others are doing the same, paying a new respect to the woods.

CHAPTER SEVEN

Taming the Unforested: Prairies, Alvars, Barrens, Cliffs, Bogs, and Fens

When we arrived, the farm in Mono had a perimeter fence of mixed vintage and was grazed to the bone. After a century and a half of hard use, the hills were worn to a summer gold of cemetery spurge and mullein. My work took me to some of the finest natural areas in North America and the contrast was stark. At a Natural Areas Association meeting in Missouri, I bought a bag of seed from a pedigreed prairie nature reserve, and I filled another bag with Ozark acorns. Close to our Mono farmhouse was a particularly bald hilltop and I spilled the seed there and walked away. A fescue took hold, and then side-oats grama and a few oaks. I have added others over the years, to test their hardiness, but the site is too dry and lime-rich. Mono was never prairie country but, it turns out, a surprising extent of Great Lakes country was.

Prairies and oak openings were always part of settler lore south of the lakes. James Fenimore Cooper set his pioneer novels in them, such as *The Prairie* in 1827: "The American prairies ... east of the Mississippi are ... exceedingly fertile ... They are susceptible of high cultivation, and are fast becoming settled. They abound in Ohio, Michigan, Illinois, and Indiana." In his 1848 book *The Oak Openings*, he described "the beautiful flowery prairies and natural groves of Michigan."[1]

Caleb Atwater wrote about the prairies of western Ohio in the first volume of the *American Journal of Science* in 1818: "To mention all the counties ... where prairies ... are found would be too tedious." He attributed them to the wet soils of Ohio's old lakebed flats but he also accepted that arid soils, grazing, and fires set by Natives helped explain them elsewhere. It slowly became clear that prairies were the result of multiple factors operating variably in different places, as interpreted as early as 1878 by Asa Gray, the Harvard botanist.[2]

In the 1930s the Ohio State botanist Edgar Transeau applied the term "prairie peninsula" to the remnant grasslands that occurred farther east, ascribing them to the intersection of "thoroughly drained" soils and repeated "pyropyrrhic" fires set by Natives. He also pointed out that the climate south of the lakes – dry summers and snow-free winters – was the same on the north side of the lakes, where there were prairie remnants. Canadian botanist John Macoun had offered one such description in 1893: "At the southern end of Sandwich [Windsor] a garden of rarities was entered ... The most interesting were *Liatris spicata, Lythrum alatum, Aletris farinosa, Polygala incarnata, Hypoxis hirsuta, Ludwigia alternifolia, Veronicastrum virginicum,* and at least a dozen others." The prairie plants were easy clues.[3]

In spite of this, north of the lakes, the prairie story was mute for a long time. Thomas Gibson, an Ontario deputy minister, was emphatic in his 1897 *Handbook of Canada*: "There are no prairies in Ontario." Museum specimens of prairie plants, like those along the Grand River, were dismissed as waifs that had fallen from railcars. It was common knowledge that "a squirrel could have run all the way from Windsor to Montreal in the trees," and a centennial history of Ontario's "lands and forests" written in 1967 would make no mention of prairies. In 2008 historian Cole Harris would still write that southern Ontario was "almost completely forested" before settlement.[4]

In the late 1960s the northern prairies started to surface again. The provincial ecologist Angus Hills got a call from a colleague saying that the Morton Salt Company in Windsor had some surplus land that he should have a look at. Hills contacted University of Toronto ecologist Paul Maycock and together they headed for Windsor, to a neighbourhood called Ojibway. There they stepped into the middle of a superb (and previously unrecognized) seven-foot-tall prairie, with old open-grown oaks scattered about. The Nature Conservancy of Canada and the province of Ontario purchased two hundred acres of it and, since then, the Ojibway Prairie Nature Reserve has expanded to a stunning six hundred acres in the heart of Windsor.[5]

The Morton family were selling these lands in Windsor – arguably the finest tall grass prairie left in North America – at the same time that the family had pledged, in its hometown of Chicago, to create from scratch and at considerable expense a new prairie at the Morton Arboretum, to experiment with prairie restoration. Maycock's students at the University of Toronto were soon searching out other remnants across Ontario. Wasyl Bakowsky, Don Faber-Langendoen, and others scoured the back roads, rail lines, and old reports, and filled in the map with their finds. They corroborated all the old stories but, to this day, it is still not widely known that prairies were so widespread toward the north and east.[6]

The French called the New World grasslands *prairies*, or meadows, and used the term on the St Lawrence, where it is remembered in places like La Prairie, south of Montreal. The British also left clues in their place names: signposts in Upper Canada included Dover Plains, Fairfield Plain, Plainville, Paris Plains, Raleigh Plains, Oakville, Oakwood, and Oak Heights. In New York State, the hamlet of Seneca Castle sits just down from Oak Corners. West of the Genesee, where the oak openings took over, and where sassafras, tulip-tree, and magnolia mixed in with the oak, hickory, and chestnut, there are crossroads with names like Oakfield and Oak Orchard.[7]

Where there had been Native nations, there had been grasslands, as far east as the Atlantic seaboard. In Ontario there were prairies from Windsor to Holland Landing and Rice Lake. Prairies and oak woodlands were nature's response to firing and grazing. Natives used fire daily, and, both deliberately and accidentally, they fired the lands around their towns, camps, and trails, and on their hunting grounds. Accounts of eastern prairies written as late as the 1800s, more than a century after forest had begun to encroach, still had them dominating many areas. Sadly, their extreme rarity today means they no longer support their original mammals or birds, but they still function as high-fidelity plant and insect habitats. They are now so small and rare that entire populations – for example, of the dependent Karner blue and frosted elfin butterflies – can be extirpated through the loss of a single site. Extinction comes easy when you are rare.[8]

The Great Lakes country was once as diverse as any temperate place on Earth, and a scan of its special places, like its prairies, cliffs, and wetlands, cannot help but remind us, as we decry the loss of biological diversity elsewhere, just what our signature nature was, and what we did with it.

Early Records of Unforested Uplands

Champlain used the word *prairie* in his earliest reports. In 1604 he described the "belles prairies" of Maine's Penobscot Bay and reported the meadows scattered with oak far up the Penobscot River, where "one would think the oaks had been planted." He named "la rivière des Prairies," on the north side of Montreal Island, after his colleague Sieur des Prairies, but it could just as well have been for its "abundant" and "vast" *prairies*. The Jesuit place name "La Prairie" is still used for the south shore facing Montreal, and it was from this *plaine* and *prairie* that the priests and traders of New France left for the interior of North America.[9]

The distant interior was, of course, transcendent prairie. Jacques Marquette described the lands west of Lake Michigan in 1670 as "beautiful plains and fields … as far as one can see." And up the Fox River, there were "prairies as far as the eye can reach" and "oak openings." Claude Allouez, coasting along southwest Lake Michigan in 1677, reported its "*grandes prairies*, which extend farther than the eye can reach. Trees are met with from time to time … [as if] planted with design."[10]

In the east, grasslands were an early target for settlers. Pierre Boucher mentions "belles et grandes prairies" in the first paragraph of his 1664 *Histoire naturelle* of New France. There were "fine prairies" near Trois-Rivières and "belles" prairies on the islands and south shore of the St Lawrence. In Iroquoia they were "admirable" in extent, and Huronia was still "almost all cleared," he reported. Boucher chose for his own seigneury the islands east of Montreal, "abounding in fish and game and *prairies*." "Prairie" was code for fine soils, abundant game, immediate pasture, and "few mosquitos," the latter a critical "inconvenience" for settlers.[11]

South of modern Rochester in 1669, the Sulpician Galinée described a Seneca town surrounded by crop fields (*un grand désert*) five miles around and, beyond them, "beautiful, broad *prairies*, on which the grass is as tall as myself … Where there are woods, these are oak plains, so open that one could easily run through them on horseback. This open country, we are told, continues eastward more than a hundred leagues [two hundred miles]. West and south it extends so far that its limit is unknown." He mapped the "grandes prairies" of the Detroit River and, north of the lakes, he walked from Burlington Bay to the Grand River, noting its "prairies seches" (dry prairies) and, near modern Burford, a "great hunting ground [on] *prairies seches*." The Norfolk plain was also open, and the base of Long Point was "prairies … terres excellentes."[12]

The Recollet Hennepin called the corridor between lakes Erie and Huron as "most agreeable and charming … a pleasant champagne [open] country." He wrote effusively about the Detroit and St Clair rivers in 1679. "The banks of the streight are vast meadows, and the prospect is terminated with some hills covered with vineyards, trees bearing good fruit, groves and forests, so well disposed that one would think nature alone could not have made, without the help of art." Baron Lahontan would similarly gush in 1687: "You cannot imagine the pleasant prospect of this straight, and of the little lake [St Clair]." There were untold "quantities of *bêtes fauves* [large game] and turkeys ... in the vast *prairies* [on] the south side of the lake [Erie]."[13]

Cadillac's Detroit project was put into action in 1701 and with him came many families who put down lasting roots. "The banks are so many vast *prairies* ... fringed with long and broad avenues of fruit trees ... You may see assembling in hundreds the shy stag and the timid hind ... the careful turkey ... the golden pheasant [greater prairie-chicken], the quail [bobwhite], the partridge [grouse], the woodcock, the teaming turtle-doves [pigeon] ... The hand of the pitiless mower has never shorn the juicy grass on which the bison of enormous height and size fatten."[14]

This was Cadillac's "earthly paradise" and he sent a hyperbolic report to Paris the next year. "All the surroundings ... are extensive pasture lands, and the grass on them is so high that a man can scarcely be seen in it." In 1749 the military engineer Joseph-Gaspard de Léry wrote that, for the settler, "it is only necessary to plough the land and to cut down some shrubs." In fact, wood was in short supply: "It is necessary to bring [it] some 25 leagues [fifty miles]." Today, the largest prairie left is part of the Walpole Island First Nation, at least two thousand acres. Parts of it are burned every spring and are said to have been burned since Walpole Island was settled in the 1800s. It is the finest tall grass prairie in North America, says ecologist Wasyl Bakowsky, and "one of the highest concentrations of rare species of any place in Canada." Walpole was unceded territory and its "three fires," or three hearths – the Ojibwa, Potawatomi, and Ottawa – maintain their prairie, as well as one of the largest marshes in the region, as part of their heritage.[15]

Patrick McNiff surveyed the area. He was loyalist from New York, an Irishman with survey skills that recommended him to Governor Haldimand. His 1791 map of southwest Ontario reported, from Windsor south to the Canard River, "a sandy barren plain" and, north of Point Pelee, "a sandy ridge producing nothing but a few trees of white oak." Of the Thames River near Chatham, he wrote: "On each side and for a distance of 6 miles upstream were extensive meadows and marshes without any wood except for a few scattered trees ... On the south side ... up to near the forks, the woodland does not extend back ... more than 30 acres ... then commenced a plain." Tiger Dunlop described the area in his *Statistical Sketches*. Upper Canada's southwest was an alluvial plain ribbed with old shore ridges, and "here and there you have an immense prairie, furnishing pasture for more cattle than are likely to graze on them for a century to come." Hardly an acre of it remained for half that long.[16]

Patrick Shirreff, the farm correspondent, headed down the Thames from London in 1833. There were "oak openings ... all the way to Delaware." Later, he said, "we left Chatham [on the Thames] ... and soon reached the plains, two miles north ... and as far as the eye could reach to the westward, destitute of trees, except small spots here and there." He visited again in October. "The plains of Chatham are, beyond all doubt, prairie, extending from Lake St. Clair on both sides of the Thames ... [and] similar to ... the Michigan prairies ... No part of Illinois seems richer. No part of this prairie is cultivated; it is so little above the level of Lake St. Clair that it is doubtful if it can be drained." Today, of course, it is all drained, and the most productive farmland in Canada. Aside from Walpole and Windsor, only a few rail-side prairie remnants persist.[17]

There are even fewer remnants of the oak savanna along the Niagara River. Hennepin described the portage around the falls as "a very fine road, with very little wood, and almost all prairies mingled with some oaks and firs on both banks." Seventy years later, Pehr Kalm visited the brow of the gorge, where there is still a trace of black oak savanna today. So, too, did Jonathan Carver in 1766: the land along the river was "very good ... grass and pasturage." Patrick Campbell would say the same in 1792: "It requires scarce any clearing, there being no more wood upon it than ... for rails, inclosures, and the other necessary purposes of farming." The battle of Queenston Heights in 1812 was fought on open ground, their densest "cover" being "small trees and stunted pines," as described by Major John Richardson."[18]

The French also encountered unforested limestone plains. In 1654 the Jesuit Le Moine, on his return from Onondaga, remarked on the "prairies ravissantes" east of Lake Ontario, in the vicinity of the Salmon River, and the "vast prairies" from there to the upper St Lawrence. These prairie-like habitats are now known as hotspots of plant and insect diversity, and are called alvars, a Baltic term first applied to them by Queen's University botanist Roland Beschel in 1967. As the water levels of the old Great Lakes rose and fell over many millennia, these limestone plains were washed clean of their overburden of glacial sediments. Farmers had little use for them and ran cattle on them. As a result, more alvars are left on the landscape today than their deeper-soiled, tillable cousins, the prairies. There are still remnants of Le Moine's prairies at the Chaumont Barrens. They were identified as unusual natural areas only in the late 1970s when botanists Stanley Smith and Charles Sheviak at the New

York State Museum visited the area and saw the prairie and alvar species there. The Nature Conservancy has since secured more than two thousand acres of this rare ecosystem.[19]

Another such site was found on Lake Erie's Marblehead peninsula in 1890, a bedrock plain that biologists called a "limestone prairie." Edwin Moseley, an educator and naturalist, described it in 1897: "The ... soil is only a few inches or a fraction of an inch deep and consists of partially decomposed vegetation and lime carbonate ... [It] becomes more parched under the summer sun than any spot in Ohio." The site at Lakeside was home to the "lakeside daisy," a beautiful flower growing only on a handful of alvars around the Great Lakes. It is a poster species for conservation because its "type location" on the Marblehead peninsula was quarried down to a single population. The aggregate company Lafarge has since built a new alvar on the floor of their Kellys Island quarry and reintroduced the daisy there. Of the original alvar, only a few acres remain.[20]

Open rocklands were more frequent north of the lakes. In 1761 Alexander Henry canoed from the French River to Sault Ste Marie. He saw the "beautiful plain" at Sault Ste Marie, "covered with luxuriant grass" (and later covered with pineries at Garden River and Kirkwood). What struck him the most, however, were the rocklands, such as the granite barrens along the French River and the flat alvar islands in the North Channel. "The lands everywhere [on] the island of La Cloche are poor," he wrote. They were visually arresting though, and in 1837 Anna Jameson said of La Cloche after a visit there: "Successive ledges of picturesque rocks, all fringed with trees and bushes, and clothed ... with a species of gray lichen nearly a foot deep." They were still just "masses of barren rock" to her, and not "nature's rock gardens" as they are called today. The lichened erratics and pitted surface rocks are now mined and trucked south to adorn urban gardens, an unregulated traffic in some of nature's most perfect miniatures, which leaves behind only scars.[21]

Nearby, on Drummond Island, are Michigan's finest alvars. Thomas McKenney, U.S. Indian Bureau chief, visited them in 1827 but he too was underwhelmed; it was "not possible for anything to be more sterile ... the picture of barrenness ... Yet it is a beautiful place for all." The bureau's survey in 1845 described the alvars as "naked rock with scattering of small trees." Today, the Drummond and Manitoulin islands are the centre of alvar diversity globally. Botanist Judith Jones pieced together the survey records from Manitoulin Island in the 1870s, and concluded: "Almost the entire Lake Huron shore from the middle of the island to the western tip and inland for 2-4 km, was ... 'no soil,' 'barren flat rock,' 'burnt,' or 'stunted timber.' The area that was open in the past was much more extensive than the alvars of today, indicating that many areas have become reforested."[22]

North of Lake Ontario, in 1852, Susanna Moodie visited a limestone plain near Shannonville, which the road from Belleville to Kingston crossed: "The trees are low and far apart, a natural growth of short grass and flowering shrubs giving it very much the appearance of a park. Clumps of butternut and hickory trees form picturesque groups." This was the Salmon River alvar, which is today largely treed with red cedar. A geologist at University College in Toronto, E.J. Chapman, studied these "plains" for a different reason; they "exhibited a polished surface equal to that of plate-glass, with fine striae running across it ... [the] result of ancient glacial action." The debate about glaciation was on the boil just then, and this proof was useful.[23]

Twenty miles south of Shannonville, there were sand barrens on Lake Ontario. The loyalist Susan Greeley wrote about them in the 1800s: "The sandbanks were a curious and interesting tract of land, about twenty-four miles in length ... The soil was a clear white sand ... covered with ... an excellent fruit, called sand cherries ... Continual gathering reduced the production till little could be obtained, and then the cranberry marshes were the resource, and when they were exhausted the wild gooseberries supplied the need ... [Here] Mr. Young came down with his foot directly on a rattlesnake ... Were there rattlesnakes in the country then? Plenty." Today the Sandbanks and Presqu'ile parks preserve some of those wild shores, but without rattlesnakes and with sand cherry uncommon.[24]

South of the Lakes

Unforested habitats always attracted notice. As early as 1654, the Jesuit Le Moine was taken to the salt springs at Onondaga Lake: "We made salt ... of which we carried a sample to Quebec." The salt was highly attractive to pigeons, which the Natives caught in nets, and to rattlesnakes. In 1743 the botanist John Bartram described the same "salt plain" where "the Indians dig holes, about 2 feet deep, [in] which ... they dip their kettles and boil the contents, until the salt remains." The springs were purchased in 1778, and commercial saltworks began in earnest in 1789. In 1792 they were still attracting wildlife, according to Patrick Campbell: "swarms [of] geese, Brants and wild ducks and swans ... [and] deer and other sorts of game." In 1807 the botanist Pursh recorded the salt-water glasswort there, at a distance from its Atlantic range and with no intervening populations, and "the only plant that grew" in the salt springs. The rare salt flora, and species like the glasswort, are now largely gone, but the salt tax levied at the time helped greatly in paying for New York's canals.[25]

At the east end of old Iroquoia lay the Albany pine barrens. Richard Smith saw them in 1769 and commented how they were as "sandy and barren as the desarts of N. Jersey," where he was from, "mere sand bearing pine trees chiefly of the pitch pine." For settlers, he said, the prospect was "forlorn, miserable and unsatisfactory." The barrens had been kept open by burning, and they shrank over time as much in the absence of fire as because of clearance. As early as the 1640s, Van der Donck wrote of the "yearly custom of burning the woods, plains and meadows" and, as late as 1769, Smith would witness the Oneida firing land around their villages. Sand barrens once covered more than two million acres of northeast North America but only a fraction persists, essentially gone now from Cape Cod, Long Island, Constance Bay, Norfolk, Scarborough, and elsewhere, and with large tracts now extant only in New Jersey and Albany.[26]

It was the prairies, however, that were most obvious to visitors. In 1751, in southwest Ohio, the surveyor Christopher Gist would report "vast and beautiful meadows of wild rye, blue grass and clover, full of turkey, deer, elk and buffalo." Closer to Lake Erie, the treeless prairies grew wetter and denser and, in 1796, Judge Jacob Burnett found it almost "impossible to ride" on horseback through the "succession of wet prairies" in Wood County south of Detroit. When he was sixteen, in 1835, Cyrus Bradley travelled the road to Sandusky. "I shall never forget my ride across those gloomy unhealthy prairies which produce nothing but long grass, horned cattle, disease, mosquitoes and rattlesnakes." North-central Ohio was open woods – oak, hickory, beech, and elm – with prairie openings. Westward, the prairies became the matrix, with scattered islands of trees. There were at least three hundred large prairies turned under for farming in Ohio.[27]

David Zeisberger, the Moravian missionary, walked from the Ohio River to the Sandusky late in 1781. "We came ... through the swamp at the head of the Scioto, and into a country altogether different ... [and] nothing but grass, which is so high and long that on horseback a man can hardly see over it ... The land is flat ... [and] rain-water can not run off ... Upon the plain there is no timber, and where there is ... timberland, it is a perfect swamp and morass." Nearing Detroit, he said, "the forest is a fine open forest ... [and] along its borders ... plains, on which nothing but high, long grass grows ... so tough and grassy that our Indians could not work it or plant it; granted ... it could be plowed." In 1810 Thomas Nuttall, the naturalist, also travelled the south shore of Lake Erie; he wrote that "an extensive prairie ... commences near Huron;

and it is here from 8 to 12 miles wide ... [and] from this place to Scioto river," sixty miles away. He described the sight as "astonishing."[28]

In 1819 the botanist John Goldie hiked the south shore of Lake Erie. Near Mercer, Pennsylvania, "I got now in amongst oaks which were generally only a few feet high – so that the country looked as if it had once been cleared ... however I believe that it is yet in its natural state." The next day was the same: "thin of trees with few bushes" but "very productive of a great variety of plants." Goldie still wanted to see a salt spring, so he walked back to the salt springs at Onondaga. "A few miles from the springs," he wrote, "the ground becomes covered with small oaks, and has a sterile appearance." Clearly, oak openings of various kinds persisted in the east.[29]

In New York, east of Tonawanda, Patrick Campbell rode across "a plain of considerable extent, the trees so thin and distant ... that we could see half a mile on all sides." This was 1792 and on each side of the Genesee River were "extensive flats without a tree or shrub ... [and with] upland on each side ... thinly timbered, with small crabs of black and white oak, chestnut and poplar." Four years later, Isaac Weld travelled the same way to the Genesee valley. Again, "the country ... [was] interspersed with open plains of great magnitude, some of them ... fifteen or twenty miles in circumference." He commented on the "buffaloes, elks and other wild graminivorous animals" that had once been "on these plains in the state of New York, but they have all disappeared ... pursued both by the Indians and white people."[30]

Buffalo, or bison, were an iconic prairie species, and these were their most northeastern haunts. Le Moine reported them south of Lake Ontario in 1654 and Lahontan south of Lake Erie in 1687, and other reports had them at the salt springs in upper New York and northern Pennsylvania, and even in the Mohawk, Susquehanna, and Delaware valleys. The last bison east of the Appalachians was killed in 1801 near Lewisburg, Pennsylvania, and in 1825 in West Virginia. They had reached these eastern limits only about 1500 AD, but, with the advent of guns, they were hunted out of all New York, Pennsylvania, and Ohio by 1803.[31]

Travelling west from Detroit, the Scot Patrick Shirreff described the terrain in 1833: "With the exception of about twenty-five miles [of prairie] next to Detroit, [it] was found to consist of oak openings ... The trees are stunted oaks, of about thirty feet in height, and so thinly scattered that a man may ... clear an acre in a day." He visited the "White Pigeon prairie," which was "of many miles extent, [and already] thickly interspersed with good farm-houses and barns." South of Chicago he finally "became fully sensible of the beauty and sublimity of the prairies ... without a tree or object of any kind ... [and] appearing like a sea." While he was in Chicago, "a treaty [was] in progress with the Pottowatamy ... nearly 8000 Indians of all ages assembled." The purpose of the negotiations was to persuade them to vacate Illinois and move west in return for $100,000.[32]

Western Lake Ontario, the Grand, and the Upper Thames

The prairies north of the lakes that were first reported by d'Aillon, Lalemant, and Galinée still dominated a century and a half later. In 1792 the touring Patrick Campbell headed west from Lake Ontario. "Towards the Grand River, the lands are so open as to have scarce a sufficiency of wood for ... farming." Near the Grand, "the plains are very extensive, with a few trees ... so thinly scattered as not to require any clearing." He also took note of other open habitats, such as the barrier beach separating Lake Ontario from Hamilton Bay: "A fine dry beach, five miles long and from two to three hundred yards broad; on this neck there grows very long grass, which the ... inhabitants cut down for hay." That day he visited Joseph Brant, who lived at the north end of the strand and rode his horses on it.[33]

This was the same year Lieutenant Governor Simcoe arrived at Niagara. By then, he had already decided "to establish a capital in the very heart of the country" on the Thames. The year before, in Quebec, he had "found in the surveyor's office an actual survey" of the area. This was Patrick McNiff's map, with its notes about black walnut, basswood, ash, oak, and maple along the Thames and, at the forks, "a very extensive plain .. where has formerly been a large Indian village." While Simcoe acknowledged that "Toronto [was] the best harbour on Lake Ontario & the Long Point the only good road on Lake Erie," he set his heart on a new London on a new Thames River and, in February 1793, he and his party set out for the site. On the way he saw "extensive meadows" along the Grand and, west of it, "fine open plains, said to be frequented by immense herds of deer."[34]

Simcoe chose the forks as his site, described by his wife, Elizabeth, as "a fine dry plain without underwood but abounding in good oak trees." Surveyors called it "open plain" and noted its Native corn fields. In 1807 George Heriot would be more eloquent: "On the east side of the fork ... there is a natural plain ... affording in its present state the appearance of a beautiful park." This was a successful trip and Simcoe immediately ordered the construction of a military road, Dundas Street, from the head of Lake Ontario to his new London.[35]

The road passed through prairie, which no traveller failed to note. Colonel Talbot wrote in 1824: "From the Indian settlement [Brantford] ... to the village of Burford, a distance of nearly 13 miles there is not an acre of woodland to be seen, and yet, in this tract alone, there are at least 100,000 acres ... interspersed with clumps of white oak, pine and poplar-trees." William Pope described it in 1834: "Timber scattered in single trees and small patches in mostly oak. Indians were formerly accustomed to set fire to the brushwood ... [so] grass might more freely grow which furnished plenty of food for deer." The Irish sportsman Thomas Magrath was there in 1832: "The whole country abounds in sunflowers of gigantic size ... and partridges without number – when you whistle, they stop to listen, and are shot." Major John Richardson called the land closer to London "an English park," and Anna Jameson agreed in 1837: "Miles of open ... oak plains ... with a park-like and beautiful effect; and still flowers, flowers everywhere."[36]

Upstream of Brantford, Dumfries Township was described by its surveyor, Adrian Marlett, in 1817 as "open plains" and "white and black oak plains," much of it "burnt." The same area was visited by the traveller Adam Fergusson, who called it "an extensive range of open, grove-like woodland, principally oak." South of Brantford, Captain Alexander Campbell would describe the land as late as 1883 as "plains ... very extensive, a few trees ... and so thinly scattered as not to require any clearing." The frequency of reports of prairie was directly proportional to the perceived benefit of such a landscape to settlers – no clearing and fast crops. Prairies were the preferred destination, and the earliest and easiest converts to European farming. Only traces remain today, along rail lines and dry river crests and bluffs. Side-oats grama grass is one local prairie specialist, found about fifteen years ago on the golf course of the Brantford Golf and Country Club and since then cared for by a fortunate coincidence of interest in maintaining its "rough" with controlled ground fires.[37]

The Toronto Plains and the Carrying Place

The open plains continued eastward. While living at York, Elizabeth Simcoe had a cabin built at Castle Frank overlooking the Don River. "There are large pine plains around it which being without underwood I can ride or walk on ... secure ... from musquitos." The open woods were the result of periodic ground fires and, in November, she noted how the air "smells & feels like smoke." She traced the same open plain west along Lake Ontario to Burlington, where "the hill [to the north] is quite like a park, a fine turf with large oak trees dispersed but no underwood. We walked two miles ... [and it] appears more fit for the reception of inhabitants than any ... I have seen, being already cleared. The Gov finds the country on the banks of the La Tranche [Thames] is like this but ... infinitely more extensive."[38]

In 1793 Lieutenant Governor Simcoe rode on horseback over the Toronto Carrying Place to Lake Simcoe. His party then canoed down the Holland River and met the Missisauga Great Sail and his family at the "landing," another sand plain with a Native encampment. The next day they canoed to another camp at De Grassi Point on the west side of Cook Bay, which Simcoe's assistant, the surveyor Aitkin, wrote up as "oak land." The headman at De Grassi, Keenees or Canise, was "dangerously ill" and Simcoe only paid his respects. They then "hoisted sail" for Kempenfelt Bay, where there was another "Indian encamping ground" and another trail north to Georgian Bay through "open, pine and oak timber." They were travelling the Native highway from the lower to the upper Great Lakes, from one well-used camp to the next, from one sand prairie and oak wood to the next.[39]

They visited De Grassi on their return but Keenees was dead and the camp was in mourning. They begged Simcoe: "We poor Indians do not know what it is, but we hope you will entreat the great spirit to remove the sickness from amongst us." Another infection, barely noted. From the landing, Simcoe took a more direct route back to York, acting on the advice of Old Sail, and it was this road that he ordered Augustus Jones to survey and the Queen's Rangers to build. Yonge Street, named for the British minister of war, would follow a straight line from York to the Native camp on the Holland Landing prairie. Simcoe ordered it surveyed as another back-up capital, a decision that William Graves explained in 1820: "The govt. is desirous of having that district respectably settled as it is in contemplation at some future time to erect the seat of government on the borders of the lake [Simcoe], the present [York] being too near the enemies frontier" (Fig. 19).[40]

Later observers would tell us more about these sites. De Grassi Point was surveyed in 1820 by Richard Birdsall, who noted "wood r.[ed] oak and popple [poplar]." He called it "Grasses point." Another survey had it as "oak plains all grown over by grasses." The botanical evidence – its prairie species – persisted, under the care of the family of Edmund Walker, the Canadian banker and intellectual who bought it in 1890. His son Edmund, the University of Toronto entomologist, grew up summering at De Grassi and used it as his point of reference for describing how, by 1957, a number of grasshopper species that had occupied open sandy habitats had disappeared while other southern grasshoppers had come in, offering "evidence of a general rising of temperature." What is left of the De Grassi prairie is still stewarded by the current generations of the family.[41]

More is known about Holland Landing and its prairie. Samuel Wilmot surveyed it in 1811; the line of Yonge Street north of the east branch of the Holland River led into "open norway [red] pine planes" all the way north past the landing. In 1829 Mary O'Brien road on horseback up Yonge Street and was overtaken by the superintendent of Indian affairs, who invited her to accompany him to the landing, where he would "issue the annual payments to the Indians. We breakfasted with the official party and immediately after walked on to the scene of action about three miles farther. Our walk was chiefly over sandy plains, producing little higher than a few stunted pines."[42]

John Goldie, the Glasgow botanist, had an eye for such habitats. In 1819 he was delayed at York because his luggage had not been forwarded on the schooner from Kingston as planned. While waiting, he walked up Yonge Street to Holland Landing. "June 27. Having gone on slowly I arrived at what is called the upper Landing Place ... a spot very interesting for the botanist – day fair, ther[mometer] 91 ... [July 4.] Since I came here I have seen a number of rare plants ... There are a species of *Asclepias* with orange flowers very handsome, a species of *Euphorbium* with white flowers, a *Ranunculus*, together with some others which were not in flower, that I had never seen before." These were prairie plants, and Holland Landing proved to be the "type" location, the first discovery anywhere, of the prairie buttercup, a common *Ranunculus* of North American prairies. (In a spring-fed fen in a river meander, Goldie discovered the linear-leaved sundew, a tiny, acid-loving, carnivorous plant. And nearby was the hairy honeysuckle, a third species new to science.)[43]

The historian Andrew Hunter summarized the site's importance. "The open space referred to by [John] Galt and other early writers was used as a camping-ground by the early Indians and fur-traders. Here could be seen encamped at all seasons of the year large numbers of Indians, often from very remote districts of the upper lakes ... for the purpose of bartering their furs at Holland Landing ... On one occasion the writer's [Hunter's] grandfather counted no less than thirty wigwams of the larger kind clustered on the commons adjoining the Landing."[44]

The prairie at the landing stayed in public ownership, a by-product of its survey as a "seat of government." It faded from memory, and in 1975 it was loaned to an energetic scout pack for the purpose of planting pine trees, which throttled out the prairie. It was rediscovered in 1980 by botanist Tony Reznicek, and recommendations were tabled and approved to clear the pine and its duff. Test clearings were made, consultations undertaken, and regulations put in place for a provincial nature reserve. But the pine is still there, on a historic Native site and prairie. One of its true rarities was eastern Canada's only occurrence of the prairie sand cherry, likely brought there by the Natives and likely now gone as well.[45]

John Goldie had studied the New Jersey sand barrens in 1817, and that was the measure against which he compared other sand plains, such as the one he crossed from Scarborough to York in 1819. "The vegetable productions here," he wrote, are "similar to what they are in New Jersey." In general, he said, the land around York is "very dry and sandy," and "after leaving York [west, towards High Park] you come into a sandy pine barren ... This as good a botanical spot as any that I ever was in." This was great praise, coming from Goldie.[46]

The Toronto sand plain was open oak and pine savanna, and so too were some of the lands toward the north. For example, the lands in Markham settled by the German Company in 1794 were "open white oak woods." In 1829 Mary O'Brien travelled the area west of Yonge Street, "leaving the York [Mill] road to traverse a plain covered with a stunted growth of pine and oak till we entered Dundas Street at the Humber." In the 1830s, Lieutenant Governor Francis Bond Head could ride his horse daily "through the pine forest and then across the Humber plains." Kathleen Lizars described the Humber plains in 1913: "A stunted growth of gnarled oaks ... dwarf cherry, sassafras and flowering shrubs rose from a ground covered with strawberry and a profusion of flowers ... [and] the startling orange lily and the masses of perennial lupine."[47]

In 1912 the Group of Seven artist J.E.H. MacDonald painted *Spring Breezes, High Park,* with its sentinel black oaks standing guard over fields of blue lupines in Toronto's High Park. In the same era, women wrote in their diaries about cutting armfuls of wood lilies in the park (Fig. 20). Starting in the 1920s, High Park was drenched in herbicides and converted to lawn. Recreation was king and the lawnmower the king's army. Before long, only a handful of lupines were left, and the wood lily was gone. The Karner blue butterfly, totally dependent on the lupine, disappeared from the park soon after.[48]

It was not until the 1970s that attention was again paid to the natural heritage of High Park. By then, fifty-four species of native plants, and six butterflies and dragonflies, had been extirpated from it, most of them prairie species. The black oak were not regenerating because of the high numbers of urban squirrels stripping them of acorns. A few steep slopes had been spared, however, and I remember sending an advisory to the city in 1987, on behalf of the province's Ministry of Natural Resources, that the park's prairie remnants warranted recognition as an "area of natural and scientific interest." The city lawyers took offence but the park staff did not, and initiated a new park master plan. Steve Varga, ecologist for the ministry, updated the park inventory and recommended restoring the site by methods like stopping the mowing, removing the exotics and shrubs, and bringing back ground fires. Varga had mapped the historic prairies stretching from the Rouge in the east to Hamilton, and there was no doubt of its modern rarity.[49]

Even framed as a revised park plan, city council was not interested, so we conspired to take advantage of Toronto's world-class-city complex. We brought in Steve Apfelbaum, an American expert on prairies, who could speak to how Chicago ran its spring burns for its urban prairies. He repeated all the same recommendations, and council approval was promptly received. The first modest ground fire was lit in March 1997 – it was a decided anticlimax for the media – and over the years since, the burns have grown larger and the prairie has started to recover. The burns are now just part of living with nature in the city. The park still has a million visitors a year but the lupines are coming back and the wood lily has emerged again. Restoration of a hundred acres of oak savanna is now a possibility and there is hope the Karner blue butterfly may one day be brought back to the park's lupines, but that will be decades off, if ever.[50]

Tony Reznicek has argued that the High Park and Humber prairies, the Holland Landing prairie, and the other sites like De Grassi Point, Kempenfelt Bay, Willow Creek and elsewhere may well date back to the Hypsithermal warm period some five thousand years ago, and that they were kept open subsequently by regular use and by periodic burns to clear away the brush and the camp debris and keep down the mosquitoes. By such means did many of the northeastern-most of North America's prairies, savannas, and pineries remain open, unforested and special places.[51]

Norfolk and Long Point Country

Norfolk is one of the longest settled parts of the north shore of Lake Erie and it has a special appeal as Canada's deep rural south. It was "belles prairies" when first noted by Galinée in 1669, and "open woods" when described by Elizabeth Simcoe more than a century later. In the same year, 1795, the surveyor William Chewett visited Long Point, Norfolk's southern tip and the longest freshwater peninsula in the world. "Long Point," he said, "from the eastern extremity, for five miles ... is formed of low, narrow ridges of sand hills ... [of] scrubby cedar, juniper, willow and small scrubby pine ... Eight miles farther to the west, the sand hills are higher, in narrow ridges and ponds of water between them, the timber is small scrubby cedar, juniper, willow, small basswood, small pines and innumerable quantities of the sand cherry ... Four miles farther to the west ... the timber is small white oak, a larger sort of pine, basswood and elm."[52]

Long Point and Turkey Point are the lakeside extremities of an ancient delta. Like the Albany sand plain, the delta was built by postglacial meltwaters, in this case flowing off the Ontario Island to the north, dumping out sandy sediments where they hit the quiet waters of proto-Lake Erie. The funnel-shaped delta starts north of Brantford and broadens south to the size of a county. Once the lake levels receded, the winds blew up parabolic dunes in some places and eroded deep blowouts in others. Scrub oak savanna established itself by 6500 BP and later, as the climate cooled and moistened, ground fires kept it open. Natives, who likely numbered in the thousands in 1600, were gone fifty years later and early visitors like Galinée saw very few. Today, the Long Point World Biosphere Reserve, the point and its adjacent sand plain, supports the largest forests in Ontario's deep south and its largest concentration of threatened species.[53]

However, it was not forest in 1650, or when the settlers came. William Hambly surveyed Norfolk in 1795: Walsingham Township, to the west, had "uneven and scrubbed timber, chiefly oak and small pines" and, farther inland, "oak plains." There were "level sandy pinery" and "oak and chestnut timber." Lieutenant Governor Simcoe appreciated it for the strategic naval importance of Long Point and its inner bay, and in 1795 he chose a site overlooking the bay, Charlotteville, as capital of the district of London. On a sketch of Turkey Point he wrote of "white oak plains extending to the River Thames." In 1807 George Heriot stated that "the townships of Woodhouse and Charlotteville ... [were] thinly timbered ... [and] cultivation is facilitated from the want of underwood."[54]

Mahlon Burwell surveyed the Talbot Road through Norfolk in 1809. He was instructed to note "particularly the white and yellow [red] pine fit or not fit for masting," which meant trees more or less than "3 ft diam." He found some "beech, maple and chestnut" but, overall, it was "small pine with sassafras," "white oak and hazle," and "open sandy plain." On a township transect, he found only four places with white pine more than 2.5 feet in diameter. Doctor John Howison visited in 1821. "The forests dwindled ... and natural groves and copses met the eye in their stead ... It may be cropped without cutting down a single tree." The land was "watered by pure, transparent and never-failing streams," he wrote. "Partridges spring from the copses and deer often bound across the path. Immense flocks of the passenger ... pigeon frequent [the area]."[55]

William Pope walked the sand plains southeast of St Thomas in 1834. "The hot sand ... penetrated through the soles of my boots ... the most miserable poor land I ever saw." However, he came back in 1842 and wrote, "The oak plains appear to be pretty much settled about here – not very arduous clearing this kind of land." Overall, he liked "the situation but not the soil. These oak openings or plains ... are much the prettiest parts of the country ... [But] locusts and grasshoppers ... ravage ... the sandy dry soils ... [and] the oak plains." Due diligence completed, he settled in 1859 near Port Ryerse.[56]

Pope described the sand plain north toward Simcoe: "Oak plains, exceeding fertile when first cleared ... [but] I should imagine very soon exhausted." The geographer David Wood has noted the suspicion with which some settlers viewed the "plains," because an absence of trees had meant sterility in their home countries. Some emigration guides even said so, and used the New Jersey and Albany pine barrens as examples. Far outweighing this, however, was the convenience of land that could be plowed directly, which was well understood by those with local experience.[57]

Notwithstanding the original open conditions in Norfolk, a hundred and fifty years of wilding yielded a great stock of merchantable timber. "One tulip tree near Kingsville yielded six thousand board feet of lumber. Chestnut trees have also been known to equal this. One thousand pipestaves have been made from one oak tree. A giant walnut in Metcalf ... measured thirty-six feet in circumference." The timber was shipped across the lake to American markets, and the cutting and slash fires helped some parts of Norfolk retain its open character into the late 1800s.[58]

In 1908 E.J. Zavitz, the pioneer of farm forestry, would call it "waste land." His crew mapped the "scrub oak with scattering white pine" and its prairie indicators, the dwarf chinquapin oak, New Jersey tea, and blue lupine. They set up Ontario's first government tree nursery and then proceeded to blanket those areas in pine, a plantation program that took decades for biologists to recognize for what it was – in the words of Ontario Wildlife Director Doug Clarke, a "cult of the little pine." Only fragments of old Norfolk survived. A recent survey by ecologists Bill Draper and Mary Gartshore showed that the sites Zavitz planted down to pine once supported at least five endangered or threatened plants, seven animals, and dozens of other rarities.[59]

Zavitz viewed the plantations differently. "These plains have lain waste for decades, and the 1500 acres [his first project] ... will be deployed with the dual aim of reforesting and improving that section which for years has been an eyesore and general drawback in the progress of the district." He acknowledged that "the scrub oak ... gives protection to the soil and improves it by adding a leaf litter," but pines could do just as well. A major investment in tree planting began, including even a Scotch Pine Experimental Group, which imported Scots pine and set the stage for Ontario to have more serious infestations of that species than anywhere in North America. This was, however, the temper of the time. Now, places like the Pinery at Grand Bend, the great sand-dune park on Lake Huron, are faced with the task of removing the planted pines that throttled the lupines, butterflies, and prairies. The hope is that, when the pine blanket is lifted, it might still be possible to reignite the dormant native habitat.[60]

The Rice Lake Plain and Peterborough

North and east, the prairies were smaller. One exception was the west end of the Oak Ridges around Rice Lake. In 1832 Catharine Traill rode north across the Rice Lake plain. "We now ascended the plains – a fine elevation of land – for many miles scantily clothed with oaks, and ... covered by large tracts of ... the finest pasture ... Exquisite flowers and shrubs adorn these plains ... The trees, too, though inferior in size ... are more picturesque ... giving a sort of park-like appearance." The "prevailing opinion," she said, was that "grazing and dairy farms" were its destined use. Five years earlier, the surveyor John Smith had reached the same conclusion: it was "capable of cultivation; but from a want of wood and water, it ... would answer best for sheep-walks." Settlers took up the land quickly, however, knowing that fire, rather than sterility, explained its open condition. Patrick Shirreff wrote that the "thinly scattered oak ... [and] stunted underwood ... [seemed] external indications of extreme sterility; but farther experience enables me to say, the appearance of the plaines is ... [due] to the herbage being annually burned."[61]

Catharine Traill raised seven children and wrote when she could, weaving her beloved plains into her stories, such as one in 1841 about a lost child: "The soil is sandy [and] thinly wooded; while the ground is covered with ... the most brilliant wild flowers, and occasional beds of blueberries and wild strawberries; [and] thickets of brush, frequently interspersed." They moved to the south shore of Rice Lake in 1849, to a home called "Oakland," and she wrote in 1852 about how things had changed in twenty years: "It was regarded as utterly unfitted for cultivation ... [and now] the plains are settled in every direction, the despised, sandy desert has become a fruitful garden." Her 1885 *Studies of Plant Life in Canada*, written in her eighties, made frequent reference to the Rice Lake plain. By then, she had not lived there for more than twenty-five years, having left after Oakland burned to the ground. Yet she wrote with nostalgia about her former prairie acquaintances, themselves the product of fire, the "azure lupines ... the splendid painted cup ... the curious yellow moccasin flower." By 1990, the blue lupine was down to a single clump or two; her painted cup was gone and her yellow moccasin a rarity.[62]

Traill recorded details. "The sand cherry abounds ... It is the smallest of the wild cherries and is far more palatable than the fruits of some of the larger trees of the genus. So eagerly is the fruit sought for by the pigeons and partridges that it is difficult to obtain any." Paul Catling, the University of Ottawa botanist, argues that the demise of passenger pigeons and the decline of partridges, both of them distribution agents for fruit, triggered the collapse of once-abundant species like sand cherry, which is now essentially gone from the Rice Lake area. Traill was philosophic: "The progress of civilization sweeps the fair ornaments from the soil. What the lover of the country loses of the beautiful is gained by the farmer in the increase of the useful, and so it must be." Unforested land ready to plow was, as she put it, "a drug in the land market."[63]

The extent of the Rice Lake plain was measured by Traill's brother Sam Strickland, when he crossed it in 1826, as "nearly twenty miles along the south shore." In the 1980s Paul Catling and friends searched the Rice Lake plain for any prairie plants, focusing on the sandiest soils at the highest elevations, which cover six hundred and fifty square miles. Catling concluded that most of that area had been prairie supporting something in the order of a single mature tree per acre but, by 1860, less than thirty years after Traill first saw it, only remnants remained. Even fewer are left today. One of them is on the Missisauga Alderville First Nation. It was surveyed in 1835 by Frederick Rubidge, who described it as "plains ... oak & pine" and "poor land, burnt pine," where the "plains end." The residents of Alderville are now restoring the black oak savanna, collecting and growing out seed to expand it. They have burned it to stimulate its dormant seed banks, knock back the shrubs, and provide a rare glimpse of the old Rice Lake plain.[64]

The site of the town of Peterborough was first called Scott's Plain, and Traill described it as an "elevated plain ... a beautiful natural park." Strickland described how the Natives assembled there to receive their annual payments in the late 1820s: "The place ... had been for years their favourite camping ground. Several hundred acres of open plain were dotted here and there with clumps of oak and pine. In the spring ... [it was] gay with wild flowers. Later ... the cardinal-plant, lobelia, lupin and tiger-lily ... adorn [it]." By 1884, what was left was filling in, "a dense growth of huckleberry bushes interspersed with a few pines," wrote historian C. Pelham Mulvaney in 1884. Like other eastern prairies on Native sites, it would stay open only as long as it had the occasional firing.[65]

The extent of habitat loss in the region's lowlands was remarkable, such as the 70 per cent loss of wetlands and 94 per cent of upland woodlands. These losses, however, were dwarfed by the special efforts made by settlers to occupy its grasslands. The native prairies and savannas of eastern North America were so uniformly easy for settlers to plow and drain that there were soon few traces of them left. In the U.S. Midwest (including Ohio and Michigan), it is calculated that the present landscape supports less than 0.2 per cent of its original tall grass prairie and less than 0.02 per cent of its oak savanna. Catling puts that figure at less than 0.1 per cent on the Rice Lake Plain – likely a generous figure for Ontario as a whole.[66]

Interior Alvars

Early visitors noticed the limestone plains around the Great Lakes shores but their interior counterparts were only encountered later. Surveyors were unsure of what to call them. They had only a cursory knowledge of geology and stone was not what they were looking for in places like Carden, northeast of Lake Simcoe. They had no way of knowing that the upper Great Lakes had once drained east across Carden through the Kirkfield outlet, and that the massive volumes of water had washed away the glacial sediments, leaving only rock. Biologists now call them alvars.

John Roche knew he was seeing something different when he surveyed Carden in 1858. Overall, he wrote, Carden was "a close thicket of brushwood and a great deal of swamp." The swamp was "tamarac and spruce" and the upland was "flat limestone rock." He mapped a distinct "plain" of "stratified limestone rock covered with a depth of soil varying from three inches to two feet." In one place there were grasses dense enough to map as "prairie." Off the plain there was a little "maple, elm and hemlock, mixed with spruce," some of it burned.[67]

Today, the Carden alvar is Ontario's second most popular birding destination. It is called by some the Serengeti of the Great Lakes because of its open country, big skies, and intriguing wildlife, which includes the endangered loggerhead shrike. The original alvar farmers were ranchers, and cattle grazing replaced the fire that had kept the alvar unforested. Since 2003 the Nature Conservancy of Canada has purchased more than six thousand acres of the Carden alvar, working closely with birding groups and the Couchiching Conservancy. Nature festivals, trails, signs, pull-overs, and wandering birders have all arrived in the past twenty years.

There are other limestone plains in eastern Ontario. The Shannonville alvar was noticed early because the main road and railway went through it, but others, like the Burnt Lands alvar twenty miles west of Ottawa, went unnoticed, even though it was thousands of acres in size. It got its name from the 1870 fire that raged from Arnprior to Gloucester. The fire's impact lasted longest here because its conifers, aspen, and birch were so flammable and its soils so thin. Settlement was attempted but farming was not feasible. Ottawa botanists began collecting at the site in the 1930s, starting with a few rare grasses. Others soon followed. Part of the alvar is owned by Canada's Department of National Defence, and in 1960 it was cut and burned again, demonstrably rejuvenating it.[68]

The limestone plains on the Bruce peninsula were similarly overlooked. The surveyor John Stoughton Dennis mapped its interior in 1855 and had little to say: "Ground rocky ... & very rough, no soil. Timber small & scrubby, cedar, balsam, Norway [red] pine, spruce & tamarack." The interior near the Crane River was "rocky, barren & level," and with the same species. South, in Lindsay, he noted the same: "Scrub on ... flat rock." The lowlands were "cedar swamp." He made careful note of the rare good timber he saw, as his survey instructions required.[69]

Modern botanists used the same terms but they mean them as compliments, as when G. Ledyard Stebbins in 1933 called the northern Bruce a "burned-over limestone barrens of a most desolate nature ... hopelessly dry." Natural wildfire had kept the alvars open, and fires became epidemic during the logging period. They scorched the Bruce and, even in the 1990s, Steve Varga would note the "fire-scarred dead wood and stumps" still common on the limestone flats. Today, the Bruce, Manitoulin, and Carden are global hotspots for alvars. They are internationally recognized as rare ecosystems occurring on an equally rare geology – freshwater limestone plains. However, they are small even here; 4,500 acres at eight sites on the Bruce, 12,000 acres at twelve sites on the Manitoulin islands, 5,500 acres at thirty sites in Michigan, and 10,000 acres at Carden. Alvars are an acquired taste, like cliffs.

They are old-growth in miniature, the beneficiaries of how useless they were to humans – and how special as a result.[70]

Cliffs

The Great Lakes below Superior are wrapped around a backbone of Niagara Escarpment, the cliff edge of a bedrock basin of limestone, sandstone, and shale laid down in an ancient sea hundreds of millions of years ago. Lake Michigan lies on the flat plain above the raised edge of its western escarpment, and the cliffs on Green Bay would have looked familiar to the French explorers who arrived there after canoeing along the North Channel of Lake Huron, where the same cliffs overhang the waters. Lake Michigan spills into Lake Huron through the complicated terrain of the Straits of Mackinac, and Huron's North Channel and Georgian Bay are cliff-bound on one side like Green Bay. All the lakes above Lake Ontario drain over the cliff at Niagara Falls, and Lake Ontario itself is framed by cliffs to the south and west.

South of Lake Ontario, the bedrock was sculpted into the Finger Lakes valleys by the same forces of ice and water that eroded the valleys on the Bruce peninsula, most of them half drowned under Georgian Bay. All of the escarpment valleys are rimmed with cliffs. The surveyor Dennis, in 1855, mapped the western Georgian Bay coast: all "limestone cliffs," "rock," and "shingle." Where he could see the clifftops, he made out a trace of "small cedar, tamarack, balsam & pine," and farther north, where the cliffs dip into the water, only "very small cedar, balsam & tamarack."[71]

In 1988 Doug Larson at the University of Guelph was counting the annual growth rings of a dead escarpment cedar, and he got a count of four hundred rings. Another had five hundred rings. Out of this grew the Cliff Ecology Research Group and the *Ancient Tree Atlas*. Cedar resists decay and, over the years, Larson's students discovered older and older cedars, eventually finding ones from thirty-five hundred years ago just lying on the talus slopes below the cliffs. Others were underwater, submerged by rising waters in Georgian Bay, and over eighty-five hundred years old.[72]

Slowly, these gnarled bonsai yielded their gerontological secrets. One of the standing dead was found to have laid down 1,567 rings. Peter Kelly and Doug Larson wrote up the personal biographies of ten of the oldest living cedars, all of them more than a thousand years and one of them 1,320 years, the oldest living tree in eastern North America. Larson says, "The most conspicuous and important finding has been that cliffs everywhere represent relict, undisturbed, and perhaps even ancient habitats." The natural processes of succession, growth, and interaction still occur uninterrupted, albeit at scales we are unused to, most of them invisible to the naked eye, like the many species of algae, fungi, and bacteria that live inside the rock itself, aging and colouring it, and operating as their own extreme life forms.[73]

The cliffs are also meccas for ferns. There are thirty-four fern species along the escarpment in Mono, more than anywhere else in Ontario. One of them is the hart's-tongue fern, a rare North American plant with its centre of distribution in Grey County, Ontario, where it was first seen in 1857 at Inglis Falls. It had been discovered fifty years earlier by the botanist Frederick Pursh, when he clambered up the escarpment just outside Syracuse. "I was quit enjoyed," were his words. Hart's-tongue is known from only ninety locations worldwide, twenty in the United States and seventy in Ontario. It is a strict calciphile, a fern growing only on rocks close to limestone cliffs. Where it survived the last glacier, and how it got here, will always be mysteries.[74]

The hart's-tongue is doing well in Mono. When first seen in 1907, Joseph Calvert found only eight plants. Thomas Taylor came back in 1934 and he counted hundreds. Clear-cutting and free-range grazing in the 1800s may have knocked them back, but they have been free to grow since and the recovery has been gratifying, reaching 18,000 individuals in 2013. Another odd species of limestone cliffs is the walking fern and, soon after Ray Lowes proposed a Bruce Trail along the Niagara Escarpment in Ontario, the University of Toronto botanist Jim Soper suggested that "the walking fern might be a good botanical symbol for the Bruce Trail ... [It] is evergreen, which reminds us that the Bruce Trail will be a green belt to be kept ever green."[75]

South in the Appalachians and north on the Shield, there are cliffs of all sizes and aspects almost everywhere. For early travellers, the cliffs and their waterfalls signalled the hard work of a portage, notwithstanding any aesthetic appeal. Scientists studied them only in their extremes. For example, when the Trans-Canada Highway was completed north of Lake Superior in 1961, Soper and Paul Maycock, also of the University of Toronto, were among the first on the road. They went directly to Old Woman Bay, where there is a spectacular cliff rising almost sheer from the water's edge. Here they described the arctic-alpine habitats that the Harvard geologist Louis Agassiz had first noted in 1848. Agassiz was Swiss and knew them well.[76]

These arctic-alpine plants at Old Woman Bay date back to when tundra persisted on the land in front of the Laurentide ice sheet in Wisconsin, the Alleghenies, and the Appalachians. The ice sheet melted back slowly to the north, and the tundra followed as far as Lake Superior, where the glacier paused in its retreat and tundra once again consolidated, from about 13,000 to 11,500 BP. After that, temperatures warmed quickly and the ice sheet collapsed rapidly. Forest rushed in, but there were still raw and unforested niches along the cold, foggy coast of Lake Superior, where trees do not grow and where arctic plants have flourished ever since.[77]

In 1973 Soper invited the New Zealand botanist David Given to join in a more thorough survey of Lake Superior cliffs. Given searched the air photos of the basin and shared his list of cliffs with me. I spent the summer of 1976 visiting some of them. At one site east of the Nipigon River and some distance from the coast, I climbed one of the cliffs straight up. I found a chimney that took me above the trees and the talus, and was promptly attacked by a northern goshawk. I got back down intact and, remarkably, had brought back a handful of a northern goldenrod, the first time it had been found anywhere in the Great Lakes region, and never previously known south of Hudson Bay. Just like that one, the vast majority of cliffs remain elusive and inviting.[78]

Where we have cliffs and talus and rock shores, we seem to be open to their beauty and have protected many of them, such as along the Niagara Escarpment and the Great Lakes coast. It therefore follows that, where we have old rock quarries, for example, we could be adding new cliffs, talus, and lakes to the landscape when the old quarries are worked out, just as we protect our native cliffs and escarpments. Many old quarries, some abandoned now for a century, have already gone native, and many others could do the same.[79]

Swamps, Marshes, Bogs, and Fens

The Great Lakes basin has unrivalled volumes of fresh water, not just in its lakes and rivers but also in its wetlands. The Black Swamp covered an area almost the size of Connecticut along the Maumee River on the old lake plain southwest of Lake Erie. An impenetrable swamp of elm, oak, cottonwood, and sycamore, it was a good ally to Canada during the War of 1812 when armies lost hope in it. In 1825 a forty-mile corduroy road was built across the swamp but it barely helped – the road was so slow that there were thirty-one inns along it, and travellers and innkeepers alike contracted malaria from mosquitoes. The swamp was slowly cleared from 1860 to 1885, wrote Robert Gordon: "The timber merchants brought great gangs of men from Canada" for the job, and cut large quantities of "giant oak, walnut and poplar." This was Ohio's final frontier and it was left to the farmers to construct, by 1920, more than three thousand miles of drainage ditches, creating an invaluable tract of black bottomland soils and incomparable farms.[80]

Of the Holland River Marsh south of Lake Simcoe, the local farmer Samuel Thompson wrote in 1834: "One summer's evening I was travelling on foot ... across the Holland River, a distance of three miles, nearly all marsh, laid with cedar logs placed crosswise to form a passable road. The ... snakes – garter chiefly but a few copperhead and black – glided on to the logs to bask ... in such numbers, that after vainly trying to step across without treading on them, I was fain to take to flight." Others like travel writer Edward Sullivan shipped down the Holland River from the landing: "[It] was only just wide enough to allow of the vessel's passing, and ... consequently the crew pushed the vessel on with long poles. Such a miserable, aguish, fetid swamp I never saw. It is said to swarm with large water-snakes, and is so quaking that even the ripple caused by the passing vessel made it tremble for several hundred yards in every direction." Also from shipboard, the Irish traveller C.H.C. called the river "dull and uninteresting ... Immense tracts of pigmy larch wood prevail, a certain indication of the worst of soils."[81]

William Hambly was the surveyor of the northeast edge of Holland Marsh, and noted in his diary:

> 20 January 1804. Wandering up [down] ... the Holland River not knowing that we had the wrong branch. The weather so extremely cold and stormy, obliged to camp in the marsh and tamarack swamp early ... everyone of the party got their feet and ears frozen.

> 21 January. ... Got assistance ... to bring one of our men which we left laying on the ice [dead].

> 22 January. Opened the line early this morning between East and North Gwillimbury and continued it through cedar and spruce swamp.[82]

In truth, Hambly never made it to the shore of Lake Simcoe at the mouth of the Holland River. As a result, the land there was never sold. Even the official county map of 1928 did not map the shoreline accurately. However, surveyed lots farther inland were sold, drained, and turned under for the lucrative black-soil farming for which the area is famous.

Eventually the marsh became known to naturalists for rarities like Leconte's sparrow, yellow and king rails, black tern, moorhen, and coot.

Richard Saunders, at the University of Toronto, wrote in 1947: "It is a real pity that some considerable part of it cannot be set aside as a nature reserve, for it is unique in this region, an island of northern life, a tamarack sphagnum bog." Saunders was ahead of his time and, as late as 1973, agency staff were still calling it a "water-logged floating mat" that should be "pot-holed with ... explosives to extend the open water" and lure waterfowl for hunters.[83]

Words like marsh, swamp, bog, and fen had been in the English language for centuries but they were not applied consistently in North America until scientists began to settle on their use in the 1970s. Europeans had studied them for generations. Marshes are the dense beds of sedges, reeds, or shrubs standing in rich waters. Swamps are high-octane forest or thicket wetlands, while bogs are nutrient- and species-poor peatlands. Fens are different again – peatlands with flowing waters, rich in species and famous for orchids and carnivorous plants. Each of them is distinct.[84]

In 1978 the farmer beside the unsold land at the mouth of the Holland River (which Hambly had failed to survey) started to ditch and drain it – to grow carrots. I knew the site and started a study of it in 1981 with biologist Kathy Lindsay. The lab at the Ontario Geological Survey analyzed our samples, which helped immensely. Long ago, the river mouth had been dry ground but it had been flooded by rising lake levels, and a peatland slowly accumulated, only a yard deep at the river but six yards deep at its east shore. Starting at the river, our site transect crossed the full range of wetlands in less than 1,200 yards; from shore marsh (pH 7.0), through fen (pH 6.2) and bog (pH 4.8), and back through thicket swamp (pH 6.1) to the lake, we observed a hundred-times difference in acidity across the peninsula and back. Nowhere else in the region was there such a concentrated package of wetland types, and such a steep gradient of change in water and peat chemistry.[85]

Bogs and fens are rare ecosystems around the lower Great Lakes, notwithstanding their abundance farther north. Overall, 30 per cent of the wetlands remain but less than 0.5 per cent of them are fens, and less than 0.5 per cent bogs. There are only four sites in southern Ontario where bog and fen occur together, and one of them is at the Holland River. Still standing regal at the site is the rare white prairie fringed-orchid, restricted to fens and wet prairies and known from only thirteen sites in Canada and sixty in the United States. Its flowers have the longest nectar spur of any native orchid, and can be pollinated only by a nocturnal hawk or sphinx moth. Fred Case, the distinguished expert on orchids, called it the "most severely endangered orchid" in Great Lakes country. To this day, the Holland River site remains unprotected, and its orchids at risk.[86]

The next closest population of white prairie fringed-orchid is at Minesing Swamp, west of Lake Simcoe in a basin along the Nottawasaga River. Samuel Thompson settled nearby in the early 1830s, "close to a large cedar swamp." Minesing is still one of the largest spring-flooded swamps in the region, surrounding the largest fen in southern Ontario. It fills a deep embayment of old Lake Algonquin, and its fen is fed by cold water flowing out of the old lake bluff. The perpetual flow sustains a fen full of orchids and carnivorous plants. One of the more transcendent rites of spring is to canoe Minesing Swamp in full flood, beyond the hackberry levees into the deep clear waters in the fen, where you can see beneath your canoe, under several feet of water, crystal red pitcher plants.[87]

To the south was the Innisifil Creek Swamp, more typical of the cedar swamps that once criss-crossed the lowlands. These were the last refuges for wildlife and young Richard Rorke spent long days hunting and trapping in the swamp between 1824 and 1848. "No moment ... can compare with a large cedar swamp for loneliness, solitude and living desolation. Your route, if you happen to know it, is impeded by fallen timber [and an] underwood of young cedars ...Timber standing at all angles ... Climb a tree and it is one universal sea of swamp ... [with] no other timber but cedars in sight, with the exception perhaps of a grove of tamarack."[88]

Drainage and other improvements have left little of Innisfil Swamp, but other swamps still stand defiant and unfrequented. One such swamp, the Greenock Swamp, lies in the heart of the Huron Tract. The area was surveyed by Allan Park Brough in 1848. He was directed to lay out a road straight from Durham to Lake Huron but, to this day, there is still a major jog in it. He wrote: "Previous to deciding upon the route for the Durham road in the township of Greenock, I explored [it] ... and found it to be almost continuous swamp, the extent of which was not fully ascertained; but it ... [is] more than 25,000 acres." Drained around its edges, about twenty thousand acres still remain, one of the few areas in Ontario's deep south wild enough to support badgers.[89]

The Bruce peninsula has attracted naturalists for more than a century, no part of it more so than its Lake Huron shores. Sherwood Fox called the Bruce "the great North American rendezvous of plants" and many botanists puzzled over how to explain such a mixed buffet from all points of the compass. John Macoun visited in 1871 and then again in 1874, 1890, and 1901.

G. Ledyard Stebbins visited in 1933 and Merritt Fernald from Harvard in 1934. The prevailing opinion was that the raw, wet limestone substrates, recently revealed above lake level and cooled by Lake Huron, were particularly receptive to all comers, including the odd species from the Rocky Mountains. Unfortunately, cottagers equally coveted the shores of Lake Huron. In 1962 Malcolm "Mac" Kirk, the Owen Sound naturalist, saw that Dorcas Bay was slated for development and he bought, for a dollar, a three-month option to purchase it. Then he turned up at the annual meeting of the Federation of Ontario Naturalists and told them what he had done, triggering a campaign to buy its first nature reserve. Journalist Fred Bodsworth publicized the bay's plight in *Maclean's* magazine, in an article titled the "Battle of the Bulldozer," and the funds were raised. Since then, it has been a close-run battle for the Huron shore. Conservation is still on the losing end but there are today a dozen small nature reserves along the Huron shore of the Bruce.[90]

The early guides advertised the great marshes of the Great Lakes-St Lawrence. Henry Small, in his *Canadian Handbook*, wrote about marshes and hunting as if they were synonymous, and he had great things to say about Lac Saint-Pierre, Rice Lake, Holland Marsh, Burlington Bay, and Long Point. William Pope had a hunting camp on Long Point, which he described in the 1840s: "The marshes ... are inhabited by immense flocks of wild fowl which resort here during the autumn to feed on the plentiful and nutritious seed of the wild rice. There are swans, geese and such prodigious quantities of ducks as to blacken the water when they settle down ... but I am told by old settlers here that they are not so numerous as they were formerly, and that is not to be wondered at as the warfare carried on against them must ... lessen their numbers." Pope wrote neither for public consumption nor to lure tourists, but he was still full of praise: "There can be no better sport to be had in the world than there may be had at Long Point."[91]

Long Point is the finest sand spit, marsh, and dune complex in the Great Lakes. It once had more than sixty thousand acres of marsh. In the days when there were navies on the lakes, Long Point was strategic and was retained by the crown. However, its tip was twenty miles out into the lake and attracted smugglers, taverns, brothels, and prize fights, more than the government could handle. James Black was sent to survey it in 1853 "with a view to the whole being disposed of at public auction." Sixteen blocks were advertised for sale in 1857 – twice – but no bidders came forward. Finally, David Tisdale, a lawyer in Simcoe, assembled a group of businessmen-sportsmen who bought 15,000 acres in 1866 and established the Long Point Company. By 1871, they controlled all sixteen blocks. They built a clubhouse and cabins in the marsh and manned it with a keeper, whose job it was to rid the place of squatters, market hunters, poachers, and smugglers. Under the keeper's watch there would be no spring duck hunt, and the fall hunt would start on 1 September each year. Licences could be purchased.[92]

In 1979 the Long Point Company donated 8,000 acres of the point and marsh to the Nature Conservancy of Canada, to be cared for by the Canadian Wildlife Service as a National Wildlife Area. The company kept 8,000 acres for safekeeping. In the winter of 1989, 490 of the deer overgrazing the point were culled, and this ushered in a spectacular renewal of habitats. Since the cull, at least twenty plant species have come back, including the white trillium, Solomon's-seal, and several shrubs. At peak migration, more than 10 per cent of the world populations of redhead and canvasback ducks use the Long Point marshes. In the spring, more than half the tundra swans in eastern North America are there. Long Point has many tales to tell, including how private ownership can sometimes avoid the tragedies of the commons, and how robust interventions can sometimes bring positive renewal.[93]

In eastern Ontario, Alfred Bog is another peatland that harbours both bog and fen. As large as a township, it occupies the bed of an old channel that was an ancestor of today's Ottawa River. Its first surveyor, in 1806, was Joseph Fortune. His notes needed interpretation, which Ted Mosquin provided in 1991. Fortune had called areas with trees "swamp" and where there were none "marsh." For bog, he used the term "barren marsh," not having seen one before. Most of the swamp he called "very low land, red spruce timber" but it was black spruce he was seeing, a good indicator of bog. He was doing his best and, after translation, Mosquin calculated that "the total size of the original Alfred bog wetland was about 105 sq. km." or 26,000 acres.

Drainage and farming have eaten away its edges and the Alfred Bog is now down to ten thousand acres. However, the high-domed bog and fen at its centre remain the largest open peatland in southern Ontario. In 1988 and 2002 two tracts were bought from their corporate owners, who gave up on their plans to extract peat. Together with other parcels, the Alfred Bog Nature Reserve is now over seventy-six hundred acres in size. It is boreal wilderness deep in the Canadian south, and home to rarities like the bog elfin butterfly, Fletcher's dragonfly, spotted turtle, white fringed-orchid, and the native rhododendron, rhodora. Incredibly, it is also home to an isolated population of moose.[94]

Across the Great Lakes lowlands, where wetlands posed obstacles or promised profits, they were drained or filled. They fared worst where cities needed space. The original Toronto harbour had cool clear streams and wide shore marshes. A fall evening would see fishermen jacklighting for salmon. The news editor Samuel Thompson tells the story of Toronto Harbour in the 1840s: "The part of the peninsula [now Toronto Island] forming the site of the present east entrance ... was crested with trees. Those trees and that bank were destroyed through the cupidity of city builders, who excavated the sand and brought it away in barges to be used in making mortar. This went on unchecked till about the year 1848, when a violent storm ... swept across the peninsula" and broke through the eastern gap.[95]

The harbour was then (as now) "under the charge of a board of commissioners." A competition was staged to seek advice on how to remedy the storm damage. Henry Youle Hind at Trinity College won the competition and his friend Sandford Fleming came second. Thompson noted: "Among the several plans submitted was one by Mr. Sandford Fleming, for carrying out into the water a number of groynes or jetties, so as to intercept the water washed down from the Scarboro' heights, and thus gradually widen the peninsula ... The chairman [of the commission], who was enfeebled by age and ill-health, resented angrily the interference of non-professional men, and refused even to put a motion on the subject. Thereupon, Mr. Allen [the city representative on the board] ... offered to pay the whole cost of the groynes out of his own pocket. Still the chairman continued obdurate, and became so offensive in his remarks that the proposition was abandoned in disgust." The gap was finally, irreversibly, breached by another storm ten years later and there has been a Toronto Island ever since.[96]

With the exception of its wharves and boathouses, the shores of Toronto Harbour stayed relatively intact and accessible until 1853, at which time construction began on a waterfront "esplanade," which was designed to provide a "recreation and pleasure ground for the residents of the city" and, more important, to accommodate the Grand Trunk Railway. Accomplishing this required an end to the past uses of the waterfront. A tender by Casimir Gzowski and company for the new railway right-of-way was accepted, as well as for five bridges that would provide public access to the shore. Unfortunately, a change in government ended the contract by mutual consent, before the bridges could be completed. The waterfront has had a poor record of public access ever since.[97]

The Grand Trunk Railway was laid down between the Gooderham Distillery and the harbour, and provided it with rail access. Serviced by both lake and rail shipping, this "industrial showcase" grew into the largest distillery in the world. It consumed six or seven hundred thousand bushels of grain a year, and its spent slop went to feed cattle penned at the mouth of the Don River. The number of cattle in the yards there grew to about ten thousand in 1883, when it was the largest cattle yard in the world outside Texas. Its sewerage discharged into the thirteen-hundred-acre Ashbridge's Marsh, polluting it so badly that it had to be filled in and rebranded as a "port." Today, as a result of infilling, the old Gooderham's – now the Distillery District – is almost half a mile away from the harbour, an extent of infill that is the result of multiple cycles of good planning, followed by infilling to serve the public interest. Each time this was expressed as a waterfront "vision," and each would lead to new infilling, and then to new public lands that would later be privatized and developed.[98]

"Privatize the profit and socialize the cost" is how this syndrome expresses itself. It is the modern equivalent of the ancient hunting-and-gathering instinct, but targeted on society itself as prey. It is so normative that it is implicit in our society. In recent years, it has been rephrased as to "privatize the upside, socialize the risks." In terms of land and resources, the method has been to use and abuse the commons at the expense of a shared public interest. With Toronto Harbour, within each infill cycle, there was rarely any public outcry, just an ongoing infill and development. Ashbridge's Marsh, the former wetland lungs of Toronto, was infilled as a centerpiece of Toronto's 1912 waterfront plan. The current vision of a Toronto waterfront and of promised public access and airport expansion is déjà vu in a long history of such visions, starting with fishermen jacklighting salmon and with sand pilfered to build the city.[99]

CHAPTER EIGHT

The True North: Three Centuries On

Great Lakes country is as large as Scandinavia, larger than Texas, four times the size of New England. Well over half of it lies on the cold hard rock of the Canadian Shield, which stretches north from Lake Huron, the Adirondacks, and Quebec City. Most people in the south think of the north - when they think of it at all - as a vague blur of summer holidays, one-industry towns, and resource dividends. However, its story of ecological change since 1600 has been as dramatic as the south's, and the area is of even greater promise today as one of nature's last great places (Fig. 21).

The story of the lower Great Lakes–St Lawrence and its arrival coast on the Atlantic was one of temperate climates, sweet soils and rich waters, and prosperous, farm-based nation-states. European newcomers shared the Iroquoian vision of settlements, farming, industry, and trade. However, there were other visions of the region, and two that stood in sharp contrast were the Laurentian and Hudsonian views. Geographically they lined up south to north - Iroquoian, Laurentian, and Hudsonian - and the last two were forged on the rugged geography *between* the Great Lakes and Hudson Bay.[1]

The Laurentian and Hudsonian visions were founded on more purely commercial goals, to achieve which a more benign respect was extended to nature and to Natives. In contrast with the south, they were non-religious, non-farming, and, at first, anti-settler visions, but this meant little in the long run, and ended with the same collapse of peoples and biota. Resource extraction for distant markets was the mission. It began on Hudson Bay and was perfected over two centuries, conferring stability, communication, and the rule of law (albeit commercial law) over much of North America. At that point, the Hudsonian vision was rebranded as the Laurentian vision and consummated in the merger of two corporate monopolies, thus retaining a larger share of the profits in the region, strengthening east-west trade, and providing the narrative for Canadian Confederation. This was the vision that long held centre stage in Canada, prior to its modern conversion to globalism.

There has never been a social narrative that has achieved lasting permanence in Canada. The narrative has shifted, and is shifting still. Geopolitically, the early face-offs between Natives and Europeans gave way to an English-French conflict, and then to a British-American conflict, all prior to the modern Canadian-American axis. Visions have come and gone, while diversity and adaptability have endured. Historian Cole Harris calls Canada the "reluctant land," defined by its "lack of definition and consensus." Notwithstanding, through all this, the entire continent has shared an ecological consensus, one that enabled massive change, independent of nation or vision.[2]

A Different Kind of Land Company

I grew up in the Iroquoian heartland but I embraced a Hudsonian point of view after years of northern studies as botanist at the Royal Ontario Museum. This took me to the Hudson plain and its Arctic coast, and to unforgettable scenes like forty polar bear enjoying a social on Bear Island, or walrus hauled out on their shoals, or seals and belugas in the river mouths. It was like going back in time – to the spruce and lichen parklands, the open coasts and plains, and the caribou and brook trout, as close an analogue of ancient Paleoindian times as exists anywhere.

The Atlantic seaboard was an arrival coast for Europeans in the 1600s, and the Hudson Bay coast played the same role, albeit one that was not so welcoming. It was (and still is) the least populated part of central North America. Its exposed seacoasts are ringed with vast tidal marshes, windswept beach ridges, and the world's most exotic palette of bogs, fens, and permafrost peatlands, a hundred miles wide before hitting the Canadian Shield. Half of Canada's largest dozen rivers drain to the bay, offering routes that would, like the St Lawrence and Hudson rivers, extend European dominion inland.[3]

It was long maintained that southern Hudson Bay and James Bay were no place for humans. In the 1960s, however, archaeologist Walter Kenyon of the Royal Ontario Museum found lances, bone awls, and flint arrowheads near Fort Albany on James Bay, and Lakehead University's Kenneth Dawson discovered pottery fragments at the mouth of the Hayes River. Then, pottery shards and chert spear points were found near Cape Henrietta Maria, the northwest tip of James Bay. In each case, it was argued, the artifacts came from elsewhere. This was challenged by John Pollock and William Noble, who discovered, at the Cape and at Hawley Lake in 1974, caribou hunting sites with chert points and hearth charcoal dating to 915 AD. Jean-Luc Pilon of the Canadian Museum of Civilization surveyed the Severn River in the 1980s and concluded that it had the "game, fuel and raw materials necessary for the manufacture of shelters and tools all in relative abundance." Full-time, long-term Native occupation was a fact, he asserted. It was clear that caribou were taken at river crossings by "some mass capture technique, such as a fence or snares." In 1988 Kenneth Lister of the Royal Ontario Museum added evidence of fish weirs on the Shamattawa River that were in full-time use before European contact. All of this validated the Native oral tradition of a millennium of occupation before contact.[4]

The first Europeans arriving on this coast resisted its appeals, and it theirs. Henry Hudson and his crew wintered on James Bay in 1610. "For the space of three moneths wee had such store of fowle of one kinde (which were partridges as white as milke) that wee killed above an hundred dozen ... The spring coming, this fowle left [and] in their places came divers sort of other fowle, as swanne, geese, duck, and teale." When the ice went out, they fished and caught, in one day, "five hundred fish, as big as good herrings, and some troutes." A Native discovered them and returned with beaver and caribou to trade, but then set fire to the woods to keep them from exploring too far afield. Hudson's crew abandoned him, his son, and five sick men, and sailed home to England where they were mercifully forgiven for their mutiny.[5]

The next year, the Royal Navy sent Thomas Button to find Hudson (unsuccessfully), and he and his crew wintered at the Nelson River. They too lived on fish, fowl (taking more than twenty thousand ptarmigan), and caribou. Then the Danish navy captain Jens Munk wintered at the mouth of the Churchill River in 1619, noting the Native camps there, one of them with a pictograph. All but two of his sixty-four men died of scurvy and, against all odds, the three of them sailed home. In 1631 the son of Bristol's mayor, Thomas James, sailed to Hudson Bay. He was not impressed. "A most shallow and perilous coast," he reported, a "land utterly barren of all goodness." He and his crew wintered on Charlton Island, at the bottom of his namesake bay, and they eked out a living – a caribou, a dozen fox, a few ptarmigan, and, in the spring, ducks, geese, cranes, and "green vetches" to cure the scurvy. On their return, they stopped at Cape Henrietta Maria and took a "dozen [caribou], young and old, very goodly beasts" and a "dozen young geese." His conclusion? "There is no passage" to the "south sea."[6]

The next visit was thirty-six years later, not inspired by China but by an improbable coincidence of French ambition, Native skill, and English finance, all in the person of coureur de bois Pierre-Esprit Radisson. As a teenager in Trois-Rivières, Radisson was abducted by the Mohawk and, after living with them for two years, returned to New France via Albany and Holland. In 1659 he and his sister's husband, Médard Des Groseilliers, set out for *le pays d'en haut*, circum-canoeing Lake Superior and learning about the fur country to the north. They returned with a convoy of three hundred Natives and a fortune in furs. A quarter of their furs were seized for trading without a licence, and Des Groseilliers was jailed. Undaunted, the two of them set their sights on Hudson Bay. Rebuffed in New France, and then sailing unsuccessfully out of Boston, they ended up in England in 1666, the year of London's great fire and great plague. King Charles II granted them an audience.

The result was a "Company of Adventurers" that, two years later, built a fort at the bottom of James Bay. When its ship *Nonsuch* returned home, it was loaded with furs, and a royal charter was granted for a "Hudson's Bay Company" (HBC) conveying to it "the sole trade and commerce ... [and] all the lands" draining into Hudson Bay, which was most of the northern half of North America. The company's first governor was Prince Rupert, the royalist champion during the English Civil War, and he was followed by the Duke of York, who became King James II, and by John Churchill, the military genius and Duke of Marlborough. This was the English ruling class, and the company was designed to profit its owners. It was tight in its dealings and maintained exceptional records.[7]

The trade out of the upper Great Lakes had belonged to New France; much of it soon flowed to Hudson Bay. The French complained that the HBC "saves the infinite expense of carrying provisions and merchandise by land ... [so] our merchants are in no position to compete." It was also irreligious, they claimed: "Prayer is not offered to God." The French urge to trade north was whetted by the stories of Awatanik, a Native who had been to Hudson Bay, home to "white bears ... little whales ... sea dogs ... wild geese, swans and ducks," and rich in beaver and moose. "The abundance of *cerfs* [caribou]," he said, "is greater ... than that of beavers." This was more detail than the French ever got from the secretive HBC. Jesuits were sent north in 1661 but did not get beyond the height of land, which they found "dry, barren and sandy, and ... covered only with rocks or with little stunted trees." The air was "brown with smoke" from fires.

A decade later, the Jesuit Charles Albanel travelled up the Saguenay and crossed to Lake Mistassini, a land "well stocked with moose and caribou" and "rich ... [in] small sturgeon, pike and whitefish." His party descended the Rupert River to James Bay ("nothing but mud and rocks"), met its Natives, saw its "grandes prairies," and heard about Akimiski Island, "abounding in all kinds of animals but especially ... its white bears" and waterfowl. "Even the Natives dread this journey," he wrote. New France was hemmed in by a difficult terrain.[8]

The French response was to drive the HBC from its posts. The Jesuit Pierre-Gabriel Marest shipped with Pierre Le Moyne d'Iberville, the great Montreal-born admiral charged with launching a sea attack on the bay. At the mouth of the Hayes and Nelson rivers, he wrote in 1695, the land was "marshy with many wet meadows ... The rivers are full of fish and game is abundant. All winter long there ... [are] partridges [ptarmigan] of which we killed at least twenty thousand. In spring and autumn ... a prodigious number of snow geese [oyes], Canada geese [outardes], ducks, Brants [bernaches] and other birds. But the best hunting is ... the caribou ... especially in the spring and autumn ... On [22 November] more than ten thousand passed by." The Natives, he observed, had "no villages nor fixed dwellings" and pursued different game in each season. Nicolas Jérémie was an officer on the same d'Iberville expedition, and he noted in the vicinity of the Churchill River "a sort of ox which we call bœufs musquez [muskox], because they smell so strongly of musk." Muskox were hunted out quickly everywhere near Hudson Bay.[9]

The French left in 1713 and the bay settled into what was criticized in England as a "sleep by the frozen sea." But the profits were steady and there was much to do. The Algonquian-speaking Cree were among the first North Americans in full-time contact with Europeans, and they fed, fuelled and transported the HBC. The Cree had their family bases in particular river systems, and hunted and fished the coasts and estuaries in the spring and fall. After contact, some of them took up roles as the "homeguards" of trading posts. Reciprocal dependencies deepened with time, and some of the homeguards became the domestics, "country wives," and orphans of the posts. The majority, however, lived off the land and were the essential workers of the commodity trade, hunting and trapping for three seasons of the year and congregating at the posts in summer to work in the fur brigades or as labourers. Leadership among them was based on their life skills and wisdom. Without the Cree, there was no Hudson's Bay Company. There was little interest in changing the culture on which its profit was based and, so, a modicum of mutual support and empathy was established between Native and newcomer.[10]

James Isham was appointed chief factor at York Factory when he was twenty-one, in 1737, after five years of service. His orders were to attract "the leading Indians to our interest with courtesy and the usual presents, and by treating the Natives with civility and dealing justly and equally with them." He sent envoys into the interior, like Anthony Henday in 1754, who travelled with Cree families to within sight of the "shining" Rockies. To draw off French trade on Lake Superior, Isham built the company's first inland post at the forks of the Albany and Kenogami rivers. This northern "Albany" never achieved the prominence of its namesake on the Hudson, but it was one of the major corridors to the Great Lakes. Isham mentored a generation of company men and was "the idol" of the Cree when he died in 1761. He willed his property to his country son.[11]

Orders arrived at HBC posts annually, and several of them in the 1730s directed the men to collect any new animals they encountered and ship specimens back to England. Any possible benefit from such "productions" was of interest, and the shipments of novelties from bayside were second only to those from "Charles Town," South Carolina. Shipwright Alexander Light was the first to respond, sending home the first North American specimens of seven species: the golden eagle, spruce grouse, snowy owl, willow ptarmigan, northern hawk owl, gyrfalcon, and porcupine. It is also probably Light who shipped back to England a live wolverine. Isham himself was just as assiduous, shipping at least fifteen new birds, including the great blue heron, snow goose, whooping crane, tundra swan, and sandhill crane. His notes offered many details, such as the measurements of a "very large" whooping crane and the rarity of passenger pigeons on the coast, though he noted of the latter that "once ... I did see some millions of them."[12]

Fuelling the Company

Native energy fuelled the HBC, and Native health was important. The company controlled who came into its world, and the arrival dates for European diseases were later as a result. There were lethal coughs, fevers, and poxes in the years 1721, 1738, 1741, and 1753-58, and venereal disease in the 1730s. "Country distemper," or tuberculosis, came early (and persists today). Something like measles arrived in 1751, and smallpox came overland from the southwest in 1781, reaching Albany in 1783. Before it hit, the homeguard Cree in the region numbered as many as seven hundred, with another fourteen hundred or more in the interior. As many as three of every four Cree were killed by the smallpox epidemic, and Samuel Hearne claimed that nine out of ten Natives west of Hudson Bay died as a result.[13]

Wildlife was as abundant in the north as the south, and the HBC tracked its harvest with care. Early on, Isham was sensitive to wasteful hunting. "Frequently Indians ... kill some scores of deer [caribou], and take only the tongues or heads ... They make such havock of what the Lord sent them plenty." But it was a land of feast or famine, and the protein was taken by any means possible, whenever possible. The Cree held that "the more they destroy the more plentiful they grow," just as the Neutral in the south had said "they must kill all they find," a conviction that was little different from the European belief that man had dominion over nature. (Anthropologist Shepard Krech has noted how contrary this is to the modern self-image of Natives as "ecological Indians." He notes: "Indians and environmentalists have opposed each other not just on waste, energy and water but on hunting and trapping." Resource users and Natives are more likely to share the same beliefs, he says, with the essential difference not a matter of principal but, rather, about who should be the primary beneficiary. Regardless of abundance, the HBC was the prime beneficiary in the north.)[14]

Caribou was the land protein that sustained the Cree for fifty generations. The barren-ground caribou arrived south of Hudson Bay each spring, following ancient trails and river crossings that took them to summer breeding grounds as far east as James Bay. Nicolas Jérémie, on the Hayes River in the 1690s, saw them twice a year: "The first time is in ... April and May, on which occasion they come from the north and go south ... The number of them is almost countless." A century later someone *did* count them. The great cartographer David Thompson was twenty-two years old in 1792 and had been a company clerk for eight years. In late May, he went "twenty miles up the [Hayes] river to shoot the rein deer as they crossed the river ... On the third morning ... we heard a noise as of distant thunder." He and his crew calculated the number of caribou. They allotted them "a full hour and a half in the morning to feed, and the same before sunset; this would give ten full hours of running, of what we thought twenty miles an hour, which they reduced to twelve ... The whole length of the herd ... [was] one hundred and eighty miles in length, by one hundred yards in breadth ... Allowing to each deer ten feet by eight feet ... the number of rein deer that passed was 3,564,000 ... without including the many small herds." Thompson's count of this one herd exceeds the total population of all the caribou now left in North America.[15]

Eastward, caribou crossed the Severn River at points between twenty and sixty miles upstream and were hunted there, and rafted down to the posts. White Seal Rapids was one of the crossings; Factor Andrew Graham reported "many thousands" taken in 1773. Their summer calving grounds extended as far east as Akimiski Island in James Bay. When it was a hunt with spears and canoes, and hedges and snares, there was a durable balance but the gun increased the kill rate, especially on the calving grounds. Captain William Coats said in the 1740s that the name Akimiski or *Agomisco* meant "where deer [caribou] herds," and that the island had "herds ... all the summer where our home Indians go to kill ... [them] for their and our uses at Albany." In 1747 the Albany factor mentioned three Cree taking more than thirty caribou on Akimiski and, the next year, nine hunters bringing in 108 tongues and 31 rumps from the island. They declined rapidly. Within a century of Thompson's count of migrating caribou, there was no such herd south of Hudson Bay and no caribou at all on Akimiski Island. There was a winter hunt farther south for woodland caribou, but that was all.[16]

The demand for protein was insatiable. Only a fraction of the harvest was recorded in the HBC books but even that trade was immense. Between 1747 and 1781, a single post recorded a trade in 18,500 caribou. Single-year reports include 2,666 caribou skins from Severn House in 1792–93 and 3,417 skins from York Factory in 1804–05. As the numbers declined, the hunt intensified. In 1811–12 neither Severn nor York Factory reported any caribou. The naturalist-doctor John Richardson recorded one of the last great crossings of the Hayes River in the fall of 1833: "The Indians, excited by the view of so many animals thronging into the river ... stabbed the poor deer wantonly, letting most of the carcasses float down the stream or putrify on the beach, for they could only use a small number of those they slew."[17]

By the 1950s, there were perhaps five thousand tundra caribou remaining south of Hudson Bay in Ontario, with about seven thousand woodland caribou southward in the interior. In 1958 Ontario asked the ecologist Teuvo Ahti, University of Helsinki, to study the woodland caribou. He found "no shortage of lichen," their main food, and habitat that could support at least seventy thousand animals. The discrepancy between potential and actual numbers, he said, was "unexplained." Ahti made no reference to the centuries of caribou hunting; the records of the HBC were not available to him, and have only recently been studied by Victor Lytwyn and others. Today, the woodland caribou, and seven of North America's twelve remaining herds of barren-ground caribou, are said to be "at risk"; however, their actual status is much debated. The issues that this debate still skirts are who has the right to kill them and who has the responsibility to protect them.[18]

For example, by 1994, the tundra herd at Pen Island near the Ontario-Manitoba border had grown to almost eleven thousand. About two thousand wandered east in November 1996, close to Peawanuck, the village twenty miles up the Winisk River from the bay. Hunters on all-terrain vehicles shot five hundred of them, too many to haul or butcher. Elders were said to be appalled but no law had been broken. After that, surveys found virtually no caribou between the Winisk River and the Manitoba border. However, in recent years, they have been summering in numbers on the tundra at Cape Henrietta Maria, part of their ancient calving grounds. By 2008, their numbers had grown to four thousand, in the most isolated part of the region. They are a telling reminder of the constancy of human behaviour and the resilience of nature.[19]

Springtime saw airborne protein arrive en masse. Snow geese, Canada geese, Brants, swans, and ducks came in prodigious numbers when the ice broke up, and were taken in bulk even before guns arrived. As early as 1631, Luke Foxe described piles of "bones of fowle" at a Native camp at the mouth of the Nelson River. Andrew Graham, the Fort Severn factor from 1761 to 1774, reported how the geese moulted in July, "at which season a great many are knocked on the head by the Indians." Factor Joseph Colen noted in 1798 that "our whole dependence at present for fresh victuals is on young ducks and moulting waterfowl killed by Indians with dogs." The birds were eaten fresh but, more important, were salted down for winter; for example, more than forty-seven hundred were salted into casks at Moose Fort in 1782. Nets and guns ushered in a more thorough hunt, and even snow buntings were taken, "very fat and reckoned a delicacy," wrote Graham. He also kept track of the ptarmigan harvest, "upwards of ten thousand caught with nets" each year near Severn. Elsewhere, in the winter of 1758, a total of 3,666 ptarmigan were shot and another 1,612 were netted for the Albany post alone, likely from points north.[20]

The other protein source was fish. Whitefish were "very numerous ... when they come from the sea into the rivers to spawn," wrote Isham in 1743, and they took "with a sean [seine] some thousands at one haw'l." The Cree built river weirs and Graham reported how they "frequently catch five or six hundred in a day, by means of weirs" in the Severn. The HBC trader George Barnston described a weir on the Winisk River in 1833, "where they bar up the river ... and have a basket on one side, in which they take in some seasons an immense number of sturgeon." Below the rapids and waterfalls, sturgeon were taken with spear, weir, and net, and the HBC tried to develop a trade in isinglass, the inner membrane of its air bladders, for use in glues and the liquor trade. The fish reached great sizes, sturgeon up to eight feet long and 310 pounds (in Lake Superior), and lake trout up to 70 pounds (in North Caribou Lake). For volume, however, it was the smaller whitefish, suckers, and pickerel that were the most dependable food for people and their dogs, with any surplus dried in the sun or smoked and stored for later use.[21]

The currency of the HBC was the beaver, and all trades were calculated in terms of "made beaver," the value of a single pelt in prime condition. Its soft underhair made the best felt, and its castoreum was in demand for perfume and for bait. Beaver trapping was winter work involving the entire family. The pelt usually belonged to the person finding the beaver house, and the flesh was shared. The Jesuit Le Jeune reported that it was Native practice to take all the beaver, male or female, young or old, but Radisson reported that the Cree left the young beaver to mature. Regardless, beaver declined, as did all the fur-bearers, whether they were targeted or incidental take. The numbers of snowshoe hare and lynx rose and fell in decadal cycles not understood at the time, and the HBC's attention turned to the lowly hare as other game declined. Some winter diaries in the late 1700s, such as those at Moose Fort in 1783-84, are little more than lists of the hare harvest. With the use of snares, "several hundreds are procured by the Company's servants ... [in] the winter, and make a considerable part of the provisions of the factory." Increasingly, it was hunger that stalked the down-cycles of the hare.[22]

During the War of 1812, the Royal Navy sent Edward Chappell to reconnoitre Hudson Bay. He dutifully reported a winter take of "90,000 partridges [ptarmigan] ... and 25,000 hares" at York Factory, as well as the caribou hunt on the river and the whaling out of Churchill. He published a trip *Narrative* in 1817 and, because the HBC kept its business to itself, it was a welcome public appraisal. He was blunt. Hudson Bay, the lesser of North America's arrival coasts, was not "an object of sufficient national importance to warrant an expenditure of the public money."[23]

The Hudsonian vision was secular and commercial, and lasted a century and a half. It did not deal in land, and it invited neither settler nor missionary. In 1821 the HBC shifted its centre of gravity to Montreal (and the Laurentians), merging with the North West Company (NWC) under the Hudson's Bay brand. The end of their hostile, competitive over-harvest permitted new approaches, such as conservation measures and a ban on the liquor trade. HBC Governor

George Simpson announced a policy to "nurse the country" and allow the beaver to "recruit" again. This ended the trade in young beaver and in summer pelts, and began a system of quotas in depleted districts and trapline allocations for particular individuals and families, to reduce harvest overlaps.[24]

The merged monopoly was trans-continental and mid-latitude – Laurentian – and set the stage for nation building. It supported "peace, order and good government" and met the sovereignty test of the Royal Proclamation in its treatment of Natives. Soon after, however, the commodity of interest became the land itself. Canada's first act of nation building after Confederation was to purchase the Hudson's Bay Company lands in 1869, for £300,000 cash and one-twentieth of its farmable acres. The Native and Métis stakeholders in the company were not consulted, and it was no accident that Louis Riel's rebellion started immediately thereafter. At issue was who owned the land and who governed it. The rebellion started when Riel physically stopped the first land surveyors sent to the Red River to start parcelling the land, the westward extension of government-as-land-company. Without permission or welcome, the surveyors showed up on the prairie behind the Riel family farm. Sixteen unarmed Métis intervened. Louis Riel put his moccasined foot on the survey chain and said "You go no farther," calmly, in English.[25]

The Northwest and Its Merchants

The old entente of the French and Algonquians in the lower Great Lakes and St Lawrence rapidly evolved into a northern and western vision. The fur trade, highly profitable at first, soon declined in the east, and the Great Lakes were wide open to the west, serving as both arrival and exit coasts for many hinterland rivers but, above all, as transit coasts throughout the region. Trade at such a distance had to be conducted over more than single-year cycles. It required interior posts, and it had to match the low costs that the HBC could deliver by provisioning its posts by sea.

The French knew about the upper lake and its native copper long before travellers like Étienne Brûlé visited. Champlain knew enough to map it in 1632 in its general size and shape, including the "sault" where it discharged east. It was called lake "supérieur" by the 1640s, and those at the "Sault de Ste. Marie" also knew about the great river that lay beyond, where Natives "till the soil … and harvest Indian corn and tobacco." Trading took Radisson and Des Groseilliers to Superior in 1659. They found its peoples "civil" and "sedentary," and they wintered southwest of Superior at Chequamegon Bay. They tested the Pigeon

River portage west and reported the copper and the "staggs, buffs, elands and castors" – the caribou, buffalo, elk, and beaver. The attraction was never more honestly expressed: "We were Cesars being nobody to contradict us."[26]

The Jesuit *Relations* describe a staged campaign of western expansion in the late 1660s. A mission was established at Chequamegon Bay, a coast servicing "more than fifty villages," including five hundred displaced Huron, for "both fishing and mutual commerce." They fished year round and it was said, "The colder the weather … the more fish one catches." In their fields within a mile of the water, "the women have found pieces of copper ... of ten, twenty and thirty *livres* [pounds] ... when digging … to plant their corn." A mission was also built at Michilimackinac, a well-populated site known for "its excellence … for raising corn" and "for its abundance of fish," many of them "monstrous" in size." Sault Ste Marie was yet another populous site, where as many as "nineteen different tribes" fished for whitefish. In 1671 a French officer at the mission there convened two thousand Natives, raised a cross, and claimed all the land "from Montreal as far as the South Sea." The French claimed the land but did not settle it, except casually for trade purposes, thus diminishing the durability of their religio-commercial approach.[27]

The great river farther west was the "Messi-Sipi" and one route to it was upriver from Green Bay, where the Jesuits set up a mission in 1669. "More than three thousand souls" pursued a sedentary life of farming there, with extraordinary access to wildlife, and it was from Green Bay that Jolliet and Marquette portaged to the Mississippi in 1673. The missions were staged steps westward, all of them located at important Native centres and all precursors to posts and forts. Green Bay and Chequamegon, for example, were the lakeheads of broad corridors into the central interior, and traders like Daniel Dulhut skilfully negotiated a rapid and peaceful expansion of trade. French daring was well rewarded, and by 1689 Lahontan had in hand a map showing the Mississippi River's connections west to the Rockies. Trade grew rapidly and fur prices declined, and in 1696 King Louis XIV revoked the traders' licences and demanded that Natives canoe their furs to New France, where more control (and taxes) could be imposed. This blunted the interior trade but the Canadiens and Métis persevered, maximizing their profits by both competing with the English and smuggling furs to them.[28]

By 1726, Sieur de La Vérendrye, a native son of Trois-Rivières, had a birch-bark map (like Lahontan's) showing the "grand portage" up the Pigeon River to Lake Winnipeg and the Saskatchewan. In 1731 he and his sons made the arduous trek and built posts on Rainy Lake and, the next year, Lake of the Woods.

His eldest son and twenty other French were killed on Lake of the Woods but the family persisted and, in 1734, built a post on the lower Red River. This opened a major route to the west, deep into the territory of the HBC and complementing the route down the Mississippi to *Nouvelle Orléans*. However, the great deeds of these merchant adventurers in the interior could not save New France on the St Lawrence, and by 1763 French interests on the continent were extinguished.

Entrepreneurs quickly took up the interior trade. Jonathan Carver, a Massachusetts surveyor, was sponsored to find new routes west. In 1766 he proceeded west from Green Bay to the upper Mississippi and the next July he was at the "grand portage" on Superior making enquiries. Lake of the Woods, he learned, had great "oakes, pines, firs, spruce" (the oaks persist today in a few groves), and Rainy Lake had "moose deer ... in great plenty, and likewise the carriboo." He returned along the north shore of Superior, all "mountainous and barren." The lake was "as pure and transparent as air" and as cold "as ice." He moved fast and recorded little. "Lake Superior is ... *moschettoe* country [and] I never saw or felt so many of those insects in my life." At Michilimackinac, he found his affairs in disarray and his work at an end. His *Travels* were hardly heroic but they were well received in London when they appeared in 1778.[29]

A more purposeful – and secretive – traveller was Alexander Henry. In 1761 he and his men canoed ten thousand pounds of goods along the south coast of Superior, noting its villages and, below its waterfalls, sturgeon "so abundant that a month's subsistence for a regiment could have been taken in an hour." At Chequamegon, Henry advanced his goods to the Ojibwa and saw them leave to hunt and trap before settling in for the winter. For food he caught "two thousand trout and whitefish, the former frequently weighing fifty pounds each, and the latter commonly from four to six." He hunted bear and boiled down "maple-sugar." The Ojibwa returned with fifteen thousand pounds of beaver and twenty-five hundred pounds of otter and marten. Henry headed east with his fifty canoe-loads of fur and, at the Ontonagon River, stopped at its famous copper boulder, which he estimated at five tons, and cut off a hundred-pound chunk for a souvenir.[30]

The hunt that winter took Henry and his men south of the "Soo." They killed a four-hundred-pound caribou – the Ojibwa had a Caribou Clan even on the south shore of Superior. Henry then canoed to the north shore of Superior, to the old French post at Michipicoten. On route, he saw the mineral veins, the sacred grave of Naniboujou, and a raw land where the details of the hunt mattered: "A few *cariboux*; and hares and partridges supplied my Sundays' dinners." Henry again advanced his goods to the local hunters and waited. Their hunt was successful, and Henry stayed for several years. He hunted on north-shore islands where caribou skeletons were "so frequent as to suggest … that want of food, in this confined situation, had been the destruction of many." The north shore of Superior was another Paleoindian landscape.[31]

In 1775 Henry set out for the west. He passed the mouth of the Nipigon River, which "annually drew [from the north] a hundred packs of beaver [10,000 pounds]," a rich harvest. He headed up the Grand Portage with a dozen canoe-loads of goods and entered the "chain of lakes … [and] carrying-places." Two weeks later, his party arrived, "exhausted," at Rainy River. Henry immediately saw the change in the land there: "Its banks are level to a great distance, and composed of a fine soil … covered with luxuriant grass. I was greatly struck with … its fitness for agricultural settlements." On Lake of the Woods, he traded with the Ojibwa, "the women bartering rice while the men were drinking. Before morning, I had purchased a hundred bags." Henry saw the pelicans and, in August, portaged out of the lake into the Winnipeg River and beyond.[32]

By the time Henry returned to Montreal the next year, he had been in his "great north-west" for fifteen years building the Laurentian trade. That same year, the Thirteen Colonies south of the lakes declared their independence, including his home state New Jersey. Trade was again disrupted, and traders had to choose. Henry chose Montreal and its traders, who were mostly highland Scots, loyalist Americans, and experienced Canadiens. They redoubled their trade in the west in direct competition with the Hudson's Bay Company and the Americans, and the new North West Company was notarized in 1779, with sixteen shares held by nine partners. Three years later, Alexander Henry was a full partner – and twenty-five years later he published his *Travels*.[33]

North of the lakes, the Natives and Métis were still central to the trade, but this was less the case in the south. In the words of Thomas McKenney, "white man had got the ascendency." McKenney was the head of a new Bureau of Indian Affairs, part of the U.S. War Department, and he led a party of 122, including 65 troops, to treat with the Ojibwa in 1826 at what is now Duluth. Their British flags and medals were exchanged for American flags and medals, and pork and flour, clothes and blankets, and whiskey were dispensed. An annuity of $2,000 was promised, in exchange for the rights to their copper and metals but leaving the Ojibwa their land. After signing the treaty, McKenney was resolved to "possess" the famous copper boulder on the Ontonagon but his troops could not lift it. It took until 1843 to transport the boulder to Detroit, where it was seized by the War Department. Two land treaties would follow, to secure their land as well, and by 1854 the Ojibwa south of Superior were on reserves.[34]

Government Land Control

A new breed started writing about the northwest. Some focused entirely on their destinations and barely noted their voyages, like Alexander Henry's son of the same name. Henry the younger's journal of 1799 *begins* at the Pigeon River. "The track ... to Lake Winnipeg being already so well known, [it] required no further description." This was the expressway of the NWC, and his notes were about repairs, portages, and whether his canoes were fastest. The first day up the portage brought him to a "prairie," kept open by long use and clearing. Other than the "sturgeon" and "berries," he registered little else before he reached the far west.[35]

The painter Paul Kane ventured north in 1846. At Fort William, the new NWC depot where the route west began, Kane joined a brigade of eight-man canoes, each with a ton of goods. Speed was of the essence, and Kane could barely keep track of the portages. (HBC Governor George Simpson passed them in his "flying canoe," the fastest transit of its day.) "The Lake of the Thousand Islands," he wrote, was "covered with ... pine." At Fort Frances, there were "vast quantities of white fish and sturgeon ... taken at the foot of the rapids," and along the Rainy River they bought "seven fine sturgeons, each ... forty or fifty pounds" from Ojibwa residents. On his return, he took note of the corn they grew on the islands in Lake of the Woods and the "sand-berries" (cherries) they gathered at the mouth of Rainy River. Kane got a berth on the "express canoe" east, and the north shore of Superior was a blur of "high mountain rock interspersed with a few trees of stunted growth." This was the same year that Britain signed the Oregon Treaty, which transferred the HBC lands south of the 49th parallel to the United States, over the protestations of the company.[36]

Not as well known as Paul Kane is Henry Youle Hind, the professor of geology at Toronto's Trinity College. The remaining land grant to the HBC was up for renewal in 1859, and Canada petitioned the Parliament in London "to consider the state" of those lands. The British dispatched an army captain, John Palliser, to survey it but Canada wanted its own advice and dispatched its own crew. Hind was asked to serve as "geologist and naturalist" on the Canadian crew in 1857 and became survey leader the next year, and author in 1860 of the two-volume survey released in London.[37]

The territory west of Lake Superior was their first charge. The party included surveyors, linemen, and engineers, and its canoes were paddled by Mohawk from Kahnawake and Ojibwa from Fort William. They were slow leaving Fort William (the Mohawk refused to share canoes with the Ojibwa – "highly ridiculous," Hind wrote) but were soon underway. He immediately noticed the rich soils of the Kaministiquia valley upstream of Fort William, with its elms, hazels, hops, and cherries. There was an open plain east of Kakabeka Falls, with "a profusion of blueberries, strawberries, raspberries, pigeon cherry and … [others,] among which the bluebell was most conspicuous." (These prairies were converted to farms but a few traces remain today, such as near the Stanley Cemetery.)[38]

The upper Kam valley was burnt, Hind wrote, and beyond was "an unbroken forest of pines dotted with … aspen and birch, and in the swamp … tamarack … The tops of a few hills showed clumps of red pine … tall above the surrounding forest … remnants of an ancient growth which probably once covered a large portion of this region, having been destroyed by fire." This was how northern stands of red pine survived unburned from earlier times; Hind was good at interpreting forest change. At Prairie Portage, he saw another burn and, at Brulé Portage, the "astonishing … remains of a magnificent white pine forest, which formerly extended over a vast area," with burnt trunks up to four feet in diameter. (Hind listed the fauna as well, such as "eagles," caribou, pigeon, and two species of plover.)[39]

"The shores of Rainy Lake are … a picture of hopeless sterility and desolate waste." Repeated fires had seared its shallow Shield soils. By contrast, the "delightful odour of the balsam poplar" welcomed him in the Rainy River lowlands. Hind was the first to notice the "vast deposit of peat" in the bogs and fens lying north and south of Rainy River, and, along the river, he noted its fine forests. "One elm tree measured three feet in diameter … Sturdy oaks, whose trunks are from eighteen inches to two feet in diameter, were found in open groves with luxuriant grasses and climbing plants … I heard more birds in ten minutes here than during the whole journey." Along the river, Hind visited "a beautiful prairie … [with] two immense mounds which appeared to be tumuli." These were the ancient Manitou Mounds, still surrounded by overgrown gardens replete with "*helianthii* [sunflowers] six and seven feet high" and "wild oats."[40]

The Lake of the Woods beyond was full of rice beds and "fine old oaks and elms." They visited the Ojibwa's Garden Island, with its fields of corn, "squashes and pumpkins," sand cherries, and passenger pigeons. The headman refused to guide them overland from there to the Red River, saying, "You do not tell us why you want to go that way, and what you want to do with those paths." The Ojibwa knew their lands were unceded, and they knew the Royal Proclamation. "If a whiteman comes to the Indian's house, he must walk through the door, and not steal in by the window … The white man comes, looks at their flowers, their trees and their rivers; others soon follow; the lands of the Indians pass from their hands, and they have nowhere a home." The boundary survey put Garden Island on the U.S. side, and the Ojibwa did lose it. The entire Lake of the Woods and Rainy River, with its fine soils, fishery, and rice beds, was another earthly paradise. Today, it is off the beaten track again, and wilding.[41]

The British survey party, under Captain Palliser, covered the same ground. Palliser was from a landed Anglo-Irish family, and he loved to travel and hunt. He had made a name for himself with his book, *Solitary Rambles*, about hunting buffalo and grizzly on the Missouri River in 1848, and he had lobbied to lead the new survey. Palliser was perfect for an imperial outing – congenial, caring, and a great shot. His party was selected by Charles Darwin, John Richardson, and Joseph Hooker, three of Britain's leading scientists. They chose botanist Eugene Bourgeau, geologist James Hector, and engineer Thomas Blakiston, a dysfunctional crew that achieved great things.

Palliser was not enamoured of the northwest. Lake Superior in June was "almost arctic, and the cold intense." Its shores were "precipitous and rugged." Up the Kam valley, he acknowledged some "rich alluvial land," as well as the "tall pines" and "reindeer (cariboo)." He admired the falls at Kakabeka, its "wreathing mist and … magnificent gorge." However, the main crossing he found "wild and rocky [with] innumerable watercourses … [and] tedious portages." The outlet of Rainy River into Lake of the Woods was "pure sand … blown sand." They paused there for Bourgeau "to botanize" (it is still a good spot) and then moved on as fast as their voyageurs could paddle. (Today, pin oak and prairie plants persist at the river mouth but Palliser's sands, except Sable Island, are under water, flooded by dams that generate power and supply Winnipeg's water.)[42]

Palliser was categorical. The "route from Lake Superior … even if modified and greatly improved by a large outlay of capital, would … be always too arduous and expensive a route of transport for emigrants … I therefore cannot recommend the imperial government to countenance or lend support to any scheme for … a thoroughfare … either by land or water." He did not even bother to describe the route, citing the "able report already laid before Parliament by a Canadian expedition." It was fortunate for Canada that Henry Hind, who surveyed the route *after* Palliser, got his report into print two years before him, and gave the route his reasoned support.[43]

Britain relinquished control to Canada in 1867. By then, there was a wealth of knowledge about the northwest but, within eighteen months, the territory had its own government, led by Louis Riel, his sympathizers, and the Métis. The U.S. consul at the Red River suggested that his State Department recognize the Riel regime. While Washington considered, Ottawa acted – sending twelve hundred troops to impose peace, order, and good government. Washington refused permission for Canada's troops to pass through the United States or use the canal at Sault Ste Marie. In the face of this, General Garnet Wolseley said he could get the Canadian troops to Red River in seventy-two days. In the end it took him ninety-six. Three weeks were needed to build a carriage trail forty-eight miles uphill from Thunder Bay to the height of land. Voyageurs estimated the size of the largest boats they could portage, and they built enough for an advance corps of three hundred and fifty.

When Wolseley got to Fort Frances, a British spy was waiting for him. William Butler had got there by way of the United States and Red River, where he had interviewed Riel and slipped away to intercept Wolseley. He kept notes. For example, Lake of the Woods was "a perfect maze ... of rich and luxuriant ... shores," and the Rainy River "rich, fertile and well wooded." Once rich in beaver and marten, he said, "it has long ceased to be rich in furs." Butler briefed Wolseley and joined the advance troops. At the portage into the Winnipeg River, they were met by Métis and Natives who, whatever their initial intent, elected to serve as guides instead – and a well-informed Riel fled before they arrived at Red River. Wolseley's odyssey went a long way toward convincing Canada that a permanent, all-Canadian route west was needed at any cost.[44]

"At any cost" meant the survey and, within twenty years, the construction of the railway that Palliser had deemed too expensive, by means that involved scandal and cost overruns and brought down governments. But it was built, and the surveys continued, mapping the land and its timber, dam sites, and potential mines. Areas with farm potential were mapped, such as the Rainy River and Kaministiquia lowlands. In rapid succession, treaties were signed and the land disbursed, where it had value, with the same efficiency that had been applied in the south.

The treaties rolled northwest following Confederation, based on the template set on lakes Superior and Huron in 1850. The Ojibwa faced a delegation headed by William B. Robinson, the son of loyalists, developer of the Welland Canal, and politician:

> In consideration of the sum of two thousand pounds ... and for the further perpetual annuity of five hundred pounds ... the said chiefs ... surrender, cede, grant and convey unto her majesty, her heirs and successors forever, all their right, title and interest in the whole of the territory ... save and except the reservations set forth ... and to allow the said chiefs and their tribes the full and free privilege to hunt over the territory now ceded by them, and to fish in the waters thereof as they have heretofore been in the habit of doing, saving and excepting only such portions of the said territory as may from time to time be sold or leased to individuals, or companies of individuals, and occupied by them.

There was no equivalent treaty with the Métis, who were by then just as attached to the land.

Scientist Surveyors

The Border Convention of 1818 encouraged an early American interest in lake surveys. For example, an American expedition left Detroit for Duluth and Green Bay in 1821 with two men interested in botany. One of them, Henry Schoolcraft, headed west again in 1831 with Zina Pitcher, later the mayor of Detroit, collecting novelties such as Pitcher's thistle, a Great Lakes endemic. The botanist Douglass Houghton, also later a mayor of Detroit, followed and is remembered with another Great Lakes endemic, Houghton's goldenrod. The south coast of Superior was well studied, but less so its north shore.[45]

In 1848 an eclectic crew of Harvard scientists led by geologist Louis Agassiz ventured north on Superior. Not far from Sault Ste Marie, they saw "flocks of pigeons," and, turning north, they trolled for lake trout, dropped in at mines, and measured red pine "five feet in diameter." Soon they left behind the southern maples and entered the boreal north, with cliffs "two hundred feet" in places and, at Agawa, pictographs of canoes and caribou. At Michipicoten the export of fish and canoes augmented a fur trade that was "very much on the decline." Native customs still held, and there was "no church, no schools, no marriage ceremony" for the hundred and fifty residents. "Caribous are found all through this region ... An Indian ... on Isle St. Ignace, killed twenty-five caribous in the course of the winter." Agassiz's book *Lake Superior* was published in Boston in 1860 and his chapter on geology was welcomed as one of the classic proofs of the theory of "terrestrial glaciers," in particular "the transportation of erratic boulders, the polishing, scratching and furrowing of the rocks, and the accumulation of unstratified, scratched and loamy drift." He also took note of the "subalpine" plants on the coast, familiar to him from the Alps.[46]

Another scientist, John Macoun, a self-taught teacher of natural history in Belleville, Ontario, read Agassiz's *Lake Superior* in 1868 and, inspired, sailed north the next summer. It was his first major field trip, and he "saw the cause at once" of the subarctic flora "close to the lake," namely its frigid waters and fog-bound shores. He shared his collections widely, gained some credibility, and shipped again for Superior two years later. On board this time was "a company of gentlemen in peculiar dress," who turned out to be the survey party for the Canadian Pacific Railway – chief engineer Sandford Fleming (Hind's friend), secretary George Grant, and a photographer. Fleming asked Macoun to join his crew, and Macoun agreed on the spot.[47]

George Grant, in his journal *Ocean to Ocean*, recounted that "among the passengers [was] a gentleman out for ... a botanical excursion ... Whatever point the steamer touched, the first man on shore was the botanist ... till recalled by the whistle that the captain ... sounded for him. They regarded him, because of his scientific failing, with ... respectful tolerance." Remarkably, given that Macoun could collect only at refuelling stops, he discovered just south of the Pic River the arctic lady's-slipper orchid, one of the four dozen arctic-alpine plants that grace the coast of Superior, at its only location in the Great Lakes basin.[48]

West of Nipigon, their steamer stopped at Silver Islet. Here "the most wonderful vein of silver in the world has been struck. Last year, thirty men took out ... $1,200,000." For fifteen years, Silver Islet was the world's largest silver mine. Beyond Thunder Bay, Fleming's party visited the "splendid farming country" up the Kam valley, and then they headed up the wagon trail that Wolseley's expedition had built to the Arctic watershed, where the Ojibwa were gathered to discuss their respective treaty, one of the so-called "numbered treaties." At Fort Frances, there were another "thousand or twelve hundred" Ojibwa conferring with the Indian commissioner. Reverend Grant was plain. "The red man ... is being civilised off the ground. In the United States they have, as a rule, dealt with him more summarily than in British America, but it comes to pretty much the same in the end."[49]

Along Rainy River, Grant made the usual comments about the "richness of the soil" and how it "could be cleared almost as easily as the prairie."

They took a steamer across Lake of the Woods and then the new wagon road west to the Red River, "utterly uninteresting" except for its "wild pigeons and prairie hens." Their conclusions were "entirely the reverse" of Palliser's. "The rugged and hitherto unknown country ... is not ... impractical for a railway ... Those vast regions of Laurentian ... rocks ... are rich in minerals beyond conception." The east would profit and "only the construction of a railway is necessary." The vision was a coast-to-coast, resource-based Canada.[50]

The land treaty they had seen being negotiated with the Ojibwa was signed in 1873 by twenty-four headmen on behalf of twenty-five hundred Natives. (The Métis signed the following year.) There was the usual cash and annuities, along with statements of intent "to open up for settlement, immigration and such other purpose as to Her Majesty may seem meet." Reserves were set aside, and schools and farm tools promised. The Ojibwa retained the "right to pursue their avocations of hunting and fishing throughout the tract surrendered ... subject to such regulations as may from time to time be made ... and saving and excepting such tracts as may, from time to time, be required or taken up for settlement, mining, lumbering or other purposes." The land was thus secured, fifty years after the south, for settlement where feasible but, much more, for the resources that could be extracted.

The Empty Forest

The resource surveys were paramilitary in their scale and speed. The fur trade and its participants were by then a minor melody lost in a new national anthem of timber, water power, mines, and farms. We know today that, almost everywhere, Earth's great forests have experienced a massive "defaunation," as Kent Redford of the Wildlife Conservation Society calls it. "Often trees remain in a forest that human activities have emptied of its large animals. The absence of these animals has profound implications." What happens when you remove almost all the caribou, beaver, wolf, and others from a forest? This is the same question asked in the south about the passenger pigeon, elk, turkey, salmon, and eel. A true north strong and free, but also free of its wildlife?[51]

In 1900 a remarkable survey was conducted, *after* two and a half centuries of aggressive wildlife harvest. The survey was ordered by the Ontario Department of Crown Lands to assess the timber, geology, and wildlife in the vast territory stretching from Temiskaming, Lake Superior, and Lake of the Woods north to the Albany and English rivers. It was a modern survey but it was new terrain and the surveyors were guided every step of the way.

Ten survey parties submitted their observations, maps, and photographs, and each one described a land exhausted by overharvest and fire.[52]

In the northeast, the Abitibi-James Bay country was still, in 1900, "occupied by Cree [who leave] the Hudson's Bay Company posts about the beginning of September to go to their different hunting grounds ... and return ... [in] June with their furs. Many of them are employed in the summer ... to transport provisions ... using large birch bark canoes." The fur-bearers were in "the following order of importance, numerically, marten, muskrat, moose, bear, mink, beaver, caribou, lynx, otter, fisher, gray fox and ... silver-gray fox." Moose, caribou, and bear were "plentiful." Waterfowl were abundant, including sandhill crane, and so were pickerel, whitefish, pike, and, "below the falls," sturgeon. Spruce and jack pine prevailed. There were rare stands of red pine, such as at Pierre Lake, but other than those "two hundred and fifty red pine," the trees were "of no value commercially." The spruce "muskeg" they considered unproductive but, within a decade, that same spruce would be the backbone of a pulp and paper industry." A "clay belt" with great farming potential was heralded (and later settled).[53]

The rest of the northeast was in worse shape. In Algoma-Missinaibi country, the fur-bearers were the same, but all declining. "Brunswick Post [reported] that only half the furs are received there in comparison with ... former years." A veteran hunter "who had formerly brought in as many as a thousand rabbit [hare] skins could this last year get but twenty." The beaver was "fast becoming an extinct animal," and the Natives had "great difficulty in keeping from starvation." Because of the European larch sawfly, "the tamarack is dead or half dead."[54]

The crew in Temagami and Temiskaming reported: "One hundred years ago, this territory was exposed to the ravages of fire, which left these clumps of timber as survivors of the pine riches that at one time existed." There were signs of caribou "everywhere" but they were "numerous" only in two valleys. "The beaver, otter, fisher and wolf are very scarce." Wolf were in one valley "only," in "the habitat of the red deer [elk]." Fish were still "in abundance."[55]

Farther west, in the Algoma highlands and Kenogami country, the fur-bearers were "bear, moose, caribou, red deer [elk], red, white and coon fox, fisher, otter, beaver, skunk, mink and muskrat." However, "the returns are greatly less than they used to be." The tracks of "caribou and red deer tracks were ... common" and fish and waterfowl were still abundant. In the upper Kenogami, "the whole country was fire swept fifty-three years ago [so] no timber of great size is to be found." Overall, "beaver are becoming very rare ...

[and] only two or three moose are killed in a year ... Caribou are fairly common ... Bear is the commonest big game."[56]

In the Ogoki-Albany country, the trade was the same but the survey reported only "a solitary beaver." There were "a few caribou tracks" but no moose or elk. Fish were still "numerous," especially the sturgeon and trout. In general, there was "little or no timber [of] commercial value. The whole country ... is very rocky and barren." It was "desolate, burnt," and with *brulés* everywhere, other than a few unburned tracts of "splendid spruce, jack pine, balsam, poplar and ... white birch."[57]

In the northwest, the Nipigon River was noted for its potential water power (since developed) and its famous brook trout (which the power dams ended). "As a fur country, it is nothing compared to what it was ... Moose, caribou and black bear are ... not at all plentiful ... The moose have been growing more plentiful, while the caribou have been disappearing ... Red deer and wolves first made their appearance near [Thunder Bay] ... three or four years ago ... driven into the district by the forest fires ... in the northern states." Fish and fowl were "numerous." Lake St Joseph reported a trade in "bear, otter, muskrat and sable, some foxes, martens and fishers," but "very few mink or beaver," only a few caribou, and moose "only very recently." Natives were reduced to eating the underbark of jack pine, it was reported. "Half of the country we traveled over is burnt, and the other half contains no marketable timber except one block of sixty acres."[58]

In the Lake of the Woods and Quetico districts, the moose were "plentiful ... [and] began to come into that country about forty years since." Caribou still occurred "in large herds ... in winter" and a few elk were "coming north ... from ... Minnesota." Wolf were "not numerous." Overall, the survey crew wrote, the constant "trapping ... from year to year keep[s] the fur-bearing animals from becoming plentiful." Lake of the Woods was still rich in elm, oak, and ironwood, and wild rice and fruit, but "much of the original timber has been killed by fire." A century before, Natives reported, "fires broke out ... [and] raged until the whole country was burnt."[59]

By 1900, the northern forest was emptying of wildlife, over-burnt, and barely able to support a family or trade. No other surveys in Great Lakes country ever used the word "starvation." The fur-bearers were largely gone, the beaver in particular, while fish and fowl held on. Much of this would be later reversed as harvests were regulated and fires suppressed. But the northern forests would never be the same.

The new economy in 1900 was timber, water power, and farming. The mineral wealth would be revealed more slowly and be the stuff of legend: first the iron and silver of Superior country and the gold, nickel, and copper of the central Shield; then the development of the world's largest mineralization zone at Sudbury; and then again, gold within a few miles of Superior's north shore. Prospectors have now discovered a new mining field even larger than Sudbury a hundred miles south of Hudson Bay. The same formula is planned – the profits will flow elsewhere, with the price paid by the land and its residents.[60]

Treaty Nine

The declines in forest, wildlife, and people went hand in hand and left Native peoples even more vulnerable. The boundary of Ontario had been extended north to the Albany and English rivers in 1889 and, following the 1900 surveys, a treaty was negotiated. In the summers of 1905 and 1906, three land commissioners, two constables, and a doctor were outfitted by the Hudson's Bay Company and canoed to each one of its fourteen posts by fur-brigade crews. Company men acted as translators and Native headmen signed the treaty in syllabic script or with an "x." By the end of 1906, eighty headmen had signed. No refusals were noted.[61]

Treaty Nine's goal was "to open for settlement, immigration, trade, travel, mining, lumbering, and such other purposes as to His Majesty may seem meet, a tract of country." The Natives agreed to "cede, release, surrender and yield up ... all their rights titles and privileges whatsoever," in exchange for "the right to pursue their usual vocations of hunting, trapping and fishing ... subject to such regulations as may from time to time be made ... for settlement, mining, lumbering, trading or other purposes." Reserves were set aside proportional to the number of families and each Native was paid "eight dollars in cash," with an annual payment of four dollars to follow. Teachers and schools would be provided. Signing ceremonies were held at each post, at which public pledges were shared to uphold the terms and the spirit of the treaty.

Ontario, Manitoba, and Quebec were soon eager to extend their boundaries farther north to Hudson Bay, and in 1912 Canada passed a law that obliged them while at the same time downloading the federal responsibility for land treaties: "The province ... will recognize the rights of the Indian inhabitants ... and will obtain surrenders of such rights in the same manner as the government of Canada." At the same time, "trusteeship of the Indians ... shall remain in the government of Canada." On this equivocal basis, preparatory work began (except in Quebec, which did not enter into treaties with Natives until 1975, to permit hydro development).[62]

Almost all that was known about the territory was still held by the Hudson's Bay Company. Agency surveys were begun about 1890 to redress the deficiency and in 1912 a summary was released, much inferior to the survey of 1900. The timber along the rivers was thin and "subject to fire," it noted. There were caribou "all over," and along the Albany sometimes "in considerable numbers." Moose had moved "as far north as the Attawapiskat river." There was a useful fishery. Akimiski Island, in James Bay, was a "favorite breeding place for ducks and geese," and "black ducks in the thousand breed in ... Hannah Bay, and the pintail and teal ... north of the Albany. A few ptarmigan were shot near Cape Henrietta Maria and, on our return, a large number of geese." Anecdotes were often all there was: "At Ekwan Point ... I counted over one hundred porpoises [belugas] passing close to the shore. Seals were often seen and numerous skeletons of walruses and seals were lying on the beach north of the Albany." The report claimed that "the fur-bearing animals ... [were] still fairly abundant," but it was the lowly hare that was "the most useful ... as it affords ... both food and clothing." The Cree were weaving blankets from hare fur, "the only furs he can afford to sacrifice to his personal use." As to health, "the greatest mortality is caused by pulmonary diseases ... and ... epidemics of measles, etc., that sometimes prove widely fatal."[63]

The wildlife, forests, and people degraded simultaneously. It was not the goal of the fur trade to leave any profit with the Natives and, by 1910, the trade hit bottom. There was not enough to sustain its workers, let alone an export trade. The approach of the HBC had been to respect Native customs and to resist both missions and schools. Perhaps that business model was always doomed, but it was to end completely when Canada took over the company's land grant in 1869. In retrospect, various models were tested in Great Lakes country: the American "life, liberty and the pursuit of happiness" (except for Natives); the British and Canadian "peace, order and good government" (especially for Natives); and the purely mercantile approach. Regardless, the result was the same – impoverishment of the land and the Native estate. Of course, there were differences: a near-total occupation and conversion of the land in the south, and only a deeply depleted natural estate in the north. However, both north and south, the trajectory was identical.[64]

The particulars of the decline in the north included an over-burnt Shield country, an over-harvest of fur-bearers, an over-kill of caribou, and an over-drowning of the land for hydro power. By 1910, the barren-ground caribou was gone south of Hudson Bay. Woodland caribou had declined by at least half, both in numbers and historic range. Its fate now lies in the balance between its predators (the wolf and human) and its ungulate brethren (the moose and deer). It will be pushed hard by the chainsaw, feller buncher, and road grader in the bush; by the gun and all-terrain vehicle in the hunt; and by pathogens like the parasitic brain worm, which the white-tailed deer took north about 1900 and has now reached as far as James Bay. The moose spread north, and the wolf increased with it, and took caribou and deer as collateral prey. Predators changed – the cougar was extirpated and the wolverine almost so – but the coyote moved in by 1900 and was everywhere other than the maritime coast by 1956. The story of any one species is highly complex. How are those that remain interacting? And what of the lakes and rivers? The Quebec hydro dams built to power New York altered the landscape forever, flooding an area of land ten times the size of New York City. The wilds of the north are more artifact than we care to admit.[65]

The decade around 1910 was perhaps the low point for nature in the north. Since then, regulation and research have recovered the wildlife. The fur trade now operates at a higher and more sustainable yield than in 1910. The wildfires that once dictated the ecology of Shield country have been suppressed since 1917, putting more wood fibre and stored carbon on the ground than at any time in history, enough to support permanent wood-harvesting communities even while the amount of wood in the forest increases. Logging is boom and bust, and industry downturns mean that even more biomass accumulates. Higher fuel-loads increase the risk of fire, especially now that the climate is warming. Fires are responsible for almost a fifth of Canada's carbon emissions, so, the logic goes, we must work even harder at fire suppression. Arguably, fire suppression has been as great a determinant of the region's modern ecology as forest harvesting. "O what a tangled web we weave."

Commissioners headed north in 1929 and 1930 to extend Treaty Nine north to Hudson Bay. Treaty Nine was the largest historic land treaty in eastern North America, and signings were staged at each of sixteen HBC posts. The communities remain isolated today and depend increasingly on external energy and food. There are limited jobs, trade, and game. Education levels are static. Substance abuse and suicide have increased. Diabetes has set in. In 1978 the factor at Severn, Chris Burke, told me his company store showed a profit that year because it sold 58,000 chocolate bars, or three per day per person. More than one in every two people is a youth under sixteen years old, and youth exercises more influence than ever. Many of them are interested in the outdoors, and spend their money on vehicles and fuel, and pursue their interests widely. In this, they are no different from youth in southern cities – buying vehicles and burning fuel in excess of what is wise. With so much more choice now, youth in the north (and south) can build more sustainable futures if they wish. Or they can perpetuate what has not worked so far. In either case, the land and its wildlife will never be as wild or abundant as it was. The hunt will continue, for minerals, fibre, energy, and game, aided and abetted by ever improving technology.

A Superior Opportunity

The south experienced such a massive withdrawal of its natural capital since 1600 that we can only stand guilty as charged and accept the verdict that – if we are to keep or restore parts of it – we will have to work long and brilliantly. Lake Superior and the north, however, are a different world, relatively free of land sales and farm clearances, and about 90 per cent still public land – part of a common wealth that is among nature's last great places. It has rewilded in the last century, and almost all of its original species and ecological systems are present and accounted for, albeit in thinner ranks. Clear-cuts, towns, mines, farms, and dams have left their mark but they are only islands of converted lands when compared with the south. It continues to be *the* bird nursery of North America, and Canada's north exports four to seven billion birds each fall, 40 per cent of all U.S. birds. The annual extent of forest cut in recent years is no more than 0.5 per cent of the productive forest and less than half its annual growth.[66]

Ghost species like the caribou may find refuge only in the remotest parts of the north, but it is a testament to increased awareness that its fate is now actively debated. Another sign of change is the growing consensus that a large part of the north – as much as half – should be conserved for nature and for nature's benefits. Historically, this is a different way of seeing the land. It is also the preference of an increasing number of northerners, if there is some way to better their own lives at the same time.[67]

Remarkable changes in public policy have occurred. Ontario, the custodian of the northern half of the Great Lakes basin, became a world leader in conservation in 1999 when it prohibited industrial development on six million additional acres of its near north, meaning that a total of 12 per cent of the territory was protected for nature. Included in this is almost all the public coast and islands of Lake Superior, Lake Nipigon, Lake Huron, and Georgian Bay. Ontario declared this its "Heritage Coast," the longest protected freshwater coast in the world - eighteen hundred miles, or two and a half million acres - the entire voyageur route from Huronia in the east to Pigeon River in the west.[68]

Then, in 2007, Prime Minister Stephen Harper declared Canada's first "national marine conservation area" in Lake Superior, another two and a half million acres of lakebed, islands, and mainland. Major tracts of the Lake Superior watershed have also been conserved by U.S. federal and state agencies, a million acres in parks and another five or six million acres in federal and state forests. Together, this is a conserved landscape in the order of *ten million acres* in and around the world's largest lakes, which hold 18 per cent of the world's fresh water. This has happened in the heart of one of the most educated and environmentally aware regions on Earth but it has gone unrecognized. Anywhere else, the public would insist that governments and communities take ownership and pride in such an extraordinary - and already completed - binational accomplishment (Fig. 22).[69]

Respecting nature's balance remains a challenge in the north. For most species, perhaps even for caribou and freshwater fish, there is still time. Intact wilderness is still present at scale. South of the Shield, wild fragments also remain, but they are outliers at the ends of its "Fifth Lines," and face all manner of futures. In the south, the challenge is "to keep what is left." In the north, it is still possible "to keep the best."

Between keeping the best and keeping what's left, northeast North America - and the Great Lakes country in particular - is more privileged than almost anywhere on Earth, able to conceive of a future that can, with good planning and generous action, accommodate on the same land base a fully urban vision (with all the intensity of the world's most anxious consumer society), a superb agricultural countryside (with half of it set aside for nature), and an unrivalled measure of wildlands on the Great Lakes coast, the Shield, and the Appalachians, Alleghenies, and Adirondacks. This is also, arguably, the trajectory that the landscapes of Great Lakes country are currently on.

PART THREE

NATURE'S PROSPECT

CHAPTER NINE

Invasives: The Unintended Consequences of the Uninvited

The twentieth century unpacked some of history's most extraordinary blessings and curses, and Nature's prospects in Great Lakes country were at a low ebb at its dawning. With the template largely set by 1900, the pressure built inexorably, imprinting its patterns on the land and water, and the city and countryside, and squeezing out ever more of the region's native identity. It was a profound deepening of the industrial revolution, uniquely supercharged with cheap energy. "The ecological peculiarity of the twentieth century is a matter of scale and intensity," writes Georgetown historian John McNeill in *Something New under the Sun.* The pace of change waxed and waned differently in different locales, but the fundamental story was one of quantitative rather than qualitative ecological change.[1]

The intensification was palpable. The global human population multiplied itself four times, and city dwellers thirteen times. Energy use and the world economy increased fifteen times. Industrial output grew forty times, and carbon dioxide emissions seventeen times. It was the most prodigal of centuries, riding high on human ingenuity, especially in resisting disease, extending lifespans, and manufacturing wealth. Like none before it, the 1900s drew down the Earth's natural capital, particularly its hydrocarbons, fresh water, timber, and ocean protein, all of them subsidies not accounted for in the spreadsheets of nations.

McNeill offers a faunal analogy. "In the twentieth century, societies often pursued the shark strategy amid a global ecology ever more unstable, and hence ever more suited for rats ... The biological success of the human species is probably not at serious risk. As a species, we are much more ratlike than sharklike. The social order, on the other hand, is probably at risk." And so too the natural order, in a new "city-state world" of displaced and reassembling peoples and biota.[2]

Globalism is the ascendant vision now, in materials, peoples, technologies, and communications, which further open the already porous borders of Great Lakes country. Even though the region has now achieved some quantitative easing of the worst effects of over-clearing, over-harvesting, and mismanagement, it may be too little too late. Fortunately, however, with these particular effects we have both clinical experience and the skills to diagnose and treat. We have no such experience with the effects of globalism, many of which are novel in the Earth's history.

The impacts of the new globalism pound their way around the globe like tsunami waves, and they reach deep into Great Lakes country. Their cultural and technological implications are in the forefront of mainstream dialogue, but their ecological consequences are largely ignored. Three pillars of globalization will be the focus in this and the next two chapters: first, the unprecedented increase in biological pollution arising from global trade; second, the twinned giants of climate change and the new city-state; and, finally, the emergent forces of restraint, conservation, and restoration.

We have considered the forensics of the blunt trauma of securing, disbursing, and converting the Great Lakes country into a new Europe. Nature paid the price and much of the continuing cost, growing like an unserviced debt, is the crescendo of ill effects arising from our global traffic in biota. I was conscious at an early age of the ruin of the countryside by Dutch elm disease, looking out the back window of our '56 Chevy, dead elms everywhere. I remember the red-headed woodpeckers, whose numbers exploded with the infinite feast of new bark beetles. I also recall the inordinate pleasure I felt when I discovered a small bottomland in the Hudson Bay lowland where elm still ruled, an untouched population far to the north of the reach of the disease.

American scientist Jared Diamond frames the last ten thousand years as follows: "Human groups with guns, germs and steel, or with earlier technological and military advantages, spreading at the expense of other groups, until either the latter groups became replaced or everyone came to share the new advantages." Such clinical language understates the impact of germs and diseases. They "replace" nothing, and four hundred years of uninvited arrivals have done little to "advantage" nature in Great Lakes country, a region with no natural borders or defences.[3]

Forest Pathogens

The elm bark beetle was first discovered in New York in 1909, no doubt an arrival in elmwood shipped from Europe. In itself, the beetle was of only passing interest, but, about twenty years later, it became host to a fungus also just arrived from Europe. Together they were the Dutch elm disease, so named because of its destruction of elms in Holland, where it was first studied. It reached Ohio by 1930 and Canada in the 1940s. It eliminated all three elm species here, although individuals still send up shoots that can even produce seed. But, unerringly, the disease takes them too before they mature, and we are left with residual patches of struggling, stunted, and dead elms. Ash and Manitoba maple try to fill their niche, unsatisfactorily.[4]

The Dutch elm disease is not a symbiotic pathogen. It is a terminator, hell-bent on eliminating its host genus, and facing no natural controls in North America. A few sentinel elms still stand in the fields, safe beyond the distance a beetle can carry the fungus. Hundreds of these elms were sampled by Henry Kock, arborist at the Guelph Arboretum, and tested for their immunity and then planted out. Other researchers are hybridizing and cloning elms, and some now suggest that elms still growing close to their interglacial refugia, with only two sets of chromosomes, may be particularly resistant. Yet the reality is that there will never again be billions of elms gracing the land. It is long gone, like the Canadian two-dollar bill, which also sported a magnificent elm.[5]

In 2000 I was at meetings in Chicago when I heard about the Asian longhorn beetle, which had arrived in 1997 as a hitchhiker on raw wood from China and was killing every broadleaf tree it met in Chicago and New York City. Chicago Mayor Richard Daley moved quickly to eradicate it. Thousands of trees were cut down in hundreds of city blocks. To get access to some backyards, security details guarded the doors while crews went through and removed the trees. I was impressed: a spectacular, inch-long black and white beetle was out to kill our broadleaf trees.[6]

I called the Canadian Food Inspection Agency (CFIA) in Ottawa. Apparently, the Chinese had problems with the beetle in their own orchards. They had conducted baiting trials to see what attracted them best and discovered that their favourite bait was the sugar maple. And the beetle had already arrived in Canada. In 1999 a forklift operator in a warehouse in the Waterloo area was sorting wood pallets of Chinese goods for shipment to retailers.

He spotted a beautiful black and white beetle, stopped his forklift, and, likely at some peril to his job, showed it to his boss and said, "I've never seen a bug like this before." Rather than firing him, his boss agreed and together they called the University of Guelph, and got through to the entomology lab, where staff dropped everything, identified it, and had the warehouse quarantined on the spot. In that case, the best defence had been sheer happenstance, and no such string of coincidences is likely to occur again.

Steve Marshall, at the University of Guelph lab, puts it succinctly. "Asian longhorns could devastate our maple forests if this species is allowed to spread out of its current urban footholds." I had asked the CFIA officer how many inspectors there were on Canada's west coast, where the pallets had arrived. He told me that the government had, at the time, two staff inspecting the shipping containers arriving on that coast. In other words, barely more than zero per cent of the shipping containers were being inspected. The beetle had showed up first at U.S. ports in 1990, and afterwards there were countless pleas from agency professionals to ban the import of raw-wood pallets. In 1998 Washington ordered China and others to kiln-dry their pallets before shipping them to the United States, and Ottawa followed suit, both countries thus assigning their security to the trade itself.[7]

Ironically, at the same time that this little miracle-in-the-warehouse was playing itself out, the beetle was already on the loose in a residential area in Toronto. It was only discovered in 2003, and more than 23,000 broadleaf trees had to be cleared out before it was safe to conclude that the beetle had not got into the nearby Humber valley, which would have connected it to the Oak Ridges and beyond. There are now so many non-native invertebrates on the North American continent that scientists have the resources to study only the ones that are likely to have transformative effects on entire landscapes, or that target entire species, genera, and families. Research can barely keep up with identifying them, let alone foretelling their effects.

The Asian longhorn beetle eats all broadleaf trees. Its conifer counterpart is the brown spruce longhorn beetle, another transformative invasive. An import from Europe, it was found killing spruce trees in Point Pleasant Park in Halifax in 1999. There was a public debate over whether or not to clear out the park's trees and try to eradicate it. On one occasion, Bill Freedman, ecologist at Dalhousie University, was asked why it had to be done. He replied: "All it takes is one knocked-up female getting out and you can say goodbye to our forest." The cutting went ahead but then, in September 2003, Hurricane Juan hit the park. Subsequent surveys found dozens of new beetle locations outside Halifax and, to contain them, six counties now have wood embargos in force. Hurricane Juan had likely blown some pregnant beetles farther than expected.[8]

In 1904, a century before these arrivals, a forester named Herman Merkel identified a fungus killing the native chestnuts in the New York Zoological Gardens in the Bronx. Experts had brought in Chinese chestnuts to breed a better chestnut, but a fungus from that stock invaded the native chestnut's vascular tissues, choking off its nutrient transport. At the time, chestnut was one of the most abundant trees in the eastern United States and southwest Ontario, and a leading source of mast food. The blight spread about twenty miles a year and, by 1950, the chestnut was finished – four billion trees in fifty years, as many as a quarter of the broadleaf trees in the U.S. east. It got to Canada in the early 1900s and killed millions. A few linger and, once in a while, a new chestnut sprouts from the roots of an old stump. The Canadian Chestnut Council is planting out disease-free trees in safe places north of their original range, and also breeding blight-resistant trees. There is still hope that chestnut will persist until we know what to do. However, some of its dependent insects, including ten species of moth, were unable to switch hosts, and are gone.[9]

In 1890 a beech-bark scale insect was brought into Halifax harbour. It later became the carrier for two non-native fungi and, together, they became the beech bark blight, which by the 1930s had killed beech trees throughout the Maritimes and New England on its march to Great Lakes country. In 2000 it hit the three-hundred-year-old beech in our bush in Mono. When the blight hits, the outer wood turns to punk, of no use to man or beast. Andrew Storer, ecologist at Michigan Tech University, found that the dying beech were of no interest to birds and caused declines in moths and ground and wood beetles. The result is another transformative loss of forest canopy and timber, and mast for wildlife. Some wildlife may shift to other foods but they definitely prefer beechnuts. Farewell the beech-maple forest of eastern North America.[10]

In 1967 a killing canker was found on the butternut in a woodlot in Wisconsin. It had been there for a few years and its fungus was described as new to science in 1979. It is almost certainly non-native. It moved fast, killing butternut of all ages, more than 90 per cent of them in Wisconsin. It reached southwest Ontario in 1991 and was killing trees in Mono by 2000. The butternut was another widespread and common tree, a great producer of mast nuts and timber, and it is now lost. The response has been to hope for some native resistance, and to list it as an endangered species.[11]

If that was not enough, a new import from China is eating the ash trees. A bug had been killing Detroit street trees for almost a decade before it was identified in 2002 as the emerald ash borer. It too arrived in raw-wood pallets and was then spread around with firewood and infected nursery stock. It is now known that the ash borer had been in agency plantations of hybrid ashes and elsewhere since 1997, but no one identified it while there was still time to stop it. Vic Mastro of the U.S. Animal and Plant Health Inspection Service can only offer that, as with the dying elms, woodpeckers may get a good feed on the dying trees. The borer will systematically kill all seventeen ash species north of Mexico – an estimated 2.7 billion trees in Canada and the United States.[12]

The ash borer flew across the Detroit River in 2002. Canada adopted a strategy of containment, removing and mulching infected and dead ash, and clearing a six-by-twenty-mile ash-free zone from Lake Erie to Lake Huron. The ash-free zone was completed in 2005, but the next year – and every year since – the borer wafted east in the winds, getting into London, Toronto, and beyond. In 2008 a quarantine was put in place in Toronto to curb its spread, and in 2011 funds were allocated to remove almost a million ash trees. The United States also started with containment and is also now reduced to cleanup. A special effort was made to lower ash densities at locations like the Mackinac Bridge in northern Michigan, which controls entry into the Upper Peninsula and boreal Canada. By 2008, however, the insect had made it across the bridges into Sault Ste Marie, Ontario. The same year, it reached the Atlantic in the east and crossed the Mississippi in the west.

The ash borer will take out entire chapters of evolution. There are twenty-six species of butterfly that depend on the ash as their host. Also gone will be the black ash of Native culture, and all the uses it served. The economic loss is estimated at $282 billion in the United States alone. "Homeland security" is an idea we limit to human threats, but the distinction between accidental and deliberate biological warfare is of no consequence to its victims.[13]

Not all invasives are terminators. Some of them pulse in synchrony with their prey. An insect called the larch sawfly was described in Europe in 1837 and showed up in Canada in 1882, where it devastated its sibling species, the tamarack. It surged across the continent and, by 1910, had knocked out the tamarack everywhere. The sawfly collapsed after that but it came back again between 1937 and 1942, and in 1951 and 1962, after the tamarack had grown back. To add to the tamarack's woes, a fungal pathogen was brought to Massachusetts from Europe in 1927 on infected larch seedlings; it reached the Canadian Maritimes in 1980.[14]

The hemlock will be next. It experienced a range collapse long ago, about 5000 BP, for reasons unknown and it took one or two millennia for it to recover. In the 1950s, a woolly adelgid insect that feeds on it arrived from Asia, having already reached the west coast in the early 1920s. It is finishing off the hemlock in the Appalachians and was found in upper New York and Pennsylvania in 2007. It is now on the south shore of Lake Ontario. Infestations lead to multiple stresses and cause death within a few years. The Canadian Forest Service calls it a "lethal pest" and the hemlock, which can live as long as nine hundred years, seems doomed. Another woolly adelgid that preys on firs also arrived from Europe in the early 1900s and it has turned out to be a terminator of the Fraser fir, an endemic conifer of the high Appalachians and a much loved Christmas tree.[15]

Introduced insects are also at work on the white pine, the provincial tree of Ontario and a link to its settlement past. Towering above the forest, they were much sought after in the days when Britain's Royal Navy was fending off Napoleon. In 1900 pine seedlings were brought from Europe infected with the white pine blister rust. Then, in the 1990s, the Eurasian pine shoot beetle showed up in Ohio, Quebec, and Ontario, joining the native pine shoot borer and white pine weevil. The larvae of all three feed and tunnel in a pine's lead shoots, which die. Growth is displaced to lateral shoots, shaping the tree more like a large shrub, perhaps still good for wildlife but not the majestic white pine of settlement days.[16]

The *Sirex* woodwasp has been the most common species of woodwasp detected at U.S. ports of entry in wooden packing materials. In its native Europe, it attacks pines almost exclusively. Its first wild occurrence here was in New York State where it was found in a Scots pine plantation in 2004. It showed up in Ontario in 2005. If it settles in on our native pines, all of them susceptible, it too may emerge as another terminator.[17]

Are the oaks still safe? The larvae of the winter moth defoliate most broadleaf trees but they like oak in particular. Winter moth was introduced from Europe in the 1950s and has caused a 40 per cent mortality among Nova Scotia red oaks. It has not arrived in Great Lakes country yet, but, like the beech bark blight, it seems to be moving south first through New England before heading west. Also afoot among the oaks is a new cadre of acorn and root weevils still poorly known.[18]

The arrivals are not slowing. One of our most admired southern shrubs, the flowering dogwood, is now failing. An anthracnose disease of unknown origins showed up in the mid-1970s on both the Pacific dogwood near Seattle and the flowering dogwood in New York. It has now spread, killing first the dogwoods in shaded forest interiors. Efforts are underway to find a resistant stock but the obituary of the dogwood was written in 1989 by Frank Santamour of the National Arboretum in Washington: "There is probably little hope for the selection and development of anthracnose-resistant plants."[19]

If we project forward, based on the last century, we see a worsening nightmare of non-native pathogens in our woods, eliminating whole species and homogenizing forests everywhere. Global trade continues to intensify, and there is no doubt that the forests of northeast North America are at greater risk from infectious non-native pests and pathogens than from any other threat, including climate change or overcutting. Sadly, North Americans remain largely oblivious to the lessons that Australia, New Zealand, Hawaii, and others – who now take more care – learned long ago. Worldwide, invasives are recognized as second to habitat destruction as the leading threat to nature, but in the Great Lakes country, where habitat destruction peaked long ago, invasives are now doing the most harm.[20]

More Bugs in the System

"Insects are the little things that run the world," says E.O. Wilson, one of the founders of conservation biology. Insects are both threatening and threatened, and entomologist David Wagner at the University of Connecticut cites the greatest threat to native insects as our impacts on habitats, including the closing of forest canopies that were once open. After this, he lists non-native invasives, many of which are other insects. Insects are global in their impact. They pollinate 70 per cent of world crop plants – including fruits, vegetables, seed crops, fibres, drugs, and biofuels. On the other hand, Cornell ecologist David Pimentel estimates that seventy thousand insect species also steal 40 per cent of the world's crop yield, despite $35 billion in pesticides applied each year. From both points of view, humans are mere spectators in the thrall of insects and fungi, seldom understanding their comings and goings, or their interactions. As the historian Alfred Crosby puts it, "humanity is the purposeful but often drunken ringmaster of a three-ring circus of organisms."[21]

Before contact, the most abundant large insect in North America was the native Rocky Mountain locust, which reached numbers in the order of 3.5 trillion in spectacular eruptions up to eight hundred miles long. They were finished by 1902. A co-dependence with bison may have doomed them; their muddy wallows were favoured egg-laying sites. Other natives are also on their way to extinction by our actions. Our lady beetles (or ladybugs) were once numerous and abundant – over ninety native species in Great Lakes country. The nine-spotted lady beetle was the most common of them, so much so that it was recognized in 1989 as the state insect of New York. Three years later, it was considered extinct. How did that happen?

Over the past century, the U.S. Department of Agriculture has introduced more than 180 non-native species of ladybugs into the United States to feed on other insects that were crop pests. About seventeen of them are now naturalized. Two of them were particularly successful, the seven-spotted and the multicoloured Asian. Coincidentally, a new soybean aphid arrived from China in 2000, and it exploded across North America, individuals breeding within a week or so of birth. The math works for aphids and it also worked for the non-native ladybugs that fed on them. I recall the day the aphids erupted north across Lake Ontario. There was a baseball game that day, 4 August 2001, at Toronto's Sky Dome. The sky was so dense with aphids that they closed the dome in the third inning. The new ladybugs exploded within weeks to feed on the aphids. They stink and bite, and invaded our homes – nothing like the native ladybugs. They spoiled so much wine in Ontario (the ladybugs were harvested with the grapes) that disposing of the vinegar became a problem. This was a scenario of non-natives interacting with other non-natives, and displacing natives. A recent five-year survey of Canadian ladybugs by citizen scientists showed that over 60 per cent of those found were the two non-native species. After no sightings for twenty years, the once-common nine-spotted lady beetle, the state insect of New York, was rediscovered only in 2011, and its future is dubious at best.[22]

The insects that eat tree leaves once played an active role in forest ecology. Spruce budworm and tent caterpillars would defoliate trees and open up a forest, and help it regenerate. This balance between trees and their native defoliators is now ended. In 1870 an announcement was made in Boston: "A year ago the larvae of a certain owlet moth ... were accidentally introduced by a Massachusetts entomologist into New England, where it is spreading with great rapidity." The Harvard professor had wanted to start an American silk industry but his gypsy moths escaped and now defoliate forests across the region. The moths prefer oaks, which can die from repeated defoliations, and thus shift forest composition to maples or other trees. The caterpillars can literally rain down from trees and overwhelm local authorities, whose responses can even make matters worse when they involve, as Steve Marshall calls it, "staggering amounts of insecticides dumped over our forested lands." Unfortunately, the preferred spray, the bacterial pathogen *Bacillus thuringiensis* (*Bt*), kills *all* moth and butterfly larvae, and its broader impacts are unclear. New York and New England states no longer spray but agencies elsewhere still do.[23]

Predictably, a half century ago, the U.S. Department of Agriculture began to import new insects to kill the gypsy moth. One of them, the *Compsilura* tachinid fly, has settled in so well that it has parasitized 180 butterfly species. At the same time, both it and eight other non-native parasites that were tested have been shown to have *no* controlling effect on their original target, gypsy moth. They are implicated, however, in a reported 81 per cent mortality of our spectacular *Cecropia* moths, and almost as much among other giant silkworm moths. The experiments continue.[24]

The affable bumble bee is known to everyone in eastern North America. They are now, however, widely parasitized by a non-native fungus *Nosema*, which arrived aboard commercially reared (and infected) bumble bees released into greenhouses to pollinate crops, especially tomatoes. The *Nosema* is now causing the collapse of native bumble bees across northeast North America. Studies in Ontario show that native bumble bees foraging near greenhouses are three times as likely to be infected with *Nosema* as those distant from greenhouses, and that another parasite, a *Crithidia*, is also infecting wild bees. Sheila Colla at York University was one of the first to raise the alarm, in 2006. "At the 45 sites I went to all through eastern North America I only found one individual ... on Lake Huron." It appears that some have all but disappeared, like the rusty-patched bumble bee, while others are holding on, like the common eastern bumble bee.[25]

Pollination is a critical evolutionary link between plants and insects, and central to our global food economy. There now exists a North American Pollination Protection Campaign, trying to bring this understanding to the public. Growers now hire pollinators from wherever they can, to pollinate their crops, orchards, and greenhouses. However, there has been a 50 to 90 per cent decline in U.S. honey bee colonies in the past twenty-five years, and in 2006 the rate of "colony collapse" – the inexplicable disappearance of bee colonies – spiked to one-third of all U.S. managed bees. Some blamed it on the constant moving of commercial bee colonies between fields. Pennsylvania State entomologist Diana Cox-Foster and others maintain that a virus discovered in 2007, the Israeli acute paralysis virus, is the cause. Others point to the debilitating effects of the parasitic varoa mites brought into the region in the late 1980s, and to the proven harmfulness of neonicotinoid insecticides, including IMD, widely used in the United States since the 1990s.[26]

Fundamentally, we know not what we do. Insects face a witch's brew: an industrialized landscape and a loss of host species; climate warming (shifting the timing of pollination); invasives and pathogens; pesticides and transgenics; and now, modified genetics. Entomologist Laurence Packer at York University worries about the latter. "Bees are more prone to extinction than almost all other organisms because of the genetic load that results from their sex determining mechanism." Bees face an "extinction vortex," he says, based on an over-production of males. Rachel Carson wrote fifty years ago that pollination was in jeopardy. "Man is more dependent on these wild pollinators than he usually realizes ... Several hundred species of wild bees take part in the pollination of cultivated crops – a hundred species visiting the flowers of alfalfa alone. Without insect pollination, most of the soil-holding and soil-enriching plants of uncultivated areas would die out." Not even Carson's alfalfa is safe today; its primary pollinator is the non-native alfalfa leaf-cutting bee, which is now infected by a non-native fungus called chalkbrood, likely brought in with honey bees, which it also infects.[27]

Consider the lowly earthworm. Charles Darwin measured them raising as much as ten tons of soil above each English acre every year, and wrote about them burying Roman ruins as they did so. Today, there are about twenty species in Great Lakes country, almost all of them from Europe. None are native to the Great Lakes basin, with the exception of a single rare mudworm. A worm moves no more than twenty-five feet each year, so the degree to which earthworms now occupy almost every acre of soil in the southern Great Lakes region is the extent to which humans have moved them around. In a study across New York and Pennsylvania, the biologist Victoria Nuzzo has reported that she "couldn't find a forest site without earthworms."[28]

Most of the earthworms are voracious ingesters of detritus and are changing our soils as a result. They churn it, homogenize it, and change its chemistry. They reduce the root fungi that plants depend on, and the diversity of native plants and the frequency of insects. Adult red-backed salamanders are large enough to eat them but they are too large for young salamanders, which go hungry. "There are significantly more non-native plants in forests with earthworms, and significantly less leaf litter," Nuzzo says. She suspects that there is a synergy of non-native plants, earthworms, slugs, and white-tailed deer which degrades native forests and particularly their understoreys. The white-tailed deer is also behaving like an invasive now. Not only has it expanded its range, but densities in eastern North America have grown from one deer per sixty acres before settlement to as high as one per twelve acres in Pennsylvania and more than one per every five acres in some U.S. National Parks. Another link in the earthworm story is the cluster fly. This obnoxious blowfly is a strict parasite on earthworms and, without doubt, arrived with the first shipments of plants – the soil bringing the worms, and the worms the cluster flies.[29]

It was estimated in one study that non-native invasives cost the United States $137 billion in the last century. Others put the cost of a single newcomer, the emerald ash borer, at $282 billion. Clearly, we have no credible estimates of their real costs or impacts. How *can* we measure it? In truth, we deliberately set out to convert the whole region to a New Europe. And now we find some of the newcomers offensive? Steadily and ceaselessly, there is a subtle diminishment of the native estate, occurring well beyond our ability to measure, or calculate, or comprehend.[30]

Pigs, Plants, and Gardening

Many introductions were as normal as packing for a trip, and early shipboard migrants knew what they were bringing. Others just came for the ride. Champlain's ship brought rats to Acadia in 1606, a familiar pest that depends on man. The house mouse, bedbug, house fly, cockroach, and earwig were other dependent species that came early, and fit in effortlessly.[31]

However, Hessian flies were a different matter. They showed up in the 1770s in wheat fields near New York City. The larvae fed on the stems of wheat and other grains, seriously reducing yields. These were revolutionary times and German troops from Hesse, fighting for England, were blamed. Was it an act of war? Prominent Americans like George Washington, Noah Webster, and Thomas Jefferson weighed in on the matter, and New York Governor George Clinton lectured on its "fatal ravages." Defeating the Hessian fly became a fleeting national cause for America. In 1788 Joseph Banks, president of the Royal Society, advised King George III to ban American wheat to keep it out of England. Was this an escalation? The next year, however, the threat of inflationary bread prices won out and the ban was lifted. The threat faded even more in 1793, when yellow fever devastated Philadelphia and attention shifted. The fly significantly affected wheat growing in New England for generations, but it was hardly an intentional act, and it soon crossed the border into Upper Canada in 1793 and Lower Canada in 1795.[32]

The celebrity of the Hessian fly did nothing to stem the flow of species. It was an accepted truth of the day that all societies could be bettered by an active trade in the new crops, animals, and trees that were being discovered at unprecedented rates worldwide. In 1854 both England and France started "acclimatization" societies, and each of their colonies followed suit. Britain's Kew Gardens, Royal Society, and Royal Navy had been doing the same since they first went global, deliberately shipping species around the world. States vied with each other, and competition was brisk. The acclimatization society in Cincinnati, Ohio, tried to bring in starlings in 1872, but it took repeated attempts by experts to finally naturalize the bird in Central Park, New York, in 1890. "Acclimatization" meant, for example, that it was an admirable goal to introduce into Central Park all the birds mentioned by William Shakespeare in his plays, including the starling.[33]

It started early. In 1539 Hernando De Soto landed in Florida fresh from Peru. He arrived with his men, horses, and three hundred pigs, and they set out to find gold on a quixotic four-year foray from one rich farming nation to the next. A few of his men made it back to tell the tale. They had found many great nations but most of those newly discovered nations had already fallen victim to new diseases just before the Spaniards' arrival. Some of De Soto's pigs had escaped and gone feral by 1541, and pigs were (and still are) vectors for disease. Although unprovable, De Soto's pigs were almost certainly carriers.[34]

Early settlers had neither the fences nor the time to corral or care for their pigs and cattle. In Upper Canada, "the cattle are turned into the woods," La Rochefoucauld would write in 1795. The settler John Langton complained that "Ohio pork can be procured cheaper; they have extensive backwoods where the pigs run almost wild." Issues arising from free-run stock were rife and every community had to develop legal means of redress. The first courts in New England made it clear that it was the farmer's responsibility to fence his crops *against* free-ranging pigs and cattle. Hogs were "the weed creatures of New England," in historian William Cronon's words, "They so rapidly became a nuisance that, as early as 1633, the Massachusetts court declared that 'it shalbe lawfull for any man to kill any swine that comes into his corne.'" Fencing laws and fencing officers have been in place ever since.[35]

Gradually the fields and pastures were fenced, but the pigs stayed wild. While the rich mast and fruit trees and crops were their special targets, the entire native vegetation fell victim. A strong tradition of hunting feral pigs developed, and the pastime is still growing today. Jack Mayer of the Savannah River National Laboratory puts it bluntly: "There is a pig bomb going off in the United States today." In 1990 there were an estimated one to two million pigs wild in nineteen states; in 2007 there were three to six million pigs wild in forty states. They are trapped and released in new haunts by enamoured sportsmen, and are the second most popular big game species in the United States, after deer.[36]

What's the matter with feral pigs? They transmit diseases like brucellosis, swine disease, *E. coli*, influenza, giardia, and pseudorabies. They destabilize soils by grubbing for food, and they wallow in anything wet. They damage tree roots and root out seedlings. They follow a "see-food diet," that is to say, they see it, they eat it. They clear out oak mast, out-competing turkey, deer, bear, and squirrel, and they prey on lambs, goats, calves, colts, fawns, poultry, rabbits, frogs, mice, salamanders, and turtles. Mayor repeats emphatically, "Pigs do it by the numbers." They are reproductively mature at five months and can have six to sixteen young in a litter. Because of this, 55 per cent of a population must be killed annually just to cap it. Hunting, fencing, immuno-contraception, and special toxins (now used in Australia) may all be needed to stabilize the pigs.[37]

The peach, which is hardly a noxious species, also came in with the Spanish and spread quickly. When Kit Carson was driving the Navajo from Arizona and New Mexico in 1863, he destroyed their peach orchards to force them out, reputedly three hundred peach groves in one place alone. The peach moved quickly inland from the Gulf of Mexico and the Atlantic seaboard, both as an invasive and an adoptee that Natives added as early as the 1500s to their orchards. Peach, apple, and cherry were quickly propagated by the Iroquois, and went wild after the Iroquois homelands were razed. The distinction between crop and weed is never great.[38]

The distinction between accidental and deliberate introductions is moot because the outcomes of either are so unpredictable. We now have no need for acclimatization societies; in the global world, everyone does it. Again, one modern version of hunting-gathering is to "privatize the profits and socialize the costs." However, when the costs are borne by nature, this gets translated into "externalize the costs." For example, a century ago, Ontario's public nurseries decided to supply Scots pine to landowners for windbreaks and a Christmas tree industry. Which genotype of Scots pine should they use? For Christmas trees, they chose a genotype that takes a dense, shrubby growth form. Landowners planted them eagerly, only to abandon most of them when they realized that Christmas trees take a lot of work. The Scots pine went feral, infesting large acreages with deformed trees. They rarely achieve the normal tree habit of other genotypes, and little else lives in their plantations.

By good fortune, agencies elsewhere in the region preferred native trees and did not subsidize the spread of Scots pine. As a result, Scots pine is a particular Ontario problem.[39]

Private nurseries also made mistakes, such as the Norway maple. The botanist John Bartram was an early acclimatizer, and his Philadelphia tree nursery introduced the Norway maple in 1756. This shade tree can survive the tough conditions of nurseries and still look good to buyers after months wrapped in rootballs. For some local authorities, Norway maple is their indestructible staple for subdivisions and roadsides. However, its heavy leaf litter complicates cleanup and its heavy shade throttles whatever grows under it. It secretes a substance that suppresses seedlings and wildflowers, and inhibits soil organisms. Feral Norway maple has seeded into many ravines in Toronto and its shade has killed off the ground cover, causing sheet erosion after heavy rains. Parks staff try to remove it and plant native trees but it is a thankless underfunded task. Norway maple is the weed tree most widely adventive into northeastern forests, and, while prohibited from sale in parts of New England, it is still a best-seller in Great Lakes nurseries.[40]

Species by species, biological pollution chokes off the native ecology. The most obvious are the plants, which dominate the Great Lakes lowlands. A third of the plant species now growing unassisted in Great Lakes country are not native here. A botanist hardly knows what to list as the most invasive: autumn olive or multiflora rose (promoted by agencies to feed wildlife); the prickly buckthorns (of cathartic fame); the purple loosestrife (a garden favourite that chokes out wetlands); Asian stilt grass (a newcomer streaking across the region); frog-bit or watermilfoil (choking our waterways); or the dog strangling vines, Eurasian thistles, spotted knapweed, reed grass, and St John's wort. Special mention goes to garlic mustard, a European now blanketing many forest floors and displacing the spring wildflowers for which the forests are famous. It also inhibits the growth of tree seedlings by interfering with their soil fungi. The list goes on, each one with its own story of virulent success as they settle on the new continent.[41]

Settlers came to the prairies early, and settlers elsewhere soon turned their land into facsimile prairies. Not satisfied with the native grasses, a program of assisted migration was instituted by the U.S. Department of Agriculture from 1870 to 1893, resulting in the testing and distribution of more than four hundred species of non-native grasses. This was the heyday of horticultural globalization, in the late 1800s and early 1900s, and it resulted in the dominant grasslands of the region today, an invented Eurasian turf of bluegrass, tall fescue, orchard grass, timothy, redtop, brome, and others – and clovers – an enduring but foreign facsimile of native prairie.[42]

Provenance – of humans and their baggage – has always been the subject of a debate that pits nativesness and naturalism against diversity and globalism. With regard to plant life, the most thoughtful debates occurred in the late 1800s and early 1900s, when agriculture and horticulture were of greatest economic and social interest across the continent. For example, there were fifteen agricultural experimental stations in the Ontario portion of the region alone in 1898, with dozens more stateside. Institutions, policies, and laws were deployed to balance the interests of those profiting from species transfers (growers and shippers) and those suffering the consequences (producers and landowners). Incidents such as the burning of donated Japanese cherry trees in Washington in 1910, because of the pests they hosted, triggered an international response, and influenced immigration policy. The bipolar response was to replant Japanese cherry trees on the White House lawn in 1912, even while adopting the Plant Quarantine Act in the same year and the Quarantine 37 in 1918 to interdict the traffic in pests and pathogens.[43]

Out of all this grew a New World naturalism in horticulture and in landscape design, which combined the native and newcomer in expansive settings. The titans of landscape design acted on this new naturalism: Frederick L. Olmsted (Central Park 1853-56, Mount Royal Park 1874, Goat Island 1885); Aldo Leopold (Curtis Prairie 1935); and Howard and Lorrie Dunington-Grubb (Royal Botanical Gardens 1929, Niagara Parks 1930s). The approach was both inclusive and bipolar, using both "clean" and "patriotic" natives, and "foreign" and delightful "oddities and freaks." People took their gardening very seriously in those days, as historian Philip Pauly writes, making individual "decisions that were by turn technical, aesthetic and ideological."[44]

Humans co-evolved with plants and are one of their most effective means of propagation and movement. Great Lakes country is changed as a result. What plants will be here after the next ice age, after a thousand centuries of acclimatization south of the ice and after the next interglacial warming releases them north again? The last two interglacials saw essentially the same North American species dominate, but the next one will be different. Based just on the volume and virulence of the non-natives, we might well picture in our mind's eye a future forest dominated by Scots pine, Norway maple, and tree-of-heaven, with understoreys of dog strangling vine, garlic mustard, and Asian stilt grass, and with new grasslands entirely. Native species will adapt or yield.[45]

Disease, Invasives, and Culture

Single organisms can change history. The potato blight started a migration of humans that has not stopped since. The New World potato was considered godsent in Europe, feeding whole new generations of rural poor. The population of Ireland grew from three million to more than eight million in the sixty years before 1840, reaching rural densities up to 475 persons per square mile. A fungus-like blight arrived in Europe in the 1830s, however, and it turned every potato into mucoid refuse. The blight hit Ireland in 1845. A million people starved to death and more than two million left in the next decade or so, most for North America. Ireland's population has yet to recover. "Irishmen who had lived by the potato died by the potato," writes historian Alfred Crosby in *The Columbian Exchange*. This was a story of two New World species played out in the Old World, which changed both worlds as a result.[46]

New diseases also prey on the wildlife, often through complex interactions of natives and non-natives. For example, type-E avian botulism is a neurotoxin now sweeping the Great Lakes and causing annual die-offs of ducks, gulls, loons, grebes, sturgeon, and other wildlife. The great black-backed gull is almost gone from Lake Ontario, and 2011 saw thousands of animals piling up on the shores of southeast Georgian Bay. This aquatic botulism was first discovered in the 1950s but did not become a problem until the 1990s, after the non-native quagga mussel and round goby exploded in numbers. The quagga filters the water column, increases light penetration, and adds phosphorus-rich feces. This spurs the growth of algae, which decompose in shallow waters and rob it of oxygen. Type-E botulism flourishes in this anoxic environment and is eaten by round goby. The quagga, goby, and algae are then eaten by the birds, fish, and other wildlife. The piping plover was essentially gone from the Great Lakes by 1986 (down to seventeen pairs), prevented from nesting by beach grooming, recreation, and development. A major binational effort brought it back, but now we learn that botulism is killing plover along Lake Michigan.[47]

In the new city-state world, pathogens can arrive from points unknown. A new fungus was found in 2006 on a bat's nose in a cave west of Albany, New York. By 2008, it had spread to more than 115 overwintering sites in the eastern Great Lakes and mid-Atlantic region; and by 2011, it was epidemic, with a 95 per cent die-off rate that now endangers four bat species in the Great Lakes region. Aberrant behaviours, such as bats flying by the cliffs in Mono in winter, are diagnostic, and regional extinctions are feared. Another fungus, likely from Africa and now spread on the feet of waterfowl, is causing lethal skin infections on frogs and declines in amphibians worldwide.[48]

Old World diseases killed at least three-quarters of New World Natives – all the regional warfare from 1600 to 1815 killed only a fraction of the number. Today, ships and planes, pallets and containers, and even our bodies are all hard at work homogenizing our pathogens, in a world with no natural borders. Too many humans and too many co-evolving organisms occupy too little space and now feed on each other. There are new pathogens directly the result of feeding meat, brains, and bone meal to animals that never ate animals before. In addition to the historic diseases, the list now includes: H5N1 avian influenza; the new prion diseases (including BSE, TME, CWD, CJD); weaponized anthrax; methicillin-resistant *Staphylococcus aureus*; vancomycin-resistant *Enterococcus*; *Clostridium difficile*; AIDS; Lyme disease; West Nile disease; SARS; and the new NDM-1 superbug from India. They all have the virulence of invasives wherever they go. Journalist and author Andrew Nikiforuk calls them "biological bombs" and "medical explosions" in his book *Pandemonium*. He paints a stark picture of a world in which the combination of unfettered free trade in organisms, and increased mobility and urban crowding, has produced a volatile environment for seven billion humans. The world, he says, requires responsible trade with responsible controls. "Accept responsibility for the biological consequences of one's actions."[49]

There is a pathology of invasiveness, and many of the traits of the human species, and of its technologies and social constructs, share the same pathological traits. New World newcomers, with their tough immune systems, metallurgy, and concepts of ownership, behaved as invasives. The host cultures and landscapes reacted just as predictably – first with a lack of recognition of the significance of the new arrivals, or any defence, and then with attempts at accommodation and retreat. We understand the pattern when it is applied to disease but we are slow to see human ideas and technologies in the same light. And yet they operate with the same virulence and irrevocability.

The key traits of invasiveness are novelty, aggression, and an ability to take advantage of disturbance. Today, and almost daily, new technologies and ideas appear in the marketplace, and their promoters vie with each other to confer on them the traits of invasives, and thus profit proportionately. Modern Western culture has excelled in this, and has parasitized Native cultures globally with viral industrialism and consumerism. Cultures that were once unique and inspiring are now interchangeable and predictable. Herb Wagner of the University of Michigan takes this to its logical conclusion: "The species *Homo sapiens* itself is without question the super invader of all time."[50]

Humans have a singular inability to move from any one place to another without bringing along a host of symbiotic, parasitic, and opportunistic hitchhikers, as well as a circus of cultural and consumer proclivities. It is as if we can never come clean. The original wilds of Great Lakes country stand in bold contrast with the world we have wrought, and we can think nostalgically of such places as natural. However, when we say we know what is "natural," we are not straying far from the same hubris that caused the problem in the first place. Brendon Larson, ecologist at the University of Waterloo, says, "We feel we can put things back in order by removing invasive species, but I'm unconvinced that there was ever such a fixed state to begin with or that humans have ever demonstrated such an ability."[51]

The necessary skill is to be familiar enough with nature that we understand how particular species, native or not, interact and succeed or fail. We can, on that basis, resist some of the invasives or soften their impact, without taking on the impossible task of eliminating them. We can also deliberately endorse and support the species that we want back on the landscape. We can recover some of our earlier biological diversity, trusting in nature in the same way that nature itself trusts in diversity, and letting it do its own magic on its own behalf. We can accept that the world can never be the same again, assume full responsibility, and get on with it.

Still, we are blessed in Great Lakes country. Many parts of it are still close to Nature's creation, which can still inspire protective instincts. Other parts of the region are, however, the ground zeros of globalization. They have suffered such a colossal cock-up for so long that we are now exploring a new "recombinant ecology," as conservation biologist Michael Soulé calls it. Original natives and adventive newcomers, together, are actively competing for new lead roles, even while the stage itself is perennially under construction. Two of the foundations of that new stage are our growing cities and our changing climates.[52]

CHAPTER TEN

Growing Cities, Changing Climates: The Next Conversion

Hurricane Hazel tore into the Great Lakes country in October 1954. I remember a neighbour loading us into the back of his pickup to test the bridge over our section of the Don River, our only way out to Yonge Street. He raced down the hill on to the bridge, spraying water in every direction. Great fun, but the headlines in the newspapers were horrific. Eighty-one people dead, and thousands homeless. Streets full of homes gone. Bridges out. Eleven inches of rain in two days.

The lessons were clear and governments woke up, as they had done in Ohio after the floods of 1913. In Ontario the rest of the watershed "conservation authorities" were put in place, to buy up the river valleys, remove all buildings from them, build dams where needed, and plant trees - millions of them - to restore the degraded lands that had been so easily torn up. Hurricane Hazel came out of the Caribbean and hit a region already saturated with rain and prone to flooding. It took a hurricane to remind people that nature meant business.

Climate ignores borders and climate change is part of the new globalism. It connects the Great Lakes to places like the Caribbean and the Gulf of Mexico, where sea waters are warming and are predicted to spawn more hurricanes as a result - and send more of them north. Even the Gulf's rising sea levels may be felt in Great Lakes country. The rise that is blamed on climate warming to date is just over one-sixteenth of an inch a year, perhaps tripling by 2100. Because 80 per cent of the low-lying coasts of the Gulf of Mexico are considered vulnerable to flooding, there is speculation that the growing, shallow Gulf will have even warmer waters, causing even more hurricanes. Such storms also cause water surges, which can spread salt-tolerant invasives like the Chinese tallow tree around the Gulf, as Hurricane Katrina did, or can open Great Lakes floodplains to invasives like Norway maple or crack willow. As ecologist Bill Platt of Louisiana State University says, "the historic state – whatever year used – is likely never to occur again."[1]

Climate is not only expressed in weather or sea levels. It is engrained into the biological fabric of the land. On Dominion Day 1974, I set up camp eighty miles north of Iroquois Falls along the Little Abitibi lakes. My work, assisted by forester John McLaren, who knew what he was doing in the bush, was to evaluate whether a park should be established there. It would be the largest park on the northern clay belt, where the paper giant Abitibi had its home mill and power dam. It was wilderness but it also had a human past, a Native graveyard, for example, and forest pests like the European sawfly. Abitibi had held off cutting for five years by the time we arrived but a logging road had been built and the company was ready to extend it north along an esker ridge, a ready-made roadbed. A month later we moved camp to the esker, which had many old red pine on it. In 1900 the surveyor M.B. Baker had written: "The timber of the district, apart from about two hundred and fifty red pine trees on the southeast corner of Montreuil Lake, is of no value." These were Baker's red pine.[2]

Eventually, the park was established, but that is another story. The red pine, up to two feet in diameter, had their own story to tell. The esker had lakes and bogs on both sides, so that the fires that had burned the area many times had not reached the pine, and they were kept safe, eighty miles north of any other surviving red pine. I cored one and it was three hundred years old. Also growing with them were wintergreen, marsh violet, and four mosses also well beyond their northern limits. How did they get here, all at their northern-most sites on the same narrow esker? By coincidence, about ten years earlier, an inquisitive naturalist had pulled a log of white pine out of a bog sixty miles south near Lake Abitibi. It, too, was far north of its modern range, so paleoecologist Jaan Terasmae at Brock University cored the bog and carbon-dated the pine. The pine was 5,800 years old, dating from the Hypsithermal Period, the warmest climate since the last glacial, proving that pine had grown far north of its modern limit when the climate was about as much warmer than average as it is today. The Montreuil esker is a living fossil, where red pine and other species held on through millennia of cooling since the Hypsithermal, as climate cooling and fires forced them out of the north.[3]

The point is that climate is engrained in the landscape. Changes to the climate creep up on organisms, like pines and humans, and on phenomena like economies and cultures, in small and easily ignored steps until, finally, they all get jammed up against the real world and force radical adjustments. When a climate shifts a few degrees, an entire landscape has to shift in its wake.

A Perpetual Worry

We have always been in awe of the weather, and in need of someone to blame. The dark days of tribalism in Europe, and of omens and entrails, lasted well into the 1600s, when the New World was being settled. Economist Emily Oster at Harvard reminds us that, when Europe's climate cooled in the 1500s and its crops failed, the Catholic inquisition blamed it on witches – almost all women – and executed hundreds of thousands between 1500 and 1700. The dependency on local harvests made for a deadly link between famine, climate, and power.[4]

In the early records from the New World, the weather featured frequently. Sometimes it was benign – a "winterless winter" on the St Lawrence in 1647, or "no winter ... to speak of" on the south shore of Lake Superior in 1661. But most of it was fearful, with special deference extended, as now, to hurricanes, tornadoes, hot summers, cold winters, droughts, and floods. Benjamin Franklin was the first to associate a volcanic eruption, in Iceland, with a cold summer in 1783. However, such eruptions were usually farther afield and as a result escaped notice, one example being the eruption of the Indonesian volcano Tambora in 1815, which we now know to have caused global crop failures and a "year without summer" in Great Lakes country in 1816.[5]

Here is a typical report from central Ontario, by Catharine Traill, to remind us how repetitive we have been on the topic. "The summer of 1845 was one of almost tropical heat ... For days together the temperature varied from ninety to ninety-six, and sometimes ninety-eight degrees [°F] in the shade ... The small creeks, and most of the springs were dried up. No rain fell for many weeks ... The fires which, as usual, had been kindled on the newly-chopped fallows ... [and put] the log-barn ... in imminent danger ... The wind carried the sparks into a thick cedar-swamp ... and there it blazed and leaped from tree to tree. The autumn rains finally extinguished the fires." Fire was thus associated with weather and, with good reason, thought of with terror.[6]

There was a clear early consensus on climate change. George Heriot expressed it in 1807: "The clearing and cultivation of lands have much contributed to the amelioration of the climate of Canada; and the number of fires kept up in the habitations in various parts of the country may likewise have a share in producing this change ... The winters in those parts of Lower Canada in the vicinity of Quebec, have remitted several degrees of their former severity. [A] priest in the island of Orleans kept, for half a century, a correct meteorological table and his successor continued it for eight years longer ... Their observations tended to prove that the medium of cold in winter had diminished eight degrees [°F] within that period."[7]

In 1853 Sam Strickland promised a further warming. "The clearing ... of the immense forests ... of Upper Canada will produce a considerable change in temperature. [Alexander von] Humboldt has clearly shown [that] as the forests of western Ontario disappear ... we may look for a rise in the minimum temperature of the spring, summer and autumnal nights. Late spring and early autumn frosts will probably become rarer." He also quoted Henry Youle Hind, who had written a pamphlet in 1851 listing the impacts of forest clearing: "the acceleration of ... spring ... [and] disappearance of snow from exposed districts." Across southern Ontario, Hind noted, sawmills were being abandoned "owing to the want of water." He measured a rise of 3°F in Toronto's mean summer temperature in the decade of most rapid forest clearing, 1840 to 1850. It became common knowledge that the climate had warmed, and even local historians did the math: "In the last 100 years, the mean annual temperature in Dufferin [County], as in the rest of southern Ontario, has increased by four or five degrees [°F] – that is, within the lifetime of some living."[8]

The whole idea of glaciation – the companion piece to climate change – was only formulated in the mid-1800s. Geologist Charles Lyell read a paper to the Geological Society of London in 1837 written by Thomas Roy, an Upper Canada surveyor, about the "Iroquois beach" in Toronto. This led to a tour of the site by Lyell himself in 1842. The bones and artifacts dug out of the old shore included those of mammoth, elk, beaver, bison, and caribou, and sparked much debate about how they got there. Louis Agassiz's 1850 book *Lake Superior* made the case for continental glaciers, which explained much of what was being found. In an 1898 paper, the University of Toronto geologist Arthur Coleman contended that the shoreline that Lyell visited was that of an old lake formed after a glacier melted, when the climate was "more rigorous than the present" and when "tamarack and spruce" dominated the area. The bones, he said, were from that time.

In 1884 Coleman discovered fossils from an even earlier time – an interglacial period – in the exposed pit-walls of the Brickyard in the Don valley in Toronto. This attracted geologists from around the world, and the fossils that Coleman found – of pawpaw, liquidambar, and Osage orange trees – proved that there had been more than one glacier, and that the earlier interglacial had been warm enough for long enough to allow southern species to live farther north than the present interglacial. Even more exciting were the bones of giant beaver, now extinct, and bison, north of the lakes. It took decades for these ideas to enter public consciousness, and as late as 1928 Coleman would make headlines in the *Montreal Gazette* when he told an audience that there had been two ice ages, that the ice had been five thousand feet thick, and that Montreal had been flooded by seawater eight thousand years ago. He also added that they could expect another glacier.[9]

It was in the 1890s that the Swedish Nobel laureate Svante Arrhenius first modelled the warming effects of carbon dioxide and water vapour in the atmosphere. This helped explain ongoing climate warming, but in 1913 it remained the considered opinion of Frederic Stupart, director of Canada's Meteorological Service, that, to that date, the "tendency towards higher annual mean and mean spring and summer temperature" was attributable to "the gradual clearing away of the vast American forests." The data, he said, conformed "exactly with the reports of early settlers." Almost a century later, in 1999, the Royal Canadian Institute updated Stupart's 1913 report on Toronto's climate. By then, climatologists Ted Munn, David Yap, and Morley Thomas took it for granted that carbon emissions were warming the climate, and focused instead on how much faster the Toronto climate was warming than the region around it. The new climate drivers were the "immense and increasing quantities of heat ... produced," and the paving of the city with buildings and dark surfaces, most of them clear of snow in the winter. The major cities of the Great Lakes and Atlantic seaboard now combust, absorb, leak, and waste so much energy that they now average 4 to 8°F (2.2 to 4.4°C) warmer than their surroundings. Downtown Toronto's average minimum temperature is now 5 to 7°F (3 to 4°C) warmer than in the 1840s, and it now has more than 190 frost-free days a year, 40 days more than just a dozen miles away at Pearson Airport or Richmond Hill, which were once in the same climate zone.[10]

There are also hotspots inside cities. Recent studies have mapped almost 15 per cent of Toronto as "heat islands" that are more than 9°F (5°C) warmer than the local average, and larger by a third than two decades ago. Urban heat waves and air-quality advisories are on the rise as cities become hotter and more polluting. The warnings extend beyond the cities, and coal-fired generators in rural Ohio and Ontario are also major contributors. Heat waves were lethal prior to air-conditioning; a heat wave in July 1936 killed more than six thousand North Americans, a quarter of them in Great Lakes cities. Today, air-conditioning protects us, but it has also moved the peak electrical demand to the summer, as summers hit record temperatures. The decade 2001 to 2010 was the warmest since standard records began in 1850 and more than 80 per cent of urban homes are now air-conditioned. This cooling accounts for more than 30 per cent of energy use, even while the outside air gets heated by the generation of that same energy. It is also less efficient to generate power in the summer, because air-cooled generators and transmission lines overheat, the lake water used to cool generators is warmer, and wind turbines run more slowly. Most of our buildings – whether historic stock or brand new high-rises – are abysmally sealed and insulated, and they leak energy both summer and winter.[11]

If there is any intention to break the link between city growth and climate warming, cities must reduce their overheating. There is a consensus that energy efficiency and conservation are the most direct means to do so. Princeton carbon modellers Stephen Pacala and Robert Socolow have calculated one of a number of global energy budgets that could curb profligate energy use, by applying available, off-the-shelf technologies, or "stabilization wedges," that would flat-line emissions. Technological innovation is not the issue. Curbing old appetites and creating new ones is the challenge, to put it in terms of our engrained hunting-and-gathering psyches.[12]

There is infinite scope for creative thinking if the challenge is accepted to retool cities. Building codes can be rewritten, incentives changed, and serious public transit built within and between cities and satellites. A century and a half ago, to build railways, the entire land base underwent a major dislocation of landowner rights to secure right-of-ways for the new rail lines. Many of those transit right-of-ways have since been lost in a blur of auto-induced forgetfulness, and similar dislocations will be needed to recreate them. In all of this, alternative design is the great hope, if and when de-energizing and containment become the goals. This is improbable, however, if city-states pursue business as usual and hope (and plan) to expand indefinitely, on more or less the old templates.

One litmus test of this will be the Toronto area, the largest urban complex in Great Lakes country. The governments of Ontario and Canada are committed to welcoming 3 million new residents to Toronto and its vicinity (the "416" and "905" area-code districts) in the next twenty-five years, and a total of more than 4.5 million to the broader Toronto-centred region. More than three-quarters of them will settle in the new cities around Toronto, which are growing more than twice as fast as the city itself. Recent public policy to "intensify" development has barely nudged the region off its historic path of "greenfield" growth, and it has forced a similar (and often inappropriate) intensification on rural areas. It advertises urban containment but, at the same time, lays plans to leapfrog its vaunted Greenbelt and build more expressways to service its gridlocked satellite cities. Even so, there are signs of change. Toronto now charges for residential water use (which others cities did long ago). It has begun to draw water from Lake Ontario to cool some of its downtown. The price of electricity is being raised, forcing people to use less. More spectacularly, Toronto has set a goal for 30 per cent tree cover by 2030, focusing on native trees that cool the city and take up carbon. A few rooftops are morphing into gardens and grasslands. Such innovation is largely in the city core, however, and the overall regional dependence on trucking and cars keeps growing. From 1994 to 2006, the number of "miles driven" increased in the Canadian portion of the region by 66 per cent, more than three times the increase south of the lakes.[13]

Urban expansion is joined at the hip with energy sprawl, both of them subsidized by cheap land. In total, Great Lakes country uses the energy equivalent of eighty or so nuclear reactors. The Great Lakes were blessed with clean and bountiful hydroelectricity but there is almost no new water to exploit inside the region. Today, more than half of its energy comes from nuclear (north of the lakes) and coal (south of the lakes). What is the extent of the land that will be needed to deliver the next few nuclear-reactors' worth of energy, if it is to come from alternative sources? Excluding transmission lines, a 1,000-MW nuclear reactor takes a few thousand acres or so. If the equivalent amount of energy is to come from fossil fuels, it takes much more land but most of that land is far away and the cost (and impact) is thus externalized, to the North American west and the Middle East, the North Sea, Mexico, and South America. Exceptions are the coalfields of Appalachia, close at hand, and the shale-gas beds under Ohio, New York, and Pennsylvania, which are coming on stream.

The solar panels that are equivalent to one nuclear reactor can take up 20,000 acres or so; the equivalent wind turbines about 175,000 acres; and the equivalent in corn ethanol, a million acres or more. In the same way that conventional fuels "externalize the costs," so too do solar, wind, and ethanol. In the case of wind, the energy output of turbines averages about 20 per cent of installed capacity. As a result, a full-time backup capacity must be installed (either fossil fuel or nuclear), and this is also part of the full cost, more so if it is built at public expense and thus forecloses on other expenditure opportunities. Full costs include as well the subsidies on energy rates and transmission lines, and suppressed land values and displaced land uses. Energy sprawl also inspires severe "not-in-my-backyard" thinking; cities are more and more averse to new energy generation inside their borders, with the exception of solar. The full costs of the new energy may be seriously debated only if and when these projects are built inside cities. The conservation option – powering down and building better – may then seem more attractive by comparison.[14]

From space at night, the planet looks to be slowly burning (Fig. 23). The Great Lakes country and Atlantic seaboard are the brightest places on Earth, the most incandescent waste of light and energy in history. Its warm glow lights the sky and even in Mono, fifty miles north of Toronto, erases half of it. Within each of those cones of artificial light thrives a seductive, non-stop city-state, increasingly dislocated from nature's rhythms through the conquest of night itself.[15]

The New City-State

The phenomena of urban growth, energy use, and climate warming cannot be separated. A century ago, the energy produced from coal, wood, and mills was more polluting and destructive for each unit of energy produced, but there are now so many more people, each using so much more. The old energy footprint was lightened tremendously by hydroelectricity, hydrocarbons, and nuclear power, all of which were great advances in clean energy in their day. They were also cheap and, over the last century, they subsidized the growth of the largest city-states in world history. More than half of the world population now lives in towns and cities. Great Lakes country has now passed the 80 per cent mark. In theory, people may want to stop climate warming but they also want to live in cities, which are the largest carbon emitters and the greatest drivers of climate warming.

The culture of rural independence that dominated the region a century ago dissolved when the rural economy could no longer deliver an average living. This happened about the same time that cheap energy arrived, and the migration of people, which had been largely rural-to-rural, changed to rural-to-urban. Today, migration is largely urban-to-urban, feeding a kind of super-tribalism that has emerged as new city-states. What does this city-state mean for the environment? From nature's point of view, it may prove beneficial for the lands and waters that have none of the resources the new city-state wants. However, for the lands and waters that are called on, for growth, energy, aggregate, water, waste disposal, and the like, there will be no respite.

City-states transcend their jurisdictions. Their citizen majorities see themselves as part of a new city-state world and set the social and economic agendas of a day on that basis. This goes largely unspoken. In Great Lakes country the new city-states are *TorBuffChester* (Toronto, Buffalo, Rochester, Hamilton, Waterloo; population of twenty million); *Chicagoland* (Chicago, Milwaukee, Gary; twelve million); *MotorCity* (Detroit, Ann Arbor, Windsor, Flint; six million); *Montreal-Quebec* (six million); and just to the east, *BosWash* (New York, Boston, Philadelphia, Washington; fifty million). To all intents and purposes, they are the western safe havens of the historic Anglo-American accord. They share their wealth with their countrysides in the same way that foreign-exchange remittances buoy up poorer economies globally. This has relieved the worst abuses to the land, abuses that resulted from rural poverty and overuse, and explains much of the rural re-wilding that is occurring. The city-states spare many parts of their regions from the worst of their impacts, as a by-product of their extraordinary magnetism and self-centredness.[16]

The long-term trajectories of city-states are, however, problematic. In theory, the efficiencies are there – such as centralized delivery of heat, cold, water, food, and energy, as well as, purportedly, economical health care, education, and governance. But there is no denying that the same ends were met, albeit more modestly, on the former landscape of dispersed rural residents. The advertised urban efficiencies are more than offset by extraordinary and conspicuous excesses, subsidized by easy energy and food, and by less-than-full cost accounting. The alleged efficiencies are cited to validate even more extreme hunting-gathering practices in pursuit of urban agendas.

Urbanites tend to be only vaguely aware of the lands around them. Again, consider the Toronto region's drive to expand. As it spreads, it is increasingly removed from its water and food sources and its building materials. Water is pumped farther and farther from Lake Ontario, and pipe-sheds are now more valued than watersheds. Most of the sewage flows back to the lakeshore for treatment, and at least a third of the processed sewage is spread on rural farm fields. Water-taking licences are essentially free, and they profit water bottlers at the expense of rural groundwaters. Each citizen uses more than ten tons of sand and gravel a year, two-thirds of it purchased on their behalf for public infrastructure. When the same level of demand is projected forward for three million new urban residents, the countryside has no alternative but to suffer new pits and quarries. No net benefits accrue to the communities where the mining occurs, in comparison to the impaired wells, dust, noise, blasting, and truck traffic that go with the mining. In Ontario, the aggregate mines – 7,000 licences and more each year – are licensed *in perpetuity*. At the same time, farm-gate food prices are at all-time lows, thus suppressing the value of farm land and leaving it vulnerable to aggregate, turbines, fill disposal, and other uses subsidized by the city-state. The land remains the resource, and the city-state the profit centre. Even so, opinion polls show the hyper-city as staunchly anti-oil, anti-coal, anti-nuclear, anti-incineration, and anti-warming, all of them basic to the success of the city-state.

Cities are like organisms. "Faster-growing cities, like teenagers, have higher metabolisms than those that have stopped growing," notes historian John McNeill. When the Canadien Louis Jolliet first described the Chicago portage southwest from Lake Michigan in 1673, it was prairie and woodland in equal measure, "abounding in catfish and sturgeon ... bison, elk, deer and turkeys." *Chicagoua*, the wild garlic, flourished in the wet prairies. A city arose here in the 1840s, built on the business of converting the prairie into grain, and selling it. The canal between Lake Michigan and the Mississippi was completed in 1848, and fifteen railways converged on Chicago by 1860. Shipping, railways, and the telegraph inspired Chicago to turn grain into a currency by inventing and trading commodity "futures" for the first time. As early as 1903, Frank Norris praised its metabolism. "Brooking no rival [Chicago] imposed its dominion upon a reach of country larger than many a kingdom ... It was Empire, the resistless subjugation of all this central world of the lakes and the prairies ... in a single generation." Chicago was the fastest growing city in the world after the U.S. Civil War, and, in McNeill's words, it "exerted a gravitational pull on timber, livestock, grain and other fruits of the land." Greater Chicagoland still exerts this pull, and is predicted to grow by 1.2 million in the next 25 years.[17]

Timber was its key early import from the north, and beef was its great export, first shipped live and then in refrigerated boxcars. Its stockyards were the largest in the world by the mid-1880s, their waste discharged into Lake Michigan along with Chicago's sewage. Fear of cholera in the water supply, and deaths from typhoid, prompted the country's largest engineering project before the Panama Canal, to reverse the flow of wastes from the lake into the Mississippi. World-class water and sewage treatment plants followed. Together, the river reversals and water-takings lowered Lake Michigan by half a foot, which was partially mitigated by diverting waters themselves diverted from the Albany River north of Lake Superior. Like all great cities, Chicago flourished as the beneficiary of a great donor landscape, and as the driver of change far beyond its borders.[18]

City-states take on particular tribal identities. Once the zenith of western industrialism, the cities of Detroit, Flint, and Toledo hollowed out as their industries aged. Employment stagnated in these centres even as affluent post-war suburbs were growing around them – green, exurban, and safe. Emigration balanced immigration, and urban ghettos began to reflect even older tribal identities. They are often cited as failed examples of smokestack industrialism, as collapsed rustbelts, but they are nonetheless cleaner and greener as a result. Their industrial engines are unlikely to be fired up again and new, more sustainable businesses are replacing them. Their economies are retooling, and their urban cores are attracting new arrivals and a new creative urbanism.

Toronto did not hollow out but went the way of Manhattan, intensifying its core into a hyper-city, a refuge for wealth surrounded by low-density city-suburbs. Its wealth and power are no longer founded on local industry; there are more jobs in the suburban cities surrounding Toronto, and the disparity is growing. The early suburbs, including Rosedale and Forest Hill, had residential densities of about five houses per acre. Today, the cities around Toronto, like Oshawa, Markham, Vaughan, Mississauga, Brampton, Burlington, and Hamilton ("905"), have intensified to more than ten homes per acre, leaving only a third of the land as soft-surface. They have estate housing on their margins but these new satellite cities are reported to have the highest non-highrise densities in North America. They were never the haphazard or low-density "sprawl" that those unfamiliar with them call them, and are arguably better planned and constructed than most of the old city.[19]

"Urban sprawl" is also code for "flight of the affluent" – to places where real estate prices seal out unwelcome neighbours. Inside Toronto, in places like the Bridle Path, or outside it, in rural retreats like Caledon, Halton Hills, and King, there are places reminiscent of the sprawl in Vermont, Connecticut, or the east side of Cleveland. They are fundamentally distinct from the dense satellite cities around Toronto, which are instead "arrival cities," as journalist Doug Saunders calls them, tied to their host city as Shenzhen is to Hongkong, or the *favelas* are to Rio de Janerio. They are nurseries of ambition, as described in 1976 by Janice Perlman in relation to the *favelas*, having "the aspirations of the bourgeoisie, the perseverance of pioneers, and the values of patriots." They are, in fact, the form of development that achieves the highest possible density of affordable, separated residences directly accessible by private transportation. They are not built around linear transit corridors because there are no transit corridors. If transit becomes necessary, the public will have to bear the cost, the land profit having already been realized.[20]

Ninety per cent of newcomers to the Toronto area now arrive from other urban centres, speaking little English and attracted to ethnic enclaves, often in the new satellite cities. Many of them live first in high-rises that serve as arrival hubs and then move to high-density suburbs where the houses have no yards and no topsoil, trees, or shade. Collectively, they are like horizontal apartment blocks, but with the added attractions of land ownership, independent access to light and air, and a place to park the vehicles on which both employment and socialization depend. At the same time, high-rise living has also exploded, in condominiums that promise the same benefits but are more dependably serviced by transit. In 2012 Toronto's city core had 148 high-rises being built, twice as many as any other North American city. In the city-state, fractional ownership is always being creatively reinvented. It was once largely horizontal and involved land, but it has now gone vertical and virtual (no land is owned by a high-rise owner), temporal (as time-shares), and even subterranean (Toronto's downtown has more than a thousand stores linked by tunnel). The manufacture and sale of land ownership is as fundamental as ever.

The new global vision is of a post-industrial, post-agricultural society based on creative, electronic, transnational urban values. "Land is not really a source of any nation's wealth anymore," claimed journalist Gwynne Dyer in 2004. "Wealth now derives mostly from industry and innovation and intellectual property." However, it is hubris to ignore the foundational importance of land. Wars over land and resources continue unabated (especially wars by other means) and the North American housing and land market remains the largest monetized market in the world. In the economic recession that began in 2008, it was the underlying valuation of land, property, and mortgages that went awry and unhinged the global financial system.[21]

North of the lakes, it appears that both urbanites and suburbanites now share a new idea of the rural countryside as a new kind of "commons" over which to further exert their self-interests. As already noted, these interests are not all benign. Around Toronto, they now include a limit to urban expansion, in the form of a 1.8-million-acre Greenbelt. Communities and landowners no longer have their old right-to-develop in most of the Greenbelt, and must protect their natural features even while also delivering goods and services such as food, aggregate, energy, and waste disposal. Ironically, it seems to be the hyper-privatized city-states that are beginning to re-establish – beyond their cities – a new kind of commons, both green and not so green in turn.[22]

A forensic goal for this book was to "follow the land" and who profits from its control, development, and sale. Two almost unconscious inventions – the manufacture of land and the social licence to develop it – remain the engines that power the new city-state. However, we have yet to fully cost or charge for the energy that powers the cities and overheats the Earth. This invites comparable questions about who owns the various energy sources, of all kinds, and who profits from their control, development, and sale. Any "commons" on that front is, no doubt, a much more remote prospect.

Milankovitch

Our global climate commons has been a relatively friendly oasis for the last half-millennium. The longer cycles of climate change were more radical, however, and they operated with nourishing regularity for more than two million years, creating a fertile ground for evolution itself, within predictable cycles of glaciers and interglacials. The Gaia hypothesis, proposed in the 1970s by scientists James Lovelock and Lynn Margulis, holds that the Earth regulates itself, as an orchestration of water, gasses, and biological processes that sustains and evolves the planet's denizens. This idea of self-regulation has climate change at its heart, and it is only a short step from there to musing about how man's land clearing and carbon burning are just Earth's way of postponing the next glacial cooling. Humans are doing a good job of this but it is an effort that will ultimately fail. A man named Milankovitch figured that out almost a century ago.[23]

One of my mentors was University of Toronto paleoecologist Jim Ritchie. The best advice he gave me was to study Quaternary geology. Drummed into us were the basics of climate change: ice cores from glaciers, deep-sea sediment cores, stratigraphy, and the network of pollen cores studied across North America. Much of what we know about climate change was known by the late 1970s, although it would take years more of compiling records and modelling trends to achieve any public awareness. We were lectured about Milutin Milankovitch, the Belgrade mathematician who first calculated the clockwork of climate change. Milankovitch had been taken prisoner by the Austro-Hungarian army in 1914, and, after he was released, he committed to paper his great work on the physical determinants of global climate. It was further elaborated in 1941 and finally translated into English in 1969, a decade after his death. Simply put, his theory was that the climatic cycles that regularly bury the north under deep glacial ice are driven by a predictable cycle of change in the influx of summer sunshine at high northern latitudes.

Milankovitch based his calculations on the interactions of three planetary cycles: the distance of the Earth from the sun (cycling every 93,400 and 400,000 years); the tilt of the Earth, which affects the angles at which sunshine strikes (cycling every 41,000 years); and the regular wobble, or precession, of the Earth's rotating axis (cycling every 25,920 years). Today, for example, the Earth comes closest to the sun during the northern-hemisphere winter. Nine thousand years ago, the Earth was closest during the northern-hemisphere summer, resulting in hotter summers and colder winters. Based on these interactions, Milankovitch calculated that the Earth experiences a glacial expansion and contraction every 100,000 years or so, with about 90 per cent of the cycle in full glacial cold and about 10 per cent of the time in warmer interglacials like today.

By 1976, scientists had discovered the same cycles in temperature-dependent oxygen isotopes in plankton-like creatures buried in sediments deep under the south Atlantic. This and other studies supported Milankovitch's theory about what triggers glaciations. What remains unclear is whether there are, within these cycles, any smoothing out of peaks and troughs by gas-producing phenomena that may act as feedback mechanisms, like carbon emissions, or by the modern reduction of the globe's chlorophyll on land and sea. Will ocean warming and acidification, at the rates occurring now, reduce chlorophyll levels further? So many questions.[24]

Another issue relates to timing; in this case, when will the current interglacial end? By Milankovitch's calculations, we should be nearing its end in the next millennium or so. Human carbon emissions may override or defer the cycle, however, and usher in a "super-interglacial," as glaciologist John Imbrie called it in 1979. Some speculate that it might be delayed for tens of thousands of years, based on the durability of greenhouse gasses in the atmosphere. Will the Milankovitch cooling thus serve as a palliative to our excessive emissions, balancing glacial cooling against climate warming? This will not happen. Nature is never in balance for long.[25]

However long the present interglacial lasts, humans will have dominated it. After that, there will be a great "shuffling of the ecological deck," as paleoecologist Herb Wright of the University of Minnesota called it. In the party-game that happens each time the climate warms and cools, there are winners and losers. But humans have definitely changed the odds for many plants and animals this time round. The chance of extinction is likely to increase in proportion to how much we have reduced them on the landscape;

with rarity comes risk. The converse is also the case, that species may dominate the next interglacial in rough proportion to how much of the landscape they occupy now. As a result, many of the winners will be the invasive non-natives. Any good game also has its random outcomes; for example, the Critchfield spruce dominated much of the forest that persisted south of the last ice sheet but even that did not guarantee its survival in the last shuffle of the postglacial deck, and it is now extinct.[26]

A Global Debate

During the last glacial, carbon dioxide in the atmosphere was about 180 parts per million. It rose slowly to 280 parts per million by about 1750 AD. This was the pattern of previous glacials. Since 1750, carbon dioxide levels have risen to 400 parts per million, most of it from burning carbon. Carbon dioxide, along with a few other gasses, acts like a greenhouse, warming the atmosphere by preventing the heat energy of the sun from re-radiating back into space. As a result, the global average temperature has warmed by about 1.3°F (0.7°C) in the past century, and the current estimate for the next century is for a 5.2°F (2.9°C) increase, based on predicted carbon dioxide levels. Aerosols and other debris from industry and from volcanoes do the opposite, cooling the atmosphere by reflecting incoming sunlight away from Earth. Atmospheric aerosols are currently in decline as we restrict their emissions, but a volcano can quickly reverse that trend. Other cycles of shorter duration, such as in ocean currents and solar radiation, also complicate the trends. As predicted, the planet is warming fastest toward the north. Glaciers are melting. Sea levels are rising.[27]

There is not much argument about this. The Intergovernmental Panel on Climate Change (IPCC) has, since 1998, communicated this widely. However, beyond this, all is chaos. Strident voices on the subject speak to the complete spectrum of hopes and fears. Others are matter-of-fact – and still alarming. I met Gord McBean while serving on a federal task force when he was head of Canada's Meteorological Service. He was one of the lead authors of IPCC reports in 1990 and 1995; in 1998 he founded the Institute for Catastrophic Loss Reduction at the University of Western Ontario. A consensus builder, he drafted a letter to Prime Minister Stephen Harper in 2006, signed by ninety scientists, that emphasized the "increasing impacts of climate change on Canada's natural ecosystems" and "the need for action and development of a strategy for adaptation to projected changes."

In person, McBean is less diplomatic. "The human forcing of climate change is now ten times more powerful than natural solar forcing. The temperature is increasing 100 times faster than during the deglaciation period. Climate change is inevitable, and we must adapt to it *and* reduce emissions." The IPCC's worst-case scenario for sea-level rise, by as much as sixteen inches in the next century, is likely to be met. The Great Lakes are warming, and ice cover decreasing, so those living downwind will face major winter storms. Forest fires will increase by 50 per cent. London, Ontario, averages eight days each summer more than 85°F (30°C), and will have sixty such days by 2100. A single storm event in August 2005 did $500 million worth of damage in southern Ontario. The insurance industry, which is founded on risk calculations, is redoing its numbers.[28]

McBean reminisces about the peak of public interest in the environment in the early 1970s, and the consensus reached to curb acid rain and ozone depletion. There was another peak in support in the 1990s with the signing of the Rio convention on climate and biodiversity. In 2003 more than fifty-five thousand people died in a heat wave in Europe, and, the next year, David Anderson, Canada's minister of the environment, stated publicly: "Global warming represents a greater long-term threat to humanity than terrorism." This was deemed politically incorrect, but in 2007 and 2008 the environment again topped the list of public concerns. Then the global economy tanked. Even the news that weather-related disasters displaced thirty-eight million people in 2010 did nothing to quell the overriding concern with jobs, debt, and the economy.[29]

Another approach is championed by Bjorn Lomborg, the "skeptical environmentalist" and statistician at the Copenhagen Business School. While quick to agree with the facts presented by the IPCC, he is just as quick to dismiss any fear-mongering he sees flowing from its findings – including the movie, book, and presentations by Al Gore. Lomborg points out that, for every warmer summer day, there would be a warmer winter day and that deaths from cold now outnumber deaths from heat worldwide. Longer growing seasons will benefit northern farming. Weather events will be more dangerous in the future anyway because, as people migrate to sea-coast cities globally, there are "more people with more assets living in harm's way." If sea levels rise by sixteen inches by 2100, it is worth reflecting that they rose twelve inches in the last 150 years, a rise that was accommodated without fanfare. As for floods and a sea-level rise, "protection is the better deal," he says, cheaper than cutting carbon emissions. And finally, he says, Don't panic. Think logically. Weigh the costs and benefits, and adapt intelligently. Lomborg used to conclude his speeches by emphasizing that "we need to stop our obsession with global warming," but even he has now admitted that a global investment of $100 billion a year in mitigation is warranted.[30]

Perhaps it is the absence, to date, of serious progress on the file in North America that frustrates so many people. Peter Raven, president of the American Association for the Advancement of Science, slammed Lomborg publicly: "He's not an environmental scientist and he doesn't understand the fields that he's talking about ... It's like a school exercise or a debating society, which really doesn't take into account the facts." Both Raven and E.O. Wilson were quoted in *Time* magazine demanding that Lomborg's book publisher drop him. They are passionate on the subject because they are biologists sensitive to the ecological consequences of climate change. Neither McBean nor Lomborg is a biologist, and their cooler disciplines take them straight to actuarial costs and benefits. Their concern is human well-being and the risks to human assets. For the biologist, however, it is clear that climate change risks almost everything in nature.[31]

On the upside, when humans get organized, they can achieve great things. Even if curbing climate change is a thousand times more difficult than acid rain and ozone depletion were, it is only a thousand times more difficult. And high energy prices may well curb emissions before public policy does. However, any triage among too-large cities, too much energy use, and too few resources may not help the patient. New fixes may require even more energy sprawl and an even heavier ecological footprint. Finally, whatever the treatment, there still remain all the other assaults on nature. Perhaps, for once, humans could come second in our pantheon of gods.[32]

Putting Earth first is one way of saying that we should put some reasonable part of the commons ahead of our selves, our tribes, and our nations. The commons should, at a minimum, embrace the native landscape and its wildlife and climate – "Standing for what we stand on," as the Kentucky philosopher Wendell Berry puts it. "Earth first" is also a statement of empirical fact. Darwin understood this when he spoke of "the clumsy, wasteful, blundering, low and horribly cruel work of nature." Humans are part of this but, objectively, Darwin understood that nature – including climate – is an impartial arbiter, and will ultimately have its way, with or without us.[33]

A Moving Landscape

Nature has its co-dependents – climate, habitat, wildlife, humans – and perhaps some of their particular abilities can shed some light on how they might act in the future. For example, the cedar along the Niagara Escarpment spent the last glacial on the highland rim of eastern Tennessee, where Gary Walker at Appalachian State University discovered its highest levels of genetic diversity. Only a subset of that diversity migrated north into its modern range, after the glacier began to melt about 18,000 BP. It showed up north of the lakes by 14,800 BP, and on Manitoulin Island by 11,500 BP. In Tennessee, where the climate is now warmer, the cedar huddles on north-facing cliffs and slopes, from which, after the next glacier, some progeny may yet again move north.[34]

How fast did the cedar move? It took three thousand years to move from Tennessee to southern Ontario – therefore, six years for each mile, a rate of seventeen miles per century. From what we see around us, this seems miraculously fast. It is also clear to us today that temperature isotherms in the future will be moving north at rates *much* faster than this. Add the fact that we have greatly reduced the amount of cedar on the landscape and interrupted its continuity of habitat, and it is almost inconceivable that cedar can keep pace with the projected northward warming.

The botanist E. Lucy Braun at Ohio State University was a great believer that the forests of eastern North America were stable communities in long-term equilibrium with their climate and soils. She postulated that the rich "mixed mesophytic" and "oak-chestnut" forests were "climax" communities that had evolved in the Appalachians and Alleghenies millions of years ago, and persisted here since. She published her masterwork in 1950, and similar studies, such as those by Paul Maycock and his lab at the University of Toronto, documented her "beech-maple" and "hemlock-white pine" forests farther north. As a result, we know what occurred here but we also know now that many of the forests they studied were, in fact, artifacts of a much more random assembly.[35]

The ecologist Henry Gleason, who grew up in the mosaic between forest and prairie in the U.S. Midwest, suggested an opposing view in 1926. Gleason claimed that the so-called climax systems were, instead, plastic assemblages of species that changed over time – and would so again – as a result of particular species arriving at particular places and succeeding or failing on their own merits. As paleoecologist Hazel Delcourt writes, "plants have formed dynamically changing communities because of the abilities of plant species to spread their propagules to new and favorable locations and to adjust their ranges in response to environmental change." The eastern broadleaf forest had only a few thousand years to assemble itself following deglaciation, during which time individual species emerged from their glacial refuges and met together on lands that had earlier been spruce woodland, tundra, or ice. Gleason was pilloried by academia and changed careers, becoming a noted plant taxonomist at the New York Botanical Garden. Only in 1959 did the Ecological Society of America award him their Eminent Ecologist Award.[36]

Pollen cores pulled from the heart of Lucy Braun's "mixed mesophytic" forest in the 1970s provided proof for Paul and Hazel Delcourt that, during the glacial maximum, the Appalachians were boreal woodlands with tundra highlands. More proof arrived with every pollen core studied. As a result, ecologists now recognize that, in the same way that species assembled after deglaciation on the basis of their individual lifestyles, so too will they continue to reproduce, migrate, and associate, independently and individually, in response to climate change, habitat fragmentation, and pests and pathogens – all simultaneously.[37]

Paleoecologists in the 1970s pooled their data from more than seventeen hundred pollen profiles from lakes, ponds, and bogs across the east. Scientists like Margaret Davis at Yale, the Delcourts at Tennessee, Thompson Webb at Brown, and John McAndrews at the Royal Ontario Museum were finally able to ask questions on a continental scale. Where did particular tree species hole up during the last glacial maximum? How fast had they moved, in what directions?

The tree species in Great Lakes country spent their glacial maximums in the U.S. south. Oaks and hickories occupied lands south and west of the Appalachians; hemlock and white pine on the continental shelf of the Carolinas; beech in the loess hills of the lower Mississippi; and chestnut on the Gulf coast plain, which was cooled by waters coming down the Mississippi from the ice sheet. Others, like the spruces, were more widespread to the north. All of them had been successful veterans of twenty or more successive glacial cycles. The Earth during its full glacials supported enough chlorophyll to pump down the carbon dioxide in the atmosphere to levels far below their levels during the interglacials. It was a very green world, with a very green ocean.[38]

The speeds calculated for tree migration are astonishing. Oak averaged seven miles per century (with maximums three times as fast); beech, nine miles per century (also with maximums three times as fast); chestnut, six miles per century; hickory, twelve to sixteen miles per century; the northern pines, eight miles (and white pine, up to twenty-two miles) per century; spruce, nine miles (and as much as 124 miles) per century; and sugar maple, up to twelve miles a century. Delcourt agrees that "such fast rates of tree migration as observed in the Quaternary fossil record cannot be explained by a simple diffusion process where a species spreads out from a central point like concentric ripples on a pond."[39]

The climate has warmed by 1.3°F (0.7°C) in the last century but we have not seen trees shift at all. Instead, they move around locally as usual, by a combination of slow frontal migration and rare dispersal events that establish new founder populations. Gravity, wind, water, and wildlife all play roles, but trees now contend with a fragmented mosaic of possible destinations, and with the remainder of the mosaic resistant because of modern uses or total conversion. As well, gravity, wind, and water act now in the absence of much dispersal of any kind by passenger pigeon, turkey, bear, or others. On human landscapes like Great Lakes country, temperature is not a main limiting factor in the movement and establishment of trees or other species.[40]

Passenger pigeons carried seed and nuts over long distances. Assisted dispersal has been generally estimated at rates up to twenty-seven yards per year by rodents, and more by birds, but blue jays have been seen to carry beechnuts for many miles and bury them, and rodents have been documented dispersing nuts up to 110 yards. Some wildlife hoard and bury acorns, and fail to retrieve them, thereby actually planting them. Some trees are adapted for such dispersal; carriers like squirrels, grackles, and blue jays often eat only the cap-end of an acorn, which has less tannin, and leave the plant embryo to germinate. Many oaks produce a larger acorn crop every few years, with low production in intervening years, and this strategy can satiate acorn predators in good years, thus leaving excess acorns to germinate. These interactions are now compromised – and some of them finished – but they all assisted migration in the past. However, even an intact Great Lakes wildlife could not help plants match the predicted rates of climate warming. And other dependencies now distract wildlife as well; today's turkey is more dependent on crop residues than on native mast, and racoons have become urban specialists because the food is easier to find.[41]

Heavy-fruited species were slower to move, and barriers like the Great Lakes obstructed them. Some of their distribution ranges at the time of contact barely wrapped around Lake Erie and Lake Ontario, with gaps in their ranges on the north side of the lakes. Examples include the bitternut and shagbark hickory, black oak, pin oak, chestnut, and witch-hazel. Eventually they would have occupied their limits as defined by temperature and soil, but, almost certainly, they were still moving when Europeans arrived. Complicating this, most people think in terms of north-south temperature gradients (it gets colder to the north), but this is not everywhere the case. South of the lakes, temperatures cool southward into the Alleghenies and Appalachians, and then warm again toward the Atlantic coast. The Ontario Island is colder than Georgian Bay to the north (Fig. 24). Nature is complex and its directions inscrutable.

If the Great Lakes were barriers to migration, then consider how much tougher the barriers are now. First, compared to 1800, the species and their propagules are so few. The production of acorns was once enough to feed wildlife and humans; now there are too few even for tree replacement in many places. Species generally move as the result of excess offspring but this is no longer the case. There are now, around the Great Lakes other than Superior, lowlands that have had as much as 90 per cent of upland forests cleared, and 70 per cent of wetlands converted, and which are now hosting major new city-states. We have left only trace corridors, where there are any at all, along waterways, moraines, and escarpments. We have also subverted the native processes, like fire, grazing, and thinning, that selected for open-ground species like the oaks, hickories, walnut, butternut, pines, and fruit trees and shrubs. Species cannot make it across such landscapes.[42]

The IPCC acknowledges that it is a challenge "to develop realistic models of plant migration." However, it claims, dispersal is not a significant issue "provided that the matrix of suitable habitats was not too fragmented." But, of course, the suitable habitats *are* too fragmented almost everywhere in central North America. Computer modellers try to predict where nature will move when climates change but their models can no longer assume that species can freely pursue their shifting climate niches. Neither can they factor in physical barriers, invasives, pathogens, pollination declines, seed set, fire suppression, or human psychology (most landowners resist their land going wild). Consider the sugar maple, an important source of timber, sugar, and fuel-wood in many rural areas. Models suggest that it must move sixty miles for each rise of 2°F (1°C) in average temperature, and the assumption is that temperatures will warm 5°F (2.9°C) over the next century. To keep up, maple would therefore have to move at a rate that is an order of magnitude more than its peak post-glacial speed of twelve miles per century. It is not credible that species can keep up with the predicted warming unassisted. If we want sugar maple to move, we will have to move it. And sugar maple is the least likely to lag behind; some land managers already see it as an aggressive native that is turning dry oak woodlands into moist shaded forests. Action of any kind may be contentious, as usual.[43]

Between invasives and climate warming, the eastern broadleaf forest is at risk. If we want it to succeed, we may have to service its needs deliberately. The paleoecologist Hazel Delcourt, writing about the Appalachian highlands, which are much more intact than the lowlands in our region, has said: "One of the biggest challenges for conservation ... will be to either provide a massive planting program that will hand-carry seedlings to favorable sites, or to provide for habitat continuity that will allow the species to adjust their ranges by natural processes." Elsewhere in the region, however, more resilience is predicted. The northern forests remain largely intact, at least spatially, balanced between cutting, growth, and fire suppression. We know the pines will grow northward, if encouraged, and black spruce has shown evidence of an enduring stability through past climate changes. So too the open peatland systems of the north, which are "complex adaptive systems," in the words of Nigel Roulet at McGill University, and may well maintain their high levels of diversity and carbon sequestration in the face of climate change. They may even benefit from the predicted increases in precipitation that come with climate warming. This kind of resilience may also express itself in novel ways in other dominantly natural landscapes, such as the Algonquin-Frontenac axis and the Adirondacks.[44]

Resiliency may also be inherent in species of broad ecological amplitude. Many of our native trees are widespread latitudinally, and Great Lakes country is at the centre or northern edge of the ranges of such trees as the sugar maple, beech, hemlock, red maple, black cherry, and red, white, and black oak. Many of these trees do well far to the south of Great Lakes country, and the same can be said for most of our common mammals and breeding birds. It has also been noted by the paleoecologist Margaret Davis that the pollen record shows that forests with long-lived trees are slower to respond to climate change. This is comforting but it also means that, when the effects of climate change do appear in the forests, it is likely that they started many decades before. In other words, by the time we notice it, it may be too late.[45]

What climates has Great Lakes country faced since the last full glacial? First, there was the putative Clovis comet at 12,900 BP and the cool Younger Dryas period that followed. Then there was the gradual warming of the Hypsithermal Period, when species and habitats succeeded farther north than now. This was followed by a less extreme Roman Warming, a Dark Age Cooling, a Medieval Warming, and a sharp Little Ice Age. We can graph the estimated minimum and maximum temperatures of these events, to roughly illustrate the changes that the region has gone through (Fig. 25). It is remarkable that the present interglacial has been book-ended by such jarring deviations, first the catastrophic Younger Dryas cooling, and second the industrial warming, not as immediately catastrophic but, in geologic terms, almost as abrupt. Biological extinctions attend each of these events, and so too human adaptation. What can we expect? The climate models for the next fifty years predict more extreme weather events and extremes in temperatures and moisture. The climate of Great Lakes country will warm but it will remain temperate, and may also experience an increase in rain and snow that, on balance, sustains its surplus of moisture, so key to its lakes and rivers and soils – and economies.

Arrayed against this backdrop, Great Lakes country is a brand-new recombinant ecology of native and non-native species, and peoples, all interacting in their individual best interests. To sustain its diversity and its native options, Delcourt argues, we must pursue multiple, deliberate actions, including the creation of a "nearly contiguous series of biological reserves ... [that] allow for dispersal of species and minimize bottlenecks to migration." At the same time, she urges a major commitment to the "removal of unwanted exotic species and replanting or seeding in desirable native species."[46]

If I want to keep the present forests and springs on the Fifth Line farm, I will have to support them. If I want to extend a welcome to southern species that climate warming might permit, like the oaks, hickories, and wild plums, I have the choice. They will not arrive on their own, no matter how much warmer it gets. Across the region, we already stock turkey, elk, Atlantic salmon, sturgeon, eel, and others, and we build new prairies, savannas, wetlands, and streams. If we do not help nature restore itself – and get creative in doing so – species will decline one by one, and be gone. It will not help to defend a status quo that never really existed.

CHAPTER ELEVEN

Restoration: A New Native Landscape

Great Lakes country has endured much but there have been substantive counterbalances to those trials, which explain why there is now more forest cover, cleaner water, more recovered biota, and a better quality of life than a century ago, even as the human footprint expands and deepens. Much was taken but it was reinvested well and has yielded an enviable dividend of social equality, cultural diversity, and ecological integrity. There may be little left of the original "paradise" but there are many ambitions afoot. Restoration is taking hold and a new natural commons is asserting itself.

In the city-state world, provenance – or nativity – may be a fading discriminant. However, for the ecologist, the provenance of biota and the authenticity of ecosystems are linked, and speak to their evolutionary origins. For the anthropologist, the provenance of peoples and the authenticity of cultures have much the same significance. The word "Native" refers to both peoples and biology because of how linked they were on the land. Both Native peoples and native species exercised a sophisticated and muscular stewardship of Great Lakes country, varying from a more dispersed influence on the Shield and Appalachians to a more forceful presence in the region's lowlands.

There was a high fidelity between three phenomena: areas of Native settlement; dry, open habitats with much dependent wildlife; and the seasonally well-drained terraces, moraines, outwash plains, and bottomlands around the Great Lakes. Years ago, ecologist Wasyl Bakowsky and I sketched a map to illustrate where prairie grasslands survived in southern Ontario. They were all on these same physiographic features, the same landforms that the archaeological and historical records agree were those selected for Native settlement (Fig. 26).[1]

Native land care was aggressive and included cropping, thinning, harvesting, and burning. Of these, fire is the particular expert Native intervention that symbolizes just how irrevocably Great Lakes country has changed. Peoples that organized themselves in settlement clusters, and knew their geography intimately, had fire as an option because they could burn without risk. For newcomers, fire was feared above all else. It was just too dangerous once settlers and their capital assets were distributed on small dispersed land parcels. Fire was replaced by the plow as the farm technology that extracted maximum protein from the land.

Anthropologist Walter Hough made the case in 1926 that fire was a key Native land-management tool, and Gordon Day reinforced the case in *Ecology* in 1953. The evidence was largely dismissed although some, like Emily Russell in 1983, admitted that Natives "undoubtedly increased the frequency of fires above the low numbers caused by lightning." Forest ecologist Marc Abrams, at Penn State, became more and more convinced as he studied oak woodlands: "Native Americans were a much more important ignition source than lightning ... promoting mast and fruit trees ... [and] the entire historical development of the eastern oak and pine forests, savannas and tallgrass prairies." So too Utah State's Charles Kay: "The dominant ecological force likely has been aboriginal burning." The earliest observers had never been reticent about the Native use of fire.[2]

The Fire Record

Open grasslands and woodlands were not invented, but they were adopted, expanded, and cared for by Natives. The New Jersey pine barrens were in place by 10,000 BP, says paleoecologist Bill Watts, but they were burned and tended thereafter for hunting and gathering. There was farming in the Little Tennessee valley by 10,000 BP, and most of its river bottoms and terraces were cleared and managed by 1000 AD, with enough charcoal remains to show, writes Hazel Delcourt, that "Native Americans used fire not only for cooking and for warmth, but also to manage the secondary scrub vegetation."[3]

In 1987 Julian Szeicz and Glen MacDonald, from McMaster University, cored lakes on the Norfolk sand plain north of Lake Erie; the pollen showed that oak savanna had settled in between 6800 and 4500 BP, coinciding with a warmer climate and Native settlement. There were nineteen encampments near the lakes – and no doubt about how the savanna was sustained. Even small villages of four hundred or so, like Crawford Lake along the Niagara

Escarpment, "fundamentally and permanently altered" their surroundings. Larger towns, even if only periodically occupied, made lasting changes to both land and water.[4]

Starting in 1524, Giovanni da Verrazano would write that the woodlands along the mid-Atlantic coast were "sparse" and the "fields ... open and free of any obstacles or trees." As well, "all along [the coast] we saw great fires because of the numerous inhabitants." On the same coast in 1605, Samuel de Champlain described its open terrain but he was not there in burning season and made only passing reference to the use of fire: "When they wish to plant [fields] they set fire to the weeds." At Massachusetts Bay the next year, he saw the Natives "cut down the trees ... burn the branches ... and sow their corn between the fallen timber." Twenty-five years later, Thomas Morton described how the Natives on the New England coast "set fire of the country in all places where they come," and William Wood wrote that it was the Native custom to burn "the wood in November when the grass is ... dried, [and] it consumes all the underwood and rubbish which otherwise would overgrow the country ... and spoil their much affected hunting." He saw what happened when fires stopped: "[After] the Indians died of the [smallpox] plague some fourteen years ago, [there] is much underwood ... because it hath not been burned."[5]

In Huronia and the Kawarthas, Champlain again witnessed an open country, with fire used to prepare fields for crops. A decade later, Gabriel Sagard saw the Huron use fire to clear trees. He was consistent in distinguishing between crop field, meadow, and forest, and he noted, for instance, how he became lost more frequently in the corn fields than in the meadows or forests. He was clear that the Huron "set fire" to their meadows (*grandes prairies*), not just to their crop fields.[6]

Adriaen Van der Donck was just as clear, in the 1640s, that the Mohawk had "a yearly custom ... of burning the woods, plains and meadows in the fall of the year ... First, to render hunting easier, as the bush and vegetable growth renders the walking difficult for the hunter, and the crackling of the dry substances ... frightens away the game. Secondly, to ... clear the woods of all dead substances and grass, which grow better the ensuing spring. Thirdly, to circumscribe and enclose the game within the lines of the fire, when it is more easily taken." The Moravian George Loskiel observed the Iroquois in about 1810 and noted the same: "These fires run on for many miles."[7]

Portaging between the Hudson River and Lake George in 1749, Pehr Kalm saw young pineries closing in on open ground and, north around Lake Champlain, vast pineries that he interpreted as the product of "the carelessness of the Indians, who frequently make great fires when they are hunting." Kalm was right to associate the fires with Natives but mistaken to call it "carelessness." He failed to understand that burning after hunting was site preparation for future hunts.[8]

On the Susquehanna River in 1769, Richard Smith described a village of displaced Oneida "setting fire to the woods." He wrote, "Much of the upland hereabouts has been burnt & looks something like a settled country." Again, in the Delaware headwaters, "the Indians either thro accident or design have burnt large spaces in the woods." In Iroquoia in 1800, John Maude noted, along the "Conhocton [river] ... the timber was principally scrub ... this degeneracy of the wood is owing to its being annually burnt by the Indians; the destructive mode of clearing a passage through the woods, and rousing the game, is now put a stop to, nothing being more destructive to the soil." But good for mast and for prairie and wildlife.[9]

North of the lakes, the Rice Lake prairie was the product of Native burning, Catharine Traill wrote. "It was to increase the growth of this [deer] grass that the Indians, at intervals of time, set fire to the Rice Lake plains ... a great feeding ground for the deer." By 1885, however, she wrote, "it must have been nearly a century ago since these plains were last burnt over – not within the memory of the oldest settler in the township." The Missisauga name for Rice Lake was "the lake of the burning plains" or Pemedashcoutayang, and their name for the plains, Pemedashdakota.[10]

Scottish farm reviewer Patrick Shirreff crossed the Rice Lake plains in 1833. "The appearance of the plaines is not owing to the quality of the soil, but to the herbage being annually burned." Later that year, in the "oak openings" near Brantford, he said, "Fire passes over the plains every year or two ... [and] prevent[s] the growth of the trees." The next year, William Pope would attribute the fires there more clearly: "Indians ... set fire to the brushwood in order to clear the land that grass might more freely grow which furnished plenty of food for deer." When Shirreff finally reached the prairies and oak openings in Michigan and Illinois in 1833, he finally understood: "They originated from, and owe their continuance to, the agency of fire. It is quite certain fire sweeps over them, at present almost every autumn ... I have no theory to offer instead of fire for the origin of prairies."[11]

Northward, among the Algonquians, Champlain would record in 1613 the Native practice along the Ottawa River: "When they wish to make a piece of ground fit for tillage, they burn the trees." Close to the busy Ottawa-Mattawa canoe route, modern tree dating has shown that the original stands of white pine and oak were subjected to, between 1721 to 1937, regular low-intensity burns on a cycle of roughly fourteen years, a frequency much greater than natural lightning fires. South in Muskoka, similar tree dating has shown a seventy-six-year fire-free period after about 1664, when the Huron and others had been displaced by the Iroquois. Reoccupation then took the fire frequency back up to about once every five to seventeen years.[12]

South of Lake Superior, the U.S. superintendent of Indian affairs, Thomas McKenney, wrote in 1826: "We often see smoke in the mountains, which doubtless comes from fires kindled by the Indians ... the fires raging for months." In the late 1990s, researchers Walter Loope and John Anderton searched the shore of lakes Superior, Michigan, and Huron for old pines. They found thirty-nine sites with pines that had fire scars they could date. The scar dates showed there had been numerous, repeated ground fires before 1910 but only one after that. From the ten oldest records, they calculated the frequency of fires before 1910 at ten times the rate of natural fires. The sites were all coastal sand flats with easy shore access, good blueberry picking, and relatively few biting insects. Most were used by Natives on their summer rounds, and corn was grown at a few. The northern Algonquians called the month of late summer the "moon of the blueberries," and it was their fires that sustained the "low sandy ... pine plains ... [and] the whortleberries" that the American surveyors John Foster and Josia Whitney wrote about in 1850 along the Superior coast.[13]

Were other sites also burned? Paul Catling has studied the role of fire in keeping limestone-plains alvars open. Some alvars are dolomite flats, fractured into clints and grikes, where surface temperatures can exceed 122°F (50°C). This precludes trees and, when you add lightning fires, may have been enough to keep them open. However, other alvars have thin soils, and support highly flammable grasslands and conifers. These sites had high numbers of deer, elk, and caribou, and were Native hunting grounds. Catling concludes that they were "highly susceptible to burning"; however, a Native role in such fires has yet to be established.[14]

It was a more open countryside in pre-contact times. Paleoecologist Ian Campbell argued in 1994 that there was no widespread use of fire by Natives but that, even excluding such fires, up to 5.2 per cent of the landscape south of the Canadian Shield in Ontario was directly "disturbed" by Native settlement, an area almost equal to the extent of the soils that were arable by Native methods. However, Natives fires were also widespread *beyond* settlements, and it is likely that as much as three times as much land was touched by regular Native firing.

Areas affected included the crop fields, the cleared fields producing fuel-wood and pole-wood, the fallow meadows, and the lands beyond the towns and camps, along the portages and on hunting grounds, where fire was used to keep the land open, tame the understoreys, and increase the wildlife. There were in addition, of course, large tracts of open, unforested wetlands and wet prairies, kept open by seasonal flood and drought.[15]

We can visualize such a landscape in three parts: first, the forested highlands standing as secure walls of wood and as hunting grounds between nations; second, on the lowlands, consolidated clusters of Native towns and villages and satellite camps, with intensive clearing, farming, and firing around them; third, areas of well-drained and sorted materials, like sand plains, ridges, moraines, and shores, that extended far away from the settlements and that were fired and thinned to keep them open for hunting and gathering. At least a quarter of the entire landscape – centred on its lowlands – was unforested, much of it effectively treeless. The Great Lakes lowlands would not be so open and unforested again until the middle of the 1800s.[16]

Old Ways Made New Again

Native farming was at the northern limits of crop hardiness here. Even so, the years between 1300 and 1475 witnessed a growing population as Natives extended that hardiness and optimized their farming, fishing, hunting, storage, and trade. And they were not the only agents of change on the landscape. Ecologists are only now calculating the impacts of single species such as the passenger pigeon, whose biomass far exceeded that of humans. The pigeon dominated the ecology of forests as bison did the prairies, influencing succession and disturbance at comparable scales. There were also deer, turkey, elk, bison (south of the lakes), caribou (to the north), grouse, squirrels, and fish in fantastic numbers. It was a rich, diverse, and naturally stimulated landscape.

When they came, Europeans cut and burned as much as they could. Natives had done the same, within the limits of their technologies and for the same reasons. Clearing and firing set back forest closure, released nutrients, and dried and warmed the soil. The open lands encouraged shrubs, forbs, and grasses that were averse to shade, and the species so favoured were the mast, nut and berry plants, and grasses that promoted wildlife. In turn, the deer, elk, turkey, pigeon, and small game succumbed to a subtle form of surrogate domestication by this customization of the land. And the open terrain, of course, favoured the hunter.

There were other benefits as well. For Gabriel Sagard on the French River in 1624, biting insects were his "worst martyrdom" but in Huronia, he wrote, there were "not many in the fields, because their district is open country." Clearing and firing reduce biting insects, and the fevers and malaria they carry, the same reason newcomers cleared and drained. Long-distance visibility was also important to where Natives located their towns, set their perimeters and defences, and maintained their neighbourhood vigil. Residents could see the sky, the weather, and whoever was coming or going, and feel safe while planting and gathering. All farmers – settler and Native alike – understood the relationship between cleared open country, less snow build-up in winter, earlier thaws, and drier ground for spring seeding. Across the region, early planting meant earlier and more secure harvests. An open countryside was the goal for both Native and newcomer.[17]

It is not just that Natives managed their lands and waters. The point is that they managed them so productively for so long, supported by a sophisticated horticulture and fire and game-harvest technologies, incrementally establishing, as the Delcourts term it, "a culturally maintained landscape mosaic." To achieve similar ends while increasing productivity, Europeans introduced land tenure, distributed labour and technology, and crop and stock monoculture. Arguably, the benefits of the new approach were narrower and more individualistic. Settlers worked hard on their own land but not on lands that were owned collectively, other than roads, schools, and churches. The community resources that were available, such as the wildlife, they just took until they were gone. This enabled settlers to raise enough protein for home and trade, raise large families, and keep to their Old World ways. It was a far more intensive land use than Natives had pursued, and the benefits flowed to the individual family. The result was a sharp increase in population, an independent citizenry, a reduced commons, and a gutted landscape.

Collateral damages included, for example, an intractable decline in the regeneration of oaks and other mast trees. William Logan, the author of *Oak*, calls the present interglacial "the age of oaks and humans," and asks why we should continue to be the agent of the oak's decline? We can ask the same of many phenomena. The motivating psychology was the same for European and Native alike but it was just that the new technologies were so much more invasive. These lessons have been taken to heart by modern conservation, albeit through the lenses of science and ecology: Respect Nature's templates. Native first. Diversity counts. Think landscape. However, perhaps in reaction to past performance, we may now be too timid. As an example, when a small burn was finally permitted to begin to restore the oak savanna in Toronto's High Park (after a decade of talk), the result was still not accepted by many. Complaints came in from well-meaning people defending the rights of the non-native black pine and Norway maple over those of the native black oak savanna and its lupines and butterflies.[18]

Earlier generations were bolder, for right or wrong. They planted hundreds of thousands of acres in pine trees. Perhaps they did so in the wrong places sometimes, but at least they acted. Today, many pine plantations are succeeding back to broadleaf trees and, in some areas, they are being restored to their earlier habitats. In the 1950s and 1960s, three million pines were planted at the Pinery Park on Lake Huron, turning what had been sand prairie and oak savanna into a pinery. In 1989 Ontario Parks took the bold step of reversing its course, to restore the health and diversity of the oak savanna that had been its natural condition for more than five millennia. Cutting and firing began to restore three thousand acres of it. The Pinery is a great example of doing the right thing for the right reasons. Its wild lupines are slowly recovering, and one day there may be enough to reintroduce the endangered Karner blue butterfly, which died out in the Pinery in 1988.[19]

The enthusiasm for prescribed burns now outruns the means to do them. In the last few years in Ontario, there have been burns at the Pinery, Rondeau Park, Ojibway Prairie, the Brantford golf course, the Norfolk sand plain, Pelee Island, the Rice Lake plain, the Niagara Gorge, and elsewhere. The Walpole Island First Nation has had the largest burns in recent years, likely greater than all the others combined. The burns are reinvigorating prairies, savannas, and wetlands, and restoring species-at-risk. Foresters in Ontario, New York, Pennsylvania, and Ohio are starting to burn oak woodlands to help them regenerate. However, there is still a love-hate relationship with fire; a wildfire in 1995 burned fifty-five hundred acres of Long Island pines and ended burns there for some time. The Nature Conservancy is a leader in prescribed burns, for example, in Ohio, where they burn at the Kitty Todd preserve (in support of the Karner blue butterfly) and at the 13,500-acre Edge of Appalachia preserve, and in Michigan. In the west, of course, fire is better accepted as the way to keep healthy prairies, and west of Lake Michigan it is almost a rite of spring to see small fires crawling across local prairies, even in the city of Chicago.

At the same time, public awareness of wildlife has also declined and some species have taken advantage. Double-crested cormorants are burying some of the islands in western Lake Erie in guano, killing the native habitats. They are not native to the Great Lakes and arrived by way of fish farms and other venues, from which they are repulsed and pushed on to the Great Lakes, where they behave like an invasive. They colonized Middle Island, part of a National Park, and their numbers soared, burying in guano the island's "fine timber," as Isaac Weld had called it in 1796. However, many well-wishers rose to their defence, and their sensitivities were long judged to be as important as the interests of Middle Island. Finally, in 2008, after fending off court challenges, Parks Canada began a cull of cormorants.

White-tailed deer are now at historic highs throughout Great Lakes country and, in many places, are beyond their habitat's carrying capacity. Deer protected in parks and suburbs can strip everything green and leave only a crisp browse line. Some of the deer carry Lyme disease, and they are also host to the parasitic brain worm that infects and kills moose, elk, and caribou. Keeping their numbers in reasonable balance should be straightforward, but nearly every time a deer cull is proposed, a predictable reaction occurs. Some culls have been abandoned in the face of protests, and, in other cases, Natives have been invited to take the deer, which somehow makes the culls more palatable. The restorative effects are spectacular on the ground. Presqu'ile on Lake Ontario, Rondeau and Long Point on Lake Erie, and the Pinery on Lake Huron are a few of the sites where, although the culls may have come late, many species were saved as a result. Slowly and quietly, nature – and how it functions – is beginning to inform our land care again.[20]

There is a shared human nature that is sufficient to explain what happened here, but there were also differences between Native and newcomer philosophies. The Huron philosopher Georges Sioui, at the University of Ottawa, characterizes European thinking as founded on the myth that people with advanced technologies are the vanguard of a long linear march of social evolution. By contrast, he maintains, Natives embraced the ecological "circle-of-life myth," in which humans occupy a place equal to that of other creatures but with special responsibilities. An ecologist is likely to take the view that both myths were the result (not the cause) of differences in available technologies and in interactions with nature, but, nevertheless, the differences were real, and when they clashed at the time of contact, they amplified the impacts of, and the responses to, new metals and weapons, disease and war, and writing and land tenure.[21]

The 1960s saw a generation of youth engage in its own vision quest, in part a reaction to business-as-usual in North America. What emerged has been ascribed by historian Claire Campbell, at Dalhousie, in some measure to the rocky shores of the Great Lakes. While David Thompson had written about the "incredible sterility" of the Georgian Bay shore, it nevertheless became a focal point for Canada's Group of Seven artists and one of Canada's premier destinations. The 1968 poem *The Pride*, by John Newlove, speaks of the native lands and peoples as "our true forbears." The myth of the "noble savage" was revived, but as the "ecologically noble savage," an idea that has become "hegemonic," in the words of Brown University anthropologist Shepard Krech, "at first a projection of Europeans and European-Americans ... [which] became a self-image [of] American Indians." This stereotype has grown in tandem with the contemporary myth of the "environment-under-siege," and together they enjoy an undeniable status of political correctness. An image that was once considered degrading now has political clout – and can be a force for good in the exercise of Native esteem. (It is now, however, also injected into battles over land and rights, where it is understandable that others take exception to it.)[22]

Is it valid to apply this stereotype backward in time to the Native peoples of Great Lakes country? It is an arguable proposition. Consider the Native fishery. Its high-energy yield warranted major investments in weirs, snares, nets, and even stream diversions. Some were so fixed, for so many years, that they became landform features. Champlain, Smith, and Marquette are a few of those who wrote about those installations, some of them near-industrial in scale, such as at the Narrows on Lake Simcoe and on the lower Fox River. These were examples of Native enterprise operating at the limits of its technologies. They were the aquatic equivalent of selective logging in forestry, and, like selective cutting, they achieved a more stable, sustainable yield.[23]

The fishing technologies of the newcomers did not achieve a sustainable harvest. Today, however, away from the lakes, the rivers and streams have been on the mend for fifty years. Restoration work by thousands of volunteers, students, and experts is now repairing two centuries of damage. The removal of natural cover left watercourses in flood after every rain, and engineering solutions like straight concrete channels, and dams, degraded them further. Currently, some of the concrete and dams is being removed or retrofitted – with bottom-draws to keep the water cool, and with ladders and other aids to help the fish past dams. Slowly, rivers are being freed again. The best of the projects are bio-engineered with live shrub and tree materials that slow and cool the water and stabilize banks. Meanders, riffles, and bank-shaded pools are rebuilt. Sources of pollution are checked. Signature projects like the cleanup of the Hudson River have brought back the dolphin, porpoise, and Atlantic sturgeon, but the systemic changes that are occurring with each of many hundreds of smaller-scale, stream-by-stream, riffle-by-riffle projects are the big story. This work is done in-stream and ground-up – from the perspective of nature – rather than top-down like much of the old engineering. Groups like Trout Unlimited and anglers have led the way, triaging between practical science, volunteer energy, and the public good.[24]

In this work, it is the condition of nativeness that is being restored. Sometimes this also involves Native people. In the 1990s, there was a battle over the construction of a new expressway in Hamilton, in the Red Hill valley where it ascends the Niagara Escarpment. There were Neutral and Paleoindian sites there, and, when the dust settled, the Six Nations of the Grand and the city of Hamilton had a $5-million deal to bring nature back to the valley, as a condition of approval of the highway. It involved the naturalization of five miles of stream, and, after a plan for a concrete drain was rejected, a new plan was implemented to restore the stream channels and vegetation and let the aquatic organisms come back. Work was also contracted to the Six Nations to restore 150 acres of land. The first plan was to install a million trees and 300,000 native plants, and to double the area of wetlands. A woodland of red oak, black cherry, bitternut and shagbark hickory, with copses of white pine and ash, was the target. All of this was good, but it got better.[25]

Among those hired by Six Nations were Mary Gartshore and Peter Carson, from Norfolk. Over the years, they had started a prairie on their own farm, helped with hundreds of similar projects, and become two of Canada's finest on-the-ground restoration ecologists. They take an aggressive nativist approach. "Our job is to put as many different native species and propagules into a site as possible, fit them with their soils, and then leave it to nature to help sort out what works and what doesn't work," says Gartshore. "And if you bring back the habitat, the fauna will show up," she adds. One native insect that had been found only once, in the U.S. southeast, showed up in the middle of a field they had restored to prairie. Gartshore and Carson had also grown weary of watering transplanted trees, and had adopted the practice of transplanting "habitat plugs" and sowing acorns and nuts directly, and letting nature do the work.

This approach resonated with the Six Nations team working on the Red Hill valley, and they followed Gartshore's lead. The younger participants learned their native materials and started finding them at the Six Nations. They learned to collect seed and start a nursery. Rather than take the approach of setting a numeric goal for trees planted and counting survival as success, the crew brought in a diverse mix of native plants, planted acorns and nuts directly, and proceeded by seeing what took and what did not, and adapting accordingly. The approach is a modern form of the old Native polyculture. It is early days yet but fish are spawning in the stream again.

On the Rice Lake plain, the Alderville First Nation has started burning and planting to restore a 110-acre black oak savanna. The project coordinator, Amanda Newell, points to the many acres of fields now planted and seeded with locally collected prairie species. "Land that was thick with cultivated oats in 2002 is now swaying with Indian grass, big bluestem, Kalm's brome and many, many prairie wildflowers." They too are ambitious for their savanna. They have already planted out many thousands of blue lupine and are looking to a future that might bring back the Karner blue butterfly to their lupines.

Walpole Island is the largest island in the St Clair River delta. It tall grass prairies and its oak savannas are the finest in North America, two thousand acres that support a hundred rare plant species, a dozen rare birds, and many rare reptiles and butterflies. Its soils would grow superb corn, which covers much of the island, but it is the pride of its First Nation (as well as its periodic burns) that keeps the land intact. To explore any part of Walpole in its summer glory is to acknowledge the accuracy of the early writings about the high-octane prairies of southwest Ontario, Ohio, and southern Michigan, so tall "a man on horseback can hardly see over it," as David Zeisberger said.

The lessons of pre-contact stewardship – polyculture, native species, promoting wildlife – are being relearned and retaught, including by Natives. The stories of caring for the land were lost to Natives just as surely as they were lost to the rest of us. But they can be relearned, and expanded from a few test plots to the landscape as a whole. There is something fundamentally good and honest about restoring a native landscape, and if we thought of ourselves more as native to this place, we would perhaps be more thoughtful and measured in our actions.

Legislating a New Commons

Government took action only after the fact. William Smith described the sad state of wildlife in his 1846 *Canadian Gazeteer*: "Bears and wolves are only to be found in the more unsettled neighbourhoods. The beaver is now seldom found ... Panther, lynx and wild cat have emigrated ... Foxes ... raccoons, otters, fishers, martens, minks and muskrats still remain in diminished numbers. Deer have become gradually destroyed ... Previous to the winter of 1842, wild turkeys were also plentiful ... Woodcocks and snipes are not so numerous ... Pigeons are [still] very plentiful ... The squirrels ... form the principal game."

The new "sportsmen" of the day knew what was happening and they tried to act. In 1845 John Prince, sportsman, judge, and member of the Legislative Assembly, proposed a new law that stated, "No person or persons shall ... hunt, shoot, take, kill or destroy any wild swan, wild goose, wild duck, teal, widgeon or snipe, between the tenth day of May and the fifteenth day of August ... No person shall hereafter trap or set traps, nets or snares for any grouse or quail, or kill, or hunt at night." The bill failed but Prince later reintroduced it. This time it passed, but it had little effect because there was no means to enforce it.[26]

Prince also spoke out during the debate on Canada's first fishing laws, the 1857 Fishing Act. He spoke against jacklighting, calling it "a dastardly and mean thing to hold a torch at the surface of the water, waiting until the fish came up, and then to stick it with a fork." Further, he said, "it was as bad to ... go out into the woods with hounds, and hunt the poor deer into the lake, and then take a canoe, paddle over to the poor animal, and shoot it." Doing so offended the new idea of sportsmanship, but it was also a cherished right. In the 1860s, Prince was appointed the first judge in northern Ontario, where he argued for a ban on Native hunting and fishing (a proposal that also failed). But again, as the legislative librarian William Houston pointed out in 1890, "it has always been, and will always be, found impossible to prevent settlers from killing game ... It is part of their food, and no system of police can ever keep them from appropriating it."[27]

South of the lakes, the first meeting of the American Ornithologist's Union was held in 1883 at New York's American Museum of Natural History. One of its first bulletins, in 1886, was on the *Destruction of Our Native Birds*, and it publicized the five million birds killed every year for women's hats in America. It proposed state laws to prohibit the killing of birds other than waterfowl and game birds. Audubon societies for youth sprang up in response throughout the eastern United States, focused on pledges neither to kill birds nor wear bird feathers.[28]

Various hunting, conservation, and fishing associations began to organize in the same decade. Their Ontario leaders convened in 1884 and recommended new laws to end the spring hunt of ducks and game birds, and suspend the bobwhite hunt. Toronto scientists and educators reorganized the Royal Canadian Institute and amalgamated it with the Natural History Society in 1885. That year, 2 per cent of all Torontonians were members. The following year, the Institute petitioned the government "for the preservation of our nature animals," and in 1890 a provincial commission was appointed, "forced upon the government by reason of public opinion, and the representations made by sportsmen," in the words of its secretary George MacCallum, physician and ornithologist from the lower Grand. His report was blunt. "On all sides, from every quarter has been heard the same sickening tale of merciless, ruthless, and remorseless slaughter." Even worse, Ontario lagged behind "all the immediately adjacent states of the Union."[29]

At the turn of the century, there were strong voices demanding that wildlife be conserved. John Muir, Ernest Thompson Seton, and President Theodore Roosevelt were a few of them, but, despite their Canadian connections, they were not as influential in Canada as civil servants and commissions. Englishman Gordon Hewitt came to Canada in 1909 as chief entomologist with the Department of Agriculture. He was soon a consulting zoologist to the government's Commission of Conservation, which was an independent voice reporting directly to Parliament. Hewitt was the advocate behind the 1916 Canada-U.S. migratory bird treaty and its 1918 legislation, which is a gold standard in bird protection. In these roles, he was the leader of a conference in Ottawa in 1919 on *The Conservation of Game, Fur-Bearing Animals and Other Wild Life*. Arthur Meighen, the Canadian minister of the interior (and later prime minister), attended and presented its closing address. Unfortunately, Hewitt died the next year at age thirty-five, and the Commission of Conservation died the same year, at the hands of the same Meighen, then prime minister. Hewitt's book *The Conservation of the Wild Life of Canada* was published posthumously. It argued that "conservation is practical foresight" and one of the "attributes that make a nation progressive."[30]

Agencies and academics rallied around this idea of "progressive conservation" – the doctrine of usefulness – in the first half of the 1900s. Aldo Leopold (before his conversion) was a famous advocate for "making land produce sustained annual crops of wild game." This was also the era of "bureaucrat as hero," which was both idealized and criticized for aggressively pursuing "conservation by law." Game wardens were sent into the field as necessary armed troops in defence of wildlife, to break centuries-old habits.[31]

Things changed again in the 1960s. "Back to the garden" was a popular lyric then, and the "wise use" philosophy had to make room for more pressing and urgent demands to protect and restore nature more aggressively. In 1964 (and not inspired by Joni Mitchell's song), Ontario provincial biologist Doug Clarke would urge the same, to "get ourselves back into paradise now, not [in the] hereafter ... We can never restore Eden, but we may retain what remains." Quietly, and largely without fanfare, citizens and agencies have pursued this goal. Bird life has been restored to the airways, and fish and mammals to their haunts, and lands and waters have been set aside for them. While writing this book on the Fifth Line of Mono, I had the company of two dozen or so turkey who trudged up the hills from their roosts in the springs, to check for any spilled feed. One day a golden eagle tore into them, causing a great uproar. That same winter, a cougar was seen dragging a deer carcass across a road close by. Who would have predicted this?[32]

Restoring the Airways

There is perhaps a greater fondness for birds than for any other life form. They are studied in more detail than may be thought rational, and they tell us as much about the land as any other organisms. From their point of view, the occupation of Great Lakes country meant two things, an incredible barrage of lead shot and a vast new open terrain of grasslands. Some birds lost and some gained.[33]

The new grasslands, whether crop or forage, attracted birds from the interior of the continent. By the mid-1800s, the region was welcoming species at the same rate as others were extirpated. The brown-headed cowbird moved in from the west in the 1870s and was common across the region by the 1920s. Cowbirds lay their eggs in other birds' nests and their young dominate at the expense of native nestlings. The evening grosbeak arrived in the 1920s, perhaps lured east by the burst of wild cherries that followed the cut-and-burn of the forests or, perhaps, by the increase in Manitoba maple, another westerner that it likes to feed on. Our favourite field bird in Mono is the bobolink, a bird that sings with unrivalled buoyancy about its pride of place. It was in the region before, in low numbers in fens and wet prairies, but the explosion in open fields meant that it became as abundant here as in the west. In the past twenty years, the bobolink has declined by a quarter, as its habitat changes to blacktop and reverts to tree cover. Its winters in South America only add to its perils.[34]

The double-crested cormorant was another Midwest bird, its territory no farther east than Minnesota and Lake of the Woods. Its population soared by the early 1950s until DDT reduced it again. After DDT was banned, it exploded by about 40 per cent a year from 1973 to 1985, and it is again a dominant Great Lakes bird. The same ban on DDT, championed by Rachel Carson in 1962 in *Silent Spring*, helped bring back all of the native raptors, and there are now more than sixty pairs of bald eagle nesting again in southern Ontario, a stunning rebound from its endangered status only a few years ago.[35]

Another westerner is the loggerhead shrike, whose unique habit of impaling its prey on hawthorns would have made it unlikely that early observers missed the "butcher bird." Pope shot one in Norfolk in 1835, and McIlwraith reported it "for the first time" near Hamilton in 1860. It became common across the Great Lakes and St Lawrence but declined after the 1940s and is now critically imperilled across the region. Its range has shrunk down to sites like the alvars at Carden, where sixteen pairs nested in 2010. Captive birds are also bred, and some of the released fledglings have returned to breed successfully, one of them in Quebec in 2010, the first time in fifteen years. It is on life support in the east, its prospects unknowable.[36]

Southern birds moved north, and are still moving north. The turkey vulture, now so common, was only known south of the lakes in the early 1800s. The mourning dove was first noted about 1850 wintering north of the lakes. The cardinal, which Sagard reported on the open Huron countryside in 1623, was gone by the time that settlers faced the region's forests two centuries later. It was found again breeding north of the lakes in 1901, at Point Pelee, and it now fully occupies the region south of the Shield. Other southerners appreciating the newfound warmth included the eastern meadowlark, Carolina wren, tufted titmouse, mockingbird, hooded warbler, and Louisiana waterthrush.[37]

Some birds are down to a handful of individuals, and may just stay that way. The piping plover was abundant along the Atlantic and on western prairie lakes. At least eight hundred pairs nested on the Great Lakes. They nested on Toronto Island, for example, and a dozen pairs nested in the 1930s at Wasaga Beach on Georgian Bay. By the 1960s, Wasaga Beach was attracting as many as a million visitors a year, many of them cruising it in their cars (Fig. 27). In 1973 the cars were moved off the beach. A nature reserve was declared on the only wild section left, at the mouth of the Nottawasaga River. By 1990, piping plover were down to eleven pairs on the Great Lakes, all of them in Michigan, and guarded by volunteers. They slowly grew to sixty pairs on the lakes, but still none in Canada. Then a pair showed up at the Wasaga Beach nature reserve in 2005; they scraped a nest but did not lay eggs. In 2008 four chicks were born and one made it through to migrate. Chicks have hatched again each year since. Fifty miles west, at Sauble Beach on Lake Huron, they also returned and have hatched from 2007 to 2012. However, in 2007 as well, four dead piping plover were found along Lake Michigan, killed by type-E botulism.[38]

Some birds that were hunted out have come back unaided. The greater sandhill crane was shot out of the south by the 1880s. A few pair hung on in

Michigan and at Walpole Island in 1920. This population has now rebounded into the tens of thousands. Farther north, hunting decimated the lesser sandhill as well but its wetland haunts were remote and it hung on. By the 1970s, the lesser sandhill was rebounding in the Hudson Bay lowland, where I enjoyed many encounters with them, and, for years, they have been increasing in numbers and moving east, now into Quebec. Matching them, the larger southern sandhills have come back to the north Huron channel, the Bruce peninsula and Manitoulin Island, and Minesing Swamp, Alfred Bog, Long Point, and Carden. Thousands of them gather each fall on Manitoulin, and south and east of Lake Michigan, to the delight of visiting birders.[39]

The birds that were deliberately brought back are the big story. Harry Lumsden, the Ontario wildlife biologist, helped the giant Canada goose to recover and calls it "one of the conspicuous conservation success stories in North America." Early on, in 1626, d'Aillon noted that the Neutral had a "great quantity of wild geese" that are "there all winter," and, six years later, Sagard noted the geese kept by the Huron. Bones of Canada geese are among those most frequently unearthed in southern archaeological sites and many of them are the giant Canada goose. This large sedentary goose was effectively gone from the wild in Ontario by 1912, hanging on in low numbers in Michigan. Lumsden recounts that a Mr Cloes, who lived near Catfish Creek in Elgin County until he was over ninety, told his nephew how, as a youth, he had driven flightless Canadas from the marshes to keep them in the barn to fatten for eating. Others were kept as live decoys for the hunt. In the 1920s, people with captive stock started releasing them; a feedmill owner in Strathroy donated some to the Toronto Riverdale Zoo, and seven of those geese were released about 1961 to become the Toronto Island flock. They bred well, and by 1961 the number of giant Canadas residing in Ontario was more than thirty-five thousand. It is now the fastest expanding bird population in Ontario, and likely the region, and numbers more than three million across North America. They were shipped worldwide, and they are now so numerous in places that they offend many people. Job well done.[40]

Trumpeter swans were another abundant species at the time of contact, found "everywhere" in the Detroit area, for example, wrote Cadillac in 1701. Others saw them too, like Champlain, Sagard, and Hennepin, and their fossil bones at eleven archaeological sites in Ontario suggest they were favoured game. They were gone by 1886, mostly shot on their wintering grounds on the Carolina coast. Harry Lumsden started working with trumpeters in 1982. He started by validating their pre-contact occurrence in the region and ended, in 2006, by declaring, "After 24 years of effort, the trumpeter swan restoration program has achieved *all* its objectives."[41]

This was an astonishing accomplishment for the volunteers, foundations, agencies, and academics who supported Lumsden in his work. He bred captive Rocky Mountain swans and then carefully released them across southern Ontario. By 2006, the population passed one thousand, with 131 breeding-age pairs. Appropriately, Huronia was at the heart of the restoration work, and Wye Marsh served as host to many of the swans. The trumpeters winter on open water in Huronia and the Great Lakes, and even venture to the Atlantic seaboard. Raised fledglings were reminded of their innate migratory behaviours by flying them beside an ultralight aircraft; ultimately, they were flown in this way from Sudbury to Indiana. Others have also bred in the Hudson Bay lowland again. Their various affairs, divorces, and bereavements have been documented in full, and they may well make it. They are not shot anymore but the lead shot and sinkers used by sportsmen are still their enemy, lining the bottoms of lakes and poisoning them when they feed. Sagard noted in 1624 that the swans were mainly seen along Georgian Bay, and it is a thrill to see them back again, and come across them in the remote bogs behind the Georgian Bay coast.[42]

The wild turkey was almost eliminated from the region as well. Every observer attested to its abundance in the south and west. They were heavily hunted and also hit hard by severe winters like the one in 1842, but they bounced back. They were finally shot out of the wild in Ontario in 1909, but they persisted in low numbers south of the lakes and, like the Canada goose, farmers kept them around. McIlwraith would report in 1884 that "most of the domestic turkeys ... are either the wild species tamed or half-breeds." Failed attempts were made to release pen-reared stock into the wild, until in 1984 the Ontario Ministry of Natural Resources and the Ontario Federation of Anglers and Hunters released seventy-four wild birds from Michigan and Missouri; eventually, more than 4,400 of them would be released from seven U.S. states at 275 sites across Ontario as far north as the Ottawa valley and St Joseph Island. By 2010, there were more than 100,000, one of the ten fastest expanding birds in Ontario.[43]

There are other birds we seem less inclined to help. Bobwhite were abundant in the south and west, and early farm practices were to their liking. They peaked about 1850 and then declined, though they are still bred by game farms. Tough winters remain their nemesis. The greater prairie-chicken went through a comparable boom and bust, and was also gone early, last seen in southern Ontario at Walpole Island in 1924, at which time it still hung on in Michigan. The spruce grouse was abundant in the south of the region but it was far too easy to hunt; it was extirpated by 1897 from everywhere south of the Algonquin highlands. It would be fine to think that, one day, these birds could also be back in numbers.

Before some bird species were even described, they were nearly hunted out. Champlain described the whooping cranes as "white cranes" (*grués blanches*), observing that along the Trent and elsewhere there were "many cranes as white as swans" (*grués, blanches comme signes*). For Cadillac, they were among the "many cranes, grey and white" in the Detroit area. Later, there would be fossil bones found in archaeological sites at Sainte-Marie in Huronia and along the Hudson Bay and James Bay coasts. The whooping crane was gone quickly from the east. Alexander Wilson said that it was still on the Atlantic coast in 1814 and McIlwraith reported a single specimen from eastern Ontario in 1817. By the time the Macouns were compiling bird records, the closest were in Manitoba.[44]

By 1954, the global population was down to twenty-one cranes migrating from the gulf coast of Texas to Wood Buffalo National Park. From this tenuous beginning, and as the result of a terrific international effort, the wild population has been nursed back to 350, with 90 adult pairs. There are another 150 captive birds that include about 30 breeding pairs. Crane numbers grow very slowly, however. The international recovery plan called for two new self-sustaining, wild populations. One of those new populations was begun in 2001, when Bill Lishman and Joe Duff flew eight hand-reared whooping cranes beside their ultralights from Wisconsin, where there had been no cranes since 1878, to Florida. They had learned the technique from Bill Carrick, the wildlife filmmaker. From a base near the Trent waterway at Lake Scugog, this "Operation Migration" has used ultralight aircraft since 2001 to lead flocks of captive-reared cranes between a summer home at the Necedah wildlife refuge in Wisconsin and a winter home on the west coast of Florida.

The Whooping Crane Recovery Team has sanctioned this approach as a method-of-choice for reintroductions. The whooping crane could be brought back to Great Lakes country, perhaps even to the great marshes along Champlain's Trent waterway, near the headquarters of Operation Migration. What we do know is that, independent of human plans, at least three of the Wisconsin whooping cranes have already strayed east on their northbound migrations and have shown up in Ontario on their own. Perhaps they will remember for themselves how to "Fly Away Home," as the movie about them calls it.[45]

Bringing the Wildlife Back

Restoring wildlife requires research, innovation, and deliberate action. The research can extend beyond the region, for example, in the case of the eel, to the international waters of the Sargasso Sea. New technology is sometimes elusive, leaving us with such thorny questions as how to deal with power dams that kill the eel on its migration. Restoration requires us to "think globally, act locally," and vice versa.[46]

The complexities can be daunting. The first restocking of Atlantic salmon into Lake Ontario was the work of Samuel Wilmot in the 1860s, but the last salmon was taken off the Scarborough Bluffs in 1898 and the work was abandoned. It took until the 1980s for it to start again. The New York Department of Environmental Conservation began stocking Atlantic salmon in 1983 and, northward, the Ontario Ministry of Natural Resources started stocking the Credit River in 1988. The hope was to once again have naturally spawning Atlantic salmon in Lake Ontario. In both countries, agencies and volunteer hatcheries cooperated in growing out young fry, and, since 2006, the "Bring Back the Salmon" project in Ontario has returned more than three and a half million Atlantic salmon to the Credit and to three other streams. More than thirty groups, and hundreds of schoolchildren, have cleared the streams and naturalized their banks. The Credit River Anglers Association planted more than four hundred thousand trees, helped remove twenty-three dams, and installed fish ladders. Many of the newly stocked fish survived their journey to Lake Ontario, and in 2007 the first of them returned to the Credit. They are now successfully reproducing.

Much research has gone into the genetics of Lake Ontario salmon. Was it genetically distinct from its ocean siblings or did it stay connected by way of the St Lawrence? Which salmon should be restocked? There are competing opinions. Early troubles raising fry from ocean stock prompted Trout Unlimited to ask Oliver Haddrath, geneticist at the Royal Ontario Museum, to examine its museum specimens of Lake Ontario salmon. Haddrath isolated genetic markers that he thought distinctive, and hoped to check them against isolated populations of salmon that were started from historic Lake Ontario transplants. His goal? "21st-century technology trying to correct 19th-century mistakes." Other researchers, however, claimed that Lake Ontario salmon could not be distinguished from ocean salmon and, so, eggs from the LaHave River in Nova Scotia were used, and others from isolated lakes in Maine and Quebec will be tested. New York State uses stock of its own. Lake Ontario will be the arbiter of all this, and providing it with choices among genetic stocks may be for the best.[47]

Fur-bearers and game were the original focus of restoration. However, recovery begins with an acceptance of loss, which was slow in coming. Doug Clarke echoed the words of Tiger Dunlop when he said, in 1961, "To the pioneer the spoils of angling and hunting were more important as morale-builders than as food supplements." The facts were hard to accept. Caribou had been resident all across northern Appalachia, the southern Shield, Manitoulin, and northern Michigan, and were hunted out early. Elk were gone from the region by 1840 in the St Lawrence basin and by 1869 south of the lakes. They were "rapidly becoming extinct" north and east of Georgian Bay by 1893. Bear were gone from the lowlands of the region by about 1890, persisting in the north and on the highlands. The eastern cougar was gone from Ohio by 1838, Ontario after 1850, and New York about 1894. Wolverine, a rare and ferocious predator, was gone by about 1890. Lynx were more frequent but were similarly depleted by the 1890s, hanging on in eastern Ontario, Manitoulin, northern Michigan, and Maine. The wolf was a common predator and, well known to Europeans, felt the special wrath of every settler. It was extirpated south of the lakes and held on only as far south as the Algonquin-Adirondacks highlands and northern Minnesota.[48]

Beaver numbered at least ten million across North America at the time of contact – and perhaps five times as many. They were the staple of the fur trade and were cleaned out at an astonishing rate, gone from Huronia and Trois-Rivières by 1635 and Iroquoia by the 1640s. After that, when war and disease ended the Native harvest north of the lakes, beaver came back and, in New France in 1653, it was said that "never were there more beavers in our lakes and rivers but never have there been fewer ... in the warehouses ... The beaver are left in peace." They recovered best on the headwaters of the region and in the myriad lakes and streams on the Shield, but they remained scarce in the lowlands, where they were more readily accessible.[49]

For the Dutch, English, and French, beaver paid the freight for their westward expansion. The first trade currency was the "made beaver," and Canada's first postage stamp had a beaver on it. It was Canada's national symbol but, by 1849, was reported as "seldom found" in the Canadas. The decline spread west and north, linked to land clearing, railways and fires, and an influx of itinerant white trappers. The Englishman Archie Belaney was one of them, and he went Native under the name Grey Owl in northeast Ontario in 1929, renouncing the beaver hunt that he had witnessed as a trapper, packer, guide, and fire ranger. "One hundred thousand square miles of country in Ontario are dry of beaver, and save for their deserted works it was as if there never had been any ... Beaver stood for something vital, something essential in this wilderness, were a component of it; they were the wilderness." Grey Owl went to England in 1935 and made his case before rapt audiences in more than forty towns and cities.[50]

Grey Owl's books were best-sellers, and a call to action. Formal traplines had been pioneered by the Hudson's Bay Company, but they were legally registered in Ontario only in 1935 and in Quebec ten years later. The beaver recovered as rapidly as it had declined. Today, the Great Lakes, New England, and northern Ontario once again have the heaviest harvests of beaver on the continent, as they had in the first century of the fur trade. The North American harvest of beaver (and of all furs) is now as high as it ever was. As Grey Owl predicted, the beaver brought health back to the land in the form of millions of ponds that watered it and its wildlife. Beaver had been gone from Pennsylvania by 1903 but, between 1915 and 1924, fifty pairs were brought from Ontario and New York, and the state now has over fifty thousand and a fur harvest again. By 1900, the number of beaver in New York was down to fifteen; beaver were brought in from Ontario and Yellowstone, and the state currently has a population of more than seventy thousand. In 1975 the beaver was adopted as official animal symbol of New York State, and in 2007 they returned to New York City itself.[51]

Another compelling personality made waterfowl his passion. Jack Miner was born in Ohio and came to southwest Ontario in 1878 when he was twelve. He worked in his family's tile and brick business and was a market hunter when he was young. He taught himself to raise bobwhite and geese, and he built a pond, to which he lured and then fed migrating waterfowl. He banded over fifty thousand ducks and forty thousand geese. By the 1920s, his ponds were a tourist attraction, and attracted agency support as well. He lectured all over North America. "Every place I lectured persons were asking: 'What has become of our wild geese that used to come here by the tens of thousands?' I answered them by saying, 'Automatic guns and systematic shooting is where they are.'"

Miner was positively acerbic about the initial Migratory Birds Convention, which was struck between Canada and the United States in 1918. It set a bag limit of 2,400 ducks and 800 geese per person each year, figures that Miner mocked, asking why anyone would need "six tons of ducks and geese in one year?" His own figures showed that ducks had "decreased eighty percent" on his watch. Miner was an evangelical conservationist, believing in the doctrine of usefulness – "Let man have dominion." People should farm the wildlife as devotedly as they farmed the soil, building ponds and bird boxes and defending useful species like ducks, geese, deer, and songbirds against their predators. He nominated raptors, crows, and wolves as predators deserving deliberate extirpation. Despite this, Miner was a powerful motivator of hands-on conservation.[52]

The elk, or *wapiti*, was once abundant across the region. They were on the species lists of every visitor to the Atlantic coast in the 1600s, and of every observer of Great Lakes prairies and alvars before 1800. They must have been magnificent. John James Audubon kept a pair on his Manhattan estate in the 1840s, purportedly from western Pennsylvania. They were long gone before attempts were made to bring them back. Elk from Yellowstone were released in the Adirondacks in 1900, but they did not persist. Pennsylvania released them into the Alleghenies in the 1920s, and there are two herds there now. North of the lakes, a pair was released on Long Point, Lake Erie, in 1909, but they wandered off the point and were shot. Another attempt was made in 1932 and 1933 when boxcars of elk were brought from Alberta to three sites in northern Ontario. In 1935 they were stocked on the Bruce peninsula. All went well until it was rumoured that an elk parasite might be harming deer and farm stock. Hunters were asked to shoot the elk on sight. We now know that it was deer that was the likely parasite carrier, of a brain nematode that harms elk, moose, and caribou in ascending order of mortality. New attempts are now underway in Ontario. From 1998 to 2001, 460 elk from Alberta were released at four sites, and they have doubled in number since. A hunt began again in 2011, and some crop damages have been reported. There still remain large parts of the Bruce peninsula and Manitoulin Island, and the Smith Falls and Chaumont plains, where they might also be restored.[53]

Cougar had ranged the entire hemisphere but were gone from Pennsylvania by 1874 and Ontario by 1884. New York saw its last wild animal in 1894, and Michigan in 1919. They took livestock, so they had to go. The standard drill when one was seen by settlers was to form a posse, gather the dogs, and track and kill it. In modern times, cougar sightings have soared, but without proof until one was killed in Quebec in 1992. Hair samples were tested for DNA, which proved they were released "pets" belonging to the South or Central America subspecies. Since then, DNA from other cougars has shown them to be of North American provenance, but again almost certainly from released pets. Cougar scat was found near a den at the Wainfleet Bog in the Niagara peninsula in 2004, there were sightings from the Flamborough Swamp to the north, and tracks from an adult and kit were seen along the Niagara Escarpment. Today, there are hundreds of credible sightings across the region. They have re-naturalized their native range, and settled in. Perhaps they will be the predator that reduces the present high deer numbers, but will we allow it?[54]

The lynx was gone from New York by the late 1890s. During the winters of 1988 to 1990, eighty-three lynx from the Yukon were released back to the Adirondacks, but roadkills and other deaths quickly eliminated them and the project failed. However, the lynx had always held out in the north Maine woods, and they showed up again in New Hampshire in 2005 and Vermont in 2007, perhaps on their way back to the Adirondacks on their own.

The early records are full of claims for the honour of who killed the last wolf in any particular jurisdiction. Gone from Ohio by 1842. Gone from Pennsylvania by about 1880, and from New York by 1893. Gone from Canada east of Quebec by 1911. Certainly enough honours to go around, but there were still a few in northern Michigan, in touch with their intact northern range, and a population in Algonquin Park, the object of classic studies by biologist Doug Pimlott from 1958 to 1965, and by his students John and Mary Theberge from 1986 to 1999. The Theberges documented the decline of Algonquin wolves, and in 1998 the Ontario minister of natural resources, John Snobelen, set up an advisory group to recommend what to do. At the same time, geneticists Paul Wilson and Brad White were developing new DNA techniques at Trent University, and showed that the Algonquin wolf was not the northern timber wolf of legend but the smaller eastern wolf, a relative of the rare red wolf of the U.S. southeast, which had been reduced to a small population along the Gulf Coast of Texas and Louisiana. Captive breeding and release has successfully restored the red wolf into North Carolina, beginning in 1987 with the release of four pairs. And here, in Algonquin Park (and elsewhere in the northeast), was its close cousin. The recommendation to Snobelen was to protect the wolf both inside and outside Algonquin, and in 2001 Ontario banned any hunting and trapping of wolf in the park and declared a moratorium on hunting and trapping it in thirty-nine surrounding townships. This was tough, but it stuck, and the Algonquin wolf population has been stable since then.[55]

In 2006 I was asked to speak in Vermont to the Society of Environmental

Journalists about how we might stitch a landscape back together so that the Canadian wolf could make it back to the Adirondacks on its own. I described what an Algonquin wolf would face: hiking south to Highway 401, then scaling its centre barricade and swimming the St Lawrence, only to face a gauntlet of stateside farms and roads between it and the Adirondacks. Still, I said, it is almost inevitable that the wolf would return to the Adirondacks, but perhaps through Maine. The question was, I said, how we would treat them when they did return.

At the same time, James Strittholt of the Conservation Biology Institute was reporting elsewhere on the coyotes in the Adirondacks. "We had a group in Montreal do some genetic work on what people thought were coyotes that were shot and killed in the region ... The animals they were thinking were coyotes had more ... wolf genes than coyote genes," said Strittholt. From DNA tests, it is now almost certain that the original wolf of the Adirondacks was the eastern wolf, not the northern timber wolf, and it never completely left the area but, instead, cross-bred and persisted with the immigrant coyote. "*Canis soup*" is what Brad White and Paul Wilson call it.[56]

Finally, and incredibly, in 2004 coyote hunters spotted – and biologist Arnie Karr photographed – a wolverine about ninety miles north of Detroit, after a hiatus of about two hundred years since the last sighting in Michigan. Where did that come from? Wildlife is full of surprises and has shown great resilience, especially in places where we have not extinguished it, where we have given it a hand, and where we have left it room to operate. The challenge almost invariably comes back to the land, and whether we will leave enough of it alone.

A New Commons: Protected Areas

The urge to protect wildlife deepened and broadened over the past century into a drive to protect the land as a whole, and to revise the land-tenure system so that nature itself held title. Land for nature was a New World invention – as ecologist Stan Rowe called it, a "needed rallying point for earth care" – and its origins were in the special circumstances of loss and settlement in the New World. Most North Americans, both Native and newcomer, had family histories of being dispossessed of what they had in their homelands, either individually or in common. Many of them had seen a New World commonwealth of wildlife and nature disappear before their eyes, over the course of individual lifetimes.[57]

The Scottish-born naturalist John Muir led the way. He is credited with inspiring U.S. National Parks in California, but his own inspiration lay in the devastation of Great Lakes country. Muir wrote in 1897 in the *Atlantic Monthly*: "The whole continent was a garden [and] the magnificent forests around the Great Lakes ... have disappeared in lumber and smoke, mostly smoke." He knew this from his time in Canada, where he had gone to avoid the military draft for the U.S. Civil War. Muir never wrote much about his years north of the border, but it was in Canada that he experienced his epiphany. With war at home and forest clearances all around, and in the solitude of a streamside swamp in Simcoe County, in old Huronia, he came on a clump of Calypso orchids. "I never before saw a plant so full of life; so perfectly spiritual. I felt as if I were in the presence of superior beings ... I sat down beside them and wept." Muir spent the next year working at a factory by a waterfalls near Meaford, tuning up its equipment and increasing its output of tool handles. The factory burned in 1866 and Muir returned home, age twenty-eight, and then headed to California for his health, to become the legendary founder of North American parks and protected areas.[58]

The first expressly "natural" park in British North America was put in place grudgingly in 1887 by Ontario Premier Oliver Mowat, a decade after a group of New Yorkers, including the architect Frederick Olmsted and the artist Frederick Church, persuaded Canada's governor general, Lord Dufferin, to propose a binational park at Niagara Falls. Protracted discussions reduced the idea to a reclaimed parkette beside the falls, Queen Victoria Park. Artists also led the way elsewhere. A.Y. Jackson, of the Group of Seven and the Ontario Society of Artists (OSA), was painting in the quartz hills of Killarney, north of Georgian Bay, when he realized that only a single lake had been spared from logging. He and the Federation of Ontario Naturalists, which had been formed just that year, lobbied the province to set aside the lake, which it did in 1932 as "O.S.A. Lake," in trust of the artists. The artistic palette, and the waters and rocklands of Georgian Bay, Killarney, and Algonquin, were the core of a new aesthetic of wilderness "shaped by the west wind."[59]

North of the lakes, parks were more often the result of committees than of artistic inspiration. It took two commissions to establish Algonquin Park in 1893, and there would be only ten more provincial or national parks established in Ontario in the next sixty years. In 1934 the Federation of Ontario Naturalists issued a paper, *Sanctuaries and the Preservation of Wild Life in Ontario*, stating: "In most civilized countries today sanctuaries are being set aside for the preservation of representative samples of the natural conditions." This took time to be accepted. The doctrine of usefulness or "multiple-use" prevailed, and those uses included logging, hunting, trapping, mining, and cottages. In 1954 a park agency was finally set up in Ontario. Public lands that had been treated as opportunities for private license would be considered for something other than their usefulness. Private lands witnessed a parallel shift, and landowners and organizations began to secure private nature reserves. All of this reshaped a new natural "commons." Today, there are 615 provincial parks and protected areas, almost 38 federal protected areas, and even more private reserves, where nature comes first – and they add up to more than 12 per cent of the Ontario Great Lakes basin. This tithing for nature reflects a sea change in civil society.[60]

In Ontario, it started with a hundred new parks between 1954 and 1970, almost all of them along highways at lakes, to service the recreation needs of the new, mobile, post-war family. Visitors quadrupled and camping grew tenfold. In 1970 Ontario naturalists joined forces with a new Wildlands League (WL) to demand formal protection zones *inside* the parks. This led to a ban on logging in Killarney and Quetico. The new Ontario park agency was no less determined. A "Blue Book" of policies was released in 1978, restricting the uses in different classes (and zones) of parks. Most ambitious of all, it set targets for the number of parks needed to "represent" the biological and geological diversity of the province. This triggered systematic natural-area assessments across Ontario. The Blue Book became a gold standard among park agencies.

In 1981 Ontario initiated a public review of how it managed the 90 per cent of the province that was public land. In this review, 254 new parks were nominated to meet the Blue Book standards. In protest, as historian Gerald Killan tells it, "commercial and industrial interests, trappers, sportsmen and some First Nations assumed a strident anti-parks posture." They particularly opposed the idea of "nature reserves," in which resource extraction would be prohibited. My own analysis at the time showed that the 152 proposed nature reserves would constitute 1.3 per cent of the land base, but the idea was resisted nonetheless. Minister Alan Pope announced the cabinet's decision in 1983: five million new acres of park were declared – an astonishing figure. However, more than a hundred candidate sites were dropped, most of them nature reserves in the south. Worse, mining, hunting, trapping, and commercial tourism would be permitted in parks where they had previously been prohibited. A change in government in 1985 resulted in a *volte-face*, however, and mining, hunting, and trapping were prohibited again, as was logging in all parks except

Algonquin. At the same time, to deal with the sites dropped in the south, a new policy was declared for these private lands, designating them "areas of natural and scientific interest" (ANSI). For these, the province would encourage private owners to conserve them, and this led in time to property-tax reductions for the owners, conservancy purchases of land from willing sellers, and land-use policies that discourage their development.[61]

A decade later, another review was undertaken of Ontario public lands, this time its mid-latitudes. Minister Chris Hodgson announced this in 1997, and suggested to me – I was working with the Federation of Ontario Naturalists – that the tone of debate would be improved if we made an effort to consolidate the voices for conservation. Of course, that was what we were doing already, through a "Partnership for Public Lands" led by the FON, the Wildlands League, and the World Wildlife Fund (WWF), with twenty-eight other groups. The issue would be logging versus parks, a "war of the woods." At the urging of an engaged citizen, John McCutcheon, the minister and the Partnership came to an early agreement that all their data and maps would be pooled, and that Partnership nominees could serve on three regional roundtables. The round tables acted as lightning rods for public complaints about government and urban environmentalists. However, new voices arose in central Ontario espousing their own brand of conservation. The Partnership undertook an analysis of a preferred protected-area system, and we took it on the road to meet the public in halls across the province. People told us where they thought the protected areas should be, and offered sound advice like, "It's the water, stupid." The lakes, rivers, shores, and wetlands of Great Lakes country were of paramount importance.

At the same time, with the WWF's Arlin Hackman at the helm, the Partnership initiated face-to-face discussions with the leaders of forest and mining companies, First Nations, and business analysts. Led by Ric Symmes, it also released an analysis of business opportunities, *Planning for Prosperity*, that identified innovations in stumpage, wood flow, and protected areas that would benefit everyone. I organized polling, which demonstrated overwhelming public support for a major breakthrough in protecting nature. The polling also showed that supporters of the party in power wanted this even more than the average voter. Results were shared with the roundtables, the new minister of natural resources, John Snobelen, Premier Mike Harris, and the media.[62]

The roundtables faced tough schedules and resistant business interests. As a result, for example, almost no new protected areas were recommended for northeast Ontario. The Partnership reacted. A petition of concerned scientists was developed by the WWF's Kevin Kavanagh. Television ads highlighted the impending failure, delivered by respected journalist Peter Trueman. Telephone and computer banks directed calls and e-mails to politicians. Behind the scenes, the key was that Premier Harris was from the north and understood the landscape. He knew that the international standard at the time was for 12 per cent of a jurisdiction to be protected, and that this could be achieved without jeopardizing resource users. It might even invigorate tourism and diversify economies. A heart-to-heart between Harris adviser David Lindsay, Monte Hummel (WWF), John McCutcheon, and me brought a nervous Christmas truce and an agreement for a last-ditch negotiation at a remote resort. Its main table was chaired by Deputy Minister Ron Vrancart and included the presidents of Abitibi, Domtar, and Tembec, Hummel and myself, Tim Gray of the Wildlands League, and Ric Symmes and Ron Reid of the Partnership. The resort was packed with operations managers and information specialists, who could respond to questions about stumpage regimes, wood volumes, and possible protected areas.

Within a week, an Ontario Forest Accord was drafted. A week later it was signed and on 29 March 1999 all the roundtable participants, negotiators, and hundreds of others joined Premier Harris and ministers Snobelen and Hodgson in a celebration. One of the outcomes was that six million new acres of forest, wetland, cliff, barrens, and water were regulated as 378 new protected areas. Naysayers said that the outcome was not what the roundtables had wanted, but the outcome *was* a response to northern residents who argued their own interests rather than the status quo. Twelve per cent of Ontario's central Shield, almost all Great Lakes country, would be protected, and now, a decade later, both Ontario and Quebec have committed to regulating 50 per cent of their far norths for conservation in the next fifteen years.[63]

On the Ontario lowlands south of the Shield, all of the current provincial and federal protected areas cover only 0.8 per cent of the land base. This was the landscape that was sold to settlers, and it has taken heroic efforts to buy it back. Conservation Authorities and their funders have secured more than 1.7 per cent of it. Towns and cities have set aside parklands, as much as twenty thousand acres in Toronto, for example. But all of this adds up to only 2.5 per cent protected for nature. Private owners and land trusts are doing more; they own the 5 per cent of the land base that has been documented as significant natural areas, where development is limited or prohibited and landowners are rebated their property taxes. These remain intact by the good graces of their private owners, and are well cared for. They hold the most promise in the south.[64]

Private Lands and the Niagara Escarpment

There are innumerable stories about natural areas cared for with grace and affection by their private owners. A few have been mentioned. The Backus family began its land assembly in 1798 in Norfolk, caring for its forest until 1956, when it was sold for conservation. The Long Point Company purchased the Long Point marshes in 1866 and donated half of it as a National Wildlife Area in 1978. Toronto's High Park and Grenadier Pond were gifts by the Toronto surveyor John G. Howard in 1873. The Krug family of furniture makers and naturalists assembled a forest at Kinghurst in 1899, and brothers Howard and Bruce donated it to the FON as a nature reserve in 1998. The Baker family bought their sugar bush in Vaughan in 1801 and cared for it well until it was bought back by the province in 2000. The Tadanac Club on eastern Georgian Bay bought the Tadanac watershed in 1884, and it is now Georgian Bay's most pristine watershed. Still, the vast majority of nature reserves remain uncounted and private, their stories never told.[65]

Some were more public. Jack Miner, the waterfowl evangelist and pond builder, said everyone should follow his lead. "Let each county establish a small ... sanctuary of not less than twenty-five nor more than one hundred acres ... [with] a dog-proof fence around it and no shooting allowed within a mile." His modest approach has been amplified hugely since then, with thousands of ponds created and with more than a thousand groups of anglers and hunters owning thousands of acres of ponds, streams, and wetlands. Ducks Unlimited, in particular, specializes in creating waterfowl habitat throughout Great Lakes country. Across the region, naturalist clubs own over ten thousand acres, and the Nature Conservancy of Canada owns more than a hundred thousand acres, secured since 1962, at more than four hundred sites in Ontario and Quebec. Since the 1990s, more than thirty local land trusts have started up north of the lakes, and more than a hundred south of the lakes, an entire new volunteer sector. The "conservation easement" was added to their tool kit, so that landowners could retain ownership but still extinguish development rights by sale or gift of an easement. Add to this tax incentives to donate both lands and easements, and the picture is clear. The protection of nature is a priority of both the public and private sectors.[66]

There are places that go unrecognized for their contribution. Among them are First Nations lands, including, to name just a few in southern Ontario, Walpole Island and its prairies and marshes; Alderville and its savannas; Cape Croker and its alvars, cliffs, and forests; Saugeen and its fens and forests;

and Wikwemikong on Manitoulin with its coasts, cliffs, and alvars. Also unrecognized are the public lands where conservation occurs coincidentally, such as those held by the military: the Meaford tank and shelling range, with its lakes, bluffs, and shores; Navy Island in the Niagara River, with its southern forests; Camp Borden and its sand barrens and pineries; the Burnt Lands alvars; and Petawawa with its pineries and peatlands. After its extirpation from Canada for sixty-two years, the endangered Kirtland's warbler came back, breeding on the Petawawa base in 2007. Military security is a good fit with nature conservation.[67]

Also taken for granted is the typical countryside, with its narrow roads and farm lanes lined with big old trees. It was farmers who planted those trees and it was incentives that encouraged them. In 1871 Ontario passed An Act to Encourage the Planting of Trees upon the Highways, which established that any tree planted by a farmer on an adjacent road right-of-way was the property of the farmer. This allowed landowners to plant trees they owned without having to fence off land to do so, and they got paid twenty-five cents for each tree that survived for three years. Tree planting caught on quickly. J. Sterling Morton, a native of Detroit living in Nebraska, held the first Arbor Day there in 1872, followed by Michigan and Pennsylvania, and then Ohio, in 1882. Ontario followed suit in 1885, encouraging schoolchildren and the public to plant trees. Between grants and Arbor Day, the early roads and lanes were planted up, a good example of how public validation can change the geography of the land.[68]

Another example is the grants for farmers after the Second World War to fence their stock out of the bush. Landowners could also get subsidized tree seedlings to plant up surplus or degraded lands. Fencing grants and tree nurseries were disbanded in the 1990s and, as a result, setbacks and tree planting have declined. However, crop prices and equipment dimensions also enter the land-care equation. When prices are high, the land is worked hard and, as farms upgrade to larger equipment, new fields are developed and others come out of production. These days, farm-gate prices have budged off their basement lows, which will intensify farming, but, at the same time, there are opportunities for tree planting, prairies, and wetlands. It is straight economics, and incentives can make the difference.

The United States (and Europe) supports landowners who meet stewardship goals such as retiring land or planting trees, grasslands, or wetlands. These fall under the rubric of providing "ecological services" that are in the public interest, and can even extend to the benefits of carbon sequestration by natural systems – nature being useful on its own terms. Such approaches deserve imitation because it will take much encouragement and many hands to restore nature. On private lands, it has been a combination of deliberate landowner efforts, modest public incentives, benign neglect, and cheap energy that has blessed nature with the time and space to recover. Now it is time to foster, through incentives, the air, water, and land services that nature also delivers.[69]

Today, the shape of the private land base is being moulded, for the first time, by public policies that favour nature. This is arguably most pronounced north of the lakes; the constitution of Canada is not embedded with the strong property and compensation rights that are part of the U.S. constitution. As a result, the community has more say in the uses to which individuals can put their land. For example, in Ontario, landowners and communities must abide by land-use policies that restrain development in designated areas. An early example of this was Premier Bill Davis's creation of a "parkway belt" that froze the use of lands around Toronto for later selective development. A more enduring example was the Niagara Escarpment.[70]

The cliffs and waterfalls of the Niagara Escarpment had been left largely undeveloped and were loved by their communities. The stone of the escarpment also made perfect crushed aggregate, an essential building material. In 1960 Ray Lowes, a metallurgist at Stelco who hailed from south Saskatchewan, convinced the Federation of Ontario Naturalists to support a new concept – that volunteers would approach landowners to ask for permission to establish a 450-mile Bruce Trail from Niagara to the Bruce peninsula. While this was underway, in 1962, a public battle broke out over quarrying. A growing Toronto needed vast amounts of aggregate; roads alone required half of it. The spark was the blasting of a hole in a magnificent cliff wall in Halton, visible to millions as they drove west on Highway 401, itself a roadway built on a deep base of crushed stone from escarpment quarries. In response, Premier John Robarts asked the advice of Len Gertler, one of the founders of Canadian urban planning at the University of Waterloo. His 1968 report proved inspirational. Gertler recommended the protection of the Niagara Escarpment through a robust mix of parks, protective land-use regulations for private lands, and strict quarry regulations. His philosophic approach was that cities should perfect the city, and that the country should stay country. Direct outcomes of this were the Niagara Escarpment Protection Act, 1970, and the Pits and Quarries Control Act, 1971, two firsts. Premier Bill Davis inherited all this in 1971.[71]

For many, it was a heavy-handed imposition of government control over their land. It was a new kind of "treaty" and the new Natives – by then resident for many generations – resisted. The hatred of appropriation without compensation runs deep on the countryside, born of the British enclosures and loyalist confiscations. The premier was burned in effigy outside a meeting hall in Grey County. Don Scott, planning director for the Bruce, got a shotgun shell in the mail. Its great public advocate was Lyn MacMillan, founder of the Coalition on the Niagara Escarpment (CONE). Lyn insisted on stronger laws to realize Gertler's vision, and hounded politicians and officials alike, finally forcing a judicial review of their stalling tactics. Local supporters stepped forward. Biologist Kathy Lindsay justified, at a public meeting in Mono, why the cliffs there should be made a park. She succeeded, and was hired as one of a crew of three to inventory the escarpment's natural areas, its ancient untouched heart, which became the "natural" and "protected" land-use zones that would have no quarries or subdivisions (67 per cent of the area). In 1985, twenty-three years after the hole was first blasted in the cliff in Halton, Premier Frank Miller's cabinet adopted the Niagara Escarpment Planning and Development Act, arguably North America's first environmental land-use plan. It was never a mere technical matter for planners and ecologists. As Ray Lowes put it: "Not all of us can study ecology, but we should all have the opportunity to walk under ancient trees on a forest floor that is rich with the things that sustain life."[72]

Today, proof of change lies in the fact that real estate prices inside the regulated plan area are higher than outside the area. Demographics have shifted, as those who wanted to live near the escarpment elected to do so. The extent of protected areas has grown from 7 per cent to about a quarter of the area. More than half of it is now forested, a green corridor crossing the landscape. There is no comparable protection for the escarpment where it occurs in Michigan or New York, but in Wisconsin there is growing interest in the Door peninsula, where the same escarpment's cliffs line Green Bay. Its rarities have now been inventoried (forty-two state-listed species at risk), and volunteer land trusts and state parks are active. In 2012 Wisconsin Governor Scott Walker signed a new law authorizing the purchase of public conservation lands along the escarpment, the first such recognition in America.

In 2003 Lyn MacMillan of CONE fame and her partner, Robert MacMillan, conserved their own 120-acre farm as a dedicated nature reserve, the most financially valuable donation of conservation lands in Canadian history. The farm is now almost totally surrounded by development. The Nature Conservancy of Canada is working with the city of Vaughan and the Toronto Region Conservation Authority to care for it as one of the last open spaces in the area. From its heights on the south flank of the Oak Ridges, you can see the approaching urban cliffs of Toronto.

The Oak Ridges and Toronto Greenbelt

The Oak Ridges are the top of the watershed north of Lake Ontario. Ancient trails crossed them to shorten the route between the lower and upper Great Lakes. One of them become Simcoe's Yonge Street. In 1829 Mary O'Brien rode up Yonge Street into the high country north of her. "We passed a line of hills which they call the Oak Ridges. These consist of small abrupt hills and valleys ... one or two which contain lakes enclosed on every side by steep banks ... [of] oak and pine." (The farm immediately south of the O'Briens' farm on the moraine was bought by the Cook brothers, who ran a mill there, and then by the MacMillans in the 1930s.)[73]

The timber from the moraine was described by Arthur Richardson. "From observations of old barn frames and of the oldest boards in existence ... some idea of the size of the trees can be obtained. For example, planks cut after 1844 ... from trees 4 1/2 feet in diameter and from 80 to 100 feet long, while trees up to five feet in diameter and over 100 feet long were [also] cut." In 1841 a single mill shipped eight hundred pine masts of this dimension. By 1851, William Smith would write about the Oak Ridges near Kettleby: "The situation is picturesque, and would be more so had a little of the timber been left standing ... The new settler ... looks upon trees as enemies, which must be destroyed on any terms, and it is not until he has been settled for some years ... that he wishes he had left a few trees to ornament his domain."[74]

By 1910, tree cover on the moraine was down to about 15 per cent, and the water table had dropped. Ralph Carman, forester at the provincial seed plant at Angus, wrote a paper in 1941 about the water situation: "This is the first time ... it has been established that such a large area of a glacial moraine had no surface drainage to the adjacent streams, and yet, owing to the nature and depth of the sand and gravel formation, it contained the ground water reservoir which fed springs in those streams and kept the flow fairly uniform all year. This reservoir has been seriously depleted ... Proper ground cover [trees] will reduce evaporation ... and make more water available for ground water storage ... Reforestation should proceed as quickly as possible."[75]

By then, the wildlife was gone. Lester Snyder inventoried King Township, in the centre of the moraine, in the 1920s: "No ... beaver ... have been noted by us. The black bear has been extirpated for some years ... A specimen of the lynx was killed west of Aurora about the winter of 1883 ... No records of [bob cat] ... Red squirrel has not been very common any year within ... experience ... It has been some years since deer were permanent residents ... Not many grouse persist." Ken Mayall, a forester, summarized the situation in King Township by the 1930s. While more than 60 per cent of the township had been forested in the year 1840, "by 1851 there were 21 sawmills in operation in the township ... By 1890 clearing and overgrazing on the highlands had continued to such an extent that much of these lands no longer retained their moisture through the summer ... Many of the small swamps ... were drained ... The lowered water table cut off the flow from many springs, ending the fish life in the springs they fed. [In 1938] only 4042 acres, or 4.9% of the township now remains in ungrazed woods." Mayall suggested the radical goal (for the time) of 15 per cent ungrazed woodland in King, a challenge that was taken up progressively and successfully.[76]

In 1943 Donald F. Putnam, geographer at the University of Toronto, wrote an appendix to Toronto's Master Plan suggesting that the Oak Ridges and the Niagara Escarpment become a "conservancy district" to protect its headwaters from "encroachment and vandalism." This, and parks on the Rouge and Humber rivers, would be "barriers ... arresting the spread of continuous bricks and mortar to uncontrolled limits." By the 1960s, the urban growth outside Toronto pushed the government of Premier John Robarts to unveil a plan for a "Toronto-centred region," calling for seven parks on the Oak Ridges. The plan was dropped, but the seed was planted. In 1988 Premier David Peterson asked former Toronto mayor David Crombie to head a commission on the future of Toronto's waterfront. Crombie dealt directly with the links between the waterfront and its headwaters in his 1990 *Watershed* report: protection of the Oak Ridges would enhance the ecological well-being of the Toronto region as a whole.[77]

On 26 March 1990 Premier Peterson visited the Rouge River at Finch Avenue and declared a Rouge Park from Lake Ontario to the Oak Ridges, the largest urban park in Canada. It was a great day and I remember helping the premier, recovering from a ski injury at the time, down to the river to be photographed beside a rare old sycamore. That July, he declared the Oak Ridges a matter of "provincial interest" but his government fell that year. The new government of Premier Bob Rae commissioned fifteen studies, and released new development guidelines, before it too was defeated. I was with the Ministry of Natural Resources at the time and my contribution was a green paper, *The Natural Heritage of Southern Ontario's Settled Landscapes*, and new mapping of the natural areas left on the moraine. The idea was that a linked, evergreen "natural heritage system" should be identified and recognized across the entire landscape, similar to how we design and operate our water and transit systems. Green infrastructure had a functional value equal to or greater to that of built infrastructure, *and* it conserved nature.[78]

The Oak Ridges was not a priority for the new government of Premier Mike Harris in 1996. Still, the land companies were grinding their way north and their advances were being thwarted. The town of Richmond Hill, in particular, faced tremendous pressures. Its northern half, where we lived at the time, included the last undeveloped east-west link in the Oak Ridges, on Yonge Street at Bond Lake. In 2000 the town council took the radical step of approving urban development on all of it. Opposition was galvanized, led by Save the Oak Ridges Moraine (STORM), Save the Rouge Valley System (SRVS), the Federation of Ontario Naturalists, and Earthroots. Demonstrations drew thousands, and shut down council meetings, forcing council to reverse its earlier decision. The developers at Bond Lake appealed the council decision to the Ontario Municipal Board, and the battle was joined. The hearing, by the spring of 2001, had run up a reported bill of $20 million in legal and consulting fees, and there were said to be another sixty contested Oak Ridges files waiting at the Ontario Municipal Board for litigation.

The Oak Ridges was also an interest of mine at the Nature Conservancy of Canada, and, in May 2001, good fortune and a day on the Oak Ridges with David Lindsay, president of the Ontario SuperBuild Corporation, led to a proposal to the premier, who assigned it to Chris Hodgson, his minister of municipal affairs. The idea was to reframe the mapping of natural cores and corridors on the moraine into land-use designations like those that had proved durable on the Niagara Escarpment. We would do this by means of a negotiation similar to the one that produced the Ontario Forest Accord. It would need a six-month freeze on development and hearings, and a negotiating table. Ron Vrancart would again act as chair. At the table, representing conservation interests, were Debbe Crandall of STORM, Ric Symmes of FON, and the author, aided by Russ Powell and Dick O'Brien for the conservation authorities, economist James McKellar of York University, and Ron Christie of the Rouge Park Alliance. Fred DeGasperis (of Metrus, remember Baker's Woods), Peter Gilgan (Mattamy), and Mario Cortellucci (Cortel Group) represented development interests, and the chairs of Durham and York regions, Roger Anderson and Bill Fisch, completed the table. Gail Beggs, the deputy minister of natural resources, who had also been at the earlier table, knew that her planners and ecologists,

Fred Johnson and Steve Varga in particular, could map out a successful outcome. We would have six months to deliver a consensus to the minister, beginning with Hodgson's declaration of a six-month freeze on all development and hearings in May 2001.

Those not at the table, like Glen De Baeremaeker of SRVS, kept the heat on. He attacked the premier for "stacking the deck with pro-development hacks." The negotiations were "doomed to failure." Worse, I had been quoted in the *Toronto Star* saying nice things about the arch-developer DeGasperis on the occasion of the purchase of Baker's Woods. These and other orchestrated remarks helped bring the main table together. I organized a public poll in Toronto, York, Durham, and Peel; more than 80 per cent supported a protective law, 87 per cent a park on Yonge Street, and 91 per cent a hiking trail. Within six months, the main table had a draft that became the basis for the Oak Ridges Moraine Conservation Act, unanimously adopted on third reading in the legislature on 14 December 2001. I was guest of the house that day and it was a pleasure to reflect on the outcome: a 480,000-acre Oak Ridges that was legislated as a dozen core areas reserved for nature (38 per cent), connected by natural links about one mile wide and by river-valley links (24 per cent), all set within a rural countryside (30 per cent), within which there were settlement areas with fixed boundaries (8 per cent). Hodgson insisted that all the boundaries be in the legislation itself so that he could state, "There will be no subdivision development on 92 percent of the entire Oak Ridges, and no one will change the core and corridor areas without legislative approval. There will be no development in any of the natural heritage or hydrological features on the moraine."[79]

Also negotiated soon afterwards was a park about a half-mile wide crossing Yonge Street in Richmond Hill, in the area that had been so contentious. An agreement guided by David Crombie was reached with the developers to forego the approved housing there in exchange for provincial lands at Seaton, south of the moraine, conditional on 60 per cent of the Seaton lands being set aside as a natural-heritage system. Minister Hodgson also set up an Oak Ridges Moraine Foundation to secure conservation lands, build a trail, help landowners, and educate the public. By 2011, the foundation had parlayed its initial investment of $15 million into more than $50 million in projects. More than 155 miles of trail were in place, including two dozen access points for disabled visitors. Four thousand acres were acquired for conservation, a good start. The much maligned Premier Harris definitely changed the geography of Ontario for the better.[80]

If the Harris government should be acknowledged, then so too should the one that followed. Dalton McGuinty became premier in 2003, and, as if genuinely irritated to see his rival succeed on these files, he acted quickly. The motivation, once again, was the overarching Toronto growth plan. Late in 2003, the *Smart Growth* exercise of the Harris regime was rebranded as a triumvirate of initiatives: *Places to Grow, Greenbelt,* and *Planning Reform.* On the first page of the announcements of each was a footnote to the work by Hemson Consulting, whose projections of major urban growth underpin government priorities independent of political stripe. The projections enumerated how and where the population would grow by almost four million, and explained that this population would need two million new housing units and two million new jobs, growth that is matched in North America only by Los Angeles and Mexico City. Ontario is the destination for more than half of new Canadians, and Canada's immigration rate is the highest in the world among countries of the Organisation for Economic Co-operation and Development (OECD).[81]

Places to Grow was the plan to build the infrastructure needed for the growth, and *Planning Reform* was the policy requiring municipalities to increase their growth to match the projections. "Greenfield" development would accommodate 60 per cent of the growth, and "intensification" 40 per cent. The *Greenbelt* would expand the Niagara Escarpment and Oak Ridges, and serve as a limit to urban growth. A task force and consultations began in 2004, led by Minister of Municipal Affairs John Gerretsen and Burlington Mayor Rob MacIsaac. They tabled their recommendations and, on 28 October, Premier McGuinty announced to an exuberant crowd at the McMichael Gallery in Kleinberg another million acres of conserved countryside extending north to Lake Simcoe, west to the outskirts of Waterloo and Guelph, and east to Durham County. Together, these three laws regulate an unprecedented natural heritage system (Fig. 28). *Planning Reform* additionally required every municipality in southern Ontario to designate a similar system "of natural heritage features and areas, linked by natural corridors which are necessary to maintain biological and geological diversity, natural functions, [and] viable populations of indigenous species and ecosystems." This consolidated two decades of innovation in using municipal official plans to conserve nature.[82]

As recently as 1999, ecologists Don Chant and Henry Regier would decry how there was "no overall environmental policy at the level of the greater Toronto region." Beyond Toronto, however, other cities had already accomplished this. Hamilton had a natural-heritage system in its official plan by the mid-1990s, based on the cooperative efforts of its planners, the local Conservation Authority, and Hamilton Field Naturalists. The Ottawa-Carleton official plan had a comparable natural-environment strategy. Even earlier, many official plans had adopted the ESA (environmentally sensitive areas) approaches of the Waterloo region, and, to the south, the Metroparks of Cleveland and Detroit offered other examples. It was only *after* many cities had already acted that the province moved to a presumptive role of leadership. Nevertheless, the new policies lent a necessary authority to the earlier efforts.[83]

Southern Ontario's present mix of public natural areas and privately conserved lands, together with restrictive land uses, property-tax reductions, and foundation supports, may arguably set the standard for developed regions in North America. It is a tripartite balance, with firm and rule-based boundaries, between: (1) the city-state, with its footprint intensifying; (2) the working landscape of farms and other resource industries, with natural features protected; and (3) conserved public lands and constrained private lands. However, it is a fragile balance. Toronto's loss of manufacturing may corrode it, as has happened stateside. Niagara Falls and St Catharines share the look of Cleveland, Flint, and Detroit. There are other canaries in the mine, such as the declining middle class and the distancing of rich and poor. City-centre schools are closing because there are too few children, even while high-rise neighbourhoods are intensifying. Outward growth – and cheap space and energy – are finite, and urban development cannot be the main engine of economic growth. Nature does not work that way. Organisms proliferate to the point where they become their own substrates, and then decline. Deceleration and de-energizing are the new frontiers, and the challenge is to find the "prosperous way down," as ecologists call it, without deepening the footprint.[84]

Seven consecutive premiers have greened Ontario over the last fifty years. They spanned the political spectrum but all understood the public demand to take better care of our natural heritage. McGuinty said when he unveiled the *Greenbelt* that it was "for clean air, safe water, and our children." But it is more than that. It is for home and native land. The test is what we leave intact or bring back – our true quality of life. Birth, youth, maturity, competition, majesty, death, and decay never stop cycling in nature. What changes is how much of each happens where, to whose benefit. Our actions dictate this, and there is more recognition of this now, of nature as a shared commons.[85]

Re-Wilding

The thinking about restoration has also gone global. Geoscientist Paul Martin, biologist David Burney at Fordham, and others have upped the ante by calling for re-wilding on a global scale – a "resurrection ecology" or a "Pleistocene re-wilding." They go so far as to suggest a global reshuffling of the deck; for example, elephants could be reintroduced to the Americas to "restart the evolution of proboscideans in the New World." Some of this is already happening. For the past twenty years *The Wilds* project has matured on ten thousand acres of reclaimed Ohio coal mines. Reputedly "North America's largest conservation facility," it supports twenty-five species of at-risk wildlife. These include the white rhino, giraffe, wild horse, cheetah, and African wild dog. Similar ventures are underway in California, Louisiana, and New Jersey, and it is estimated that there are more than seventy-seven thousand large ungulates from Asia and Africa, as well as kangaroos, free to roam these days on various private Texas ranches. The approach goes far beyond the restoration of native North America.[86]

"Jump-start our diminishing biodiversity" is the call-to-arms. Josh Donlan, ecologist at Cornell University, paints the global picture. "Africa's large mammals are dying, stranded on a continent where wars are waging over scarce resources ... We outline a bold plan for preserving some of our global megafaunal heritage ... [by] the restoration of large wild vertebrates into North America." Ironically, though we can barely convince ourselves to let cougar and bison roam freely again, we are now talking about lions and elephants. As with acclimatization societies, such ventures can have unforeseen outcomes. To date, global species transfers, like cross-type blood transfusions, have been fraught with unplanned repercussions, most of them negative. Species are conglomerate organisms and we have learned that they and their dependents, while quite peaceful in their own homes, can have unintended consequences when relocated elsewhere – diseases, pathogens, and insects galore. What we do not know outweighs what we do know. The precautionary approach might be to restore our native species first, on a preferential basis.[87]

More faithful to New World nature has been the work on "greater ecosystems." One of the first and best of these was the Wildlands Project, started in 1992. Dave Foreman, the direct-action advocate and founder of Earth First, said, "What we seek is nothing less than the full flowering of the natural biological diversity of North America." The vision is one of unbroken natural corridors from Georgia to Gaspé, and from Algonquin to the Adirondacks. It speaks to the "re-introduction of all extirpated species," to reconnect native species wherever they once were. As Michael Soulé, co-founder of the Society for Conservation Biology, puts it, "the key is thinking big, both in space and time." Gary Snyder, the American poet, harkened back to the words of eighth-century Buddhists that "everything is connected," and Reed Noss, the astute conservation thinker at the University of Central Florida, proposed strategies for cranking up every known approach to conservation and restoration – to scales not considered before. The Wildlife Project was a catalyst for creative thinking and it inspired many similar endeavours. Of course, it is problematic at the large scales contemplated. Reed Noss admits that the "areas apparently needed to maintain viable populations [of large carnivores] over centuries are so large as to strain credibility; they certainly strain political acceptance."[88]

The Wildlands Project was a top-down vision, and it invited pushback. I recall a gathering in rural Montana of people working on the Yellowstone-to-Yukon (Y2Y) initiative. The on-the-ground feedback was that there was limited interest in hooking up Yellowstone to the Yukon, but, instead, there was a great deal of interest in hooking up the mountain to the north of the valley with the one to the south, because the benefits were obvious, and at comprehensible scales. Thinking too big – let alone globally – can obscure local possibilities. The obstacles to getting the wolf to the Adirondacks seemed insurmountable but then it turns out that they had never left. Finding a way for lynx to move from Quebec's Gaspé to New England seemed improbable, but lynx are suddenly found in Maine anyway. Linking Niagara to the Bruce was unlikely but thirty years later it is reality. Concepts of natural cores and corridors, community by community, can be implemented in stages, and then become what is expected. We may argue about issues like reintroducing large carnivores or Eurasian megafauna, but, on the ground, the last fifty years in this part of North America have been right on cue. A re-wilding *is* taking place.

"Conservation blueprints," "ecoregional assessments," and "big pictures" have been developed for Great Lakes country. They have identified and mapped the species and habitats that are priorities to conserve, the places that are already protected, and the lands that need care to get the job done. Species by species, habitat by habitat, acre by acre, we can thoughtfully decide what conservation actions to take. At this juncture, we have the intelligent design, in the form of adequate foresight. What is needed is to bring the necessary resources to bear, as fast as possible, to act on those designs (Fig. 29).[89]

The Great Lakes country has long been partitioned, first by Natives and then by newcomers, at multiple scales. James Lovelock postulates a three-part landscape for a future Britain: one part for city, industry, and built systems; one part for growing food; and the third for nature and green infrastructure. Here we can do better for nature because we still have some real wilds left. We can limit our cities to a smaller fraction, and partition the rest between working landscapes and protected wildlands. We know from the "blueprints" and "big pictures" that, for example, more than a third of lowland Ontario and two-thirds of the whole Great Lakes country remain in natural cover. The lowlands may be skeletonized but they are still structured as functioning systems that thread their way up and down valleys and rivers, shores and cliffs, bulking up in lowland wetlands and highland forests. There is a great payback in taking care of what is left, retiring some of it for long service, and building on it, as every spring builds on each winter.[90]

We are now deliberately staying out of natural areas and helping wildlife restore itself. We are naturalizing streams, removing dams and ponds, and putting back pools and meanders. We are bringing back prairies and savannas, and planting new ones. We are planting forest again, as well as plantations. We are tolerating more predators. With its elements intact, it is intelligent design to let nature do its thing. The assembly rules are the same as for built systems. Keep all the parts and keep them in good condition, both species and spaces. Find more parts, some of which may have gone astray. Multiply the parts, both species and spaces, and intensify their distribution, so that they can connect efficiently and economically. Let waters flow and let some fires go. Let predators prey and wildlife move. Take care of the small scales and the large scale will take care of itself. Notwithstanding their modern depletion, the number of species worldwide may, at present, be as high as it ever was in the geological record. The Earth and its biota, and evolution and restoration, are going full steam, whatever we might think of the results.[91]

Back on the farm in Mono, the area bottomed out at about 15 per cent natural cover in 1910, before cheap fuel and an end to poverty made it feasible for people to stop cropping and grazing and cutting too hard. Farming like that was industrial and our own farm was post-industrial, a tabula rasa for nature. It required more of everything natural, and the simplest of restoration lessons was to "bulk up." What was here we needed more of; what was gone, we wanted back; and what we could help, we would. There is a three-way partitioning of the farm as well. Around the buildings we exercise our polycultural inclinations - vegetable garden, orchard and fruit, and honey bees - and make attempts at a little crest of prairie, a Shield rock wall, and a wetland hollow. A blank slate. We plant far beyond pre-contact hardiness limits, testing what may be possible. People have been migrating species for ever, and on our farm we chose to do it with natives, a dozen southern oaks and hickories, chestnut, magnolia, tulip-tree, pumpkin ash, hop-tree, redbud, and sycamore, which can make it now through the warming highland winters.

The working part of the farm is fenced and in non-native pasture and crops. There are level fields, and fields that grow stones. There are steep slopes and a bottom for grazing. Much of it should never have been cleared and, when we came, it was all cemetery spurge, a sure sign of over-grazing. We eased up on the cattle, planted nitrogen-fixers to build soil, and grew windrows to hold the snow and water the ground. The spurge is now gone and the fields are a haven for grassland birds.

The third part of the farm is "maple beech hemlock," as it was when Benson surveyed it, with basswood in its bottoms and cedar in its springs. We fenced out the cattle, and we planted oak, pine, and ash to grow out the bush and shield it. The springs now gather as a stream again and downstream there are beaver. A few pre-settlement maple remain but the veteran beech all died of the blight. The bush has no yew, or trilliums, or wild garlic, which did not survive the grazing, but it is now on the mend and has the feel of the wild.

We began this tale on the Fifth Line and took it back to the open shores of ancient lakes where we hunted and gathered, and then farmed and built nation-states. Native land care had profound effects and was ended by disease and displacement. A century and a half of war and wilding followed, and what was thought pristine in the 1800s we now understand was largely new. Old World newcomers extended the hunter-gatherer-grower psyche and its economies into every part of the region, and they kept arriving until the place was transformed totally, into a highly severed and high-octane mosaic of global dreams, homogenized trade, city-states, and changed climate.

Hope is cheap and, therefore, inexhaustible. However, an objective scan of Great Lakes country yields grounds for optimism. Climate change threatens, but the predictions are for gentler change than elsewhere. Stressed resources and straining economies will settle down into some new balance as the era of cheap energy slowly wanes. Cheap energy has sheltered the region's forests from the demands of fuel and fibre, and they recovered as a result. Plowed lands and grazing livestock have declined, and we have put fences between our fields and natural areas. The use of pesticides, herbicides, and fertilizers peaked, and is declining. The quality of the water in our lakes and streams has improved. So has the quality of our air, in terms of sulphur, nitrogen dioxide, benzene, and particulates. Public demand and government regulation have combined to clean the air and water, and keep forests, streams, and natural areas intact. We have extended the rights of species beyond a mere orderly harvest to existential rights for those at risk. Given some modicum of affluence and education, we seem to be able to learn.[92]

But more can be done. A curb on our excesses would improve our futures. In support of nature, we can multiply its spaces and species, interdict the worse of the invasives, anticipate climate change, and re-wild the place. Certainly, it will be different. When any single strand of life is ended – a chestnut or a passenger pigeon – all its possibilities also end, but that does not mean that there are fewer possibilities, just different ones. Nature is always full on, it never repeats itself. We are its beneficiaries to the degree that we keep ourselves close to it and, in this good fortune, the Great Lakes country may well be anomalous on the modern stage, with cause to be both glad and fearful. As William Shakespeare wrote four centuries ago, "Nature's bequest gives nothing, but doth lend."

Nature Never Repeats Itself

There is growing doubt these days about Nature and what it has in store for us. Youth are especially sensitive to this, and more power to them. Of course, we care most about whether it will bite back and take its revenge, but, even so, a good part of our sympathy lies with Nature itself, and its prospects. At the same time, most people's understanding of their place in Nature has rarely been so slight. More of us than ever before live in cities, far from the madding land, and think of Nature, if at all, essentially as a commodity. There has never been a time when global consumerism has forced such a rapid conversion of Nature into artifact. And to further obscure our sightlines, we now live permanently and electronically in fast forward, in deficit, indoors.

The Great Lakes country was a place like none other when newcomers first saw it, a land of many resident nations all speaking differing but related languages, much like Europe in the same period. The differences between Native and newcomer were few but they were transformative, starting with the Europeans' resistant immune systems and their advanced metallurgy. Another was the written word, which swamped the oral and wampum record, and without which there could be no pretence of law or land ownership. On the other hand, in terms of land care, self-governance, and even gender equity, it is arguable that this part of North America had achieved an advantageous social and ecological balance.

Newcomers called it an earthly paradise but, as Radisson said, "we were Cesars," and all efforts were soon turned to profiting from that paradise, especially in its rich lowlands. This required the full weight of war and would reveal the region as an invaluable, open, and borderless thoroughfare of continental commerce. The warfare went on until 1815, after which lawfare took over and, by means of surveys, treaties, land sales, and, south of the lakes, lawful expulsions, completed the conversion of land to commodity. This was the foundation of the region's wealth, and its modern ecology owes as much to that manufacture of land-as-property as to anything else. Great Lakes country was thus transformed from a Native village world, by means of both warfare and lawfare, into the city-state world of today.

The early record is full of details of the region's superabundant wildlife and its great lakes and rivers, and forests and prairies. Also buried in the records is the story of a landscape that wilded itself – rapidly and dramatically – after Native land care ceased and before the flood of Europeans arrived a century and a half later. It was that newly wilded country that became the iconic landscape of record, where settlers cut the forests and sacrificed to build their new Europe. Yet another massive change was the extirpation, extinction, and decimation of the native wildlife of Great Lakes country, and the introduction of non-native species in such numbers – and some of them of such virulence – that the landscape could never be the same again. The template once set, its imprint deepened and widened over successive generations, reaching its nadir in the early 1900s.

Great Lakes country is now split between two nation-states, each with narratives born in its own sweat and tears, but it could yet have a unique future as the shared and cared-for land where ecological balance comes first to North America. It still has a surplus of fresh water, nature in abundance, a benign climate, and four seasons, each one refreshing the one before it. It also has a public more educated and informed with each new generation, and benefits from the wealth of our ancestors still invested in the region. Today it is transforming yet again. We are bringing in new organisms, goods, and resources at record speeds, and we are changing the climate itself. We are migrating into ever larger city-states but we are also deliberately re-wilding signature parts of our landscape. We have begun to evolve as residents of the place and, now that we are affluent, we are showing more sensitivity. There is a whole new narrative of individuals and groups and agencies bringing back Nature's places and species, and its watersheds and native habitats, as a new commons with a new semblance of ecological balance, if our demands on it can be contained.

The Great Lakes country is my home place, and the challenge is to look at it dispassionately as an object of ecological forensics. Scientists like James Lovelock tell us to look at the Earth volumetrically, as the self-regulating sum of organisms, landscapes, water, and atmosphere all orchestrated within systems we are just beginning to recognize. Where does man fit in? Lovelock is sympathetic with the view of E.O. Wilson that humankind is the tribal omnivore that happened to acquire intelligence and thus appropriate too much of the Earth's resources. "Genes hold culture on a leash," Wilson says, and, from this point of view, we might well reflect on a few of them that have been selected over two million years of exercising that omnivory, such as the "selfish" gene and the "altruism" gene. Every living thing arrived here after the last ice sheet melted, and, in the two-million-year story of the human species, this interglacial is barely a heartbeat. As anthropologist Michael Alvard writes, "we retain many of the physiological and psychological tools we evolved in the previous two million years." What, in the affairs of man and nature, are those tools and tendencies, and how did they play out in Great Lakes country?[1]

Hunting, Gathering, and Growing

One metaphor is that of the "hunter-gatherer," referring loosely to those various motivations that lead individuals (and cultures) to seek selective advantage and material security. The "selfish gene" is an even looser metaphor for these primordial behaviours. (By contrast, the "grower" instinct is an ultra-modern behaviour that has had only ten thousand years to mellow the human condition.) Society lionizes its successful "hunter-gatherers," often regardless of their social or environmental effects. In 1785 Joseph Brant and the Mohawk were championed in London for just those instincts. Our founders and forebears wear the same crown. These instincts are at play today in all walks of life and, in finance and in urban and resource development, can have costs for Nature that far outweigh any targeted suite of benefits. Of course, none of this is hard-wired, as the ecologist Tom Nudds is quick to say. What we need now is a new "prudent predator," one that can intelligently moderate the drive to dominate so as to sustain both the hunter and hunted, and the gatherer and gathered. In any such balance, of course, humans remain the keystone species; on the modern landscape, we are it.[2]

A growing number of people, however, are learning to "hunt and gather" differently. There are still targets and rewards – and the chase – but to more altruistic ends. Youth, naturalists, hikers, birders, artists of all kinds, anglers, hunters, farmers, recyclers, and, now, even the builders of the new city-states seem to understand the new frontiers – buildings that touch lightly on the land and last longer, training a whooping crane to follow an ultralight, or influencing a government to protect a natural area. These are people who can imagine restoring a trumpeter swan, a Lake Ontario salmon, or an oak savanna. They can imagine that acid rain can be curbed, and do it. They are working on carbon emissions, and they are thinking about how the city might be a garden and its residents ecological natives. Retooling and cooling the city can happen even while it is intensified, up-skilled, and perfected. Energy sprawl can be recalculated on the same basis as urban sprawl, based on full-cost accounting. Fundamentally, we can recalculate the carrying capacity of Great Lakes country, in pursuit of a future more durable than the one we inherited.[3]

A hyper-expression of the "hunter" can occur in organisms newly arrived in new habitats. In particular, Old World diseases, invasives, and pathogens have all run amok here. Great Lakes country is an open and borderless crossroads that plays host to a remarkable range of new arrivals, and its biological homogenization continues. The World Conservation Union ranks these migrants – and invasives in particular – as the greatest threat to biological diversity, after habitat loss. Habitat loss in the region is now largely complete, so the threat of invasives now ranks first here. Two-thirds of the region's lowlands are dominated by European species, with the Great Lakes themselves among the most affected freshwaters in the world. Forest pests and pathogens are the number-one threat to the remaining forests in Great Lakes country.[4]

In the city-state world, invasiveness and homogeneity are traits that are deliberately selected and inserted into new products, so that they can optimally seek out fertile new markets and saturate them. "Edge-tooles and weapons" were the first new technologies in the New World, as John Brereton wrote in 1602. Close behind was the written word, the law, and the manufacture of land. Such novelties always have steep transactional costs, which in the case of land tenure included an ecological collapse in return for a land-based egalitarianism that was uniquely attractive in its day and affluent enough to support the renewal the region witnessed in the last half-century.[5]

The Circle of Relations

"Altruism," if it exists at all, may be a latent gene that is expressed only if affluence is assured. This is perhaps the case in Great Lakes country today, with its economy steady and its ecology on the mend, and with discretionary capacity to reflect on our relationship with Nature. Some of the Native cultures in the region may also have achieved this state, albeit modestly, and have expressed its possibilities as a "circle of relations." This idea of responsible interconnectedness has few equivalents in the English language. David Crombie listed the keys to the emerging city-state as "clean, green, usable, diverse, open, accessible, connected, affordable and attractive." Another fine mantra has been to "reduce, reuse and recycle." These codes have their roots in ecology and, to the degree they are acted on, can help lead an honourable retreat into a more stable state. Self-interest intersects with ecology when it comes to the place where we live.[6]

In a Great Lakes country that is open to the globe, responsible inter-connectedness may also be driven by new forms of full-cost accounting, or "natural capital accounting," as economist Robert Costanza and others call it. The global accounting of carbon emissions is one such ledger, prompting nations to calculate the costs of stabilizing their emissions. Are "steady-state economies" in our future? Herman Daly, economist at the University of Maryland, has spoken out since the days of the Club of Rome about the inevitability of the steady-state economy as "an open subsystem of a finite, nongrowing and materially closed total system - the biosphere." Ideally, Daly says, it "neither depletes the environment beyond its regenerative capacity, nor pollutes it beyond its absorptive capacity." In these terms, he says, "progress in the steady state is no longer to get bigger, but to get better." In today's world, Europe, Japan, and even Great Lakes country may be pioneers of steady-state economics, or at least of new and unfamiliar slow-growth economies.[7]

A steady-state ecology, however, is another proposition entirely. In Great Lakes country, despite its revival in the last century, Nature remains in deficit, and challenged. It can be left to its own or we can make deliberate investments in its renewal. As the ecologist Daniel Botkin says, "Nature in the twenty-first century will be a nature that we make." The same can be said for climate change; we can always accommodate and adapt, but we can also be a positive force for Nature, once again writ large.[8]

Perhaps it is time to fear Nature once again, and let it motivate us. Nature is an impartial judge and it forces compliance on its own terms. It does not mourn the comings and goings of species or systems, and it intersects dispassionately with history. The ecologist Stan Rowe expressed this bluntly: "History ends in ecology, or nothing." In this, he was echoing Aldo Leopold: "Many historical events, hitherto explained solely in terms of human enterprise, were actually biotic interactions between people and land."[9]

Most of us are still newcomers here, and barely conscious of our home place. It may look good and inspire us, especially our youth, but youth has no memory and, in any half-generation, little seems to change. What is clearer to our elders - and to those curious enough to exhume the story's details - is that almost everything has changed. In all the maelstrom of causes and effects, one of the highest goals of human endeavour is to see pattern in the streams of constant change. One of those patterns is that Nature never repeats itself, a fact that may seem the sad trapping of a tragedy but also, by good fortune, confers a freedom of choice that we will need - profoundly - in the century ahead.

NOTES

Introduction

1 Hunter 1948: 14-16. Victory over Iroquois: Tanner 1987: 34; Leitch 1975: 32.

2 Leitch 1975: 28; Trigger 1987: 87.

3 The Ontario Island, or Dundalk Highlands, showed above the decaying Wisconsinan glacier *c.* 15,000 BP (Before Present, i.e., 1950; Taylor 1913). No archaeological sites are located on it (Sadler and Howard 2003: 325; Campbell and Campbell 1994: 22-3, maps 1a,b). The Mono survey (Benson 1820) followed a standard township plan (Ladell 1993: 93; Harris et al. 1975).

4 Armstrong 2000.

5 Local history: Steve Brown, Dufferin County Museum, pers. comm. 2007; and Bower Family and Laverty manuscripts in Dufferin County Museum Family Archives.

6 In Ontario the standard one-and-a-half-storey farmhouse was encouraged by a lower 1807 tax mill rate (McIlwraith 1997: 112). House built 1849: Shelly Anderson, pers. comm. 2003.

7 Brown 1995.

8 Elmer Coleman, pers. comm. 1999. Dates, ages from Relessey cemetery.

9 Ibid. Bert McCutcheon, pers. comm. 1980s.

10 Mono Township Council 1974: 28-31.

11 Population increase: Hemson Consulting 2005. Forensics is the study of motive, means, and opportunity.

12 Wayne Grady describes its natural history vividly in *The Great Lakes* (2007).

13 Detroit was the first place white women and children settled, as Cadillac noted: "Iroquois ... looked upon this move as the most important that could be made

to prove to them that we wished to settle there in earnest" (Cadillac 1702; B.4 in Lajeunesse 1960: 20-2). Sir William Lee to General Bunberry, 9 August 1759, in Kirby 1972: 44. Ickworth Park was landscaped by Capability Brown, famous for his naturalistic parklands.

14 Quammen 2008: 513. Louis Dollo's 1893 "law of irreversibility," as it applies to biology.

Chapter One

1 Forty-six species of fern and fern ally; Jalava et al.1996: 189-94.

2 Elk bones had been found in a cave to the south, also 150 years after their extirpation (Churcher and Fenton 1968).

3 Rocky Mountain pika, *Ochotona princeps*; giant pika (extinct), *O. whartonii*: Hafner 1993; Mead and Grady 1996.

4 Churcher and Dods 1979; Mead and Grady 1996.

5 Barnett 1992; Chapman and Putnam 1984.

6 Figs. 21.40 and 21.43 in Barnett 1992: 1048, 1051.

7 Keeshig-Tobias 2003; Blasco et al. 2003; Janusas et al. 2004. Drowned shoreline features off ocean coasts illustrated sea-level rise of 125 metres after deglaciation (Daly 1934: 157-64), since verified by C^{14} dating.

8 See Fig. 21.24 in Barnett 1992: 1031; and Fig. 2 in Dadswell 1974: 8. Compare the map of archaeological sites in Ontario in Sadler and Howard 2003: 325 with the map of high water levels, Fig. 2, in Dadswell 1974: 8; and with the map of low-water levels, Fig. 1.56h, in Barnett 1992: 1073. Also Jackson et al. 2000. Many Paleoindian sites were later flooded by rising lake levels (Jackson 2004: 37). 14,000 BP: Wisconsin (Waters et al. 2011b).

9 Storck 2004: 44, 58, 97, 107. Caribou now also from the Hiscock site just south of Lake Ontario.

10 Storck 2004: 199, 205; Stewart 2004. Caribou (*Rangifer terandus*), snowshoe or arctic hare (*Lepus americanus, L. arcticus*), arctic fox (*Alopex lagopus*). For putative caribou movements in the area, see Dibb 2004: Fig. 5.16. Farther east, fifteen Paleoindian hunt camps have been located on the Rice Lake Plain (Jackson 2004: Fig. 2.13). On a ridge now 100 feet under Lake Huron, evidence shows caribou hunting at a low-water level (O'Shea and Meadows 2009).

11 Harington 1988; Karrow 2004: 13.

12 North American humans arrived from Asia by way of the Pacific coast, which connected to Asia in the late glacial period, dating to 14,300 BP at the earliest by human coprolites in dry Oregon caves (Gilbert et al. 2008), and from central Texas

about 15,500 BP (Waters et al. 2011a). Mastodon hunting occurred contemporaneously in Washington (13,800 BP) and in Wisconsin (14,200 BP, 14,800 BP) (Waters et al. 2011b). Mastodons, dated to the full glacial era, 19,700 BP, in Tennessee: the Delcourts found mastodon molars with walnut shell and spruce cone, set in a fossil bed with hickory nuts, an acorn, tulip tree seeds, and the pollen of hazelnut, sugar maple, and beech (Delcourt 2002: 126; King and Saunders 1984). Paleoindians: Haynes 2002; Storck 2004: 220-1; Milner 2004: 27. Mastodon butchering: 11,400 BP Heisler site in south Michigan (Daniel Fisher, University of Michigan, Museum of Paleontology, Ann Arbor).

13 The dates that follow were converted from radiocarbon dates (RBP) to calibrated calendric ages before present (BP) using CAPPAL_2007_HULU, quickcal 2007 version 1.5. If the date and impact of the Clovis comet prove accurate, many of the following terminal dates should approximate 12,900 BP. Mastodon (*Mammut americanum*), regionally extinct by 13,000 BP; mammoth (*Mammuthus primigenius* and *M. columbi*), regionally extinct by 12,800 BP (10,340 RBP) in Ohio and with later terminal dates of 12,100 RBP in New York and 12,200 RBP in Michigan; woodland muskox (*Symbos cavifrons*), with extinction date 13,000 BP in Kalamazoo, Michigan; shrub ox (*Euceratherium* sp.), terminal date for extinction 16,000 BP (13,280 RBP), Leamington, Ontario; fugitive deer (*Sangamona fugitiva*), last date 10,800 BP (9440 RBP) in Missouri; stag moose (*Cervalces scottii*), the size of a modern moose, regionally extinct 12,000 BP (10,230 RBP) in Ohio; flat-headed peccary (*Platygonus compressus*), terminal date for extinction 13,600 (11,710 RBP) in Ohio and 13,800 BP (11, 900 RBP) in Pennsylvania; long-nosed peccary (*Mylohyus nasutus*), from Pennsylvania; giant short-faced bear (*Arctodus simus*), with terminal date 13,600 BP (11,710 RBP) in Ohio; tapir (*Tapirus veroensis*), from Pennsylvania; wild horse (*Equus complicatus*), latest date 9100 BP (8150-8000 RBP) in Alberta; giant beaver (*Castoroides ohioensis*), "most common just south of the Great Lakes" and with regional extinction date of 12,000 BP (10,230 RBP) in Ohio; dire wolf (*Canis dirus*); ground sloth (*Megalonyx jeffersonii*), first described by Thomas Jefferson from bones collected in a West Virginia cave, with a regional extinction date 12,000 BP (10,230 RBP) in Ohio. Refer, Anderson 1984. For Appalachian specifics, see Guilday 1984. For Ohio species, see McDonald 1994. For shrub ox, see Morris, McAndrews, and Seymour 1993. Also Karrow et al. 2007.

14 Wallace 1962: 149-50. Eighteen species (Guilday 1984), plus shrub ox and giant pika referenced above. McAndrews and Jackson 1988.

15 Guthrie 2006; Ellis and Deller 1990: 63; Culver et al. 2000. Bison bones estimated older than 12,800 BP from Toronto brickyard, and dated in the Lake of the Woods area of northwest Ontario at 3600 BP: McAndrews 1982. And from 12,100 BP in

Syracuse, New York: Paleaontological Research Institute, Ithaca, New York. Bison fossils have not yet been found from this period in Ohio (McDonald 1994).

16 Hunter 1768; Lyell 1832: 155; Lyell 1853; Dawkins 1874.

17 Martin 1973: 972; Kay 2002; Krech 1999: 16, 29–43; Haynes 1984: 351; Martin 2005: 145; Kay 2002: 242, 246. Limited evidence: Ellis and Deller 1990. Clovis have been associated with proboscidean bones at Burning Tree, Ohio (mastodon, 14,400 BP), and Hiscock, New York (mastodon, 10,100–14,200 BP) (Haynes 2002), and with mastodon bones at the Heisler site in Michigan at least 11,400 BP (Daniel C. Fisher, University of Michigan, Museum of Paleontology, Ann Arbor).

18 Firestone et al. 2007; Haynes 1984: 349, Fig. 16.3; Haynes 2005.

19 Broeker et al. 2010.

20 Species moving most rapidly were r-selected, or pioneer, species with winged or tufted seeds that disperse fast and far, like aspen and white spruce. Later came k-selected, or late-successional, species like oak, beech, and maple. Delcourt 2002: 149, 172, 198, 200.

21 Notable "geographic overlap between major biotic assemblages" (Remington 1968): e.g., Carolinian life zone in Ontario (Fox and Soper 1952–54); tension zone in Michigan (Voss 1972: 22). Aquatics: Dadswell 1974. Insects: Scudder 1979: 159. Also, Gleason 1926, Matthews 1979.

22 The northern Great Lakes-St Lawrence region has mixed forests of pines, hemlock, birch, sugar maple, beech, red oak, basswood, elm, cedar, and ash (Rowe 1959). Its southern half was described as early as 1898 by Merriam as an area where "sassafras, tulip tree, hackberry, sycamore, sweet gum, rose magnolia, redbud, persimmon, and short-leaf pine first make their [northernmost] appearance … together with the opossum, gray fox, fox squirrel, cardinal, Carolina wren, tufted tit, gnatcatcher, summer tanager and yellow-breasted chat. Chestnuts, hickorynuts, hazel-nuts, and walnuts grow wild in abundance."

23 Vegetation: willow (*Salix*), birch (*Betula*), alder (*Alnus*), juniper (*Juniperus*), wormwood (*Artemisia*), sedges (Cyperaceae), grasses (Poaceae), spruce (*Picea*), jack pine (*Pinus banksiana*), red pine (*P. resinosa*), balsam fir (*Abies balsamea*), white pine (*P. strobus*), hemlock (*Tsuga*), beech (*Fagus*), oak (*Quercus*), elm (*Ulmus*), ash (*Fraxinus*), and maple (*Acer*); refer, Karrow and Warner 1990; Wright 1964; Holloway and Bryant 1985. Range extensions: Terasmae and Anderson 1970; Fig. A115 in Riley 2003: 159; and stand of red pine on Pierre Lake, northeast of Cochrane, Ontario (also in Fig. A115]. Little Ice Age: Fagan 2000.

24 Delcourt and Delcourt 1981; Johnston and Cassavoy 1978; Neumann 2002: 147; Bogue 2000: 5–7.

25 Lake sturgeon, *Acipenser fulvescens*); whitefish, *Coregonus clupaeformis*: Ellis et al. 1990. Cootes Paradise wild rice: Crawford and Smith 2003: 204. Fox River: *Jesuit Relations* (JR) 55: 193–201.

26 Wright 1972.

27 Shetrone 1930; Pauketat 2009; Iseminger 2010.

28 Shetrone 1930; Woodward and McDonald 2002 ; Spence et al. 1990: 165–6; Lajeunesse 1960: xxxviii, Fig. 3; Ellis and Ferris 1990. An enigmatic mound on a terrace above the Miramichi River in New Brunswick has woven textiles and copper but no corn, and pre-dates sites to the west, including Serpent Mounds.

29 Woodward and McDonald 2002. Native sophistication gave rise to theories that early European contacts explained such finds; for example, Grave Creek yielded a scripted disk that joined other such tablets to inspire a literature on the subject: including the Grave Creek Tablet (1838), Shepherd Tablet (1832), Cincinnati Tablet (1841), Wilson-Braxton Tablet (1931), and Lakin A and B Tablets (1949). See speculations such as by Campbell 1898.

30 Milner 2004; Smith 1992; Yarnell 1964. Sunflower, *Helianthus annuus*; Jerusalem artichoke, *H. tuberosus*; chenopod, *Chenopodium* spp.; purslane, *Portulacca oleracea*; knotweed, *Polygonum erectum*; squash, *Cucurbita pepo*. Squash: Smith 1992: chapter 4.

31 Kay and Simmons 2002: xvii; Winterhalder 1981; Trigger 1987: 118; Neumann 2002: 158–64. Acorns, *Quercus* spp.; hickory nuts and pecans, *Carya* spp.; walnuts, *Juglans* spp.; chestnut, *Castanea dentata*; beechnuts, *Fagus sylvatica*; hazelnuts, *Corylus* spp. There were no bison east of the Mississippi until after 1000 AD; they were not part of the eastern mound-builder culture (Shaler 1900: 183).

32 Milner 2004: 87; Trigger 1987: 118; Spence et al. 1990: 142; Wright 1972: 50.

33 Tuck 1971: 13; Neumann 2002: 143; Milner 2004: 145; Pauketat 2009; Iseminger 2010. The Seneca said that, when they arrived, they found the land already "cleared by a race of inhabitants who preceded" them (Seaver 1824: 95). Proto-Iroquoians included the Owasca, Pickering, and Glen Meyer (Snow 1994: 19.) Detroit mounds: Graustein 1950–51: 66 (1810). *Chunkey* was a field sport challenging competitors to aim spears or arrows through the centres of artfully rounded, flattened, and rolling stone disks; an early newcomer spectator was the Jesuit Jacques Gravier who, in 1700, saw it played at a town along the lower Mississippi (JR 65: 147).

34 Crawford and Smith 2003; Wright 1994: 32. Also Federoff 2003.

35 Engelbrecht 2003: 23; Crawford and Smith 2003: 195, 217; Neumann 2002: 150–1; Agosta 1996: 11; Delcourt 2002: 192. Iroquoians expanded into southwest Ontario between 1300 and 1550 AD (Murphy and Ferris 1990: 255–6). Population explosion: Warrick 2008: 244.

36 *Dehesa* in Spain, *montado* in Portugal: Mann 2005: 197–201; Logan 2005: 122–6; Janzen 1998; Glavin 2006: 247–60. The Cahuilla of California: Bean and Saubel 1972: 121–31.

37 Galinée, *au milieu d'un grand désert d'environ 2 lieues de tour*: Coyne 1903: 22, 23. John Burrows cited in Parker 1910: 19.

38 Ibid., 42. Native cultivars of corn were also summarized by Sturtevant 1919.

39 Erichsen-Brown 1989; also Yarnell 1964, Turner 1981, Crawford and Smith 2003: 239. Oaks (*Quercus* spp.), chestnut (*Castanea dentata*), hickories (*Carya* spp.), walnut and butternut (*Juglans* spp.) and hazelnuts (*Corylus* spp.), onions (*Allium* spp.), serviceberry (*Amelanchier* spp.), hog-peanut (*Amphicarpa bracteata*), groundnut (*Apios americana*), milkweed (*Asclepias syriaca*), New Jersey tea (*Ceanothus americanus*), bergamot (*Monarda* spp.), groundcherry (*Physalis heterophylla*), mayapple (*Podophyllum peltatum*), sumac (*Rhus glabra*), currants and gooseberries (*Ribes* spp.), raspberries (*Rubus* spp.), arrowhead (*Sagittaria latifolia*), bulrush (*Scirpus* spp.), cattail (*Typha latifolia*), blueberries (*Vaccinium* spp.), nannyberry (*Viburnum americanum*). Transplanting and, thus, the selection, of plants occurred along portage routes (e.g., asexual canada onion, *Allium canadense*: Dore 1971), in appropriate habitats (e.g., wild rice, *Zizania* aquatica) and between settlements (e.g., sweet flag, *Acorus calamus*; wild plum, *Prunus americana*: Gilmore 1931; and walnut and pawpaw, *Asimina triloba*).

40 Pring, Quinn, and Quinn 1983: 212–30 (1603). Lafitau, in Fenton 1941: 503, 516, 519 (wild ginseng is now endangered). Scurvy stalked New France for another century. The identity of *annedda* disappeared with Stadacona. It was likely eastern white cedar (Rousseau 1954). Erichsen-Brown (1979: 1) disagrees: "Beauchamp translates the Onondaga name for the hemlock, O-Ne-Tah, as meaning 'greens on a stick.' Cartier … translated the Laurentian Iroquois word 'haneda' as 'greens on a stick' and gave the name 'annedda' to the tree that cured his crew of scurvy." Both species occurred around Stadacona and have the most vitamin c of eastern North American evergreens. See Fenton 1941: 506; Cook 1993: 80, 94, 100; Thevet 1986: 8 (1557).

41 Heidenreich and Burgar 1999: 66; Warrick 2008: 102. The Doncaster Site, St Michael's College, University of Toronto.

42 These dispersed archaeological sites "almost invariably produce carbonized remains of cultigens which may include corn, beans, squash, sunflowers and tobacco … prolific quantities of bones of white tail deer, black bear, ground hog, squirrel, beaver, raccoon, muskrat, elk, dog and other mammals. Fish remains … include all the common species such as perch, bass, sucker and catfish … a variety of ducks, geese, grouse and pigeons." Ramsden 1990: 380. Also, Trigger 1987: 122–6, 148.

43 Compare maps of earlier sites (Williamson 1990: 292, Fig. 9.1; Murphy and Ferris 1990: 252, Fig. 7.34) with map of later Neutral sites (Lennox and Fitzgerald 1990: 406, Fig. 13.1). The Neutral village of Onghiara became Niagara and Niagara-on-the-Lake (Kirby 1972: 9). St Lawrence: Jamieson 1990: 387, Fig. 12.1. Iroquoia: Engelbrecht 2003: xiv, 90, 158. Neumann (2002: 151-5) suggests that shifts in climate altered energy flow and population numbers in eastern North America. One decline from high population levels was at the beginning of the Hopewell period for about 700 years until 900 AD, evidenced in a decrease in settlement sites and variety of artifacts. This was followed by an increase in populations from 900 to 1300 AD.

44 Stable populations and birth control: Warrick 2008: 245. Three children: Snow 1994: 54, 74; Wright 1994.

45 Williamson 1990: 292, 294; Guilday 1984: 251. Eastern Ontario: Pendergast 1966, Catling et al. 2008: Fig. 2. Pollen record from Crawford Lake, Ontario, shows a decline in forest biomass from 1400 AD to 1800 AD, corresponding to the Little Ice Age, and a shift from beech- to oak-dominated forests and then white pine (Campbell and McAndrews 1993). Carneiro (1979) timed skilled stone-axe users cutting down a four-foot-diameter tree in 115 hours and an acre and a half in 153 eight-hours days. Pennsylvania village sites: Black et al. 2006.

46 Campbell and McAndrews 1991, 1993; Snow 1994: 21. McAndrews (1976: 2) identifies how "prehistoric ... forest clearance activities initiated a succession from maple and beech to oak and pine." Most important: Delcourt 2002: 169.

47 5 per cent: Campbell and Campbell 1994.

48 Churcher and Fenton 1968: 16; Guilday 1984: 251. Inclusion of Canada geese: McAndrews and Turton 2007.

49 Trigger 1987: 69; Tuck 1978: 324; Sioui 1992: 42, 51-4. The Neutral were reported to have a supreme headman (D'Aillon 1627: 2) and a capital city (mouth of Kettle Creek; Coyne 1895), in contrast to other Iroquoians, who were guided by multiple headmen and war lords. Slavery had long been part of Native cultures, with slaves considered an entire class – the *"panis"* – by the Jesuits (JR 69: 301).

50 New Netherland in 1627: letter from de Rasieres to Samuel Blommaert (original in royal library at the Hague, communicated by Dr Campbell to the New York Historical Society).

51 Canoes: "Bark canoes ... are constructed of a single sheet of bark stripped from the elm, hickory or chestnut" (Smith 1906: 48). "The Iroquois canows are so dull and large, that they cannot sail near so quick as those made of birch-bark. The former are made of elm bark" (Lahontan 1905: 138 [1683-89]). There were also dugout canoes of white pine, tulip-tree, and cedar in the south (Kalm 1966: 108, 333 [1748-49])

and, northward, dugouts of white pine, black walnut, butternut, and basswood (Strickland 1970: 49). Women's role: Mary Jemison, a white captive of the Seneca in 1758, recorded: "Our labor was not severe ... probably not harder than that of white women ... and their cares certainly not half as numerous ... no masters to oversee or drive us, so that we could work as leisurely as we pleased" (Seaver 1824: 46). Nettle, *Urtica*; hemp, *Apocynum*. Nets: Bogue 2000: 7. Animals raised: Trigger 1960: 17. *Outarde* was applied to the Canada goose, *Branta canadensis*, starting with Champlain (Biggar 1922, vol. 1, pt. 3, 360: 1605). Posted fields: Parker 1910: 29. Corn as Huron staple: Crawford and Smith 2003: 214; Dean 1994: 7. Annual cycle of food use: White 1991: 44.

52 John Casselman, Queen's University, to Brodie Club, Toronto, 6 May 2008 (Casselman and Cairns 2009).

53 Neumann 2002: 147. Delaware River: Gray 1956: 9. Marquette: JR 54: 217.

54 Brébeuf 1635: 108; Van der Donck 1841: 79–81. Tuck (1971: 79) reports a longhouse at Howlett Hill 334 feet by 23 feet, with doors at the ends and middle. Chaumont: JR 42: 87. Threat of fire: Ragueneau 1650: 254. As recounted in the next chapter, in 1616 Champlain lay siege to an Iroquois town and urged his Native allies to torch it, which they failed to do. He interpreted this as lack of will but firing a town might have been beyond the acceptable norms of warfare, inviting a doomsday response.

55 Champlain said they moved their villages "after ten, twenty or thirty years," and Sagard said "ten, fifteen, or thirty years" (Biggar 1929, vol. 3, 124; Sagard 1939: 92; Peron 1639: 139; Heidenreich 1971: 213.) Lamberville in 1682 explained the need for moving (JR 62: 54).

56 St Lawrence towns and camps in the 1530s (Cook 1993: 57) estimated at 5,000 (Heidenreich 1990: 475) and 8,000 (Warrick 2008: 203).

57 Warrick estimated the combined Huron-Petun population in 1615 at 31,500, based on persons per hearth per unit area "from excavated village plans" (2008: 221, 244). The estimate of Huron numbers by Champlain in 1615 was 32,000, by other Jesuits 35,000 (JR 40: 223). The estimate by the soul-counter Brébeuf in 1635 was 30,000. Sagard counted more, "two or three thousand warriors [and] ordinary people who may number about thirty or forty thousand." There is consistency among estimates (Warrick 2008: 74, Table 5.1). Biggar 1929, vol. 3, pt. 1, 122; Brébeuf 1635: 111; Sagard 1939: 92. Also, Wright 1966: 81; Trigger 1985: 231–41; Trigger 1987: 32, 94, 98.

58 The Petun: Warrick 2008: 221; Wright 1966: 81; Jones 1908: 78.

59 D'Aillon; Johnston 1964: 6 (1627); Coyne 1895. Sagard reported the Neutral as more numerous than the Huron, with two to three times the number of warriors (1939: 157). Brébeuf said they had 4,000 warriors (twice the number of Huron warriors) and

a population of 12,000 in forty towns and villages. Wright estimated a population of about 30,000 (1966: 81). In total, in 1672 the Jesuit Claude Dablon estimated the historic Huron, Petun, and Neutral population at 80,000 (Jones 1908: 424) and Snow estimated 90,000 to 95,000 (1994: 1, 88).

60 Engelbrecht 2003: 157–8; Warrick 2008: 82, Table 5.2. Lahontan's estimate in 1684 was 50,000–70,000 (1905: 58).

61 Brébeuf: JR 10: 313. Green Bay: JR 55: 193–201.

62 Epidemic region: Dobyns 1983: 324. Dates of outbreaks: ibid., 270, 313–27; Howland 1903: 98; Kirkconnell 1921; Trigger 1985: 231–41; Warrick 2008; Cook 1993: 119. See Garcilaso 1951: 300, 315, 325, 570 (1540s "scourge," "pestilence," Green Bay: JR 55: 201).

63 Eastern seaboard Algonquian agriculturalists in 1600 were estimated at 80 per cent of the population of 70,000 to 100,000 in New England alone (Cronon 1983: 42).

64 Snow (1994: 50) and Warrick (2008: 201) maintain that the Five Nations were confederated sometime around 1536. Jennings (1984: 8) suggests a date between 1450 and 1500 AD, in response to early European contacts elsewhere. Others claim earlier dates (Mann and Fields 1997).

65 Colden 1747: 3 (1727). Along the Atlantic, white wampum were made from the shells of periwinkle (*Littorina littorea*), knobbed whelk (*Busycon carica*), and channelled whelk (*Busycotypus canaliculatum*). Purple beads were made from the dark purple spot on the shell of northern quahog (*Mercenaria mercenaria*). St Lawrence beads from the freshwater mussel genus *Unio* were also "most precious," the *esnoguy* of Cartier (1993: 62), and beads may have also been made from river snails (*Pleurocera* spp., *Goniobasis* spp.) See http://www.mccord-museum.qc.ca/en/collection/artifacts/ M11085&section=196.

66 Hudson: Juet, in Purchas 1625: 518–95. Van der Donck 1841 (1640s); Jogues: in JR 28: 111 (1643).

67 Tuck 1971: 213; Mann 2005: 264.

68 Trigger 1960: 16; Wright 1966: 79; Kinietz 1940: 59; Becker 1995: 325; Heidenreich 1971: 111, 214; Trigger 1987: 62, 171, 304. *Cahiagué* population estimated at 5,000 (Wright 1966: 81) and more than 2,000 (Warrick 2008: 207). The Mohawk term *tkaronto* means "where the trees stand in the water," describing the fish weir at the Narrows on Lake Couchiching, carbon-dated as in use 4000 BP. The word emerged as *Lac de Taronto* on French maps of Lake Simcoe, then as *Passage de Taronto* for the Carrying Place from Lake Simcoe, then *Riviere Taronto* for the Humber River, and then *Fort Toronto* for the French fort east of the mouth of the Humber. It then appeared in the *Toronto Purchase*, Governor Dorchester's treaty with the Missisauga for the portage and the harbour on Lake Ontario. *Toronto* officially displaced the name York in 1834. Rayburn 1994.

69 Cord fibres: hemp, *Apocynum cannabinum*; swamp milkweed, *Asclepias incarnata*; nettle, *Urtica dioica* var. *procera*; basswood, *Tilia americana*: Kinietz 1940: 47; Tooker 1968: 84; Heidenreich 1971: 200; Erichsen-Brown 1979.

70 Heidenreich 1971: 228; Biggar 1929, vol. 3, pt. 1, 125, 130 (1615); Sioui 1992: 12, 26-48. The Noisy River's Lavender Falls exhibit one such stratum of chert nodules.

71 Colden 1747: 2 (1727); White 1991: xv. Others were less idealizing, such as Isaac Weld at Detroit in 1797, who wrote of the Iroquois: "No people on earth have a higher opinion of their own consequence; indeed, they esteem themselves superior to every other race of men" and "the English settlers … cannot banish wholly from their minds ... that the Indians are an inferior race" (1807, vol. 2, 180, 200 [1796]). Reciprocated racism of both the overly venomous and overly idealistic types was, unfortunately, the social construct that clouded most policy and business.

72 Morgan 1851; Morgan 1877; and Trigger 1985: 39-43, 110, referring to Wilson 1862, Dawson 1880, and Hale 1883. Tooker (1988) noted the dissimilarities between the U.S. constitution and Iroquois governance: one based on majority rule, the other on consensus; senators elected vs. headmen appointed. Tooker claimed the writers of the constitution ignored native political systems (ibid., 311), but it was the observations of Jefferson, Franklin, Paine, Adams, and others that gave rise to the "influence thesis." The term "noble savage" was first used by the lawyer and traveller Marc Lescarbot in 1609, speaking of the Natives of New France (Ellingson 2001: 20-2). The phrase was revived in modern times and its sentiment has seldom varied from the meaning of Lahontan (*bon sauvage*): Colden, Morgan and others.

73 Trigger 1987: 104; Richard Cartwright, in Talman 1946: 45.

74 Métis: Fischer 2008: 507; Colden 1747: 203 (1727); Kalm 1966: 457 (1749). White abductees: White 1991: 271-83.

Chapter Two

1 Baker et al. 1994: 20, Map 20; and Hayes 2002: 72, Map 70.

2 Cook 1993: 76. Trigger (1985: 122) notes a Bristol voyage in 1505 that returned with specimens of the extinct Carolina parakeet (*Conuropis carolinensis*). Refer also to the Cabot Project (http://www.bristol.ac.uk/history/research/cabot.html).

3 *Sagana*, and stories of its wealth, were passed on to John III of Portugal: Cook 1993: 131. New England: Quinn 1994. For "Arcadia," *Dictionary of Canadian Biography*, vol. 1, 659.

4 Axtell 1994: 154-5. Atlantean: Cunliffe 2001. Crossings: Trigger 1985: 135-41. Chinese: Menzies 2003.

5 Verrazano 1970: 133-43; Sturtevant 1919 (1870s).

6 Cook 1993: 24–7, 69; Wright 1994; Trigger 1987: 185. Beans: Sturtevant 1919 (1870s). Justifications of Christian sovereignty over infidels included Aristotle's doctrine of "natural servitude," with the consequence that Amerindians did not qualify for *dominium* (Green and Dickason 1989: 152, 188). Porpoise, *Phocoena phocoena*.

7 Cook 1993: 59, 61, 62.

8 Cook 1993: 65; Heidenreich 1990: 475; Jamieson 1990: 386; Trigger 1987: 194; Rousseau 1954. Donnacona was, with Cartier, interviewed by André Thevet, who publicized the New World (1986).

9 Cook 1993: xl.

10 Algonquin: Innis 1956: 21. Huron: JR 22: 215. Mohawks, or climate change: Warrick 2008: 198–201. Withdrawal: Sioui 1992: 43. Also, Trigger 1994; Trigger 1987: 214.

11 Dobyns 1983; Fenton 1940; Sioui 1992: 3; Trigger 1987: 218. De Soto: Garcilaso 1951: 53, 147, 260, 270, 300, 315, 325, 570. Nothing was left of De Soto's lower Mississippi nations when La Salle visited in 1682. Epidemic in Saint-Malo: letter of 3 March 1534, in Cook 1993: 119. The disease could have travelled upriver and left no physical evidence (but see Warrick 2008: 200).

12 1550; by 1610, it was noted that ships competed to be earliest into the Gulf, and that this year was the earliest arrival in "sixty years"; Biggar 1925, vol. 2, pt. 1, 117. 1578: Trigger 1987: 209. Also, Innis 1954, 1956.

13 Fischer 2008, chapters 1, 2, 3; Cunliffe 2001. King's pleasure: Charlevoix, 1744; Heidenreich and Ritch 2010: 137. See and explore: Champlain, 1632 (ibid., 227).

14 *Géographe du roi*: Lescarbot, 1612; Tyrrell 1931: 281 (1690s). Newfoundland: Fischer 2008: 110.

15 Heidenreich and Ritch 2010: 255–9; Biggar 1922, vol. 1, pt. 2, 98–101; Fischer 2008: 108.

16 Biggar 1922, vol. 1, pt. 2, 122, 124, 128, 133, 143, 155, 156, 163; pt. 3, 231; Heidenreich and Ritch 2010: xv, 287, 297, 301, 313, 325, 327, 335, 400. Mistranslating *salubre* was Richard Haklyut's work, published by Samuel Purchas in 1625.

17 Biggar 1925, vol. 2, pt. 1, 12, 22. In all, Champlain crossed the Atlantic twenty-seven times (Fischer 2008).

18 Biggar 1925, vol. 2, pt. 1, 99, 110, 244–8.

19 Robert Juet's Journal of Hudson's 1609 voyage: in Purchas 1625: 581–95.

20 Jurgens 1966.

21 Biggar 1925, vol. 2, pt. 1, 269, 276, 287. Yellow puccoon (*Lithospermum caroliniense*) and butterfly weed (*Asclepias tuberosa*) both occur on the sands at Constance Bay, as do about fifteen other prairie species.

22 Ibid., 339–45. Champlain 1612, 1613: maps 70, 75 in Hayes 2002: 52, 54.

23 Biggar 1929, vol. 3, pt. 1, 44. Champlain's 1632 map annotated the north shore as a "place where natives dry raspberries and blueberries each year" (Campbell 2005: 25).

Forest growth in the absence of fire along Georgian Bay has reduced blueberries (also see records of Tadanac Club since 1883; Martin Abell, pers. comm. 2007).

24 Biggar 1929, vol. 3, pt. 1, 50, 51, 56; Trigger 1987: 304; Trigger 1963. A *lieue* was about three miles in 1600s (Jones 1908: 114-15).

25 *"Pays fort deserté, beau et agreable"*: Sagard 1939: 69-70, 90-1, end map (1623-24). "Great distance," perhaps eight to ten miles.

26 Biggar 1929, vol. 3, pt. 1, 217; Trigger 1987: 306; Cranston 1949.

27 Biggar 1929, vol. 3, pt. 1, 59, Plate IV, 74. The Onondaga town was located in modern Syracuse, New York (Fischer 2008: 616).

28 Biggar 1929, vol. 3, pt. 1, 98. The Ottawa (Chippewa) of Nawash include their descendants. Cape Croker supports some of the finest escarpment cliffs and forests, prairies, and shores on Lake Huron. Brulé travelled widely to the south and, later, toward Lake Superior. He was sent back to France in 1626 but returned with the English ships that took Quebec in 1629; he then went back to Huronia, where he was executed in 1633 (Cranston 1949; Trigger 1985: 196).

29 Golden chains: JR 14: 127. Justice of God: JR 12: 85.

30 Trigger 1987: 337, 353, 413, and Map 18.

31 JR 24: 27; Trigger 1985: 207; Trigger 1987: 37, 350, 416, 619, 630, 633; Tanner 1987: 29.

32 Champlain 1632: Refer, Murray 2006: 27. Champlain's 1632 *Voyages* included observations of raptors, game birds, waterfowl and shorebirds, landbirds, fish, and mammals (this time *"eslans, cerfs, dains, caribou,"* namely, moose, elk, deer, caribou, and excluding buffalo). Biggar 1929, vol. 3, pt. 2, 253-6; Snow 1994: 82.

33 Brébeuf 1635: 100, 102; JR 7: 217-21.

34 JR 12: 261, 15: 31, 19: 93, 39: 127; Trigger 1987: 530. Jesuit culpability: JR 7: 127; 12: 261; 15: 31, 151; 19: 93.

35 Kidd 1949; Trigger 1985: 252.

36 Warrick 2008: 245; Snow and Strna 1989. The 1634 epidemic was considered measles by Brébeuf (1635: 104) and Dobyns (1983: 315). Lalemant: JR 17: 222, 223. Following epidemics: smallpox in 1661-63 in Iroquoia (JR 47: 193; 48: 79); "contagion" in 1668 in Seneca country (JR 54: 78) and in 1679 "as far as the [Lake] Nipissingue where most of the Nipissiriniens had died" (Dulhut 1697: 189).

37 95 per cent: Dobyns 1966. 75 per cent; Fenn 2001. Tanner (1987: 169-74) lists the region's native epidemics: 1633-34 (measles); 1636-37 (scarlet fever and influenza); 1639-40 (smallpox); 1641 (?); 1645 (?); 1649 ("loathsome fever"); 1669-70 (?); 1676-79 (influenza? and smallpox); 1690-91 (smallpox); 1731-33 (smallpox); 1752 (smallpox); 1755 (?); 1762-64 (smallpox); 1781-83 (smallpox); 1787-88 (smallpox); 1801 (smallpox); 1831-34 (Asian cholera); 1849 (cholera). Absolute numbers: Lovell 1992: 426.

38 Plague, *Yersinia pestis (Pasteurella pestis)*, is a bacterium exhibiting in three forms –bubonic, pneumonic, and septicemic plague. Duncan et al. (2005) suggest that about 10 per cent of Europeans have a genetic mutation known as the *CCR5-Δ*, which confers immunity to the HIV virus, as a result of the plagues that swept Europe from the Middle Ages on. The proportion of people carrying this resistance is high in Europe and particularly Scandinavia, where it is 14–15 per cent. Some research suggests that alcohol tolerance relates to frequency of enzymes that break down alcohol (dehydrogenases), which were selected for in Eurasians on the basis of long exposure to alcohol (Long and Knowler 1998).

39 JR 22: 265; 24: 271, 295; 26: 71; 27: 25; Heidenreich 1990: 489; White 1991: xv; Trigger 1987: 623, 632.

40 *Genocide* was a term coined in 1943 by Polish jurist Raphael Lemkin, referring to lethal depredations between nations or peoples. Applied here to the Iroquois campaigns against the Huron, Petun, and Neutral; the English campaign against the Pontiac rebellion; and the American campaign against the Iroquois and western confederacy. These were nation-on-nation campaigns and shared an intent, if not an outcome, of extirpation. Refer, United Nations Convention on the Prevention and Punishment of the Crime of Genocide. *Total war*, a term coined to characterize the First and Second World Wars, was the title of a 1935 book by German General Erich Ludendorff.

41 "A new style of warfare": Trigger 1987: 660–4, 725–8. To intercept trade: Hunt 1940: 91.

42 Trigger 1987: 762–6.

43 Ragueneau 1650. In less than one hour: Pouliot 1966: 562; 5,000; JR 35: 87.

44 The cannon: Kidd 1949, Plate II. *C'est un people efface de dessus la terres*: Ragueneau 1651: 97.

45 Ragueneau 1650.

46 The *Jesuit Relations* document the extent and effects of Iroquois raids, such as the one on Lac Saint-Jean: JR 46: 287.

47 Marquette: JR 54: 185–9, 231. Village world: White 1991: 14–24, 32–3, 42, 47, 135, 308.

48 Jesuits: Tuck 1971: 171. Tuscarora were forced out of North Carolina and joined the Five Nations in 1722–23.

49 War impacts: see Freedman 1989: 297–317. Huronia: see also Heidenreich 1971: 63.

50 Norumbega: Biggar 1922, vol. 1, pt. 3, 281, 283 (1604). Saco, Plymouth, Nauset: Prins 1994: 104; Biggar 1922, vol. 1, pt. 3, 328, 329, plates LXXIII, LXXIV (1605). Crops: Biggar 1922, vol. 1, pt. 3, 341, 351 (1605). Native squash or marrow, *petites citrouilles* (*Cucurbita pepo*); *pourpié* or purslane (*Portulaca oleracea*), rich in Omega-3 fatty acids; and *artichaut* or Jerusalem artichoke (*Helianthus tuberosus*; see Byrne and McAndrews 1975).

51 At least 100,000: Cronon 1983: 42: those in 1600 in New England alone estimated at 70,000 to 100,000. Portrayals of the coast: Axtell 1994: 154-5; Baker et al. 1994: xxv; Mann 2005: 39, 44-5. Voyages: Quinn and Quinn 1983: 1.

52 The Bible and its sanction: Bobrick 2001: 218-21, 269. See G. MacBeath, "The Atlantic Region," in *Dictionary of Canadian Biography*, vol. 1, 23.

53 Quinn and Quinn 1983: chapter 2, 139-203 (1602). Gabriel Archer, too, wrote up the Gosnold voyage, noting its open "champaine" countryside and large population: "We perceived much smoake" and "this coast is very full of people" (ibid., chapter 1, 112-38 [1602]). Heidenreich and Ritch 2010: 53-5.

54 Quinn and Quinn 1983: chapter 4, 212-30 (1603); chapter 6, 248-311 (1605). Serviceberry, *Amelanchier* spp.; beach plum, likely *Prunus maritima*.

55 J. Rousseau and G.W. Brown, "The Indians of Northeastern North America," in *Dictionary of Canadian Biography*, vol. 1, 6; Wood 1977: 32, 75, 112, 113 (1629-33). John Tradescant, English botanist, collected plants in Virginia 1628-37, returning with trees like tulip-tree and magnolia.

56 Williams 1973: 167, 237, 175 (1631-43).

57 Died in heaps: Morton 1669; 11 November 1620, in Bradford 1856: 49 (1620). Room for us: Mann 2005: 56.

58 Gardener 1833: 154-5 (1642). Cited in Cronon 1983: 162.

59 Van der Donck 1841: 2; Bogaert 1988: xiii-xix.

60 Population numbers: Warrick 2008: 242, etc.; Gray 1956: 11-20.

61 Jennings 1965: 188.

62 Iroquois raids: JR 46: 219-21. Boucher: Montizambert 1883: 80.

63 Jesuits: JR 46: 277-9. Non-Iroquois comprised at least a third of the Seneca by 1673: JR 57: 27; Colden 1747: 52 (1727). The Christian Mohawk at La Prairie later moved past the Lachine rapids to Kahnawake, and those near Mount Royal later moved to Lake of Two Mountains (Kanesatake). Nicolas: Gagnon 2011: 27.

64 Coyne 1903: 39, 41, 66-7, 77.

65 Ibid., 82-3. At the Rouge, Denonville's "Christian Indians," who had been sent ahead to provision the army returning from Seneca country in 1687, harvested two hundred deer in a drive (1687, in Robinson 1933: 56).

66 Hennepin 1905: 44, 54, 55, 319 (1678-80). Pehr Kalm sketched the gorge with conifers ringing its cliffs and with open, unforested lands above the gorge (1966: 704b). Niagara Falls was a biodiversity hotspot renowned for its cliffs, talus slopes, herpetofauna, winter birds, and black oak savanna along the gorge. Since the 1990s, some remnants of savanna have been restored with prescribed burns and the removal of invasive plants. Rare species now include sixteen nationally or provincially rare plants, for example, but more than forty-five species of rare plants have been extirpated from

the gorge in the last century, more than any other natural area in Canada (Varga and Kor 1993). Native harvest of dead animals below the falls is also mentioned by Galinée (Coyne 1903 [1669]) and Lahontan 1905: 137 (1683–89).

67 Hennepin 1905: 96, 99, 111 (1678-80). The rapids exiting Lake Huron were also noted by in 1831 by Strickland: "At the entrance to the river the current runs very swiftly for about the distance of a thousand yards, at the rate of seven miles an hour." It was only a shift in the wind "from the southwest, which enabled us, by the help of a tow-rope, to ascend the current" (Strickland 1970: 111, 123). Declining water levels in Lake Huron have been attributed to channel dredging through the sill at the exit of Lake Huron.

68 La Salle would later explore the Mississippi to the Gulf, establishing posts along the way, from 1681 to 1683 (Hennepin 1905: 116, 117, 146, 147, 331). Hennepin said corn would not grow at Sault Ste Marie, but Galinée saw "wheat, and Indian corn, pease" growing there (Coyne 1903: 85, map).

69 Lahontan 1905: 7, 8 (1684); Siggins 2008: 6-12. The English text of Lahontan has been checked against Lahontan's original French text, and a few French words added for clarification (from Ouellet [1990]).

70 Sioui 1992: 63-4; Lahontan 1905: 141, 148 (1684–89).

71 Ibid., 421, 434; Sioui 1992: 66-81.

Chapter Three

1 Seneca farms were diversified operations by then, with "plenty of horses, black cattel, fowl and hogs" (Lahontan 1905: 131). Colden 1747: 79 (1727).

2 War on Hudson and James bays: Tyrrell 1931.

3 Colden 1747: 191 (1747).

4 Early interior sites were religious missions, then military posts. There are contemporary descriptions of the Native villages, for example, of the Huron at Detroit: "This is the most industrious nation that can be seen. They scarcely ever dance, and are always at work. They raise a very large amount of Indian corn, pease, beans; some grow wheat. They construct their huts entirely of bark, very strong and very solid; very lofty and very long, and arched like arbors. Their fort is strongly encircled with pickets and bastions, well redoubled, and has strong gates ... The Indian corn grows there to a height of ten to twelve feet; the fields are very clean, and very extensive; not the smallest weed is to be seen in them" (Lajeunesse 1960: 24–6 [1718]). See also White 1991: 147–89.

5 Bartram 1895: 42 (1743).

6 Colden 1747: 17 (1727); O'Toole 2005. The previous year, 1709, was the year of the Great Frost in Europe, a severe cooling perhaps the result of low sun-spot activity.

7 Colden 1747: 94; White 1991: 60-75.

8 Colden 1747: 94 (1747); O'Toole 2005: chapters 3 and 4 and p. 90.

9 Johnson's will established a trust for Molly's children, based on his "close connections" and "the long uninterrupted friendship" between him and Molly. His estate was confiscated and his family dispersed during and after the American Revolution. O'Toole 2005: 322; Gray 2002: 24.

10 Census of the Inhabitants of Detroit, 1750, C7 in Lajeunesse 1960: 56.

11 Bartram 1895: 40, 42 (1743).

12 Kalm 1966, vol. 1, 153, 154; and vol. 2, 504 (1748-50).

13 O'Toole 2005: 110-218; White 1991.

14 William Johnson to General Amherst, 29 July 1761, and response of 9 August 1761, in Howland 1903: 36-7. Also, O'Toole 2005: 236, 238, 248; White 1991: 350-5.

15 Neolin's mission was carried on by Tecumseh's younger brother, Tenskwatawa, also called the Prophet.

16 Cave 1999; Wallace 1970: 114-21; Wright 1992: 135; White 1991: 269-79; Trent 1763: 400; Bouquet 1763; Amherst 1763; Tanner 1987: 48-353; O'Toole 2005: 249, 254-5.

17 O'Toole 2005: 256.

18 Jennings 1984: chapter 2.

19 Colden 1747: 99, 101 (1747); Wright 1992: 116.

20 Sir William Johnson to the Lords of Trade, 30 October 1764, in Taylor 2006: 36; Henry 1969: 23 (1761).

21 Coyne 1903: 77; Lajeunesse 1960: A2, A8, pp. 8, 11.

22 Taylor 2006: 37, 39-40 (Johnson to Goldsbrow Banyar, 27 April 1767). Johnson council practices: Cruikshank 1925, vol. 3, 254. Johnson's lands were confiscated during and after the American Revolution (Gray 2002: 24.) Others say Johnson owned 170,000 acres (O'Toole 2005: 282). Pratt-Yorke opinion: Pease 1838-39, in Johnston 1964: xxxii.

23 Tanner 1987: Map 12, 54-6; Snow 1994: 145. See Sioui 1992: 109 for discussion of lands exempted from Proclamation. The Quebec Act of 1774 was one of the "intolerable acts" cited by American rebels (Harris 2008: 125).

24 Surtees 1994; Green and Dickason 1989: 99-124.

25 Taylor 2006: 78-81.

26 Trigger 1987: 3; with the exception of Newfoundland.

27 Smith 1906: 49, 64 (1769). After Brant's first wife died, he married her half-sister, Susanna. Upon Susanna's death in 1778, he married Catherine Croghan, of the Mohawk Turtle Clan.

28 Fenn 2001.

29 Tilghman 1876: 88; Taylor 2006: 78, 83, 84.

30 Wallace 1970: 134-9; Taylor 2006: 90. See Seaver 1824: 68, for Mary Jemison's support of Brant.

31 Letter of August 1777, in O'Toole 2005: 326.

32 Orders of George Washington to General John Sullivan, 31 May 1779. And orders of George Washington to General John Sullivan, 15 September 1779, in Washington 1732-99.

33 Sullivan: in Cook 1887: 301 (1779). 128 houses: Parker 1910: 20; Wright 1992: 139; Ke-che-ah-gah-me-qua 1850; Axtell 1981: 152, 181.

34 Sullivan, 1779, "The Devastation of the Genesee County," 30 September 1779, in Cook 1887: 305 (1779).

35 Wallace 1970: 134-44. Smallpox: Harris 1903: 433.

36 Refugee camps: Taylor 2006: 101. Molly Brant's influence: Captain Malcom Fraser, cited in Feister and Pulis 1996: 313. Burials: Innis 1965: 78 (1792).

37 Boundary: Hayes 2002: 124. Haldimand to Baron von Riedesel, 26 April 1783, quoted in Stone 1868 and cited in Taylor 2006: 112. MacLean to Haldimand, 18 May 1783, in Haldimand Papers, MG 21, no. 21763. Taylor 2006: 113.

38 McMaster 1907: 307.

39 There are only three copies of Mitchell's 1775 map, in London, Washington, and Maine. Mitchell was a botanist, a founder of Kew Gardens, and is commemorated by the partridge-berry genus *Mitchella*. Hayes 2002: 124.

40 Ford 1904-37; Taylor 2006: 145.

41 Taylor 2006: 158-9.

42 Ibid., 163-5.

43 See Good Peter speech, 25 June 1785, in Hough 1861: 91-2.

44 The Laki eruption was first associated with climate cooling by Benjamin Franklin while he was in Paris negotiating the Treaty of Paris. Philadelphia, likely yellow fever: George Hammond to Lord Grenville, 12 October 1793, in Cruikshank 1924, vol. 2, 87 (1793). The role of pigeons: Barton 1883: ix; Brickell 1737: 186, cited in Schorger 1973: 32.

45 The 1782 Detroit census had 1,290 people on the east shore alone, including 179 slaves, and 4,600 livestock. Shipping: Weld 1807, vol. 2, 185. Maumee: General Wayne, cited in Kaatz 1955: 4. Native numbers c. 3,000: Cruikshank 1925, vol. 3, 74. Also, Day 1953: 334.

46 Benn 1998: 79; Taylor 2006: 259.

47 Bliss 1885; Gray 1956: 73-4. Powell, later chief justice of Upper Canada, was the sole judge of common pleas in the Western District at the time. Most of the remaining Delaware were driven west to Oklahoma.

48 Land sales: Taylor 2006: 201.

49 Hamilton 1776: D7 in Lajeunesse 1960: 84-5.

50 Surtees 1994: 103, Map 6.3.

51 Robert Paudash, Missisauga headman at Rice Lake, was recorded in 1904 describing the history of Mohawk attacks in the mid-1600s, after which "a great council of war decided to attack the Mohawks, and, if possible, to drive them away." A major battle took place at Rice Lake, "in which no less than one thousand warriors were slain." J.H. Burnham, recorder, in Guillet 1957: 9–11.

52 Hungry years: Kirby 1972: 73; Talman 1946: lv–lviii; Campbell 1937: 123, 125. Winter 1790: Hind 1863, vol. 1, 86.

53 Lajeunesse 1960: Fig. 9, lxxiii–lxxiv, 74.

54 1,344,000 acres and treaty, 19 May 1790: G17 in Lajeunesse 1960: 171. Sale of the Huron Church Reserve, 1800: H23 in Lajeunesse 1960: 2050. McKee: Nelson 1999: 138.

55 Western tribes: Johnston 1964: xxxvii. The Grand: "Substance of Brant's Wishes" and Haldimand's reply, March 1783, B7 in Johnston 1964: 44–5. Sir John Johnson, 1783: in Taylor 2006: 130; Ladell 1993: 63. Missisauga unease: Guillet 1957: 9–11. The Iroquois were beaten in battle three times in 1696 by the Ojibwa and Missisauga (Tanner 1987: 34) and there was another battle in 1712–17 at the base of the Blue Mountains, where the Ojibwa defeated the Mohawk on the beach (Leitch 1975: 32).

56 "Sale of Grand River Lands by the Missisaugas to the Crown, May 22, 1784," B11 in Johnston 1964: 48–9. The payment price is also reported as an equivalent "worth of trade goods" by Surtees (1994: 102), and elsewhere as an annuity of £1,180 (History of Canadian Indians, Marianopolis College, http://www.faculty.marianopolis.edu/c.belanger/QuebecHistory/encyclopedia/HistoryofCanadianIndians-1763-1840.htm).

57 Land grant size, 570,000 acres: Johnston 1964: xl.

58 Campbell 1937: 178.

59 Heckewelder 1876: 104, cited in Nelson 1999: 20.

60 Taylor 2006: 254–5.

61 Cruikshank 1923, vol. 1, 1924, and vol. 2, 336 (1793); 1925, vol. 3, 53, 61–3.

62 Cruikshank 1924, vol. 2, 16 (1793); Taylor 2006: 275, 276.

63 Brant built his home at Burlington Beach on an old Native site, using red cedar from the St Lawrence. Jones's survey was completed by 1 February 1791; B26 in Johnston 1964: 50. In a February meeting, Brant and eight Six Nations chiefs agreed to the survey and signed the map, now believed lost. See 1795 map, Cruikshank 1926, vol. 4, opposite 106.

64 Simcoe: Cruikshank 1924, vol. 2, 58 (1793). Simcoe Patent, 1793: Leitch 1975: 35. By the Royal Proclamation, only lands that were the subject of a treaty could be granted; there continue to be Six Nations claims for lands upriver.

65 Cruikshank 1924, vol. 2, 58, 59 (1793).

66 Ibid., 59, 114 (1793). Brant's power of attorney 1796: C12 in Johnston 1964: 79. Justice John Osler, Ontario High Court, 11 July 1973 ([1973] 3 O.R. at 677).

67 Taylor 2006: 334.

68 The threat was made by Brant in Philadelphia, and reported to Robert Prescott, governor of Canada; see Robert Liston to Robert Prescott, 1797, C15 in Johnston 1964: 85. Also, Johnston 1994: 173; Taylor 2006: 336; memoir of William Dummer Powell, 1797, C21 in Johnston 1964: 89–90; "Formal Transfer of the Grand River Tracts," C27 in Johnston 1964: 97–8.

69 Campbell 1937 (1792). Rouchefoucault also mentioned the "two negroes" (Smith 1917: 48 [1795]). In 1793 Simcoe limited slavery in Upper Canada; adult slaves then living in the colony were to remain slave property, but further import of slaves was prohibited and any children born to slaves were to be freed once they reached the age of twenty-five (Lajeunesse 1960: lxviii, 74).

70 Queen Anne's original silver communion service was buried on Boyd Hunter's land during the American Revolution and later retrieved and shared with Molly Brant's Mohawks at Tyendinaga.

71 Ke-che-ah-gah-me-qua 1850.

72 Wood 2000: 24; Harris 2008: 309.

73 Hull and Brock quotes: Casselman 1902: 50, 71. American prisoners at Queenston Heights, and U.S. casualties of 500: Benn 1998: 96.

74 Casselman 1902: 204-14. John Richardson was born in Queenston, raised in Amherstburg, served at Detroit and the defence of Queenston, and fell prisoner to the Americans at the battle of the Thames, which began on his seventeenth birthday. He was Canada's first novelist, famous for *Wacousta* and the poem *Tecumseh*.

75 Fitzgibbon 1984: 72, 95; Benn 1998: 114, 177; Taylor 2010.

76 Johnston 1994; Weaver 1994. The Grand River Navigation Company failed in 1861 (Benn 1998: 189).

77 In 1900 the capital accounts of the Cape Croker and Saugeen bands totalled $707,980, with a further 20,674 acres identified for auction (Robertson 1971: 5,528). 1847 immigration: O'Gallacher 2008: 52. Sir Charles Trevelyan, Britain's assistant secretary to the Treasury, called the migrants "surplus population," and the potato famine "the judgement of God."

78 Ogden 1799. Native population in 1840: Strickland 1970: 79 (1825-52). Other population figures: Robertson 1971: 11 and Wood 2000: 139, 161.

79 Langton 1926: 11, 25 (1830s).

80 Polished: Shirreff 1835: 123 (1833-34). Notables: Strickland 1970 (1825-52); Traill 1836 (1836); Moodie 1913 (1852) and 1959 (1853); Dunlop 1832; Jameson 1972 (1837).

81 Langton 1926: 48, 65, 145 (1830s). Langton became county warden, member of the provincial Parliament, and, after Confederation, Canada's auditor general and deputy minister of finance.

82 Snow 1994: 221; Wood 2000: 9–11, 166. Six Nations: see chapter 4, n.40.

Chapter Four

1 Post-1977: Winchester 2003; Catchpole and Faurer 1985.

2 War as politics: Carl von Clausewitz, *On War* (1832). Lawfare: Dunlap 2001; Qiao Liang and Wang Xiangsui 1999, also referring to the offensive projection of law for political-military ends.

3 Surtees 1994.

4 1805 payment for the Toronto Purchase was £1,700 cash and goods, including cloth, blankets, fifteen laced hats, ribbon, brass kettles, mirrors, tobacco, fishhooks, powder, shot, tools, and ninety-six gallons of rum. Eight headmen signed the treaty (Kyte 1954: 7). 1794 map, Dundas and Yonge streets: Cruikshank 1925, vol. 3, 142; Ke-che-ah-gah-me-qua 1850: 18.

5 Miller 2006; Green and Dickason 1989: 81, 108.

6 Surtees 1994.

7 Malthus's *Essay on Population* was first published in 1798.

8 Malthus 1826; "Malthus" 1965.

9 John Locke argued for enclosure of the commons in his 1690 *Second Treatise of Government*. Half of modern Scotland owned by 600 landowning families: Monbiot 1995; Harris et al. 1975; Milani 1971: 9.

10 C.H.C. 1846: 143. England never favoured convict transport to Newfoundland because of that colony's importance as a nursery for seamen; a single shipload arrived in 1789.

11 London *Monthly Review*, 97 (1822): 200–1.

12 Mitchell 1950: 22.

13 Strickland 1970: 140 (1831).

14 Lizars and Lizars 1896. The company sold its last land holdings in 1951 and ceased operations.

15 Dunlop 1832: 66, 77–9, 81, 147.

16 Harris 2008: 233, 287. About 45,000 stayed in Lower Canada. By 1851, there were 220,000 anglophones in Lower Canada, who constituted a majority of Montrealers and close to a majority overall. The average Canadian family then had seven children.

17 Graham 1962: 209.

18 Sir George Prevost to Lord Liverpool, colonial secretary, 11 December 1811.

19 Irish visitor: C.H.C. 1846: 82.

20 Ermatinger 1859: 18, 23-4. By 1827, Talbot's records showed 650,000 acres in twenty-eight townships under his control (Jameson 1972, vol. 2, 193).

21 Dunlop 1832: 108.

22 Graham 1962: 100.

23 Fitzpatrick 1931-44, vol. 7, 65. Abraham Lincoln was accredited as an Illinois surveyor in 1833.

24 Snow 2010: 83, 204.

25 Ladell 1993: 75; Gordon 1969: 15.

26 Shock troops of settlement: Ladell 1993: 9; McIlwraith 1997, chapter 4.

27 Talman 1946: liii. On marginal lands, like the District of Parry Sound, the land was often free (Macfie 2004). Friends of government: Cruikshank 1931, vol. 5, 153.

28 Lambert 1967: 19-21; Wood 2000: 94. Aristocracy: Cruikshank 1923, vol. 1, 264; ibid., 1926, vol. 4, 116; ibid., 1931, vol. 5, 173.

29 Lambert, 1st Earl of Durham: Wood 2000: 163-4. Slowing land conversion: Harris 2008: 287.

30 McIlwraith 1997: 61; Barnes 2003: 54-6; McKenney 1827: 87.

31 Chewett's map of the footpaths north of Lake Erie: Cruikshank 1925, vol. 3, 142. McNiff 1791: in Gentilcore and Head 1984: 66-7; Guillet 1966: 42; Macfee 2004.

32 Keefer 1863; Lizars 1913: 56; Wood 2000: 124-5.

33 Requirements for settlers could be harsher; those on the roads from Owen Sound to the Fishing Islands and Saugeen had to "cut and remove all the timber from the center of the road to the depth of ninety feet" within one year (Robertson 1971: 31, 532, 552).

34 Tolls remain common south of the lakes but, in Canada, privatized highways and tolls were usually temporary (such as to pay off the Burlington Skyway in the 1960s) until 1999 when tolls (to Brazilian owners) were revived for Highway 407. Mitchell 1950: 72; Guillet 1933: 536-7, 540; Guillet 1966: 57; Guillet 1970: 112; Kyte 1954: 77.

35 Harris 2008: 108.

36 Harris 1966: 25, endpiece map, and Fig. 3.1. The Island of Montreal belonged to Lauzon, one of the Compagnie.

37 Negative comments: e.g., Weld 1807, vol. 2, 8 (1797).

38 Green and Dickason 1989: 118, citing Taschereau J. (1887) before the Supreme Court of Canada.

39 "Absolute exclusive right": Chief Justice William Ritchie in a key Canadian case on the Royal Proclamation in 1888. He also stated: "The Crown owns the soil of all the unpatented lands, the Indians possessing only the right of occupancy." Green and Dickason 1989: 103, 113-14. Historian D. Snow distils the French regime's failed alternative to POGG as "cannon, catholicism and command" (2010: 43).

40 The twenty-first-century Caledonia land dispute has precedents in Iroquois entrepreneurs like Joseph Brant. Since 2006, in the *Hamilton Spectator* and *Macleans*, S. Buist, J. Walters, J. Burman, P. Legall, and J. Kirby have reported on the Caledonia land dispute. Their stories about Ken Hill and Jerry Montour, and their exercise of corporate ambition through Six Nations interests in Grand River Enterprises, Canada's fourth- largest cigarette manufacturer, and SixNet, the Internet gambling operation at the same site in Ohsweken, tell of a continuing wild west and of modern Six Nations entrepreneurial instincts. The disputed lands were part of lands sold by Six Nations along the Grand in the 1840s but were of recent interest as a possible casino site, following failed attempts to set up casinos in Brownsville, Pennsylvania, and Niagara Falls, New York. In 2006 elected Six Nations Band Chief David General warned his community not to be enticed "to the dark side [by] big money and tobacco." He went on to report allegations "that he [Ken Hill] brought the tires, the pallets and the vehicles that were burned there and that it's his equipment that dug up Highway 6. People have thanked him over the radio for bringing in the gravel and trucks that formed the barricade." This example of aggressive Native lawfare has been adopted into mainstream media political correctness.

41 Armstrong 1968: 18. Provincial Policy Statement, 2005, section 3 of the Planning Act, revision 2011; Board of Adjudicators, Ontario Municipal Board.

42 Four million: Hemson 2005.

43 The fifth and fourteenth constitutional amendments. John Locke, in a 1690 essay, first invoked the trinity of life, liberty, and property as the natural rights of free men. Bobrick 2001: 288–95.

44 Hall 2002: 658–848.

45 Sax 2005.

46 Durand 2001. And http://www.wildlandsandwoodlands.org.

47 Armstrong 1968. Adams founded the Town Planning Institute of Canada in 1919 (Canadian Institute of Planners).

48 Reaman 1957: 106, 234.

49 Implementing action 6.5.3, Parkway Belt West Plan.

50 As an example, Charles Sauriol, first director of Nature Conservancy of Canada, from 1978 to 1983, helped secure fifty-one properties (5,080 acres) on the Niagara Escarpment, matching provincial funds with those donated by the Richard and Jean Ivey Fund.

51 Larson et al. 1999: 95.

52 Vaughan now requires developers to pay a development charge on new residential units to fund the purchase and protection of woodlots.

53 Wilson 2002: 50

Chapter Five

1 Passenger pigeon, *Ectopistes migratorius*. The estimate of one in four birds is Schorger's, for the United States (1973: 199–205), extrapolated to North America by Mann (2005: 316). Also, Leopold 1966: 116–19.

2 Champlain, *un nombre infini*: Biggar 1922, vol. 1, pt. 3, 332. Sagard, *une infinité des tourterelles*: Sagard 1939: 381. Weld 1807, vol. 2, 43 (1796). Wilson: reported by Howison 1821: 160 (1821). Flight over Niagara: King 1866: 121–2 (1866). Schorger 1973: 201–2; Anonymous (Small) 1971: 134, 168; Muir 1997: 78–82 (1813).

3 Van der Donck 1841: 51; Harris 1903: 449–51; Gunn 1903. Jones was interpreter of choice for Iroquois land sales south of the lakes, such as the 1788 sale of land east of Genesee. He and Sarah Whitmore, also a Pennsylvanian child abductee, led a heroic life on the western frontier, spurning any return east. Late in his life, the Seneca, as a gift, gave him a square mile of what later became Buffalo.

4 Thompson 1968: 53; Fox 1952: 96; Robertson 1971: 79.

5 Mackinaw: McIlwraith 1894: 184. New York, Pennsylvania: Schorger 1973: 90. Leopold 1966.

6 Schorger 1973: chapter 3. A study of stomach contents showed 9.4 per cent animal food, the remainder vegetable (Cottam and Knappen 1939). Peabody 1841, vol. 3, 194. Also, Schorger 1973: 48–9. The report of pigeons clearing out infestations of "green caterpillars" may refer to leaf-feeding loopers in the family *Geometridae*, or possibly the eastern tent caterpillar.

7 Neumann 2002: 158–64. Ontario sites: Sadler and Howard 2003: 10. Onondaga sites: Tuck 1971.

8 Neumann 2002: 170; Weld 1807, vol. 2, 44–5; Dunlop 1832: 91, 92.

9 Clarke 1964. European defaunation, especially in medieval times, was the pattern revisited here: Hoffman 2005.

10 Darwin's "entangled bank" was guided by the "laws acting around us" (Quammen 2008: 513). William Whewell coined the word "scientist" in 1840 at the request of Samuel Taylor Coleridge but it was not widely used until the end of the nineteenth century. E.O. Wilson of Harvard used the word "biodiversity" as title of a conference proceedings in 1988 and it entered the vernacular, but Wilson himself went full circle by titling his autobiography *Naturalist*.

11 Quinn and Quinn 1983: 112–38, 160–1, 170, 212–30. Heath hen, *Tympanuchus cupido cupido*: Krech 1999: 112.

12 Horseshoe crab, *Limulus polyphemus*; turkey, *Meleagris gallopavo*; porpoise, *Phocoena phocoena*. Biggar 1922, vol. 1, pt. 3, 358–61. The king's gifts: Fischer 2008: 202, 227.

13 Quinn and Quinn 1983: 26, 481-93 (1605), 347-51.

14 Wood 1865: 42-6, 50, 65, 106; Wood 1977: 53-7. Atlantic salmon, *Salmo salar*; striped bass, *Morone saxatilis*. Whaling: Rosier, in Quinn and Quinn 1983: 303.

15 Morton 1637: 76, 80; Heath 2007; Quinn and Quinn 1983: 15; Williams 1973: 163-84.

16 Robert Juet's notes on Hudson's voyage: Jameson 1959; http://www.ianchadwick. com/hudson/hudson_03.htm.

17 Van der Donck 1841: 42-53, 57, 97-8. Collective Mohawk seine netting: Engelbrecht 2003: 17.

18 Cook 1993: 4, 5. Great auk, *Pinguinus impennis*.

19 Ibid., 46, 48, 49, 74, 75. Carp, likely redhorse, *Moxostoma* sp.; bream likely a sunfish. Based on interviews with Cartier and others, Thevet emphasized in 1557 the whales in the St Lawrence and the seals around Newfoundland: "the sea there abounds in [fish] more than any other place in the universe, especially in seals" (1986: 55, 97, 123).

20 Cook 1993: 57, 58, 62,74. *Cerfz... daims*, trans. as elk and deer by Ganong (1909: 209). Elk were "common about the Saguenay" as late as 1823, after which they were hunted out (Hind 1863: vol. 1, 224). Saintonge: Hakluyt 1903-05.

21 Champlain's *orignas, cerfs, biches, dains* were interpreted by Biggar (i.e., Ganong) as "moose, stags, hinds, deer" (meaning moose, elk, female elk, white-tailed deer) and by Slafter (i.e., Otis) as "*orignacs*, stags, hinds, does" (meaning, moose, elk, deer, female deer). Elsewhere, Champlain's *eslās* and *eslan* were translated by Biggar as "moose" and by Slafter as "elk." Champlain later mentions, in 1611 at Mount Royal, a quartet of ungulates, specifically the *cerfs, daims, cheureuls, caribous*, the latter for the first time and with no mention of *orignas* or moose. Champlain admitted his difficulty identifying these ungulates in 1613 after his men brought nine different animals to their camp at the Lachine Rapids: "These stags are not at all like ours, and there are different kinds of them, some larger and others smaller." By 1632, his *Voyages* were clear, noting, for example, south of the St Lawrence near the Rivière du Sud "numbers of moose [*eslans*] and caribou [*caribaux*] nearly as large as stags [*cerfs, elk*]." Biggar 1922, vol. 1, pt. 2, 146 (Heidenreich and Ritch 2010: 315); Biggar 1925, vol. 2, 45, 177, 305; Biggar 1933, vol. 5, pt. 2, 189; Ganong 1909; Slafter 1880.

22 Biggar 1925, vol. 2, pt. 1, 24, 44, 90, 181, and plates 3 and 7. The Lachine Rapids Islands, including Heron Island, are now protected by the Nature Conservancy of Canada.

23 Pike were known to Europeans but some of the larger ones were no doubt muskellunge, *Esox masquinongy*, a New World species (Biggar 1932, vol. 4, pt. 1, 238-9). Nets: Biggar 1929, vol. 3, pt. 1, 166; Bogue suggests these were gill nets (2000: 5-7). Trip down the Trent: Biggar 1929, vol. 3, pt. 1, 45-6, 61-2, 82, 83, and plate 5 on 85. The reference is likely to whooping crane (*Grus americana*), based on the description and

on fossil bones from Sainte-Marie (Sadler and Howard 2003: 127). Deer drives with built enclosures were noted by d'Aillon in 1626 among the Neutral (Coyne 1895) and by archaeologist Williamson on the Caradoc sand plain (1990: 314, 316). Canada geese are associated with Iroquoian farming by McAndrews and Turton 2007.

24 Carolina parakeet, *Conuropsis carolininensis*, of which bones have been found at an archaeological site in southwest Ontario (Sadler and Howard 2003: 10, 243). Biggar 1929, vol. 3, pt. 1, 83.

25 Sagard 1939: 42, 69-70, 90-5, 186, 189, 230-2, 235 (1623-24). Lake sturgeon, *Acipenser fulvescens*; lake whitefish, *Coregonus clupeaformis*; burbot, or ling, *Lota lota*.

26 The cardinal was a northern record, "birds with plumage all red or crimson [*entierement rouge ou incarnate*], which they call *stinondoa*." It likely reflects the open countryside of Huronia. The wilding of southern Ontario displaced it, and it was only after its deforestation by settlers that the cardinal returned in the late 1800s (Sagard 1939: 217-21). Passenger pigeons: Sagard-Theodat 1866, pt. 3, 674. Mammals: Sagard 1939: 222-7, 233-4.

27 D'Aillon: Johnston 1964: 5-6. Lalemant: JR 21: 196-7.

28 JR 5: 21, 6: 309. Travel food: John Casselman, presentation to Brodie Club, Toronto, 6 May 2008. Quebec City harvest: JR 28: 239. Fifty thousand barrels: Gagnon 2011: 228.

29 Simon: JR 48: 152-79. In 1660 one sealer "killed 220 seals on isle rouge," downstream of Quebec (JR 45: 109).

30 Bison: JR 42: 37. Onondaga: Tuck 1971: 4-5. Dablon: JR 43: 261, also Engelbrecht 2003: 16; Bogue 2000: 23. Raffeix, 1671: JR 56: 49-51.

31 Le Moine: JR 41: 93, 126-9. Chaumont: JR 42: 60-9, 207.

32 Champlain's 1832 map located *lieu où il y a force cerfs* in this area. Lett 1884 (cited by Seton 1929, vol. 3, 14-15).

33 *Serfs, biches, ours, schenontons, chats sauvages, et castors*: Galinée regularly noted as ungulates *cerfs, chevreuils*, and *biches* (elk and deer) around lakes Erie and Ontario, as well as *orignaux* (moose) northward on Huron and along the Ottawa (Coyne 1903: 51, 52, 53, 81-7). Charlevoix 1761: 4 (1721).

34 Galinée: Coyne 1903: 72-3, 81-7. Fishing: see Bogue 2000: 5-7. There were "two thousand souls" at Sault Ste Marie in 1642 (JR 23: 225). *Élans*: Tailhan 1864: 126, mistranslated as "elk" by Jaenen 1996. Manitoulin Native elders have oral traditions of caribou but not elk (J. Jones and R. Tasker, pers. comms., March 2009 and November 2010). St. Joseph Island was originally "Isles aux Cariboux" (Cruikshank 1926, vol. 4, 246, 327). Disease: JR 30: 281.

35 JR 54: 185-89, 207, 215, 231; JR 55: 193-201; JR 56: 121.

36 Gagnon 2011: 21, 27, 279, 329.

37 Hennepin 1903: 57, 63, 97, 314, 315, 321, 324, 329, 522, 523, 524 (1678-80).

38 Boucher: Montizambert 1883: 15, 23, 25, 35-7, 40, 44, 46. Herring (cisco), *Coreogonus artedii*.

39 Lahontan 1905: 50, 103, 106, 109, 111-15 (1684-86). Lahontan's French edition did not mentioned elk north of Montreal but his English edition did.

40 Lahontan 1905: 138-40, 320 (1687-89). French in italics from Ouellet 1990.

41 Lahontan 1905: 147-8, 156, 161 (1687-89). Joutel: Engelbrecht 2003: 18.

42 Cadillac 1904. And Cadillac 1701: B2 in Lajeunesse 1960: 18-19.

43 Kalm 1966, vol. 1, 127, 325, 326, 342, 344, 351 (1748-49). Albany fur trade: Barnes 2003: 54; White 1991: 125.

44 Kalm 1966, vol. 1, 352, 353, 369 (1749).

45 Kalm to John Bartram, 2 September 1750, in Bartram 1895: 88, 92 (1750); first description of Niagara Falls in English. Timber rattlesnakes: Kalm 1966, vol. 2, 708. St John's-wort (*Hypericum kalmianum*), a Great Lakes plant species endemic only on the shores of lakes Erie, Huron, and Michigan and the Ottawa River. Niagara Falls is the only place where Kalm visited the range of the species. Linnaeus erroneously published its type location as "in Virginia," which Kalm never visited.

46 Kalm 1966, vol. 2, 494, 522 (1749).

47 Henry 1969: 19, 20, 30, 54, 56, 61-3, 70, 146, 165, 166, 201 (1761-66). Eastern cougar (*Felis concolor couguar*) is now considered extinct.

48 Lake Erie water snake (*Nerodia sipedon insularum*): Carver 1813: 92, 100 (1766-68).

49 Cruikshank 1923, vol. 1, 387-8.

50 Smith 1906: 34, 41, 45, 46, 68 (1769); Taylor 2006: 35; Cooper 1850: 289 (1848).

51 Simcoe: Cruikshank 1925, vol. 3, 54. The deer ran: Jesse McQuigg quoted in Kingman 1987: 36. Servos: Kirby 1972: 67.

52 Campbell 1937: 147-78 (1792). Sturgeon no longer spawn in the Grand but oral tradition, like that of Paul General of the Six Nations, establishes them south of present-day Paris and upstream as far as Glen Morris: Jack Imhof, pers. comm., 2008. Isinglass was a clarifying agent in jellies, glues, and glass, even in the windows of early automobiles.

53 Campbell 1937: 152 (1792). Horned bladderwort (*Utriculalria cornuta*): Zenkert 1934: 7.

54 Cruikshank 1923, vol. 1, 289-93; Gray 1956.

55 Zeisberger and turtles: Bliss 1885, vol. 2, 258-9, 313, 413, 459, 481. Elma Gray (1956) translated "turtle" here as "soft-shelled river turtles," *Apalone spinifera*, and the Thames still provides habitat for these now-rare turtles.

56 Innis 1965 (1791).

57 Ibid., 75-7, 96, 107, 161, 169 (1792-95).

58 Ibid., 94 (1793). Matthews reported that loyalists from America brought their hogs with them across the Niagara River: "Their hogs throve so well on the acorn mast

covering the floor of the oak forest that farmers often 'killed them out of the woods, well fatted on nuts'" (1965: 129). John Maude wrote about the snakes at the Onondaga reserve in Iroquoia: "This part of the country is notoriously infested with snakes, especially with rattlesnakes. Hogs hunt for and pursue rattlesnakes with eagerness and avidity, and eat them as greedily" (1826: 41–2).

59 The botanist John Goldie's only faunal observation in his 1819 diary in Upper Canada was of three snakes at the bottom of the gorge at Horseshoe Falls, "two of them striped [likely timber rattlers, *Crotalus horridus horridus*] and one of what is called the milk kind [milk snake, *Lampropeltis triangulum triangulum*]."

60 Innis 1965: 81 (1792).

61 Ibid., 104, 106, 110, 187 (1793). Eastern tiger swallowtails, *Papilio glaucus*, search wet ground for nutrients like sodium. Atlantic salmon spawned in Lake Ontario streams until 1898, extirpated by overfishing, obstructing dams, and stream siltation. It is now being reintroduced into Lake Ontario streams in the United States and Canada but must compete with popular, non-native Pacific and hybrid salmon in same streams. Bouchette was Samuel Holland's nephew (Bouchette 1831, in Robinson 1933: 185).

62 Innis 1965: 111, 165 (1794–96).

63 Ibid., 117, 129, 155, 170 (1794–95). Calamus, sweet flag, *Acorus calamus*, a known medicinal with a similar history of use in Europe.

64 Smith 1917: 21, 22, 49 (1795–97). Mrs Simcoe reports the same descent (Innis 1995: 162).

65 Weld 1807, vol. 1 (1796–97).

66 Ibid., vol. 2, 44–5, 128 (1797).

67 Ibid., vol. 2, 124–5 (1797). 108 fish per second: Zubrow and Buerger 1980.

68 Weld 1807, vol. 2, 139, 144, 147, 148, 152–6 (1797). The land parcels containing the sand dunes west of Point Abino were assembled by the Marcy family of Buffalo, and are now owned, with similar conservation intent, by the DiCienzo family of Niagara Falls. Larson et al. 1999: 143.

69 Weld 1807, vol. 2, 161–2 (1797). Northern redbelly snake, *Storeria occipitomaculata*; eastern hognose snake, *Heterodon platyrhinos*. Middle Island was purchased in 1998 by the Nature Conservancy of Canada and donated to Canada as a National Park. It was colonized by double-crested cormorants, *Phalocrocorax auritus*, which are not native breeders in the Great Lakes but can now eat the modern suite of smaller fish. Middle Island's unique hackberry forest and rare ground flora and breeding birds are being buried in cormorant guano. Control of the cormorants on Middle Island by Parks Canada began, under protest, in 2008. Massasauga rattlesnakes were also reported from Pelee Island (Hooper 1967).

70 Maude 1826: 67, 69, 150.

71 Heriot 1807: 49, 57. Belugas have high levels of PCBs, DDT, mirex, mercury, lead, and PAHs, all known for their toxic effects and for interfering with immunity and reproduction. Snares or weirs: Hind 1863, vol. 2, 90.

72 Heriot 1807: 81, 116, 117.

73 Ibid.,137, 139. Lynde Creek: Higgins 1972: 124; Kirby 1972: 146.

74 Quinepenon, speech, 6 September 1806, RG 10 (Upper Canada Civil Control, Indian Affairs), 1: 294, in Taylor 2006: 132.

75 Cronon 1983: 159.

76 Maude 1826: 59; Cooper 1823, vol. 2, 41.

77 Dunlop 1832: 85, 88-94, 183. Poaching: Loo 2006: 13.

78 Dunlop 1832: 94-6.

79 Wilmot; Bogue 2000: 21-5. Magrath 1953: 177; Wood 2000: 6.

80 Magrath 1953: 107, 128, 169, 172. Also in York, in 1800: "A flock of wolves ... came into the town. One man lost 17 sheep; several other lost in proportion" (J. Willcocks to R. Willcocks, 3 November 1800, in Guillet 1933: 116).

81 Rorke 1987: 24, 49-52, 68, 80, 88 (1824-68); Wood 2000: 18.

82 Langton 1926: 34, 35 (1833).

83 Shirreff 1835: 214, 218, 246, 390 (1833-34). A sentiment shared by David Wilkie in his 1834 visit to Toronto: "Pigeons were scarce, woodcocks still more rare [and on the bay] we saw little game and shot less" (Wilkie 1937).

84 Romney 1988; Theberge 1988.

85 Black 1934 (1820-22). This black ratsnake (*Elaphe obsoleta*) was killed by Sylvester Richmond, likely of Hallowell, Prince Edward County. The species is no longer extant between the Frontenac Axis and the Niagara frontier but was so formerly, possibly as late as 1958 in Toronto (Johnson 1989). Elk: Seton 1929, vol. 3, 14-15. At Collingwood: Grant 1873: 12.

86 Only six or seven years of Pope's diaries have been discovered: Barrett 1976: 85, 149, 150-52, 159, 163. Toothwort, *Dentaria* spp.

87 Ibid., vol. 1, 188, 297-8, and vol. 2, 115. Seton noticed this misidentification of wolverine (1929, vol. 3). Uxbridge: Higgins 1972: 34.

88 Strickland 1970: 173, 179, 188 (1825-52). Gray or timber wolf, *Canis lupus*; eastern wolf, *Canis lycaon*. The smaller western coyote (*Canis latrans*) arrived in Ontario in 1919 and Massachusetts in the 1950s. The wolf bounty was $15 to $20 in the United States at this time, and "the wolves are quickly extirpated" (Jameson 1972, vol. 2, 212 [1837]).

89 Traill 1836: 112; Traill 1969: 157, 161. 1807 Act for the Preservation of Salmon: Lizars 1913: 115, 118. Another law was passed in 1823; Wood 2000: 19. The first closed fishing season in Ontario was legislated in 1885 for brook trout, followed in 1903 by a prohibition on the sale of game fish, intended to aid the licensed commercial fishery.

90 Jameson 1972, vol. 2, 6, 334 (1837). The English at the time applied "turtle" to sea-living turtles; "terrapin" to those in fresh or brackish water; and "tortoise" to those on land (Goldsmith 1822). Jameson could have meant snapping turtle, *Chelydra serpentina*, or spiny softshell turtle, *Apalone spinifera*. She also reported "terrapin [on] every log floating on the water" in the Thames (1972, vol. 2, 281), where David Zeisberger also noted them and where they still occur (Gray 1956). Softshells were reported from Toronto in 1858 (Ure 1858) and have been reported by fishers (Roots 1999: 197) and by Toronto Region Conservation Authority staff (Leslie Street Spit, Toronto). It is a threatened species in Canada.

91 Jameson 1972, vol. 2, 211-12; vol. 3, 4, 6, 178, 253 (1837); Henry 1969: 20. Sturgeon are still in healthy numbers in Mississagi River. Jameson also noted a sturgeon fishery near Penetanguishene in Gloucester Bay, "which are caught and cured in large quantities by the neighboring settlers; some weigh ninety and one hundred pounds" (Jameson 1972, vol. 3, 348).

92 Jameson 1972, vol. 3, 321; vol. 2, 7. Most of the protected public lands along the eastern Georgian Bay coast were set aside by Ontario's "Lands for Life" program, with additional lands protected by the Georgian Bay Land Trust and the Nature Conservancy of Canada (Jalava et al. 2005); Sullivan 1852: 54. Yonge Street paving: see Haight 1986: 153.

93 Kane 1968: 2, 4.

94 Haight 1986: 41-2, 76-6. Pike, *Esox lucius*; mullet, likely *Moxostoma macrolepidotum*; sucker, *Cyprinus hudsonius*; pickerel, *Stizostedion vitreum vitreum*; muskellunge, *Esox masquinongy*.

95 McIlwraith 1860; McIlwraith 1894: 169, 179, 181, 182, 222, 306, 347, 413. William Pope shot a shrike ("called by Wilson the loggerhead shrike") in Norfolk in 1835, one of three he had seen: Barrett 1976: 163.

96 Weld 1855: 80-3.

97 Thoreau 1906: VII, 24 January 1855, and VIII, 23 March 1856. See Cronon 1983: 4.

98 Thomas Mason, "Feby 29, 64. Settlement of the Northern Townships of the Trent Valley," in Guillet 1957: 79-81 (punctuation added).

99 In 1885 eighteen fishing boats manned by seventy fishermen sailed out of Southampton. Robertson 1971: 21-4, 463, 519.

100 Hamilton 1893: 19, 30, 109; Campbell 2005: 75.

101 Richardson 1847: 102, 132. "Walton" refers to Izaak Walton and the pastoral art of fishing he personified.

102 Anonymous (Small) 1971: 25, 113, 126, 128, 156, 160, 166.

103 Syndrome: Pauly 1995.

104 Catling 2001.

105 8 per cent of the landscape, etc.: Ellsworth and McComb 2003. Hartford, MI, numbers: Hewitt 1921: 20.

106 Forget et al. 2004. Notes on sand cherry: Traill 1906: 69, 165; Chewett 1795: 77; and choke cherry: Thompson 1968: 52–3 (1833–53). White oak group, *Quercus* sect. *Quercus*, red and black oak group, *Quercus* sect. *Lobatae*: USDA 1974: 699.

107 Pokeweed, *Phytolacca americana*: Schorger 1973: 86.

108 Pawpaw, *Asimina triloba*.

109 Udall 1963: 54.

110 Bogue 2000: 25–7, 208–9.

111 Harvest levels: Bogue 2000: 46, Kinnunen 2003. Ballast flushing: Mittelstaedt 2008: A3. Best-researched: Bogue 2000: 45. Lake trout, *Salvelinus namaycush*; ciscoes, *Coregonus* spp.; sculpins, *Cottus* spp.; *Myxocephalus* spp. Governments of Canada and the United States 2009: 2.

112 Sea lamprey, *Petromyzon marinus*, controlled with lampricides TFM (3-trifluoromethyl-4-nitrophenol) in streams and granular Bayluscide in lentic systems. Rainbow smelt, *Osmerus mordax*.

113 No sturgeon recovery was recommended in 2007 by the Canadian Zonal Peer Review Meeting – Recovery Potential Assessment for Lake Sturgeon-Great Lakes-Upper St. Lawrence Populations, 5–7 November 2007, Sault Ste Marie, ON. Crowder et al 1996; Sly 1991.

114 Quoted by H. Hoag, 31 March 2007, *Globe and Mail* (F7); John Casselman, presentation to Brodie Club, Toronto, 6 May 2008. Japanese eel bladder worm, *Anguillicola crassus*. Eel listed as an endangered species by Ontario in 2011; recovery plans are under development.

115 Hoyle and Mathers 2002.

116 Scott 1957.

117 Productivity in 1900: Zubrow and Buerger 1980. 1915–1971: Hartman 1973. Lake trout, *Salvelinus namaycush*; alewife, *Alosa pseudoharengus*; rainbow smelt, *Osmerus mordax*; ciscoes, *Coregonus* spp.; sculpins, *Cottus* spp.; *Myxocephalus* spp.; carp, *Cyprinus carpio*; northern cisco, *Coregonus artedi*; blue pike, *Stizostedion vitreum glaucum*; walley, *Stizostedion vitreum vitreum*.

118 By a foot: Crowder et al. 1996; Regier 1968. Also, Scott 1963 and Sweeney 1969.

119 Colborn et al. 1990: 228.

120 Hartman 1973; Regier and Hartman 1974. Zebra mussel, *Dreissena polymorpha*; quagga mussel, *Dreissena rostriformis bugensis*; round goby, *Neogobius melanstomus*.

121 Crowder et al. 1996. Amphipod, *Diporeia* spp. Species displacement has included more than 99 per cent of the native freshwater mussels of the lower Great Lakes (Governments of Canada and the United States 2009: 6, 13). Boutique chemicals: ibid., 4.

122 Eshenroder and Krueger 2002. Lake trout: Governments of Canada and the United States (2009: 6).

123 Governments of Canada and the United States of America 2009.

124 Varga et al. 1991: 111, Table 10.

Chapter Six

1 Benson 1820; Wood 1961. 1915: Mono 1974: 13.

2 Larson et al. 1999; Snell 1987. U.S. states: Dahl 1990.

3 North American consumption of lumber on a per-capita basis peaked from 1870 to 1907, declined to about a fifth of this rate by 1932, during the Depression, and rose to rates that were half-as-high in the years after the Second World War. The year 1910 also marks the high point, in terms of acres, of land cultivation in Great Lakes country.

4 Snell 1987; Riley 1999; Larson et al. 1999. Ancient Forest Exploration and Research, http://www.ancientforest.org/.

5 Positive changes in Ontario: property-tax relief for woodland owners; protection of "significant woodlands" by the Planning Act; subsidies for tree planting by Trees Canada, Trees Ontario, the Ontario Forestry Association, conservation authorities, Ontario Hydro, and others; restoration support, such as by the Oak Ridges Moraine Foundation. The closure of provincial tree nurseries stands out as a continuing barrier to tree planting by landowners.

6 Cook 1993: 51, 57, 60. Cartier also noted maple syrup (Thevet 1986: 17) (1557). Boucher confirmed that, on Montreal Island, "most of the trees are oak" and that the woods are "clear and not incumbered with undergrowth" (Montizambert 1883: 22).

7 St Lawrence: Biggar 1922, vol. 1, pt. 2, 122, 131, 139, 140, 145. Heidenreich and Ritch 2010: 297, 307, 309, 314. Most islands between Lac Saint-Pierre and Montreal were grazed and cultivated. In the 1980s the Nature Conservancy of Canada created the vision of "une fleuve, un parc"; a partnership of groups has since purchased the majority of the islands to conserve them. East coast: Biggar 1922, vol. 1, pt. 3, 329, 398. Sassafras, *Sassafras albidum*.

8 Biggar 1925, vol. 2, 76, 77, 91, 176, 273, Plate 11. Champlain lost his astrolabe on the portage above Gould's Landing, the last point at which he made a reading of latitude. It was found at Green Lake in 1867 by E.G. Lee, age fourteen. After time in the United States it was repatriated to the Canadian National Museum in 1989. Gillies Grove: owned by the Nature Conservancy of Canada on behalf of the people of the Ottawa valley, and uncut by its owners, the Gillies family and the McLaughlin family, both logging enterprises. Ontario's tallest white pine, at 165 feet, grows here. The Ottawa valley was also noted for its oaks, such as those observed on the

islands at Chaudière Falls by Nicholas Garry, deputy governor of the Hudson's Bay Company, in 1821 (Siggins 2008: 47).

9 Biggar 1929, vol. 3, pt. 1, 50–1, 58–60, 63. Grape, *Vitis riparia*; plums, *Prunus americana*, *P. nigra*; wild apples, *Crataegus* spp. or *Malus coronaria*; mayapple, *Podophyllum peltatum*.

10 Sagard 1939: 91, 108, 240. Lalemant: JR 21: 194–7.

11 Talon 1665, A.I.2, in Jaenen 1996. Baie-Saint-Paul: Tyrrell 1931: 286; Lahontan 1905, vol. 1, 35 (1684).

12 Port Dover: Coyne 1903: 52, 53, 82, 83, map (1669). Dablon: JR 43: 257, 259, 325 (1656). Hennepin 1903: 109.

13 Mulberry, *Morus rubra*; hazel, filberts, *Corylus* spp.; magnolia, *Magnolia acuminata*; tulip-tree, *Liriodendron tulipifera*; honey locust, *Gleditsia triacanthos*; pawpaw, *Asimina triloba*. Cadillac 1701: 18 (1701); Cadillac 1904: Nouvel: JR 60: 215–17 (1676). Green Bay: JR 55: 193–201 (1670).

14 La Salle: Robinson 1933: 38, Jaenen 1996: 156. Pouchot: Hough 1866: 121. Henry 1969: 171–3. Where the portage ended at the mouth of the Humber, Henry's captors crafted an elm-bark canoe to deliver him to William Johnson at Fort Niagara. The Happy Valley forest, where the portage crosses the Oak Ridges Moraine, is a project of the Nature Conservancy of Canada and partners. Many travellers portaged it: Brûlé, in 1615 (?); La Salle, in 1680–83; Dulhut and Henry, in 1764; and Simcoe in 1793 (Robertson 2010). The Happy Valley is a "core natural area" of the Oak Ridges Conservation Plan.

15 Lorimer 1977; Williams 1973: 138, 168, 169 (1631–43); Wood 1977: 38 (1629–33).

16 Bogaert 1988: 1, 7, 9, 11, 12 (1634–35).

17 Van der Donck 1841: 22, 23 (1640s). Blue indian figs, *Opuntia humifusa* (?); artichokes, *Helianthus tuberosus*; ground-acorns, perhaps *Quercus prinoides*; ground beans, *Apios americana*; wild onions, *Allium* spp.

18 Lahontan 1905, vol. 1, 131, 319 (1687–89). Boucher: Montizambert 1883: 22 (1664).

19 Bartram 1895: 37, 39, 57, 62 (1743). Ginseng, *Panax quinquefolius*; maidenhair fern, *Adiantum pedatum*.

20 Kalm 1966: 351, 357, 400, 436, 488, 510, 598 (1749). Ginseng: now fewer than 150 occurrences in Canada and endangered through overharvesting. Exports of wild ginseng are prohibited, and it is now grown commercially.

21 Smith 1906: 21, 25, 34, 36, 40, 41, 53 (1769).

22 Ibid., 52–5 (1769).

23 Bliss 1885, vol. 1, 105. French travellers: Simon Desjardins et al., in *Castorland Journal*, trans. and ed. by F.B. Hough, cited in Taylor 2006: 383. Pursh 1923: 35 (1807). McKenney 1827: 73 (1826).

24 Instructions to Governor Murray, 7 December 1763; instructions to Governor Carleton, 2 January 1775: Ontario Archives, *Report*, 1906: 7, 58. Simcoe's opposition to reserving pine: Cruikshank 1931, vol. 5, 181, 183.

25 Lower 1938: 16; Logan 2005: 221; Lambert 1967: 32. Of the Montmorency sawmills, "the offal of this work which is let float away with the tide wd. produce a large income to a man if in Ireland" (Graves 1951: 26).

26 Campbell 1937: 140-1, 149, 155-6. Chestnut were not otherwise noted from north of Lake Ontario.

27 Innis 1965: 61, 65, 69, 70, 72, 73, 190.

28 Ibid., 74-7, 96. Robinson 1911: 169; Rogers 1765: 174.

29 Mrs Simcoe: Innis 1965: 82, 94 – fringed gentian, *Gentiana crinita*; cardinal flower, *Lobelia cardinalis*; milkweed, *Asclepias syriaca*; sweet grass, *Hierochloe odorata*; cranberry, *Vaccinium macrocarpon*; chestnut, *Castanea dentata*. Governor Simcoe: Cruikshank 1923, vol. 1, 288, 290 (1793). Burning springs, 1656: JR 43: 326. The first oil well in North America was dug by J.M. Williams at Oil Springs, Ontario, in 1858, followed a year later by the Drake well in Pennsylvania.

30 Simcoe: Cruikshank 1923, vol. 1, 153, 339; Cruikshank 1924, vol. 2, opposite 56 (1793); Aitkin 1788; Robinson 1933: 167; Innis 1965: 95, 101 (1793). Land purchase: Toronto Purchase in 1787, Ontario Crown Land Surveys, Plan 1092, Peterborough. The copy of the map in the Archives of Ontario was signed by William Chewett and by Missisauga headmen in 1805. Presumably Chewett did the original survey of 1787, or it might have been surveyor John Collins, who conducted the negotiation of the Toronto Purchase at the portage on the Bay of Quinte in 1787, signed by three Native headmen. Another plan of the Toronto harbour and the proposed townsite was completed in 1788 (Kyte 1954: 7, 31). Simcoe's name "York" was from Shakespeare's *King Henry VI*: "Let's harbor here in York."

31 Innis 1965: 101-3 (1793). Cottonwood, *Populus deltoides*; beach pea, *Lathyrus maritimus*, last seen on Toronto Islands in 1939.

32 Cruikshank 1924, vol. 2, 70-9 (1793). Seven years later, John Stegmann surveyed the Happy Valley forest where it crossed the Oak Ridges: north on 7th line into Happy Valley forest ("Broken timber, pine maple & oak") and north on Weston road in the same area ("Pine, hemlock and oak," and "on high hill–pine & oak") (Stegmann 1800: 418-20).

33 Smith 1917: 17, 25, 54, 55, 81, 83 (1795-97).

34 Weld 1897, vol. 1, 42, 52, 110, 123 (1797). Ancient cedars: Kelly and Larson 2007: 58.

35 Heriot 1807: 132, 136, 146, 148, 149, 152, 154, 156, 174.

36 Ibid., 155.

37 Kalm 1966, vol. 2, 447, 461, 467 (1749). Likely *Sarracenia purpurea* and *Gaultheria procumbens*.

38 Michaux 1819, cited in Zenkert 1934: 6. White oak: commented on by Ellsworth and McComb 2003. Magnolia, cucumber-tree, *Magnolia acuminata*; kentucky coffee-tree, *Gymnocladus dioica*; black maple, *Acer nigrum*.

39 Dwarf lake iris, *Iris lacustris*; Huron tansy, *Tanacetun huronense*. Graustein 1950-51: 22-72; Voss 1978.

40 Reznicek 1980.

41 Goldie 1819: viii, 4-7, 10; Fox 1944; Suffling 1987. Hairy beardtongue, *Penstemon hirsutus*. High-rise buildings were proposed for the site of Ganatsekiagon but public opposition saw it returned to public ownership. The unexcavated archaeological site was used by Huron, Seneca, and Missisauga, and by various explorers, governors, and missionaries who visited. A "very fine" road led from there to Lake Simcoe and the upper Great Lakes (Coyne 1903: 82-3).

42 The Rouge River slopes at the old Dundas Street are dominated by oak today but the understorey, which the surveyor J. Galbraith described in 1833 as "briars," "hazel," and "brush," the result of a fire in 1802, has now closed in; the hairy beardtongue has dwindled or disappeared. Galbraith 1833. Fire of 1802: R.D.H.P. Valley Conservation Report 1956; Varga et al. 1991. For 1793 map: Smith 1793. In 2011 Parks Canada began planning for a Rouge National Park.

43 Galbraith also called them "pine barrens" and "pine plains" (1833; 1833b). Goldie 1819: 11, 36. Goldie settled in Ayr, Ontario. His family established the Galt foundries, mills, and an insurance company.

44 Rafinesque 1944: 337 (1802-33). The word "ecology" was coined by German biologist Ernst Haeckel in 1866.

45 Kent, "Tour of the Western Circuit," 1798, cited in Taylor 2006: 383; Bartlett 1842.

46 Howison 1821: 11-13, 21 (1821).

47 Wood 2000: 13, 14, 85, 108; Cronon 1983: 121.

48 Graham 1939 (1820s).

49 Dunlop 1832: 106, 111.

50 Geddes: Pursh 1923: 109.

51 Magrath 1953: 90, 94-6. Even northward, along Georgian Bay, elms could reach diameters of seven or eight feet: A.H.R. 1924: 9.

52 Shirreff 1835: 33, 58, 84, 90, 98, 119, 127 (1833-34). "Canada" thistle, *Cirsium arvense*. Strickland reported farm fields half overrun with this same "common corn-thistle" in the Darlington area, 1825 (1970: 32).

53 Ibid., 162, 191, 195, 197, 202 (1833-34). Lower Canada's bog iron near Trois-Rivières was used by late 1600s; Upper Canada's first ironworks were set up in 1809 at Normandale. Tiger Dunlop also remarked the "papoa" "growing wild in the woods" at Long Point (1832: 111).

54 Head 1829: 192.

55 Burden et al. 1986; O'Brien 1976; Larson et al. 1999: 88-90.

56 Langton 1926: 23 (1833). Harrison: "Reminiscences of Robert Harrison, Asphodel Township," cited in Guillet 1957: 268 (1832). Logging was big business. In the course of a single day, 280 rafts came down the Otonobee through Peterborough, worked by 1,150 men. See *Peterborough Review*, 17 July 1864, cited in Guillet 1957: 267.

57 Strickland 1970, vol. 1, 15-19, 62, 162-3.

58 Ibid., 253-7, 290-1, and vol. 2, 122 (1831).

59 Ibid.; Reaman 1957: 150; Wood 2000: 109.

60 Tenche Cox, 1790s, cited in Mathews 1965: 21.

61 Strickland 1970, vol. 1, 274, 285 (1831).

62 Traill 1836: 53, 56, 77, 195, letters XIII, XIV (1832-33). Mrs Traill was a descendant of Catharine Parr, sixth wife of Henry VIII. Cholera killed six thousand in Lower Canada that year.

63 Ibid., 113 (1832); Traill 1838.

64 Traill 1836: 158, 234 (1832).

65 Traill 1999: 145.

66 Moodie 1913: 166, 337, 341, 372 (1852).

67 J.W. Dunbar Moodie, "The Land Jobber," *Roughing It in the Bush*, 2nd ed. (1852). Moodie 1959: 34 (1854).

68 Jameson 1972, vol. 1, 2, 7, 16, 66 (1837).

69 Ibid., vol. 1, 137-9, 176; vol. 1, 95 (1837).

70 Ibid., vol. 2, 103, 185, 194, 221-13, 229 (1837).

71 Sullivan 1853: 46.

72 King 1866 (1860s).

73 Haight 1986: 8, 23, 61, 106, 111.

74 Ibid., 125, 136, 152. Edwin Guillet reports 1,449 water-wheeled sawmills in southern Ontario in 1854 (1933: 248). The second, improved Welland Canal was started in 1845 and built courtesy of the Irish potato famines, the work of "between two and three thousand Irishmen ... indeed I believe none other, save Irishmen, ever think of offering their services" (C.H.C. 1846: 206.). Upper Canada College land endowment: Guillet 1946: 26. Reported deposits: Mitchell 1950: 64.

75 The Camp Borden area, concessions 5/6, 6/7, and 7/8, was "pine plain" from Lot 17 all the way to Lot 30 (Black 1822: 10). Benson 1820: Thompson 1968: 26, 34, 45 (1833-53). The pinery fire of 1849 is described by Rorke (1987: 91-2). The Beattie Family pinery was purchased by the Nature Conservancy of Canada in 1995 and was regulated in 1997 as the Beattie Pinery Provincial Nature Reserve (Varga and Schmelefske 1992). As late as 1906, there remained a large stand of red pine on the Angus plain, owned

by J.B. Smith and inspected by E.J. Zavitz; it was offered to the province for $3 per acre, for seven thousand acres, "but the Minister of Agriculture felt the price was too high" (Lambert 1967: 192).

76 Thompson 1968: 48 (1833-53). The remaining Minesing Swamp is about fifteen thousand acres in size, of which eleven thousand acres have been purchased (over thirty years) by the Nature Conservancy of Canada, with the Nottawasaga Valley Conservation Authority acting as the steward of this RAMSAR wetland (RAMSAR was an international treaty on wetland preservation signed in Ramsar, Iran, in 1971). In 2007 a stewardship intern found here Canada's first occurrence of Hine's emerald dragonfly (*Somatochlora hineana*), a U.S. endangered species.

77 Ibid., 52-3 (1833-53). See Catling 2001.

78 Thompson 1968: 69-70 (1833).

79 Logan 2005: 219; Lower 1938: 92-3. Most favoured: U.S.-French Convention of 1800.

80 Legget 1975: 105.

81 Lambert 1967: 41-5; Harris 2008: 279.

82 Innis, cited in Lower 1938: xvii. Also Lower 1938: 103-16, 134.

83 Rail lines: see Lower 1938: 184, Map 3. Ezra Eddy was an American lumberman who came north. In Ottawa, at age twenty-four, he started processing mill waste into washboards, tubs, and pails; he built a match factory in 1870 and sawmills in 1872; and he pioneered chemical pulping in the manufacture of paper in the late 1880s.

84 Grant 1882.

85 Traill 1836: 197 (1833); Traill 1969: 225 (1853).

86 Magrath 1953: 16; Traill 1836: 198-9 (1833).

87 Mathews 1965: 16.

88 *Pittsburgh, Its Industry and Commerce* (1870), 5, 6.

89 Bonnycastle 1842: 120 (1826-41); Pringle 1972 (1830s); Jameson 1972, vol. 2, 102 (1837). Also Weld 1855: 99.

90 Ontario Royal Commission on Forestry 1947: 5; Wood 2000: 14.

91 Hamilton 1893: 126, 129.

92 Thompson 1968: 236 (1834). John A. Macdonald to J.S. Macdonald, 1871, cited in Lambert 1967: 119. Wildfires were integral to rejuvenating boreal forest, and the historic record is full of "dark days" in southern settlements, the darkest and longest in 1716, 1780, 1785, and 1814 (Pyne 2007).

93 Kohl 1861, vol. 2, 41-3.

94 Weld 1855: 84-8.

95 In comparison with 1855 survey records, the slash fires resulted in significant declines in cedar, hemlock, red pine, sugar maple, and beech (Riley et al. 1996). Lymburner: Fox 1952: 191.

96 Pyne 2007: 143, 149; Bell 1882.

97 Richardson 1928: 69.

98 N.W. Beckwith, *Canadian Monthly*, June 1872, 527. Campbell 2005: 81.

99 Zavitz 1909: 1; Lambert 1967: 177.

100 Lambert 1967: 168; Kirkwood 2011.

101 Ibid., 280; Saunders 1932. In 2009 an agreement was reached to increase the area of Algonquin Park protected from logging to over 50 per cent, but no action was taken.

102 Tully 1904. See also other Toronto scientists: Hind 1851; Stupart 1913, 1917; Zavitz 1909: 22.

103 Zavitz 1909: 24.

104 Howe et al. 1913: 1, 3, 5, 10, 11, 31, 33, opposite 63. Howe also authored the "Forest Conditions in Nova Scotia" in 1912.

105 Ibid., 3, 5, 14, 16.

106 McKibben 1995.

107 Guelph Conference, *Conservation and Post-War Rehabilitation*.

108 Richardson 1944: v-xxvi. Richardson also organized a reconstruction meeting in Kingston in 1945. Irwin 1943: Irwin was editor of *Save Ontario Forests*.

109 Zavitz 1909: 6-17, 24, pt. 2. Below potential: OMNR 2001: 30; and Bacher 2011. Big picture: see Riley et al. 2003. Conservation blueprint: see Henson et al. 2005.

110 Lambert 1967: 192. W.E. Saunders, in Rutter 1949. Rondeau downburst: Larson et al. 1999: 25.

111 The Ontario Heritage Foundation, the Ministry of Natural Resources, and the Long Point Conservation Authority were signatories to the first conservation agreement on Backus, expiring 2010. The Nature Conservancy of Canada bought Backus in 2011, as well as 3,400 acres nearby, through the generosity of the W. Garfield Weston Foundation.

112 Forest birds: see regional references in Riley and Mohr 1994.

113 Keynes, in his "General Theory," 1936: Wilson 2002.

114 In Quebec, private land conservation can be recognized under the Natural Heritage Conservation Act; and in Ontario, under the Managed Forest and the Conservation Land Tax Incentive Programs. New York offers income-tax reductions to offset 25 per cent of property taxes for lands donated as conservation easements. Also in Ontario, the Forestry Act empowers municipalities, counties, and regional municipalities to pass bylaws "restricting and regulating the destruction of trees by cutting, burning or other means" but not to prohibit tree cutting.

115 Larson et al. 1999: 140.

Chapter Seven

1 Cooper 1827: i; Cooper 1848: 380. Also, Chapman and Pleznac 1982.

2 Atwater 1818: 116–25; Gray 1878: 92–4; Pauly 2007: 88–90; Gordon 1969: 7.

3 Transeau 1935: 423, 424, 426; Gordon 1969. See also Brewer and Vankat 2004; Macoun 1893.

4 No prairies: Gibson 1897: 215. U.S. equivalent: "A squirrel might travel from bough to bough for a thousand miles without seeing a flicker of sunshine on the ground" (Day 1953). Discounted museum (Herriot) collections: Boivin 1980: 121. Centennial history: Lambert 1967. Completely forested: Harris 2008: 306.

5 Bevan 1977. In the provincial nature reserve, shrub removal has occurred regularly, starting in 1982, and partial burns have occurred almost ever other year since 1978.

6 Bakowsky 1993; Faber-Langendoen and Maycock 1987.

7 Bakowsky and Riley 1994; Bakowsky 1993; Fenton 1941: 504.

8 Lajeunesse 1960; Reznicek 1983.

9 Biggar 1922, vol. 1, pt. 3, 290, 291 (1604). JR 12: 135; 18: 226; 24: 229, 253, 265; 55: 33. Lower Ottawa River *prairies* also noted by Heriot ("on either side, bordered by meadows," 1807: 108). In 1749 Pehr Kalm described some meadows at La Prairie kept open by spring floods and ice scour. Iroquois for meadow, *Kentaké* (Kentucky).

10 JR 54: 185–9; 55: 14, 193–201; 60: 155–6.

11 Montizambert 1883: 18, 22, 23, 26–8, 77.

12 Coyne 1903: 23, 25, 60, 61, 82, 83. And see Lajeunesse 1960.

13 Hennepin 1903: 59, 109 (1678–80); Lahontan 1905: 139, 320 (1687).

14 Cadillac 1701: 18; Cadillac 1702; B.4 in Lajeunesse 1960: 20–2, 240–2. Bison on the west side of the river only.

15 Cadillac 1904: De Léry 1749; C.1/C.4 in Lajeanesse 1960: 43, 47, 259; Bakowsky 1993.

16 Lumsden 1966; McNiff 1791; Lauriston 1952; Dunlop 1832: 114. Major Richardson was with the 1813 army retreat up the Thames and described the Moravian Delaware village as "in a small plain" (Casselman 1902: 208, 234–7).

17 Shirreff 1835: 190, 195, 203 (1833–34). Robert Gourlay described the Sandwich area in 1822 as "a plain, and timber most abounding is white, red and black oak, ash, elm, hickory, poplar, maple and chestnut" (1966: 176; see Milani 1971). Robert Stevenson called the land downstream of Chatham in 1843 the "richest I ever saw in any country. Six or seven feet deep of earth that would do for a garden, and ... grass plains stretching for miles ... the grass, particularly that called blue joint [*Calamagrostis canadensis*], furnishes excellent pasture and hay" (Guillet 1963).

18 Hennepin 1683: 71-1; Carver 1813: 102 (1766-68). Kalm 1966: opposite 705 (1750). Campbell 1937 (1792). Queenston Heights: Richardson, in Casselman 1902: 112.

19 Le Moine: JR 41: 126-9. Beschel 1967, elaborated by Catling et al. 1975; Slack et al. 1988; Reschke et al. 1999; Brownell and Riley 2000; Catling and Brownell 1995. New York alvars: see Gilman 1998.

20 Lakeside daisy, *Hymenoxys herbacea*: Weed 1890; Moseley 1897; Cusick 1988.

21 Henry 1969: 36, 61 (1761); McKenney 1827: 168; Jameson 1972, vol. 3, 258 (1837).

22 Since 1989, Ontario Parks and the Nature Conservancy of Canada, helped by the W. Garfield Weston Foundation, the Ohio Chapter of the Nature Conservancy, and private donors, secured more than eighteen thousand acres of alvar and twenty-five miles of coast, at Belanger Bay, Misery Bay, and Gore Bay. Drummond Island: McKenney 1827: 168; General Land Office 1890.

23 Type location of the endemic juniper sedge, *Carex juniperorum*: Moodie 1959: 108. Salmon River alvar: Brownell and Riley 2000: 209; Chapman 1860.

24 Talman 1946: 99-100.

25 Le Moine, and glasswort; Pursh 1923: 65. Pigeons, rattlesnakes: JR 42: 97; 43: 153; Campbell 1937: 212; Bartram 1895: 45. Glasswort, *Salicornia europaea*.

26 Smith was referring to the large and now-threatened New Jersey pine barrens (Smith 1906: 15, 17, 20, 23, 64). Albany pine barrens: Pursh 1923: 55; Barnes 2003: 3-6; 21; Campbell 1937: 234. The Albany barrens were forty thousand acres but are now reduced to three thousand acres, much of it conserved as the Albany Pine Bush Preserve. The pitch pine (*Pinus rigida*) and shrub oak plain are home to the endangered Karner blue butterfly, described in 1941 by entomologist Vladimir Nabakov, author of *Lolita*. The barrens are sustained by burning and the removal of invasives.

27 Gist quoted in Williams 1913. Burnett, quoted in Gordon 1969. Bradley 1906, cited in Sears 1926: 137. Gordon 1969: 54, 55.

28 Bliss 1885: 19, 32; Grautstein 1950-51: 53.

29 Goldie 1819: 41, 43, 56, 59.

30 Campbell 1837: 186-90; Weld 1807, vol. 2, 313-20.

31 Roe 1951: 248-54; Matthiessen 1987: 63. Since the last glaciation there have been no buffalo north of the Great Lakes. Fossil bison bones from near Kenora date to 3600 BP, when the warmer-than-present climate supported a pine-poplar woodland (McAndrews 1982).

32 Shirreff 1835: 218, 243-4.

33 Campbell 1937: 157, 161, 178. The strand was breached later, to provide ship access to Hamilton Bay.

34 Niagara-on-the-Lake prairies: "the country resembled Ickworth Park" (Sir William Lee, 1759, in Kirby 1972: 44); and "open turf" (Mrs Simcoe's description, in Innis 1965: 75). Simcoe: Cruikshank 1923, vol. 1, 18, 90, 288, 289; McNiff 1791.

35 Mrs Simcoe: Innis 1965: 89. Surveyors: McNiff and Jones 1795; Heriot 1807: 182. In 1817 Robert Gourlay called it the "Westminster Plains" (Gourlay 1966: 302), and it was still "oak plains" in 1850 (Steevens 1850). Smith initiated road work with "100 men" in 1793 (Innis 1965: 107; Smith 1793: 195; Cruikshank 1924, vol. 2, 89).

36 Pope 1834; Wood 2000: 106-7; Magrath 1953: 79; Talbot 1824, vol. 1; Richardson 1847: 123; Jameson 1972, vol. 2, 139 (1837). Also Robertson 1996: 4.

37 Wood 1958: 142; Wood 1961; Fergusson 1834; Campbell 1883. Shirreff described a farm in Dumfries seven miles north of Brantford: "Oak openings or plains ... The crops ... equal to any I had met with in America " (1835: 159). Side-oats grama grass, *Bouteloua curtipendula*.

38 Innis 1965: 110, 183, 186 (1793-95). Of the Burlington slopes, those at the Royal Botanical Gardens north of Cootes Paradise remain intact, but largely succeeding to red oak forest. Pilot burns have been conducted in the past few years to restore the site.

39 Aitkin 1793; Cruikshank 1924, vol. 2, 72. Simcoe had met Canise earlier in 1793 when he paid his respects at York and played with his son (Innis 1965: 105). Simcoe named Holland River and Landing after Samuel Holland, Dutch-born surveyor general of British North America.

40 Cruikshank 1924, vol. 2, 72. Kempenfelt Bay "Indian encampment": in Wilmot 1808, vol. 2, 181. Mrs Simcoe attributed her husband's return route to Old Sail (Innis 1965: 108). Graves 1951: 12.

41 Birdsall 1820: 10; Heidenreich 2007. Early farmers grazed De Grassi, and the Walkers also grazed it with sheep until 1938. In the late 1950s an effort was made to cut out invading seedlings. In 1972 Tony Reznicek, University of Michigan, brought its rarity to the attention of the family: the only red oak-white pine savanna in Simcoe County, still supporting little and big bluestem grass, Indian grass, and three rare sedges, among others. In 1973 a tennis court was built on part of it. Staff of the Ontario Ministry of Natural Resources inventoried it as an area of natural and scientific interest (ANSI), and the family agreed to try to restore a twenty-seven-acre site. Prescribed burns were conducted in 1999, 2001, and 2005, to stimulate oak regeneration and any dormant "seed bank" of prairie species. Reznicek and Maycock 1983. The two sand-prairie grasshoppers no longer at De Grassi by 1957 were *Circotettix verruculatus* and *Melanoplus fasciatus* (Walker 1957).

42 Wilmot 1811: 1-11; Miller 1968: 56, 57.

43 Asclepias or butterfly weed, *Asclepias tuberosa*; euphorbium, *Euphorbia corollata*; ranunculus, *Ranunculus rhomboideus*. Linear-leaved sundew, *Drosera linearis*; hairy honeysuckle, *Lonicera hirsuta*. Goldie 1819: 11, 16; Reznicek 1980.

44 Hunter 1948, pt. 2, 3.

45 Gould 1986; Reznicek 1980; Reznicek 1982. The surveyed town, St Albans, was in Gwillimbury Township (Mrs Simcoe's maiden name was Gwillim). Some lands were sold, but the core was intact when Reznicek rediscovered it. It was regulated as a Provincial Nature Reserve in 1994. Few pine have been removed, and no attempt has been made to stimulate its fading seed bank with ground fire. Some prairie species hang on, including the flowering spurge, *Euphorbia corollata*; prairie buttercup, *Ranunculus rhomboideus*; and prairie sand cherry, *Prunus pumila* var. *besseyi*.

46 Goldie 1819: 11, 16. The New Jersey pine barren once dominated the coastal plain and had many open sand barrens and acid bogs. It was designated the Pinelands National Reserve (the first in the United States) in 1978 and a UNESCO World Biosphere Reserve in 1983. Land use is controlled by a state-federal agency, the New Jersey Pinelands Commission.

47 Miller 1968: 73 (1829); Lizars 1913: 138. Markham: Cruikshank 1925, vol. 3, 192.

48 Wood lily, *Lilium philadelphicum* var. *andinum*; Karner blue, *Lycaeides melissa samuelis*. Among the butterflies now gone were the spicebush swallowtail, *Pterourus troilus*, on its host sassafras, and the scrub-oak hairstreak, *Satyrium edwardsii*, on its host black oak.

49 Varga 1999. In the Hamilton area, Anthony Goodban mapped 15,000 acres above and below the escarpment that early surveyors said were prairie or savanna, of which one acre of high-quality habitat survived (Goodban et al. 1996).

50 Wainio et al. 1976; Varga 1989; City of Toronto Department of Parks and Recreation 1992; Apfelbaum et al. 1993.

51 Reznicek 1982.

52 Coyne 1903: 52; Simcoe 1795; Chewett 1795: 77.

53 Szeicz and MacDonald 1991; Shirreff 1835; Draper et al. 2002.

54 Hambly 1795–96: 5–11; Heriot 1807: 175; Cruikshank 1926, vol. 4, opposite 102. Charlotteville was abandoned after 1816 and became one of the first places Zavitz started planting pine trees (Zavitz 1909, pt. 2, 5).

55 Howison 1821: 153–9; Burwell 1809: 185–96.

56 Barrett 1976: 85, 91.

57 Pope 1834; Wood 1961.

58 ODLF 1963.

59 Norfolk wasteland: Zavitz 1908; Norfolk Field Station No. 1, photograph, AO, RG-1-448-1; and AO, RG-1-448-1, A05582, "Trees and Bark Studies," photo of large

chestnut. Wild lupine, *Lupinus perennis*; dwarf chinquapin oak, *Quercus prinoides*; New Jersey tea, *Ceanothus americanus*. Karner blue; *Lycaeides melissa samueli*; frosted elfin, *Callophrys irus*. C.D.H. (Doug) Clarke, Ontario provincial biologist, pers. comm., at Brodie Club, Toronto, 1970s. Survey: Draper et al. 2002: 19.

60 Zavitz 1926; Zavitz 1909: 8.

61 Traill 1836: 58 (1832). Smith 1827, 29–36, in Guillet 1957: 31. Shirreff 1835: 124 (1833).

62 Traill 1994: 73 (*A Canadian Scene*, 1841), 198, 209 (*Forest Gleanings*, 1852). Traill 1906. Lupine, *Lupinus perennis*; painted cup, *Castilleja coccinea*; yellow mocassin, *Cypripedium calceolus (s.l.)*

63 Traill 1994: 199 (*Forest Gleanings*, 1852); Traill 1906: 69, 165; Catling 2001. In her 1855 *Canadian Settler's Guide* she noted that, on "those parts called plains, the abundance of wild fruits is yet greater than on the forest clearings." There was a tea-substitute, New Jersey tea, and she offered recipes for wild rice from Rice Lake: "The deer come down at night to feed on the rice-beds, and there the hunter often shoots them" (1969: 73, 105, 137). Lake levels stabilized by mill-dams ended the rice-beds.

64 Strickland 1970, vol. 1, 61; Catling et al. 1992; and Paul M. Catling, University of Ottawa, pers. comm. Since 2000 the Alderville First Nation has set aside 120 acres for restoration, part of a Rice Lake Plain Joint Initiative that also engages the Nature Conservancy of Canada, the Ganaraska and Lower Trent conservation authorities, the Northumberland County and Land Trust, and Ontario Parks. Almost one thousand new acres of the Rice Lake plain have been set aside for conservation and restoration, some of them now cleared and burned to restore prairie, such as at the Red Cloud Cemetery and the Ganaraska Forest. Rubidge 1835: 182.

65 Traill 1836: 86, 90 (1832); Strickland 1970: 66–7; Mulvaney et al. 1884; Guillet 1957: xlii.

66 U.S. Midwest: Roberson et al. 1997; Nuzzo 1986. Ontario: Catling et al. 1992; Bakowsky and Riley 1992.

67 Roche 1858.

68 Brunton 1986; Catling and Brownell 1998.

69 Dennis 1855b; 1855a: 198–219.

70 Stebbins 1935; Riley et al. 1996. Hotspot: Brownell and Riley 2000; Michigan Natural Features Inventory 1998. Quarries, invasives, and fire suppression remain the key threats.

71 Dennis 1855b; 1855a: 89.

72 Kelly and Larson 2007: 44, 56.

73 Cryptoendoliths; Larson et al. 2000: 109–10, 284; Wilson 2002: 4–5.

74 Pursh 1923: 44. Hart's-tongue fern, *Phyllitis scolopendrium* var. *americana*.

75 J.F. Calvert was an educator in London, Ontario, and T.M.C. Taylor was a botanist at the University of Toronto. Soper 1954; Soper 1962. Walking fern, *Camptosus rhizophyllus*.

76 Soper and Maycock 1963; Agassiz 1974: 153-4; Given and Soper 1981.

77 Saarnisto 1974; Riley 2003: 40-3; Watts 1979.

78 Northern goldenrod, *Solidago multirdiata*. Given and Soper 1981.

79 Quarry rehabilitation regulations often require burying quarry walls with fill material, rather than leaving intact cliffs or talus slopes.

80 Colborn et al. 1990: 144; Kaatz 1955; Gordon 1969: 24.

81 Thompson 1968: 54; Sullivan 1852: 52; C.H.C. 1846: 169. Head reported at Kempelfelt Bay in 1828 "green snakes … as numerous as earth worms in England after a shower of rain" (1829: 256).

82 Hambly 1804.

83 Saunders 1947: 169; Riley and Lindsay 1997: 4.

84 Jeglum et al. 1974; Riley 1989, 2011.

85 Riley and Lindsay 1997: 4.

86 Riley 1989; Case 1987. Prairie fringed-orchid, *Platanthera leucophaea*.

87 Thompson 1968: 55 (1834). Most of the Minesing Swamp, about ten thousand acres of which is left, has been purchased in the past thirty years by the Nature Conservancy of Canada on behalf of the Nottawasaga Valley Conservation Authority.

88 Rorke 1987: 28, 55 (1824-48).

89 Robertson 1971: 14.

90 Fox 1952: xvii. J. Bruce Falls, president of the Federation of Ontario Naturalists, asked Aird Lewis to chair a Natural Areas Fund Committee to purchase Dorcas Bay, and the committee succeeded, later founding the Nature Conservancy of Canada to serve as nature's real estate agents. Founders were Falls, Lewis, Antoon DeVos, David Fowle, Bill Gunn, and John Livingston.

91 Anonymous 1971; Barrett 1976: 156. The St Lawrence islands from Lac Saint-Pierre to Montreal have been gradually secured for conservation over the past thirty years by a project of the Nature Conservancy of Canada, *Un fleuve un parc*, helped by the government of Quebec, Environment Canada, and other groups and supporters.

92 Barrett 2000: 143.

93 In 1986 Long Point was designated a UNESCO World Biosphere Reserve. For recovery comparisons, see Reznicek and Catling 1998; Oldham and Reznicek 2006.

94 Fortune 1806-07: Mosquin 1991; Cuddy 1983. Neither white nor red spruce occurs at Alfred Bog. The Nature Conservancy of Canada acted on behalf of the conservation community, the Ottawa Field Naturalists' Club, and federal and provincial governments to purchase two large tracts for a Provincial Nature Reserve. Bog elfin butterfly, *Callophrys lanoraieensis*; Fletcher's dragonfly, *Williamsoni fletcheri*; spotted turtle, *Clemmys guttata*; white fringed-orchid, *Platanthera blephariglottis*; rhodora, *Rhododendron canadense*.

95 Snell 1987; Colborn et al. 1990: 144; Thompson 1968: 200–5 (1834).

96 Hinds won £100 for first prise, Fleming £75 for second. Both appear in supplement to the *Canadian Journal*, 1854, illustrated with the best early survey of the original Toronto islands and waterfront.

97 Thompson 1968; Kos-Rabcewicz-Zubrowski and Greening 1959: 88. By 1867, the Grand Trunk Railway was the largest railway system in the world, at 1,277 miles.

98 "Industrial showcase": Byers 2009.

99 Whillans 1999.

Chapter Eight

1 Hudsonian vision, 1670s to 1760s, based on English trade. Laurentian vision, based on French-British Montreal commerce: Innis 1956; Creighton 1956.

2 Harris 2008: 473. "Massive change" is not just a modern motif, *ergo* Mau 2004: "Now that we can do anything, what will we do?"

3 McAndrews et al. 1982; Riley 2003, 2011.

4 Pilon 1987: 71, 139; Lister 1988. James Isham illustrated the caribou hedge and snares that were in use in 1743 (Rich 1949: 153). "Other": analogous cultures such as the Barren Ground Naskapi of Labrador (Henriksen 1989).

5 One of Hudson's crew, Abacuck Prickett, left a record of the voyage (1811). The "partridges" were ptarmigan.

6 James 1973: 30, 33, 91, 104, 121–2 (1631). Vetch, beach pea, *Lathyrus maritimus*.

7 Schooling 1920. Christopher Wren, architect of St Paul's Cathedral, London, was one of the original shareholders in the company (Tyrrell 1931: 377).

8 Innis 1956: 45–8; JR 56: 177. Awatanik (1660): JR 45: 217–33 (1661); JR 46: 277–9. Albanel: JR 56: 159–207. Akimiski Island, or *Ouabaskou*, or *Agameske*, or white bear" island: JR 56: 304.

9 Marest: Tyrrell 1931: 64, 70; Bishop 1994: 126–7, 280. Musk-ox: Rousseau 1969; Tyrrell 1931: 262, 355; Banfield 1974. Samuel Hearne reported muskox "within nine miles of Prince of Wales's Fort" and Graham said they were "plentiful" just north and west of the Churchill River. Muskox pelts were stacked with the moose and buffalo pelts, and not recorded specifically. Williams 1969: 19, 35.

10 Rich 1949: cii; Lytwyn 2002. Traditions held; as late as the 1960s a public stoning took place at Severn, forcing a factor off the end of the dock; pers. comm., Chris Burke, Hudson Bay factor, Severn, 1978.

11 Rich 1949: cii, 125, 325; MacGregor 1954.

12 Houston et al. 2003: 11, 13, 34–9; type specimens of golden eagle, *Aquila chrysaetos*;

spruce grouse, *Falcipennis canadensis*; snowy owl, *Bubo scandiacus*; willow ptarmigan, *Lagopus lagopus*; northern hawk owl, *Surnia ulula*; gyrfalcon, *Falco rusticolus*; porcupine, *Erethizon dorsatum*; great blue heron, *Ardea herodias*; snow goose, *Chen caerulescens*; whooping crane, *Grus americana*; tundra swan, *Cygnus columbianus*; sandhill crane; *Grus canadesis*. Passenger pigeon were shipped to England from Severn in 1771, and were "numerous" on the Albany in 1840 and "common" at Moose Factory in 1860 (Schorger 1973: 261). Rich 1949: 125.

13 Lytwyn 2002: 24, 160–9; Hearne, cited in Williams 1969: l. Harris calls the smallpox "the background that, more than any other, underlies the modern history of western Canada" (2008: 382) A "measles and chincough" brought to the Red River in 1820 by the "colonists … was so fatal among the natives that one in fifty of the population … [died] all the way from Lac La Pluie [Rainy Lake] to Athabasca" (Wentzel 1807–24, vol. 1, 130).

14 Rich 1949: 81; Krech 1999: 205, 213–14, 222–9. Most natives accept this, says David Lester, U.S. Council of Energy Resource Tribes: "The debate is pretty much over as to whether [natives] should engage in economic development."

15 Jeremie 1926: 22; Glover 1962: 86–7; Banfield 1954: 12. Canada's population of caribou was down to perhaps a quarter-million in 1964 and rebounded to about two million. Pre-contact numbers of barren-ground caribou were as many as thirty million (Banfield 1974: 388; Loo 2006: 132). Barren-ground caribou, *Rangifer tarandus groenlandicus*; woodland caribou, *Rangifer tarandus caribou*.

16 Coats 1852: 43; Lytwyn 2002: 97–9, 104, 106.

17 Caribou harvest at York Factory and Severn House, and John Richardson: Lytwyn 2002: 152, 185, 186.

18 Brokx 1965: 80; Ahti and Hepburn 1967: 58; Sarkadi 2007; Lytwyn 2002.

19 1994: Scholten 1994. Magoun et al. 2005: Fig. 9. "Main caribou calving grounds": Lytwyn 2002: 97.

20 Fox 1965: 216; Williams 1969: 41, 84, 109; Lytwyn 2002: 111. Colen, cited in Lytwyn 2002: 92. Moose Fort: Rich 1954: 151. Andrew Graham shipped home from Severn in 1771 four new birds: great grey owl, *Strix nebulosa*; boreal chickadee, *Parus hudsonicus*; blackpoll warbler, *Dendroica striata*; and white-crowned sparrow, *Zonotrichia leucophrys* (Houston et al. 2003: 64). Graham shared at least ten handwritten copies of his *Observations on Hudson's Bay 1767–91* with contemporaries, some of whom published parts of it as their own (Williams 1969).

21 Lister 1988: 75; Wagner 1969: 122. Barnston, cited in Lytwyn 2002: 94–5; Rich 1949: 169. I benefited myself from a Cree weir in the Shagamu River in 1977. Fish weights: MacKay 1963; Dean 1994: 17.

22 Rich 1949: 129. Snowshoe hare, *Lepus americanus*; lynx, *Lynx canadensis*. HBC records permitted calculation of decadal cycles in lynx and hare, regular from 1820 to 1910, after which numbers stayed low (Elton and Nicholson 1942: 230).

23 Chappell 1817: 38, 39, 144, 153, 225.

24 Loo 2006: 93, 96; Krech 1999: 173–209. Krech surveyed the beaver harvest of six Algonquian groups on the Shield at six time periods from the 1600s to the 1800s. Among the three earliest, "the concept of conservation seems to have been largely absent," while the later three started new traditions of restraint and hunting territories. Based on adoption of conservation practices and trapping territories, the beaver population has rebounded to more than fifteen million (est. at fifty million in pre-contact North America). There were fewer than a dozen missions in the Canadian northwest before 1840 (Harris 2008: 396).

25 John Stoughton Dennis, of Upper Canada, was the surveyor sent to Red River. Thomas Scott, executed during Riel's uprising, was a surveyor. In 2003 the HBC was the largest retailer in Canada, with seventy thousand employees and sales of $7.4 billion. Howard 1970: 91. Liquor-trade ban: Rogers 1994: 307.

26 Brûlé 1621; Jurgens 1966; Hayes 2002: 55; Nute 1944: 20–3. Radisson's account of 1659–60 journey: B.III.1, in Jaenen 1996: 123 (see also JR 44: 237; JR 45: 163).

27 Chequamegon: JR 54: 13, 151, 165. Michilimackinac: JR 55: 101, 157–9. Sault Ste Marie: JR 54: 12, 131; JR 55: 107–15. Copper: JR 54: 163.

28 Messi-Sipi, Allouez, Marquette: JR 54: 185–9, 204, 215, 231. Compare Lahontan's map (1905: 284), with Ojibwa linear maps (Dewdney 1975).

29 Carver 1813: 70, 73, 83, 85, 87. Bur oak, *Quercus macrocarpa*, and northern pin oak, *Q. ellipsoidalis*, persist at sites like Oak Point at the mouth of the Rainy River, where there is also black cherry, *Prunus serotina*, a northwest range disjunction of almost two hundred miles. See Maycock et al. 1980.

30 Henry 1969: 186, 190, 192, 195. Pierre Boucher reported the copper boulder, and its Native miners, in 1664 (Montizambert 1883: 82–3; and see Henry 1969: 197n.).

31 Henry 1969: 202, 210, 222 (1767). Naniboujou is the hero of Algonquin creation myths. Ojibwa Caribou Clan (and common elk): McKenny 1827: 255.

32 McKenny 1827: 233–44 (1767). In 1804 the United States put a duty of 20–25 per cent on goods taken up the Pigeon River even though it was a shared border. The traders immediately moved to the Kaministikwia River and the United States lost the trade. Today, the number of pelicans on Lake of the Woods is fifteen thousand or so.

33 Masson 1960: 181. The trade was profitable; in 1791 £16,000 of expenditures yielded £88,000 on the London fur exchange (Siggins 2008: 35).

34 McKenney 1827: 180, 209, 255, 295, 313, 343, 350, 464, 477, 481. The Ontonagon boulder, reduced to 3,700 pounds of 95 per cent pure copper, was moved to the Smithsonian Institute in 1860; its return has long been sought by the Ojibwa.

35 Gough 1988: 1–12.

36 Kane 1968: 34–43, 318–22. Simpson's "flying canoe" travelled from York Factory to the Pacific, almost thirty-two hundred miles, in sixty-five days or so, but the speed grew in the telling, down to a reported crossing in thirty-eight days (Cowie 1913: 122).

37 Hind 1971; Morton 1980.

38 Hind 1971, vol. 1, 33, 36, 37. Hind also reported "butternut," not known that far northwest; it may have been bitternut hickory, *Carya cordiformis*. Neither occurs there now. The 1860 land surveys around Stanley indicate more than six square miles of sandy grass prairie: Bakowsky 1995, and Bakowsky, pers. comm., April 2009.

39 Hind 1971, vol. 1, 39, 40, 49, 53, 55, 63–4.

40 Ibid., 80, 81, 87, 89. One of the peatlands is the deepest large peatland in Onario, and many others are now parks. The Jesuits called the peatlands to the south the "trembling lands" in 1661 (JR 46: 141).

41 Hind 1971, vol. 1, 97, 99, 101, 103. Hind noted an infestation of "grasshoppers," likely the Rocky Mountain locust (*Melanoplus spretus*), now extinct. A native revolt, an "Indian outbreak," occurred in 1890 to reclaim Garden Island from the fishing company that had it, and a "posee" was "dispatched" to deal with the situation (*New York Times*, 14 August 1890). It is now a "recreation area" with a small unoccupied Native reserve. The sophisticated scrolls and maps of the Ojibwa were mimicked by the first linear maps of the west by the French (Dewdney 1975; compare Lahontan 1905: 284). The Ojibwa grew many crops, even spreading wild rice in appropriate habitats (Chapeske 2002). Later, the Dawson Trail would be built from Lake of the Woods west (Hind 1971, vol. 2, 214; Davidson-Hunt 2003).

42 Northern pin oak, *Quercus ellipsoidalis*. Spry 1968: 53, 58, 80. The Sable Island nature reserve has the largest sand dunes in northwest Ontario and nesting beaches for the endangered piping plover.

43 Ibid., 7–8.

44 Butler 1968: 159 (1870).

45 Pitcher's thistle, *Cirsium pitcheri*; Houghton's goldenrod, *Solidago houghtonii*. Voss 1978.

46 Agassiz 1850: 39, 52, 56, 64, 67, 74, 153, 406, 412. The furs taken at the Pic River post over the previous two years were, in order: muskrats, 4,449; marten, 699; mink, 699; otter, 316; lynx, 298; beaver, 151; ermine, 150; fisher, 149; bear, 41; fox, 39; wolverine, 1. No wolf pelts or caribou, moose, or deer hides.

47 Macoun 1979: 44. His collections would form the core of the Canadian Museum of Nature.

48 Grant 1873: 21–3. Arctic lady's-slipper, *Cypripedium passerinum*. Rediscovered in 1964 by University of Toronto botanist Jim Soper and sought out by many since, including myself in 1976. A campground in Pukaskwa National Park was built in its habitat. Arctic-alpine plant species on Lake Superior: Given and Soper 1981.

49 Grant 1873: 33–4, 46. "World's largest silver mine": Nute 1944: 168.

50 Grant 1873: 48, 50, 58–9, 353.

51 Redford 1992; Christensen 2004.

52 Legislative Assembly of Ontario 1901.

53 Ibid., 6, 8, 24, 26, 37, 50, 51. The name, Iroquois Falls, remembers the northern raids by the Iroquois.

54 Ibid., 55, 61, 73, 81. European larch sawfly, *Pristiphora erichsonii*. Tamarack was a preferred species for rail ties for the Canadian Pacific Railway, finished locally by 1918 (Kirkconnell 1919).

55 Legislative Assembly of Ontario 1901: 88, 91, 95.

56 Ibid., 121, 128, 137, 156–7.

57 Ibid., 159, 172, 178.

58 Ibid., 198, 206, 215, 230.

59 Ibid., 253, 256–9.

60 The "Ring of Fire" area of mineralization has given rise to Ontario's Far North Act and to enhanced government surveys (OMNR 2010).

61 One of the land commissioners was Duncan C. Scott, the Canadian poet who was recruited by John A. Macdonald into the Department of Indian Affairs, eventually rising to deputy superintendent.

62 Miller 1912: 6, 8. Quebec's boundary was first extended north to the Eastmain in 1898, and then to Hudson Bay and Ungava in 1912.

63 In 1920 HBC archivists in London began to respond to research requests. In 1975 the HBC donated its archives to Manitoba, making them publicly accessible. Miller 1912: 6, 8, 15, 16, 79, 133, 185, 198. "The [hare] skins are cut into strips ... [and] sewn together at the ends, and twisted into ropes, which are woven loosely into blankets and rough coats that very effectually keep out the most extreme cold."

64 The year 1906 marked an increase in competition for declining resources, when Revillon Frères (now Revlon) set up posts. Western religion came one hundred and fifty years after the HBC established its posts: a Methodist mission at Moose Factory in the 1840s, followed by Oblates at summer missions to Albany and Attawapiskat in the 1840s, and full-time missions at Albany in 1892, Attawapiskat 1893, and Winisk 1924. An Anglican mission was started at York Factory about 1846, followed by others at

Churchill and Severn. A full-time Anglican mission began at Moose Factory in 1851 and was competitive at Albany so that, in the 1950s, the majority of residents left to set up the Anglican community of Kashechewan across the river. By the 1970s, there were multiple evangelical missions at Severn and elsewhere. Oblates and Anglicans ran residential schools in Albany (closed in 1964), as did Anglicans in Moose Factory (Renison 1957).

65 Peterson 1957; Bergerud et al. 2007. The interactions of moose, wolf, white-tailed deer, and caribou, and their changing distributions and ranges, are beginning to be understood (Strickland 2009). Range decline: Ontario Woodland Caribou Recovery Team 2008. There are twenty dams on the Moose River system, for example, many of them peaking dams, which flush their impoundments downriver (Seyler 1997: 4).

66 The last two decades have seen in Ontario an "overall increase in northern birds" and "forest birds." Noteworthy has been the decline in insectivores, likely reflecting declines in insects (Cadman et al. 2007: 32, 36, 42, 48). The 2010 forest harvest in northern Ontario was 40-50 per cent less than the amount of fibre accruing through overall annual growth.

67 Severn HBC store: C. Burke, pers. comm., 1978. 50 per cent: see Canadian Boreal Initiative Framework, http://www.borealcanada.ca/framework-full-e.php. The Ontario Far North Act requires that 50 per cent of the north be identified for conservation, and Quebec's Plan Nord has committed to the same target.

68 Blancher and Wells 2005.

69 The Great Lakes basin currently has four of Canada's thirteen UNESCO world biosphere reserves - Long Point, Niagara Escarpment, Georgian Bay, and Frontenac Arch - and the Oak Ridges Moraine has been nominated for the same status. George Francis, University of Waterloo, advanced the concept of a Lake Superior Biosphere Reserve through the Canada/MAB Working Group on Biosphere Reserves in the 1990s, but "in the US portion of the basin, local hostility towards the United Nations generally (and also towards the U.S. federal government) ... made the further pursuit of the nomination unfeasible" (1999 MS, "Lake Superior Biosphere Reserve").

Chapter Nine

1 McNeill 2000: xxiv, 4, 360.

2 City-state world: updating the "global village" of Marshall McLuhan and "village world" of Richard White.

3 Diamond 1999: 429.

4 Asian fungus *Ophiostoma ulmi* carried by European elm bark beetle *Scolytus multistriatus* and related shothole borer *S. mali,* as well as the native elm bark beetle

Hylurgopinus rufipes. White elm, *Ulmus americana*, rock elm, *U. thomasii*, slippery elm, *U. rubra.* Manitoba maple, *Acer negundo*, was native southwest of lakes Huron and Michigan and, in Ontario, was observed as native in 1869 by John Macoun near Fort William along the Kam River; not native farther east, where agencies promoted it for windrow plantings.

5 Kock: University of Guelph *Elm Recovery Project Newsletter.* Diploid elms: Whittemore and Olsen 2011.

6 Asian longhorn beetle, *Anoplophora glabripennis*: Marshall 2006.

7 Ibid., 36.

8 Brown spruce longhorn beetle, *Tetropium fuscum.*

9 Chestnut blight fungus, *Cryphonectria (Endothia) parasitica*: Jaynes 1979: 111; Little 1995; McKeen 1995; the National Recovery Plan for American Chestnut, December 2001; Simberloff 2007.

10 The beech scale is *Cryptococcus fagisuga*, carrier of the invasive fungi, primarily *Nectria coccinea* var. *faginata* and *N. galligena.* See Ehrlich 1934.

11 Butternut blight fungus *Sirococcus clavigignenti-juglandacearum.* See Furnier et al. 1999.

12 Vic Mastro, USDA, Animal and Plant Health Inspection Service, October 2007, presentation to Natural Areas Conference, Cleveland, Ohio. Mastro et al. 2005.

13 Poland and McCullough 2006: 120. Or $100 billion (Mastro et al. 2005).

14 Tamarack sawfly, *Pristiphoa erichsonii*: Legislative Assembly of Ontario 1901; Girardin et al. 2002; Coppel and Leius 1955; Girardin et al. 2001. Fungal pathogen, *Lachnellula willkommii.* Some remote tamarack were not touched; there were aged tamaracks 550 years old in the Hudson Bay lowland in the 1970s.

15 Davis 1981a; Bhiry and Filion 1996. Hemlock woolly adelgid, *Adelges tsugae*; balsam woolly adelgid, *Adelges piceae.* By 2010, the ancient hemlock at the Joyce Kilmer Memorial Forest in the southern Appalachians were all dead.

16 White pine blister rust, *Cronartium ribicola*; managed by reducing its necessary alternating hosts, currants and gooseberries (*Ribes* spp.) and barberry (*Berberis* spp.). Eurasian pine shoot beetle, *Tomicus piniperda.* Eastern pine shoot borer, *Eucosma gloriole*; eastern white pine weevil, *Pissodes strobe*, respectively.

17 *Sirex* woodwasp, *Sirex noctilio.*

18 Winter moth, *Operophtera brumata.* New acorn and root weevils, *Curculio* spp., *Conotrachelus* spp., and *Cyrtepistomus castaneus*, the Japanese oak weevil; Lombardo and McCarthy 2008.

19 Flowering dogwood, *Cornus florida*; and anthracnose fungus (*Discula destructiva*): Dughtrey 1993; Santamour et al. 1989; Holzmueller et al. 2006.

20 Threats summarized as HIPPO: Habitat destruction, Invasive species, Pollution, Population, and Overharvesting (Wilson 2002: 50).

21 Wilson 1987; Wagner 2007; Pimentel et al. 1997; Crosby 1993: xiii.

22 Bird 1961; Marshall 2006: 278. Now-rare, native nine-spotted lady beetle, *Coccinella novemnotata.* Introduced ladybugs: multicoloured Asian lady beetle, *Harmonia axyridis,* and seven-spotted lady beetle, *Coccinella septempunctata.* The soybean aphid is *Aphis glycines.* See USDA Research Bulletin, http://www.ars.usda.gov/research/publications/publications.htm?SEQ_NO_115=134771.

23 Spruce budworm, *Choristoneura fumiferana;* eastern, forest, and northern tent caterpillars (*Malacosoma americanum, M. disstria, M. californicum pluviale*): Dean 1994; Marshall 2006: 170. Owlet moth, *Porthetria (Lymantria) dispar*: Forbush and Fernald 1896. Also, Pauly 2007: 136–7.

24 The tachinid fly, *Compsilura concinnata. Hyalophora cecropia,* and other giant silkworm moths of the *Saturnidae.* Elkinton and Boettner 2004; Wagner 2005; Stirling and Simberloff 2000. D.L. Wagner, presentation to Natural Areas Conference, Cleveland, Ohio, October 2007.

25 Two native bumble bees: rusty-patched bumble bee, *Bombus affinis,* and common eastern bumble bee, *B. impatiens. Nosema bombi* and *Crithidia bombi,* are imported on non-native bumble bees. Colla et al. 2006; Otterstatter and Thompson 2008; Cameron et al. 2010; York University press release, 28 May 2007.

26 Cox-Foster et al. 2007, and White Paper on "Importation of Non-Native Bumble Bees into North America." Varoa, *Varroa destructor.* Neonicotinoid and IMD insecticides: Northwest Michigan's Horticultural Research Station Weekly Update, 24 April 2008; Henry et al. 2012. Decline in insectivorous birds: Cadman et al. 2007: 38; Herriot 2009: 149–88.

27 Witch's brew: Abu-Asab et al. 2001; Haughton et al. 2003; Packer and Owen 2001; Zayed and Packer 2001; Gilpin and Soulé 1986; Carson 1962: 73 (the bee is *Megachile rotundata;* the fungi *Ascosphaera apis*). Also, Status of Pollinators in North America, 2007.

28 Darwin 1881. Ontario has nineteen species, Ohio twenty-two, New York eighteen; see Reynolds 1977. Victoria Nuzzo, Natural Area Consultants, presentation to Natural Areas Conference, Cleveland, Ohio, October 2007.

29 Aquatic mudworm, *Sparganophilus eisen*: Reynolds 1977. Victoria Nuzzo, Natural Area Consultants, presentation to Natural Areas Conference, Cleveland, Ohio, October 2007. Decline in diversity: Holdsworth et al. 2007. Deer numbers: Gubanyi et al. 2008: 121. Key driver: Wiegmann and Waller 2006. Cluster fly, *Pollenia rudis*: Marshall 2006: 481.

30 Perrings et al. 2002.

31 Rat, *Rattus norvegicus,* in Acadia: Marc Lescarbot, *Nova Francia.* House mouse, *Mus musculus;* cockroaches, *Periplaneta americana, P. australasiae, Blatta orientalis,*

B. germanica; bedbug, *Cimex lectularius*; house fly, *Musca domestica*; earwig, *Forficula auricularia*; as well as the non-native mosquito, *Aedes aegypti*.

32 Hessian flies, *Mayetiola destructor*, probably from southern Russia (see Pauly 2007: 35-50). Philadelphia: possibly an avian flu associated with passenger pigeons. End of wheat growing: Cronon 1983: 153. Upper Canada: Cruikshank 1925, vol. 3, 216. Lower Canada: Innis 1965 (1795).

33 Shtilmark 2003. The drug manufacturer Eugene Scheiffelin took on the Shakespearean cause.

34 Diamond 1999: 210; Garcilaso 1951: 530.

35 Smith 1917: 73 (1795); Langton 1926: 129 (1830s); Cronon 1983: 135-50.

36 John J. Mayer, presentation to Natural Areas Conference, Cleveland, Ohio, October 2007; Mayer and Brisbin 1991.

37 Porcine diseases: brucellosis (*Brucella suis*, which can cause recurrent flu-like condition in humans); *E. coli*; swine disease (*Streptococcus suis*); giardia (*Giardia duodenalis*); avian influenza; and pseudorabies (a herpes virus).

38 Carson: see Austin 2007: 274. Weeds and crop plants: see Larson et al. 2004. Iroquois cultivation: Parker 1910. Peach wild on beaches of Lake Erie: Casselman 1902: 291.

39 Scots pine, *Pinus sylvestris*, includes as many as twenty subspecies/genotypes. Some were imported from Germany to Zavitz's tree nursery at the Ontario Agricultural College in Guelph in 1904, "seventy-eight cents per thousand f.o.b. Hamburg, Germany" (Zavitz 1909: 28). Between 1906 and 1912, millions were distributed, recommended for farm windbreaks, such as in Wisconsin in the 1930s (Trenk 1934) and in Ontario until the 1970s (OMNR 1973). Dropped as a recommended species in Ontario in the 1980s (OMAF).

40 Norway maple, *Acer platanoides*. Variably sold as red maple, crimson king, Schwedler's maple, or other names. For impacts, see http://www.fs.fed.us/database/feis/plants/tree/acepla/all.html#IMPACTS. Webb et al. 2000.

41 Autumn olive and multiflora rose (*Eleagnus angustifolia* and *Rosa multiflora*, the latter producing up to a million seeds per plant per year); the buckthorns (*Rhamnus cathrartica* and *R. frangula*); purple loosestrife (*Lythrum salicaria*); Asian stilt grass (*Microstegium vimineum*, perhaps soon to enter Canada); European frog-bit (*Hydrocharis morsus-ranae*) and Eurasian watermilfoil (*Myriophyllum spicatum*); dog strangling vines (*Vincetoxicum nigrum* and *V. hirundinaria*, in Ontario before 1900 and spreading massively); Eurasian thistle (*Cirsium arvense*); spotted knapweed (*Centaurea maculosa*); reed grass (*Phragmites australis*); St John's-wort (*Hypericum perforatum*); garlic mustard (*Alliaria petiolata*). White et al. 1993; McKnight 1993; Stinson et al. 2006; Meekins and McCarthy 1999; Nuzzo 1993. Also, Invasive and

Exotic Species Compendium, Natural Areas Association; National Invasive Species Council; and USDA National Invasive Species Information Center.

42 Pauly 2007: 115-26. Bluegrass (*Poa pratensis*), tall fescue (*Festuca arundinacea*), orchard grass (*Dactylis glomerata*), timothy (*Phleum pratensis*), redtop (*Agrostis*), smooth brome (*Bromus inermis*), clover (*Trifolium*).

43 Ibid., 136-56. Experimental stations: Thirtieth Annual Report of the Fruit-Growers Association of Ontario, 1898.

44 Pauly 2007: 170-3.

45 To be objective rather than offended, terms like "novel ecosystems" are now applied (Hobbs et al. 2006).

46 Potato blight, *Phytophthora infestans*; potato, *Solanum tuberosum*. Crosby 1972: 183.

47 *Clostridium botulinum* neurotoxin type-E botulism. "Fish exposed to BONT/E show prolonged moribund states and express changes in behaviour and pigmentation, both of which ... could increase the likelihood of consumption by fish-eating birds. Thus ... live fish can represent a significant transport vector for BONT/E from its point of origin in the ecosystem to fish-eating birds" (Yule et al. 2006).

48 White-nose syndrome, *Geomyces destructans*; little brown bat, *Myotis lucifugus*; Blehert 2008; Frick et al. 2010; Foley et al. 2011. Frogs: chytrid fungus, *Batrachocytrium dendrobatidis*, possibly from Africa when clawed frogs were imported for human pregnancy tests (Mitchell 2008), now spread by waterfowl (Garmyn et al. 2012).

49 Nikiforuk 2006. H5N1 avian influenza (poultry virus, from Asia); new prion diseases, implicated in forced cannibalism by ungulates (transmissible spongiform encephalopathies, TSEs; bovine spongiform encephalopathy, BSE; transmissible mink encephalopathy, TME; chronic wasting disease, CWD; and Creutzbeldt-Jakob disease, CJD); weaponized anthrax (*Bacillus anthracis*, as if the original anthrax was not enough); methicillin-resistant *Staphylococcus aureus* (MRSA); vancomycin-resistant *Enterococcus* (VRE); crypto (*Cryptosporidium*); autoimmune deficiency syndrome (AIDS); Lyme disease (deer-hiking ticks carrying the bacterial spirochete *Borrelia burgdorferi*: Margos et al. 2008); West Nile disease (the bird killer, from Uganda); and severe acute respiratory syndrome (SARS, from China). The two "hospital diseases" (MRSA and *Clostridium difficile*) alone, in Canada in 2007, killed more than eight thousand individuals, more than the combined mortality from breast cancer and car accidents combined.

50 Wagner 1993: 3. Huang, at MIT, deals with the relationship of modern Shanghai to its expropriated, traditional countryside (2008).

51 Larson 2008: 17; Larson 2007a, b.

52 Soulé 1990.

Chapter Ten

1 Chinese tallow tree, *Tiadica sebifera*, spread into Gulf lowlands (Batista and Platt 2003). W.J. ("Bill") Platt, Louisiana State University, presentation to Natural Areas Conference, Cleveland, Ohio, October 2007. Crack willow, *Salix fragilis*.

2 Legislative Assembly of Ontario. 1901: 16, 24.

3 Wintergreen, *Gaultheria procumbens*; marsh violet, *Viola cucullata*; and four mosses. Terasmae and Anderson 1970; Bergeron and Brisson 1990.

4 Papal bull by Pope Innocent VIII, 1484: "It has ... come to Our ears [that] many persons of both sexes ... have blasted the produce of the earth." Oster 2004.

5 JR 30: 161; 46: 139. Tambora lowered global average temperatures 1.8°F (1°C) (Winchster 2003: 291).

6 Traill 1969: 202.

7 Heriot 1807: 266.

8 Strickland 1970, vol. 2, 23, 30; Hind 1851: 18, 25-7; Leitch 1975: 23.

9 Pawpaw, *Asimina triloba*; Osage orange, *Maclura pomifera*; and liquidambar, *Liquidambar styraciflua*. Coleman 1913: 71. The fossil and pollen assemblage from the Sangamonian interglacial of 125,000 BP indicates a mean July temperature 2°C (3.6°F) warmer than today (Westgate et al. 1999: 20). *Montreal Gazette*, 1929, vol. 157 (282); Lyell 1845, vol. 2, 103-6; Agassiz 1850: chapter 10; Coleman 1898-99.

10 Tully 1904; Stupart 1913, 1917; Munn et al. 1999.

11 Expanding heat island: C. Pérez, 2008, http://www.urbanheatislands.com/toronto, based on 18 July 1985 and 4 July 2004. The year 1998 was also the strongest El Niño year on record in over a century.

12 Wedges: Pacala and Socolow 2004. Global energy consumption is projected to increase 50 per cent by 2035.

13 Growth rates by 2041: Hemson 2013. Vehicle distances driven: Governments of Canada and the United States 2009: 8. Leapfrog: Doyle 2009.

14 20 per cent of installed capacity: UK Centre for Policy Studies, *Wind Chill*, 2008 (www.cps.org.uk/publications/reports/wind-chill-why-wind-energy-will-not-fill-the-uk-s-energy-gap/). Subsidies: for example, Ontario's Feed-In Tariff Program for private green-energy producers. Ontario's Green Energy Act (2009) also removed municipal controls over green-energy developments. Energy sprawl: McDonald et al. 2009.

15 Rich and Longcore 2006; Bidwell et al. 2007.

16 City-state world: see chapter 9, n.2.

17 JR 58: 105-7; McNeill 2000: 126-7, 291-4; Cronon 1991: 394.

18 The canals connecting the Mississippi with the Great Lakes are potential

transmission sites for the invasive bighead and silver carp (*Hypophthalmichthys nobilis*, and *H. molitrix*), both now in the Chicago connector canals.

19 Toronto proper (area code 416) has a population of 2.5 million, with 1.5 million jobs. The cities around Toronto (905) have a population of 4 million, with 1.8 million jobs. The latter cities are projected to take up 80 per cent of the now-to-2031 growth of the overall 416-905 region (Hemson 2005).

20 Arrival cities: Saunders 2010. *Favelas*: Perlman 1976. Three tracked measures of growth: population, jobs, and residential units (Hemson 2005). Of these, delivery of new jobs ("goods" jobs rather than "service" jobs) is the most difficult. Herman Daly lists three challenges to limiting economic growth: redistribution of wealth, population control, and reducing current consumption (2009).

21 Dyer 2004: 163.

22 The compensation of landowners for the environmental good and services they provide is part of the rural-benefits package of the European Union. In the United States, farmers are directly compensated for *not* planting crops, for example. Canada lags in this area, other than organizing pilot projects in Alternate Land Use Systems (ALUS). The motives are variously viewed as environmental or as replacing crop subsidies no longer acceptable internationally.

23 Lovelock 2006; Ruddiman and McIntyre 1981; Ruddiman et al. 2005.

24 Hays et al. 1976; Kawamura et al. 2007; Ritchie et al. 1983.

25 Super-interglacial: Imbrie and Imbrie 1979. Attention has also turned to cycles in "cosmic ray flux," by which celestial particles force cloud condensation and change temperatures (Veizer 2005).

26 Critchfield spruce, *Picea critchfieldii*; Delcourt 2002: 153.

27 Best estimate, averaging best low and best high scenarios postulated by the IPCC, Climate Change 2001 and 2007.

28 Remarks, 15 November 2007, Georgetown, Ontario.

29 Displacement: Internal Displacement Monitoring Centre, Norwegian Refugee Council, 2011.

30 Lomborg 2007: 50, 60, 76; Gore 2006. Lomborg remarks: 28 November 2007, Toronto, Ontario. $100 billion: *The Guardian*, 30 August 2010.

31 Raven: ABC's *In Conversation* (2002).

32 Stabilization models: Pacala and Socolow 2004. But actions can be unpredictable; hydrochlorofluorocarbons (HCFSs) used to replace ozone-depleting CFCs are potent greenhouse gasses.

33 Charles Darwin to Joseph Hooker, 13 July 1856 (http://www.darwinproject.ac.uk/entry-1924).

34 Walker 1987; Kelly and Larson 2007: 29.

35 Braun 1950. Various studies by Paul Maycock, especially Maycock 1979.

36 Gleason 1926; Gleason and Cronquist 1991: vi; Delcourt 2002: 154, 199; Hunter et al. 1988.

37 Delcourt 2002: 135-9.

38 Gulf of Mexico: Brunner 1982. Fig. 1 in Hunter et al. 1988. Pump down: Lovelock 2006: 53.

39 Delcourt and Delcourt 1987, 1991; Davis 1983; Davis 1981b; Woods and Davis 1989. Comparable figures for Europe: Huntley and Birks 1983, Delcourt 2002: 172.

40 IPCC, Climate Change 2001; Huntley 1991.

41 Woods and Davis 1989; Delcourt and Delcourt 1991: 27; Vander Wall 2001; Steele et al. 1993; Catling 2001.

42 Snell 1987. And Colborn et al. 1990: 144.

43 IPCC, Climate Change 2001; Moroff 1949: 21; IPCC 2007.

44 Delcourt 2002: 207. Stable boreal forests: IPCC, Climate Change 2001. Peatlands: Riley 2011: 16.

45 Davis and Botkin 1985.

46 Delcourt 2002: 207, 213; Delcourt and Delcourt 1991: 212.

Chapter Eleven

1 Bakowsky and Riley 1994.

2 Hough 1926; Day 1953: 334-8; Stewart 1951; Russell 1983; Abrams 1992; Abrams and Nowacki 2008; Kay 2007.

3 Watts 1979; Delcourt 2002: 186.

4 Szeicz and MacDonald 1991. Crawford Lake: Ekdahl et al. 2004.

5 Verrazano 1970: 133-43; Biggar 1922, vol. 1, pt. 3, 352 (1605) and 401, 405 (1606). Also, Morton 1637: 52-4; Wood 1977: 38.

6 Biggar 1929, vol. 3, pt. 1, 156; Sagard 1939: 90, 103, 104, 325 (corn fields, meadows, forests; *champs de bled, prairies, forests*).

7 Van der Donck 1841: 21 (1640s); Engelbrecht 2003: 9.

8 Kalm 1966, vol. 1, 374, and vol. 2, 597-8.

9 Smith 1906: 64, 72. Maude (1826: 59) was west of Bath, in upper New York State.

10 Traill 1906: 210 (Traill 1836: 62). Traill identified the deer grass as Indian grass, *Sorghastrum nutans*, and big bluestem, *Andropogon gerardii*: Traill 1906: 210-11. Martin at al. 1986; Traill 1999: 104.

11 Shirreff 1835: 159-60; 243-4; Pope 1834.

12 Biggar 1925, vol. 1, pt. 1, 276; Pyne 2007: 41, 92-3. Research by Richard Guyette and Daniel Dey, Ontario Forest Research Institute.

13 McKenney 1827: 359; Loope and Anderton 1998; Tanner 1987: maps of village sites; Anderton 1999. Summer camps: Tanner 1987.

14 Claudia Schaefer compared Bruce peninsula alvars using survey records and 1930 and 1978 air photos; forest closed in on more than half the alvars in the absence of fire. Unburned alvars had cedar older than five hundred years. Judith Jones made similar observations on Manitoulin. Catling concluded that prescribed burns on alvars were "an appropriate management consideration [if it can avoid] certain fire-susceptible features such as ancient trees and arthropod populations." Schaefer 1996; Jones and Reschke 2005; Catling and Brownell 1998.

15 Campbell and Campbell 1994.

16 "Unforested" refers to less than 25 per cent tree cover (http://www.carbon.cfs.nrcan. gc.ca/ForestInventory_e.html). Lieth and Whittaker 1975.

17 *Mon plus grand martyre*: Sagard 1939: 394. *Leur païs est decouuert, et pour la pluspart deserté*: Sagard 1939: 221. Long-distance visibility: Storck 2004: 79. The ague, mostly native malaria, was "a fever ... more or less epidemic every year during the autumnal season in all low and moist situations in every part of the continent" (Currie 1811).

18 Delcourt and Delcourt 1991: 87; Logan 2005: 91.

19 OMNR Press Release, 7 April 1992.

20 White-tailed deer currently number in excess of thirty million in North America, about as many as at the time of contact (Krech 1999: 153). Lyme disease in Europe was documented almost a century before North America; its origins are likely Eurasian (Margos et al. 2008).

21 Sioui 1992: xx, 10. James Der Derian, at Brown University, adds: "If you have the technological superiority, and you believe in your ethical superiority, these factors combine to a very nasty effect" (Mau 2004: 179).

22 Campbell 2005: 105–6; Krech 1999: 26–7; Nadasky 2005: 312. The idea of the "noble savage" originated with French lawyer Marc Lescarbot in 1609, ostensibly in admiration of the Mi'kmaq ("they are truly noble," in *Nova Francia*), and from poet John Dryden in 1665 ("I am as free as nature first made man ... when wild in woods the noble savage ran," in *The Conquest of Granada*). The concept was gently fanned by Lahontan (as *le bon sauvage*) and later inflamed as "a sarcastic emblem of racial inferiority" by Americans like John Crawfurd in 1859. A new veneer was added when it was re-released (and simultaneously debunked) as the "ecologically noble savage" by Kent Redford in 1990. It has enjoyed a resurgence as a modern Native self-image (Lescarbot 1609; Lahontan 1905; Redford 1990; Ellingson 2001). Margaret Atwood calls it part of the "long-standing white-into-Indian project" (1995).

23 Landform features: Neumann 2002: 147.

24 Palmer et al. 2005.

25 Paleoindian site: Storck 2004: 44; Ron Williamson, pers. comm., 17 February 2009.

26 Smith 1972 (1846); Douglas 1980: xxxiv. Much earlier, in 1762, General Thomas Gage, military governor of Canada, had declared a closed season on ruffed grouse, but his edict was ignored (Foster 1978: 10).

27 Sadler and Howard 2003: 279. "There was no skill": Douglas 1980: 155; Hamilton 1893: 152.

28 Matthiessen 1987: 167.

29 Morton 1980; Foster 1978: 10; Killan 1993: 6-7. The Royal Canadian Institute was chartered by Queen Victoria in 1851. A week after MacCallum tabled his report, Premier Mowat appointed the commission that would later recommend the creation of Algonquin Park.

30 Foster 1978: 3, 14, 144-8, 161, 201-19; Hewitt 1921. Commission of Conservation, 1909-20.

31 Loo 2006: 18-24, 183; Leopold 1933: 3.

32 Clarke 1964: 198.

33 Cadman et al. 1987; Cadman et al. 2007.

34 Breeding Bird Survey data 1987-2007: Cadman et al. 2007.

35 DDT, an organochlorine insecticide.

36 Barrett 1976: 163; McIlwraith 1894. In 2011 Carden had thirteen breeding pairs (Wildlife Preservation Canada).

37 Snyder 1957; Cadman et al. 1987; Sagard 1939: 218 (*entierement rouge ou incarnate*).

38 Eleven eggs in three nests at Sauble, 1 June 2009. The parabolic sand dunes behind Wasaga are the largest in Ontario, untouched in comparison with the beach and protected as parkland.

39 Lesser sandhill, *Grus canadensis rowani*; greater sandhill, *G.c. tabida*. Michigan sandhills rebounded to eight thousand birds by 1987 and more than this frequent the Baker Sanctuary alone, and thousands more the Jasper-Pulaski area in northwest Indiana. Lumsden 1971; Riley 1982; Cadman et al. 1987; Cadman et al. 2007: 33; Pedlar and Ross 1997.

40 D'Aillon: Johnston 1964: 5-6; Lumsden 1981; Sadler and Howard 2003.

41 Carolina coast: Larson 1903; Lumsden 1984.

42 Sagard 1939: 221.

43 McIlwraith 1894: 181.

44 McIlwraith 1894: 116; Macoun and Macoun 1909: 145; Biggar 1929, vol. 3, pt. 1, 62, 82. Fossils: Sadler and Howard 2003: 127. Early East Coast records of cranes without note of dominant colour: Cartier (1535); Xanctoigne (1542); Archer and Brereton (1602); Sagard (1623); d'Aillon (1626); Williams (1630s); Adriaen Van der Donck (1640s).

45 Lishman 1996. The Hudson Bay lowland is the logical place for a second breeding population.

46 See chapter 5.

47 Oosthoek 2007; Wilson and Daniels 2010.

48 Clarke 1961: 116; Matthiessen 1987: 63; Trigger 1987. Last specimen of wolverine in Grey County 1890: Peterson 1957. The pressure on wolf was unrelenting; thirty-three thousand wolves were culled in Ontario in ten years in the 1930s and 1940s alone (Loo 2006: 157–60).

49 Ten million: Seton 1909: 452; Huronia, Trois-Rivières, and Iroquoia: JR 8: 57; Trigger 1987. Also none in southwest Ontario "in the memory of man" by 1780s: Servos, in Kirby 1972. "Never were there": JR 40: 211.

50 Innis 1956; Ray 1987: 23. Seldom found: Smith 1852, vol. 1, Wa-Sha-Quon-Asin (Grey Owl) 1934: 47; Smith 1990: 83–5. The period 1900–19 saw the "lowest levels" of beaver across all North America: Novak 1987: 302.

51 Distefano 1987; Novak 1987: Figures 2, 8. Historic trends: Obbard et al. 1987: Figures 4, 26. Present Ontario harvest: 160,000 beaver pelts. The hunter and angler groups in Ontario federated in 1941.

52 Miner 1929: 6–14; Loo 2006: 63. Miner's killing of raptors spurred the wrath of naturalists, including Toronto's Brodie Club; pole trapping of raptors was stopped as a result, contrary to Miner's urging for "an incessant campaign against predatory animals and birds" (Hewitt 1921: 293). Miner advocated the creation of a national park at Point Pelee, on condition that its duck hunt and fur trapping continue, which they did until 1989 (Foster 1978: 194).

53 The deer nematode, or parasitic brain worm, *Parelaphostrongylus tenuis*, causes low mortality in white-tailed deer, higher mortality in elk, and serious mortality in moose and, especially, caribou. Pre-contact cohabitation of elk with deer may have been possible because of a stronger immunity in the extirpated eastern elk, and perhaps through partitioning the landscape, with the elk preferring open ground and porous soils that were freer from nematodes (Prestwood and Smith 1969; McIntosh et al. 2007).

54 Not possible to distinguish genetically between eastern and western North American cougars: Culver et al. 2000; Rosatte 2011.

55 Eastern wolf, *Canis lycaon*: Wilson et al. 2000; Voight and Berg 1987. The modern eastern coyote is a hybrid between the original western coyote (*Canis latrans*) and the eastern wolf (*C. lycaon*), a "coywolf" (*C. latrans* X *lycaon*).

56 Stritholt, in *All Points North*, June 2006. Plattsburg, New York: Paquet et al. 1999; White et al. 2001.

57 Rowe 1976.

58 Muir 1897: 701-9; Muir 1997: 839. Near the Holland River: Theberge and Theberge 1976. Muir was in Mono in the summer of 1864 and noted: "Much of Adjala and Mono is very uneven and somewhat sandy; many fields here are composed of abrupt gravel hillocks; inhabitants are nearly all Irish ... Botany was a term they had not heard before."

59 Killan 1993: 31; Campbell 2005: 39, 42, 214. The FON federated in 1931.

60 Provincial Parks, Conservation Reserves, Wilderness Areas, etc.; National Parks, Marine Areas, National Wildlife Areas, Heritage Rivers, Migratory Bird Sanctuaries, Conservation Authority lands (Henson et al. 2005: 87; Gray et al. 2009).

61 Killan 1993; Killan 1997. 1.3 per cent: part of environmental-non-government-organization response to Monzen Report. Property-tax reductions: see Conservation Land Act, Conservation Land Tax Incentive Program, Managed Forest Tax Incentive Program. *Legacy 2000* was a partnership of Ontario Parks and Nature Conservancy of Canada in 1996 to secure natural areas. Programs like the federal Natural Area program continue to match private dollars to achieve public conservation interests. Land-use policies: Ontario *Provincial Policy Statements*.

62 More than two-thirds of the lands nominated by Partnership for Public Lands regulated as protected areas (Riley et al. 1999).

63 Forest Accord: *Room to Grow*, OMNR 2002. Far north: Ontario Far North Act (2010) and parallel Quebec promise (OMNR 2010; Canadian Boreal Initiative).

64 Henson et al. 2005: 87-8 (n.d.). Toronto's twenty thousand acres: Reeves 1999: 237.

65 Many of old Toronto's parks were citizen gifts: Howard of High Park; R. Home Smith of the lower Humber; Susan Marie Denton of Dentonia Park; Alice Kilgour of Sunnybrook Park.

66 Miner 1929: 14.

67 Richard 2008.

68 McIlveen 2007; Lambert 1967: 183. Sterling Morton's son was one of the founders of the Morton Salt Company, later owner of prairies in Windsor, Ontario (Woodliffe 2008).

69 U.S. programs: Conservation Reserve Program; Wetland Reserve Program. Canada: Greencover Program; Alternate Land Use Services (Prince Edward Island, Manitoba, and Norfolk, Ontario); Payments for Ecological Goods and Services (Huron County, Ontario).

70 The Parkway Belt Planning and Development Act, 1973 is now the Ontario Planning and Development Act, 1994. Land-use policies: Ontario *Provincial Policy Statements*. Plans: Niagara Escarpment, Oak Ridges Moraine, Greenbelt.

71 Lowes discussed the idea in 1959 with the Hamilton Field Naturalists, including fellow member Robert Bateman. The "gap" is bridged today and part of the Bruce Trail.

72 First escarpment surveys: Cuddy et al. 1976. Second survey: Riley et al. 1996. Cliff ecology: Larson et al. 2000, 2004.

73 Mary O'Brien was a sister of Anthony Gapper, who, from the Gapper farm in Richmond Hill, collected mammals in the 1820s; Gapper's red-backed vole, *Clethrionomys gapperi*, was new to science but is no longer in Ontario south of the Bruce and Shield. Miller 1968: xii, 42 (1829); Gapper 1830; Dobbyn 1994: 60; Reaman 1971: 263.

74 Richardson 1944: 41; Smith 1852: 283-4.

75 Carman 1941.

76 Snyder 1930; Mayall 1939. In 1991 township forest cover reached 22 per cent, a level of restoration that allowed King to sell itself as a high-end destination for horse and nature lovers.

77 Toronto City Planning Board 1943: 17, cited by Reeves 1999: 233; Crombie 1990.

78 Rouge park: Varga et al. 1991. The Rouge Park that day was 10,500 acres, since grown to 11,600 acres and, in 2012, declared a candidate National Urban Park. The site of Ganatsekiagon in the park was saved from development but no archaeology has been underaken, although Huron, Seneca, and Missisauga lived there and all early travellers visited it. A portage led from there to Lake Simcoe. Natural heritage systems: Riley and Mohr 1994.

79 *Toronto Star*, 3 and 14 July 2001. Comparison figures for 472,000-acre Niagara Escarpment Plan area: natural (33 per cent), protection (34 per cent), rural (25 per cent), and urban/recreation/resource extraction (7 per cent).

80 Nature Conservancy of Canada and Oak Ridges Land Trust have each secured about three thousand acres by purchase/easement.

81 The 2010 net migration per 1,000 population was, for Canada +9, and for the United States +3 (Population Reference Bureau 2010 [Washington, D.C.]).

82 Hemson Consulting Ltd 2005; Ontario Provincial Policy Statement, under section 3 of the Planning Act, effective 1 March 2005. The requirement for 40 per cent intensification also applies to rural communities, where it forces greenfield development. Plans to leapfrog the *Greenbelt* are behind amendment 1 to the Places to Grow Act, which envisions adding to Simcoe County as many as a million more residents on as many as 29,000 urban acres, contrary to the 2008 Lake Simcoe Protection Act (see V. Doyle to Ontario Growth Secretariat, 26 September 2009).

83 Chant and Regier 1999; Fraser and Neary 2004. Cleveland Metroparks include 19,000 acres, and the Cleveland Museum of Natural History is notable for conserving a system of representative nature preserves.

84 Czucz et al. 2010; Hulchanski et al. 2010.

85 John Robarts, William Davis, Frank Miller, David Peterson, Bob Rae, Michael Harris, and Dalton McGuinty.

86 Martin 2005: 209.

87 Donlan et al. 2005; Burney et al. 2002.

88 Articles by Dave Foreman, Michael Soulé, Reed Noss, Gary Snyder, in *The Wildlands Project*, 1992. Noss et al. 1996.

89 Riley et al. 2003; Henson et al. 2005; Groves 2003.

90 Southern Ontario natural cover: conservation blueprint – 34 per cent (Henson et al. 2005); big picture – 35 per cent (Riley et al. 2003; Lovelock 2006: 133).

91 Riley and Mohr 1994. Species numbers worldwide: Rob Ross, Paleontological Research Institute, Ithaca, New York, pers. comm., October 2007. For example, about 64 per cent of all known species are insects and 95 per cent of all insect species are now extinct. The remainder, 5 per cent, are still extant, the greatest diversity of any time in the fossil record.

92 Hayward 2006; Munn et al. 1999. Understudied pesticides may still undermine human health and cause insect and insectivore, and hence trophic, declines.

Afterword

1 Lovelock 2006; Wilson 1978: 167; Wilson 1996: 183–99. *The Selfish Gene*, Richard Dawkins, 1976. Altruism gene: Wilson 1978: 149–67; Alvard 2002: 34, 40. See also Rockström et al. 2009 for itemization of "non-negotiable planetary pre-conditions" for a stable Earth.

2 Nudds 1987; Wilson 1992: 401.

3 Mann 2005: 326; Cook 1992.

4 Dextrase 1996. Threats: habitat destruction, invasive species, pollution, population growth, and over-harvesting. Wilson 2002: 50.

5 Quinn and Quinn 1983.

6 Sioui 1992: 8–19, 106; Crombie 1990.

7 Daly 2006; Daly 1992; Daly and Farley 2004; Costanza et al. 1997; Czucz et al. 2010.

8 Botkin 1990: 193; Huntley 1991; Peters and Darling 1985. See Mann 2005: 326.

9 Rowe 1990: 7; Leopold 1966: 205.

REFERENCES

Abrams, M.D. 1992. "Fire and the development of oak forest." *Bioscience* 42 (5): 346-53.

Abrams, M.D., and G.W. Nowacki. 2008. "Native Americans as active and passive promoters of mast and fruit trees in the eastern USA." *The Holocene* 18: 1123-37.

Abu-Asab, M.S., P.M. Peterson, S.G. Shetler, and S.S. Orli. 2001. "Earlier plant plowing in spring as a response to global warming in the Washington, DC, area." *Biodiversity Conservation* 10: 597-612.

Agassiz, L. 1974 (orig. 1850). *Lake Superior*. New York: Robert E. Krieger Publishing.

Agosta, W. 1996. *Bombadier Beetles and Fever Trees: A Close-Up Look at Chemical Warfare and Signals in Animals and Plants*. Reading, MA: Helix Books.

A.H.R. (A.H. Ross). 1924. *Reminiscences of North Sydenham*. Owen Sound, ON: Richardson, Bond and Wright.

Ahti, T., and R.L. Hepburn. 1967. "Preliminary studies on Woodland caribou range, especially on lichen stands, in Ontario." Ontario Department of Lands and Forests, *Research Report (Wildlife)* 74.

Aitkin, A.D. October 1793. "Sketch of the communication from York on Lake Ontario to Glouscester or Matchidash Bay Lake Huron." Archives of Ontario, Simcoe Map Collection, P.72. In E.A. Cruikshank, ed. *The Correspondence of Lieut. Governor John Graves Simcoe*, vol. 2, 1793-94. Toronto: Ontario Historical Society 1924.

Alvard, M.S. 2002. "Evolutionary theory, conservation, and human environmental impact." In C.E. Kay and R.T. Simmons, ed., *Wilderness and Political Ecology*. Salt Lake City: University of Utah Press. 28-43.

Amherst, J. 16 July 1763. Letter to Colonel Bouquet. http://www.nativeweb.org/pages/legal/amherst/lord_jeff.html.

Anderson, E. 1984. "Who's who in the Pleistocene: a mammalian bestiary." In P.S. Martin and R.G. Klein, eds., *Quaternary Extinctions*. Tucson: University of Arizona Press. 40-89.

Anderton, J.B. 1999. "Native American, fire-maintained blueberry patches in the coastal pine forests of the northern Great Lakes." *Great Lakes Geographer* 6 (1, 2): 29-39.

Anonymous (H.B. Small.) 1971 (orig. 1866). *The Canadian Handbook and Tourist's Guide*. Toronto: Coles Publications.

Anonymous. Manuscript on the Bower Family. Dufferin County Museum Family Archives.

Apfelbaum, S.I., J. Larson, A.W.H. Haney, et al. 1993. "Analysis of the historic and existing ecological conditions of significant oak woodlands at High Park, Toronto, Canada." Brodhead, WI: Applied Ecological Services.

Armstrong, A.H. 1968. "Thomas Adams and the Commission of Conservation." In L.O. Gertler, ed., *Planning the Canadian Environment*. Montreal: Harvest House. 17-35.

Armstrong, F.H. 2000. "George Jervis Goodhue." *Dictionary of Canadian Biography*, vol. 9, http://www.biographi.ca.

Atwater, C. 1818. "On the prairies and barrens of the west." *American Journal of Science* 1: 116-25.

Atwood, M. 1995. *Strange Things: The Malevolent North in Canadian Literature*. Oxford: Clarendon Press.

Austin, M.H. 2007 (orig. 1924). *The Land of Journey's Ending*. Sante Fe, NM: Sunstone Press.

Axtell, J. 1981. *The European and the Indian*. New York: Oxford University Press.

- 1994. "The exploration of Norumbega: Native perspectives." In E.W. Baker, E.A. Churchill, R. D'Abate, et al., eds., *American Beginnings: Exploration, Culture, and Cartography in the Land of Norumbega*. Lincoln: University of Nebraska Press. 150-65.

Bacher, J. 2011. *Two Billion Trees and Counting*. Toronto: Dundurn Press.

Baker, E.W., E.A. Churchill, R. D'Abate, et al., eds. 1994. *American Beginnings: Exploration, Culture, and Cartography in the Land of Norumbega*. Lincoln: University of Nebraska Press.

Bakowsky, W.D. 1993. "A review and assessment of prairie and savanna in site regions 7 and 6." Ontario Ministry of Natural Resources. Ontario: Gore and Storrie.

Bakowsky, W.D. 1995. "Rare communities of Ontario: western grassland and oak woodland relicts of northwestern Ontario." *NHIC Newsletter* 2 (3): 2-4.

Bakowsky, W.D., and J.L. Riley. 1994. "A survey of the prairies and savannas of southern Ontario. In R.G. Wickett, P.D. Lewis, A. Woodliffe, et al., eds., *Spirit of the Land, Our Prairie Legacy*. Windsor, ON: Dept. Parks and Recreation. 7-16.

Banfield, A.W.F. 1954. "Preliminary investigation of the Barren Ground caribou."

Department of Northern Affairs and Natural Resources, Ottawa, *Wildlife Management Bulletin*, 1: 10A.

- 1974. *The Mammals of Canada*. Toronto: University of Toronto Press.

Barnes, J.K. 2003. *Natural History of the Albany Pine Bush*. Albany, NY: New York State Museum.

Barnett, P.J. 1992. "Quaternary geology of Ontario." In P.C. Thurston, H.R. Williams, R.H. Sutcliffe, and G.M. Stott, eds., *Geology of Ontario*. Toronto: Ontario Geological Survey, Special Vol. 4. 1011-88.

Barrett, H. 1976. *The 19th Century Journals & Paintings of William Pope*. Toronto: M.F. Fehely Publishers.

Barrett, H.B. 2000. *Lore & Legends of Long Point*. Port Dover, ON: Patterson's Creek Press.

Bartlett, W.H. 1842. *Canadian Scenery Illustrated*. 2 vols. London: George Virtue.

Barton, B.S (O. Salvin, ed.). 1883. *Barton's Fragments of the Natural History of Pennsylvania*. London.

Bartram, J. 1895. *Observations on the Inhabitants, Climate, Soil, Rivers, Productions, Animals in His Travels from Pensilvania to Onondago, Oswego and the Lake Ontario*. London: J. Whiston and B. White.

Batista, W.B., and W.J. Platt. 2003. "Tree population response to hurricane disturbance." *Journal of Ecology* 91: 197-212.

Bean, L.J., and K.S. Saubel. 1972. *Temalpakh. Cahuilla Indian Knowledge*. Banning, CA: Malki Museum Press.

Becker, M.D. 1995. "Farmers and hunters of the eastern woodlands: a regional overview." In R.B. Morrison and C.R. Wilson, eds., *Native Peoples: The Canadian Experience*. Toronto: McClelland and Stewart. 317-22.

Bell, R. 1882. "The geographical distribution of the forest trees of Canada." *Montreal Horticultural Society Report 7. Montreal Gazette*.

Benn, C. 1998. *The Iroquois in the War of 1812*. Toronto: University of Toronto Press.

Benson, S.M. 1820. "Field notes of the Township of Essa." Ontario Crown Land Surveys, Field Note Book 2006. Peterborough, ON: OMNR.

- 19 June 1820. "Field notes of the Township of Mono East of Hurontario Street." Ontario Crown Land Surveys, Field Note Book 532. Peterborough, ON: OMNR.

Bergeron, Y., and J. Brisson. 1990. "Fire regime in red pine stands at the northern limit of the species' range." *Ecology* 71 (4): 1352-64.

Bergerud, A.T., S.N. Luttich, and L. Camps. 2007. *A Return of Caribou to Ungava*. Montreal and Kingston, ON: McGill-Queen's University Press.

Beschel, R.E. 1967. "Field trip no. 1 to the Kingston region." Canadian Botanical Association Annual Meeting.

Bevan, L. 1977. "The Windsor prairie." *Nature Canada* 6 (3): 7-12.

Bhiry, N., and L. Filion. 1996. "Mid-Holocene hemlock decline in eastern North America linked with phytophagous insect activity." *Quaternary Research* 45: 312-20.

Bidwell, R.G.S., R. Dick, P. Goering, et al. 2007. "Canadian dark sky initiatives." International Conference on the Quality of the Night Sky, Santa Cruz de la Palma, Canary Islands, Spain. 145-52.

Biggar, H.P., ed. 1922-33. *The Works of Samuel de Champlain*. Vols. 1-5. Toronto: Champlain Society.

Bird, R.D. 1961. "Ecology of the aspen parkland of western Canada in relation to land use." Canada Department of Agriculture, Research Branch. Publication 1066.

Birdsall, R. 1820. "Township of Innisfil." Ontario Crown Land Surveys, Field Note Book 474. Peterborough, ON: OMNR.

Bishop, C.A. 1994. "Northern Algonquians, 1550–1760." In E.S. Rogers and D.B. Smith, eds., *Aboriginal Ontario*. Toronto: Dundurn Press. 275-306.

Black, B.A., C.M. Ruffner, and M.D. Abrams. 2006. "Native American influences on the forest composition of the Allegheny plateau, northwest Pennsylvania." *Canadian Journal of Forest Research* 36: 1266-75.

Black, H. 1822. "Tosorontio Township." Ontario Crown Land Surveys, Field Note Book 474. Peterborough, ON: OMNR.

Black, R.D. 1934. "Charles Fothergill's notes on the natural history of eastern Canada, 1816-1837." *Royal Canadian Institute Transactions* 43 (20, pt. 1): 141-68.

Blancher, P. and J. Wells. 2005. "The boreal forest region: North America's bird nursery." Canadian Boreal Initiative and Boreal Songbird Initiative, Ottawa.

Blasco, S., A. Promaine, J. Shearer, et al. (Geological Survey of Canada). 2003. "Rediscovering past landscapes." Canadian Archaeological Association 36th Annual Conference, 2003, McMaster University, Hamilton, ON.

Blehert, D.S., A.C. Hicks, et al. 2008. "Bat white-nose syndrome: an emerging fungal pathogen." *Sciencexpress* 30 October 2008.

Bliss, E.F. (ed. and trans.) 1885. *Diary of David Zeisberger*. 2 vols. Cincinnati, OH: R. Clarke.

Bobrick, B. 2001. *Wide as the Waters*. New York: Penguin Books.

Bogaert, H.M. van den. (trans. and ed. C.T. Gehring and W.A. Starna). 1988. Syracuse, NY: Syracuse University Press.

Bogue, M.B. 2000. *Fishing the Great Lakes: An Environmental History 1783-1933*. Madison: University of Wisconsin Press.

Boivin, B. 1980. "Survey of Canadian herbaria." *Provancheria* 10.

Bonnycastle, R.H. 1842. *The Canadas in 1841*. Vol. 1. London: Henry Colburn.

Botkin, D. 1990. *Discordant Harmonies: A New Ecology for the Twenty-First Century*. New York: Oxford University Press.

Bouquet, H. 13 July 1763. Letter to General Amherst. http://www.nativeweb.org/pages/legal/amherst/lord_jeff.html.

"Bower, James, 6th child of James Bower, copied by Hugh Bower." Original MS in Red Deer, AB; copy in Dufferin Museum Family Archives, Rosemont, ON.

Bradford, W. 1856. "History of Plymouth Plantation." *Massachusetts Historical Society Collections*, series 4, vol. 3.

Bradley, C.P. 1906. "Journal of Cyrus P. Bradley." *Ohio Archaeological and Historical Quarterly* 15: 1-236.

Braun, E.L. 1950. *Deciduous Forests of Eastern North America*. Philadelphia: Blakiston.

Brébeuf, J. 1635. "Relation of what occurred among the Hurons in the year 1635." In E. Kenton, ed., *The Jesuit Relations and Allied Documents*. New York: Vanguard Press 1954. 98-117.

Brewer, L.G., and J.L. Vankat. 2004. "Description of the oak openings of northwestern Ohio at the time of Europe-American settlement." *Ohio Journal of Science* 104 (4): 76-85.

Brickell, J. 1737. *The Natural History of North Carolina*. Dublin: James Carson.

Broecker, W.S., G.H. Denton, L.R. Edwards, et al. 2010. "Putting the Younger Dryas cold event into context." *Quaternary Science Reviews* 29: 1078-81.

Brokx, P.A.J. 1965. "The Hudson Bay lowland as caribou habitat." MSC thesis, University of Guelph.

Brown, S.J. 1995. "Relessey: Mono Township and Relessey Cemetery Board." Mono, ON.

Brown, Steve. Dufferin County Museum. Pers. comm., April 2007.

Brownell, V.R., and J.L. Riley. 2000. "The alvars of Ontario: significant alvar natural areas in the Ontario Great Lakes Region." Don Mills, ON: Federation of Ontario Naturalists.

Brunner, C.A. 1982. "Paleoceanography of surface waters in the Gulf of Mexico during the Late Quaternary." *Quaternary Research* 17: 105-19.

Brunton, D.F. 1986. "A life science inventory of the Burnt Lands." Carleton Place, ON: OMNR.

Burden, E.T., J.H. McAndrews, and G. Norris. 1986. "Palynology of Indian and European forest clearance and farming in lake sediment cores from Awenda Provincial Park, Ontario." *Canadian Journal of Earth Sciences* 23: 43-54.

Burke, C. Pers. comm., 1978.

Burney, D.A., D.W. Steadman, and P.S. Martin. 2002. "Evolution's second chance." *Wild Earth* 12 (2): 12-15.

Burwell, M. 1809. "Talbot Road through Middleton." Ontario Crown Lake Survey Records Field Notes. Vol. 16. Peterborough, ON: OMNR.

Butler, W.F. 1968 (orig. 1872). *The Great Lone Land*. Edmonton: M.G. Hurtig.

Byers, M. 2009. *The York Club. A Centennial History*. Toronto: York Club.

Byrne, R., and J.H. McAndrews. 1975. "Pre-Columbian purslane in the New World." *Nature* 253: 726-27.

Cadillac, L. de. 1701. "Description of the Detroit River by M. de Lamothe, the commandant there." In E.J. Lajeunesse, ed., *Windsor Border Region*. Toronto: Champlain Society and University of Toronto Press 1960. B.2.

– 1702. "Extracts from Cadillac's description of Detroit in 1702." In E.J. Lajeunesse, ed., *The Windsor Border Region*. Toronto: Champlain Society and University of Toronto Press 1960. B.4.

– 1904. "Account of Detroit." *Michigan Pioneer and Historical Collections* 33: 131-51, http://clarke.cmich.edu/resource_tab/information_and_exhibits/i_arrived_at_detroit/cadillac.html.

Cadman, M.D., D.A. Sutherland, G.G. Beck, et al., eds. 2007. "Atlas of the breeding birds of Ontario, 2001-2005." Bird Studies Canada, Environment Canada, Ontario Field Ornithologists, OMNR, and Ontario Nature.

Cadman, M.D., P.F.J. Eagles, and F.M. Helleiner. 1987. *Atlas of the Breeding Birds of Ontario*. Waterloo, ON: University of Waterloo Press.

Cameron, S.A., J.D. Lozier, et al. 2010. "Patterns of widespread decline in North American bumble bees." PNAS, http://www.doi:10.1073/pnas.1014743108.

Campbell, Alexander. 1883. Letter in *The History of the County of Brant*. Toronto: Warner, Beers.

Campbell, C.E. 2005. *Shaped by the West Wind: Nature and History in Georgian Bay*. Vancouver: UBC Press.

Campbell, I.D., and C. Campbell. 1994. "The impact of Late Woodland land use on the forest landscape of southern Ontario." *Great Lakes Geographer* 1 (1): 21-9.

Campbell, I.D., and J.H. McAndrews. 1991. "Cluster analysis of Late Holocene pollen trends in Ontario." *Canadian Journal of Botany* 69: 1719-30.

– 1993. "Forest disequilibrium caused by rapid Little Ice Age cooling." *Nature* 366: 336-8.

Campbell, J. 1898 (22 January). "The oldest written records of the League of the Iroquois." *Canadian Institute Transactions*, 11/12, Semi-Centennial Memorial Volume. Toronto: Murray Printing. 245-72.

Campbell, P. 1937. *Travels in the Interior Inhabited Parts of North America in the Years 1791 and 1792*. Ed. H.H. Langton. Toronto: Champlain Society.

Carman, R.S. 1941. "The Glacial Pot Hole area, Durham County, Ontario." *Forestry Chronicle*, September: 110-20.

Carneiro, R.L. 1979. "Tree felling with the stone axe." In C. Kramer, ed., *Ethnoarchaeology: Implications of Ethnography for Archaeology*. New York:Columbia University Press. 21-58.

Carson, R. 1962. *Silent Spring*. Boston: Houghton-Mifflin.

Carver, J. 1813. *Three Years' Travels throughout the Interior Parks of North America.* Walpole, NH: Isaiah Thomas and Co.

Case, F.W. Jr. 1987. "Orchids of the western Great Lakes region." Cranbrook Institute of Science, *Bulletin* 48.

Casselman, A.C. 1902. *Richardson's War of 1812.* Toronto: Historical Publishing Co.

Casselman, J.M., and D.K. Cairns, eds. 2009. "Eels at the edge." *American Fisheries Society Symposium Series* 58: 1-460.

Catchpole, A.J.W., and M. Faurer. 1985. "Ship's log-books, sea ice and the cold summer of 1816 in Hudson Bay and its approaches." *Arctic* 38: 121-37.

Catling, Paul. Pers. comm., Department of Biology, University of Ottawa.

Catling, P.M. 2001. "Extinction and the importance of history and dependence in conservation." *Biodiversity* 2 (3): 2-14.

Catling, P.M., H. Goulet, and B. Kostiuk. 2008. "Decline of two open Champlain Sea dune systems in eastern Ontario and their characteristic and restricted plants and insects." *Canadian Field-Naturalist* 122: 99-117.

Catling, P.M., J.E. Cruise, K.L. McIntosh, and S.M. McKay. 1975. "Alvar vegetation in southern Ontario." *Ontario Field Biologist* 29 (2): 1-25.

Catling, P.M., and V.R. Brownell. 1995. "A review of the alvars of the Great Lakes region: distribution, composition, biogeography and protection." *Canadian Field-Naturalist* 109: 143-71.

- 1998. "Importance of fire in alvar ecosystems - evidence from the Burnt Lands, eastern Ontario." *Canadian Field-Naturalist* 112 (4): 661-7.

Catling, P.M., V.R. Catling, and S.M. McKay-Kuja. 1992. "The extent, floristic composition and maintenance of the Rice Lake plains, Ontario, based on historical records." *Canadian Field-Naturalist* 106: 73-86.

Cave, A.A. 1999. "The Delaware prophet Neolin: a reappraisal. *Ethnohistory* 46 (2): 265-90.

Champlain, Samuel de. 1612, 1613. Maps 70, 75. In D. Hayes, *Historical Atlas of Canada.* Vancouver: Douglas and McIntyre 2002. 52, 54.

- 1632. "Carte de la nouvelle france: augmentee depuis la derniere servant as la navigation faicte en son vray meridian." National Museum of Canada 51970.

Chant, D.A., and H.A. Regier. 1999. "Discussion and conclusions." In B.I. Roots, D.A. Chant, and C.E. Heidenreich, eds., *Special Places: The Changing Ecosystems of the Toronto Region.* Vancouver: UBC Press. 295-303.

Chapeskie, A. 2002. "Liberating Canada from settler mythology." In J. Bird, L. Land, and M. Macadam, eds., *Nation to Nation.* Toronto: Irwin Publishing. 74-84.

Chapman, E.J. 1860. "On the geology of Belleville and the surrounding district."*Canadian Journal* 5 (25): 41-8.

Chapman, K.A. and R.J. Pleznac. 1982. *Public Prairies of Michigan.* Kalamazoo, MI: Zemlick.

Chapman, L.J., and D.F. Putnam. 1984. "The physiography of Ontario." *Ontario Geological Survey*, Special Vol. 2.

Chappell, E. 1817. *Narrative of a Voyage to Hudson's Bay.* London: J. Mawman.

Charlevoix, P.F.X. 1761. *Journal of a Voyage to North America.* London: R. and J. Dodsley.

C.H.C. 1846. *It Blows, It Snows; A Winter's Rambles through Canada.* Dublin: P.W. Brady.

Cheadle, W.B. 1931 (orig. 1865). *Cheadle's Journal of Trip across Canada 1862–1863.* Ottawa: Graphic Publishers.

Chewett, W. 1795. "Report of Long Point etc." Ontario Crown Land Survey Records, vol. 1. Peterborough, ON: OMNR.

Christensen, J. 2004. "Win-win illusions." *Conservation Practice* 5 (1): 12–18.

Churcher, C.S., and M.B. Fenton. 1968. "Vertebrate remains from the Dickson limestone quarry, Halton County, Ontario, Canada." *National Speleological Society Bulletin* 30: 11–16.

Churcher, C.S., and R.R. Dods. 1979. "*Ochotona* and other vertebrates of possible Illinoian age from Kelso cave, Halton County, Ontario." *Canadian Journal of Earth Sciences* 16: 1613–20.

City of Toronto, Department of Parks and Recreation. 1992. "High Park proposals for restoration and management."

Clarke, C.H.D. 1961. "Wildlife in perspective." In *Resources for Tomorrow. Conference Background Papers.* Ottawa: Queen's Printer.

– 1964. "A philosophy of conservation." In J.R. Dymond, ed., *Fish and Wildlife.* Toronto: Longmans. 187–98.

– 1970s. Pers. comm., Brodie Club.

Coats, W. 1852. *The Geography of Hudson's Bay* (ed. J. Barrow). London: Hakluyt Society.

Colborn, T.E., A. Davidson, S.N. Green, et al. 1990. *Great Lakes. Great Legacy?* Washington, DC: Conservation Foundation; and Ottawa: Institute for Research on Public Policy.

Colden, C. 1747 (repr. 1972). *The History of the Five Indian Nations of Canada.* Toronto: Coles Publishing.

Coleman, A.P. 1898–99. "The Iroquois Beach." Royal Canadian Institute *Transactions* 6: 29–44.

– 1913. "Geology of the Toronto region." In J.H. Faull, ed., *The Natural History of the Toronto Region.* Toronto: Royal Canadian Institute. 51–81.

Coleman, Elmer. Pers. comm., 4 April 1999.

Colla, S.R., and L. Packer. 2008. "Evidence for decline in eastern North American bumblebees (Hymenoptera: Apidae), with special focus on *Bombus affinis* Cresson."

Biodiversity and Conservation 17 (6): 1379-91.

Cannon, W.B. 1915. *Bodily Changes in Pain, Hunger, Fear and Rage.* New York: D. Appleton and Co.

Cook, F., ed. 1887. *Journals of the Military Expedition of Major General John Sullivan against the Six Nations of Indians in 1779.* Auburn, NY: Knapp, Peck and Thomson.

Cook, R. 14 October 1992. "1492 and all that: making a garden out of the wilderness." Seventh Annual Robarts Lecture, York University, Toronto. http://www.yorku.ca/robarts/projects/lectures/pdf/rl_cook.pdf.

- ed., 1993. *The Voyages of Jacques Cartier.* Toronto: University of Toronto Press.

- 1998. "Canada: an environment without a history. Themes and issues in North American environmental history." 24-26 April 1998, University of Toronto.

Cooper, J.F. 1823 (repr. 1962). *The Pioneers.* New York: Washington Square Press.

- 1827. *The Prairie.* 3 vols. London: Henry Colburn.

- 1848. *The Oak Openings, or Bee-Hunter.* London: Bentley.

Cooper, S.F. 1850. *Rural Hours, by a Lady.* New York: Putnam.

Coppel, H.C., and K. Leius. 1955. "History of the larch sawfly." *Entomologist* 87: 103-11.

Costanza, R., R. d'Arge, R. de Groot, et al. 1997. "The value of the world's ecosystem services and natural capital." *Nature* 387: 253-60.

Cottam, C., and P. Knappen. 1939. "Food of some uncommon North American birds." *Auk* 66: 155-8.

Cox-Foster, D.L., S. Conlan, E.C. Holmes, et al. 2007. A metagenomic survey of microbes in honey bee colony collapse disorder. *Science* 318: 283-7.

Coyne, J.H. 1895. *The Country of the Neutrals from Champlain to Talbot.* St Thomas, ON: Times Print.

- 1903. "Explorations of the Great Lakes 1669-1670, by Dollier de Casson and De Bréhant de Galinée." *Ontario Historical Society, Papers and Records* 4: i-xxxvii, 1-89.

Craig, G.M., ed. 1955. *Early Travellers in the Canadas 1791-1867.* Toronto: Macmillan.

Cranston, J.H. 1949. *Etienne Brûle: Immortal Scoundrel.* Toronto: Ryerson Press.

Crawford, G.W., and D.G. Smith. 2003. "Paleoethnobotany in the northeast." In P.E. Minnis, ed., *People and Plants in Ancient Eastern North America.* Washington, DC: Smithsonian Books. 172-257.

Creighton, Donald. *The Empire of the St. Lawrence: A Study in Commerce and Politics; Originally Published as* The Commercial Empire of the St. Lawrence, 1760-1850. Toronto: Macmillan 1956.

Crombie, D. 1990. *Watershed: Interim Report of the Royal Commission on the Future of the Toronto Waterfront.* Toronto: Waterfront Regeneration Trust.

Cronon, W. 1983. *Changes in the Land: Indians, Colonists, and the Ecology of New England.* New York: Hill and Wang.

- 1991. *Nature's Metropolis. Chicago and the Great West*. New York: W.W. Norton and Co.

Crosby, A.W. 1972. *The Columbian Exchange: Biological and Cultural Consequences of 1492*. Westport, CT: Greenwood Press.

- 1993. *Germs, Seeds and Animals: Studies in Ecological History*. New York: M.E. Sharpe.

Crowder, A.A., J.P. Smol, R. Ralrymple, et al. 1996. "Rates of natural and anthropogenic change in shoreline habitats in the Kingston basin, Lake Ontario." *Canadian Journal of Fisheries and Aquatic Sciences* 53 (supplement 1): 121-35.

Cruikshank, E.A. 1923-31. *The Correspondence of Lieut. Governor John Graves Simcoe*. Vols. 1-4. Toronto: Ontario Historical Society.

Cuddy, D. 1983. "Alfred Bog." *Trail & Landscape* 17 (3): 145-63.

Cuddy, D.G., K.M. Lindsay, and I.D. Macdonald. 1976. "Significant natural areas along the Niagara Escarpment." OMNR, Parks Planning Branch.

Culver, M., W.E. Johnson, J. Pecon-Slattery, et al. 2000. "Genomic ancestry of the American puma (*Puma concolor*)." *Journal of Heredity* 91: 186-97.

Cunliffe, B. 2001. *Facing the Ocean*. New York: Oxford University Press.

Currie, W. 1811. *A View of the Diseases Most Prevalent in the U.S.A.* Philadelphia: J. and A.Y. Humphreys.

Cusick, A.W. 1988. "Alvar landforms and plant communities in Ohio." Columbus: Ohio Department of Natural Resources.

Czucz, B., J.P. Gathman, and G.R. McPherson. 2010. "The impending peak and decline of petroleum production." *Conservation Biology* 24 (4): 948-56.

Dadswell, M.J. 1974. "Distribution, ecology and postglacial dispersal of certain crustaceans and fishes in eastern North America." National Museum of Natural Sciences, *Publications in Zoology* 11.

Dahl, T.E. 1990. "Wetland losses in the United States - 1780s to 1980s." Washington, DC: U.S. Department of the Interior, Fish and Wildlife Service.

Daly, H.E. 1992. *Steady-State Economics*. 2nd ed. Washington, DC: Island Press.

- 2006. "Steady-state economics." In M.J. Groom, G.K. Meffe, and C.R. Carrol, eds., *Principles of Conservation Biology*. Sunderland, MA: Sinauer Associates. 139-40.

- 2009. "Three anathemas on limiting economic growth." *Conservation Biology* 23 (2): 252-3.

Daly, H.E., and J. Farley. 2004. *Ecological Economics*. Washington, DC.: Island Press.

Daly, R.A. 1934. *The Changing World of the Ice Age*. New Haven, CT: Yale University Press.

Darwin, C. 1881. *The Formation of Vegetable Mould through the Actions of Worms, with Observations on their Habits*. New York: Appleton.

Davidson-Hunt, I.J. 2003. "Indigenous lands management, cultural landscapes and Anishinaabe people of Shoal Lake, northwestern Ontario, Canada." *Environments* 31 (1): 21-41

Davis, M.B. 1981a. "Outbreaks of forest pathogens in Quaternary history." *Proceedings of the IV International Palynological Conference* 3: 216-27.

- 1981b. "Quaternary history and the stability of forest communities." In D.C. West et al., eds., *Forest Succession: Concepts and Application*. New York, Springer-Verlag. 132-53.

- 1983. "Quaternary history of deciduous forests of eastern North America and Europe." *Annals of the Missouri Botanical Gardens* 70 (3): 550-63.

Davis, M.B., and D.B. Botkin. 1985. "Sensitivity of cool-temperature forests and their fossil pollen record to rapid temperature change." *Quaternary Research* 23: 327-40.

Dawkins, W.B. 1874. *Cave Hunting: Researches on the Evidence of Caves respecting the Early Inhabitants of Europe*. London: Macmillan.

Dawson, J.W. 1880. *Fossil Men and Their Modern Representatives*. Montreal: Dawson.

Day, G.M. 1953. "The Indian as an ecological factor in the northeastern forest." *Ecology* 34 (2): 329-46.

Dean, W.G. 1994. "The Ontario landscape, *circa* A.D. 1600." In E.S. Rogers and D.B. Smith, eds., *Aboriginal Ontario*. Toronto: Dundurn Press. 17.

Delcourt, H.R. 2002. *Forests in Peril*. Blacksburg, VA: McDonald and Woodward.

Delcourt, H.R., and P.A. Delcourt. 1991. *Quaternary Ecology*. New York: Chapman and Hall.

Delcourt, P.A., and H.R. Delcourt. 1981. "Vegetation maps for eastern North America: 40,000 yrs. BP to the present." In R.C. Romans, ed., *Geobotany II*. New York: Plenum Press. 123-65.

- 1987. "Long-term forest dynamics of the temperate zone." *Ecological Studies* 63.

De Léry, J.P.C. 1749. In E.J. Lajeunesse, ed. *The Windsor Border Region*. Toronto: Champlain Society and University of Toronto Press 1960; and http://www.clarke.cmich.edu/detroit/delery1749.htm. c.1, c.4.

Dennis, J.S. 1855a. "Field Notes of Lindsay Saugeen Peninsula." Ontario Crown Land Surveys, Field Note Book 3259. Peterborough, ON: OMNR.

- 1855b. "Field Notes of St. Edmunds Saugeen Peninsula." Ontario Crown Land Surveys, Field Note Book 3258. Peterborough, ON: OMNR.

Denonville, M. 1687. *New York Colonial Documents, Vol. IX*. Cited in P.J. Robinson, *Toronto during the French Regime*. Toronto: Ryerson Press 1933. 368-9.

Dewdney, S. 1975. *The Sacred Scrolls of the Southern Ojibway*. Toronto: University of Toronto Press.

Dextrase, A. 1996. "Alien species in the Great Lakes of North America: problems, solutions and outstanding issues." In C.D.A. Rubec and G.O. Lee, eds., *Conserving Vitality and Diversity. Proceeding of the World Conservation Congress Workshop on Alien Invasive Species*. 63-81.

Diamond, J. 1999. *Guns, Germs and Steel*. New York: W.W. Norton.

Dibb, G.C. 2004. "The Madine phase." In L.J. Jackson and A. Hinshelwood, eds., *The Late Palaeo-Indian Great Lakes*. Gatineau, QC: Canadian Museum of Civilization, *Archaeology Paper* 165. 117–61.

Dictionary of Canadian Biography. http://www.biographi.ca. *See also* individual biographies.

Dickason, O.P., and L.C. Green. 1989. *The Law of Nations and the New World*. Edmonton: University of Alberta Press.

Distefano, J.J. 1987. "Wild furbearer management in the northeastern United States." In M. Novak, J.A. Baker, et al., eds., *Wild Furbearer Management and Conservation in North America*. Toronto: OMNR and Ontario Tappers Association. 1077–90.

Dobbyn, J. 1994. *Atlas of the Mammals of Ontario*. Don Mills, ON: Federation of Ontario Naturalists.

Dobyns, H.F. 1966. "Estimating aboriginal American population: an appraisal of techniques with a New Hemispheric estimate." *Current Anthropology* 7: 395–416.

– 1983. *Their Number Become Thinned*. Knoxville: University of Tennessee Press.

Donlan, J., H.W. Greene, J. Berger, et al. 2005. "Re-wilding North America." *Nature* 436: 913–14.

Dore, W.G. 1971. "Canada onion: its method of spread into Canada." *Naturaliste canadien* 98: 385–400.

Douglas, R.A. 1980. *John Prince*. Toronto: Champlain Society.

Doyle, V. 2009. "Comments on Ontario Growth Secretariat report 'Simcoe area: a strategic vision for growth.'"

Draper, W.B., M.E. Gartshore, and J.M. Bowles. 2002. "Life science inventory and evaluation of St. Williams Crown Forest." Vol. 1. OMNR.

Dughtrey, M. 1993. "Dogwood anthracnose: native fungus or exotic invader." In B.N. McKnight, ed., *Biological Polution*. Indianapolis, IN: Indiana Academy of Science. 23–33.

Dulhut, D.G. 1697. In C.J. Jaenen, *The French Regime in the Upper Country of Canada during the Seventeenth Century*. Toronto: Champlain Society 1996. B.vii.1.

Duncan, S.R., S. Scott, and C.J. Duncan. 2005. "Reappraisal of the historical selective pressures for the *CCR5-Δ32* mutation." *Medical Humanities* 42: 205–8.

Dunlap, C.J. 2001. "Law and military interventions: preserving humanitarian values in 21st century conflicts." Working Paper. Boston, MA: Kennedy School of Government, Harvard University.

Dunlop, W. ("A Backwoodsman") 1832. *Statistical Sketches of Upper Canada. For the Use of Emigrants*. London: John Murray. Repr. 1967 as *Tiger Dunlop's Upper Canada* (Toronto: McClelland and Stewart).

Durand, B. 2001. "BioMap. Guiding land conservation for biodiversity in Massachusetts." Executive Office of Environmental Affairs, MA.

Dyer, G. 2004. "On conventional war." In B. Mau, *Massive Change*. New York: Phaidon Press 2004. 162–3.

Ehrlich, J. 1934. "The beech bark disease, a *Nectria* disease of *Fagus*, following *Cryptococcus fagi* (Baer.)" *Canadian Journal of Research* 10: 593–692.

Ekdahl, E.J., J.L. Teranes, T.P. Guilderson, et al. 2004. "Prehistorical record of cultural eutrophication from Crawford Lake, Canada." *Geology* 32 (9): 745–8.

Elkinton, J.S., and G.H. Boettner. 2004. "The effects of *Compsilura concinnata*, an introduced generalist tachinid." In R.G. Van Driesche and R. Reardon, eds., *Assessing Host Ranges for Parasitoids and Predators Used for Classical Biological Control*. Morgantown, WV: U.S. Dept. of Agriculture, Forest Health Technology Enterprise. 4–14.

Ellingson, T. 2001. *The Myth of the Noble Savage*. Berkeley: University of California Press.

Ellis, C.J., and D.B. Deller. 1990. "Paleo-Indians." In C.J. Ellis and N. Ferris, eds., *The Archaeology of Southern Ontario to A.D. 1650*. London Chapter, Ontario Archaeological Society, *Occasional Publications* 5. 37–63.

Ellis, C.J., I.T. Kenyon, and M.W. Spence. 1990. "The Archaic." In C.J. Ellis and N. Ferris, eds., *The Archaeology of Southern Ontario to A.D. 1650*. London Chapter, Ontario Archaeological Society, *Occasional Publications* 5. 65–124.

Ellsworth, J.W., and B.C. McComb. 2003. "Potential effects of passenger pigeon flocks on the structure and composition of presettlement forests in eastern North America." *Conservation Biology* 17 (6): 1548–58.

Elton, C.S., and M. Nicholson. 1942. "The ten-year cycle in numbers of lynx in Canada." *Journal of Animal Ecology* 11: 215–44.

Engelbrecht, W. 2003. *Iroquoia*. Syracuse, NY: Syracuse University Press.

Erichsen-Brown, C. 1989. *Medicinal and Other Uses of North American Plants*. New York: Dover Publications. (1979 title, *Use of Plants for the Past 500 Years*.)

Ermatinger, E. 1859. *Life of Colonel Talbot, and the Talbot Settlement*. St Thomas, ON: McLaughlin's Home Journal Office.

Eshenroder, R.L., and C.C. Krueger. 2002. "Reintroduction of native fishes to the Great Lakes proper: a research theme area." Great Lakes Fishery Commission, Board of Technical Experts.

Faber-Langendoen, D. and P.F. Maycock. 1987. "Composition and soil-environment analysis of prairies on Walpole Island, southwestern Ontario." *Canadian Journal of Botany* 65: 2410–19.

Fagan, B.M. 2000. *The Little Ice Age: How Climate Made History 1300–1850*. New York: Basic Books.

Federoff, N.V. 2003. "Prehistoric GM corn." *Science* 302: 1148-59.

Feister, L.M., and B. Pulis. 1996. "Molly Brant." In R.S. Grumen, ed., *Northeastern Indian Lives, 1632-1816.* Amherst, MA: University of Massachusetts Press.

Fenn, E. 2001. *Pox Americana: The Great Smallpox Epidemic of 1775-82.* New York: Hill and Wang.

Fenton, W.N. 1940. "Problems arising from the historic northeastern portion of the Iroquois." *Smithsonian Miscellaneous Collections* 100: 159-252.

- 1941. "Contacts between Iroquois herbalism and colonial medicine." In *Smithsonian Institution Annual Report,* Washington, DC. 503-26.

Fergusson, A. 1834. *Practical Notes Made during a Tour in Canada (1831).* Edinburgh: Blackwood.

Firestone, R.B., A. West, J.P. Kennett, et al. 2007. "Evidence for an extraterrestrial impact 12,900 years ago that contributed to the megafaunal extinctions and the Younger Dryas cooling." National Academy of Sciences *Proceedings* 104: 16016-21.

Fischer, D.H. 2008. *Champlain's Dream.* Toronto: Knopf Canada.

FitzGibbon, M.A. 1894. *A Veteran of 1812.* Toronto: William Briggs.

Fitzpatrick, J.C., ed. 1931-44. *Writings of George Washington from the Original Manuscript Sources, 1745-1799.* Vol. 7. Washington, DC: Government Printing Office. 65.

Foley, J., D. Clifford, et al. 2011. "Investigating and managing the rapid emergence of white-nose syndrome." *Conservation Biology* 25 (2): 223-31.

Forbush, E.H., and C.H. Fernald. 1896. *The Gypsy Moth.* Boston: Massachusetts State Board of Agriculture.

Ford, W.C., ed. 1904-37. *Journals of the Continental Congress, 1774-1789.* Vol. 25. Washington, DC: Government Printing Office. 687.

Forget, P.-M., J.E. Lambert, P.E. Hulme, et al., eds. 2004. *Seed Fate: Predation, Dispersal and Seedling Establishment.* Newbury, UK: CAB International Publishing.

Fortune, J. 1806-07. "Fieldbook of Caledonia." Ontario Crown Land Surveys. Peterborough, ON: OMNR.

Foster, J. 1978. *Working for Wildlife: The Beginning of Preservation in Canada.* Toronto: University of Toronto Press.

Fox, L. 1965 (orig. 1635). *North-West Fox or Fox from the North-West Passage.* New York: S.R. Publishers.

Fox, W.S. 1944. "John Goldie, botanist, in southern Ontario, 1819." *Western Ontario History Nuggets* 4: 1-6.

- 1952. *The Bruce Beckons.* Toronto: University of Toronto Press.

Fox, W.S., and J.H. Soper. 1952-54. "The distribution of some trees and shrubs of the Carolinian zone of southern Ontario." Pts. 1-3. Royal Canadian Institute *Transactions* 29 (2): 65-84, 30 (1): 1-34, 30 (2): 99-130.

Franklin, B. "Papers of Benjamin Franklin. American Philosophical Society." http://www.franklinpapers.org/franklin/framedVolumes.jsp.

Fraser, D.M., and B.P. Neary. 2004. *The State of Greenlands in Protection in South-Central Ontario*. Toronto: Neptis Foundation.

Freedman, B. 1989. *Environmental Ecology*. New York: Academic Press.

Frick, W.F., J.F. Pollock, et al. 2010. "An emerging disease causing regional population collapse of a common North American bat species." *Science* 329: 679-82.

Furnier, G. R., A.M. Stolz, R.M. Mustaphi, et al. 1999. "Genetic evidence that butternut canker was recently introduced into North America." *Canadian Journal of Botany* 77: 783-5.

Gagnon, F.-M. 2011. *The Codex Canadensis and the Writings of Louis Nicolas*. Montreal and Kingston, ON: McGill-Queen's University Press.

Galbraith, J. 1833a. "Field notes, broken fronts in Pickering." Ontario Crown Lands Surveys, Field Notes. Peterborough, ON, OMNR.

- 1833b. "Survey of the fifty concession line in the township of Scarborough, lot. no. 35 to lot no. 1, March 1833." Ontario Crown Lands Surveys, Field Notes. Peterborough, ON: OMNR.

Ganong, W.F. 1909. "Identity of animals and plants mentioned by the early voyagers to eastern Canada and Newfoundland." Royal Society of Canada *Transactions*, serial 3, 3 (2): 197-242.

Gapper, A. 1830. "Observations on the quadrupeds found in the district of Upper Canada extending between York and Lake Simcoe." *Zoological Journal* 5 (18): 201-7.

Garcilaso de la Vega (El Inca). 1951 (orig. 1605). (Trans. J.G. and J.J. Varner.) *The Florida of the Inca*. Austin: University of Texas Press.

Gardener, L. 1833. "Leift Lion Gardener: his relation of the Pequot warres." Massachusetts Historical Society *Collections*, 3rd series (3): 154-5.

Garmyn, A., P. VanRooji, et al. 2012. "Waterfowl: potential environmental reservoirs of the chytrid fungus *Batrachochytrium dendrobatidis*." *PLos One*, http://www.doi:10.1371/journal.pone.0035038.

General Land Office 1890. "Transcriptions of surveyors' field notes for Michigan." State Archives of Michigan.

Gentilcore, R.L., and C.G. Head. 1984. *Ontario's History in Maps*. Toronto: University of Toronto Press.

Gibson, T.W. 1897. "Unalienated lands of the public domain of Ontario." In *Handbook of Canada*. Toronto: Publication Committee of the Local Executive.

Gilbert, M.T.P., D.L. Jenkins, et al. 9 May 2008. DNA from Pre-Clovis human coprolites in Oregon, North America." *Science* 320: 786-9.

Gilman, B. 1998. "Alvars of New York." Canandaigua, NY: Finger Lakes Community College.

Gilmore, M.R. 1931. "Dispersal by Indians as a factor in the extension of discontinuous distribution of certain species of native plants." Michigan Academy of Science, Arts and Letters *Papers* 13: 89-94.

Gilpin, M., and M.E. Soulé. 1986. "Minimum viable populations: processes of species extinction." In M.E. Soulé, ed., *Conservation Biology: The Science of Scarcity and Diversity*. Sunderland, MA: Sinauer. 19-34.

Girardin M.-P., J. Tardif, and Y. Bergeron. 2001. "Radial growth analysis of *Larix laricina* from the Lac Duparquet area, Quebec." *Ecoscience* 8: 127-38.

- 2002. "Dynamics of eastern larch stands and its relationships with larch sawfly outbreaks in the northern Clay Belt of Quebec." *Canadian Journal of Forest Research* 32: 206-16.

Given, D.R., and J.H. Soper. 1981. "The arctic-alpine element of the vascular flora at Lake Superior." National Museum of Natural Sciences, Ottawa. *Publications in Botany* 10.

Glavine, T. 2006. *Waiting for the Macaws*. Toronto: Viking Canada.

Gleason, H.A. 1926. "The individualistic concept of the plant association." *Bulletin of the Torrey Botanical Club* 53 (1): 7-26.

Gleason, H.A., and A. Cronquist. 1991. *Manual of Vascular Plants of Northeastern United States and Adjacent Canada*. New York: New York Botanical Garden.

Glover, R. 1962. *David Thompson's Narrative 1784-1812*. Toronto: Champlain Society.

Goldie, J. 1819. "Diary of a journey through Upper Canada and some of the New England States. Privately published by his granddaughter Theresa Goldie Falkner." Toronto Public Library.

Goldsmith, O. 1822. *A History of the Earth and Animated Nature*. 4 vols. London: Henry Fisher. Vol. 4, book 5.

Goodban, A., W.D. Bakowsky, and B.D. Bricker. 1996. "The historical and present extent and floristic composition of prairie and savanna vegetation in the vicinity of Hamilton, Ontario." In C. Warwick, ed., *Proceedings of the 15th North American Prairie Conference, October 1996*. St Charles, IL. 87-103.

Gordon, R.B. 1969. "The natural vegetation of Ohio in pioneer days." *Bulletin of the Ohio Biological Survey* 3 (2): 1-113.

Gore, A. 2006. *An Inconvenient Truth*. New York: Rodale Press.

Gough, B.M. 1988 (orig. 1897). *The Journal of Alexander Henry the Younger 1799-1814*. Toronto: Champlain Society.

Gould, J. 1986. "A biological inventory and evaluation of the Holland Landing prairie relict." Parks and Recreational Areas Section, OFER 8804, OMNR.

Gourlay, R. 1966 (orig. 1822) *Statistical Account of Upper Canada*. East Ardsley, UK: S.R. Publishers.

Governments of Canada and the United States of America. 2009. *State of the Great Lakes 2009: Highlights*. Environment Canada and the U.S. Environmental Protection Agency.

Grady, W. 2007. *The Great Lakes. The Natural History of a Changing Region*. Vancouver: Greystone Books.

Graham, J.S. 1939. *A Scotch-Irish-Canadian Yankee*. New York: G.P. Putnam's Sons.

Graham, W.H. 1962. *The Tiger of Canada West*. Toronto: Clarke, Irwin and Co.

Grant, G. 1873. *Ocean to Ocean: Sandford Fleming's Expedition through Canada in 1872*. Toronto: James Campbell and Son.

Grant, G.M., ed. 1882. *Picturesque Canada*. 2 vols. Toronto: Art Publishing Co.

Graustein, J.E., ed. 1950-51. *Nuttall's Travels into the Old Northwest*. Waltham, MA: Chronica Botanica Co.

Graves, W. 1951. "Diary of William Graves." *Ontario History* 63 (1): 1-26.

Gray, A. 1878. "Forest geography and archaeology." *American Journal of Science* (3rd series) 16: 9-94.

Gray, C. 2002. *Flint & Feather*. Toronto: Harper-Collins.

Gray, E.E. 1956. *Wilderness Christians*. Toronto: Macmillan.

Gray, P.A., D. Paleczny, T.J. Beechey, et al. 2009. *Ontario's Natural Heritage Areas*. Peterborough, ON: Queen's Printer Ontario.

Green, L.C., and O.P. Dickason. 1989. *The Law of Nations and the New World*. Edmonton: University of Alberta Press.

Groves, C.R. 2003. *Drafting a Conservation Blueprint*. Washington, DC: Island Press.

Gubanyi, J.A., J.A. Savidge, S.E. Hygnstrom, et al. 2008. "Deer impact on vegetation in natural areas in southeastern Nebraska." *Natural Areas Journal* 28: 121-9.

Guelph Conference. 1942. *Conservation and Post-War Rehabilitation*. Toronto.

Guilday, J.E. 1984. "Pleistocene extinction and environmental change: case study of the Appalachians." In P.S. Martin and R.G. Klein, eds., *Quaternary Extinctions*. Tucson: University of Arizona Press. 250-8

Guillet, E.C. 1933. *Early Life in Upper Canada*. Toronto: Ontario Publishing Co.

- 1957. *The Valley of the Trent*. Toronto: Champlain Society.

- 1966. *The Story of Canadian Roads*. Toronto: University of Toronto Press.

- 1970 (orig. 1963). *The Pioneer Farmer and Backwoodsman*. 2 vols. Toronto: University of Toronto Press.

Gunn, S.E. 1903. "Sarah Whitmore's captivity." *Publications of the Buffalo Historical Society* 6: 515-26.

Guthrie, R.D. 2006. "New carbon dates link climatic change with human colonization and Pleistocene extinctions." *Nature* 441: 207-9.

Hafner, D.J. 1993. "North American pike (*Ochotona princeps*) as a late Quaternary biogeographic indicator species." *Quaternary Research* 39: 373-80.

Haight, C. 1986 (orig. 1885.) *Country Life in Canada*. Belleville, ON: Mika Publishing Co.

Hakluyt, R., ed. 1903-05. *The Principal Navigations Voyages Traffiques & Discoveries of the English Nation*. Glasgow: James MacLehose. Extra Series VIII.

Hale, H. 1883. *The Iroquois Book of Rites*. Philadelphia: Brinton.

Hall, K.L. 2002. *The Oxford Companion to American Law*. New York: Oxford University Press.

Hambly, W. 30 November 1795-16 May 1796. "Walsingham East Line." Ontario Crown Land Survey Records Field Notes. Vol. 16. Peterborough, ON: OMNR.

- 1804. "Diary while executing the survey of East and North Gwillimbury." Ontario Crown Land Surveys, Field Note Book 432. Peterborough, ON: OMNR.

Hamilton, J.C. 1893. *The Georgian Bay*. Toronto: James Bain and Son.

Harington, C. R. 1988. "Marine mammals of the Champlain Sea." In N.R. Gadd, ed., "The Late Quaternary development of the Champlain Sea basin." Geological Association of Canada, Special Paper 35. 225-40.

Harris, G.H. 1903. "The Life of Horatio Jones." *Publications of the Buffalo Historical Society* 6: 383-514.

Harris, R.C. 1966. *The Seigneurial System in Early Canada*. Madison, WI: University of Wisconsin Press.

- 2008. *The Reluctant Land*. Vancouver: UBC Press.

Harris, R.C., P. Roulston, and C. DeFreitas. 1975. "The settlement of Mono Township." *Canadian Geographer* 19 (1): 1-17.

Harrison, R. 27 October 1902. "Reminiscences of Robert Harrison, Asphodel Township." In E.C. Guillet, ed., *The Valley of the Trent*. Toronto: Champlain Society 1957. 268-74.

Hartman, W.L. 1973. "Effects of exploitation, environmental change, and new species on the fish habitats and resources of Lake Erie." Great Lakes Fishery Commission *Technical Report* 22.

Haughton, A.J., G.T. Champion, C. Hawes, et al. 2003. "Invertebrate responses to the management of genetically modified herbicide-tolerant and conventional spring crops. II. Within field epigeal and aerial arthropods." Royal Society of London Series B-Biological Sciences, *Philosophical Transactions* 358: 863–1877.

Hayes, D. 2002. *Historical Atlas of Canada*. Vancouver: Douglas and McIntyre.

Haynes, C.V. Jr. 1984. "Stratigraphy and Pleistocene extinction in the United States." In P.S. Martin and R.G. Klein, eds., *Quaternary Extinctions*. Tucson: University of Arizona Press. 345-53.

- 2005. "TBD." In R. Bonnichsen, B.T. Lepper, D. Stanford, and R.R. Waters, eds., *Paleoamerican Origins: Beyond Clovis*. College Station, TX: Texas A&M University Press. 113-32.

Haynes, G. 2002. *The Early Settlement of North America: The Clovis Era*. Cambridge: Cambridge University Press

Hays, J.D., J. Imbrie, and N.J. Shackleton. 1976. "Variations in the earth's orbit: pacemaker of the ice ages." *Science* 194 (4270): 1121-32.

Hayward, S.F. 2006. *11th Annual Index of Leading Environmental Indicators 2006*. San Francisco, CA: Pacific Research Institute.

Head, G. 1829. *Forest Scenes and Incidents in the Wilds of North America*. London: John Murray.

Heath, W. 2007. "Thomas Morton: from merry old England to New England." *Journal of American Studies* 41: 135-68.

Heckewelder, J. 1876. *History, Manners, and Customs of the Indian Nations Who Once Inhabited Pennsylvania and the Neighbouring States*. Philadelphia: Historical Society of Pennsylvania.

Heidenreich, C.E. 1971. *Huronia: A History and Geography of the Huron Indians, 1600-1650*. Toronto: McClelland and Stewart.

- 1990. "History of the St. Lawrence-Great Lakes area to AD 1650." In C.J. Ellis and N. Ferris, eds., *The Archaeology of Southern Ontario to AD 1650*. London Chapter, Ontario Archaeological Society, *Occasional Publications* 5. 475-92.

- 2007. "The De Grassi Point oak-pine savanna." *Bluestem Banner, Tallgrass Ontario, London* 7 (1): 2-3.

Heidenreich, C.E., and K.J. Ritch. 2010. *Samuel Champlain before 6004*. Toronto: Champlain Society.

Heidenreich, C.E., and R.W.C. Burgar. 1999. "Native settlement to 1847." In B.I. Roots, D.A. Chant, and C.E. Heidenreich, eds., *Special Places: The Changing Ecosystems of the Toronto Region*. Toronto: UBC Press. 63-75.

Hemson Consulting Ltd. 2013. "Greater Golden Horseshoe Growth Forecasts to 2041," https://www.hemson.com/wp-content/uploads/2016/03/HEMSON-Greater-Golden-Horseshoe-Growth-Forecasts-to-2041-Technical-Report-Addendum-and-Rev.-Appendix-B-Jun2013.pdf.

Hennepin, L. 1683. *Description de la Louisiane*. Paris: Veuve Sebastien Huré.

- 1903 (orig. 1699). *A New Discovery of a Vast Country in America*. London: Henry Bonwicke. Repr. (under editorship of R.G. Thwaites) in 1974 by McClurg and Co. of Chicago and Coles Publishing of Toronto.

Henriksen, G. 1989. "Hunters in the Barrens: The Naskapi on the Edge of the White Man's World." Memorial University, *Newfoundland Social and Economic Studies* 12.

Henry, A. 1969. *Travels and Adventures in Canada and the Indian Territories*. Edmonton: M.G. Hurtig.

Henry, M., M. Beguin, et al. 2012. "A common pesticide decreases foraging success and survival in honey bees." *Science* 335 (6076).

Henson, B.L., K.E. Brodribb, and J.L. Riley. 2005. *Great Lakes Conservation Blueprint for Terrestrial Biodiversity*. Toronto: Nature Conservancy of Canada; and Peterborough, ON: Ontario Natural Heritage Information Centre.

Heriot, G. 1807 (repr. 1971). *Travels through the Canadas*. Edmonton: M.G. Hurtig.

Hewitt, C.G. 1921. *The Conservation of the Wild Life of Canada*. New York: Charles Scribner and Sons.

Higgins, W.H. 1972. *The Life and Times of Joseph Gould*. Toronto: Fitzhenry and Whiteside.

Hind, H.Y. 1851. *A Comparative View of the Climate of Western Ontario*. Toronto: Brewer, McPhail and Co.

– 1863. *Explorations in the Interior of the Labrador Peninsula, the Country of the Montagnais and Nasquapee Indians*. 2 vols. London: Longman Green.

– 1971 (orig. 1860). *Narrative of the Canadian Red River Exploring Expedition of 1857 and of the Assiniboine and Saskatchewan Exploring Expedition of 1858*. 2 vols. Tokyo: Charles E. Tuttle.

Hobbs, R.J., S. Arico, J. Aronson, et al. 2006. "Novel ecosystems: theoretical and management aspects of the new ecological world order." *Global Ecology and Biography* 15: 1–7.

Hoffman, R.C. 2005. "A brief history of aquatic resource use in medieval Europe." *Helgoland Marine Research* 59: 22–30.

Holdsworth, A.R., L.E. Frelich, and P.B. Reich. 2007. "Effects of earthworm invasion on plant species richness in northern hardwood forests." *Conservation Biology* 21: 997–1008.

Holloway, R.G., and V.M. Bryant Jr. 1985. "Late-Quaternary pollen records and vegetational history of the Great Lakes region: United States and Canada." In V.M. Bryant Jr. and R.G. Holloway, eds., *Pollen Records of Late-Quaternary North American Sediments*. Dallas, TX: American Association of Stratigraphic Palynologists Foundation. 205–45.

Holzmueller, E., S. Jose, M. Jenkins, et al. 2006. "Dogwood anthracnose in eastern hardwood forests." *Journal of Forestry* 104: 21–6.

Hooper, M.M. 1967. *Pelee Island, Then and Now*. Scudder, ON.

Hough, F.B., ed. 1861. *Proceedings of the Commissioners of Indian Affairs Appointed by Law for the Extinguishment of Indian Titles in the State of New York*. Vol. 1. Albany, NY: J. Munsell.

– ed. and trans. 1866. *Memoir upon the Late War in North America, between the French and English, 1755–60, by Pierre Pouchot*. Vol. 2. Roxbury, MA: W.E. Woodward.

Hough, W. 1926. "Fire as an agent in human culture." *US National Museum Bulletin* 139: 1–270.

Houston, S., T. Ball, and M. Houston. 2003. *Eighteenth-Century Naturalists of Hudson Bay*. Montreal and Kingston, ON: McGill-Queen's University Press.

Howard, J.K. 1970. *The Strange Empire of Louis Riel*. Toronto: Swan Publishing Co.

Howe, C.D., J.H. White, and B.E. Fernow. 1913. *Trent Watershed Survey*. Toronto: Bryant Press.

Howison, J. 1821. *Sketches of Upper Canada*. London: G. and W.B. Whittaker.

Howland, H.R. 1903. "Historical Papers." *Publications of the Buffalo Historical Society* 6: 17-164.

Hoyle, J.A., and A. Mathers. 2002. "Lake Ontario Commercial Fishery." In *Lake Ontario Fish Communities and Fisheries: 2001 Annual Report of the Lake Ontario Management Unit*. Picton, ON: OMNR. PII.

Huang, Y. 2008. *Capitalism with Chinese Characters. Entrepreneurship and the State*. Cambrdge: Cambridge University Press.

Hulchanski, D.J., et al. 2010. "The Three Cities within Toronto, 1970-2005." Cities Centre, University of Toronto, update, *Research Bulletin* 41.

Hunt, G.T. 1940. *The Wars of the Iroquois: A Study in Intertribal Trade Relations*. Madison: University of Wisconsin Press.

Hunter, A.F. 1948 (corrected repr. of 1909 edition). *A History of Simcoe County*. 2 pts. Barrie, ON: Historical Committee of Simcoe County.

Hunter, M.L., G.L. Jacobson, and T. Webb. 1988. "Paleoecology and the coarse-filter approach to maintaining biological diversity." *Conservation Biology* 2 (4): 375-85.

Hunter, W. 1768. "Observations on the bones, commonly supposed to be elephant's bones, which have been found near the river Ohio in America." *Philosophical Transactions of the Royal Society* 58: 34-45.

Huntley, B. 1991. "How plants respond to climate change; migration rates, individualism and the consequences for plant communities." *Annals of Botany* 67: 15-22.

Huntley, B., and H.J.B. Birks. 1983. *An Atlas of Past and Present Pollen Maps for Europe: 0-13000 Years Ago*. Cambridge, MA: Cambridge University Press.

Imbrie, J., and K.P. Imbrie. 1979. *Ice Ages: Solving the Mystery*. Short Hills, NJ: Enslow.

Innis, H.A. 1954. *The Cod Fisheries*. Toronto: University of Toronto Press.

- 1956 (rev. ed.). *The Fur Trade in Canada*. Toronto: University of Toronto Press.

Innis, M.Q. 1965. *Mrs. Simcoe's Diary*. Toronto: Macmillan.

IPCC (Intergovernmental Panel on Climate Change). 2001. *Climate Change 2001: Working Group II: Impacts, Adaptation and Vulnerability* (5.2.4.1).

- 2007. *Fourth Assessment Report (AR4). Climate Change 2007*.

Irwin, J.C.W. 1943. "Forestry problems in reconstruction."

Iseminger, W. 2010. *Cahokia Mounds. America's First City*. Charleston, SC: History Press.

Jackson, L.J. 2004. "Changing our view of lake Palaeo-Indian in southern Ontario." In L.J. Jackson and A. Hinshelwood, eds., *The Late Palaeo-Indian Great Lakes*. Gatineau, QC: Canadian Museum of Civilization, *Archaeology Paper* 165. 25-56.

Jackson, L.J., C. Ellis, A.V. Morgan, and J.H. McAndrews. 2000. "Glacial Lake levels and eastern Great Lakes Palaeoindians." *Geoarchaeology* 15: 415-40.

Jaenen, C.J. 1996. *The French Regime in the Upper Country of Canada during the Seventeenth Century*. Toronto: Champlain Society.

Jalava, J.V., and J.L. Riley. 1996. "Mono Cliffs." In J.L. Riley, J.V. Jalava, and S. Varga, *Ecological Survey of the Niagara Escarpment Biosphere Reserve*. Vol. 1. Peterborough, ON: OMNR. 189-94.

Jalava, J.V., W.L. Cooper, and J.L. Riley. 2005. *Ecological Survey of the Eastern Georgian Bay Coast*. Toronto: Nature Conservancy of Canada; and Peterborough, ON: OMNR.

James, T. 1973. *The Dangerous Voyage of Captain Thomas James*. Toronto: Coles Publishing.

Jamieson, J.B. 1990. "The archaeology of the St. Lawrence Iroquoians." In C.J. Ellis and N. Ferris, eds., *The Archaeology of Southern Ontario to AD 1650*. London Chapter, Ontario Archaeological Society, *Occasional Publications* 5. 385-404.

Jameson, J.F. 1959. *Narratives of New Netherland, 1609-1664*. New York: Barnes and Noble.

Jameson, Mrs (A.B.). 1972 (orig. 1838). *Winter Studies and Summer Rambles*. 3 vols. Toronto: Coles Publishing.

Janusas, S.E., S.M. Blasco, S. McClellan, et al. 2004. "Prehistoric drainage and archaeological implications across the submerged Niagara Escarpment north of Tobermory, Ontario." In L.J. Jackson and A. Hinshelwood, eds., *The Late Palaeo-Indian Great Lakes*. Gatineau, QC: Canadian Museum of Civilization, *Archaeology Paper* 165. 303-14.

Janzen, D. 1998. "Gardenification of wildland nature and the human footprint." *Science* 279: 1312.

Jaynes, R.A. 1979. "Nut Tree Culture in North America." Hamden, CT: Northern Nut Growers Association.

Jeglum, J.K., A.N. Boissonneau, and V.F. Haavisto. 1974. *Toward a Wetland Classification for Ontario*. Sault Ste Marie, ON: Canadian Forestry Service. Information Report O-X-215.

Jennings, F. April 1965. "The Delaware interregnum." *Pennsylvania Magazine of History and Biography* 89 (2): 174-98.

– 1984. *The Ambiguous Iroquois Empire*. New York: W.W. Norton.

Jérémie, N. 1926. *Twenty Years of York Factory, 1694-1714*. Trans. and ed. by R. Douglas and H.N. Wallace. Ottawa: Thornburn and Abbott.

Jesuit Relations and Allied Documents, 1610-1791 (JR). Ed. R.G. Thwaites. 1896-1901. 73 vols. Cleveland, OH: Burrows Bros.

Johnson, B. 1989. *Familiar Amphibians & Reptiles of Ontario.* Toronto: Natural Heritage.

Johnston, C.M 1964. *The Valley of the Six Nations.* Toronto: Champlain Society.

–1994. "The Six Nations in the Grand River Valley, 1784-1847." In E.S. Rogers and D.B. Smith, eds., *Aboriginal Ontario.* Toronto: Dundurn Press.

Johnston, R.B., and K.A. Cassavoy. 1978. "The fishweirs at Atherley Narrows, Ontario." *American Antiquity* 43: 697-709.

Jones, A.E. 1908. "Sendake Ehen, or Old Huronia." *Fifth Report of the Bureau of the Archives for the Province of Ontario.*

Jones, J., and C. Reschke. 2005. "The role of fire in Great Lakes alvar landscapes." *Michigan Botanist* 44: 13-27.

JR. *See* Jesuit Relations and Allied Documents.

Jurgens, O. 1966. "Étienne Brûlé." *Dictionary of Canadian Biography,* vol. 1, http://www.biographi.ca.

Kaatz, M.R. 1955. "The Black Swamp." *Annals of the Association of American Geographers* 45: 1-35.

Kalm, P. 1966. *Peter Kalm's Travels in North America.* Ed. A.B. Benson. 2 vols. New York: Dover Publications.

Kane, P. 1968 (orig. 1858). *Wanderings of an Artist.* Edmonton: M.G. Hurtig.

Karrow, P.F. 2004. "Ontario geological events and environmental change in the time of the late Palaeo-Indian and early Archaic cultures." In L.J. Jackson and A. Hinshelwood, eds., *Late Palaeo-Indian Great Lakes.* Gatineau, QC: Canadian Museum of Civilization, *Archaeology Paper* 165. 1-23.

Karrow, P.F., and B.G. Warner. 1990. "The geological and biological environment for human occupation in southern Ontario." In C.J. Ellis and N. Ferris, eds., *The Archaeology of Southern Ontario to AD 1650.* London Chapter, Ontario Archaeological Society, *Occasional Publications* 5. 5-37.

Karrow, P.F., T.F. Morris, J.H. McAndrews, et al. 2007. "A diverse late-glacial (Mackinaw Phase) biota from Leamington, Ontario." *Canadian Journal of Earth Sciences* 44: 287-96.

Kawamura, K., et al. 2007. "Northern hemisphere forcing of climatic cycles in Antarctica over the past 360,000 years." *Nature* 448 (7156): 912-17.

Kay, C.E. 2002. "Afterward: false gods, ecological myths, and biological reality." InC.E. Kay and R.T. Simmons, eds., *Wilderness and Political Ecology.* Salt Lake City: University of Utah Press. 238-62.

– 2007. "Are lightning fires unnatural?" In R.E. Masters and K.E.M. Galley, eds., *Proceedings of 23rd Tall Timbers Fire Ecology Conference.* Tallahassee, FL: Tall Timbers Research Station. 16-28.

Kay, C.E., and R.T. Simmons, eds. 2002. *Wilderness and Political Ecology.* Salt Lake City: University of Utah Press.

Ke-che-ah-gah-me-qua. 1850. *Captain Joseph Brant*. In possession of B.H. Rothwell, Brantford, ON.

Keefer, T.C. 1863. "Travel and transportation." In *Eighty Years' Progress of British North America* (1863), edited and published by the *British American Magazine*, Toronto.

Keeshig-Tobias, L. 2003. "The oral history of Fathom Five." Canadian Archaeological Association 36th Annual Conference, 7-10 May 2003, McMaster University, Hamilton, ON.

Kelly, P.E., and D.W. Larson. 2007. *The Last Stand*. Toronto: Natural Heritage Books / Dundurn Group.

Kidd, K.E. 1949. *The Excavation of Ste Marie I*. Toronto: University of Toronto Press.

Killan, G. 1993. *Protected Places*. Toronto: Queen's Printer / Dundurn Press.

- 1997. *Ontario's Provincial Parks System*. Toronto: Quetico Foundation.

King, J.E., and J.J. Saunders. 1984. "Environmental insularity and the extinction of the American mastodon." In P.S. Martin and R.G. Klein, eds., *Quaternary Extinctions*. Tucson: University of Arizona Press. 315-39.

King, W.R. 1866. *The Sportsman and Naturalist in Canada*. London: Hurst and Blackett.

Kingman, L.W. 1987 (orig. 1907). *Early Owego*. Interlaken, NY: Heart of Lakes Publishing.

Kinietz, W.V. 1940. *The Indians of the Western Great Lakes, 1615-1760*. Ann Arbor: University of Michigan Press.

Kinnunen, R.E. 2003. "Great Lakes commercial fisheries." Michigan Sea Grant Extension, University of Michigan.

Kirby, W. 1972 (orig. 1896). *Annals of Niagara*. London: Edward Phelps.

Kirkconnell, T.W. 1919. "The flora of Kapuskasing and vicinity." *Canadian Field-Naturalist* 33: 33.

Kirkconnell, W. 1967 (orig. 1921). *History of Victoria County*. Lindsay, ON: Victoria County Council.

Kirkwood, V. 2011. "A family treasure full of history." *Forestory* 2 (2): 3-5.

Kohl, J.G. 1861. *Travels in Canada, and through the States of New York and Pennsylvania*. London: George Manwaring.

Kos-Rabcewicz-Zubrowski, L., and W.E. Greening. 1959. *Sir Casimir Stanislaus Gzowski*. Toronto: Burns and MacEachern.

Krech, S. 1999. *The Ecological Indian: Myth and History*. New York: W.W. Norton.

Kyte, E.C., ed. 1954. *Old Toronto*. Toronto: Macmillan.

Ladell, J.L. 1993. *They Left Their Mark*. Toronto: Dundurn Press.

Lahontan, Baron. 1905 (orig. 1703). *New Voyages to North-America*. 2 vols. London: H. Bonwicke. Repr. under editorship of R.G. Thwaites and published by McClurg and Co. of Chicago.

Lajeunesse, E.J., ed. 1960. *The Windsor Border Region*. Toronto: Champlain Society / University of Toronto Press.

Lalemant, J. 1640. "Father Jérôme Lalemant's account of the mission of the angels to the Attiwandaronks." In C.M. Johnston, *The Valley of the Six Nations*. Toronto: Champlain Society 1964. A.3.

– 1660. "Relation of what occurred in the mission … the summer of the year 1660." In E. Kenton, ed., *The Jesuit Relations and Allied Documents*. New York: Vanguard Press 1954. 301-13.

Lambert, R.S. (with P. Pross). 1967. *Renewing Nature's Wealth*. Toronto: Ontario Department of Lands and Forests.

Langton, W.A., ed. 1926. *Early Days in Upper Canada: Letters of John Langton*. Toronto: Macmillan.

Larson, B.M., J.L. Riley, E.A. Snell, et al. 1999. *The Woodland Heritage of Southern Ontario*. Don Mills, ON: Federation of Ontario Naturalists.

Larson, B.M.H. 2007a. "An alien approach to invasive species: objectivity and society in invasion biology." *Biological Invasions* 9: 947-56.

– 2007b. "Thirteen ways of looking at invasive species." In D.R. Clements and S.J. Darbyshire, eds., *Invasive Plants: Inventories, Strategies and Actions*. Canadian Weed Science Society, *Topics in Canadian Weed Science* 5. 131-56.

– 2008. "Friend, foe, wonder, peril." *Alternatives Journal* 31 (1): 14-17.

Larson, D.W., U. Matthes, and P.E. Kelly. 2000. *Cliff Ecology*. Cambridge: Cambridge University Press.

Larson, D.W., U. Matthes, P.E. Kelly, et al. 2004. *The Urban Cliff Revolution*. Markham, ON: Fitzhenry and Whiteside.

Lauriston, V. 1952. *Romantic Kent: More than Three Centuries of History 1626-1952*. Chatham, ON: Shepherd Printing Co.

Lawson, J. 1903 (orig. 1714). *History of North Carolina*. Repr. Charlotte, NC: Observer Printing House.

Legget, R.F. 1975. *Ottawa Waterway: Gateway to a Continent*. Toronto: University of Toronto Press.

Legislative Assembly of Ontario. 1901. *Report of the Survey and Exploration of Northern Ontario 1900*. In possession of L.K. Cameron, Toronto.

Leitch, A. 1975. *Into the High County*. Orangeville, ON: County of Dufferin, Ontario.

Lennox, P.A., and W.R. Fitzgerald. 1990. "The culture history and archaeology of the Neutral Iroquoians." In C.J. Ellis and N. Ferris, eds., *The Archaeology of Southern Ontario to A.D. 1650*. London Chapter, Ontario Archaeological Society, *Occasional Publications* 5. 405-56.

Leopold, A. 1933. *Game Management.* New York: Charles Scribner and Sons.

- 1966. *A Sand County Almanac.* New York: Oxford University Press.

Lescarbot, M. 1609. *Nova Francia. A Description of Acadia, 1606.* Trans. P. Erondelle, 1928. New York: Harper.

Lett, W.P. 1884. "The deer of the Ottawa valley." *Transactions of the Ottawa Field-Naturalist's Club* 5: 101-17.

Lieth, H., and R.H. Whittaker, eds., 1975. *Primary Productivity of the Biosphere.* New York: Springer-Verlag.

Lishman, W. 1996. *Father Goose: One Man, a Gaggle of Geese, and Their Real Life Incredible Journey South.* New York: Crown.

Lister, K.R. 1988. "Provisioned at fishing stations: fish and the native occupation of the Hudson Bay Lowland." In C.S. Reid, ed., *Boreal Forest and Sub-Arctic Archaeology.* Ontario Archaeological Association, *Occasional Publications* 6. 72-99.

Little, C.E. 1995. *The Dying of the Trees.* New York: Penguin Books.

Lizars, K.M. 1913. *The Valley of the Humber, 1615-1913.* Toronto: William Briggs.

Lizars, R., and K.M. Lizars 1896. *In the Days of the Canada Company.* Toronto: William Briggs.

Logan, W.B. 2005. *Oak: The Frame of Civilization.* New York: WW. Norton and Co.

Lombardo, J.A., and B.C. McCarthy. 2008. "Forest management and Curculionid weevil diversity in mixed oak forests of southeastern Ohio." *Natural Areas Journal* 28: 363-9.

Lomborg, B. 2007. *Cool It.* New York: Alfred A. Knopf.

Long, J.C., W.C. Knowler, et al. 1998. "Evidence for genetic linkage to alcohol dependence on chromosomes 4 and 11 from an autosome-wide scan in an American Indian population." *American Journal of Medical Genetics* 81: 216-21.

Loo, T. 2006. *States of Nature: Conserving Canada's Wildlife in the Twentieth Century.* Vancouver: UBC Press.

Loope, W.L., and J.B. Anderton. 1998. "Human vs. lightning ignition of presettlement surface forest in coastal pine forests of the upper Great Lakes." *American Midland Naturalist* 140: 206-18.

Lorimer, C.G. 1977. "The presettlement forest and natural disturbance cycle of northeastern Maine." *Ecology* 58: 139-48.

Lovell, W.G. 1992. "Heavy shadows and black night: disease and depopulation in colonial Spanish America." *Annals of the Association of American Geographers* 82: 426-43.

Lovelock, J. 2006. *The Revenge of Gaia.* New York and London: Penguin Books.

Lower, A.R.M. 1938. *The North American Assault on the Canadian Forest.* Toronto: Ryerson Press.

Lumsden, H.G. 1966. "The prairie chicken in southwestern Ontario." *Canadian Field-Naturalist* 80: 33-44.

- 1971. "The status of the sandhill crane in northern Ontario." *Canadian Field-Naturalist* 85: 285-93.

- 1981. "History of breeding Canada geese in southwestern Ontario." *Ontario Field Biologist* 35: 49-56.

- 1984. "The pre-settlement breeding distribution of trumpeter, *Cygnus buccinator,* and tundra swans, *C. columbianus,* in eastern Canada." *Canadian Field-Naturalist* 98: 415-24.

Lyell, C. 1832. *Principles of Geology.* Vol. 1. London: John Murray.

- 1845. *Travels in North America.* Vol. 2. London: John Murray.

- 1853. *Manual of Elementary Geology.* 4th ed. New York: Appleton.

Lytwyn, V.P. 2002. *Muskekowuck Athinuwick: Original People of the Great Swampy Land.* Winnipeg: University of Manitoba Press.

Macfie, J. 2004. *Up the Great North Road.* Erin, ON: Boston Mills Press.

MacGregor, J.G. 1954. *Behold the Shining Mountains. The Travels of Anthony Henday.* Edmonton: Applied Art Products.

MacKay, H.H. 1963. *Fishes of Ontario.* Toronto: Ontario Department of Lands and Forests.

Macoun, J. 1893. "Notes on the flora of the Niagara peninsula and shore of Lake Erie." *Journal and Proceedings of the Hamilton Association* 9: 78-86.

- 1979 (orig. 1922). "Autobiography of John Macoun 1831-1920." Ottawa: Ottawa Field-Naturalists Club.

Macoun, J., and J.A. Macoun. 1909. *Catalogue of Canadian Birds.* Ottawa: Department of Mines.

Magoun, A.J., K.F. Abraham, J.E. Thompson, J.C. Ray, et al. 2005. "Distribution and relative abundance of caribou in the Hudson plains ecozone of Ontario." *Rangifer* 16: 105-21.

Magrath, T.W. 1953 (orig. 1833). *Authentic Letters from Upper Canada.* Toronto: Macmillan.

Malthus, T.R. 1826 (6th ed., orig. 1798 anon.). *An Essay on the Principle of Population.* London: John Murray. Book 3, chapter 4.

"Malthus, T.R." 1965. *Encyclopaedia Britannica* 14: 717-18.

Mann, B. and J.L. Fields. 1997. "A sign in the sky: dating the league of the Haudenosaunee." *American Indian Culture and Research Journal* 21: 105-63.

Mann, C.C. 2005. *1491.* New York: Alfred A. Knopf.

Marshall, S.A. 2006. *Insects: Their Natural History and Diversity.* Richmond Hill, ON: Firefly Books.

Martin, N.D., D.S. McGillis, and C. Milne. 1986. *Gore's Landing and the Rice Lake Plains.* Bewdley, ON: Clay Publishing.

Martin, P.S. 1973. "The discovery of America." *Science* 179: 969–74.

– 2005. *Twilight of the Mammoths*. Berkeley, CA: University of California Press.

Mason, T. ("A. Parsonage"). "'Feby 29, 64' Settlement of the Northern Townships of the Trent Valley." In E.C. Guillet, *The Valley of the Trent*. Toronto: Champlain Society 1957. 79–81.

Masson, L.R. 1960. *Les Bourgeois de la Compagnie Nord-Ouest*. Vol. 2. New York: Antiquarian Press.

Mastro, V. 2007. "USDA Animal and Plant Health Inspection Service," Presentation to Natural Areas Conference, Cleveland, OH. October.

Mastro, V., R. Reardon, and G. Parra (comp.) 2005. "Emerald ash borer research and technology development meeting." USDA Forest Service Forest Health Technology Enterprise Team Meeting, Proceedings of 26–27 September 2005, Radisson Hotel, Pittsburg, PA.

Mathews, H.C. 1965. *The Mark of Honour*. Toronto: University of Toronto Press.

Matthews, J.V. Jr. 1979. "Tertiary and Quaternary environments." In H.V. Danks, ed., *Canada and Its Insect Fauna*. Memoirs of the Entomological Society of Canada, Ottawa. 32–86.

Matthiessen, P. 1987. *Wildlife in America*. New York: Viking Penguin.

Mau, B. 2004. *Massive Change*. New York: Phaidon Press.

Maude, J. 1826. *Visit to the Falls of Niagara in 1800*. London: Longman and Co.

Mayall, K.M. 1939. "The natural resources of King Township, Ontario, 1938." Royal Canadian Institute *Transactions* 48 (vol. 22, pt. 2): 217–58.

Maycock, P.F. 1979. *A Preliminary Survey of the Vegetation of Ontario with Special Reference to the Establishment of Nature Reserves*. Toronto: OMNR, Parks and Natural Heritage Policy Branch, Site Region Matricies.

Maycock, P.F., D.R. Gregory, and A.A. Reznicek. 1980. "Hill's oak (*Quercus ellipsoidalis*) in Canada." *Canadian Field-Naturalist* 94: 277–85.

Mayer, J.J. and I.L. Brisbin Jr. 1991. *The Wild Pigs of the United States: Their History, Morphology and Current Status*. Athens: University of Georgia Press.

Mayer, John J. 2007. "Wild pigs." Presentation to Annual Natural Areas Association Conference, Cleveland, OH. October.

McAndrews, J.H. 1976. "Fossil history of man's impact on the Canadian flora: an example from southern Ontario." Canadian Botanical Association *Bulletin*, supplement to vol. 9 (1): 1–6.

– 1982. "Holocene environment of a fossil bison from Kenora, Ontario." *Ontario Archaeology* 37: 41–51.

McAndrews, J.H., and C.L. Turton. 2007. "Canada geese dispersed cultigen pollen grains from prehistoric Iroquoian fields to Crawford Lake, Ontario, Canada." *Palynology* 31: 9–18.

McAndrews, J.H., J.L. Riley, and A.M. Davis. 1982. "Vegetation history of the Hudson Bay Lowland: a postglacial pollen diagram from the Sutton Ridge." *Naturaliste canadien* 109: 597–608.

McDonald, H.G. 1994. "Late Pleistocene vertebrate fauna in Ohio." In W.S. Dancey, ed., *The First Discovery of America*. Columbus, OH: Ohio Archaeological Council. 23–39.

McDonald, R.I., J. Fargione, J. Kiesecker, et al. 2009. "Energy sprawl or energy efficiency: climate policy impacts on natural habitat for the United States of America." *PoS ONE* 4, no. 8: e6802. http://www.doi:10.1371/journal.pone.0006802.

McIlveen, W.D. 2007. "Rural roadside trees." *Field Botanists of Ontario Newsletter* 19 (3/4): 13–14.

McIlwraith, T. July, 1860. "List of birds observed in the vicinity of Hamilton, C.W." *Canadian Journal of Industry, Science, and Art* 28: 387–96.

– 1894 (2nd ed.) *The Birds of Ontario*. Toronto: William Briggs.

McIlwraith, T.F. 1997. *Looking for Old Ontario*. Toronto: University of Toronto Press.

McIntosh, T., et al. 2007. "Evidence of *Parelaphostrongylus tenuis* infections in free-ranging elk (*Cervus elaphus*) in southern Ontario." *Canadian Veterinarian Journal* 48 (11): 1146–54. McKeen, C.D. 1995. "Chestnut blight in Ontario: past and present status." *Canadian Journal of Plant Pathology* 17: 295–304.

McKenney, T.L. 1827. *Sketches of a Tour to the Lakes*. Baltimore, MD: Fielding Lucas Jr.

McKibben, B. April 1995. "An Explosion of Green." *Atlantic Monthly*, April 1995: 61–83.

McKnight, B.N., ed. 1993. *Biological Pollution*. Indianapolis, IN: Indiana Academy of Science.

McMaster, J.B. 1907. "The struggle for commercial independence." In *The Cambridge Modern History*. Vol. 7. New York: Macmillan. 305–34.

McNeill, J.R. 2000. *Something New under the Sun: An Environmental History of the Twentieth-Century World*. New York: W.W. Morton.

McNiff, P. 1791. "A plan of Lake Erie Detroit River part of Lake St Clair and River La Tranche." In R.L. Gentilcore and C.G. Head, *Ontario's History in Maps*. Toronto: University of Toronto Press 1984. 66–7.

McNiff, P., and A. Jones. 1795. "Survey of the River Tranche or Thames." In R.L. Gentilcore and C.G. Head, *Ontario's History in Maps*. Toronto: University of Toronto Press 1984. 232–3.

Mead, J.I., and F. Grady. 1996. "*Ochotona* (Lagomorpha) from late Quatenary cave deposits in eastern North America." *Quaternary Research* 45: 93–101.

Meekins, J.F., and B.C. McCarthy. 1999. "Competitive ability of *Alliaria petiolata* (garlic mustard, Brassicaceae), an invasive, nonindigenous forest herb." *International Journal of Plant Sciences* 160: 743–52.

Menzies, G. 2003. *1421*. New York: William Morrow / HarperCollins Publishers.

Mercier, F. 1654. "Relation of what occurred in the mission of the Fathers of the Society of Jesus ... of the year 1654. In E. Kenton, ed., *The Jesuit Relations and Allied Documents*. New York: Vanguard Press. 244-59.

Merriam, C.H. 1898. "Life zones and crop zones of the United States." USDA Division, Biological Survey, *Bulletin* 10. Washington, DC.

Michaux, A. 1819. *North American Sylva* (English trans.). Paris and Philadelphia: C.D Hautel.

Michigan Natural Features Inventory. 1998. "Alvars of Michigan." Lansing, MI: Nature Conservancy.

Milani, L.D. 1971. *Robert Gourlay: Gadfly*. Thornhill, ON: Ampersand Press.

Miller, A.S. 1968. *The Journals of Mary O'Brien*. Toronto: Macmillan.

Miller, R.J. 2006. *Native America, Discovered and Conquered: Thomas Jefferson, Lewis & Clark, and Manifest Destiny*. Westport, CT: Praeger Publishing.

Miller, W.G. (comp. and ed.). 1912. *Reports on the District of Patricia Recently Added to the Province of Ontario*. In *Report of the Bureau of Mines 1912*, vol. 21, pt. 2. In possession of L.K. Cameron, Toronto.

Milner, G.R. 2004. *The Moundbuilders*. New York: Thames and Hudson.

Miner, J. 1929. *Jack Miner on Current Topics*. Toronto: Ryerson Press.

Mitchell, J. 1950. *The Settlement of York County*. Municipal Corporation of the County of York, ON.

Mitchell, S. 2008. "Fascinating frogs." *Landscope* 24 (1): 10-15.

Mittelstaedt, M. 2008. "Entering Great Lakes? Flush first." A3. *Globe and Mail*. 19 January.

Monbiot, G. 1995. "A land reform manifesto." *The Guardian*, London. 22 February.

Mono Township Council. 1974. *The Green Hills*. Mono, ON.

Montizambert, E.L. 1883. *Canada in the Seventeenth Century*. Montreal: George E. Desbarats and Co.

Moodie, S. 1913 (orig. 1852). *Roughing It in the Bush*. Toronto: Bell and Cockburn.

– 1959 (orig. 1853). *Life in the Clearings*. Toronto: Macmillan.

Morgan, L.H. 1851. *The League of the Ho-de-no-sau-nee or Iroquois*. New York: Sage and Brother Publishers.

– 1877. *Ancient Society*. New York: Henry Holt and Co.

Moroff, R.A. 1949. "The climate of New York State." *Cornell Extension Bulletin 764*, Ithaca, NY.

Morris, T.F., J.H. McAndrews, and K.L. Seymour. 1993. "Glacial Lake arcona – Whittlesey transition near Leamington, Ontario; geology, plant and muskox fossils." *Canadian Journal of Earth Sciences* 30: 2436-7.

Morton, N. 1669. *New-England's Memoriall*. Cambridge, MA: John Usher.

Morton, W.L. 1980. *Henry Youle Hind, 1823–1908.* Toronto: University of Toronto Press.

Moseley, E.L. 1897. "Climatic influences of Lake Erie on vegetation." *American Naturalist* 31: 60–3.

Mosquin, T. 1991. *The Alfred Bog: An Ecological Study.* Toronto: Nature Conservancy of Canada.

Muir, J. 1897. *The American Forests.* In *Our National Parks.* Boston: Houghton Mifflin 1901.

– 1997. *John Muir: Nature Writings.* W. Cronon, ed. New York: Library of America.

Mulvaney, C.P., C.M. Ryan, and C.R. Stewart. 1884. *The History of the County of Peterborough.* Cited in E.C. Guillet, *The Valley of the Trent.* Toronto: Champlain Society 1957.

Munn, R.E., M. Thomas, and D. Yap. 1999. "Climate." In B.I. Roots, D.A. Chant, and C.E. Heidenreich, eds., *Special Places: The Changing Ecosystems of the Toronto Region.* Toronto: UBC Press. 33–49.

Murphy, C., and N. Ferris. 1990. "The late Woodland western basin tradition of southwestern Ontario." In C.J. Ellis and N. Ferris, eds., *The Archaeology of Southern Ontario to AD 1650.* London Chapter, Ontario Archaeological Society, *Occasional Publications* 5. 189–278.

Murray, J.S. 2006. *Terra Nostra, 1550–1950.* Montreal and Kingston, ON: McGill-Queen's University Press.

Nadasky, P. 2005. "Transcending the debate over the ecologically noble Indian: indigenous people and environmentalism." *Ethnohistory* 52 (2): 291–331.

Nelson, L.L. 1999. *A Man of Distinction among Them.* Kent, OH: Kent State University Press.

Neumann, T.W. 2002. "The role of prehistoric peoples in shaping ecosystems in the eastern United States." In C.E. Kay and R.T. Simmons, eds., *Wilderness and Political Ecology.* Salt Lake City: University of Utah Press. 141–78.

Nikiforuk, A. 2006. *Pendemonium. Bird Flu, Mad Cow Disease, and Other Biological Plagues of the 21st Century.* Toronto: Viking Canada / Penguin Group.

Noss, R.F., H.B. Quigley, M.G. Hornocker, et al. 1996. "Conservation biology and carnivore conservation in the Rocky Mountains." *Conservation Biology* 10: 949–63.

Novak, M. 1987. "Beaver." In M. Novak, J.A. Baker, et al., eds., *Wild Furbearer Management and Conservation in North America.* Toronto: OMNR / Ontario Tappers Association. 283–312.

Nudds, T. 1987. "The prudent predator." In M. Novak, J.A. Baker, et al., *Wild Furbearer Management and Conservation in North America.* Toronto: OMNR / Ontario Tappers Association. 113–18.

Nute, G.L. 1944. *Lake Superior.* New York: Bobbs-Merrill Co.

Nuzzo, V. 1986. "Extent and status of Midwest oak savanna: presettlement and 1985."

Natural Areas Journal 6: 6-36.

- 1993. "Distribution and spread of the invasive biennial *Alliaria petiolata* (garlic mustard)." In B.N. McKnight, ed., *Biological Pollution*. Indianapolis, IN: Indiana Academy of Science. 137-45.

- 2007. "Natural area consultants." Presentation to Natural Areas Conference, Cleveland, OH. October.

Obbard, M.E., et al. 1987. "Furbearer harvests in North America." In M. Novak, J.A. Baker, et al., eds., *Wild Furbearer Management and Conservation in North America*. Toronto: OMNR / Ontario Tappers Association. 1007-34.

O'Brien, R.M. 1976. "An archaeological survey of Methodist Point Park Reserve." *Research Report* 9, Ontario Ministry of Culture and Recreation, Toronto.

ODLF (Ontario Department of Lands and Forests). 1963. *Lake Erie Forest District History*. Peterborough, ON: OMNR.

O'Gallacher, M. 2008. "Children of the famine." *The Beaver*, Special Edition, February/ March.

Ogden, J.C. 1799. *A Tour through Upper and Lower Canada, by a Citizen of the United States*. Litchfield, CT.

Oldham, M.J., and A.A. Reznicek. 2006. "Rare plant field surveys on Long Point." Natural Heritage Information Centre *Newsletter* 11: 10-11.

OMAF (Ontario Ministry of Agriculture and Food.) *Windbreaks on the Farm*. Publication 527.

OMNR (Ontario Ministry of Natural Resources). 1973. *The Farm Windbreak* (pamphlet).

- 2001. "Critical review of historical and current tree planting programs on private lands in Ontario." Peterborough, ON: OMNR.

- 2002. *Room to Grow: Final Report of the Ontario Forest Accord Advisory Board on Implementation of the Accord*. Toronto: OMNR. March.

- 2010. *Science for a Changing Far North: Report of the Far North Science Advisory Panel*.

Ontario Royal Commission on Forestry *Report*. 1947. In possession of Baptist Johnson, Toronto.

Ontario Woodland Caribou Recovery Team. 2008. *Woodland Caribou (Rangifer tarandus caribou) Forest-Dwelling, Boreal Population) in Ontario*. Peterborough, ON: OMNR.

Oosthoek, S. 2007. "Raising the dead." *On Nature* 47 (4): 26-42.

O'Shea, J.M., and G.A. Meadows. 2009. "Evidence for early hunters beneath the Great Lakes." PNAS, http://www.doi: 10.1073/pnas.0902785106.

Oster, E. 2004. "Witchcraft, weather and economic growth in Renaissance Europe." *Journal of Economic Perspectives* 18 (1): 215–28.

O'Toole, F. 2005. *White Savage*. New York: Farrar, Straus and Giroux.

Otterstatter, M.C., and J.D. Thompson. 2008. "Does pathogen spillover from commercially reared bumble bees threaten wild pollinators?" *PLOS One* 7:e2771, http://www.doi:10.1371/journal.pone.0002771.

Ouellet, R. 1990. *Lahontan: Oeuvres complètes*. 2 vols. Montreal: Les Presses de l'Université de Montréal.

Pacala, S., and R. Socolow. 2004. "Stabilization wedges: solving the climate problem for the next 50 years with current technologies." *Science* 305: 968-72.

Packer, L., and R. Owen. 2001. "Population genetic aspects of pollinator decline." *Conservation Ecology* 5: 4, http://www.consecol.org/vol5/iss1/art4/.

Palliser, J. 1853. *Solitary Rambles and Adventures of a Hunter in the Prairies*. London: John Murray.

Palmer, M.A., et al. 2005. "Standards for ecologically successful river restoration." *Journal of Applied Ecology* 42: 208–17.

Paquet, P.C., J.R. Strittholt, and N.L. Stauss. 1999. *Wolf Reintroduction Feasibility in the Adirondack Park*. Convallis, OR: Conservation Biology Institute.

Parker, A.C. 1910. "Iroquois uses of maize and other food plants." *New York State Museum Bulletin* 144.

Pauketat, T.R. 2009. *Cahokia. Ancient America's Great City of the Mississippi*. New York: Viking/Penguin Group.

Pauly, D. 1995. "Anecdotes and the shifting baseline syndrome of fisheries." *Trends in Ecology and Evolution* 10 (10): 430.

Pauly, P.J. 2007. *Fruits and Plains: The Horticultural Transformation of America*. Cambridge, MA: Harvard University Press.

Peabody, W.B.O. 1841. "A report on the birds of Massachusetts made to the legislature in the session of 1838-9." *Journal of the Boston Society of Natural History* 3: 194.

Pease, T.C. 1838-39. "The Ordinance of 1787." *Mississippi Valley Historical Review* 25: 175. Cited in C.M. Johnston, *The Valley of the Six Nations*. Toronto: Champlain Society 1964. xxxii.

Pedlar, J.H., and R.K. Ross. 1997. "An update on the status of the sandhill crane in northern and central Ontario." *Ontario Birds* 15 (1): 5-12.

Pendergast, J.F. 1966. "Three prehistoric Iroquois components in eastern Ontario: The Salem, Grays Creek, and Beckstead sites." National Museum of Canada, *Bulletin* 208, Ottawa.

Perlman, J. 1976. *The Myth of Marginality*. Berkeley and Los Angeles: University of California Press.

Peron, F. 1639. "Letter of Father François du Peron, of the Society of Jesus, to Father Joseph Imbert du Peron, his brother." In E. Kenton, ed., *The Jesuit Relations and Allied Documents*. New York: Vanguard Press 1954. 137-43.

Perrings, C., M. Wiliamson, E.B. Barbier, et al. 2002. "Biological invasion risks and the public good: an economic perspective." *Conservation Biology* 6: 1.

Peters, R.L., and J.D.S. Darling. 1985. "The greenhouse effect and nature reserves." *BioScience* 35 (11): 707-17.

Peterson, R.L. 1957. "Changes in the mammalian fauna of Ontario. In F.A. Urquhart, ed., *Changes in the Fauna of Ontario*. Toronto: University of Toronto Press. 43-58.

Pilon, J.-L. 1987. "Washahoe Inninou Dahtsuounoaou: ecological and cultural adaptation along the Severn River in the Hudson Bay lowlands of Ontario." Ontario Ministry of Citizenship and Culture, *Conservation Archaeology Report* 10.

Pimentel, D., X. Huang, A. Cardova, et al. 1997. "Impact of population growth on food supplies and environment." *Population and Environment* 19: 9-14.

Pittsburgh, Its Industry and Commerce. 1870. Pittsburgh: Barr and Meyers.

Platt, W.J. ("Bill"). 2007. "Hurricane Katrina." Presentation to Annual Natural Areas Association Conference, Cleveland, OH. October.

Poland, T.M., and D.G. McCullough. 2006. "Emerald ash borer: invasion of the urban forest and the threat to North America's ash resources." *Journal of Forestry* April/May: 118-24.

Pope, W. 1834. "Journal, Part II. May 16, 1834-July 21, 1834." *Western Ontario Historical Nuggets* 18: 24-49.

Post, J.D. 1977. *The Last Great Subsistence Crisis in the Western World*. Baltimore, MD: Johns Hopkins University Press.

Pouliot, L. 1966. "Paul Ragueneau." *Dictionary of Canadian Biography*, vol. 1, http://www.biographi.ca.

Prestwood, A.K., and J.F. Smith. 1969. "Distribution of meningeal worm (*Pneumostrongylus tenuis*) in deer in the southeastern United States." *Journal of Parasitology* 55 (4): 720-5.

Prevost, Sir George. Letter to Lord Liverpool, colonial secretary, 11 December 1811. http://www.glengarrylightinfantry.ca/index.php.

Prickett, A. 1811. *A Larger Discourse of the Same Voyage, and the Success Thereof*. New York: New York Historical Society / I. Riley Publishers.

Pringle, J.F. 1972 (orig. 1890). *Lunenburgh, or the Old Eastern District*. Bellevillle, ON: Mika Silk Screening.

Prins, H.E.L. 1994. "Children of Gluskap." In E.W. Baker, E.A. Churchill, R. D'Abate, et al., *American Beginnings: Exploration, Culture, and Cartography in the Land of Norumbega*. Lincoln: University of Nebraska Press. 95-117.

Purchas, S. 1625. *Purchas His Pilgrimes*. London: Fetherstone.

Pursh, F. 1923. *Journal of a Botanical Excursion in the Northeastern Parts of the States of Pennsylvania and New York*. Syracuse, NY: Onondaga Historical Association / Dehler Press.

Pyne, S.J. 2007. *Awful Splendour: A Fire History of Canada*. Vancouver: UBC Press.

Qiao Liang, and Wang Xiangsui. 1999. *Unrestricted Warfare. People's Liberation Army.* Beijing: Literature and Arts Publishing House.

Quammen, D. 2008. *On the Origin of Species: The Illustrated Edition.* (1st ed.) New York: Stirling Publishing.

Quen, J. 1656. "Relation of what Occurred in the Mission … in the Years 1655." In E. Kenton, ed., *The Jesuit Relations and Allied Documents.* New York: Vanguard Press 1954. 260–79.

Quinn, D.B. 1994. "The early cartography of Maine in the setting of early European exploration of New England and the Maritimes." In E.W. Baker, E.A. Churchill, R. D'Abate, et al. eds., *American Beginnings: Exploration, Culture, and Cartography in the Land of Norumbega.* Lincoln: University of Nebraska Press. 37–59.

Quinn, D.B., and A.M. Quinn. 1983. *The English New England Voyages 1602–1608.* London: Hakluyt Society.

Raffeix, P. 1688. "Le Lac Ontario avec les Lieux circonvoisins & particulierement les cinque nations Iroquoises. Paris." In R.L. Gentilcore and C.G. Head, *Ontario's History in Maps.* Toronto: University of Toronto Press 1984.

Rafinesque, C.S. 1944. "A life of travels." *Chronica Botanica* 8 (2): 291–360. Waltham, MA.

Ragueneau, P. 1650. "Of the removal of the House of Sainte Marie to the Island of St. Joseph." In E. Kenton, *The Jesuit Relations and Allied Documents.* New York: Vanguard Press 1954. 225–43.

- 1651. *Jesuit Relation of 1649–50. Chapter VIII. Of the Devastation of the Country of the Hurons in the Spring of the Year 1650.* Paris: Sebastien et Gabriel Cramoisy.

Ramsden, P.G. 1990. "The Hurons: archaeology and culture history." In C.J. Ellis and N. Ferris, eds., *The Archaeology of Southern Ontario to A.D. 1650.* London Chapter, Ontario Archaeological Society, *Occasional Publications* 5. 361

Ray, A.J. 1987. "The fur trade in North America." In M. Novak, J.A. Baker, et al., eds., *Wild Furbearer Management and Conservation in North America.* Toronto: OMNR / Ontario Tappers Association. 21–30.

Rayburn, A. 1994. "The real story of how Toronto got its name." *Canadian Geographic,* September/October: 68–70.

R.D.H.P. Valley Conservation Report 1956. Toronto: Ontario Department of Planning and Development.

Reaman, G.E. 1957. *The Trail of the Black Walnut.* Toronto: McClelland and Stewart.

- 1971. *A History of Vaughan Township.* Toronto: University of Toronto Press.

Redford, K.H. 1990. "The ecological noble savage." *Orion Nature Quarterly* 9 (3): 25–9.

- 1992. "The empty forest." *BioScience* 42 (6): 412–22.

Reeves, W. 1999. "From acquisition to restoration." In B.I. Roots, D.A. Chant, and C.E.

Heidenreich, eds., *Special Places: The Changing Ecosystems of the Toronto Region.* Toronto: UBC Press. 229-41.

Regier, H. 1968. "The ecology and management of the walleye in Lake Erie." Great Lake Fishery Commission.

Regier, H.A., and W.L. Hartman. 1974. "Lake Erie's fish community: 150 years of stresses." *Bulletin of the Conservation Council of Ontario* 21 (4): 4-7.

Remington, C.L. 1968. "Suture zones of hybrid interaction between recently joined biotas." *Evolutionary Biology* 2: 321-428.

Renison, R.J. 1957. *One Day at a Time.* Toronto: Kingswood House.

Reschke, C., R. Reid, J. Jones, T. Feeney, and H. Potter. 1999. *Conserving Great Lakes Alvars: Final Technical Report of the International Alvar Conservation Initiative.* Nature Conservancy.

Reynolds, J.W. 1977. *The Earthworms (Lumbricidae and Spharganophilidae) of Ontario.* Toronto: Royal Ontario Museum.

Reznicek, A.A. 1980. "John Goldie's 1819 collecting site near Lake Simcoe, Ontario." *Canadian Field-Naturalist* 94: 439-42.

- 1982. "Association of relict prairie flora with Indian trails in central Ontario." In R. Brewer, ed., *Proceedings of the 8th North American Prairie Conference, Western Michigan University, Kalamazoo, MI.* 33-8.

Reznicek, A.A., and P.F. Maycock. 1983. "Composition of an isolated prairie in central Ontario." *Canadian Journal of Botany* 61: 3107-16.

Reznicek, A.A., and P.M. Catling. 1998. "Flora of Long Point, Regional Municipality of Haldimand, Norfolk, Ontario." *Michigan Botanist* 28 (3): 99-175.

Rich, C., and T. Longcore. 2006. *Ecological Consequences of Artificial Night Lighting.* Washington, DC: Island Press.

Rich, E.E. 1949. *James Isham's Observations on Hudsons Bay, 1743.* Toronto: Champlain Society.

- 1954. *Moose Fort Journals 1783-85.* London: Hudson's Bay Record Society.

Richard, T. 2008. "Confirmed occurrence and nesting of Kirtland's Warbler at CFB Petawawa, Ontario." *Ontario Birds* 26 (1): 2-15.

Richardson, A.H. 1928. *Forestry in Ontario.* Ontario Department of Forestry.

- 1944. *A Report on the Ganaraska Watershed.* Toronto: T.E. Bowman.

Richardson, J. 1847. *Eight Years in Canada.* Montreal: H.H. Cunningham.

Riley, J.L. 1982. "Habitats of sandhill cranes in the southern Hudson Bay lowland, Ontario." *Canadian Field-Naturalist* 96: 51-5.

- 1989. "Southern Ontario bogs and fens off the Canadian Shield." In M.J. Bardecki and N. Patterson, eds., *Wetlands: Inertia or Momentum.* Conference Proceedings, Federation of Ontario Naturalists, Don Mills, ON. 335-67.

- 1999. "Southern Ontario woodlands." In A. Kettle (comp.), *Southern Ontario Woodlands*. Federation of Ontario Naturalists, Don Mills, ON. 9-22.

- 2003. *Flora of the Hudson Bay Lowland and Its Postglacial Origins*. Ottawa: National Research Council Press.

- 2011. *Wetlands of the Hudson Bay Lowland: An Ontario Overview*. Toronto: Nature Conservancy of Canada.

Riley, J.L., A. Blasutti, T. Iacobelli, et al. 1999. "Conservation suitability mapping across the Lands for Life planning process in Ontario, Canada." ESRI ARC News: 27.

Riley, J.L., J.V. Jalava, and S. Varga. 1996. *Ecological Survey of the Niagara Escarpment Biosphere Reserve*. 2 vols. Peterborough, ON: OMNR, South-Central Region. Open File Site Report SR9601.

Riley, J.L., and K.M. Lindsay. 1997. "Life science inventory of the Holland Rivermouth Fen Provincial Nature Reserve. OMNR, Ontario Parks, Open File Ecological Report.

Riley, J.L., M. McMurtry, P.J. Sorrill, et al. 2003. *Big Picture 2002. Identifying Key Natural Heritage Areas and Linkages*. Nature Conservancy of Canada / Peterborough, ON: Ontario Natural Heritage Information Centre.

Riley, J.L., and P. Mohr. 1994. "The natural heritage of southern Ontario's settled landscapes." OMNR, Technical Report TR-001, Aurora, ON.

Ritchie, J.C., L.C. Cwynar, and R.W. Spear. 1983. "Evidence from north-west Canada for an early Holocene Milankovitch thermal maximum." *Nature* 305: 126-8.

Robertson, H. 2010. *Walking into Wilderness*. Winnipeg: Heartland Associates.

Robertson, K.R., R.C. Anderson, and M.W. Schwartz. 1997. "The tallgrass prairie mosaic." In M.W. Schwartz, ed., *Conservation in Highly Fragmented Landscapes*. New York: Chapman and Hall. 55-87.

Robertson, M. 1996. *Wild Life of the Burford Plain*. Scotland, ON: Taylor Made Printing.

Robertson, N. 1971 (orig. 1909). *The History of the County of Bruce*. Owen Sound, ON: Bruce County Historical Society.

Robinson. J.R. 1911. *The Diary of Mrs. John Graves Simcoe*. Toronto: William Briggs.

Robinson, P.J. 1933. *Toronto during the French Regime*. Toronto: Ryerson Press.

Roche, J.K. 1858. "Plan of the township of Carden." Ontario Crown Land Surveys, Field Note Book 1023, and Plan O.V.7. Peterborough, ON: OMNR.

Rockström, J., W. Steffen, K. Noone, et al. 2009. "Planetary boundaries: exploring the safe operating space for humanity." *Ecology and Society* 14 (2): 32, http://www.ecologyandsociety.org/vol14/iss2/art32/.

Roe, F.G. 1970 (2nd ed.) *The North American Buffalo*. Toronto: University of Toronto Press.

Rogers, E.S. 1994. "Northern Algonquians and the Hudson's Bay Company, 1821-1890." In E.S. Rogers and D.B. Smith, eds., *Aboriginal Ontario*. Toronto: Dundurn Press. 307-33.

Rogers, R. 1765. *A Concise Account of North America*. London: Printed for the author.

Romney, P. 1988. "Charles Fothergill." *Dictionary of Canadian Biography*, vol. 7, http://www.biographi.ca.

Roots, B.I., D.A. Chant, and C.E. Heidenreich, eds., 1999. *Special Places: The Changing Ecosystems of the Toronto Region*. Toronto: UBC Press.

Rorke, R. 1987. *Forty Years in the Forest: Reminiscences from the Pen of a Backwoodsman, 1820-1868*. Ed. P.E.K. Armstrong. Tecumseth and West Gwillimbury Historical Society, ON.

Rosatte, R. 2011. "Evidence confirms the presence of cougars (*Puma concolor*) in Ontario." *Canadian Field-Naturalist* 125: 116.

Ross, Rob. Pers. comm., Paleontological Research Institute, Ithaca, NY, October 2007.

Rousseau, J. 1954. "L'annedda et l'arbre de vie. " *Revue d'Histoire de l'Amerique Françaises* 8: 171-213.

- 1969. "Nicolas Jérémie. " *Dictionary of Canadian Biography*, vol. 2, http://www.biographi.ca.

Rowe, J.S. 1959. "Forest regions of Canada." Canada Department of Northern Affairs and National Resources, *Bulletin* 123.

- 1976. "The significance of natural areas." In *Natural Areas. Proceedings of a Symposium at the Thirteenth Annual Meeting of the Canadian Botanical Association*. 3-7.

- 1990. *Home Place: Essays on Ecology*. Edmonton: NeWest Publishers.

Rubidge, F.P. June 1835. "No.15 Alnwick." Ontario Crown Land Survey Records, vol. 18. Peterborough, ON: OMNR.

Ruddiman, W.F., and A. McIntyre. 1981. "Oceanic mechanisms for amplification of the 23,000-year ice-volume cycle." *Science* 212: 617-27.

Ruddiman, W.F., S.J. Vavrus, and J.E. Kutzbach. 2005. "A test of the overdue-glaciation hypothesis." *Quaternary Science Review* 24: 11.

Russell, E.W.B. 1983. "Indian-set fires in the forests of the northeastern United States." *Ecology* 64 (1): 78-88.

Rutter, R.J., ed. 1949. *W.E. Saunders: Naturalist*. Toronto: Federation of Ontario Naturalists / University of Toronto Press.

Saarnisto, M. 1974. "The deglaciation history of the Lake Superior region." *Quaternary Research* 4: 316-39.

Sadler, D.C., and H.G. Howard. 2003. "Birds from the ground: the record of archaeology in Ontario." *Occasional Papers in Anthropology* 15, Trent University, Peterborough, ON.

Sagard, G. 1939. *The Long Journey to the Country of the Hurons*. Toronto: Champlain Society.

Sagard-Theodat, G. 1866. *Histoire du Canada*. 4 vols. Paris: Librairie Tross.

Santamour, F.S., A.J. McArdle, and P.V. Strider. 1989. "Susceptibility of flowering dogwood of various provenances to dogwood anthradnose." *Plant Diseases* 73: 590-1.

Sarkadi, L. 2007. "Caribou in decline." *Canadian Geographic* 127 (6): 56-64.

Saunders, D. 2010. *Arrival City*. Toronto: Knopf Canada.

Saunders, R.M. 1947. *Flashing Wings*. Toronto: McClelland and Stewart.

Saunders, W.E. 1932. "Notes on the mammals of Ontario." Royal Canadian Institute *Transactions* 40 (18): 271-309.

Sax, J.L. 2005. "Why America has a property rights movement." *University of Illinois Law Review* 2005: 513-20.

Schaefer, C. 1996. "Plant community structure and environmental conditions of alvars of the Bruce peninsula, Ontario." MSc thesis, University of Guelph.

Scholten, S.J. 1994. "Aerial survey of the Pen Islands caribou herd for 1994." Peterborough, ON: OMNR.

Schooling, W. 1920. *The Hudson's Bay Company 1670-1920*. London: Hudson's Bay House.

Schorger, A.W. 1973. *The Passenger Pigeon*. Norman: University of Oklahoma Press.

Scott, W.B. 1957. "Changes in the fish fauna of Ontario." In F.A. Urquhart, ed., *Changes in the Fauna of Ontario*. Toronto: University of Toronto Press. 19-25.

- 1963. "A review of the changes in the fish fauna of Ontario." Royal Canadian Institute *Transactions* 44 (2): 111-25.

Scudder, G.G.E. 1979. "Present patterns in the fauna and flora of Canada." In H.V. Danks, ed., *Canada and Its Insect Fauna*. Entomological Society of Canada *Memoirs* 108: 87-179.

Sears, P.B. 1926. "The natural vegetation of Ohio. II. The prairies of Ohio." *Ohio Journal of Science* 26: 128-46.

Seaver, J.E. 1824. *A Narrative of the Life of Mary Jamison*. Canandaigua, NY: J.D. Bemis and Co. (repr. 1950, American Scenic and Historic Preservation Society, NY).

Seton, E.T. 1909. *Life-Histories of Northern Animals*. New York: Charles Scribner and Sons.

- 1929. *Lives of Game Animals*. Vol. 3. Garden City, NY: Doubleday.

Seyler, J. 1997. "Biology of selected riverine fish species in the Moose River basin." Timmins, ON: OMNR, Northeast Science and Technology. IR-024.

Shaler, N.S. 1900. *Nature and Man in America*. New York: Charles Scribners.

Shetrone, H.C. 1930. *The Mound-Builders*. New York: A. Appleton and Co.

Shirreff, P. 1835. *A Tour through North America*. Edinburgh: Oliver and Boyd.

Shtilmark, F. 2003. *History of the Russian Zapovedniks 1985-1995*. Edinburgh: Russian Nature Press.

Siggins, M. 2008. *Marie-Anne. The Extraordinary Life of Louis Riel's Grandmother*. Toronto: McClelland and Stewart.

Simberloff, D. 20 June 2007. "Given the stakes, our *modus operandi* dealing with invasive species should be 'guilty until proven innocent.'" *Conservation Magazine* 8: 18-19.

Simcoe, Mrs J.G. 1795 (?). "Sketch Map of Upper Canada showing the routes Lt. Gov. J.G. Simcoe took on trips between March 1792 and September 1795." Repr. St Catharines, ON: Stonehouse Publications.

Sioui, G.E. 1992. *For an Amerindian Autohistory: An Essay on the Foundations of a Social Ethic*. (Introduction by B.G. Trigger.) Montreal and Kingston, ON: McGill-Queen's University Press.

Slack, N.G., C. Reschke, and B. Gilman. 1988. "*Scorpidium turgescens* rediscovered in New York State." *Bryologist* 91 (3): 217-18.

Slafter, E.F., ed. 1880. *Voyages of Samuel de Champlain*. Trans. C.P. Otis. 3 vols. Boston: Prince Society.

Sly, P.G. 1991. "The effects of land use and cultural development on the Lake Ontario ecosystem since 1750." *Hydrobiologia* 213: 1-75.

Smith, B.D. 1992. *Rivers of Change*. Washington, DC: Smithsonian Institution Press.

Smith, D.B. 1990. *From the Land of Shadows: The Making of Grey Owl*. Saskatoon, SK: Western Producer Prairie Books.

Smith, D.W. February 1793. "Thames - its banks." Crown Land Survey Records, vol. 1. Peterborough, ON: OMNR.

- 1793. "A sketch showing the situation of 230 acres." Copy in Map Library, University of Toronto Library.

- 1917 (orig. 1799). *La Rochefoucault-Liancourt's Travels in Canada 1795*. In *Thirteenth Report of the Bureau of Archives for the Province of Ontario*. Toronto: T. Wilgrass.

Smith, R. 1906. *A Tour of Four Great Rivers*. Ed. F.W. Halsey. New York: Charles Scribner and Sons.

Smith, W.H. 1852. *Canada: Past, Present and Future*. 2 vols. Toronto: Thomas Maclear.

- 1972 (orig. 1846). *Canadian Gazeteer*. Toronto: Coles Publishing.

Snell, E. 1987. "Wetland distribution and conversion in southern Ontario." *Working Paper* 48, Inland Waters and Lands Directorate, Environment Canada, Burlington, ON.

Snow, D. 2010. *Death or Victory*. Toronto: Allen Lane Canada / Penguin Group.

Snow, D.R. 1994. *The Iroquois*. Oxford: Blackwell.

Snow, D.R., and W.A. Strna. 1989. "Sixteenth-century depopulation: a view from the Mohawk valley." *American Anthropologist* 91: 142-9.

Snyder, L.L. 1930. "A faunal investigation of King Township, York County, Ontario. II. The mammals of King Township. III. The summer birds of King Township." Royal Canadian Institute *Transactions* 38 (17): 173-81, 183-202.

- 1957. "Changes in the avifauna of Ontario." In F.A. Urquhart, ed., *Changes in the Fauna of Ontario*. Toronto: University of Toronto Press. 26-42.

Soper, J.H. 1954. "The Hart's-tongue fern in Ontario." *American Fern Journal* 44 (4): 129-47.

- 1962. "The Walking Fern." *Federation of Ontario Naturalists Bulletin* 98: 14-17.

Soper, J.H., and P.F. Maycock. 1963. "A community of arctic-alpine plants on the east shore of Lake Superior." *Canadian Journal of Botany* 41: 183-98.

Soulé, M.E. 1990. "The onslaught of invasive species, and other challenges in the coming decades." *Conservation Biology* 4: 233-9.

Spence, M.W., R.H. Pihl, and C.R. Murphy. 1990. "Cultural complexes of the early and middle Woodland periods." In C.J. Ellis and N. Ferris, eds., *The Archaeology of Southern Ontario to A.D. 1650*. London Chapter, Ontario Archaeological Society, *Occasional Publications* 5. 125-70.

Spry, E.M. 1968. *The Papers of the Palliser Expedition 1857-1860*. Toronto: Champlain Society.

National Research Council Committee on the Status of Pollinators in North America. 2007. *Status of Pollinators in North America*. Washington, DC: National Academies Press.

Stebbins, G.L. 1935. "Some observations on the flora of the Bruce peninsula, Ontario." *Rhodora* 37: 63-74.

Steele, M.A., T. Knowles, K. Bridle, et al. 1993. "Tannins and partial consumption of acorns: implications for dispersal of oaks by seed predators." *American Midland Naturalist* 130: 229-38.

Steevens, M. 1850. "Sketch of part of the London Township." University of Western Ontario Library, London, ON.

Stegmann, J. 1800. "Field notes of the Township of King." Ontario Crown Land Survey Records, vol. 3. Peterborough, ON: OMNR. 407-29.

Stewart, A.M. 2004. "Intensity of land-use around the Holland marsh." In L.J. Jackson and A. Hinshelwood, eds., *The Late Palaeo-Indian Great Lakes*. Gatineau, QC: Canadian Museum of Civilization, *Archaeology Paper* 165. 85-116.

Stewart, O.C. 1951. "Burning and natural vegetation in the United States." *Geographical Review* 41: 317-20.

Stinson, K.A., S.A. Campbell, J.R. Powell, et al. 2006. "Invasive plant suppresses the growth of native tree seedlings by disrupting belowground mutualisms." *PLOSBIOL* 4 (5): e140, http://www.doi:10.1371/journal.pbio.0040140.

Stirling, P., and D. Simberloff. 2000. "The frequency and strength of non-target effects of invertebrate biological control agents." In P. Follett and J. Duan, eds., *Nontarget Effects of Biological Control*. Norwell, MA: Kluwer Academic Publishers. 31-43.

Stone, W.L., ed. 1868. *Memoirs, and Letters and Journals of Major General Riedesel*. Albany, NY: J. Munsell.

Storck, P.L. 2004. *Journey to the Ice Age*. Vancouver: UBC Press.

Strickland, D. 2009. "What originally prevented, and what later permitted, the great northern expansion of white-tailed deer." *Occasional Papers from Oxtongue Lake* 1: 1-40.

Strickland, S. 1970 (orig. 1853). *Twenty-Seven Years in Canada West.* 2 vols. Edmonton: M.G. Hurtig.

Stupart, R.F. 1913. "The climate of Toronto." In J.H. Faull, ed., *The Natural History of the Toronto Region.* Toronto: Royal Canadian Institute. 82-90.

- 1917. "Is the climate changing?" *Journal of the Royal Astronomical Society, Canada* 11 (6): 197-207.

Sturtevant, E.L. 1919. *Sturtevant's Notes on Edible Plants.* (U.P. Hendrik, ed.). New York State, Department of Agriculture, 27th Annual Report, vol. 2, pt. 2. Albany, NY: J.B. Lyon Co.

Suffling, R. 1987. "John Goldie, early Canadian botanist 1793-1886." *Waterloo Historical Society* 75: 98-116.

Sullivan, E.R. 1852. *Rambles and Scrambles in North & South America.* London: Richard Bentley.

Surtees, R.J. 1994. "Land cessions, 1763-1830." In E.S. Rogers and D.B. Smith, eds., *Aboriginal Ontario.* Toronto: Dundurn Press. 93-121.

Sweeney, R.A., ed. 1969. "Proceedings of the Conference on Changes in the Biota of Lakes Erie and Ontario." *Bulletin of the Buffalo Society of Natural Sciences* 25 (1): 1-84.

Szeicz, J.M., and G.M. MacDonald. 1991. "Postglacial vegetation history of oak savanna in southern Ontario." *Canadian Journal of Botany* 69: 1507-19.

Tailhan, R.P.J., ed. 1864. *Mémoire sur les Moeurs, Coustumes et Relligion des Sauvages de l'Amérique septentrionale par Nicholas Perrot.* Leipzig and Paris: Librairie A. Franck.

Talbot E.A. 1824. *Five Years Residence in the Canadas.* Vol. 1. London: Longman, Hurst, Rees, Orme, Brown and Green.

Talman, J.J. 1946. *Loyalist Narratives from Upper Canada.* Toronto: Champlain Society.

Tanner, H.H., ed. 1987. *Atlas of Great Lakes Indian History.* Norman: University of Oklahoma Press.

Taylor, A. 2006. *The Divided Ground.* New York: Vintage Books.

- 2010. *The Civil War of 1812.* New York: Vintage Books.

Taylor, F. 1913. "The moraine systems of southwestern Ontario: Royal Canadian Institute *Transactions* 23 (10), pt. 1: 57-79.

Tenche Cox. 1790s. Cited in H.C. Mathews, *The Mark of Honour.* Toronto: University of Toronto Press.

Terasmae, J., and T.W. Anderson. 1970. "Hypsithermal range extension of white pine (*Pinus strobus* L.) in Quebec, Canada." *Canadian Journal of Earth Sciences* 7: 406-13.

Theberge, E. 1988. "Fothergill: Canada's pioneer naturalist emerges from oblivion." *The Beaver* 68 (1): 12-18.

Theberge, E., and J. Theberge. 1976. "John Muir's Ontario valley." *Ontario Naturalist* 16 (2): 4-9.

Thevet, A. 1986 (orig. 1557). *André Thevet's North America*. R. Schlesinger and A.P. Stabler (trans. and ed.). Montreal and Kingston, ON: McGill-Queen's University Press.

Thompson, S. 1968 (orig. 1884). *Reminiscences of a Canadian Pioneer*. Toronto: McClelland and Stewart.

Thoreau, H.D. 1906 (orig. 1855). (Edited by Bradford Torrey and Francis H. Allen.) *The Journal of Henry D. Thoreau*. 2 vols. (VII, 24 January 1855; VIII, 23 March 1856).

Tilghman, O. 1876. *Memoir of Tench Tilghman*. Albany, NY: J. Munsell.

Tooker, E. 1968. *An Ethnography of the Huron Indians*. Huronia Historical Development Council and Ontario Dept. of Education, in cooperation with Smithsonian Institution, Washington, DC.

- 1988. "The United States constitution and the Iroquois League." *Ethnohistory* 35 (4): 305-36.

Toronto City Planning Board. 1943. *Second Annual Report*. Toronto.

"Toronto purchase in 1787." Ontario Crown Land Surveys, Plan 1092. Peterborough, ON: OMNR.

Traill, C.P. 1836. *The Backwoods of Canada*. London: Charles Knight.

- 1838. "Canadian lumberers." *Chamber's Edinburgh Journal* 7: 380-1.

- 1906 (orig. 1885). *Studies of Plant Life in Canada*. Toronto: William Briggs.

- 1969 (orig. 1855). *The Canadian Settler's Guide*. Toronto: McClelland and Stewart.

- 1994 (ed. M.A. Peterman and C. Ballstadt). *Forest and Other Gleanings*. Ottawa: University of Ottawa Press.

- 1999 (ed. E. Thompson). *Pearls & Pebbles* Toronto: Natural Heritage Books.

Transeau, E.N. 1935. "The prairie pensinsula." *Ecology* 10: 423-37.

Trenk, F.B. 1934. *The Farm Windbreak* (pamphlet). College of Agriculture, University of Wisconsin, Madison, WI.

Trent, W. 24 May 1763. "Journal of William Trent." Ed. A.T. Volwiler. 1924. *Mississippi Valley Historical Review* 11: 28-57, 115-42, 390-413, http://www.nativeweb.org/pages/legal/amherst/lord_jeff.html.

Trigger, B.G. 1960. "The destruction of Huronia: a study in economic and cultural change, 1609-1650." *Royal Canadian Institute Transactions* 33, 68 (1): 14-45.

- 1963. "Settlement as an aspect of Iroquoian adaptation at the time of contact." *American Anthropologist* 65 (1): 86-101.

- 1985. *Natives and Newcomers: Canada's Heroic Age Reconsidered*. Montreal and Kingston, ON: McGill-Queen's University Press.

- 1987. *The Children of Aataentsic: A History of the Huron People to 1660*. Montreal and Kingston, ON: McGill-Queen's University Press.

- 1994. "The original Iroquoians: Huron, Petun and Neutral." In E.S. Rogers and D.B. Smith, eds., *Aboriginal Ontario*. Toronto: Dundurn Press. 41-63.

Tuck, J.A. 1971. *Onondaga Iroquois Prehistory*. Syracuse, NY: Syracuse University Press York.

- 1978. "Northern Iroquoian prehistory." In B.G. Trigger, ed., *Handbook of North American Indians* 15 (Northeast). Washington, DC: Smithsonian Institution. 322-33.

Tully, K. 1904 (pub. 1905). "The fluctuations of Lake Ontario." Royal Canadian Institute *Transactions* 16 (8, pt. 1): 1-10.

Turner, N. 1981. "A gift for the taking: the untapped potential of some food plants of North American native peoples." *Canadian Journal of Botany* 59: 2331-57.

Tyrrell, J.B. 1931. *Documents relating to the Early History of Hudson Bay*. Toronto: Champlain Society.

Udall, S.L. 1963. *The Quiet Crisis*. New York: Holt, Rinehart and Winston.

Ure, G.P. 1858. *The handbook of Toronto*. Toronto: Lovel and Gibson.

USDA (U.S. Department of Agriculture). Forest Service. 1974. "Seeds of woody plants in the United States." *Agriculture Handbook* 450. Washington, DC.

Van der Donck, A. 1841 (orig. 1655). *A Description of the New Netherlands*. Trans. Jeremiah Johnson. *Collections of the New-York Historical Society*, 2nd series, vol. 1, 125-242. Re-edited by T.F. O'Donnell 1968. Syracuse, NY: Syracuse University Press.

Vander Wall, S.B. 2001. "The evolutionary ecology of nut dispersal." *Botanical Review* 67: 74-117.

Varga, S. 1989. "A botanical inventory and evaluation of the High Park oak woodlands Area of Natural and Scientific Interest." OMNR, Open File Ecological Report 8907. Richmond Hill, ON.

- 1999. "The savannahs of High Park." In B.I. Roots, D.A. Chant, and C.E. Heidenreich, eds., *Special Places: The Changing Ecosystems of the Toronto Region*. Toronto: UBC Press, 260.

Varga, S., J. Jalava, and J.L. Riley. 1991. "Ecological survey of the Rouge Valley Park." OMNR, Open File Ecological Report 9104. Aurora, ON.

Varga, S., and J. Schmelefske. 1992. "Biological inventory and evaluation of the Alliston Pinery Area of Natural and Scientific Interest." OMNR, Southern Region, Aurora, ON. Open File Ecological Report 8909.

Varga, S., and P.S.G. Kor. 1993. "Reconnaissance survey of the Niagara Gorge Area of Natural and Scientific Interest." OMNR.

Veizer, J. 2005. "Celestrial climate driver: a perspective from four billion years of the carbon cycle." *Geoscience Canada* 32 (1): 13-28.

Verrazano, G. 1970. "The written record of the voyage of 1524 of Giovanni da Verrazano." In L.C. Wroth, ed., *The Voyages of Giovanni da Verrazano, 1524-1528*. New Haven, CT:

Yale University Press. http://www.nationalhumanitiescenter.org/pds/amerbegin/contact/text4/verrazzano.pdf.

Voigt, D.R., and W.E. Berg. 1987. "Coyote." In M. Novak, J.A. Baker, et al., eds., *Wild Furbearer Management and Conservation in North America*. Toronto: OMNR / Ontario Tappers Association. 345-57.

Voss, E.G. 1972. "Michigan Flora. Pt.1." Ann Arbor, MI: Cranbrook Institute of Science / *University of Michigan Herbarium Bulletin 55*.

- 1978. "Botanical Beachcombers and Explorers." *University of Michigan Herbarium* 13.

Wagner, D.L. 2005. *Caterpillars of Eastern North America*. Princeton, NJ: Princeton University Press.

- 2007. "Consequences of introduced and invasive species on imperiled invertebrates." Natural Areas Conference, Cleveland, OH. October.

Wagner, G.E. 2003. "Eastern woodlands anthropogenic ecology." In P.E. Minnis, ed., *People and Plants in Ancient Eastern North America*. Washington, DC: Smithsonian Books. 126-71.

Wagner, W.H. Jr. 1993. "Problems with biotic invasives: a biologist's viewpoint." In B.N. McKnight, ed., *Biological Pollution*. Indianapolis, IN: Indiana Academy of Science. 1-8.

Wainio, A., J. Barrie, J. Rowsell, et al. 1976. "An ecological study of Grenadier Pond and the surrounding areas of High Park – Toronto."

Walker, E.M. 1957. "Changes in the insect fauna of Ontario." In F.A. Urquhart, ed., *Changes in the Fauna of Ontario*. Toronto: University of Toronto Press. 4-12.

Wallace, A.F.C. 1970. *The Death and Rebirth of the Seneca*. New York: A.A. Knopf.

Wallace, A.R. 1962 (orig. 1876). *The Geographical Distribution of Animals*. Vol. 1. New York: Hafner. 149-50.

Wallace, P.A.W. 1965. *Indian Paths of Pennsylvania*. Harrisburg: Pennsylvania Historical and Museum Commission.

Warrick, G. 2008. *A Population History of the Huron-Petun, AD 500-1650*. Cambridge: Cambridge University Press.

Wa-Sha-Quon-Asin (Grey Owl). 1934. *Pilgrims of the Wild*. London: Lovat Dickson.

Washington, G. 1732-99. *The Writings of George Washington from the Original Manuscript Sources*. Electronic Text Center, University of Virginia Library.

Waters, M.R., J. Forman, et al. 2011. "The Buttermilk Creek complex and the origins of Clovis at the Debra L. Friedkin site, Texas." *Science* 331 (25): 1599–1603.

Waters, M.R., T.W. Stafford Jr, et al. 2011. "Pre-Clovis mastodon hunting 13,800 years ago at the Manis site, Washington." *Science* 334: 351.

Watts, W.A. 1979. "Late Quaternary vegetation of central Appalachia and the New Jersey coastal plain." *Ecological Monographs* 49 (4): 427-69.

Weaver, S.M. 1994. "The Iroquois: the consolidation of the Grand River Reserve in the mid-nineteenth Century, 1847-1875." In E.S. Rogers and D.B. Smith, eds., *Aboriginal Ontario*. Toronto: Dundurn Press. 182-212.

Webb, M. Undated MS. Dufferin County Museum Family Archives.

Webb, S.L., M. Dwyer, C.K. Kaunzinger, and P.H. Wyckoff. 2000. "The myth of the resilient forest: case study of the invasive Norway maple (*Acer platanoides*)." *Rhodora* 102: 332-54.

Weed, C.M. 1890. "The Lakeside daisy." *Journal Columbus Horticultural Society* 5: 72-3.

Weld, C.R. 1855. *A Vacation Tour in the United States and Canada*. London: Longman, Brown, Green.

Weld, I. Jr. 1807. *Travels through the States of North America and the Provinces of Upper and Lower Canada*. 4th ed. 2 vols. London: Stockdale.

Wentzel, W.F. "Letters, 1807-1824." In L.R. Masson, *Les Bourgeois de la Compagnie Nord-Ouest*. Vol. 1. New York: Antiquarian Press 1960. 69-144.

West, D.C., H.H. Shugart, and D.B. Botkin, eds. 1981. *Forest Succession*. New York: Springer-Verlag.

Westgate, J.A., P.H. von Bitter, N. Eyles, et al. 1999. "The physical setting." In B.I. Roots, D.A. Chant, and C.E. Heidenreich, eds., *Special Places: The Changing Ecosystems of the Toronto Region*. Toronto: UBC Press. 11-31.

Whillans, T. 1999. "Waterfront ecosystems: restoring is remembering." In B.I. Roots, D.A. Chant, and C.E. Heidenreich, eds., *Special Places. The Changing Ecosystems of the Toronto Region*. Toronto: UBC Press. 245-8.

White, B., P. Wilson, A. Johnson, et al. 2001. "Status of the eastern wolf (*Canis lycaon*)." Peterborough, ON: Natural Resources DNA Profiling and Forensic Centre, Trent University.

White, D.J., E. Haber, and C. Keddy. 1993. "Invasive plants of natural habitats in Canada: an integrated review of wetland and upland species and legislation governing their control." Ottawa: Canadian Wildlife Service.

White, R. 1991. *The Middle Ground: Indians, Empires and Republics in the Great Lakes Region, 1650-1815*. New York: Cambridge University Press.

Whittemore, A.T., and R.T. Olsen. 2011. "*Ulmus americana* is a polyploid complex." *American Journal of Botany* 98 (4): 1-7.

Wiegmann, S., and D. Waller. 2006. "Fifty years of change in northern upland forest understories: identity and traits of 'winner' and 'loser' plant species." *Biological Conservation* 129: 109-23.

Wildlands Project. 1992. *Wild Earth*. Canton, NY.

Wilkie, D. 1937. "Sketches of a summer trip to New York and the Canadas." In E.C. Guillet, *Pioneer Life in the County of York*. Toronto: Hess-Trade Typesetting 1946. 142-6.

Williams, B. 1913. *History of Clermont and Brown Counties, Ohio.* Milford, OH: Hobart Publishing Co.

Williams, G. 1969. *Andrew Graham's Observations on Hudson's Bay 1767-1791.* London: Hudson's Bay Record Society.

Williams, R. 1973. *A Key into the Language of America.* Detroit: Wayne State University Press.

Williamson, R.F. 1990. "The early Iroquoian period of southern Ontario." In C.J. Ellis and N. Ferris, eds., *The Archaeology of Southern Ontario to A.D. 1650.* London Chapter, Ontario Archaeological Society, *Occasional Publications* 5: 291-320.

Wilmot, S.G. 1808. "Field notes … of a line for a road between the head of Kempenfelt Bay on Lake Simcoe and Penetanguishene Bay on Lake Huron." Ontario Crown Land Survey Records, vol. 2, 181.

Wilmot, S.L. February/March 1811. "Field Notes of the Village of Gwillimbury." Ontario Crown Land Surveys, Field Note Book 436. Peterborough, ON: OMNR.

Wilson, C., and M. Daniels. 2010. "Atlantic salmon in Lake Ontario: genetic evidence regarding the distinctiveness of the historical population." Peterborough, ON: Ontario Ministry of Natural Resources.

Wilson, D. 1862. *Prehistoric Man.* London: Macmillan.

Wilson, E.O. 1978. *On Human Nature.* Cambridge, MA: Harvard University Press.

- 1987. "The little things that run the world." *Conservation Biology* 1: 344-6.

- 1992. *The Diversity of Life.* Cambridge, MA: Belknap Press.

- 1996. *In Search of Nature.* Washington, DC: Island Press.

- 2002. *The Future of Life.* New York: Vintage Books / Random House.

Wilson, E.O., and F.M. Peter, eds. 1988. *Biodiversity.* Washington, DC: National Academy Press.

Wilson, P.J., et al. 2000. "The relationship of the red wolf and eastern Canadian wolf provides evidence for a common evolutionary history, independent of the gray wolf." *Canadian Journal of Zoology* 78: 2156-66.

Winchester, S. 2003. *Krakatoa.* New York: HarperCollins.

Winterhalder, B. 1981. "Foraging strategies in the boreal forest." In B. Winterhalder and E.A. Smith, eds., *Hunter-Gatherer Foraging Strategies.* Chicago: University of Chicago Press. 66-98.

Wood, J.D. 1958. "The historical geography of Dumfries Township, Upper Canada." MA thesis, University of Toronto.

- 1961. "The woodland-oak plains transition zone in the settlement of western Upper Canada." *Canadian Geographer* 5 (1): 43-7.

- 2000. *Making Ontario: Agricultural Colonization and Landscape Re-Creation before the Railway.* Montreal and Kingston, ON: McGill-Queen's University Press.

Wood, W. 1865 (orig. 1634). *Wood's New England's Prospect*. Boston: Prince Society.

- 1977. *New England's Prospect*. Amherst, MA: University of Massachusetts Press.

Woodliffe, A. 2008. "Arbour Day assists in the demise of prairie." *Bluestem Banner* 8: 5.

Woods, K.D., and M.B. Davis. 1989. "Paleoecology of range limits: beech in the Upper Peninsula of Michigan." *Ecology* 70 (3): 681-96.

Woodward, S.L. and J.N. McDonald. 2002. *Indian Mounds of the Middle Ohio Valley*. Blacksburg, VA: McDonald and Woodward Publishing Co.

Wright, H.E. Jr. 1964. "Aspects of the early postglacial forest succession in the Great Lakes region." *Ecology* 45: 439-48.

Wright, J.V. 1966. "The Ontario Iroquois tradition." National Museum of Canada. *Bulletin* 210.

- 1972. *Ontario Prehistory*. Ottawa: National Museum of Man.

- 1994. "Before European contact." In E.S. Rogers and D.B. Smith, eds., *Aboriginal Ontario*. Toronto: Dundurn Press. 32.

Wright, R. 1992. *Stolen Continent*. Toronto: Viking Press, Toronto.

Wroth, L.C., ed. 1970. *The Voyages of Giovanni da Verrazano, 1524-1528*. New Haven, CT: Yale University Press.

Yarnell, R.A. 1964 (repr. 1970). "Aboriginal relationships between culture and plant life in the Upper Great Lakes region." Museum of Anthropology, *Anthropology Paper* 23. University of Michigan, Ann Arbor, MI.

Yule, A.M., I.K. Barker, J.W. Austin, et al. 2006. "Toxicity of *Clostridium botulinum* Type E neurotoxin to Great Lakes fish." *Journal of Wildlife Diseases* 42 (3): 479-93.

Zavitz, E.J. 1909. "Report on the Reforestation of Waste Lands in Southern Ontario." Ontario Department of Agriculture. In possession of L.K. Cameron, Toronto.

- 1926. Appendix 36. Report of the Forestry Branch. In *Report of the Minister of Lands, Forests and Mines of the Province of Ontario*. *The Legislative Assembly of Ontario*.

Zayed, A., and L. Packer. 2001. "High levels of diploid male production in a primitively eusocial bee." *Heredity* 87: 631-6.

Zenkert, C.A. 1934. "The flora of the Niagara frontier region." *Bulletin of the Buffalo Society of Natural Sciences* 16.

Zubrow, E.B.W., and P.T. Buerger. 1980. "The Martin Site of Grand Island: the Archaic and Woodland occupation of western New York." Department of Anthropology, University at Buffalo, NY.

INDEX

Selected species are indexed; for others, *see* wildlife, observer lists; and trees and plants, observer lists